FORGED
IN FIRE

FORGED
IN FIRE

A HISTORY AND TOUR GUIDE
OF THE WAR IN THE EAST,
FROM MANASSAS TO ANTIETAM, 1861–1862

Jim Miles

CUMBERLAND HOUSE

NASHVILLE, TENNESSEE

TIPS FOR ENJOYING THE TOUR GUIDES

The driving tours to historic sites have been exhaustively researched, but readers should be aware that highways and streets are occasionally altered and that names and designated numbers of roads are frequently changed. That is why we have included written directions, mileage, and general maps. These should enable you to circumvent any changes that might be made to the tour route in coming years.

Remember that odometers can vary considerably. Our 0.1 might be your 0.2, so please take this into account. (All distances refer to miles.) When in doubt about where you are, do not hesitate to ask local residents for directions. While preparing these guides, we were frequently misplaced (i.e., lost).

For safety's sake, it is best to tour the campaign with a companion. While one drives, the other can read and direct. It is also advisable to read the touring information before hitting the road. Familiarization with the tours will enable you to choose beforehand the sites you would like to visit. Traffic in metropolitan areas can be fast and hazardous, so please exercise caution in stopping to view a historic site and in reentering the traffic flow.

By all means, be respectful of private property. Do not trespass on land or call on the residents of a private historic home. It is extremely difficult to live in or on a part of history, and there are too many vandals and arsonists around for homeowners to be tolerant of uninvited visitors. Fortunately, many historic homes are open as part of community tours around Christmas and during the spring. Check calendars of events for specific dates.

Copyright © 2000 by Jim Miles

Published by
Cumberland House Publishing, Inc.
431 Harding Industrial Drive
Nashville, Tennessee 37211

Cover design by Bateman Design, Nashville, Tennessee

Library of Congress Cataloging-in-Publication Data

Miles, Jim.
    Forged in fire : a history and tour guide of the war in the East from Manassas to Antietam,
      1861–1862 / Jim Miles.
          p.   cm. — (The Civil War explorer series)
    Includes bibliographical references (p.) and index.
    ISBN 1-58182-089-5 (pbk. : alk. paper)
    1. Virginia—History—Civil War, 1861–1865—Campaigns. 2. United States—History—
Civil War, 1861–1865—Campaigns. 3. Virginia—History—Civil War, 1861–1865—
Battlefields—Guidebooks. 4. United States—History—Civil War, 1861–1865—Battlefields—
Guidebooks. 5. Historic sites—Virginia—Guidebooks. I. Title.
E470.2.M55 2000
973.7'3—dc21   00-027354

Printed in the United States of America.

1 2 3 4 5 6 7 8—04 03 02 01 00

To my brother Ray, who helped me survive my youth,
and to his family: Wave, Susan, and Adam.
I love you all.

CONTENTS

INTRODUCTION

I T IS WITH GREAT trepidation and a sense of humbleness that I begin a four-volume history of the Civil War in the East and a comprehensive tour guide to military events in Virginia, West Virginia, Maryland, and Pennsylvania. Many excellent histories have been written about this theater, and I would not pretend that mine is more than a survey. This is, however, the first attempt to map out driving tours of every Civil War campaign in the region.

The task is daunting. For four years Confederate and Federal armies campaigned extensively in the eastern theater, particularly in northern and central Virginia. Because fragments of campaigns from different years overlap or extend in an inconvenient direction, devising practical tours that include all the significant sites in one campaign without unduly infringing upon later campaigns required a great deal of study.

The eastern portion of the Civil War Explorer Series will be composed of four books: *Forged in Fire, The Storm Tide, The Killing Time,* and *Into the Valley.* This book, the first in the series, starts with Lincoln's election and carries the war through its first two years. Battles and campaigns include First Manassas, Ball's Bluff, the clash between the *Virginia* and the *Monitor,* the Peninsula campaign, the Seven Days' battles, Second Manassas, and Antietam.

The tours start in Portsmouth, Norfolk, Hampton, and Newport News for the clash of the ironclads, then proceed up the peninsula through Big Bethel, Yorktown, and Williamsburg to the outskirts of Richmond and the battlefield of Seven Pines–Fair Oaks.

An extensive tour follows of the Confederacy's capital and the target of numerous Federal campaigns, Richmond. Examined are the capitol, the White House of the Confederacy, the incredible Tredegar-Valentine Riverside complex, Hollywood Cemetery—where many generals and thousands of enlisted men lie—numerous outstanding museums, and a forest of statues.

Next is a guide to Robert E. Lee's brilliant and savage Seven Days' battles—which includes preserved portions of the battlefields of Mechanicsville, Gaines's Mill, Malvern Hill, and McClellan's refuge at Harrison's

Landing—which then crosses the historic James River to swing north to Drewry's Bluff, where Confederate artillery stopped the Union navy.

From Richmond a long driving tour explores the Second Manassas campaign, first following the route of the Virginia Central Railroad, which funneled tens of thousands of Confederate soldiers to battlefields farther north and supplied Southern armies throughout most of the four years of war. This tour includes Yellow Tavern, where Jeb Stuart was mortally wounded, and Trevilian Station, site of another great cavalry battle, both later events of the Civil War but best included here.

The Orange and Alexandria Railroad is encountered at Gordonsville, a Confederate assembly site, and continues across the famed Rapidan River and past the battlefield of Cedar Mountain to Culpeper, one of Virginia's most frequently occupied cities. The route crosses the Rappahannock River to follow a maze of minor roads that retrace Stonewall Jackson's magnificent flanking movement around John Pope through narrow Thoroughfare Gap to Bristoe Station and Manassas, where the battlefield of Second Manassas will be comprehensively toured.

From Manassas I advise traveling to Alexandria for a tour of that important Civil War port. You may then follow the Federal route through Fairfax and Centreville to the field of First Manassas.

From Manassas we follow Robert E. Lee's invasion route into the North, first following Stonewall's roundabout trail to Chantilly, then north to Dranesville Tavern and Leesburg, where the earlier battle of Ball's Bluff will be examined. The Potomac River is crossed at White's Ferry as we forge past many of the river's historic fords to explore the numerous historic attractions of Frederick, including the battlefield of Monocacy, again a later campaign but best seen on this route. South Mountain is crossed at the three gaps where vastly outnumbered Confederates fought desperately to slow McClellan while Lee gathered his scattered armies, and the tour ends at Boonsboro.

A separate tour explores the events of America's bloodiest day at Antietam—the legendary sites of the Dunker Church, the Cornfield, Bloody Lane, and Burnside's Bridge. From Sharpsburg another tour follows the Union forces that reoccupied Harpers Ferry, where John Brown had rebelled three years earlier and Stonewall had captured a position he had commanded during the first year of the war. The history of Brown and the Civil War legacy of Harpers Ferry are closely examined.

In the remaining volumes of this series, *The Storm Tide* is largely concerned with one year, 1863, and explores the campaigns of Fredericksburg, Chancellorsville, Gettysburg, Bristoe Station, and Mine Run. *The Killing Time* follows Lee and Grant from the spring of 1864 to the end of the war in April 1865. The Shenandoah Valley was so important to the Civil War that we examine that beautiful region in book four, *Into the Valley,* which will include Jackson's Valley campaign of 1862 and the devastating Federal campaigns of 1864.

The tours in each book will take travelers to every significant Civil War battlefield and site in the East, from First Manassas to Appomattox. Extraordinary rivers will be crossed, mountain barriers surmounted, and a great deal of road time consumed. The countryside is beautiful, and the battlefields and monuments are inspiring. These are the routes traveled by the soldiers, and this was the geography that determined the campaigns and battlefields of this war. Although today's journeys are made in great comfort, such was not the case for our forefathers. Their perseverance and bravery are humbling. We honor their sacrifice by remembering them along the way. We also learn a great deal about our past and ourselves, and we will have the adventure of a lifetime.

The history of Virginia is so vast that we will concentrate solely on the Civil War. Throw in the natural beauty and extensive history of the state and adjacent areas, and there are enough attractions to occupy a historic traveler for years.

These tours cover not only developed battlefields operated by the federal and state governments, but also those maintained by city and county governments. They can range from large forts to tiny plots (like Chantilly) and fields marked by isolated monuments (like Cedar Mountain). Dozens of museums and hundreds of statues and monuments are included in these tours. A number of cemeteries—official national cemeteries for the Federal dead and city and battlefield cemeteries where Confederate casualties were concentrated—are pinpointed as well as burial grounds that contain the graves of generals and other Civil War notables. There are many large stone and brick coastal forts (like Monroe, Wool, and Norfolk) and many earthen works protecting river approaches to Washington, Richmond, and several other locations. Courthouses and other public buildings, homes, churches, and commercial structures with a Civil War history are also described.

Many Civil War sites in Virginia, West Virginia, Maryland, and Pennsylvania are open to the public. Visiting hours and fees vary and can change with little or no notice, so call ahead and check Web sites. Many significant Civil War sites are privately owned and closed to the public. Considerate visitors will view such sites from sidewalks or the road. It is very difficult and expensive to maintain historical property, and owners are entitled to their privacy. Do not trespass. Many private homes are open for formal tours around Christmas and during the spring, so watch for announcements.

There are a number of preservation groups raising funds and enlisting public and private support for the preservation and development of important Civil War sites. As a result of their efforts, additional land and structures are continually being added to the protected list. Support these organizations with your money and participation.

It is easy to get lost on rural roads and city streets, so we advise travelers to purchase maps beforehand and to plot out the portions of the tours they wish to travel. I prefer official state county maps for rural areas, and a large *recent* city map will get you through larger communities.

Allow plenty of time for traveling and visiting sites. I always find that the journey is the most rewarding part of an outing. I also habitually underestimate the time necessary to complete a history trip.

Take a partner to read the book's directions and your maps. No driver can safely direct and drive, and besides, you need someone to fight with when you get turned around. Historic routes are often natural travel routes. As a result many historic sites are bisected by major highways. Be very careful exiting and entering these thoroughfares.

Unfortunately, traveling today can be dangerous. The possibility of car jacking, robberies, and assault cannot be dismissed. Be a wary traveler. Develop a strong sense of situational awareness and know what is going on around you. Know where you are at all times. Keep a watch on who is around you. Try to stay in groups. Always lock your car—even historic cemeteries have become dangerous. A cellular phone is a very good companion for long trips. If you are not comfortable in a particular place, keep going.

Having listed these alarming precautions, let me assure you that the vast majority of people you will encounter on these trips are friendly and helpful, glad to help educate a traveler with a thirst for exploring history. I have never felt threatened during my tens of thousands of miles traveling historic routes.

Don't be a slave to these tours. They are completely Civil War oriented, and there are a myriad of historical attractions in Virginia and the other eastern states. Visit the MacArthur Memorial in Norfolk, Colonial Williamsburg, and the homes and museums of Virginia's presidents. These and so many other attractions are widely advertised. If tracing a particular campaign is not of interest to you, drive directly to the battlefields and spend your time there. Follow the campaigns that do interest you.

Forged in Fire covers a huge area geographically because the initial campaigns ranged from Hampton Roads to Alexandria, and from Richmond to Antietam. The early armies covered a lot of ground, and so will we. Enjoy the ride.

FORGED IN FIRE

1

From Fort Sumter to the Battle of First Manassas

FOLLOWING ABRAHAM LINCOLN'S ELECTION to the presidency of the United States on November 6, 1860, South Carolina seceded on December 20. On the day following Christmas, Maj. Robert Anderson abandoned Charleston's vulnerable Fort Moultrie and occupied Fort Sumter in the center of the harbor. On December 30 President James Buchanan refused to surrender the fort to South Carolina authorities. After being fired on, a relief ship, *Star of the West,* turned back on January 9, the same day Mississippi left the Union, followed a day later by Florida and Alabama. A call went out for an alliance of the fourteen slave states, and a convention was arranged to meet in Montgomery, Alabama, on February 4. Georgia joined her sister states on January 19, with Louisiana leaving the Union on January 26 and Texas on February 1. On January 21 Southern senators and congressmen delivered their farewell addresses to the Congress.

Seceded states soon began seizing U.S. forts and arsenals throughout the South. When seventy-one-year-old Bvt. Maj. Gen. David E. Twiggs, one of the four highest ranking officers in the U.S. Army, surrendered all military facilities in Texas, he was dismissed as a traitor, which prompted him to challenge President Buchanan to a duel.

By February 8, delegates in Montgomery had passed the Provisional Constitution of the Confederate States of America and turned to the selection of a president. Two leading candidates, Howell Cobb and Robert Toombs, both from the vital state of Georgia, had political enemies, and Toombs had gotten drunk at the convention. The members chose Jefferson Davis of Mississippi, a West Point graduate and former secretary of war who would have preferred to lead the Confederacy's armies, but he accepted this responsibility. In March, Davis called for one hundred thousand men to

When a lone Republican arrived at nearby Fairfax County Courthouse to vote for Lincoln in 1860, he was seized by citizens, coated with printer's ink, and sent home.

15

create a Confederate army, but added that the new nation wanted peace and would fight only if attacked.

Taking his own oath of office on March 3, Lincoln also stated a desire for peace; however, he contended that the Union was still whole. "In your hands, my dissatisfied fellow-countrymen," the president said, "and not in mine is the momentous issue of civil war."

Lincoln determined to supply Fort Sumter rather than send reinforcements and so informed South Carolina Gov. Francis Pickens, who relayed the message to Davis and the local Confederate commander, Brig. Gen. P. G. T. Beauregard, a Louisianan with considerable ambition and ego, who commanded nearly fifty cannon and six thousand troops in Charleston.

Meeting on April 9, every member of the Confederate cabinet save one advised that Fort Sumter be attacked. A day later Beauregard issued Anderson an ultimatum demanding his surrender. The Union commander's reply promised surrender on April 15 with certain conditions. For example, should he be resupplied, the fort would not capitulate. Accepting this reply as less than concrete, Beauregard opened fire at 4:30 A.M. on April 12. Although Union supply ships arrived at the mouth of Charleston Harbor, they refused to venture into the gunfire. Out of food and gunpowder, Anderson surrendered on April 13 after a thirty-four-hour bombardment. The garrison was allowed to evacuate honorably. Not a man on either side had

The Great Emancipator ■ Abraham Lincoln

Born in Kentucky in 1809, Abraham Lincoln was raised at various places there and in Indiana. After self-educating himself and holding a series of jobs, he won election to the Illinois legislature and became a lawyer in 1836. A U.S. representative for the Whig Party during the Mexican War, Lincoln opposed the conflict. He became a Republican in 1858 and ran for the chair in the U.S. Senate then occupied by Stephen A. Douglas. A series of highly publicized debates made Lincoln a national figure. He won the popular vote in the election, but the Illinois legislature sent Douglas back to Washington.

At the Republican Convention in 1860, Lincoln won the party's nomination for president after his managers worked a deal that would make rival Simon Cameron secretary of war. Opposing Lincoln was

Stephen Douglas for the Northern Democrats, former vice president John C. Breckinridge for the Southern Democrats, and John Bell for the National Constitutional Union Party. Although banned from most southern ballots, Lincoln won the majority of the electoral votes.

Before the new president was inaugurated, a number of southern states seceded and formed the Confederacy. Lincoln insisted secession was illegal and took a conciliatory stance toward the South. He refused to surrender Fort Sumter, and after it was captured he called for seventy-five thousand volunteers to put down the rebellion, a move that led other states to secede.

Lincoln conducted an effective war, slowly but steadily conquering large portions of the South. He persisted in changing generals until he discovered

effective ones and greatly expanded the nation's war-making ability. Lincoln managed to prevent foreign governments from interceding in the war, particularly with the Emancipation Proclamation, which changed the focus of the war from Southern independence to slavery. Critics accused Lincoln of suspending civil liberties and the writ of habeas corpus, resulting in the illegal imprisonment of opponents, but his actions managed to keep the North unified.

In 1864 Lincoln overcame a challenge by the Radical Republicans (through John C. Frémont) and defeated the Democratic challenger, former Union army commander George B. McClellan. He pressed the war to a successful conclusion just a few months later. After Richmond was evacuated in early April 1865, Lincoln toured the city. On April 14,

while attending the play *Our American Cousin* with his wife, Mary, at Ford's Theatre, the president was mortally wounded by John Wilkes Booth. Lincoln died the following morning, the first American president to be assassinated. He is buried in Springfield, Illinois.

The Confederate flag was raised over Fort Sumter (left) after the surrender by Robert W. Anderson. The officers of the garrison (right—front row, left to right, Abner Doubleday, Anderson, Samuel W. Crawford, John G. Foster; standing, left to right, Truman Seymour, George W. Snyder, Jefferson C. Davis, Richard K. Meade, and Theodore Talbot) were photographed by Charleston cameraman George Cook two months before the bombardment. Six of the nine men would be generals by the end of the war, and one would resign from the army to fight for the South.

been killed during the shelling; the only casualty occurred during a gun salute to the fort's flag as the garrison prepared to depart.

Following Sumter's surrender, the nation was consumed by a war frenzy. Large spontaneous public demonstrations and loud posturing resulted as harsh recriminations flew. The *New York Times* expressed the desire "to conquer, to subjugate" the Southern states. In Montgomery, Confederate Secretary of War Leroy P. Walker proclaimed that the new nation's flag would fly over the Capitol in Washington "before the first of May."

The leaders allowed for the possibility of reconciliation. "Separation is not, of necessity, final," Jefferson Davis stated. His counterpart Lincoln sincerely desired "that our present difficulties might be settled. I will not say that all hope is yet gone." Lincoln considered the United States indissoluble and felt compelled to fight to preserve it. Davis, however, accepting the absolute right of secession, concluded, "All we ask is to be left alone." This Lincoln could not allow. Convinced the Union of American states could not be broken up, Lincoln resolved to use force to reunite his beloved nation.

Both sides were convinced that the affair would be decided in one great battle, a gallant clash of knights that would produce great glory but little bloodshed.

On April 16 Lincoln issued a call for seventy-five thousand volunteers to serve for three months "in order to suppress" the revolt in seven Southern states "and cause the laws to be duly executed." The president then asked loyal Americans to support his attempt to "maintain the honor, the integrity, and the existence of our Noble Union."

Green troops drilled in camps that were quickly established in answer to the call for men issued by both North and South.

Lincoln allowed the states of the Confederacy twenty days to disband their forces. Unstated was the threat of military action to crush the rebellion. On April 20 Lincoln declared a blockade of Southern ports, a decidedly aggressive move.

Northern response was a grand show of patriotic fervor that united the region and quickly surpassed the requested number of volunteers. The South responded as well, but with outrage and defiance. Chances of peace dissolved as Southern men flocked to join military units to protect their homes from naked Northern aggression.

Three border states—Kentucky, Missouri, and Maryland—refused to furnish men for Lincoln's program. Not only did a state convention in Richmond pass an ordinance of secession on April 17, but on the following day Virginia Gov. John Letcher dispatched a company of militia commanded by Capt. Ashby Turner to seize the U.S. Arsenal at Harpers Ferry.

Harpers Ferry was indefensible, surrounded by ridges from which an enemy could shell the position at will. The small Federal garrison there torched fifteen thousand firearms and fled across the Potomac River to Maryland. The damage was poorly done, for Virginia found five thousand usable rifles, intact machinery for making more, and considerable parts for just that purpose. Harpers Ferry would change hands many times over the next four years.

Another vital establishment in Virginia was the Gosport Navy Yard outside Norfolk. Its Federal commander, Como. Charles S. McCauley, was old and distressed by the circumstances. When informed that state troops were near, he sortied only three ships ready for sea and ordered that the remainder be burned or scuttled. These vessels settled on the bottom of the Elizabeth River, but one would still prove useful to the Confederacy. As a Richmond newspaper claimed, "We have material enough to build a Navy of iron-plated ships."

Most of the yard's facilities were undamaged—a welcome gift to a region with few shipbuilding or maintenance resources. Also seized were more than one thousand heavy cannon that would soon reinforce shore defenses all across the Confederacy.

If aggression were to occur, Virginia was the obvious theater of conflict. Thousands of Southern men joined local companies that were mated to regiments and trained in their states, then shipped rapidly up the rails to the Old Dominion. John B. Jones, a newspaperman in Richmond, thought twenty-five thousand men would appear in a week, but two days later he altered his estimate to fifty thousand. "Martial music is heard everywhere, day and night," he declared, "and all the trappings and paraphernalia of war's decorations are in great demand."

The Confederacy's Only President ■ Jefferson Davis

Born in Kentucky in 1808, Jefferson Davis attended West Point, graduating in 1828. He spent five years in service before retiring and marrying the daughter of Zachary Taylor, his commander. Shortly after he assumed the life of a Louisiana planter, his wife died, as almost did he, of yellow fever. He later married Varina Howell. Entering politics, Davis became a U.S. Representative. During the war with Mexico he led the First Mississippi to distinction, but rejected the rank of brigadier general

LIBRARY OF CONGRESS

to return to civilian life. Davis was elected to the U.S. Senate, then became Franklin Pierce's secretary of war before returning to the Senate. A strong supporter of states' rights and secession, he resigned his seat on January 2, 1861, at Mississippi's secession, and made one last powerful speech.

Davis became Mississippi's military commander with the rank of major general. When problems developed at the Montgomery Convention, he became the compromise candidate for provisional president on February 9, 1861, and was inaugurated on February 18. Davis won a six-year term as the Confederacy's president in November 1861 and was again sworn into office, this time on George Washington's birthday near the great equestrian statue on the grounds of the Virginia capitol.

It was no secret that Davis would have preferred a military commission to his political situation. As a result, he constantly meddled in military affairs, ignoring his several secretaries of war and creating considerable friction with army leaders. Davis

reached First Manassas as the battle ended and arrived at Seven Pines while the combat was ongiong. At Mechanicsville, Lee all but ordered him off the field.

Davis openly battled with several of his highest-ranking generals, most notably Joseph E. Johnston and P. G. T. Beauregard. He consistently defended several poor field commanders, most notably western commanders Braxton Bragg, John Pemberton, and John Bell Hood, which led to grave Confederate reverses.

Davis fared as badly with the Confederacy's politicians. The Confederate Congress, particularly the Senate, opposed what were seen as Davis's attempts to force his will upon the government. State governors, including Zebulon Vance of North Carolina and Joseph Brown of Georgia, opposed Davis's efforts to concentrate power in the national government. Supporters of states' rights bedeviled the president more than any Northern general.

After four long years of struggle, Richmond fell on April 3, 1865, and Davis attempted to escape with his

family to the Trans-Mississippi, where he hoped to continue the war. Captured on May 10 near Irwinville, Georgia, he began a two-year imprisonment. His initial shackling and close imprisonment in Fort Monroe generated a wave of sympathy not only in the South but around the world. Although at the close of the war Davis had been widely despised across the Confederacy, he emerged from confinement in 1867 as a revered figure.

The former Confederate president engaged in the insurance business in Memphis before choosing a retirement home, Beauvoir, on the Mississippi coast. There he wrote *The Rise and Fall of the Confederate Government,* published in 1881, in which he resumed fighting the Civil War. This was a bitter war of words in which he blamed Johnston, Beauregard, and others for the Confederacy's defeat. Unlike many former Confederates, Davis never attempted to regain his U.S. citizenship. He died in 1889 and was buried in New Orleans. Three years later Davis was reinterred in Richmond's Hollywood Cemetery.

Capt. Edward Porter Alexander was infuriated by the quality of soldiers he was assigned to build his observation towers. "Some of them are so stupid that I have to knock them down & jump on them & stamp & pound them before I can get an idea into their heads," he swore.

By April 29, sixty-two thousand Southerners had completed their military training and fifteen thousand were en route to Virginia. The Confederates were so united that Davis claimed there could not "be a reasonable doubt of our final success." If the North attacked, he concluded, Confederates would "struggle for our inherent right to freedom, independence, and self-government."

Tennessee allied itself with Confederate ranks on May 1 and seceded June 8. Arkansas joined the Southern union on May 6. Last was North Carolina, which seceded on May 6. By May 29 the Confederacy had relocated its capital from distant Montgomery to Richmond to be closer to the scene of anticipated military activity and to display its support for the rich and populous Virginia

The North was also preparing for the conflict. Within weeks of the capitulation of Fort Sumter, Washington was alive with activity. Every street was barricaded, and constantly mutating rumors had hosts of Confederates approaching to seize the capital. The city of 60,000 was defended by only 1,000 of the country's 13,000 regular army soldiers, who were spread thinly across the country (primarily in Indian territory) and by 1,500 militia, many of them Southern sympathizers.

Lucius C. Chittenden arrived from Vermont to accept his position of register of the treasury to find the stoutly built Treasury Building being fortified and clerks receiving rifles and ammunition. Lincoln and his cabinet were to gather there in case of attack.

Washington, only ten miles square, was isolated from the Northern states. The city faced Virginia across the Potomac River, and the other three sides were surrounded by Maryland, an ostensibly neutral border state. Should Maryland secede, the capital of the United States—its heart, soul, and brain—would be untenable.

South Carolina's militias invested every fortification along the state's coast, including Charleston's Castle Pinckney.

BATTLES AND LEADERS

From the Northern camps, the troops marched to demarcation points that led to Washington, a city fearful of the sudden arrival of a Southern army.

Lincoln doubted Maryland's loyalty. In the recent election only 3,000 of 92,000 votes cast there were for him. The strategic city of Baltimore gave barely 1,000 of 31,000 ballots for the president. Economics bound the state to the South and sentiment for secession ran deep in some sectors, particularly in Baltimore. Nevertheless, there is a great gulf between an election and secession. Many citizens supported the Union, including Gov. Thomas H. Hicks.

Responding to Lincoln's original call for troops, Pennsylvania had dispatched several hundred poorly trained soldiers to Washington. They encountered trouble in Baltimore in the form of showers of rocks and verbal abuse by hostile mobs. But Lincoln needed more men—and quickly.

The solution was in Massachusetts where Brig. Gen. Benjamin F. Butler, until lately a politically connected lawyer, had drilled four regiments for several months. Receiving orders to move south, he dispatched two regiments to hold Fort Monroe, which commanded strategic Hampton Roads. Leaving one regiment in Boston to complete training, Butler sent the Sixth Massachusetts under Col. Edward F. Jones toward Washington. They arrived in New York City via rail on April 18 to a grand reception. Thousands of spectators cheered wildly as the men paraded down Broadway to a decidedly unmilitary meal at the Astor Hotel. Reaching Philadelphia the following morning, Colonel Jones learned of the Pennsylvania troops' ordeal in Baltimore and issued ammunition to his eight hundred soldiers.

While Alexandria was a hotbed of secession—only 106 of 1,089 voters had rejected Virginia's ordinance—Robert E. Lee was apparently not one of them. A pharmacist remembered Lee's comment that he was "one of those dull creatures that cannot see the good of secession."

Baltimore had a transportation problem normal for this era. The Philadelphia, Wilmington, and Baltimore Railroad from the north terminated at President Street Station. From there railcars were hitched to teams of horses and hauled through the city to Camden Street Station, where the rails of the Baltimore and Ohio Railroad led south and east.

The first seven cars filled with armed and alert Union soldiers peacefully made the transition, but a mob of eight thousand citizens stopped the final three cars at Pratt Street. The troops were forced to disembark and march through the jeering, hostile crowd. Oaths gave way to bricks, stones, and clubs, and the more militant wrestled soldiers for their rifles.

Suddenly civilians started firing pistols into the troops, killing one. An officer ordered his men to fire on the mob, an action that opened an avenue of escape. When the troops reached Colonel Jones at Camden Street Station, he deployed to attack the crowd. Other officers convinced him to board the train instead, and they were soon in Washington. Lincoln met

The Beast ■ Benjamin Franklin Butler

Born in Deerfield, New Hampshire, on November 5, 1818, Benjamin Franklin Butler spent most of his life in Lowell, Massachusetts. Short and aggressive, Butler attended Colby College in Maine, graduating in 1838. He taught in Lowell, then studied law and practiced in Lowell and Boston. He was elected to the Massachusetts house in 1853 and the state senate in 1859. As a delegate to the 1860 Democratic Convention in Charleston, he cast fifty-seven consecutive votes for the nomination of Jefferson Davis for president of the United States. When southerners walked out, Butler joined them. When they met again in Baltimore, he helped nominate John C. Breckinridge.

Despite these apparent leanings toward the South and states' rights, Butler became a brigadier of Massachusetts militia. A week before Fort Sumter was fired on, civil disturbances in Baltimore wrecked the railroad and isolated Washington, D.C., from the North. Butler embarked his Eighth Massachusetts in Philadelphia and steamed for Annapolis, where it boarded trains to relieve what was a

virtual siege of the U.S. capital. He then outmaneuvered Confederate sympathizers by seizing Fort Hill, which commanded Baltimore, and held Maryland for the Union, an unauthorized move that won him brief censure.

Butler's amateur military career was off to a surprisingly good start. In appreciation for his service, Abraham Lincoln appointed him a major general on May 16, 1861. From his post at Fort Monroe, Butler was beaten at the battle of Big Bethel, then coined the term "contrabands of war" to label slaves who entered the Union lines. As they were the property of Secessionists, he argued, the government was entitled to seize, protect, and care for them and utilize their labor. In August, Butler organized the successful movement to Hatteras, North Carolina, which established a Federal base on the Confederate Atlantic coast.

On May 1, 1862, after returning to New England to recruit troops, Butler officially took command as military governor of occupied New Orleans. He became immediately

embroiled in controversy by hanging William Mumford for desecrating a U.S. flag. Then, angered that local ladies were demonstrating their contempt for the occupiers by such acts as dumping chamber pots from upper windows onto them, Butler issued the infamous "Woman's Order," which branded females who committed such acts as prostitutes. Jefferson Davis called him an "outlaw," and Southerners referred to him as "Beast Butler."

Butler's administration was effective but corrupt. Family and friends profited enormously, earning him another nickname, "Spoons," for his alleged habit of appropriating any silver in sight. He was relieved in December 1862 by Nathaniel Banks.

In 1864 Butler was given two corps, called the Army of the James, which was to operate in conjunction with Ulysses S. Grant's grand design to destroy Robert E. Lee. While Grant sidestepped to Petersburg, Butler was to drive from the flank and take Petersburg. Instead, a handful of soldiers under P. G. T. Beauregard bottled him up at Bermuda Hundred.

Butler entered Congress in 1866 as a leading Radical Republican, advocating severe punishment for men such as Jefferson Davis, his former comrade, for their part in the rebellion. He helped impeach President Andrew Johnson, who was almost turned out of office. Butler left the House in 1875 but returned in 1878 in his third political incarnation—as a member of the Greenback Party. He was its presidential candidate in 1884 and was elected governor of Massachusetts in 1886. Butler died on January 11, 1893, and is buried in Lowell.

The route to Washington led through Baltimore, a city with strong Southern sympathies, which was occupied by Northern troops to protect the capital's lifeline of troops and supplies.

Jones at the station, saying, "Thank God you have come," as he wrung the colonel's hand. Jones had lost three killed, twenty hurt, and several missing. Twelve civilians had been killed.

To prevent the Federal government from using its territory for hostile purposes again, the people of Maryland concluded that they should destroy the four railroad bridges leading into Baltimore. After this was accomplished, Washington authorities quickly devised a new route. The Seventh New York and Rhode Island troops would be shipped south to Annapolis, twenty miles south of Baltimore, and march forty miles to the capital.

Southern sympathizers in Maryland objected to this route. They sent a delegation, including Maj. George W. Brown and police marshal George P. Kane, to protest the transportation of any additional Federal troops through their neutral state.

"I *must* have troops for the defense of the capital," Lincoln told the group. "Our men are not moles and can't dig under the earth; they are not birds and can't fly through the air. There is no way but to march them across, and that they must do. Keep your rowdies in Baltimore and there will be no bloodshed." The last comment was an acknowledgment that he had lost control of Baltimore.

The new route, while more reliable, was frustratingly slow. As the days stretched out, Lincoln paced and muttered, "Why don't they come? Why don't they come?"

Calming Lincoln was General in Chief Winfield Scott. The seventy-five-year-old Mexican War hero had served in the army for fifty-three years, twenty as the country's highest-ranking officer. Despite his being in poor health, he steadily prepared Washington's defenses, planned future strategy, and was confident of ultimate success. He raised several local military units, including one composed of older citizens called the Silver Grays.

As Washington seemed threatened from south and north alike, the trickle of Southerners resigning from the army became a torrent. Over 300 West Point–trained officers—one-third of the country's military leadership, including brilliant men such as P. G. T. Beauregard and Joseph E. Johnston—decided to follow their conscience and fight for their home states. The navy lost almost as heavily—373 of 1,554.

Scott had favored Robert E. Lee for twenty years, since Lee had served as an engineer on the general's staff in Mexico. Scott and Lincoln agreed that Lee should command the Union armies, and on April 18 Lee

Helping repair the railroad bridges damaged by Secessionists in Maryland was a young Scottish immigrant named Andrew Carnegie.

Irwin McDowell did not smoke, drink, or use caffeinated beverages, but he did eat. "At dinner he was such a Gargantuan feeder and so absorbed in the dishes before him that he had but little time for conversation," an officer wrote. "While he drank neither wine nor spirits, he fairly gobbled the larger part of every dish within reach, and wound up with an entire watermelon, which he said was 'monstrous fine!'"

McDowell was determined that the Union army would not abuse private property. After Mrs. Robert E. Lee wrote him on May 30, 1861, to protest his use of her ancestral home, he promptly answered that he used a tent and not the mansion. Further, he established a military commission to prosecute those who damaged private property. His command was not to search houses without specific orders, nor were soldiers to arrest Southern sympathizers without cause. He instructed officers to document structures occupied, crops and other property destroyed, and land appropriated for camps and forts. Citizens had the right to apply for restitution. This "civil" Civil War would not last long.

received the offer. Lee regarded secession "as anarchy" and expressed a willingness to sacrifice every slave to preserve the Union, but he declined this opportunity, asking, "How can I draw my sword upon Virginia, my native state?" He retired to his home, Arlington House, within sight of the Capitol across the Potomac, in peace, he hoped, vowing "save in defense will draw my sword on none."

At their parting Scott said, "Lee, you have made the greatest mistake of your life, but I feared it would be so." Scott had previously told a Virginia delegation, come to discuss his own anticipated resignation: "I have served my country, under the flag of the Union, for more than fifty years, and so long as God permits me to live, I will defend that flag with my sword, even if my own native state assails it."

Scott was branded a traitor in the South. The family of another Virginian who remained with the Union, George H. Thomas (who later distinguished himself at Chickamauga and Nashville), turned his portrait to the wall and never mentioned his name again.

Secessionists in Baltimore continued to grow stronger and bolder, a situation that enraged Benjamin Butler. From Philadelphia on April 20, Butler and the Eighth Massachusetts entrained for Perryville where they boarded a ferry on the Susquehanna River and steamed for Annapolis. Butler intended to use the Annapolis and Elk Ridge Railroad to intersect the Baltimore and Ohio south of Baltimore at Annapolis Junction, but he had to first repair an ancient locomotive (Secessionists had removed all working engines to Baltimore) and repair the tracks.

On April 25 Scott issued a proclamation stating that an attack on Washington "may be expected at any moment." Instead Butler arrived, an event accompanied by gleeful celebration from troops and residents alike. Lincoln "smiled all over," an aide noted. Baltimore had been bypassed and up to fifteen thousand soldiers a day reached Washington.

To escape the influence of Secessionists in Baltimore, Governor Hicks convened the state legislature in Frederick, fifty miles west of Baltimore and eighteen miles from Harpers Ferry on the Baltimore and Ohio Railroad and athwart the route to the vital Shenandoah Valley.

Scott planned to secure the route by seizing Relay House, a railroad junction eight miles from Baltimore. Reinforcements were also dispatched to Fort McHenry and another position commanding the city, Fort Morris. Work crews would rebuild the demolished railroad bridges, and Lincoln suspended the writ of habeas corpus along the route and permitted preventive arrests.

With the Sixth Massachusetts, Butler occupied Relay House on May 5 without difficulty and fortified the position. Then, without orders, he decided to seize Baltimore as well. On May 13 he sent a train to Frederick and arrested several Secessionists as a feint. The train then reversed direction back through Relay House and on to Baltimore. A raging storm covered the arrival at Camden Street Station, and at dawn the citizens awoke to spot one thousand soldiers and artillery frowning down at the city from Federal Hill, which overlooked the harbor. For this daring success Butler was reprimanded for the unauthorized maneuver and removed from command.

During the crisis, Scott had formulated a strategy for winning the war. It combined Lincoln's blockade, which would eliminate the South's export of cotton and the importation of European weapons, with a thrust down the Mississippi River to divide the Confederacy.

James Jackson, who killed Elmer Ellsworth for removing a Confederate flag from his hotel, possessed a relic of John Brown's Harpers Ferry raid: part of an ear severed from one of the raiders.

The First Union Martyr ■ Elmer Ellsworth

Elmer E. Ellsworth had organized a militia unit in Chicago in 1860 and outfitted it with red baggy-trousered uniforms (one of many units that imitated the colorful French Zouaves that had fought in the Crimean War). Strenuous practice transformed them into America's premier drill team, displaying hundreds of precision moves with their bayoneted muskets.

Known as the U.S. Zouaves Cadets, the unit toured American cities during the summer of 1860, challenging all militia outfits to drill battle. The resulting publicity made Ellsworth the darling of the nation, including Lincoln, who considered him "the greatest little man I ever met."

After Ellsworth campaigned for Lincoln in the 1860 election, the president-elect picked the young celebrity to accompany him to Washington for the inauguration, a journey that, considering the mood in the country, was fraught with danger. While serving as Lincoln's bodyguard and confidant, Ellsworth caught the measles from Willie and Tad, the president's young sons.

When war broke out, Ellsworth raised a volunteer regiment from New York City's Fire Department. "I want men who can go into a fight now," he wrote on April 17, 1861. Within two weeks his Fire Zouaves were in Washington. Learning that an assault force was being prepared to seize Alexandria and the Virginia side of the Potomac River the moment Virginia seceded, Ellsworth wrangled the role of shock troops for his regiment.

Virginia left the Union on May 23, and early the next morning Ellsworth landed from a steamer on the docks of Alexandria, dressed in a handsome new uniform with a gold medal penned to his chest with the Latin inscription "Nor for ourselves alone but for country." Confederate forces, forewarned and ordered not to fight, withdrew immediately.

Ellsworth sent a company to secure the railroad station while he and a few men started up King Street to seize the telegraph office. Spotting a large Confederate flag waving from the Marshall House hotel, Ellsworth, with Cpl. Francis E. Brownell and correspondent Edward H. House, ran up to the fourth floor and cut it down. Returning downstairs, they encountered the inn's owner, James W. Jackson, armed with a double-barreled shotgun. Brownell deflected the barrel with his musket, but Jackson's shot hit Ellsworth full in the chest, ruining the splendid uniform and driving the gold medal deep into his chest.

"He dropped forward with the heavy, horrible headlong weight which always comes with sudden death," House wrote.

Jackson emptied the second barrel at Brownell, but it missed as the corporal fired into the innkeeper's face then bayoneted the body, which tumbled down the stairs.

Ellsworth was the first Union officer killed in the war and became a martyr to the North while Jackson became a martyr to the South. Hundreds of thousands would follow, but Ellsworth's death shocked the North. "My boy! My boy!" Lincoln exclaimed when he viewed the body. "Was it necessary that this sacrifice be made?"

LESLIE'S

Ellsworth's body lay in state at the White House on May 25, 1861, and the cabinet and other noted political and military leaders attended the funeral. A second ceremony was held at city hall in New York City, where thousands gathered. Ellsworth was buried in his hometown, Mechanicsville, New York, on the banks of the Hudson River.

The young man was lionized in the North, his name given to babies, towns, and streets. Songs and poems were written to honor him, and many editorials, sermons, and speeches featured the officer. The slogan Remember Fort Sumter! was supplanted by Remember Ellsworth! Enlistments soared, particularly in the many Zouave regiments that were immediately popular. Ellsworth's slug-torn jacket toured the North, and photos of Brownell (promoted to second lieutenant) standing on the Confederate flag taken from the inn sold well.

LESLIE'S

Virginia's Other Government

In August 1863 the head of Virginia's Restored Government, Francis H. Pierpont, arrived in Alexandria. He had been in charge of West Virginia, which became a state in June. Pierpont had been provisional governor of Union Virginia, representing areas such as Alexandria and Hampton Roads, which were under Federal control. His "general assembly" met in the Alexandria city council chamber. Although they abolished slavery, the body and its governor had no power.

The plan was immediately assailed and ridiculed by the impatient public, particularly newspaper editors, who demanded a quick, massive invasion of Virginia. The North would come to realize that this plan, the only one proposed by an experienced military professional, would not only work, but was the only feasible option available to quash the rebellion.

On May 6 Jefferson Davis appointed Robert E. Lee as his chief military adviser. Together they decided that P. G. T. Beauregard, a Southern hero for his reduction of Fort Sumter, would command the army being concentrated around Manassas Junction, an important point south of the Union capital where the Orange and Alexandria Railroad, which connected Washington and Richmond via Gordonsville, intersected the Manassas Gap Railroad, which led across the Bull Run Mountains at Thoroughfare Gap and the Blue Ridge Mountains at Manassas Gap to the rich Shenandoah Valley. His force would initially be known as the Army of the Potomac. Beauregard, appointed on May 31, arrived the following day and immediately applied his engineering skills to defending the junction.

Davis and Lee also appointed fifty-three-year-old Maj. Gen. Joseph E. Johnston to command an army massing in the Shenandoah Valley to protect Virginia's western border. Beauregard and Johnston were separated by

Alexandria

Alexandria suffered great damage during its four-year occupation. Homes and other structures were sacrificed for the construction of extensive fortifications, and the land was denuded of trees cut for the forts and fuel. Prices soared, newspapers were censored, and a pass system was rigidly enforced. The biggest commercial enterprises were taverns. Soldiers were everywhere, often drunk and unruly, particularly following the defeats at First and Second Manassas. The crime rate soared, and murders and robbery became common occurrences. After a newspaper criticized the arrest of a minister for failing to offer the official prayer for Lincoln, its office was burned, one of many arson fires that plagued the city. During the winter of 1862, twenty-two prominent citizens were arrested.

By mid-1862 Alexandria, the terminus of the Orange and Alexandria Railroad and a major Potomac River port, had become a supply and hospital center. Facilities for thirty locomotives were built at the O&A depot. Wounded arriving from the battlefields of northern Virginia in 450 wagons were cared for in warehouses, homes, commercial buildings, and four churches. The initial fourteen general hospitals, the largest with five hundred beds, was later increased to twenty-six.

Low morale among Union soldiers created a disgraceful desertion rate, and many of them wound up in Alexandria. From October until December 1862, thirty thousand stragglers were rounded up into camps established there.

The threat of cavalry raids, particularly later in the war by John S. Mosby, forced the Federals to construct a number of wooden stockades around depots and other vital sites. Forests were leveled for timber

needed in the fortifications and to create abatis.

Civilians attempting to make money by smuggling liquor to Union troops were a constant problem. The wharf and Long Bridge, leading to Washington, D.C., were constantly watched. Bottles of wine were found in the supposed coffins of dead soldiers, and three "fat" women were found to have twenty-three canteens, fifteen bottles, and one jug hidden beneath their skirts. They admitted that it was their fourth trip.

City services ceased, leading to filthy conditions that bred epidemics of typhoid fever, diphtheria, and smallpox.

Like Harpers Ferry to the west, Alexandria became a refuge for escaped slaves. More than seven thousand contrabands entered the Union lines here.

An ammunition magazine exploded on June 9, 1863, killing twenty-three soldiers, including one man who was blown fifty yards away.

US ARMY MILITARY HISTORY INSTITUTE

Forts were constructed in Alexandria and Arlington to protect the Union capital at Washington, D.C. By the end of the war sixty enclosed forts completed the ring of iron around the city. This battery at Arlington's Fort C. F. Smith was manned by Company F, Second New York Artillery.

fifty miles and the Blue Ridge Mountains, but they could rapidly reinforce each other via the Manassas Gap Railroad.

In Washington, Lincoln and Scott created a military department that included Washington, Pennsylvania, Maryland, and Delaware. In command they placed sixty-eight-year-old Maj. Gen. Robert Patterson, a colleague of Scott's from the Mexican War. The pressure this placed on him soon led to his replacement by fifty-eight-year-old Col. Joseph K. F. Mansfield.

The choice for a field general was also a problem. Scott and three other regular army generals were too old and infirm to campaign vigorously. Influential Ohio Gov. William Dennison lobbied for two of his state's favorites. His first choice, George B. McClellan, quickly rose from major general of state militia to major general in the regular army and was placed in command of the Middle West. Dennison also pushed forty-two-year-old Acting Maj. Irwin McDowell, who was promoted to brigadier and made top field commander in the East. His thirty-thousand-man army was being marshaled around Washington.

These moves were made none too soon, for on May 23 Virginia's voters ratified the ordinance of secession, and that important state joined the Confederacy. Scott and Mansfield reacted with decisive and immediate action. At 2 A.M. on the following morning they sent eleven regiments across the Potomac River to seize a buffer zone in Virginia.

The first column, composed of three New York regiments, crossed upstream of Washington on a road laid atop the Potomac Aqueduct that connected Georgetown with Arlington. It advanced two miles to sever the Loudoun and Hampshire Railroad that ran from Alexandria to Leesburg.

Two columns crossed on the Long Bridge from Washington to Arlington. One column, under Maj. Gen. Charles Sandford, a New York militiaman, occupied Arlington Heights, which Confederates had used to observe activity in the capital itself, and advanced to the Columbia turnpike. Sandford established the headquarters for the defense of Washington in Arlington House, the Custis-Lee mansion.

The final column, led by Col. Orlando B. Willcox, turned south from Long Bridge to capture Alexandria with the First Michigan. The Eleventh New York Zouaves under Col. Elmer Ellsworth were to land at Alexandria on three steamers escorted by the warship *Pawnee* in order to trap seven hundred Confederate militia guarding the city. An officer from the *Pawnee,* however, allowed the Confederate force, under Col. A. S. Taylor,

The Confederates in Alexandria had little choice but to withdraw when the first Federals arrived. Due to supply problems, they had but two rounds of ammunition each.

During the Civil War, 530 million pounds of coal, 412 million pounds of oats, 412 million pounds of hay, and 81 million pounds of corn passed through Alexandria.

The Marshall House hotel in Alexandria was the scene of Elmer Ellsworth's death.

Federals frequently complained of the quality of medical care they received in Alexandria. One drunken doctor was fired but simply began "a fresh career of cutting off your wrong leg," complained one woman.

A Federal chaplain wrote thirty letters a day for wounded soldiers and mailed thirteen hundred letters in a year. He described one "slightly wounded" soldier who told the folks back home that he had bones poking out of every part of his body before the surgery that pulled him through. With a straight face the chaplain asked, "But shan't I add that you are better now?"

No, was the reply, "That's not important."

an unauthorized truce that enabled it to withdraw. They marched out one end of town to entrain on the Orange and Alexandria Railroad while Federal troops entered the opposite side of the city. Only thirty-five Confederate cavalrymen were captured. Ellsworth was killed by the innkeeper of the Marshall House after the regimental commander removed a Confederate flag from the inn's roof.

On the following day Union troops began erecting what would become the world's most extensive system of fortifications to protect Washington, D.C., a city trapped by geography in a hostile land.

Skirmishes soon erupted all across northern Virginia. In late May, Federals attacked Confederate batteries on Aquia Creek. A cavalry clash took place near Fairfax Court House on June 1. A Union probe through Falls Church to Vienna on June 17 was driven off by the First South Carolina.

Virginia was vulnerable not only from attack in the north, but also from the east and west. To the west, threats could come from over the Allegheny Mountains, originating in Ohio and Pennsylvania, into the Shenandoah Valley. To the east were hundreds of miles of lightly defended waterways.

The tidewater region of Virginia's long eastern coast is dominated by Chesapeake Bay. It is fed by four great rivers—the Potomac, Rappahannock, York, and James—which form three long peninsulas. To Virginians *the* peninsula was the historic one between the James and the York, which leads directly to Richmond, sixty miles distant.

In the meantime, Benjamin Butler was quickly back in favor. The public and newspapers alike lauded his accomplishments in Maryland, and Secretary of War Simon Cameron and Secretary of the Treasury Samuel Chase admired him. Butler's politics also carried considerable weight. He was an influential Democrat who had strongly supported the Republican Lincoln.

Against his will, Scott reinstated Butler and gave him the Department of Virginia and North Carolina with headquarters at the tip of the peninsula at Fort Monroe, which the Massachusetts general had earlier reinforced. The installation was safely isolated from the mainland and presented a base for land operations on the peninsula. The site also threatened Confederate use of the James and York Rivers and Chesapeake Bay.

Butler arrived at his new assignment on May 22 to find two thousand men, who were quickly reinforced to seventy-five hundred. He immediately occupied nearby Newport News without bloodshed, then chaffed under Scott's admonition to advance no farther.

Confederate headquarters on the peninsula was eighteen miles north at historic Yorktown on the York River and was under the command of the colorful fifty-one-year-old Brig. Gen. John B. Magruder, who had won three commendations in Mexico. To establish a forward base he sent fourteen hundred of his twenty-five hundred troops—the First North Carolina under Col. Daniel Harvey Hill, another Mexican War standout—to the village of Big Bethel at Marsh Creek, only eight miles northeast of Fort Monroe.

Hill arrived on June 7 and set his men to working for the next two days building earthworks and clearing trees from both sides of Back River, where the primary road from Fort Monroe to Yorktown crossed. Marshy terrain on his left was unsuitable for infantry, so he posted only sharp-shooters to cover it. Behind some buildings on the right was high ground, where he placed a cannon and 208 men. The primary position north of the river contained earthworks with four cannon, and more fortifications covered a ford east of the bridge.

In Fort Monroe, Butler had learned of Hill's advance and itched to take action to protect Newport News. Without the permission or knowledge of Scott, he sent two separate columns on a night march that would converge at dawn to attack New Bethel. Brig. Gen. Ebenezer Pierce of Massachusetts would lead the four-thousand-man expedition. One-half of the force consisted of the Fifth New York Zouaves and Third New York; the other the Seventh New York, First Vermont, and Fourth Massachusetts. The First and Second New York were held in reserve.

The crossroads community of Centreville, Virginia, served as headquarters for both armies just before the clash at Manassas.

When Richmond, the Confederate capital, fell in April 1865, Federal authorities ordered all of Alexandria's bells pealed and all the guns in the city's forts fired salutes.

Union occupation troops speedily destroyed every commercial sign in the Alexandria area that contained the word *Southern*.

Modern-day Alexandria's premier landmark, the towering George Washington Masonic National Memorial, occupies the hilltop site of Fort Ellsworth.

On the afternoon of July 16, 1861, McDowell's army advanced toward Fairfax Court House along a recently constructed military road into Virginia.

Gen. Nathan Evans was a gruff man who never traveled without his "barrelita," a gallon drum of whiskey strapped to the back of an orderly and from which the general took generous swigs. A staff officer called Evans "at the same time about the best drinker, the most eloquent swearer, and the most magnificent bragger I ever saw."

Their advance at 1 A.M. on June 10 was soon detected by Confederate scouts. The march would have been an ambitious undertaking for veterans, but these were barely trained troops. Although they wrapped white cloth around their arms for recognition by friendly forces, a firefight broke out when the two columns encountered each other at Bethel, resulting in twenty-one casualties. Officers argued that with the element of surprise lost, the attack should be canceled, but Price insisted that the plan be followed.

Advancing at 8 A.M. the raw Union volunteers were unnerved by the sight of occupied enemy trenches. Many thought it unfair that the Confederates refused to meet them in a "fair" stand-up fight. Their first taste of artillery fire at 9:15 was unpleasant, leading one Confederate to report that the Yankees "did some pretty scientific dodging." One Federal revealed that cannonballs whistled by "as if they meant something nasty."

Union artillery was useless against the defenses as Pierce deployed a long line of battle designed to envelop the Confederate flanks. Col. Abram Duryée encountered severe fire near the ford on the Union right. "At every boom of the cannon we would drop flat on our faces and rise instantly," said one Zouave, "but they came so fast after that many of us did not take the trouble."

On Pierce's left the Third New York advanced under Col. Frederick Townsend. Rough terrain separated one company, which was fired upon by the main body. Then, believing the Confederates had turned their flank, the regiment retreated.

Pierce ordered troops from the First Vermont and Fourth Massachusetts to try the left again. They forded the river and attacked, urged on by Maj. Theodore Winthrop who shouted, "Rally, boys, rally!" until a bullet hit him in the chest. The advance ended with his death, and much of the army lost its organization. After two hours of battle, Pierce felt compelled to retreat, which was a ragged procession.

Confederate casualties were one killed and ten wounded; the Federals lost eighteen dead and seventy wounded. The recruits had gained their first taste of combat, and most were appalled by the maimed bodies, screaming wounded, and stench of the battlefield.

Although Pierce was relieved for his role in the skirmish, Butler was blamed by the army and the public, who now criticized the Massachusetts man for his political connections and lack of military training. It was the first of many tragedies perpetuated by political generals—men who received their rank through political influence—in this war. On the Confederate side, both Magruder and Hill found themselves promoted to brigadier general.

On the opposite side of the Old Dominion, Col. Thomas J. Jackson arrived to train Confederate recruits at Harpers Ferry on April 29. The former artillery and physics instructor at Virginia Military Institute was eccentric and energetic, but he found himself subordinated two weeks later with the arrival of Joseph Johnston. By the end of June, Johnston had

A woman approached Confederate Gen. Richard Ewell with what she felt was important information, but Ewell had no patience with heroines.

"You'll get killed," he shouted. "You'll be a *dead damsel* in less than a minute. Get away from here! Get away!"

When she refused to leave, Ewell turned to John B. Gordon, whose wife was never far from the front during the four years of war, and said: "I tell you, sir, women would make a grand brigade—if it was not for snakes and spiders! They don't mind bullets—women are not afraid of bullets; but one big black-snake would put a whole army to flight."

For forgetting the countersign a Confederate colonel was arrested.

Napoleon in Gray ■ Pierre Gustave Toutant Beauregard

Pierre Gustave Toutant Beauregard, born near New Orleans on May 18, 1818, finished second in the class of 1838 at the U.S. Military Academy, where he was dubbed "Little Napoleon" for his admiration of the French military genius. The brilliant engineer served under Winfield Scott in Mexico and was twice wounded and breveted. Appointed commandant of West Point in January 1861, Beauregard was removed within a week for no stated reason, but his dismissal was undoubtedly attributable to his Southern origins and beliefs.

Beauregard resigned his commission in February and became a brigadier in Confederate service on March 1. No Southerner saw more important or varied service than the "Little Creole." He commanded Charleston when orders were received to bombard Fort Sumter in April 1861, then created the Army of the Potomac and two months later became its second in command under Joseph E. Johnston. Beauregard exercised field command at First Manassas while Johnston fed him reinforcements, winning the first battle of the war and the rank of full general.

After bitter arguments with Jefferson Davis over credit for the victory at First Manassas and leadership of Confederate forces in Virginia, Beauregard was sent west in 1862. There he engineered the massing of Confederate forces that allowed Albert Sidney Johnston to launch his attack against Ulysses S. Grant at Shiloh in April. Beauregard took control when Johnston was killed and was criticized for not pressing the offensive against Grant's exhausted army. He retained command of the Army of Tennessee until relieved for taking unauthorized leave.

Beauregard served next in Charleston, where in 1863 and 1864 he rebuffed powerful Union naval attacks against the city. Recalled to Virginia in May 1864, he bottled up Benjamin F. Butler at Bermuda Hundred, then divined Grant's intention to strike southeast of Richmond and stopped him at Petersburg until Robert E. Lee tardily arrived. After attempting to usurp Lee's soldiers for an invasion of the North in September, Beauregard was made overall commander of the West, where he was unable to influence John Bell Hood's disastrous attack into Tennessee. Subsequently, he had no forces available to stem William T. Sherman's March to the Sea. Beauregard ended the war as he began it, under Johnston in North Carolina, where he was surrendered to Sherman after Bentonville.

Beauregard rejected job offers from the Egyptian and Rumanian governments and became the president of two railroad companies before serving as adjutant general of Louisiana. He died on February 20, 1893, and is buried in Metairie Cemetery in New Orleans.

NATIONAL ARCHIVES

Union Col. Israel Richardson was married to a shrew who accompanied him into the field. Her will was so pronounced that a soldier claimed, "Mrs. Richardson had gone up to the command of the brigade at the same time that the Colonel had." She once ordered a regimental quartermaster dismissed for misappropriating the honey from a hive she had secured for the headquarters personnel. The man was sent home.

A scouting party from the First Ohio Infantry advances toward Fairfax Court House. The artist, Alfred Waud, depicted several of the men with havelocks, but these were eventually discarded.

trained four infantry brigades, an equal number of batteries, and a cavalry led by Col. James Ewell Brown "Jeb" Stuart. The brigades were commanded by Jackson, Brig. Gen. Barnard E. Bee, Col. Arnold Elzey, and Col. Francis Bartow. This ten-thousand-man force, known as the Army of the Shenandoah, was soon withdrawn to Winchester, which Johnston considered more defensible. Johnston always seemed to find another place more defensible than where he was.

Before Confederate Col. William N. Pendleton fired his first hostile shot of the war, he shouted, "Fire, boys! and may God have mercy on their guilty souls!"

Robert Patterson took command of a Union army organized at Chambersburg, Pennsylvania, to threaten Johnston. The elderly officer slowly advanced on abandoned Harpers Ferry and occupied it with excitement.

The Man Who Lost the First Major Battle ■ Irwin McDowell

Irwin McDowell, born on October 15, 1818, in Columbus, Ohio, was educated in France before entering West Point in 1834. After graduation in 1838, he taught tactics for four years at the U.S. Military Academy, educating many future Confederate foes. Breveted for bravery at Buena Vista in Mexico, he was the adjutant general of the army in 1861. His patron, Secretary of the Treasury Salmon P. Chase, aided McDowell's promotion to regular army brigadier on May 14, 1861, despite the fact that he had never commanded a single soldier in

the field. He had a good plan at First Manassas but fought the battle poorly.

Replaced by George B. McClellan, McDowell was nonetheless made a major general in 1862, commanding a corps of volunteers in the Army of the Potomac that was charged with the defense of Washington, D.C., while McClellan was on the peninsula. McDowell's actions at Second Manassas brought renewed criticism and accusations of the same offenses that resulted in Fitz John Porter's court-martial. McDowell testified on Porter's behalf, to little avail, but

McDowell and Pope were absolved of blame when a court of inquiry cleared their names.

McDowell endured two years without any military duties before he was given command of the Department of the Pacific on July 1, 1864. He was promoted to regular army major general in 1872 and commanded other regional departments before his retirement in 1882. He died in San Francisco on May 4, 1885, and is buried at the Presidio.

At Fairfax Court House, McDowell's men skirmished with one of Beauregard's advance guards and occupied the area. The courthouse building has changed little since it saw considerable Civil War traffic.

Despite promises to Scott, Patterson failed to check Johnston. Instead, he maneuvered to Martinsburg in early July, but no battle resulted. On July 2 Patterson and Jackson skirmished at Falling Waters, on the Potomac, before the Confederates withdrew. Patterson reached Bunker Hill, just a few miles from Winchester, but believing Johnston had forty-two thousand men and sixty cannon, his moves were tentative. He ignored direct orders to attack and was relieved of command a week after Manassas.

During the Mexican War, P. G. T. Beauregard was the American officer who met the surrender flag at Mexico City.

Irwin McDowell, who was thought brusque and inattentive by both the public and by his colleagues, was widely disliked and disrespected. His superiors and the people demanded that he attack immediately, before the summer was over, and win the expected climatic battle. No one except McDowell seemed to realize that his force was manifestly unprepared.

McDowell's green recruits were poorly trained, and their commanders were equally inexperienced or were encumbered by advanced age. Supplies of weapons, ammunition, and equipment were inadequate. Maps of northern Virginia were nonexistent, and McDowell lacked sufficient cavalry that could provide scouting information. What was needed more than any other commodity was "a little time," as the general said.

Perversely, while Scott agreed that additional time was required to ready the army, he and his staff constantly delayed forwarding troops across the Potomac. On June 10 Lincoln, under constant pressure from the press, politicians, and the public, ordered Scott to attack. Scott relayed the message. When McDowell protested, he was told, "You are green, it is true, but they are green also; you are all green alike."

McDowell submitted several plans of attack that were rejected before one proved acceptable to his military and political superiors. Designed primarily to push the Confederates farther from the capital, the scheme called for a three-pronged western advance along parallel routes through Fairfax Court House, occupied by Rebel scouts, and on to the Confederate line along Bull Run Creek, twenty-five miles south of Washington. While two columns focused Beauregard's attention in the center, the third would cross on the Union left, cutting the railroad to Richmond. Flanked, the Confederates would be forced to retreat from Manassas Junction to the Rappahannock River forty miles farther south. The plan was designed to avoid a pitched battle, which McDowell knew his troops were unprepared to fight. He feared that Johnston would move swiftly via

P. G. T. Beauregard was not familiar with the word *modest*. His soldiers "have the most unbounded confidence in me," he wrote. "Oh, that I had the genius of a Napoleon, to be more worthy of our cause and of their confidence!"

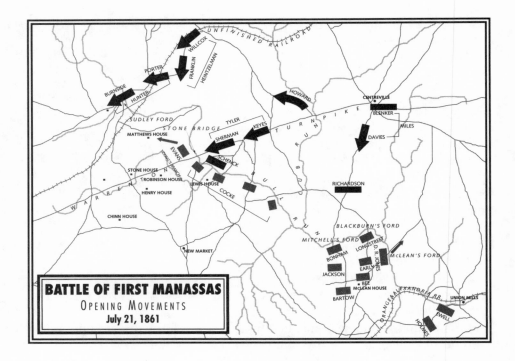

BATTLE OF FIRST MANASSAS
OPENING MOVEMENTS
July 21, 1861

Federal soldiers attacking the Confederate lines at Big Bethel on June 10, 1861, were outraged that the enemy had constructed earthworks. "They were completely in ambush," declared one Federal, "and within the embankment of one of the strongest fortifications in this section of the country."

The Yankees felt this was an unfair tactic, a belief widespread in the officer corps of both armies through the early years of the war. Slugging it out in open fields, as Napoleon's armies had, was believed to be the "proper" method of fighting. This tactic was responsible for horrendous casualties and was not supplanted by trench warfare until 1864 during the Atlanta campaign in the west and the battles between Lee and Grant in the east.

the railroad and attack his right flank, but Scott trusted Patterson to fix Johnston at Winchester.

McDowell intended to start the campaign on July 8, but he delayed the move when he received an additional division, raising his troop level to thirty-five thousand and making it the largest army in American history. (In Mexico, Scott had commanded only thirteen thousand men.) McDowell began his march early on the afternoon of July 16.

Beauregard vacillated between taking the offensive with his six brigades and remaining on the defensive, but Davis and Lee forbade an attack as they rushed reinforcements forward from Richmond. The Confederate position at Centreville was fortified, but that line could be easily flanked. Bull Run was a better defensive position. The south bank of the creek between Manassas Junction and Centreville was five feet high, and the stream was crossed by a lone stone bridge on the Warrenton turnpike. The problem was that there were a number of fords Beauregard would have to defend.

Two and a half miles upstream of the stone bridge was Sudley Ford, reached by rough country roads that Beauregard assumed McDowell was unaware of, so it was left undefended. Because the bridge seemed too obvious a target, it was lightly held by Col. Nathan Evans, a hard-drinking, boastful fighter commanding Louisiana troops. The next three fords downstream, hampered by heavy woods and undergrowth, were protected by Col. Philip St. George Cocke's brigade. Two and a half miles down from the stone bridge were two good adjacent fords and beyond were flat, open plains leading to Manassas Junction. This obvious target was defended by half the Confederate army. The first ford, Mitchell's, was screened by Brig. Gen. Milledge L. Bonham's brigade, and at Blackburn's Ford, a half mile away and visible from Mitchell's, was posted Brig. Gen. James Longstreet's brigade. Half a mile farther down, at McLean's Ford, was Brig. Gen. David R. Jones's brigade. Behind it were reserves commanded by Brig. Gen. Jubal A. Early, whose headquarters was near Wilmer McLean's house. Another mile and a half downstream were Union Mills Ford and the Orange and Alexandria Railroad bridge, covered by Brig. Gen. Richard S. Ewell's brigade. The stone bridge and the lower fords were commanded by the heights of Henry Hill, which the Warrenton turnpike passed along Young's Branch, with Matthews Hill to the north. Union possession of the road and Henry Hill would cut Beauregard off from Manassas Junction.

Five of Beauregard's seven brigades were posted along the five miles of Bull Run between the stone bridge and Union Mills. When McDowell attacked at one crossing, Beauregard planned to cross his other brigades and cut off the Federal army's route of retreat to Washington. This would require close cooperation among his inexperienced officers and troops. His signal officer, Capt. Edward Porter Alexander, constructed four towers behind the lines from which Union movements and Beauregard's orders could be quickly flashed from one position to another with wigwag flags.

Beauregard thought McDowell would strike across Mitchell's Ford and attack Bonham. When that occurred, Longstreet would cross at Blackburn's Ford and hit the Federal left while Jones crossed the creek at McLean's Ford and struck the Union flank and rear.

The Confederate fortifications erected at Manassas Junction were photographed in March 1862 after the Southerners withdrew. The works had changed little since the 1861 battle.

LIBRARY OF CONGRESS

Col. Dixon S. Miles, left out of the battle, drank throughout the day. He launched an unauthorized attack with two regiments at Blackburn's Ford (which was soon repulsed), raged at subordinates, and refused the counsel of officers who attempted to tell him of the disaster that had befallen McDowell. While finally putting men into position as a rear guard, he came across the Twelfth New York, routed at Blackburn's Ford three days earlier. "Stay there, damn you," he told the regiment, "and die there." Learning of his inebriated condition, McDowell relieved him. A little over a year later, Miles was again embroiled in controversy.

Before the battle of First Manassas, South Carolinian Col. Joseph B. Kershaw thought Bull Run was too unromantic a name for a battle and wanted to change it.

Before resigning and leaving Washington on May 21, Capt. Thomas Jordan had organized a Confederate spy ring that often involved society leader Rose O'Neal Greenhow, who obtained information at parties from Union officers and their proud wives. Coded messages were then given to beautiful young women who charmed their way past young guards at the bridges connecting Washington with Virginia.

On July 10 Bettie Duval arrived to see Bonham with a message secreted in her hair. McDowell would start for Manassas Junction on July 16, the missive revealed. On the appointed day Greenhow sent information, only hours old, that the Federals had departed.

The Union advance was not as rapid as McDowell would have hoped. It was slowed by narrow, primitive roads blocked with thousands of trees cut by the Confederates and by swampy areas that bogged down artillery and supply wagons. The Federal troops suffered in the humid heat with inadequate water. Many dropped out by the hundreds for water, to pick blackberries, to seek shade beneath the trees, or to ransack and even burn roadside homes and stores. Camp was not made until 10 P.M., after an advance of only six miles.

In the morning the center column, led by Brig. Gen. David Hunter's division, quickly occupied Fairfax Court House. It was met there by the right column division under Brig. Gen. Daniel Tyler. The left division, Brig. Gen. Samuel P. Heintzelman's, slowed to a crawl as its brigades crossed a narrow, shallow run in single file over a single log.

McDowell's orders on July 17 were for Tyler to occupy Centreville, followed by Hunter and the reserves under Col. Dixon S. Miles. They would feint an attack after arriving at Bull Run, but McDowell's orders emphasized, "Do *not* bring on an engagement."

Frustrated after receiving no word from the left, McDowell rode through the night to reach Heintzelman early in the morning. At dawn he realized that the terrain on his left was unsuitable for crossing large bodies of troops. He had no choice but to send Heintzelman to Centreville also.

At first light Tyler and his lead brigade under Col. Israel Richardson scouted Blackburn's and Mitchell's Fords. From a slope on the north bank they saw open fields stretching all the way to Manassas Junction. The creek banks were tangled with undergrowth, but the Federals saw only one Confederate battery and a few enemy soldiers. Encouraged, they called up two 20-pounders to engage the artillery and deployed two companies of the First Massachusetts as skirmishers.

The ford at Sudley Springs was photographed in early 1862, showing where McDowell's army crossed Bull Run to get to the battle and also to get away from it.

BATTLES AND LEADERS

For the first time, railroads were used to shuttle troops from one battle front to another, as Edmund Kirby Smith's troops were shifted from the Shenandoah Valley to Manassas Junction to meet the invaders. They arrived just in time to turn the battle in the Southerners' favor.

After an hour's action the Federals discovered the woods were occupied by invisible Confederate sharpshooters. Against the advice of his officers, Tyler ordered Richardson's brigade to attack. When three regiments and one battery had finished deploying, Tyler elected to withdraw, but the Twelfth New York had already advanced into the scrub to discover "the bushes seemed to be alive with Rebels," a Federal wrote, and a "murderous" volley exploded from the forest.

Tyler had encountered half the Confederate army, which had been as surprised by the fight as had the Federals. The Southern troops had been snoozing beneath the trees when the 20-pounders cut loose. The rattled Rebels fumbled into line, and Longstreet was required to pace behind them with his sword drawn to keep some from running. Early quickly sent reinforcements as Beauregard appeared personally on the scene.

The Twelfth New York withdrew in disorder, which quickly became a rout to the safety of the brigade and left the First Massachusetts exposed. Spotting the opportunity, Longstreet sent the First and Seventh Virginia to splash across the creek and attack. The Bay State men and other Federals nearby dove to the ground to escape the fire. His blood up, Richardson issued orders for an assault by his full brigade, which Tyler countermanded with instructions to retreat. The Confederates also withdrew to their side of the creek.

The Eighteenth Mississippi had a pet rooster named Kilby, which would come when called and perch on men's shoulders.

37

LESLIE'S

Opening the battle of Manassas, the main Federal column of eighteen thousand men moved against the Confederates at 9:30 A.M. on Sunday morning, July 21, 1861. McDowell, however, had already made his first mistake: his army was exhausted from two days of marching and the men had only had a few hours' sleep before the attacks began.

McDowell, outraged by the scope of the attack and its effects, severely criticized Tyler as other Federal brigades arrived to see their comrades in flight. Tyler had lost 19 dead, 38 wounded, and 26 missing, to 53 Southern casualties

For the next two days McDowell camped around Centreville. His original plans shattered by the topography and Confederate dispositions on the left, he sent his cavalry out to scout the situation. After they reported that the terrain at Sudley Ford was suitable for crossing, McDowell determined to ford the creek there and feint at the Stone Bridge. It was originally slated for July 20, but a twenty-four-hour delay was necessitated by the slow arrival of supply trains.

Not only did supplies arrive but the finest citizens of Washington rode out on horseback and in buggies to view the proceedings. Senators, congressmen, and their ladies looked about from beneath parasols and ate from large picnic baskets. Among the sightseers was Secretary of War Simon Cameron and Rep. John A. Logan, who later picked up a rifle and fought as an infantryman.

For this stage of the war, the affair at Blackburn's Ford constituted a serious battle. Informed by telegraph of the clash, Johnston set his Shenandoah army into motion. An exhausting march brought the four brigades to Piedmont Station on July 19, where they entrained for Manas-

Union Brig. Gen. William B. Franklin oversaw the construction of the Capitol dome, left uncompleted when the war began.

sas Junction. Jackson's Virginia brigade started first, arriving at Manassas Junction later that same day, having covered sixty miles in twenty-eight hours. The engines were immediately turned around for Bartow's Georgians, who arrived at dawn on July 20. Next was Bee, a South Carolinian leading men from several states. Last was Brig. Gen. Edmund Kirby Smith's brigade. Stuart's cavalry rode from the Shenandoah.

The operation was completed by July 21 despite worn tracks and engines. The trains traveled so slowly and wrecked with such frequency that many suspected the engineers were trying to sabotage the operation. One conductor was executed.

The small brigade of Brig. Gen. Theophilus H. Holmes soon reported from Aquia Creek on the Potomac. Fresh from South Carolina was the Hampton Legion, led by Col. Wade Hampton who had personally raised and equipped his combined unit of infantry, artillery, and cavalry.

Beauregard appreciated the reinforcements but dreaded the arrival of Johnston, his superior. He must have been surprised when Johnston left the Creole in field command, explaining that he knew the land and troops. Relieved, Beauregard prepared to strike McDowell across the fords at dawn on July 21. He sent Bartow and Bee to reinforce Longstreet at Blackburn's while Holmes bolstered Ewell at Union Mills and Jackson became a reserve at Mitchell's. Few troops were at the Stone Bridge and none farther to the Confederate left at Sudley Ford.

Beauregard's orders were confusing, inexact, and contradictory. He referred to divisions when he had previously established a system of brigades, and no one knew which brigades belonged to which divisions. He also devised two corps that were not really corps and neglected to tell Holmes that he might command one of them. Beauregard's attack involved only two brigades—the remainder were kept in reserve. Finally,

Keeping soldiers disciplined while under fire for the first time was a difficult chore. As William Tecumseh Sherman's brigade neared the front, he noticed men ducking from the passage of shells. "Keep cool," he urged them. "If you heard the projectile, it has already passed," he told them. Suddenly a shell zipped by, and Sherman ducked to hug the neck of his horse. As the men laughed and catcalled, Sherman joined them saying, "Well, boys, you may dodge the big ones."

The General Who Outfitted His Own Force ■ Wade Hampton

Born in Charleston, South Carolina, on March 28, 1818, Wade Hampton received his education at South Carolina College, graduating in 1836. Considered the largest property and slaveholder in the South, he spent nine years in the state legislature. When the Civil War started, Hampton organized, equipped, and led the Hampton Legion—an integrated force consisting of infantry, cavalry, and artillery—to Virginia. It fought well at First Manassas, where Hampton was wounded.

After service on the peninsula, Hampton made brigadier on May 23, 1862, just before being wounded again at Seven Pines. In July he started the second phase of his military career, commanding a brigade of cavalry under Jeb Stuart. He participated in the daring cavalier's exploits through 1864, being seriously wounded again at Gettysburg and earning the rank of major general. With the death of Stuart at Yellow Tavern in 1864, Hampton led the Army of Northern Virginia's Cav-

alry Corps. He fought valiantly to defeat Philip H. Sheridan at Trevilian Station and successfully held off Federal cavalry around Richmond and Petersburg. His most famous exploit occurred in September 1864, when he rustled twenty-five hundred cattle from the Federals in the "Great Beefsteak Raid." In January 1865, he joined Joseph E. Johnston and the Army of Tennessee in North Carolina, fighting at Bentonville and surrendering to William T. Sherman in April. He became a lieutenant general on

February 15, 1865, one of only three military "amateurs" to do so in the Confederacy.

Hampton returned to politics, fighting Reconstruction in South Carolina as fiercely as he had fought Yankees in Virginia. He served two terms as governor and two terms in the U.S. Senate. Hampton died April 11, 1902, in Columbia, and is buried there.

When a bullet destroyed one Rebel's canteen, he reached behind with his hand and felt a warm liquid flowing down his back. Thinking himself mortally wounded, he fainted.

Ambrose E. Burnside's Rhode Islanders assaulted the Confederate position atop Matthews Hill, but fell back in the face of a fierce fire and did little during the rest of the battle.

the orders were not issued until five in the morning, and his hastily recruited couriers had difficulty locating the recipients.

The Federals heard the whistles blowing at the junction, but they believed that only small units were arriving from Richmond. Some thought the whistles were a ruse.

Things were more organized across the creek in Centreville where McDowell met with his officers at 8 P.M. Apparently as punishment, Tyler was relegated to creating a diversion at the Stone Bridge and middle fords to freeze the Confederates in place. When the real battle developed he would cross and join the action. In the center, Hunter and Heintzelman would ford at Sudley and attack Beauregard's left flank. Miles was left in reserve. McDowell hoped to capture Gainesville and cut the Manassas Gap Railroad before Johnston arrived with reinforcements. The troops would march at 2 A.M. and attack at dawn.

Tyler had one valid objection to the plan. Demonstrating at the Stone Bridge would draw Confederates upstream from Mitchell's and Blackburn's Fords, toward McDowell. Tyler thought the feint should be at Blackburn's, but the commander rejected the idea. When Tyler, apprehensive of Johnston's whereabouts, as were others, broached the subject, McDowell replied, "You know as well as I do."

The night before the battle, William Woodward, of the Fifth Virginia, had a premonition of his death. A bullet killed him beside the Henry house.

Few soldiers, Union or Confederate, slept soundly that night. They contemplated their fates and wrote thousands of last letters home.

40

Tyler's force was the first to move out, an hour late, and it was only then that McDowell realized that Tyler had the shortest distance to the Stone Bridge. At that point Tyler was ordered off the narrow lanes so Hunter and Heintzelman could start for Sudley. The pace was slow in the dark forest lanes on rough, circuitous roads. Hours were lost by wrong turns at unmarked forks. Tyler opened with artillery at the Stone Bridge at 6 A.M., expecting the other divisions to be in position. They arrived three hours later.

The Federals had skirmishers feeling their way through the dense forest and thickets, using axes, picks, and shovels to clear paths. The worst obstacles were again thousands of trees the Confederates had felled across every passage in the previous weeks. Porter manhandled a three-ton 30-pounder James rifle through the wilderness and across precarious bridges. When it fired to signal the start of the assault, everyone for miles around heard it.

To conceal his small numbers at the Stone Bridge, Evans kept his force in the woods. He had decided that the attack to his front was a feint when the signal stations proved their worth. Relaying reports from scouts that large Federal forces were approaching Sudley Ford, Evans left four companies and marched to deploy atop Matthews Hill to address the threat to his left flank. From this vantage point his men were concealed by trees and could observe Sudley Ford a mile distant across open fields.

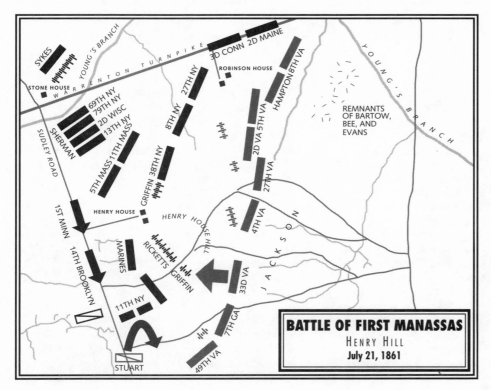

BATTLE OF FIRST MANASSAS
HENRY HILL
July 21, 1861

On Matthews Hill, Confederate Maj. Roberdeau Wheat was struck by a bullet that entered one side, cut completely through his chest, and exited the other side. He was wrapped in the Louisiana Tigers' regimental flag and borne to the rear, where doctors told him that his wound was fatal because one, and perhaps both, of his lungs had been penetrated. To his protest, "I don't feel like dying yet," the surgeons explained that they had never seen anyone recover from such a terrible wound.

"Well, then," Wheat replied, "I will put my case upon record."

He did and returned to fight again, but Wheat was killed less than a year later at Gaines's Mill.

Like most officers and enlisted men, Barnard Bee feared missing the battle. Joining Nathan Evans's desperate battle on Matthews Hill, Bee was delighted, exclaiming, "Here is the battlefield, and we are in for it!"

The previous evening Francis Bartow had gently reminded his men that "battle and fighting mean death, and probably before sunrise some of us will be dead."

Both Bee and Bartow were killed in action at Manassas.

With Evans was the Fourth South Carolina, the First Louisiana Special Battalion under Maj. Chatham Roberdeau Wheat, and two cannon.

The Second Rhode Island was the lead regiment of Col. Ambrose Burnside's brigade, with Hunter accompanying it, when the first Confederate volley stunned the Federals. As the column halted, their commander was killed and Hunter was badly wounded. Burnside assumed command and deployed the remainder of his brigade, but Evans's fire decimated their ranks and killed Burnside's horse. The fierce fire convinced Burnside that he faced six regiments and two full batteries. As Col. Andrew Porter's brigade extended Burnside's right, Wheat's five hundred men charged in a maniacal fury, screaming savagely and waving huge Bowie knives. A bullet pierced Wheat's chest and fifty others were wounded, but the Federal line was thrown into confusion, which bought time for Beauregard to rush in reinforcements.

As the Federal line continued to expand and overlap the Confederate left flank, the signal station reported that another division, Heintzelman's, was crossing at Sudley Ford. Bee arrived to form on the Confederate right, followed immediately by Bartow, but both brigades were exhausted by the six-mile march and suffered from the heat and thirst. Hundreds of men fell out to pick ripe blackberries for their juice as bullets buzzed overhead. Bee's Fourth Alabama and Eleventh Mississippi and Bartow's Seventh and

A Commanding General First and Last ■ Joseph E. Johnston

Joseph Eggleston Johnston, born in Farmville, Virginia, on February 3, 1807, was a classmate of Robert E. Lee in the West Point class of 1829. He was twice wounded in combat with the Seminoles and five times while fighting the Mexicans, where he was twice breveted. Johnston was a brigadier when he resigned from the army after the secession of his home state.

Commanding Confederate troops in Virginia in 1861, Johnston rushed his men by rail to Manassas, where they turned the tide for the South in the first major battle of the war. Almost a year later, in March 1862, Johnston demonstrated his skill in executing deft withdrawals (a cursed habit, his critics maintained), first from Centreville, then Manassas, and again down the peninsula before George B. McClellan's mas-

sive force. With the Union army within sight of Richmond, Johnston launched a furious, confused attack at Seven Pines to blunt the Federal advance. While reconnoitering at twilight, Johnston exercised his propensity for attracting projectiles and was seriously wounded. His replacement was Robert E. Lee.

Transferred to recuperate and take nominal command of the Confederate West, Johnston was ineffective in stemming the Union tide that flowed through Tennessee and down the Mississippi River. He failed to save Vicksburg through inaction, and after Braxton Bragg's retreat from Chattanooga, Jefferson Davis grudgingly appointed Johnston, an old and bitter enemy, to command the Army of Tennessee.

Johnston kept the army intact but retreated to Atlanta's outskirts with-

out initiating a major battle to stop William T. Sherman's relentless advance. Davis, distressed by Johnston's reticence to communicate his plans, dismissed Johnston from command with the Union army at the outskirts of Atlanta.

Eight months later, with the Army of Tennessee reduced to tatters by John Bell Hood's reckless campaign to draw Sherman out of Georgia, Johnston was returned to command. He rushed the army to North Carolina and threw his lean ranks against Sherman at Bentonville. The Federal commander, caught unaware, fought hard to regain the advantage. Two weeks after Lee surrendered to Ulysses S. Grant, Johnston capitulated to Sherman.

Johnston entered the insurance business in Savannah and Richmond after the war, then was appointed to be U.S. Railroad Commissioner. He

stoutly defended his actions in the war through his book, *Narrative of Military Operations.* In 1891 Johnston died of pneumonia soon after attending Sherman's funeral, where he stood hatless in the rain to pay his respects. He is buried in Green Mount Cemetery in Baltimore.

LIBRARY OF CONGRESS

BATTLES AND LEADERS

Confederates under Brig. Gen. Barnard E. Bee and Cols. Nathan Evans and Francis Bartow (carrying the flag at the far left) bought time during the battle for the rest of the army to be assembled in the field by Gen. Joseph E. Johnston (in the right foreground) to protect the left flank of the Southern line. Bee and Bartow fell while rallying their commands.

Eighth Georgia regiments advanced the line a thousand yards toward the Federals while Bee's artillery, under Capt. John D. Imboden, deployed on Henry Ridge, behind Matthews Hill. The five thousand Confederates were quickly outnumbered three to one. At 10:30 A.M. the Confederates boldly attacked Burnside and Porter but met fierce resistance.

"The balls just poured on us," remembered a Georgian, "struck our muskets and hats and bodies."

"It was a whirlwind of bullets," another said. "Our men fell constantly. The deadly missiles rained like hail among the boughs and trees."

"I felt that I was in the presence of death," another Georgian wrote.

The Georgians particularly suffered as they charged across open fields before gaining a thicket where they opened on the Union cannon.

South Carolina and Alabama troops under Bee attacked Burnside across a barren hill. "Our brave men fell in great numbers," recalled Alabama Capt. Thomas Goldsby, "but they died as the brave love to die—with faces to the foe." One company lost thirty of one hundred men, and gallant Confederate officers paid a heavy toll. Bee's horse was killed, and every officer in the Fourth Alabama was killed or wounded. One officer's horse was felled by eight bullets, then hit by five more before the rider

Under fire for the first time, one of Francis Bartow's Georgians thought: "This is unfair; somebody is to blame for getting us all killed. I didn't come out here to fight this way; I wish the earth would crack open and let me drop in."

Rallying troops atop Henry Hill, Barnard Bee encountered a small knot of soldiers and asked, "What regiment is this?"

"Why, General," replied one of Bee's men, "don't you know your own troops? This is all that is left of the Fourth Alabama."

Asking if they would follow him for another attack, they shouted, "To the death!"

43

The Federals' flanking action was stymied by the quick and resolute action of three Confederate brigade commanders. Col. Francis S. Bartow (above) of Georgia and Brig. Gen. Barnard E. Bee (below) of South Carolina wheeled their men in conjunction with Col. Nathan G. Evans's brigade to blunt the Union attack on the left side of the Southern line. Evans survived, but both Bartow and Bee were mortally wounded during the engagement.

rolled clear. Bee, drawing ahead of Bartow and Evans, received fire from the front and both flanks.

The Confederates had accomplished all they could, stopping McDowell for two hours. They were forced off Matthews Hill and across Young's Branch and the Warrenton turnpike, losing men with every step of the withdrawal. Spotting gray-clad soldiers crossing near the Stone Bridge to their right, the Rebels briefly thought reinforcements had arrived and moved to form beside them. When the breeze stirred a Confederate flag, the approaching troops, the Second Wisconsin and part of Col. William T. Sherman's thirty-four-hundred-man brigade, "opened a murderous fire upon our flank," said one South Carolinian.

Those Federals were part of Tyler's command, ordered by McDowell at 11 A.M. to attack the Confederate right flank. McDowell had spotted distant dust clouds signaling Confederate reinforcements and urgently ordered his troops to clear the Stone Bridge. Col. Erasmus D. Keyes's Federal brigade followed Sherman and aligned with Hunter and Heintzelman. After fighting bravely against overwhelming numbers—three brigades against two divisions—the Confederates panicked, running up Henry Hill.

From Matthews Hill, Sherman, Burnside, and Porter watched with satisfaction as the Confederates broke and ran. After reorganizing, McDowell would order them to advance as his third division began crossing Bull Run. The Manassas Gap Railroad was only three miles distant, and when it was cut, the Federals believed, Johnston would be unable to reinforce Beauregard. They would then capture Manassas Junction and sever the Orange and Alexandria Railroad.

"Victory! Victory!" McDowell shouted to his men. "The day is ours!"

Back at headquarters at the McLean house near Mitchell's Ford, Beauregard spent several hours frozen with indecision. He had dispatched five brigades across the fords, but fortunately for him, confusing orders had prevented his anticipated attack. While there were no sounds of battle on his right, the din of combat to the left grew alarmingly. Tardily, at 9:30 A.M. he had sent the three brigades of Bee, Bartow, and Jackson to the left. He directed brigades to the north side of Bull Run to attack Centreville, then learned from Alexander that a half-mile-long column of Federals was approaching Sudley Ford. This prompted Beauregard to order Ewell, Holmes, Longstreet, and David Jones back to the Confederate side of Bull Run.

After bearing Beauregard's confusion for several hours, Johnston decided to act. Around noon he pointed to the left and told Beauregard, "The battle is there. I am going," adding that the left needed reinforcements.

Beauregard had bombastically declared that his troops compared him to Napoleon, but he later admitted that his "heart for a moment failed me." After earlier wishing for death, he rallied and "solemnly pledged my life that I would that day conquer or die!" He ordered Holmes, Early, and

Bonham to reinforce the left and again sent Longstreet, Ewell, and Jones across the creek for a counterattack. As his units moved into action, Beauregard belatedly followed Johnston.

At Henry Hill the retreating Confederates found the six-hundred-man Hampton Legion, designated by Bee as a reserve. The bloodied Southerners raced through the legion and up the hill, leaving Hampton to face most of McDowell's army. After a short stand, the South Carolinians were ripped by artillery fire and retreated behind Henry Hill.

Having broken the Confederate resistance, McDowell paused to regroup, particularly the remnants of Burnside's and Porter's brigades, which had been committed piecemeal and savaged in detail throughout the morning. Holding Burnside in reserve, McDowell placed Keyes on the left, Sherman in the center, and Porter, Orlando Willcox, and William Franklin to the right, with Schenck's brigade and artillery at the Stone Bridge. McDowell deployed eleven thousand men and twenty-four pieces of artillery to continue the assault. At 2 P.M. he ordered his army forward.

Jackson's brigade had waited through the morning to support Longstreet's planned attack across Bull Run, but at noon Jackson marched

Also at the front was visionary photographer Mathew Brady. "I know well enough that I cannot take a photograph of a battle," he said, "but I can get a little glimpse of some corner somewhere that will be worthwhile. We are making history now, and every picture that we get will be valuable."

Brady was correct that his work would become historic. The public was soon viewing photographs of famous places on the battlefield, including sobering images of dead soldiers.

The Immortal Stonewall ■ Thomas Jonathan Jackson

Thomas Jonathan "Stonewall" Jackson, born on January 21, 1824, in Clarksburg, Virginia, was a member of the West Point class of 1846 that produced twenty-three other general officers for Civil War armies. In Mexico he won brevet promotions to captain and major, then resigned in 1852 to teach physics and artillery at the Virginia Military Institute in Lexington. In 1859 his cadets stood guard at John Brown's hanging.

Jackson briefly commanded state troops at Harpers Ferry until relieved by Joseph E. Johnston. As a Confederate brigadier general, Jackson transported his brigade via rail to fight at First Manassas, where his performance earned him the famous moniker.

Promoted to major general in October, Jackson was sent to the Shenandoah Valley the following month. In the spring of 1862 two Federal armies were dispatched to the Shenandoah to threaten Richmond from the north while George B. McClellan advanced up the penin-

sula. In a dazzling offensive, Jackson defeated John C. Frémont at Staunton on May 8, then turned on Nathaniel P. Banks and drove him across the Potomac River after battles at Front Royal and Winchester on May 23–25. To prevent a feared attack against Washington, James Shields, with a portion of Irwin McDowell's force, was sent to attack Jackson from the east while Frémont advanced from the west. Jackson managed to defeat the Federal forces in detail, punishing Frémont at Cross Keys on June 8, then marching for Port Republic, where he flogged Shields the next day.

Lee then ordered Jackson to march east and participate in the Seven Days' battles. There Stonewall's reputation suffered as he failed to carry out his orders at Mechanicsville, tardily attacked at Gaines's Mill, and unaccountably failed to advance across the Chickahominy River and White Oak Swamp to attack McClellan's rear. Each of these unaccount-

able lapses may have allowed the Federal army to survive.

Nonplused, Lee next directed Stonewall to central Virginia to challenge John Pope's march on Richmond. He managed to win the poorly conducted battle at Cedar Mountain, then marched around Pope's flank and hit his rear, destroying his supply depot and railroad communications. Jackson then disappeared but induced Pope to attack his strong position at Second Manassas, setting up a decisive Union defeat.

During the Antietam campaign Jackson skillfully captured Harpers Ferry before leading the Confederate left flank at Antietam, a battle saved by one of his divisions led by A. P. Hill

Jackson was commissioned a lieutenant general on October 10, 1862, and received command of the Second Corps. He held the right flank at Fredericksburg in December and was with Lee at Chancellorsville when the vastly superior army of Joseph Hooker appeared. Jackson

was dispatched on a brilliant sweeping move around the Federal right that rolled up half of Hooker's army. At the very pinnacle of his career, Jackson was wounded by his own troops as he scouted Union lines. He developed pneumonia and died on May 10, 1863, at Guinea Station. Stonewall is buried near his home in Lexington, Virginia.

BATTLES AND LEADERS

After the battle, Wilmer McLean inspected the damage to his home, which had been struck by artillery. One shell nearly killed Beauregard there as he sat at a meal. Considering his position between Washington and Richmond, McLean decided that the area would be the scene of conflict again. He was correct. In a year a greater battle would occur on the same ground, and Confederate and Federal forces used the property for much of the next four years.

McLean elected to relocate his family to a remote, peaceful corner of Virginia that should be safe from military operations. He was again correct, at least until the last two days of the war. He purchased a home in remote Appomattox Court House. On April 9, 1865, Robert E. Lee surrendered his army to U. S. Grant in McLean's parlor.

In the early days of the Civil War there was no standardization of uniforms, which were variously furnished by states, cities, and private citizens. At Bull Run, Confederates and Federals wore many colors besides blue and gray, making identification of friend and foe uncertain. Confederates in blue were instructed to tie strips of white cloth to their uniforms, but Gen. Thomas Jonathan Jackson felt further identification was needed. When meeting an unknown unit, his men were to slap their left breast with their right hands and shout, "Our homes!"

"We presented the appearance of so many lunatics," a soldier wrote. "They failed to tell us that while we were going through this Masonic performance, we thus gave the other fellow an opportunity to blow our brains out, if we had any."

BATTLES AND LEADERS

The fighting at Henry Hill turned the battle in favor of the Confederates. Jeb Stuart's cavalry (facing page) and Thomas J. Jackson's infantry threw back the Federal assault, and a series of confused charges and countercharges exhausted the strength of both armies. Newly arriving reinforcements bolstered the Southern ranks and routed the Northerners from the field.

his men to the sounds of battle without orders. Once there the initiative seemed to elude him. As fighting raged at Young's Branch, Jackson and Imboden's artillery formed a static line behind the crest. It will always remain a mystery why the combative Jackson chose to wait instead of immediately joining the fight.

"The firing in our front was terrific," one of Jackson's men remembered, "and why we did not render immediate and timely assistance to Bee I could never learn."

Bee appeared and told Jackson, "General, they are beating us back."

With his customary calm Jackson replied, "Sir, we'll give them the bayonet."

Bee rallied the thin remains of his command and led them back down Henry Hill to attack again. We will never know whether he urged his men to rally with Jackson's troops or whether he condemned the Virginians for taking no part in the battle, but he shouted, "There stands Jackson like a stone wall. Rally behind the Virginians." Bee's force was shattered by fierce artillery fire and fled. Attempting to rally them once more, Bee fell, dying soon afterward.

Johnston and Beauregard arrived then to find Jackson, Hampton, and what was left of Evans's and Bartow's brigades. Johnston personally reformed the Fourth Alabama around their colors as Evans and Bartow reorganized their units. Johnston agreed to ride a mile to the rear to Portici, a prominent house at an elevated position that gave him a good view

HARPERS

Beauregard ordered Jeb Stuart to "bring your command into action at once and . . . attack where the firing is hottest." Stuart led two companies of the First Virginia Cavalry in two charges against the Eleventh New York Zouaves, ending their effectiveness on the field and ensuring the Southern victory.

Nathan George "Shanks" Evans was born in Marion, South Carolina, on February 3, 1824. After graduation from the U.S. Military Academy in 1848, he spent thirteen years in the cavalry on frontier service. Evans resigned from the army on February 27, 1861. He observed the shelling of Fort Sumter, and in July led a small brigade on the extreme left of the Confederate line at First Manassas. Discovering Irwin McDowell's flanking move, he blunted the Federal advance, allowing P. G. T. Beauregard and Joseph E. Johnston to meet the threat. Although a brigadier by the fall, the hard-drinking and difficult Evans had been shunted to Leesburg, Virginia, on the upper Potomac River. Despite his reputed drunkenness, Evans's forces destroyed the Union incursion at Ball's Bluff.

Evans was transferred to South Carolina, where he stopped a Union thrust at Secessionville, and returned to Virginia to lead troops at Second Manassas, South Mountain, and Antietam. In a dispute over captured ambulances, Evans relieved John Bell Hood of command. Transferred to North Carolina, Evans quarreled with several of his regimental commanders and arrested one, who promptly charged Evans with drunkenness. Both were acquitted. Evans went next to Mississippi with Johnston, where he was arrested on charges of disobedience but again was acquitted. Beauregard considered Evans incompetent and relieved him of command until March 1864. That April he was hurt in a fall from his horse and never held command again.

Before his death on November 23, 1868, Evans claimed to have reformed himself and was principal of a high school in Midway, Alabama. He is buried in Cokesbury, South Carolina.

of the entire battlefield, to direct reinforcements—Early, Bonham, and Stuart's cavalry—into position while Beauregard managed the battle.

Scattered Confederate commands arrived and were fed into the line. Two Virginia regiments, one led by elderly former governor William "Extra Billy" Smith, allowed Beauregard to extend his left as Federal strength grew opposite him. He sent Stuart's cavalry into the woods on the extreme left. Soon Beauregard had sixty-five hundred men and thirteen cannon on Henry Hill. Although badly outnumbered, the Confederates were steady under professional leadership. Beauregard rode up and down the line encouraging the troops. When one horse was killed beneath him, he found another.

His deployment complete, McDowell sent two batteries, James B. Ricketts's and Charles Griffin's, up Henry Hill to soften the Confederate line for an assault, a classic Napoleonic tactic. Jackson alerted Beauregard of the threat and prepared his brigade to meet it, telling his men, "When their heads are seen above the hill, let the whole line rise, move forward with a shout, and trust to the bayonet." Officers heard him mutter, "I am tired of this long-range work."

Ordered forward by Maj. William F. Barry, McDowell's chief of artillery, Griffin pointed out that his guns would be beyond infantry support and vulnerable to capture. Barry promised that the Eleventh New York Fire Zouaves would advance with him. Griffin doubted that the initiates could withstand a Confederate assault, but Barry asserted that they would and repeated McDowell's order. Griffin left saying, "I will go, but mark my words, they will not support us."

Ricketts's battery followed Griffin to an area three hundred yards from the Confederate line. Its eleven guns, shortly reinforced by two more, had barely gone into action when bullets began felling gunners and horses. Believing the fire came from the Henry house, Ricketts's battery fired on the structure. In an upstairs bedroom, where Judith Henry, an elderly widow, cowered with her daughter and a servant, a shell penetrated and exploded, amputating one of the widow's feet and causing other mortal wounds.

Berry personally located the Eleventh New York and led it, with the Fourteenth Brooklyn Chasseurs and a battalion of marines, to support the artillery. "Up, up, not a single enemy in sight," wrote a New Yorker, "not a shot from this side. Up, up till we gained the top."

The Virginians rose at Jackson's order and fired as the Zouaves reached the battery. "We mowed them down," remembered a Confederate. Some Federals fought back but most withdrew behind the guns.

Stuart gained the Union right flank and led two companies in a brief attack. The sudden onslaught by horsed Rebels unnerved the Zouaves, who retreated or refused to move forward to support the artillery. Barry could not rally the New Yorkers or a body of marines, and nearby Federal regiments refused to take the initiative.

Confederate Col. Arthur C. Cummings, commanding the Thirty-third Virginia, seized the moment. Ignoring Jackson's orders to remain on the defensive, he charged his blue-uniformed regiment for the Union flank at

The Stone Bridge (below) spanning Bull Run marked the shortest avenue of escape from the battlefield for many Federals as well as the sightseers from Washington.

LIBRARY OF CONGRESS

Judith Henry was the widow of Dr. Isaac Henry, who had served in the U.S. Navy aboard the frigate *Constellation*. At their home near Manassas Junction, which they called Spring Hill Farm, they had a son, John, and a daughter, Ellen. When the battle began on the morning of July 21, the two plus a hired black servant, Lucy Griffith, were attending the bedridden woman.

As the first shots were fired, John, Ellen, and Lucy started to carry the widow Henry to safety at nearby Portici, where Johnston would establish his headquarters. Turned back by the intensity of the battle, they first took refuge in their springhouse, which occupied a less vulnerable position, but Mrs. Henry begged to be returned to her own bed.

When Union artillery opened on the house, John was outside and Ellen and Lucy crawled under Mrs. Henry's bed. Ellen next ducked inside the brick chimney, where she was deafened by nearby explosions that reverberated in the cavity. A round then penetrated the upstairs bedroom, destroying the bed and throwing the widow to the floor with a severed foot and other serious wounds. Although suffering intense pain for several hours, Mrs. Henry attempted to comfort her daughter. When Mrs. Henry died, John ran outside and threw himself on the ground, where the battle still raged, shouting, "They've killed my mother!"

LIBRARY OF CONGRESS

The Union rear guard deployed near Centreville to cover the retreating Federal army. Saber-waving Col. Louis Blenker's New Yorkers maintained their position just south of the town.

2 P.M. Artilleryman Griffin studied the approaching troops for a moment before deciding they were Confederates. As he prepared to fire two canister-loaded cannon, Barry intervened.

"Those are your battery support!" he shouted.

Griffin replied, "They are Confederates!" moments before the approaching troops loosed a volley from seventy yards. "That was the last of us," Griffin would recall.

The gunners were decimated, half the horses needed to haul the guns away were slaughtered, and the infantry ran in panic. Ricketts was wounded, and Griffin ordered the guns abandoned. Only three were saved.

From atop Henry Hill, Jackson launched his brigade in pursuit, joined by troops to his right on Beauregard's orders. Enough Federals stood fast that attack and counterattack dominated the following two hours.

Casualties mounted as troops swept up and down the slope under constant artillery fire. The abandoned Federal cannon were captured and recaptured.

"The cannonballs struck all around us," a Confederate remembered, "the shells burst at our feet, and the Miniés sung their song of death around our ears."

At one point Griffin and the Thirty-eighth New York were hauling three of his guns to Union lines when they were struck by the Fifth Virginia led

A Tough First Manassas ■ James Brewerton Ricketts

Born June 21, 1817, in New York City, James Ricketts graduated from West Point in 1839 and received no brevets in Mexico despite active duty. His Civil War service was widely varied. Commanding a battery at First Manassas, he was shot four times and captured, along with six 10-pound Parrotts, after being ordered too close to Confederate lines without support.

Imprisoned for six months in Richmond hospitals, Ricketts returned in January 1862 and became a brigadier of volunteers on April 30. At Cedar Mountain his division protected Nathaniel Banks's retreat. After participation at Second Manassas, Ricketts had two horses killed under him at Antietam. Serving at the court-martial of Fitz John Porter, Ricketts, like others, was self-serving.

Ricketts sat out 1863 with injuries suffered at Antietam, but he led a division at the Wilderness with Ulysses S. Grant in May 1864 and fought at Spotsylvania and Cold Harbor—where he was breveted—and at Petersburg. Sent to reinforce Lew Wallace with 3,350 men when Jubal Early threatened Washington, Ricketts's men did most of the fighting. He then accompanied Philip H. Sheridan to the Shenandoah Valley, where he was seriously wounded in the chest while leading his corps. Ricketts returned to command only two days before Lee surrendered. He was made a major general in the regular army and retired two years later due to his numerous injuries. Ricketts died in Washington on September 27, 1887, and is buried at Arlington.

After losing the Federal guns at Henry Hill, Union Maj. William F. Barry and Capt. Charles Griffin encountered each other along Bull Run as they watered their horses.

"Major, do you think the Zouaves will support us?" taunted Griffin, referring to the brightly garbed Southern brigade that had undermined the Union position. Barry had believed the unit was the colorfully bedecked New York Fire Zouaves and had countermanded Griffin's orders to fire upon the approaching force.

"I was mistaken," Barry replied quietly.

"Do you think that was our support?" Griffin continued.

"I was mistaken," Barry repeated.

"Yes, you were mistaken all around," Griffin retorted, riding off.

by Beauregard, who shouted, "Give them the bayonet! Give it to them freely!" Griffin lost the guns, but in turn Beauregard was hurled back by another counterattack. An exploding shell disemboweled the Confederate commander's horse.

Elsewhere on the battlefield, Bartow was struck in the chest while commanding his remaining Georgians. Calling upon his men to defend their banner, he implored them, "They have killed me, but boys, *never* give it up."

McDowell squandered his temporary superiority in numbers. He apparently forgot about Schenck's brigade at the Stone Bridge, and Keyes's brigade, behind Young's Branch, took little part in the combat. Instead of launching a large-scale attack that could have broken Beauregard's line, McDowell committed his regiments one by one. They were savaged in turn. Hundreds of men were felled by the heat, some dying of sunstroke.

Sherman wasted his brigade in similar fashion. The gray-clad Second Wisconsin was upon Jackson before his men decided they were Yankees. As they withdrew, Sherman sent in the Seventy-ninth New York, which in turn delayed firing because the Confederate Stars and Bars, particularly on a windless day, could easily be confused with the Stars and Stripes. The New Yorkers had lowered their guns when a breeze caught the flag. "We were met by a terrible raking fire," one said, "against which we could only stagger." Their commander, Col. James Cameron, the brother of Secretary of War Simon Cameron, was killed.

Organization is paramount in battle, and as each regiment staggered back in disorder, unit cohesion and discipline were steadily degraded.

Col. Oliver O. Howard brought McDowell's last fresh brigade, three Maine regiments and one from Vermont, onto the field just before 4 P.M. Ordered by McDowell to attack on the run, the men no longer had it in them, having marched from Sudley Ford with full packs. One soldier thought a fourth of his regiment had fallen out from the heat before it was under fire.

Howard led half the brigade against the Confederate left, but they were met by a withering fire. Terrified by their initial taste of combat and stepping over mounds of dead and maimed soldiers from earlier attacks, many men forgot their training. Inexperienced men left ramrods in their barrels and sent them flying across the field or neglected to use percussion caps and rammed home charge after charge without noticing that they had not fired a single shot. Orders were drowned out or simply not comprehended or obeyed.

When the first two regiments withdrew, Howard led the other two into the melee only to be met by fresh Confederate reinforcements under Brig. Gen. Edmund Kirby Smith on their right flank and massed Confederate artillery. The Federals fled behind Young's Branch.

Smith had detrained at Manassas Junction at 12:30 and marched toward the front, directed by streams of wounded and the growing sound of battle. The choking dust thrown up by fifty thousand marching, fighting men made it "impossible to see more than a few feet ahead," one soldier remembered. At Portici, Johnston's simple instruction had been, "Go where the firing is hottest."

That was now the Confederate left, threatened by Howard. A bullet immediately hit Smith in the chest, leaving Col. Arnold Elzey of the First Maryland to lead the attack. Elzey had said he would earn six feet of dirt or a general's sword belt that day, and he won the latter. The brigade emerged from the woods and hit Howard's right. When Jubal Early's brigade joined the assault, McDowell's flank collapsed.

"A panic had seized all the troops in sight," Howard noted later. They dropped rifles and packs and streamed for the rear shouting, "The enemy is upon us!"

When Beauregard ordered a general assault at 4:30, the Union army dissolved, and there was nothing that could be done to stem its flight. McDowell and his officers worked frantically to piece the Federal line together, but the stampede was contagious. Fresh troops just arriving, never fired on and fearful at the prospect, saw veterans of a day's fight racing for Sudley Ford and joined the rout. McDowell deployed a battalion of regular army troops under Maj. George Sykes to cover the retreat.

The sight astounded Federal officers, including Lt. Emory Upton, who said: "One glance told the tale; a tale of defeat, and a confused, disorderly and disgraceful retreat. The road was filled with wagons, artillery, retreating

The Stone House on the Warrenton turnpike marked the end of the left flank of the Confederate line and figured prominently in both battles at Manassas Junction.

After arriving on the battlefield, Jefferson Davis sent a telegram to his wife, Varina, in Richmond. She was the first to learn of the great victory and of the death of Francis Bartow. Mrs. Davis shared the news with her friends, then went to inform Mrs. Bartow. While Leroy P. Walker, the Confederate secretary of war, waited anxiously for word of the battle, Attorney General Judah P. Benjamin happened by Mrs. Davis's hotel and learned of the president's victory telegraph. He carried the news to the War Department, where the Cabinet was overjoyed, if a little miffed at being kept in the dark.

Hundreds of Washington's finest citizens filtered into the area near Manassas in the days before the climatic battle. Senators, congressmen, judges, gentlemen, and their finely attired women all rode out on horses or in buggies, often accompanied by servants and carrying large picnic baskets. Illinois Congressman John Logan came to fight as a private in the ranks. Secretary of War Simon Cameron perhaps had real business on the field where his brother would soon die. Ohio Congressman Albert G. Riddle attempted unsuccessfully to rally the routed troops.

"Many distinguished citizens came over from Washington to witness the grand performance of their army," a Confederate wrote home, "many of whom were captured and frightened to death by our advancing army." In addition to rifles and cannon, Southerners found slippers and parasols on the ground.

The Union General with a Medal of Honor ■ Orlando Bolivar Willcox

Orlando Bolivar Willcox was born on April 16, 1823, in Detroit, Michigan, and graduated from the U.S. Military Academy in 1847. He saw garrison duty until 1857 when he resigned to practice law. Willcox rejoined the army as a colonel in 1861 in time to lead a brigade at First Manassas, where he was wounded and captured.

Imprisoned for a year, Willcox was exchanged for Confederate privateers threatened with execution. He was appointed a brigadier and led a division at Antietam, Fredericksburg, Knoxville, and from the Wilderness to Appomattox, becoming a major general of volunteers and the regular army.

Willcox returned to his law practice in January 1866 but was reappointed a colonel in July. He spent ten years in San Francisco, then fought Apaches in Arizona, where a town was named for him. While living in Washington, D.C., from 1887 until 1905, Willcox wrote two novels under a pseudonym. In 1895 he was awarded the Medal of Honor for "most distinguished gallantry" at First Manassas. He died in Ontario, Canada, on May 10, 1907, and is buried at Arlington.

A Confederate soldier noticed that Union prisoners had written "Richmond or hell" across their caps.

cavalry and infantry in one confused mass, each seemingly bent on looking out for number one and letting the rest do the same."

"The plain was covered with the retreating groups," McDowell marveled, "and they seemed to infect those with whom they came in contact. The retreat soon became a rout, and this soon degenerated still further into a panic."

Stuart's pursuit was soon halted by the sheer numbers of prisoners he took. Other cavalry crossed Bull Run at Lewis Ford to cut off McDowell's retreat from Sudley Ford to the Warrenton turnpike, but Beauregard recalled them because of rumors that the Federals were threatening Union Mills far downstream. When the report proved false, the Federals escaped via Sudley and the Stone Bridge.

Johnston sent Longstreet and Bonham across Bull Run at Mitchell's and Blackburn's Fords to Centreville to sever McDowell's primary retreat route, but the nonexistent threat caused them to be ordered back. When they renewed the chase, a fresh Federal brigade under Col. Israel Richardson stopped them.

The Confederates were exhausted from marching and fighting all day. Realizing their condition, Beauregard called off the pursuit. A squadron of Col. R. C. W. Radford's Thirtieth Virginia Cavalry did encounter Keyes's brigade at the Warrenton turnpike. They were turned back by fire from a regular army battery but not before Confederate Capt. Delaware Kemper shelled the bridge spanning Cub Run. The first shot, fired by elderly, feisty Edmund Ruffin, who was also given the honor at Fort Sumter, hit the center of the Stone Bridge and blew a wagon onto its side, blocking the span just as two Union columns approached. The men panicked, throwing down their rifles and abandoning the wagons as they waded across the branch.

Federal prisoners from the battle were held as far south as Charleston. The New York Fire Zouaves below, whose line was broken by Stuart's cavalry, were imprisoned in Fort Moultrie.

HARPER'S

Union soldiers wandered back to Washington for days after the battle. Rather than return to their camps, they preferred venues of easy leisure. New leadership, however, brought better discipline.

"Then a scene of confusion ensued which beggars description," wrote Keyes. "Cavalry horses without riders, artillery horses disengaged from the guns with traces flying, wrecked baggage-wagons, and pieces of artillery drawn by six horses without drivers, flying at their utmost speed and whacking against other vehicles. . . . The rush produced a noise like a hurricane at sea."

Confederates recovered valuable materiel for weeks. "Baggage lay as thick as the rocks on the Pike," one soldier noted. "Wagons were broken in every fence corner, guns, trunks, clothes, &c blocked up the road." The Federals lost twenty-seven cannon, including the 30-pounder Parrott rifle, over a thousand artillery rounds, half a million rounds for the five hundred rifles abandoned, and all manner of equipment, rations, and hospital supplies.

Late in the day Jefferson Davis arrived at the battlefield to confer with Johnston. They agreed that the men were too exhausted, hungry, and short on ammunition to pursue the Federal army farther. Rain also began to pour, as it would often do following a major battle, and the roads were quickly rendered into quagmires.

Davis sent a telegram trumpeting the victory to Richmond: "Night has closed upon a hard-fought field," it read. "Our forces have won a glorious victory."

"The day is lost," McDowell wired his superiors. "Save Washington and the remnants of this army." Writing a day later he described a "most unaccountable transformation into a mob of a finely-appointed and admirably-led army."

A soldier of the Seventy-ninth New York wrote of the fighting at First Manassas, "He who had a big, or even a little tree, behind which to shelter himself, was looked upon with envy."

William Tecumseh Sherman was disgusted with the discipline shown by the raw Union troops. He wrote: "They fell into disorder—an incessant clamor of tongues, one saying they were not properly supported, another that they could not tell friend from foe. Each private thinks for himself. If he wants to go for water, he asks leave of no one." Sherman continued, "He takes the oats and corn, and even burns the house of his enemy," which is a fascinating comment, considering Sherman's future actions. He thought that "no curse could be greater than invasion by a volunteer army."

Sherman believed that McDowell and the other officers did their best to control their men, "but for us to say we commanded that army is no such thing. They did as they pleased."

In conclusion, the Ohioan decided that the recruits "are not good soldiers. They brag, but don't perform, complain sadly if they don't get everything they want, and a march of a few miles uses them up. It will take a long time to overcome these things, and what is in store for us in the future I know not."

Another result of the battle was the design of a new Confederate flag, a standard to be displayed in the field that was clearly distinguishable from the Stars and Stripes. Johnston and Beauregard designed a red square with a blue Saint Andrew's cross containing a white star to represent each Confederate state. It became the Confederate battle flag.

McDowell established a defensive position at Centreville with his reserves, but most of his army fled for the capital. At dawn of July 22 they had all reached Alexandria and poured across the Long Bridge. The weaponless, mud-caked stragglers appalled the residents.

Walt Whitman, reporting for a Brooklyn newspaper, watched the "shame faced" men arrive, looking "baffled, humiliated, panic-struck. They come along in disorderly mobs, some in squads, stragglers, companies . . . defeated soldiers—queer-looking objects, strange eyes and faces, drench'd, and fearfully worn, hungry, haggard, blister'd in the feet. Good people hurry up something for their grub. They put wash-kettles on the fire, for soup, for coffee. They set tables on the sidewalks—wagonloads of bread are purchas'd, swiftly cut into stout chunks."

Women fed the men throughout the day, "and there in the rain they stand, active, silent, white-hair'd, and give food, though the tears stream down their cheeks almost without intermission, the whole time."

Fed, the soldiers fell asleep "anywhere, on the steps of houses, up close by the basements or fences, on the sidewalk, aside on some vacant lot, and deeply sleep."

Beauregard's ego allowed him to accept full responsibility for the victory. Although he ultimately directed the battle with great energy and skill,

All Quiet on the Potomac Tonight ▪ Thaddeus Oliver

Thaddeus Oliver was born on Christmas Day 1826 in Jeffersonville, Georgia. He taught school in Buena Vista while studying law and passed the bar. On April 15, 1861, Private Oliver left with the Second Georgia to fight in Virginia. While sitting around a campfire one night, he was inspired to write this classic poem, which he dashed off in an hour. Oliver returned home in November 1862 to raise a company of the Sixty-third Georgia, which joined the Army of Tennessee. Wounded in fighting around Charleston, South Carolina, Oliver died there in a hospital in 1864.

"All quiet along the Potomac tonight."
Except now and then a stray picket
Is shot as he walks on his beat to and
    fro,
By a rifleman hid in the thicket
'Tis nothing—a private or two now
    and then

Will not count on the news of the
    battle,
Not an officer lost—only one of the
    men—
Moaning out, all alone in the death
    rattle.

"All quiet along the Potomac tonight,"
Where the soldiers lie peacefully
    dreaming;
Their tents, in the rays of the clear
    autumn moon
Or the light of the watchfires, are
    gleaming.
A tremulous sigh, as the gentle night
    wind
Through the forest leaves slowly is
    creeping,
While the stars up above, with their
    glittering eyes,
Keep guard, for the army is sleeping.

There is only the sound of the one
    sentry's tread,

As he tramps from the rock to the
    fountain,
And thinks of the two in the low
    trundle bed,
Far away in the cot on the mountain.
His musket falls slack—his face, dark
    and grim,
Grows gentle with memories tender,
As he mutters a prayer for his children
    asleep—
For their mother, may heaven defend
    her.

The moon seems to shine as brightly
    as then,
That night, when the love yet unspoken,
Leaped up to his lips, and when low
    murmured vows
Were pledged to be ever unbroken.
Then drawing his sleeve roughly over
    his eyes,
He dashed off tears that are welling,
He gathers his gun close up to its
    place,

As if to keep down the heart's
    swelling.

He passes the fountain, the blasted
    pine tree—
The footstep is lagging and weary,
Yet onward he goes, through the
    broad belt of light,
Towards the shade of the forest so
    dreary.
Hark, was it the night-wind that
    rustled the leaves?
Was it the moonlight so wondrously
    flashing?
It looked like a rifle—ha, Mary,
    Goodbye.
And the life blood is ebbing and
    splashing.

"All quiet along the Potomac tonight"
no sound save the rush of the river;
While soft falls the dew on the face of
    the dead—
The picket's off duty forever.

What the Southerners lacked in materiel they compensated for with bluff and bravado, such as so-called Quaker guns, which were logs painted black and emplaced to resemble artillery. Such phantom ordnance confounded Union armies across northern Virginia during the first year of the war.

LIBRARY OF CONGRESS

he almost lost it through indecision and chaotic orders, which apparently only he understood. Beauregard and Davis, however, soon quarreled about rank and became enemies. Johnston, feeling he deserved more recognition than he received for reinforcing Beauregard and shaming him into taking action, quarreled with both. Many later felt that Johnston should have acted earlier, a character flaw that afflicted him throughout the war: He moved too cautiously and indecisively. Many Southern officers found further fame in the war, among them Johnston, Beauregard, Jackson, Longstreet, Ewell, A. P. Hill, Kirby Smith, Stuart, Early, and Imboden. Promising officers such as Bee and Bartow became martyrs, sanctified at the time but largely forgotten by history.

About 60,000 men had been on the field, certainly the largest battle North America had ever witnessed. The Confederates had suffered 387 men killed, 1,582 wounded, and 13 missing. A quarter of the casualties were suffered by Jackson's brigade. Many brave officers were lost by both sides.

"It's damn bad" was Lincoln's response to the disaster. Some 470 Union men were killed, 1,071 wounded, and 1,791 missing. The Federal army had started the battle with a good plan, but it was poorly led on the battlefield.

The same citizens who had forced Lincoln into premature action now castigated him for moving before the army was prepared. A congressional investigation absolved McDowell of blame for the debacle, but his career never recovered. A number of Federal careers, however, were made and lost at Manassas, among them Sherman's and Burnside's.

Ever the professional, Scott moved immediately to rebuild the army. Only days later, July 25, he appointed George B. McClellan, who had won a small battle in the western Virginia mountains shortly before Bull Run, to command Union forces.

Manassas had other results. The horrible tales of the battle vanquished the notion of war as a romantic and noble adventure. The belief that the war would be decided quickly by one bloodless battle was also shattered. The participants, in victory and defeat, resolved to redouble their efforts and win the war whatever the cost.

For thirty years following the Civil War, officers argued over their part in important battles. Affirming that he and not Beauregard was responsible for the victory at First Manassas, Joseph E. Johnston stated, "I gave every order of importance."

A Tour of the First Manassas Campaign

THE FIRST MANASSAS tour is not a fun journey. The twenty miles that required Irwin McDowell's green army two days to cover will still take hours in the dreadful suburban Washington traffic. Some will elect to tour Alexandria then hop on Interstate 66 to zip to the battlefield of First Manassas, but the Fairfax County Courthouse is worth a visit, and there are other historic sites with Civil War significance along the route.

A related, although modest, trip can be mounted to explore one of the Civil War's lost campaigns, the Confederate effort to blockade Washington, D.C., during the winter of 1861–62. To the south along the Potomac River are a few sites related to the Southern batteries that nearly closed the capital to shipping.

This tour begins in downtown Alexandria at the Ramsey house (1724, 221 King Street, 703-838-4200), the city's visitors center since 1956. Walking tours originate here to explore Alexandria, an old city established in 1749. Located directly across the Potomac River from Washington, D.C., this important port city was so strategic to the defense of the capital that it remained in Confederate hands only a matter of hours before Federal troops seized it in a nearly bloodless coup on May 24, 1861. Unlike large portions of the South, Alexandria was spared wholesale destruction while serving as an extensive Federal port, supply base, and hospital center. The docks bustled with activity as troops came and went. This was the primary departure point for George McClellan's Peninsula campaign, which employed 389 ships—ferryboats, side-wheelers, barges, schooners, canal boats, and essentially any vessel that could float—to transport over a hundred thousand men and innumerable tons of supplies.

Visit the waterfront, less than three blocks away, to get a feel for the importance of the port and its strategic position. Many important Civil War sites in Alexandria are within walking distance of the Ramsey house. Obtain maps, walking tour information, and brochures and set out.

On the opposite corner, at 107 South Fairfax, is the Stabler-Leadbeater Apothecary, built in 1792, operated until 1933, and now a museum and shop. Col. Robert E. Lee was shopping in the store in 1859 when Lt. Jeb Stuart arrived with orders directing Lee to travel immediately to Harpers Ferry to quell the insurrection of John Brown. A metal plaque on the exterior wall describes the event.

A block south and four blocks west, at South Washington and Prince, in the center of the city, is the

Virginia Infantry Monument, a stone obelisk that marks the site where seven hundred volunteers marched off to fight for the South. A Confederate statue, a dejected bronze image, was modeled by John A. Elder on a figure in his painting, *Appomattox*.

Two blocks north, at Washington and Cameron, is Christ Episcopal Church (1767). George Washington was a regular worshiper, and Robert E. Lee was confirmed here and rejoined the congregation after moving to Arlington house. Two pews are marked Washington and Lee. Legend holds that after morning services here on April 21, 1861, representatives of Virginia Gov. John Letcher met with Lee to offer him command of the state's military forces. A museum at the church records that Federal soldiers broke tombstones and stole Washington's brass pew marker. In the churchyard cemetery a mound topped by a marble tablet covers a mass grave of thirty-four Confederates who died in Union hospitals.

Four blocks north is the boyhood home of Robert E. Lee (1795, 607 Oronoco). The structure was a museum at one time but was recently sold for use as a private home. At some time in the future it may be a museum again. After financial reverses, Richard Henry "Lighthorse Harry" Lee moved his family here in 1812, having left the ancestral estate at Stratford. He also lived at other addresses in Alexandria (611 Cameron Street; 407 North Washington). The elder Lee died in coastal Georgia after an absence of five years. Robert E. Lee lived here until leaving for West Point in 1823. He witnessed the burning of Alexandria's warehouses and other property by the British in 1814 and met Lafayette when the famous Frenchman visited to pay his respects to Lee's mother. In this house on July 7, 1804, Mary "Molly" Fitzhugh Lee married George Washington Parke Custis, Martha Washington's grandson. Twenty years later, their daughter, Mary Anne Randolph Custis, married Robert E. Lee, a distant cousin and a former resident of the same house, which is an interesting coincidence. Across the street is the Lee-Fendall house (1785, 614 Oronoco Street, 703-548-1789), a Civil War hospital. Home to thirty-seven different Lees, at one time Robert E. Lee's father owned it, and the young Lee frequently visited family here.

Lee received his primary education at the Free School (400 block of South Washington Street). At

Robert E. Lee's boyhood home in Alexandria, Virginia.

the Hallowell School (established 1824, 609 Oronoco Street) Lee prepared for West Point.

In May 1869 Lee met with President U. S. Grant in Washington, where he stayed, but a reception was held in Lee's honor at 121 North Fairfax Street. The reception line was so long that Lee shook hands for two hours.

Other interesting Civil War sites in Alexandria include the Lyceum (1839, 201 South Washington Street, 703-838-4994), used as a Federal hospital. It is now a city museum. A display on the Marshall House incident—in which Elmer Ellsworth was killed—includes a fragment of the flag that sparked the event. The Atheneum (1851, 201 Prince Street, 703-548-0035), originally the Bank of Old Dominion, became a Union commissary. Legend has Lee being informed that he had been chosen to lead Virginia's military forces at the Hooe-Lloyd house (220 North Washington Street), the home of a Lee cousin. Local lore has the owner of Snowden house (619 South Lee Street) and other prominent residents of Alexandria being forced to ride in front of railroad engines heading into the interior of Virginia in 1864 to prevent John S. Mosby from attacking the trains.

The *Alexandria Gazette-Packet* (established in 1784, published at 717 Asaph Street) was burned by Federal occupation troops for its pro-Secessionist views. It continued publishing underground as the *Local News*. Odd Fellows Hall (218 North Columbus Street) was the site of the first reunion of Mosby's Rangers on January 16, 1895. It was the only such affair that Mosby attended; his Republican Party membership caused considerable conflict between him and former Confederates. The pastor of Saint Paul's Episcopal Church (228 South Pitt Street) was arrested during Union occupation.

There was considerable opposition to secession in northwestern Virginia, where Unionists organized the Restored Government of Virginia in Wheeling before moving to Alexandria during the Federal occupation. Its governor, Francis H. Pierpont, made his headquarters at the Stone house (418 Prince Street).

Alexandria National Cemetery (established 1862, Wilkes and Payne Streets), one of the first, contains the remains of 3,750 Union soldiers, most of them wounded or sick men who died in the city's many hospitals, particularly during Grant's 1864 Overland campaign. A controversy resulted following the war when 230 black soldiers were reinterred here from the Freedmen's Cemetery. In 1879 the United Daughters of the Confederacy (UDC) reinterred the remains of 30 Confederate soldiers in a mass grave on the grounds of Christ Church. Prominently marked at the front of the five-acre cemetery are the graves of U.S. marshalls who drowned in the pursuit of John Wilkes Booth. The cemetery was added to the National Register of Historic Places in 1981.

Adjacent is Christ Church Cemetery, which contains the graves of the Confederacy's highest-ranking general when the war started, Samuel Cooper, and diplomat James M. Mason, whose seizure from the British ship *Trent* by the Union navy nearly brought Great Britain into the war. This is also the resting place of Confederate naval officer Sidney Smith Lee, brother of Robert E. Lee and father of Fitzhugh Lee, a Confederate cavalry general and a governor of Virginia.

In nearby Saint Paul's Cemetery is the grave of Wilmer McLean. It was said that the Civil War began in his front yard in Manassas and ended in his parlor at Appomattox Court House. Here also lies Abraham Myers, the first quartermaster of the Confederacy, whose wife allegedly had a spat with Jefferson Davis's wife, Varina. Also buried here is Confederate Col. Julius A. de Lagnel, who was wounded and captured at Rich Mountain in western Virginia in July 1861.

Ivy Hill Cemetery (King Street, Route 7) contains the grave of Frank Stringfellow, one of Jeb Stuart's scouts.

This replica of a Union headquarters building houses the museum at Fort Ward.

On Royal Street is the site of the Marshall House, now occupied by a modern hotel. Here James W. Jackson shot Col. Elmer E. Ellsworth for removing a Confederate flag and was in turn killed by Cpl. Francis E. Brownell.

Historic Falls Church (1769, 115 East Fairfax Street at Washington Street, on U.S. 29–Route 211) suffered during the Civil War when it was repeatedly occupied by Union soldiers who used the structure as a hospital and stable. By war's end the interior had been gutted. The stone baptismal font was stolen in 1863 by a soldier who planned to ship it north, but locals managed to recover and hide it. It was returned to the church in 1876. Tablets inscribed with the Lord's Prayer, the Ten Commandments, and the Apostles' Creed were destroyed by Federal soldiers. The church was repaired following the war with most of the expenses, thirteen hundred dollars, paid by the U.S. government.

Near the fence is the grave of a Mr. Reed, a Baptist minister executed as a spy in 1863 by Mosby. A marker at the end of the front walk honors an unknown Confederate soldier. Thaddeus Lowe operated balloons from this area.

North of Falls Church is Freedom Hill Fort, a unique fortification different from the artillery positions usually preserved. Completed on January 11, 1865, it was a fortified picket post that housed one hundred men of the Fifth Pennsylvania Heavy Artillery and protected Union camps against raiders such as Mosby. The hilltop position had a commanding view of the area for miles since the area had been cleared for timber to be used in constructing forts and for firewood. It has been preserved, restored, and interpreted with historical markers. To reach Freedom Hill Fort, at the intersection of the Leesburg Pike–Route 7 and Dolly Madison Boulevard–Route 123, turn west on the latter and turn right on Old Court House Road to the fort on the left.

Several miles north of Alexandria, a mile west of Arlington Heights and just northwest of Falls Church, is Munson's Hill, which was fortified by Confederates after the battle of First Manassas until early 1862. From here, Southerners had a good view of the dome of the Federal Capitol and observed the frantically erected fortifications around Washington. The world's first antiaircraft fire was directed from here at a Federal observation balloon operating from Arlington Heights. Munson's and Upton's (near Wilson Boulevard) Hills, twelve to fifteen miles beyond Fairfax Court House, were a mile apart and within sight of each other. They were held by two regiments of Longstreet's infantry when his headquarters was at the town of Falls Church, and included a few cannon and Stuart's cavalry on the flanks. Pickets were positioned only a mile from the Union lines, and constant skirmishing ensued. After Union forces occupied the area, Fort Ramsay was built on Upton's Hill and Fort Munson on Munson's Hill, where Lincoln and the cabinet observed McClellan's grand review of the Army of the Potomac on November 20, 1861.

From the Ramsay house drive west on King Street–Route 7. Drive straight to follow West 7 in front of the towering George Washington National Masonic Memorial. Turn right onto Kenwood at the sign for the Fort Ward Museum, then turn left onto West Braddock Road at a second sign for the fort. Turn right into Fort Ward.

The Masonic Monument occupies Shooters Hill, a Civil War fortification. This is one of the best surviving examples of the extensive defenses that once surrounded Washington from the Potomac River south of Alexandria to the river above Georgetown and eventually across the land approaches in Maryland. These fortifications consisted of thirty-three forts, twenty-five batteries, and seven blockhouses armed with nine hundred assorted artillery pieces, including large smoothbores, powerful rifles, and

massive mortars. All were connected by miles of rifle pits and infantry works. A total of thirty-seven miles of fortifications were constructed, and many miles of military roads were established to allow quick communication between threatened points.

Modeled on Frenchman Sébastian Le Prestre Vauban's seventeenth-century fieldworks, the line was started in May 1861 but work proceeded slowly until the defeat at First Manassas, which immediately stimulated additional work. Predictably, the fortifications were expanded again following Second Manassas. By the end of 1862, Washington was one of the most heavily fortified cities in the world. Maj. Gen. John G. Barnard, chief engineer of the defenses of Washington, directed the work.

Fort Ward, started in September 1861, was named for Comdr. James K. Ward, the first Federal naval officer killed in the war. It became the fifth largest fort in the system. While Confederates were entrenched on nearby Munson's Hill, fieldworks were thrown up on high ground to defend the Little River turnpike (Route 236) and the Leesburg turnpike (Route 7) on September 1, 1861, and enlarged following Second Manassas.

When the Civil War ended, the five bastions of Fort Ward had thirty-six embrasures and twenty-nine guns, including a 100-pounder Parrott, which could lay down a crossfire on any attacker. There were also bombproofs for ammunition storage, three barracks for troops, officers quarters, a mess, and a stable. Northern Virginia was denuded of trees to supply lumber for the forts and to provide clear lines of fire. After the war, Fort Ward's woodwork was salvaged and sold for eighty-eight dollars.

Donated to the city of Alexandria in 1961, Fort Ward was opened to the public in 1964 as a forty-five-acre park containing 95 percent of the original works. The museum is a replica of a typical Union headquarters and officers quarters building, based on a Mathew Brady photograph of one erected in Alexandria. The excellent displays explain the purpose, construction, and location of Washington's defenses, the life of garrison soldiers, and the operation of artillery through maps, sketches, pictures, shells, musical instruments, medical equipment, shoulder weapons, and other artifacts. There are special exhibits about the Ellsworth-Jackson incident and the role of black soldiers in the war.

A walking tour takes visitors through a recreated 1865 gate erected by the Corps of Engineers, which constructed all the forts. The restored northwest bastion has emplacements, platforms, heavy artillery, two bombproofs, and abatis. An officers hut has also been recreated.

Return to the road and turn left onto West Braddock. Turn right onto Quaker and pass the site of Fort Williams. Turn right onto Route 236, which is Duke but shortly becomes historic Little River Turnpike, an important Civil War thoroughfare, and Main Street in Fairfax. After 11.8 miles the Fairfax Museum and Visitors Center is on the left.

The museum explores the history of northern Virginia and has a number of Civil War displays, including Stuart's sword, and other memorabilia of Stuart and Mosby. The visitors center has an excellent tour guide titled *A Historic Treasure, Old Town Fairfax, Virginia, Journey Through Time.*

Fairfax Courthouse witnessed a great deal of Civil War activity, including the repeated advance and retreat of Union armies and a famous raid by John S. Mosby and his partisan rangers.

Across the street is the Farr Homeplace (1885, 10230 Main Street). The original Farr home was torched by Union soldiers after Richard R. Farr and a servant fired on Union troops. Farr later rode with Mosby and constructed the house following the war.

Turn left back onto Main Street–Little River Turnpike. Just after the road jogs to the right, turn left and go straight through the light onto West. Immediately across the highway is the courthouse complex on your left, and parking is available on both sides of the road.

The historic Fairfax Court House (1800) contains the original will of George and Martha Washington. On the grounds are two boat howitzers captured by Confederates at First Manassas (and facing north) and the Marr Monument. The first serious skirmish of the Civil War occurred here at 3 A.M. on June 1, 1861, when Federal cavalry raided the town, which was defended by the Warrenton Rifles. As Confederate Capt. John Quincy Marr, a VMI graduate and professor, led his troops, a spent bullet struck him in the chest and killed him without penetrating him. Marr was found the following morning in a field eight hundred feet southwest of the courthouse. He was the first Confederate officer killed in the Civil War. The courthouse was used as headquarters by a number of different officers, both Confederate and Federal, and the cupola served as an observation and signaling station. Mosby captured a Union telegraph operator here.

In Willcox's Tavern, which stood north across Main Street from the courthouse, Jefferson Davis met with Joseph E. Johnston, P. G. T. Beauregard, and Gustavus W. Smith on October 1–2, 1861. They agreed that the Confederate army was in no shape to take the offensive. Legend contends that Beauregard designed the famous Confederate battle flag there. The flag used at First Manassas had caused considerable confusion among both Confederate and Federal troops because it was so similar to the Stars and Stripes. The Cary sisters of Fairfax were commissioned to sew the first three new flags.

The historic courthouse occupies the corner of Main–Little River Turnpike and Chain Bridge Road. North up Chain Bridge Road are two Civil War sites. To the right is the Ford Building (1835, 3977 Chain Bridge Road), an office building that was the

1863 home of Antonia Ford, a beautiful, charming twenty-two-year-old woman. She listened intently to conversations between the Federal officers who frequently visited, including McDowell, McClellan, and John Pope, and passed the intelligence on to Confederate authorities. She allegedly learned that McDowell was advancing on Manassas and forwarded the intelligence.

Impressed with Miss Ford's exploits, Stuart sent her a commission as "my honorary aide-de-camp," which she proudly hid in her home. Following Mosby's raid, the head of the U.S. Secret Service, Gen. Lafayette C. Baker, suspected the Fords of espionage. He dispatched female agent Frankie Abel to cultivate Antonia's confidence. The ruse worked, and Antonia showed Abel her "commission." Antonia and her father were imprisoned in the Old Capital Prison in Washington. Her father was shortly released, but Antonia languished until May 20, 1863, and was arrested again when she refused to take the oath of allegiance. Maj. Joseph C. Willard, Union provost marshal and owner of Washington's famed Willard Hotel, who had arrested and imprisoned Antonia, fell in love with her. Seven months later he had her released, and they were married on March 16, 1864. Due to the harsh prison conditions she endured, Antonio died only seven years later. It is a unique, if bizarre, love story.

The Moore house (1840, 3950 Chain Bridge Road) is on the left farther down the road. Mosby unsuccessfully searched this house for Federal Col. Sir Percy Wyndham, who had dared call the Confederate raider a horse thief. Mosby retorted that every horse he seized had a Federal trooper armed with two pistols and a saber sitting on it. Unfortunately, Wyndham was absent.

On Chain Bridge Road south of Route 236 is the Joshua Gunnell house (1835, 4023 Chain Bridge Road). During a June 1, 1861, skirmish on Main Street, former Virginia governor William "Extra Billy" Smith, a guest, ran from this house to take command of the Warren Rifles when Marr was killed. Two years later, when Mosby raided on March 9, 1863, Federal Lt. Col. Robert Johnstone, commanding in Wyndham's absence, was housed here. Hearing a commotion outside, Johnstone threw open a second-floor window and demanded to know what was happening. When derisive laughter met his request, Johnstone perceived the situation and ran out the back of the house and hid under an outhouse, losing his nightshirt in the process. The two Confederates sent to the house were delayed by Johnstone's wife, who met them swinging and scratching. Johnstone escaped Confederate capture but was afterward known as "Outhouse Johnstone."

The city of Fairfax has recently invested in its heritage, purchasing Blenheim (1850, 3610 Old Lee Highway) and twelve surrounding acres in the center of town. The brick Georgian–Greek Revival structure was abandoned by its owners during the Civil War and used for more than a year as a Federal hospital and convalescence home. Its treasure is found on the walls of a stairway and two rooms of an attic that still exhibit dozens of vivid signatures and graffiti made by Union soldiers. The earliest of more than fifty items is dated March 1862 and the last is marked June 30, 1863. Some of the drawings are pornogaphic, and a few of those were destroyed by past residents. A large drawing of a warship is prominent, and a sketch of John S. Mosby and other inscriptions are covered by wallpaper. Done in pencil, charcoal, and crayon, the graffiti contain various phrases—some in German—including "Death to the Rebels," word and number games, and a verse from "The Star-Spangled Banner."

There are presently no earthworks preserved for public viewing, but that may soon change. At the intersection of Route 28 and Old Centreville Road is a parcel of land containing two trenches. One of these, a Confederate fortification shaped like an *L,* is all that remains of the five-mile defensive line constructed during the winter of 1861–62, a lone remnant of the

Southern army's first winter camp. The trench is 110 yards long and five to six feet deep. The work was reversed and used by Federals. Works like these boasted the Quaker artillery that so embarrassed McClellan on the peninsula.

The second trench was a Union work, 133 yards long and two to three feet deep. John Pope's army occupied it in late August–early September 1862, following the rout at Second Manassas, until the battle of Chantilly, which forced him to retreat to Washington, as did George Gordon Meade following the battle of Bristoe Station in October 1863. Developers plan to preserve the Confederate work and build townhouses over the Federal.

Chain Bridge Road is Route 123 south of Fairfax and leads to Saint Mary's Catholic Church (1758). After the battles of Second Manassas and Chantilly, many wounded soldiers were transported here for care under Clara Barton, future founder of the Red Cross. It was her first exposure to the horrors of war. The fields surrounding the church were outdoor wards for the wounded.

Southeast of Fairfax, at the intersection of Route 645 (Burke Lake Road) and Route 652 (Burke Road), is the site of Burke's Station. Stuart used the Federal military telegraph office there to send a message complaining of the substandard mules he had captured.

In eastern Fairfax County, the area around Lewinville Church, where two skirmishes occurred in 1861, is being developed. After visiting the site, Julia Ward Howe wrote "The Battle Hymn of the Republic."

Continue south on West a short distance and turn right onto Page, then turn right onto Judicial, and turn right on Main to the City Cemetery (10565 Main Street) on the right.

At the front of the cemetery is a Confederate monument, a large granite obelisk dedicated on October 1, 1890, by Gov. William Fitzhugh Lee. It honors Fairfax's ninety-six Confederate war dead and the two hundred Southern casualties who were gathered from across the county and buried beneath the monument. Also interred here are eleven of Mosby's Rangers. One, Ned Hurst, was wounded seven times but killed nineteen Federals. Another raider, John N. Ballard, lost a leg in a skirmish in Prince William County in June 1863, and his artificial leg was crushed during a later cavalry clash. After Union Col. Ulric Dahlgren was killed on a raid against Richmond, Ballard received the Yankee raider's artificial limb. The most famous burial is James W. Jackson, killed May 24, 1861, after shooting Elmer Ellsworth in Alexandria. Jackson was shot and bayoneted by Cpl. Francis E. Brownell of the First Zouaves, which earned him the Medal of Honor. Brownell's uniform is displayed in the Manassas National Battlefield Visitors Center. This was the site of a Union stockade during the war.

To see the Dr. William Gunnell house (1835, 10520 Main Street), turn right onto Main Street here and the house will be on your left. It was in this house that Mosby captured Brig. Gen. Edwin Stoughton on the night of March 9, 1863. The general, who had attended a champagne party earlier that night, was sound asleep when Mosby entered his bedroom. The Confederate ranger raised Stoughton's nightshirt and soundly slapped the general's buttocks,

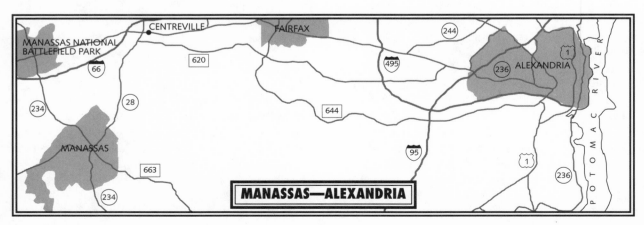

MANASSAS—ALEXANDRIA

The famous Stone Bridge at the Manassas battlefield was recreated after its destruction during the war.

Intense fighting swirled around the Stone House during First and Second Mannassas.

then commanded him, "Get up, General, and come with me."

"What is this!" Stoughton shouted. "Do you know who I am?"

"I reckon I do, General," Mosby replied. "Did you ever hear of Mosby?"

"Yes, have you caught him?"

"No, but he has caught you."

Note the stone monument in front of the house that commemorates the event. Mosby and his twenty-eight men captured thirty-eight other Union soldiers and fifty-eight horses.

Upon learning of the raid, Lincoln reportedly said something to the effect of, "Well, I can make more generals, but I do regret losing the horses."

Northeast of Fairfax is Blenheim (1850, 3610 Old Lee Highway), which was occupied by Federal soldiers who carved or wrote their names, regiments, and sketches into the wooden attic walls.

In some manner get back on Main Street heading west toward Manassas. Turn left onto U.S. 29–Lee Highway and continue to the intersection of U.S. 29 with Route 28–Centreville Road.

McDowell concentrated his troops at Centreville before advancing against Beauregard at First Manassas. For six months following that battle, from fall 1861 until spring 1862, the community was the center of the Confederate line facing Washington. Over forty-five thousand soldiers manned eight miles of fortifications on the heights around Centreville, which was a crossroads town with a scattering of houses and churches. The strength of the position led McClellan to develop a plan to approach Richmond from the southeast rather than the north. When Johnston ordered the line abandoned early in 1862, the vast camps and considerable stores were torched. After Centreville's occupation by Federal forces, McClellan was mocked because correspondents found obvious evidence that one hundred thousand men had not been stationed here. Further embarrassment was provided by Quaker guns, which were merely charred logs that poked out of many embrasures.

Centreville was also important to the Federals. After Second Manassas, John Pope took refuge within a line of Union works until the battle of Chantilly, which was an effort to cut Pope off from Washington or to force him to retreat into Washington's defenses. At the end of the Bristoe campaign, following Gettysburg in 1863, George G. Meade also sought safety here. Mosby operated in the area during the last two years of the war.

Discipline deteriorated within Confederate ranks in the dreary months following First Manassas. When two of Maj. Roberdeau Wheat's Louisiana Zouaves, Dennis Corcoran and Michael O'Brien, beat an officer, an example had to be made. The two men were executed on December 9, 1861, with the entire army watching. The execution site is a little southwest of Centreville. In 1979 the remains were exhumed and reinterred at Saint John's Episcopal

Church, near the fence in the northwest corner of the cemetery. To reach the church, backtrack on Route 29 and turn left on Braddock Road to Mount Gilead Road and turn right. The church will be on the right.

Centreville was once surrounded by miles of earthworks, including several substantial forts, but extensive urbanization has destroyed most of them.

Continue on U.S. 29–Lee Highway to cross Cub Run, where a Confederate artillery shell wrecked a wagon and blocked the Stone Bridge, causing a great panic among the Federals retreating from First Manassas. Most abandoned their equipment and fled in haste, leaving behind cannon, caissons, wagons, and the carriages of civilians who were caught in the mad rush.

After crossing Bull Run, beside the famous Stone Bridge, turn right into the parking area and walk back to view the beautiful span, which was the primary avenue of escape for two separate Union armies a year apart. This is a reproduction of the original, which did not survive the war. From a spot near Cub Run, McDowell swung far to the northwest, his men making a slow march on the rough roads and over hundreds of trees felled by the Confederates. It had taken the raw soldiers two days to cover the short distance from Washington. A trail leads from the bridge north to Farm Ford, where Sherman crossed his brigade during First Manassas.

Turn right from the parking area at the Stone Bridge onto U.S. 29–Lee Highway, then turn right onto Route 234–Sudley Springs Road and park in the lot near Sudley Methodist Church.

A trail leads to Sudley Springs Ford, where McDowell crossed to start the battle of First Manassas. Details about the springs and church can be found in the Second Manassas tour.

Return on Route 234 and turn right into Tour Stop No. 3, Dogan Ridge. Ignore that Second Manassas site and cross the road to the east to explore Matthews Hill, where the earliest fighting at First Manassas occurred.

Informed by an observer in a tower that masses of Union troops were crossing at Sudley Springs Ford, Col. Nathan Evans ignored the weak demonstration

The only statue at Manassas is of Thomas J. "Stonewall" Jackson, who played pivotal roles in both battles fought on these fields.

at the Stone Bridge and hurried his small force to Matthews Hill, where he slowed Ambrose Burnside's division. Although reinforced by Barnard Bee and Francis Bartow, the Confederates were battered back over Buck Hill to the south and then across Young's Branch and past the Stone House to the slopes of Henry Hill. Artillery pieces along the trail represent those used during First Manassas and Second Manassas by both armies. The Matthews house and others are ruins.

Continue back on Route 234 toward U.S. 29, but turn left into the parking lot for the Stone House just before the intersection.

This is the Henry P. Matthew house, located at the base of Buck Hill. Henry Hill rises to the south of the highway. The Stone House witnessed hot combat during both battles, when it served as a hospital. It was struck by many shells and bullets, and several are seen recreated in the walls. During summers and busy weekends the house is staffed and interpretive displays, tours, and special programs are featured.

Remain on Route 234 to cross U.S. 29 and turn left into the Manassas National Battlefield Park Visitors Center.

This park originated when the Sons of Confederate Veterans (SCV) bought 130 acres on Henry Hill, where they organized a Confederate memorial park. In 1940 it was deeded to the National Park Service, which purchased additional land, including important sites associated with Second Manassas. The park now contains 3,025 acres. Walking tours of Henry Hill originate from the visitors center several times daily. Among the artifacts displayed in the visitors center is the uniform of Cpl. Francis Brownell, who killed James Jackson at the Marshall House.

After viewing the displays in the newly renovated center, which includes a video and a fiber-optic map exploring the battles fought here, start your tour at the great equestrian statue of Thomas Jonathan Jackson, who, properly or not, is considered the Confederate hero of First Manassas. He gained his immortal nickname "Stonewall" here.

The general is mounted on Little Sorrel, a Yankee horse he seized from a train at Harpers Ferry. Although Jackson purchased the mount for his wife,

This monument honors the first Confederate general to die during the war—Barnard E. Bee of South Carolina, who also bestowed Jackson with his famous nickname, Stonewall.

The Civil War's first monument was erected just months after First Manassas to honor Francis Bartow, a Georgian killed while leading his troops. Only the stub of the monument remains today.

he decided to keep it for himself when he noticed how calm the horse was. Jackson was riding Little Sorrel when he was mortally wounded at Chancellorsville, and the horse was sent to North Carolina to live with Jackson's widow. Little Sorrel died at age thirty-six, having lived longer than his famous owner. Jackson is depicted riding the famed horse here, on Richmond's Monument Boulevard, and on the great stone monolith of Stone Mountain, Georgia. Little Sorrel was stuffed and can be viewed today at the Virginia Military Institute in Lexington, where Stonewall taught artillery tactics and physics. The bones of the noble beast were buried at Jackson's statue there in 1997.

Greater heroes of the battle were Barnard E. Bee and Francis S. Bartow, whose troops died while Jackson stood like a wall. They are recognized with modest stone monuments and metal plaques erected by the UDC in the 1930s near where the generals were killed making valiant assaults to hold off the Federals. Ironically, Bartow was honored by the war's first monument. Just six weeks after the battle, on September 4, 1861, a slab of white marble, engraved with his name and famous words, was erected at a ceremony attended by more than a thousand people, including three Georgia regiments. By spring 1862 the monument had been all but destroyed by Confederate souvenir hunters and angry Federals. The stub can be seen beneath a cedar tree near the other monuments.

On Henry Hill, Johnston and Beauregard organized the scattered Confederate units, all green ninety-day recruits. Beauregard led them into battle as Johnston rode to Portici to direct the flood of reinforcements arriving on the field. McDowell had thirty-five thousand troops in the field, while the Confederates started with twenty-two thousand and received ten thousand reinforcements during the fighting.

Numerous cannon and interpretive markers line the path to the Henry house and illustrate well the famous actions of First Manassas that were fought on the slopes of this historic ridge. The Henry house was destroyed by artillery fire during the battle and reconstructed later. Near the house is the Henry family cemetery, where rests the body of the eighty-five-year-old invalid widow Judith Carter Henry, killed July 21, 1861, during the battle. Her bible is displayed in the visitors center.

Also notable is the Bull Run Monument, a pyramid of brown sandstone blocks adorned with artillery shells. It was one of the first Civil War monuments, erected on June 10, 1865, by Union Brig. Gen. William Gamble's cavalry and dedicated to the "Patriots" who fought at First Manassas. This obelisk is identical to the Second Manassas Monument in the Deep Cut.

Two walking tours begin at the visitors center. The most ambitious is the five-mile Stone Bridge Trail, which starts in the area of the Jackson statue, the Confederate battle line, and Jackson's guns. The route follows farm roads, which Southern soldiers traversed, to Tour Stop 2, the site of the Van Pelt house. This ground was the extreme left of Beauregard's original line, covering the fords of Bull Run, which McDowell flanked far to the left at Sudley Ford. Tour Stop 3 is the Stone Bridge, and the trail continues to Tour Stop 4, Farm Ford, which was used

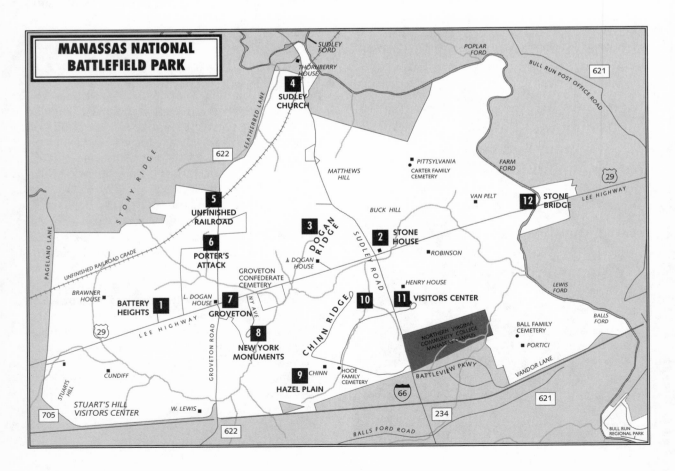

The home of widow Judith Henry, destroyed by an exploding shell that also killed her, has been reconstructed.

often by both armies during the war and by William Tecumseh Sherman's brigade at First Manassas.

From here the trail follows the Union advance. Tour Stop 5 highlights the ruins of the Carter house (Pittsylvania) on Van Pelt Ridge, where the Confederates fought to counter McDowell's advance then withdrew to Matthews Hill. The Stovall Marker is Tour Stop 6, on the Confederate right, where Georgia Pvt. George T. Stovall died carrying his brother off the battlefield. The trail continues to Tour Stop 7, Matthews Hill, a Union position marked by a row of cannon. Continue over Buck Hill to the Stone House, Tour Stop 8, and up Henry Hill to the Henry house at Tour Stop 9, which faces the Confederate line.

The second walking tour is the one-mile Henry Hill Walking Trail, which starts at Tour Stop 1, the forward position taken by Ricketts's Union battery, represented by a line of artillery pieces and scene of one of the turning points of the battle. Tour Stop 2 is a position that was held by the Seventh Georgia, whose veterans later erected six stone markers at positions held by the regiment. Francis Bartow died leading the Seventh and Eighth Georgia. Tour Stop 3 is at the Henry House Monument, erected in 1865 by Federal soldiers to honor their casualties. The reconstructed Henry farmhouse and graveyard is Tour Stop 4. Visible from Tour Stop 5 is Matthews Hill, where fifteen thousand Northerners advanced against Confederate John Imboden and his four artillery pieces, which covered the retreat of Southern infantry from Matthews Hill.

Tour Stop 6 is a lane and fence line on the Robinson farm, past which the Confederates retreated. At Tour Stop 7 are the remains of the Robinson house, a chimney and foundation, where Wade Hampton's South Carolina Legion bought time before being forced back. Robinson, a freed slave, saw his property destroyed by Union troops during the battle of Second Manassas. In 1873 Congress awarded him $1,249 in damages. Tour Stop 8 is the area where Johnston and Beauregard rallied the remnants of their command and were reinforced by Jackson and thirteen cannon. Before he died here, Bernard Bee bestowed the famous nickname on Jackson. From Tour Stop 10 Jackson attacked Griffin's battery, at Tour Stop 11, which was overrun because the battery commander believed the attackers were his infantry support. For hours the battle at Tour Stop 12 was charge and countercharge. Tour Stop 13 is Chinn Ridge, viewed after a short car trip.

From the visitors center drive back to Route 234 and turn left, along the base of Bald Hill, which was part

Judith Henry was the only civilian killed during the battle of First Manassas. Her grave is atop Henry Hill, near her restored homeplace.

of the Confederate line, and turn right onto the park road to drive along Chinn Ridge.

Late in the day the battle had spilled across the Manassas-Sudley road and the Warrenton turnpike to this area. As Confederate reinforcements continued to arrive on the field they were directed here, to the Confederate left. An attack broke O. O. Howard's Federal troops and began the Union rout about 4 P.M., after ten hours of combat.

Beauregard established his headquarters in 1861 at Liberia (1825), which has been donated to the city of Manassas, although full restoration will require millions of dollars. He utilized the home, and staff quarters were maintained in tents on the grounds. This was also the site of Confederate Camp Picket. The home was a hospital during the battle of First Manassas on July 19, and at the close of the day Jefferson Davis met with Johnston and Beauregard here. They agreed that the Confederates were in no shape to pursue the beaten Federal army to Washington. By June 1862 Union Gen. Irwin McDowell occupied the home. Because McDowell had been injured by a fall from a horse and could not travel, President Lincoln and Secretary of State William Seward visited the general, surely making this the only structure visited by both presidents during the war (at least until Lincoln explored the Confederate White House in April 1865).

Portici (1799), from which Johnston directed reinforcements to the battlefield, lies in ruins at the end of Vandor Lane. Shelling during the battle drove pregnant Mrs. Fannie Lewis from her home to a ditch, where she delivered Johnston Beauregard Lewis. Portici saw service as a hospital and was the scene of a brisk cavalry battle on August 30, 1862, during Second Manassas. It was burned by Federal soldiers.

Signal Hill has received recent improvements. This was the site where Capt. Edward Porter Alexander, atop an observation tower, signaled Evans, "Look out for your left, you are turned," which initiated the fighting at First Manassas. The incident is considered the first modern battlefield signal message. In 1996 a monument, the only one to the Confederate Signal Corps, was dedicated here. Another attraction is earthworks that accommodated twelve cannon.

Yorkshire Acres Subdivision is the site of Wilmer McLean's home, Yorkshire, destroyed during the war. On July 18, 1861, Beauregard trans-

The First Manassas Monument, adjacent to the Henry house, was one of the first Civil War monuments.

ferred his headquarters there, and during the battle Union artillery destroyed the family china as they ate dinner. Wounded soldiers soon filled the interior. After Second Manassas intruded on their home, McLean resolved to move his family to a place far removed from danger. He purchased a home in remote Appomattox Court House, but three years later Lee surrendered to Grant in his parlor.

The fords where Confederates and Federals clashed before First Manassas—Ball's Ford, Island Ford, Mitchell's Ford, Blackburn's Ford, and the railroad bridge near Union Mills—lie downstream of the Stone Bridge and are not accessible to the public. Earthworks remain at Mitchell's Ford, and the original stone piers of the Orange and Alexandria Railroad bridge remain. The span was important to Union operations throughout the war and was destroyed several times, first by Stuart prior to First Manassas and again by Jackson just before Second Manassas. Constant threats by Stuart and Mosby induced the Federals to prefabricate sections for the bridge that could be hauled to the piers and quickly assembled.

Just north of Manassas Battlefield Park is Blooms Crossing, where the Georgia Cemetery contains the graves of seventy-five Georgia and Louisiana troops. Also here are the Connor house, which was Joseph E. Johnston's field headquarters, and Camp Carondelet, site of a grand military ball on February 14, 1862.

Important Civil War sites in Manassas are examined closely on the Second Manassas tour, including an excellent city museum, a cemetery, several monuments, and fortifications. Manassas Junction was an important rail center, controlling traffic to the strategic Shenandoah Valley via the Manassas Gap Railroad. The Orange and Alexandria Railroad ultimately led to Richmond, skirting the direct route, which was hampered by a wilderness of forests, streams, and swamps. Throughout most of the war, Manassas was seen as the first stop on the one-hundred-mile journey to Richmond.

THE ROUTE south from Alexandria is the appropriately designated U.S. 1. Known since colonial days as the Potomac Path and Kings Highway, it was the major overland transportation route between the North and the South for several centuries. During the American Revolution the army of George Washington and Rochambeau and another commanded by Lafayette marched via it to Yorktown in 1781. Along the route is Fort Willard, George Washington's estate and burial site at Mount Vernon, George Mason's plantation home at Gunston Hall, Henry "Lighthorse Harry" Lee's home site at Leesylvania, Polich Church, and the historic communities of Occoquan, Woodbridge, Dumfries, and Quantico.

From U.S. 1 south of Alexandria turn right on Fort Hunt Road, right on Belle Haven Road up the hill,

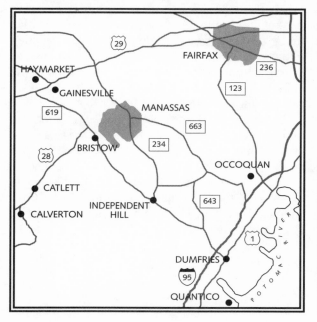

right on Radcliff, and left on Fort Drive to Fort Willard Circle.

This site was donated to Fairfax County, which has developed a park to preserve Fort Willard in a natural state. It may be restored at some future date. Parapets, ditches, magazine, and even earthen gun platforms are in good shape. Guarding the Kings Highway and the Accotink road, Fort Willard contained fourteen guns, including 24-pounder siege guns and 4.5-inch rifles. A guardhouse, three twenty-by-one-hundred-foot barracks, officers quarters, cook house, one bombproof, and one magazine completed the facility.

Eight miles south of Alexandria off U.S. 1 is Mount Vernon, which contains the graves of George and Martha Washington, their restored mansion and outbuildings, thirty acres of gardens, and a museum with many of the Washingtons' personal possessions. Federals and Confederates alike claimed Washington as their patron saint, both sides believing he would have endorsed their stand. Soldiers traveling on the King's Highway invariably made a slight detour to pay their respects to this most honored of American heroes.

The interior of Polich Church (1774, 9301 Richmond Highway), sixteen miles south of Alexandria on U.S. 1, was torn out when Federal troops stabled horses in it. Soldiers carved their initials into the sandstone walls and stole the baptismal font. It was missing for years until found on a nearby farm, where it had been used as a watering trough.

Fort Belvoir, entered from U.S. 1, features the U.S. Army Engineering Museum (Sixteenth Street and Belvoir Road), which includes Civil War displays.

Occoquan, established in 1765, was a thriving industrial community during the Civil War. In the early months, with Washington and Alexandria blockaded, mail between the North and the South passed through here. The Hammill Hotel (200 Union Street, corner of Union and Commerce Streets) was brigade headquarters for Wade Hampton during the war's first winter, before the Confederates were forced to withdraw to Ballywack Creek.

Visitors are drawn to Occoquan today by its numerous shops and restaurants. A good guide to the primary historical structures is available in the brochure *Ghosts of Historic Occoquan, Virginia, A "Spirited" History,* available from the Prince William

County Conference and Visitors Bureau. The Mill House Museum (Mill Street, 703-491-7525) provides a good orientation.

A series of Confederate batteries constructed on high bluffs along the Potomac River in Prince William County during the fall of 1861 closed the Potomac River to Union traffic early in the war, isolating Alexandria and Washington and limiting Federal strategy. Various plans were made to capture the batteries, but the Confederate withdrawal in early 1862 from Centreville-Manassas caused the positions to be abandoned.

Batteries were erected at the creek entrances to Occoquan and Dumfries (Newport), Freestone Point, Cockpit Point, Possum Point, and Evansport (Quantico). The most powerful guns were placed on either side of the mouth of Quantico Creek. The bluff there was high and projected into the river, which enabled gunners to keep Federal ships under fire for a longer period of time. The largest battery was at Rising Hill, now occupied by Walter Hall (1900) on the marine corps installation.

The site of the batteries on the high bluffs at Freestone Point is part of Leesylvania State Park (16236 Neabsco Road, Woodbridge, Virginia, 22191-4504, 703-670-0372, closed from November to March), which was the ancestral home of Henry Lee II, Robert E. Lee's grandfather, and the birthplace of Lee's father, Henry "Lighthorse Harry" Lee. His grandparents are buried here. Four hiking trails pass the sites of the house, which overlooked the Potomac River and was burned in 1790, and the site of the batteries. A new visitors center and interpretive signs help explain the Confederate blockade of Washington. The entrance to the park is on U.S. 1 at Woodbridge.

Two surviving batteries are threatened by development—a heavy battery at Cockpit Point, and the smallest, Freestone, used as a diversion.

Several brigades of Confederate troops camped in the area to protect the batteries during the winter of 1861–62. Primary campgrounds were at Neabsco, Montclair on Route 234, and Minnieville at Cardinal Drive and Minnieville Road.

Dumfries, established in 1749 as the first town in Prince William County, was a wealthy port that once rivaled Washington, D.C., Alexandria, Baltimore, and New York City, primarily because of the tobacco trade. Designated the county seat in 1762, the community declined after the creek silted. The Henderson house (1785, 200 Fairfax Street) was a Civil War hospital and boasts a hole in its southwest corner caused by a cannonball. The Old Stage Coach Inn (U.S. 1) was a Civil War staging area. Information can be gathered at the Weems Botts Museum (pre-1798, 300 Duke Street, 703-221-3346).

On December 12, 1862, Hampton surprised and captured a Federal wagon train at Dumfries. Two weeks later, on December 26, 1862, Stuart departed on the last of three great cavalry raids he led that year. The Dumfries raid, made with eighteen hundred troopers, left Fredericksburg for a two-pronged attack against a major Federal supply base located here. The assault, carried out by Brig. Gens. Fitzhugh Lee and W. H. F. Rooney Lee, was repulsed, and the expedition returned to Confederate lines through Occoquan, Burkes Station, Fairfax Court House, Warrenton, and Culpeper, arriving on New Year's Day 1863. Stuart netted two hundred prisoners, an equal number of horses and mules, and twenty wagonloads of equipment, mostly captured on December 27 by Fitzhugh Lee from a Union wagon train at Chopawamsic, several miles south of Dumfries.

Historic Greenwood Presbyterian Church (1850, Route 215) was the only church the Federals did not desecrate. A local resident and Englishman had given the land and money for the construction of the building, and he persuaded Union authorities that it was the property of a neutral. Buried in the cemetery is Bradford Hoskins, another Englishman, killed while fighting under Mosby.

About halfway between the Manassas battlefield and U.S. 1 to the south, on Route 610 in Headly, is Bethel Baptist Church (1850), a wooden church severely damaged by its war service as a hospital.

Just to the north of Bethel, at the intersection of Routes 610 and 663 is the wooden Bacon Race Meeting House (1845), the site of a supply depot for Hampton's brigade and a battalion of reserve artillery under Maj. Stephen D. Lee during the winter of 1861–62.

2

The Battle of Ball's Bluff

C IRCUMSTANCES MAKE YOUR presence here necessary," Winfield Scott's telegram read. "Come hither without delay." George B. McClellan received the message at his headquarters in northwestern Virginia, 150 miles from Washington, and rode to the nearest station on the Baltimore and Ohio Railroad. Arriving in the Union capital on the afternoon of July 22, he found the city filled with drunken, demoralized soldiers and civilians consumed with fears of a Rebel attack. Famed newspaper editor Horace Greeley of the *New York Tribune* admitted he was unable to sleep at night. The Confederates were only twenty-five miles to the southwest at Centreville.

McClellan rode to the White House the next morning to meet with Lincoln. There he learned that his new duties were to lead the troops around Washington, defend the capital, and attack Richmond. His tour of the city found some fortifications to the south of the Potomac in Virginia, but none protecting the overland approaches from Maryland.

Of the fifty-one thousand troops suddenly at his disposal, McClellan wrote, "I find no army to command." Two-thirds were poorly trained and led, "cowering, some perfectly raw, others dispirited." He considered Washington vulnerable to one regiment of Confederate cavalry.

McClellan always felt up to a challenge. As he wrote his wife, Ellen, "By some strange operation of magic I seem to have become the power of the land." And he immediately set to solving the problem.

To restore discipline in the demoralized ranks he appointed Brig. Gen. Andrew Porter to provost marshal, with one thousand regular army troops as military police. They cleaned out the saloons, gambling houses, and brothels and barred the sale of alcohol to soldiers. Civilians were banned from the army's camps, and both men and officers absent from camp without permission were arrested.

There were immediate challenges to his program. Several regiments that had signed up for three years' service threatened mutiny after the first recruits, Lincoln's three-month volunteers, started for home. When the Second Maine declined to answer roll call one morning, Porter arrested sixty-three ringleaders and sentenced them to confinement at Fort Jefferson in the distant Dry Tortugas in Florida.

Next was the Seventy-ninth New York Highlanders who had been decimated at Manassas. Mistakingly believing they would receive leaves to return home and recruit, on August 14 most of the regiment refused orders. Porter sent hundreds of MPs to surround the camp with canister-loaded cannon. Thirty-five were arrested, and the remainder carried out their duties. McClellan, however, was not finished with them. He confiscated their regimental colors and promised their return when the unit proved itself worthy. Several months later they did and he did, and thereafter the regiment worshiped their commander.

Another problem was reorganizing the army. A medical director was needed to establish sanitation standards for the camps, and a quartermaster general was necessary to organize supplies for more than one hundred thousand soldiers. McClellan's personal staff soon soared to sixty-five officers. As his chief of staff, a position McClellan found useful in the grand European armies he had studied, he appointed his father-in-law, Col. Randolph Marcy.

Trained as an engineer at West Point, McClellan oversaw the start of a vast set of fortifications to defend Washington. It consisted of forty-eight forts and redoubts that extended in a thirty-seven-mile perimeter from Alexandria north to the Chain Bridge. At points along the Maryland side, the works were eight miles from Washington.

McClellan's greatest fear was Joseph E. Johnston, who in early August advanced to Fairfax Court House, only fifteen miles to the west, and entrenched. This fear was heightened in that McClellan consistently overestimated enemy strength. He had seventy thousand soldiers to Johnston's forty thousand, but the Federal commander was convinced that the Confederates outnumbered him by four to one.

Johnston had his own problems, but these were not as imaginary as his counterpart's. Besides not having the troops McClellan believed he did, the Confederate commander needed additional soldiers, ammunition, and food. "Our army was more disorganized by victory than that of the United States by defeat," he declared. Thus despite their proximity, the Confederates were not presently a threat.

BATTLES AND LEADERS

Union provost guards took control of the demoralized stragglers in Washington following the defeat at Manassas.

LIBRARY OF CONGRESS

Newly promoted Gen. George B. McClellan was largely responsible for creating the system of defenses that made the Federal capital at Washington virtually impregnable.

By September 1861, McClellan felt Washington was sufficiently defended, allowing him to give his full attention to training an army that could take the war to the Confederates. In July, Lincoln had called for a half-million volunteers to serve a three-year enlistment. During the next two months, ten thousand recruits arrived in Washington every week. On August 20, McClellan named his force the Army of the Potomac, which included all troops around Washington and in Maryland, Delaware, and the Shenandoah Valley.

The green soldiers trained relentlessly, learning to march, maneuver, and deploy, first as companies then in larger units—regiments, brigades, and divisions. Each division of roughly ten thousand men consisted of three infantry brigades, one regiment of cavalry, and four artillery batteries. The men spent a great deal of time practicing with bayonets but rarely fired their muskets. McClellan thought individual marksmanship was not important in massed formations.

Finding competent officers was a challenge. Brigade commanders and higher ranks were adequate, since most were West Point graduates, but from the regimental level down, many positions were held by political appointees and, worse, elected officers. Brig. Gen. George Gordon Meade considered these men "ignorant, inefficient and worthless." In response, McClellan instituted a board of review for all officers. Over the next eight months 310 officers resigned or were dismissed. Meanwhile Lincoln created dozens of brigadiers.

McClellan spent twelve hours a day touring his constantly expanding camps to learn about his troops and inspire them. "Little Mac," as he was called because of his short stature, was difficult to miss; his soldiers learned

At a dinner in late 1861, renowned diarist Mary Chesnut was conversing with people who knew the family of Joseph E. Johnston. Of Johnston's brother Sid, Hamilton Boykin said, "Never in his life could he make up his mind that everything was so exactly right, that the time to act had come. There was always something to fit that would not fit. Joe Johnston is that, too. Wade Hampton brought him here to hunt—he is Mrs. Hampton's cousin. We all like him—but as to hunting, there he made a dead failure. He was a capital shot, better than Wade or I, and we are not so bad—that you'll allow. But then with Colonel Johnston—I think he was colonel then—the bird flew too high or too low—the dogs were too far or too near—things never did suit exactly. He was too fussy, too hard to please, too cautious, too much afraid to miss and risk his fine reputation for a crack shot. Wade and I waded through the mud and water briars and bushes and came home with a heavy bag. We shot right and left—happy-go-lucky. Joe Johnston did not shoot at all. The exactly right time and place never came.

"Unless his ways are changed, he'll never fight a battle—you'll see. Oh, yes—he is as brave as Caesar. An accomplished soldier? Yes—who denies it? You'll see. I know Sid, and I've hunted with Joe. He is too particular—things are never all straight. You must go it rash—at a venture to win—&c&c&c."

This assessment became an accurate prophecy of Johnston's actions, or rather inactions, in Virginia, Mississippi, and Georgia.

to look for his "tail," a traveling retinue of twenty personal staffers, and the general's big horse, Dan Webster. McClellan loved parade reviews, starting with small units and culminating in a grand exhibition of eighty thousand infantry and cavalry, accompanied by artillery and numerous bands. The spectacles served to raise both civilian and military morale, and all learned to adore the new commander, who reveled in the attention.

McClellan and Scott increasingly clashed. Scott wanted to keep regular army soldiers together to serve as dependable units in emergencies, a role they had performed well in the rout following Manassas. McClellan believed they should be distributed throughout the volunteer army to leaven the raw recruits.

McClellan's soon-to-be legendary caution also grated on Scott. The old soldier realized that the South had the same weaknesses and shortages that the North faced, perhaps more so, and he believed Johnston could be successfully attacked with the present Union strength. McClellan, however, heartily disagreed. His chief of intelligence was Allan Pinkerton, who had organized one of America's first private detective agencies and had worked with the general in the 1850s at the Illinois Central Railroad. He proved to be an excellent spy catcher, cracking the ring led by Rose Greenhow, but his estimates of the enemy's troop strength were outrageously inaccurate. Questioning Confederate deserters, Unionist residents of northern Virginia, and runaway slaves, he informed McClellan that Johnston had "not less than 150,000" troops when the Southern leader could count only 50,000. While McClellan feared a Confederate attack on the capital, Scott dismissed the notion.

Alexandria was ringed with Federal camps. The view below is of the city from the camp of the Fortieth New York Infantry.

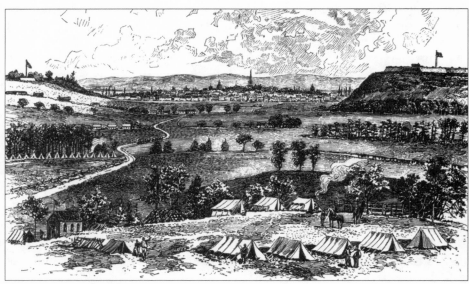

Despite the Union occupation of Alexandria and Arlington, the Confederate works on Munson's Hill allowed a clear view of all activities within Washington, D.C.

"He understands nothing, appreciates nothing," McClellan wrote to Ellen. "Scott is the most dangerous antagonist I have."

Elderly, ailing, and tiring of McClellan's disrespect, Scott offered his resignation to Lincoln, who rejected it. The situation, however, continued to worsen as McClellan went over Scott's head directly to the president, the secretary of war, and other cabinet officers.

For some months Lincoln met McClellan late at night in the general's office on Lafayette Square to discuss the military situation. Lincoln had done some legal work for McClellan back in Illinois, and the general enjoyed the president's homespun humor, but to his confidants McClellan shared his reservations about the commander in chief.

By August, Lincoln demanded a definite plan for conducting the war. The rebellion could be destroyed with "one blow," McClellan promised, provided he was given the necessary soldiers: 273,000 or more, he estimated. By October he had over 100,000, and the public and press were lobbying for an immediate campaign in the pleasant fall weather.

"I intend to be careful," McClellan wrote Lincoln. "Don't let them hurry me, is all I ask."

"You shall have your own way," came the president's reassurance.

After Bull Run, P. G. T. Beauregard had written a letter to Confederate congressmen in Richmond implying that he could have captured Washington had he been supplied better. When the legislators asked President Davis about this assertion, the chief executive politely informed the general that his failure to pursue had nothing to do with supplies. Beauregard switched topics and informed the president that friends were urging him to run for president against Davis, who had been provisional president since the Montgomery convention early in the year.

In his official report of the battle, Beauregard claimed full credit for the victory, including getting Johnston's forces to the field. Davis also challenged this boast, giving tribute to Johnston and accusing Beauregard of attempting to "exalt yourself at my expense."

Beauregard struck next in the Richmond newspapers with a letter that defended his actions. The general also challenged the War Department to give him independent command of his forces. Such pressure led Secretary of War Judah P. Benjamin to quip that Beauregard did not understand that he was second to Johnston "in command of the whole army and not first in command of half the army."

Beauregard's appeal of this matter to Davis prompted his transfer as second in command to another Johnston, this one Albert Sydney Johnston

Confederate forts were erected along the Potomac and created an effective blockade of the Federal capital. One of the powerful batteries was built at Shipping Point (above left), about thirty-three miles from Washington at the entrance to the Quantico (or Dumfries) Creek. Another was erected at Mathias Point (above right).

in the West, where the bantam Beauregard's curious career would continue. After coordinating the Confederate assault at Shiloh, the hero of Fort Sumter and Manassas commanded the Army of Tennessee after Johnston's death, at least until Davis removed him for leaving the troops to visit a health spa without permission.

Meanwhile, all quiet on the eastern front continued for three months after Manassas.

Joseph E. Johnston soon did what he would continue to do with great skill and questionable judgment for the remainder of the war: withdraw. On

The Baltimore and Ohio Railroad

The Baltimore and Ohio Railroad was the most important transportation link between the Mid-Atlantic Coast and the Ohio Valley during the Civil War. In an age where coal provided heat and energy, it was vital to keep vast quantities of coal rumbling daily from the Appalachian mines to Washington and Baltimore. The route traversed a very rugged region.

Initially the railroad—whose line followed the Potomac River, which divided Federal and Confederate territory—attempted to remain neutral. When Maryland remained in the Union, the line requested that the Federal government protect the road that passed through Confederate territory in northwestern Virginia, particularly near Harpers Ferry. Increasing Confed-

erate raids tied up an ever-growing number of Federal troops needed to protect the line and repair ruined rails.

After arriving in Harpers Ferry on April 30, 1861, Thomas J. Jackson studied the train activity, which crossed the Potomac River on a double-tracked bridge. The railroad had twin tracks for the thirty-one-mile stretch between Martinsburg to the west and Point of Rocks, Maryland, to the east. The railroad bridge across the Potomac at Harpers Ferry was the center of this line.

Jackson, complaining that the heavy traffic interfered with his soldiers' training and rest, restricted rail movement to between 11 A.M. and 1 P.M. Understandably, rail traffic was extremely heavy throughout those two hours. On May 23, at 11 A.M., Jackson barri-

caded the eastbound tracks at Point of Rocks and the westbound traffic at Martinsburg, then destroyed the rails at each end. With little effort, he had captured 42 locomotives and 386 cars, mainly coal gondolas, sorely needed by the poorly provisioned Southern railroad network.

Four small engines steamed up a thirty-mile spur line to Winchester, then were hauled twenty miles along a wagon road to the Manassas Gap Railroad at Strasburg, which connected with the Orange and Alexandria and Virginia Central.

On June 14, Jackson was ordered to evacuate Harpers Ferry. At 4 A.M. explosives dropped the B&O Railroad bridge and the wagon bridge over the Potomac River. Several days later the

Winchester and Potomac Railroad bridge across the Shenandoah was destroyed and a large locomotive thrown into the water. The remainder of the engines and rolling stock was sent to Martinsburg for disposition.

It was at this time that Jackson noticed a horse on one of the Federal freight cars. Always scrupulous in official matters, Jackson paid the Confederate quartermaster for the little nag, which he intended to send to his wife, Anna, in Winchester. The general, however, grew fond of the horse and decided to keep it. Little Sorrel saw Jackson through First Manassas, the Valley campaign, the Seven Days' battles, Antietam, Fredericksburg, and Chancellorsville, where the general was killed riding the horse.

September 27 he returned to Fairfax Court House, leaving behind Quaker guns in the abandoned defenses at Munson's Hill near Washington. On October 17 he continued his retrograde movement to Centreville, where he concentrated his forty-one thousand men on a line that extended to Manassas.

These moves delighted McClellan, who was able to expand his defensive zone in front of Washington along the Potomac River. The last Confederate stronghold along the Potomac was at Leesburg, thirty-five miles upriver. McClellan thought he could manipulate a Confederate withdrawal there without a fight.

This chapter of the story starts with Edward D. Baker, who had practiced law with Lincoln in Springfield, Illinois. Baker had led a regiment to Mexico in 1846, then moved west, joining the Republican Party and entering politics, soon becoming a senator from Oregon. In Washington, D.C., Baker, a spellbinding speaker, became an early supporter of the Lincoln administration. Within months he was urged to command the First California Regiment (formed with many New Yorkers and Pennsylvanians). Because Baker was busy in the Capitol, Isaac Wister, another old law partner, handled the recruiting.

Charles P. Stone of Massachusetts, an 1845 graduate of West Point who had won two brevets in Mexico, met Baker in California in 1856. On January 1, 1861, General in Chief Scott appointed Stone a colonel, the first of several million volunteers who would serve during the Civil War.

South Carolinian Nathan Evans finished second from the bottom of his class at the U.S. Military Academy in 1848 but was known as a cunning

---

The Chesapeake and Ohio Canal

The Appalachian Mountains were a formidable barrier to transportation between the Atlantic Coast and the Ohio and Mississippi Valleys, and the Potomac River was only navigable to Washington, D.C. To facilitate the transportation of grain and coal, the Chesapeake and Ohio Canal was proposed to connect Georgetown with Cumberland, Maryland. It was hoped that in the future the canal would be extended to connect with the Ohio and Mississippi Rivers.

The canal, 184.5 miles in length, would have seventy-four locks to overcome the 605-foot difference in elevation between Georgetown and Cumberland. Initially projected to be constructed in three years, this first great national project required twenty-two years and twenty-two million dollars to complete. One hundred sixty culverts were built over the canal and eleven aqueducts carried the canal over larger streams. The six-foot-deep channel accommodated canal boats that were ninety-three feet long, fourteen and a half feet wide, and drew four and a half feet. Beside the canal was a twelve-foot-wide tow path, a high earthen bank on which walked the mules that hauled the boats. More than six thousand laborers and seven hundred horses, mules, and oxen labored to build the canal, which followed the route of the Potomac River. Labor shortages, disputes over pay and working conditions, insufficient construction materials (stone, timber, cement, and rubble), and rugged terrain delayed completion of the canal. By the time it was operational, the railroad had beaten the canal to Cumberland by eight years. The working life of the canal was similarly cursed. Frequent floods and rail competition prevented the canal from fulfilling its potential and eventually killed the enterprise.

The C&O Canal saw a peak Civil War traffic of five hundred boats a year, its cargo primarily coal from Cumberland and flour and corn from the Midwest. This was an invaluable supplement to the supplies brought by the Baltimore and Ohio Railroad to Federal armies and the large eastern cities. Confederates made efforts throughout the Civil War to disrupt both the railroad and the canal, but the well-constructed stone canal was notoriously difficult to disable for any length of time.

The C&O is now a vast national park. People hike, bike, canoe, and ride horses along its entire length. Many locks and other structures have been restored, although floods continue to plague the system. Rangers and historic displays are located at several sites, and there are picnicking and camping facilities. Mule-drawn canal boat rides are offered at Georgetown and Great Falls. A number of important Civil War sites—including Harpers Ferry, Point of Rocks, and several fords—are located along the C&O. They are featured in the Antietam and Harpers Ferry tours in this book.

officer who had shown bold initiative in delaying McDowell at First Manassas. For his skill and "unshakable courage," Evans received command of the Seventh Brigade of Beauregard's First Corps of the Confederate Army of the Potomac, consisting of the Eighth Virginia and Thirteenth, Seventeenth, and Eighteenth Mississippi. The brigade was deployed to defend the region around Leesburg, located in northern Virginia.

Leesburg had a population of four thousand in a border area whose residents sympathized with both sides in the war. On the Potomac River, a few miles east of the town, were the one-hundred-foot-high cliffs known as Ball's Bluff, which dominated large Harrison's Island and the Maryland shore opposite. The strategic position of Harpers Ferry was twenty-five miles upstream. Between that point and Washington was only one bridge, at Berlin (modern Brunswick, Maryland), which had been burned by Confederate cavalry in June. At the northern edge of Harrison's Island was Smart's Mill Ford, and five miles farther downstream was Edward's Ferry.

Since Virginia's secession, the border between the Confederate States and the United States had been the Potomac River. Evans guarded the Confederate left flank in Virginia, picketing the fords and ferries and a turnpike that followed the Potomac from Leesburg to Alexandria. Two miles east of Leesburg the Confederates constructed Fort Evans, a substantial earthwork that enclosed one and a half acres.

McClellan's defensive plan placed Stone in Maryland opposite Evans. By May 17 Stone was appointed brigadier general of volunteers, and promotion to major general soon followed. He then commanded a division officially titled a Corps of Observation, consisting of the California Regiment, the Tammany Regiment (Forty-second New York), and the Fifteenth and Twentieth Massachusetts, which patrolled the Potomac from Point of Rocks, ten miles upstream of Leesburg, to Edward's Ferry. Baker commanded a brigade with the rank of colonel. Upriver, the responsibility for the Potomac from Point of Rocks to Harpers Ferry rested upon Col. John W. Geary's regiment; downstream from Edward's Ferry to Washington was the division of Maj. Gen. Nathaniel Banks; and in Virginia, opposite Washington, were Federal divisions under Gens. W. F. Smith and George A. McCall.

Despite the calm that had descended upon the Virginia front since the battle of Manassas, McClellan fretted whether Evans would cross the Potomac and strike toward either Washington or Baltimore or would reinforce Johnston at Centreville. The Federals were ignorant of the topogra-

Not all Southern batteries were as formidable as they appeared. In late September 1861 Confederates believed thier forward positions were susceptible to Federal attack and began to pull back. So-called Quaker guns were employed to deter immediate attack.

BATTLES AND LEADERS

phy of the area surrounding Leesburg, the disposition of Southern forces, and their number. McClellan estimated there were twenty-seven thousand Rebels there; in fact Evans counted only two thousand.

In the meantime, public and political pressure mounted on McClellan to take action, *any* action, to break the stalemate and redeem Northern honor for the debacle of Manassas. To determine if he could frighten Evans into decamping for Centreville, McClellan sent McCall's three thousand men from Washington upstream to Dranesville, twelve miles from Leesburg, which was accomplished on October 19. To exert further pressure on Evans, McClellan ordered Stone, "Perhaps a slight demonstration on your part would have the effect to move them, though great discretion recommended." (Stone had previously been instructed to exploit any opportunity to disperse or capture small groups of Confederates.)

On the afternoon of October 20, Stone dispatched the ten thousand men of Brig. Gen. Willis A. Gorman's brigade to Edward's Ferry from Poolesville, eight miles east of Leesburg. He shelled the Virginia shore, then sent one hundred men across to search for Confederates. Finding none, they returned.

To determine if Evans had vacated Leesburg, Stone ordered twenty men across the river from Harrison's Island to Ball's Bluff, three miles upstream from Edward's Ferry. Night fell as they advanced to within two miles of Leesburg, where they spotted thirty tents, but curiously no campfires. Actually, they had seen a cluster of haystacks, not tents.

Stone decided to destroy this Southern "camp." He sent Col. Charles Devens, commanding the Fifteenth Massachusetts, and half his regiment, three hundred men in five companies, with cover provided by one hundred men under Col. William R. Lee of the Twentieth Massachusetts, to Ball's Bluff. Devens started at midnight, but with only three small boats to transport his troops across the swift, rain-swollen Potomac, it was 4 A.M. before he led his men up the steep, wooded slope via a single narrow path.

Devens found an eight-acre open field atop the bluff. Beyond it was thick forest penetrated by one road and bordered by a stout rail fence, with a second field beyond. Discovering the true nature of the Confederate "camp," Devens sent word back to Stone at Edward's Ferry, where two companies had been passed across as a feint. Stone ordered the remainder of the Sixteenth Massachusetts to reinforce Devens and scout the terrain. He sent Baker to take command of the Tammany Regiment and the Twentieth Massachusetts at Ball's Bluff. Baker's ensuing actions, however, seem to prove that his intention was to cross all his troops to Virginia and initiate battle, which was contrary to his orders.

When a skirmish finally developed near Ball's Bluff, Confederate Capt. W. C. Duff alerted Evans, then opened fire on Devens with forty men. Evans faced a dilemma. A Union division threatened from downstream at Dranesville, and crossings were reported from Gorman at Edward's Ferry and now at Ball's Bluff. Evans elected to move his headquarters to Fort

Evans, from which he could monitor developments at Edward's Ferry and Ball's Bluff. He also reinforced Duff with two companies of infantry and seventy cavalry under Lt. Col. Walter H. Jenifer. Steady fighting developed as the two small forces pushed each other back and forth.

At 10 A.M. Evans decided that the action at Edward's Ferry was a feint and concentrated his forces against Ball's Bluff, where Union troops were massing, albeit slowly. The Federals were conveyed from Maryland to Harrison's Island by seven tiny boats. They then marched across the island and were ferried to the Virginia shore.

Baker unaccountably tarried several hours before getting to the island, where he spent additional hours micromanaging the crossing. He wasted an hour attempting unsuccessfully to haul a canal boat from the nearby Chesapeake and Ohio Canal and more time transporting two howitzers and a 12-pounder Parrott rifle. The larger cannon was so heavy it had to be dismantled, carried up the slope, and reassembled. It performed well, but positioned ahead of the infantry, the gunners were cut down from eighty yards.

The Federals fighting had no overall commander as the Californians and New Yorkers crossed the Potomac. Stone sent a dispatch to Baker demanding regular reports, but Baker, absent from the battlefield, had no idea what was happening, a fact he neglected to tell Stone. From Edward's Ferry, Stone telegraphed McClellan that Gorman hoped to turn the Confederate right flank, but that force went nowhere as Evans rushed the Eighteenth and Seventeenth Mississippi to Ball's Bluff, leaving little to contest Gorman. Stone had 2,250 men on the Virginia shore at Edward's Ferry but offered no help, stopped by the Fifteenth Mississippi, which blocked the road with a masked battery. He thought there were 10,000 more Confederates in Leesburg.

The Politician at Ball's Bluff ■ Edward Dickinson Baker

BATTLES AND LEADERS

Edward Dickinson Baker was born in England on February 24, 1811, and immigrated to America four years later. Apprenticed to a weaver at age fourteen, by nineteen he was practicing law. In 1835 Baker moved to Springfield, Illinois, and became a law partner with Abraham Lincoln. A noted orator, he entered the statehouse at age twenty-six and the Illinois senate three years later. Baker defeated Lincoln for a position in the U.S. House before forming a company for service in the Black Hawk War. He organized and led a regiment to Mexico in 1846, where he became a colonel. After moving to California in 1852 to practice law, the lifelong Whig joined the Republican Party and moved again, to Oregon in 1860, when the state legislature there asked him to represent the Beaver State in the U.S. Senate. In Washington, D.C., Baker, a charming, spellbinding speaker, became an early supporter of President Lincoln.

Within months Baker was urged to command the First California Regiment (formed with many New Yorkers and Pennsylvanians). He accepted the command but refused the ranks of brigadier and major general of volunteers because he would have been forced to resign from the Senate. While Baker was busy in Congress, others actually led the regiment. His officers included his brother, son, and nephew. In his only combat command, Baker made foolish decisions that led to his death and the destruction of his command at Ball's Bluff on October 21, 1861. His death was mourned in the White House and across the nation. Baker is buried at the Presidio in San Francisco.

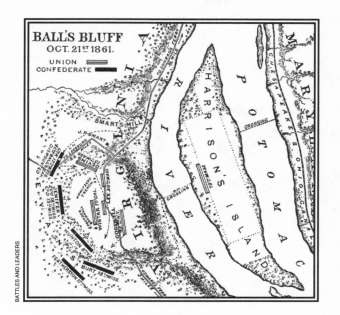

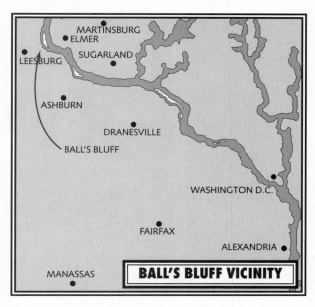

When Baker reached the battlefield at 2 P.M., one officer muttered, "Thank God . . . We have been waiting eight hours." Lee passed command to Baker, who proceeded to weaken the Union position. The Federals had been holding their own from behind the fence at the edge of the woods, forcing the Confederates to advance over open ground, but Baker drew them back to form a line in the middle of an open field. Baker was no tactician. A rugged cliff and the Potomac River were immediately to his rear, and his men were in the open with no protection. He also positioned four reserve companies in the center of the line, where they could only shoot their comrades in front of them but were close enough to be hit by the Confederates. Worse still was a hill to the left that commanded his position.

Baker queried his subordinates about this disposition, but when the only professional soldier present, Col. Milton Cogswell, commanding the New Yorkers, stated that their entire force needed to occupy the threatening hill immediately, Baker ignored him. Minutes later the Confederates seized the ridge, rendering the Union line untenable. Baker concentrated his cannon on the hill, but Confederate fire quickly drove the gunners away.

Union casualties mounted, particularly among the officers, convincing Baker that he was outnumbered three to one. Rather than address the problem, however, the politician reverted to form, bravely pacing his line, heedless of Rebel fire, encouraging his men as a desperate situation steadily deteriorated. Spotting Confederates advancing on his left, Baker decided it was Gorman with reinforcements. Finally, at 5 P.M. he sent an aide to Stone saying, "We are fixed," and asked for reinforcements. Before the messenger left the field, Confederates broke the Union line and killed Baker.

Lee took command until Cogswell appeared and made the only reasonable decision: The Federals must fight their way downstream to Edward's

The new Union commander, George B. McClellan, suggested "a slight demonstration" to dislodge the Southerners from Leesburg, Virginia. From across the Potomac, at Edward's Ferry, Maryland, Brig. Gen. Charles P. Stone ordered a light shelling and began the series of events that climaxed with the assault at Ball's Bluff.

Ferry. At six he ordered the line forward. A few men stepped off, but Devens and other officers shouted orders for the men to "stand firm." The few Northerners who charged were decimated, and at that moment Confederate Col. Winfield S. Featherstone launched an assault shouting, "Charge, Mississippians! Charge! Drive them into the Potomac or into eternity!" The Southerners rose, fired a volley, and advanced.

Seeing disaster relentlessly approaching, Union officers ordered their men to retreat to the ferry. The order was not necessary as Yankee soldiers raced for the river, most scrambling down the slope, some leaping from the top, impaling themselves on the bayonets of those below, breaking their necks, or injuring the men they fell upon. At the Potomac they fought for space aboard boats, displacing the wounded and overloading the vessels. One boat, crowded with one hundred men, twice its capacity, was swamped in midriver—only one soldier was known to have survived. Other boats sank or drifted downstream after Confederates shot the occupants.

With the boats gone, a few Federals huddled against the bank, but hundreds more jumped into the river, most fully clothed, others hurriedly stripping. Officers urged men to throw their rifles into the river; a few attempted to swim across with their weapons. Some soldiers helped comrades who could not swim through the dangerous current; others grabbed swimmers and both went under.

When the Confederates reached the cliff, they began firing with deadly earnest at the Yankees packed on the riverbank and at those struggling in the river. No Federals seemed willing to ask for surrender, and the Rebels seemed equally adamant about not offering quarter. The surface of the river teemed with desperately swimming men, and the water was

After the shelling, Stone dispatched a patrol to the Virginia side of the river. On the evening of October 20, twenty men of the Fifteenth Massachusetts landed at the base of a steep bank known as Ball's Bluff—a rocky bluff almost one hundred feet high and covered with tangles of mountain laurel. The area had been named after a previous landowner, the family of George Washington's mother, Mary Ball Washington.

BATTLES AND LEADERS

churned to froth by Southern bullets. The fire was so intense that some swimmers were seen to return to the Virginia shore even when halfway to Harrison's Island. They said the bluff was ablaze with muzzle flashes.

"Here was a horrible scene," Union Capt. William Bartlett wrote his mother days later. "Men crowded together, the wounded and the dying. The water was full of human beings, struggling with each other and the water, the surface of which looked like a pond when it rains from the withering volleys that the enemy were pouring down from the top of the bank."

Union Capt. Francis Young related: "Tumbling down the steep heights, the enemy following, murdering, and taking prisoners. Hundreds plunged into the rapid current, and the shrieks of the drowning added to the horror. All was terror, confusion and dismay."

It was a scene worthy of hell: the Federals suffering heavy casualties and the survivors left terrified, exhausted, and screaming in fear and pain, dying on the shore and in the water as bodies floated downstream. The Confederate ranks maintained a demonic, constant loading, firing, cheering.

Remarkably, the Confederates did not pursue a complete victory. After darkness fell they left two companies on guard and withdrew to camp near Leesburg, where local women fed the victorious soldiers. Hearing of the victory, Evans returned to Leesburg. Hours later a Confederate crept down the bank and discovered large numbers of Federals still remaining. Sending word to Fort Evans, 40 Southerners returned and ordered the Union survivors to surrender. They marched 325 prisoners to Leesburg.

Meanwhile, Stone and McClellan thought their forces were winning the battle. McClellan said that he might want to take Leesburg that day, and Stone believed it could be accomplished with support from McCall at Dranesville. McClellan, however, neglected to inform Stone that McCall had been recalled twelve hours earlier. Stating his only source of concern, Stone concluded, "We are a little short of boats."

At 4 P.M. Stone had reported the battle going well. At 6:45 he telegraphed: "Colonel Baker has been killed." A follow-up message at 9:45 stated: "I deeply regret to report a repulse. Our loss is severe."

Progress of the battle had been followed closely in Washington, only thirty-five miles downstream. At the end of the day Lincoln entered McClellan's headquarters to read the latest dispatches. Informed of the death of his old friend Baker, the president stood stunned for several minutes then stumbled out of the house, tears staining his cheeks.

Stone arrived at Harrison's Island at 9 P.M., passing through the wounded and the demoralized remains of his division. Only then did he receive Baker's request for reinforcements from the man who bore the colonel's body. At 10 P.M. Lincoln demanded of Stone, "Bring me information . . . give me a correct understanding of affairs." Stone replied that it was "impossible to give full particulars of what is yet inexplicable to me. Our troops were reported in good condition and position until fifteen minutes of the death of Colonel Baker."

Union casualties were appalling. With an estimated 1,600 soldiers in combat, 200 were killed, 158 wounded, and 714 captured—over 1,000 total casualties. Confederate losses were 155—36 killed, 117 wounded, 2 captured. Stone and McClellan maintained until their deaths that the Confederates outnumbered them three to one. In reality, the forces were equal in number.

The North was shocked by the sudden defeat, the second in a war that had seen only two sizable battles. "How weary I am of this business," McClellan wrote his wife. "Care after care, blunder after blunder, trick upon trick." The Union regiments involved defended their own conduct and condemned the others for the defeat. Both sides, fearing renewed combat by superior forces, withdrew and entrenched. There were hourly alarms that the armies were on the march, but all was quiet along the Potomac again.

News of the defeat, arguably the most complete of the war, spread quickly over telegraph lines despite Secretary of State William Seward's unsuccessful attempt to censor information about the battle. City after city was angered and demoralized by the details, bringing swift condemnation upon both the Union government and the military for what the public considered "murder" and *Harper's Weekly* called a "great military crime." The horror continued as bodies of Union dead washed ashore for a week, some at Washington itself. McClellan proclaimed to his men: "Soldiers! We have seen our last retreat! We have seen our last defeat!"

Jenifer attempted to claim the credit for the victory until Evans corrected him. Evans's role, however, was disparaged for managing the battle from Fort Evans, and rumors persisted that he had been drunk. Despite the controversies, Evans was promoted to brigadier, received a gold medal from the state of South Carolina, and remained a Southern hero for the coming winter. In retrospect, Ball's Bluff was a small battle, but at the time it was considered extremely important by both sides and allowed the South to claim another great victory.

The battle inspired a number of poets, as many early actions of this war did. Willie Lincoln, the president's ten-year-old son, wrote "Lines on the Death of Colonel Baker," which was published by a magazine, but the most memorable verse was penned by Henry S. Washburn in memory of

2d Lt. John W. Grout, killed in the disaster: "We shall meet, but we will miss him, / There will be one vacant chair."

On October 25 senators demanded satisfaction. McClellan shifted responsibility to Scott, blaming him for the uncoordinated mess. Congress then forced Lincoln to accept Scott's previously tendered resignation.

Scott faced the situation with dignity. He suggested that Lincoln replace him with Maj. Gen. Henry W. Halleck, an acclaimed military tactician commanding the Department of Missouri. For the time being the president rejected the advice and asked McClellan if he could handle the responsibility of managing half a million soldiers scattered across half a continent.

"I can do it all," the egotistical little general replied, and he received the appointment on November 1. McClellan had the gall to see Scott off at the railroad station. The elderly general visited his daughter, then proceeded to France for medical care.

During the fall, McClellan planned an advance on Johnston's line, which stretched from Centreville to Manassas, but by Thanksgiving he had decided to bypass the strong Confederate fortifications for a grander adventure. Embarking his army aboard a fleet of ships at Annapolis, he would steam down Chesapeake Bay and land at Urbanna on the Rappahannock River, then march overland 60 miles to the northeast to besiege Richmond. This plan would cut in half the 110-mile advance required via Centreville-Manassas, and McClellan hoped to reach the Confederate capital without having to fight a major battle. Perhaps he could occupy the city

As the battle took shape in an open field atop Ball's Bluff, both sides were reinforced until they were nearly equal in strength, but the Confederates were largely veterans of the battle of Manassas and the Federals were experiencing their first fighting.

Federal Col. Edward D. Baker was in the thick of the fight. Although he had led a regiment during the Mexican War, he had little battlefield experience and made several tactical errors atop Ball's Bluff. Shortly after 4:30 P.M. he was killed in front of his troops.

before Johnston, forced to abandon his lines near Washington, could rush in confusion to defend Richmond. The Urbanna plan would also give the Federal army weeks of needed drill before the hundreds of ships could be assembled to transport one hundred thousand men, artillery, horses, and supplies.

McClellan avoided Lincoln, however, and failed to inform him of the plan, although he discussed it with Secretary of the Treasury Salmon P. Chase and others. A staunch Democrat, as were many West Pointers, McClellan openly showed his disrespect for Lincoln and other Republican leaders, "a set of men unscrupulous and false," he thought. In this case familiarity had definitely bred contempt. McClellan considered Lincoln a military amateur, and he detested civilian interference with the work of professional military commanders—like himself.

After a month of silence from his general in chief, Lincoln sent over his own plans for attacking Johnston near Manassas. For a week McClellan did not deign to reply, then on December 10 he rejected the plan, claiming recently received intelligence indicated that Johnston had been reinforced to the same strength as the Union army.

"I have now my mind actually turned towards another plan of campaign that I do not think at all anticipated by the enemy, nor by many of our own people," McClellan reported. Beyond that mysterious statement, he refused to explain further.

The Confederate Secretary of State ■ Judah Philip Benjamin

Born in the Virgin Islands in 1811, Judah Philip Benjamin, a lawyer and politician, resigned his Senate seat in 1861 and returned to Louisiana. Although he had once challenged Jefferson Davis to a duel, the president of the Confederacy appointed Benjamin the attorney general in February 1861, then head of the War Department in September. His brief tenure there earned him censure for the losses of coastal North Carolina,

Forts Henry and Donelson in Tennessee, and the Cumberland Gap. Forced by Congress to remove Benjamin, Davis immediately made him secretary of state, where his talents were well applied.

Although failing to gain recognition for the Confederacy from any European powers (largely a military failure), Benjamin wrangled loans that kept the Confederacy financially afloat.

Fleeing Richmond before the Federal occupation in April 1865, Benjamin managed to reach Florida and sailed to the West Indies in a small boat. In London, he became Queen's Counsel, where he served until 1883. Benjamin died in Paris a year later.

LIBRARY OF CONGRESS

Both sides tried to recover Baker's body. Amid the hand-to-hand fighting that ensued, the colonel's sword-wielding adjutant, Capt. Frederick Harvey, thwarted the Confederate effort.

The seasons meanwhile had progressed to a time when active field campaigning was impossible. The first snow had fallen, and McClellan's two hundred thousand soldiers had constructed log huts in which to spend the winter. Military endeavors were limited to reconnaissance. A large scouting force sent up the Potomac River clashed with a Confederate brigade at Dranesville, twelve miles from Ball's Bluff. The Federals claimed victory, inflicting 180 casualties to their own 66.

On November 8, U.S. warships intercepted the British steamer *Trent* and seized two Confederate commissioners en route to England. Fearing a foreign conflict in the midst of a growing civil war, Lincoln released the Southern agents. A number of politicians, however, read this as weakness, spurring senators and representatives to form an opposition group known as the Radical Republicans.

While these events unfolded, McClellan fell seriously ill with typhoid fever and took to his bed for a month as rumors spread that he was at death's door. Taking advantage of the general's infirmity, Congress convened the Joint Committee on the Conduct of the War to investigate the military disasters at Bull Run and Ball's Bluff and "the conduct of the present war" in general. Led by fanatical Ohio Sen. Benjamin F. Wade, the committee obviously hoped to influence military policy and was unwilling to allow anything, including the Constitution, to stand in its way of defeating and inflicting severe punishment on the rebellious South.

The joint committee met in secret but leaked biased accounts to the press. Witnesses were not allowed legal counsel, and the committee

The Federal troops were routed and hurled back to the brink of the bluff. Men threw themselves into the Potomac while the Confederates maintained a steady fire. As many as one hundred Union soldiers drowned. Their bodies were pulled from the water over the next several days.

LIBRARY OF CONGRESS

accepted the most outrageous testimony as the truth. Correctly believing most West Point officers to be Democrats, all those leaders were automatically under suspicion, in addition to anyone who was not a rabid abolitionist. McClellan was particularly scrutinized because he saw the important goal of the war as restoring the Union, not ending slavery. Since the general was ill, the committee summoned his officers.

On January 6, committee members thought they had sufficient evidence of McClellan's treasonous intent and met with Lincoln to demand that he order the general to attack Johnston. Attorney General Edward Bates urged the president to "command the commanders."

Although Lincoln defended McClellan, he did question his inactivity. The chief executive flirted with taking the field himself. He ordered Halleck in Missouri and Don Carlos Buell in Kentucky to coordinate campaigns, despite the season. "Delay is ruining us," Lincoln admonished them. When Halleck and Buell reported insufficient troops to take the offensive, Lincoln found the situation "exceeding discouraging. As everywhere else, nothing can be done."

The president was soon forced to dismiss Secretary of War Simon Cameron for improperly awarding government contracts, which had furnished the army with bad food, guns that would not fire, and uniforms that fell apart. The corruption filled an eleven-hundred-page report. Cameron's replacement was Edwin Stanton, a Machiavellian schemer who worked eighteen hours a day and terrorized all around him.

On January 10, Lincoln visited Q.M. Gen. Montgomery C. Meigs and asked plaintively, "General, what shall I do?" The people were out of patience, he said, the treasury was broke, and his general was ill. Noting that the Confederates might attack before McClellan recovered, Meigs suggested that Lincoln might need to replace the general.

Encouraged, two days later Lincoln gathered his cabinet and Gens. Irwin McDowell and William B. Franklin and made a classic statement: "If General McClellan does not want to use the Army, I would like to *borrow* it, provided I could see how it could be made to do something."

McDowell suggested a direct overland attack against Johnston, apparently seeing no irony in his suggestion. Franklin, previously briefed on the Urbanna plan, ventured it. While these plans were debated, McClellan made a miraculous recovery. Informed of the meeting by Stanton, who was playing the president against the general, McClellan staggered in, thin, pale, and upset by the nature of the conference.

McClellan remained quiet until Chase demanded to know his plan of attack. Even then he said little, but what little he said was insulting, stating that some present "were incompetent to form a valuable opinion, and others [were] incapable of keeping a secret." So the general piously announced that he had a plan but would not reveal it. Incredibly, Lincoln acquiesced to the condescending statement, seemingly satisfied that his general was back on the job, but McClellan made some very powerful enemies—Chase, Seward, Meigs, and Postmaster General Montgomery Blair.

Word of McClellan's revival spread, resulting in a six-hour audience with the Joint Committee on the Conduct of the War. The general's conceit was not affected by the congressmen, who also bristled at his contemptuous demeanor. Asked why he had failed to attack, McClellan explained that he had to secure a retreat route before advancing. That comment revealed "infernal, unmitigated cowardice," thought Sen. Zachariah Chandler.

Lincoln used his position to protect McClellan, which led the joint committee to persecute Stone for the debacle at Ball's Bluff. Accepting rumor and innuendo at face value, Stone was accused of improperly conferring with Confederates under flags of truce and exchanging suspicious messages between the lines. Uninformed of the charges against him, Stone was shocked when he was arrested at midnight on February 8 under orders from Stanton and later imprisoned in New York City forts for 189 days without charges.

McClellan understood this lesson in real politics and was rendered more cautious than before, realizing that a loss would mean his dismissal and perhaps imprisonment. On January 27, Lincoln demanded that McClellan move "against the insurgent forces." On January 31, Lincoln was more specific: The general was to attack the Confederates southwest of Manassas Junction along the Orange and Alexandria Railroad.

Lincoln's Secretary of War ■ Edwin McMasters Stanton

Edwin McMasters Stanton, born in Ohio in 1814, became a notable lawyer in Washington and California before serving as attorney general at the end of the James Buchanan administration. He opposed slavery but believed the rights of states should be respected. As such, Stanton was a Democrat who supported Buchanan's policies, the Dred Scott decision, and John C. Breckinridge for president in 1860. He retired from public office and openly criticized Abraham Lincoln's actions, but despite these negatives Stanton was appointed secretary of war a year later, on January 15, 1862.

Lacking military experience, Stanton was an enthusiastic and competent administrator who particularly targeted waste and fraud in the rapidly expanding military of the Civil War. He was able to cooperate with Congress and his generals, and was sufficiently tough that when George B. McClellan, a close friend, faltered during the Seven Days' battles and neglected to pursue Lee following Antietam, he supported the general's dismissal.

After the war, Stanton became a leader of the Radical Republicans and an enemy of President Andrew Johnson, who decided to dismiss him. Meanwhile, Congress passed the Tenure of Office Act to thwart Johnson, but the president believed the law was unconstitutional and stood by his decision, for which he was impeached and nearly removed from office. Stanton resigned on May 26, 1868, and returned to his legal practice. Ulysses S. Grant appointed him to the Supreme Court in 1869, but Stanton died before taking the oath of office.

LIBRARY OF CONGRESS

Ball's Bluff ■ By Herman Melville

One noonday, at my window in the
  town,
I saw a sight—saddest that eyes can
  see—
Young soldiers marching lustily
Unto the wars,
With fifes, flags in mottled pageantry;
While all the porches, walks, and
  doors
Were rich with ladies cheering royally.

They moved like July morning on the
  wave;
Their hearts were fresh as clover in its
  prime
(It was the breezy summer time);
Life throbbed so strong,
How should they dream that Death in
  a rosy clime
Would come to thin their shining
  throng?
Youth feels immortal, like the gods
  sublime.

Weeks passed; and at my window,
  leaving bed,
By night I mused, of easeful sleep
  bereft,
On those brave boys (Ah War thy
  theft);
Some marching feet
Found pause at last by cliffs Potomac
  cleft;
Wakeful I mused, while in the street
Far footfalls died away till none were
  left.

Having forced McClellan's hand, Lincoln was informed of the Urbanna plan three months after its original formulation. On February 3, McClellan dispatched a twenty-two-page letter to the president explaining why his water route was preferable to Lincoln's overland campaign.

McClellan was certain that his plan would be successful, but Lincoln feared that the absence of the Army of the Potomac would leave Washington open for capture by the Confederates. Before approving the Urbanna plan, the president required McClellan to open the lower Potomac River by eliminating Southern batteries and clearing the upper Potomac to reopen the Baltimore and Ohio Railroad northwest of Harpers Ferry.

It was a time of considerable activity. Maj. Gen. George H. Thomas had crushed a Confederate advance at Mill Springs, Kentucky, leaving Tennessee open to invasion through the Cumberland Gap. Maj. Gen. Ulysses S. Grant captured Forts Henry and Donelson, and the ensuing occupation of Nashville and the remainder of western Tennessee invited a Union advance to the borders of Georgia, Alabama, and Mississippi. Finally, Brig. Gen. Ambrose Burnside established a bridgehead on the Confederacy's eastern coast by capturing Roanoke Island, North Carolina. These successes, during months in which conventional wisdom decreed armies could not campaign, led Congress, the joint committee, and the public to exert tremendous pressure on McClellan and on Lincoln to motivate his recalcitrant general.

Lincoln, however, suffered an unmeasurable tragedy when his son Willie died on February 20 of fever. This deeply touched McClellan, who offered the president his sincerest condolences and thanked him for his

After the defeat at Ball's Bluff, there was little Federal activity along the Potomac until two foraging parties encountered one another near Dranesville, Virginia. This time the Federals inflicted heavy losses on the Southerners. Among the beaten was Jeb Stuart, who rarely experienced such setbacks.

LESLIE'S

support. "I am pushing to prompt completion the measures of which we have spoken," he wrote, "and I beg that you will not allow military affairs to give you a moment's trouble."

McClellan developed a plan to achieve both objectives simultaneously, hoping to prevent Johnston, in the center at Centreville, from moving to thwart either operation. Brig. Gen. Joseph Hooker would cross the Potomac with four thousand troops from Maryland and attack the batteries obstructing the lower river near Evansport. Upstream, twenty-three thousand men with McClellan in attendance would bridge the river at Harpers Ferry, capture Winchester in the Shenandoah Valley, and protect the workers repairing the railroad.

At Harpers Ferry a pontoon bridge was thrown across the river and soldiers began crossing. Mindful of the disaster at Ball's Bluff, where Union troops were trapped against the river, a larger, sturdier bridge, composed of canal boats, was designed to carry the bulk of the infantry, artillery, and supply-wagon traffic. The canal boats were secured and taken down the canal, but they proved to be six inches too wide to fit through the lock that connected the canal to the Potomac. No one had thought to measure the boats or the lock. Frustrated and overcautious as usual, McClellan canceled both operations on February 27.

Tardy George ■ By George H. Boker

A number of people besides Lincoln, Stanton, and Halleck tired of McClellan's extensive delays before committing to military action. Their frustration was summed up in a poem by George H. Boker, written in January 1862 long before McClellan's major sins were committed:

What are you waiting for, George, I
  pray?—
To scour your cross-belts with fresh
  pipe-clay?
To burnish your buttons, to brighten
  your guns;
To wait you for May-day and warm
  Spring suns?
Are you blowing your fingers because
  they are cold,
Or catching your breath ere you take a
  hold?
Is the mud knee-deep in valley and
  gorge?
What are you waiting for, tardy George?

Want you a thousand more cannon
  made,
To add to the thousand now arrayed?
Want you more men, more money to
  pay?
Are not two millions enough per day?
Wait you for gold and credit to go,
Before we shall see your martial show;
Till Treasury Notes will not pay to forge?
What are you waiting for, tardy George?

Are you waiting for your hair to turn,
Your heart to soften, your bowels to
  yearn
A little more towards "our Southern
  friends,"
As at home and abroad they work their
  ends?
"Our Southern friends!" whom you
  hold so dear
That you do no harm and give no fear,
As you tenderly take them by the
  gorge?
What are you waiting for, tardy George?

Now that you've marshaled your whole
  command,
Planned what you would, and changed
  what you planned;
Practiced with shot and practiced with
  shell,
Know to a hair where every one fell,
Made signs by day and signals by
  night;
Was it all done to keep out of a fight?
Is the whole matter too heavy a
  charge?
What are you waiting for, tardy George?

Shall we have more speeches, more
  reviews?
Or are you waiting to hear the news;
To hold up your hands in mute surprise
When France and England shall
  "recognize"?
Are you too grand to fight traitors
  small?
Must you have a Nation to cope
  withal?

Well, hammer the anvil and blow the
  forge:
You'll soon have a dozen, tardy George!

Suppose for a moment, George, my
  friend—
Just for a moment—you condescend
To use the means that are in your hands,
The eager muskets, and guns, and brands;
Take one bold step on the Southern sod,
And leave the issue to watchful God!
For now the Nation raises its gorge,
Waiting and watching you, tardy George!

I should not much wonder, George, my
  boy,
If Stanton gets in his head a toy,
And some fine morning, ere you are out,
He sends you all "to the right about"—
You and Jomini, and all the crew
Who think that war is nothing to do
But drill, and cipher, and hammer, and
  forge—
What are you waiting for, tardy George?

Lincoln, his cabinet, Congress, and the public were shocked and out-raged that such an important mission was defeated by such a simple prob-lem. Chase cleverly noted that the project "died of lockjaw."

Earlier on the day McClellan ended his campaigns, Lincoln and Stan-ton authorized the chartering of the vast fleet of transports needed to ship McClellan's army to Urbanna. Later Lincoln summoned McClellan's chief of staff and complained bitterly: "Why in the nation, General Marcy, wouldn't the general have known whether a boat would go through that lock before spending a million dollars getting them there? I am no engi-neer, but it seems to me that if I wished to know whether a boat would go

The General with the "Slows" ■ George Brinton McClellan

George Brinton McClellan, born in Philadelphia on December 3, 1826, attended prep school and the Univer-sity of Pennsylvania before graduat-ing from the U.S. Military Academy in 1846, ranked second in a class of fifty-nine that produced twenty-nine other Civil War generals, including Thomas J. "Stonewall" Jackson. A second lieutenant of engineers in Mexico under Winfield Scott, McClel-lan was repeatedly commended for bravery and skill at constructing roads and bridges under combat conditions. He taught three years at West Point and translated a French manual on bayonet tactics. McClellan performed many engineering and surveying duties and traveled to the Crimean War to study European operations. Leaving the army in 1855, he became chief engineer for the Illinois Central Railroad and was president of the Ohio and Mississippi Railroad in Cincinnati when the Civil War started.

On April 23, 1861, Gov. William Dennison made McClellan a major general of Ohio volunteers with com-mand of all the state's forces. By repu-tation alone Lincoln promoted McClellan to major general in the regu-lar army three weeks later, outranked only by the ancient general in chief Winfield Scott, who had received his position when McClellan was fourteen. McClellan helped hold Kentucky in the

Union and led forces into northwestern Virginia, defeating Robert E. Lee at Rich Mountain, protecting the Balti-more and Ohio Railroad, and securing that part of the state for the Union.

When Irwin McDowell stumbled at First Manassas, Lincoln turned to McClellan and gave him command of the Army of the Potomac. He was made general in chief on November 1, 1861, following Scott's resigna-tion, which McClellan had engineered.

McClellan exhibited great skills in training, disciplining, supplying, and preparing armies, but he was overly cautious and exceedingly slow to move. He also had an enormous ego and held his superiors in absolute contempt. Con-vinced that his force was always vastly outnumbered by his enemies, McClellan had to be coerced into action. He was blamed for the Union debacle at Ball's Bluff, then allowed a larger operation devised to break the Confederate block-ade of the Potomac River to fail because of poor planning. As the spring of 1862 approached, McClellan refused to advance against Joseph E. Johnston until the Confederates had evacuated Centreville and Manassas.

The massive Peninsula campaign started well, then quickly bogged down, first before Yorktown and then at the gates of Richmond. McClel-lan's leisurely pace allowed Johnston to stop him at Seven Pines, then

Robert E. Lee pounded him relent-lessly during the Seven Days, which McClellan left to be poorly fought by his subordinates while he supervised the "change of base," or retreat, to the James River. From Harrison's Landing, McClellan refused to resume the offensive despite repeated entreaties from Lincoln and the new general in chief, Henry W. Halleck, and negotiated for reinforcements until he was relieved.

Ordered to unite his troops with John Pope's army, McClellan moved criminally slowly, even while Pope was being defeated at Second Manas-sas. After Pope's failure, Lincoln felt he had no option but to restore McClellan to command. The general quickly reorganized the army and pur-sued Lee into Maryland, but his offen-sive at South Mountain was so deliberate that it gave Lee time to cap-ture Harpers Ferry and consolidate his inferior force at Sharpsburg. McClel-lan's attack there was uncoordinated, and when success seemed certain, he threw victory away by refusing to commit his numerous reserves.

McClellan allowed Lee to withdraw into Virginia unmolested and would not cross the Potomac for two months. Again, despite numerous pleas and threats, he would not be hurried. On November 7, 1862, he was relieved for the second and final time.

The general returned home to Tren-ton, New Jersey, to await orders that never arrived. He resigned from the army to run against Lincoln as the Democratic nominee for president in 1864, but only carried three states. Nonetheless, McClellan made a for-tune in business, served as governor of New Jersey, and died on October 29, 1885. He is buried at Riverview Cemetery in Trenton.

McClellan was worshiped by his men primarily because he kept them well supplied and avoided costly bat-tles, but he also denied them victory. He blamed every failure on lack of support from his superiors and mas-sive Confederate forces, although both excuses were unwarranted. McClellan seemed so fearful of losing his reputation that he could never fight a major battle to conclusion.

LIBRARY OF CONGRESS

The lethary of the armies during the winter of 1861–62 wore heavily on the expectations of the public, which expected the war to be over quickly. McClellan had created an army, but he had done nothing with it. For his part, Beauregard was content to wait for his opponent to act.

through a hole or lock, common sense would teach me to go and measure it. Everything seems to fail. The impression daily gaining ground is that the general does not intend to do anything." Marcy soon wired his son-in-law that the president "was in a hell of a rage."

The joint committee was similarly flustered and took the opportunity to urge Lincoln to either fire McClellan or require an immediate offensive.

"If I remove McClellan," Lincoln asked the committee, "whom shall I put in command?"

"Well, anybody," rejoined Senator Wade.

"Wade, anybody will do for you," was the president's reply, "but not for me. I must have somebody. I must use the tool I have."

Lincoln might have felt better had he known that his counterpart, Jefferson Davis, was suffering the same dilemma in Richmond. The public, newspapers, and Congress wanted action as Union victories mounted in Kentucky, Tennessee, and North Carolina. Considering the fourteen-hundred-mile border between North and South and the thirty-five hundred miles of coastline that had to be defended by half the numbers Lincoln had, Davis could consider no action but remain on the defensive.

Back in September, Johnston and Beauregard had suggested an offensive across the Potomac River into Maryland. They requested

Before Lincoln declared a blockade of the Southern coast on April 19, 1861, Jefferson Davis had offered letters of marque and reprisal to the owners of private vessels, which allowed them to engage and capture Northern shipping for the navyless Confederacy. Although privateering had been outlawed by most nations in 1856, the United States had not signed the agreement. Despite this, Lincoln insisted that any ship molesting American vessels would be considered a pirate and the crew members hanged.

On May 18, 1861, letters were granted to the *Savannah,* a fifty-three-ton schooner with one 18-pounder cannon and a nineteen-man crew under Capt. Thomas Baker. On June 3, she seized the brig *Joseph,* carrying sugar from Cuba to Philadelphia. Later in the day the USS *Perry* captured the *Savannah.*

Davis urged Lincoln to treat the crew as prisoners of war. Lincoln failed to reply, leading Davis to select the Confederacy's thirteen highest-ranking Union prisoners as hostages, to be executed if the crew of the *Savannah* was hanged. Ten colonels and three captains were selected, six of them captured at Ball's Bluff. Since the *Savannah*'s crew was being held in New York City jails, these officers were moved to the Richmond city jail where rats swarmed at night through the seventeen-by-eleven-and-a-half-foot cell. The officers seemed to have been most horrified by the fact that their jailer, described as a "coarse, ruffianly, drunken sot," read their mail.

Cooler heads prevailed. On January 31, 1862, the Union officers were transferred to the War Department. Five days later the Confederate privateers were also returned to prison.

twenty thousand additional troops, but Davis believed they could not be spared from the other theaters. Johnston and Davis, veteran adversaries, sparred throughout the fall and winter, with Secretary of War Judah Benjamin joining in to make it a three-way fight.

On February 19, Johnston was summoned to Richmond for a conference dominated by bad military news. The Federals were advancing through Tennessee, and from their new base in North Carolina they threatened Norfolk. Johnston proceeded to add his own cloud. When the rainy season passed and the roads dried out, he explained, his position at Manassas would not be defensible. Recommending retreat, Johnston had no idea where the withdrawal would end. After seven months around Manassas, he had failed to reconnoiter the terrain south of Bull Run. Davis found this fact "inexplicable" and charged that Johnston "had neglected the primary duty of a commander."

While Davis was inaugurated to a six-year term as president of the Confederacy on February 22, Johnston prepared to evacuate Manassas Junction. His immediate motivation had occurred before his departure from Richmond. Leaving the meeting, Johnston found the city abuzz with news that Manassas would be abandoned. If citizens in the street knew, Johnston believed, then surely McClellan knew. As the general ordered surplus supplies shipped south, he purposefully kept the Confederate government in the dark to prevent further leaks.

During the ten months the Southern army had occupied Manassas Junction, a city of cabins had been erected. Johnston complained that every volunteer had brought a trunk with him. The Confederate commissary department had stocked twice as many rations as Johnston had requested. The army had also constructed a large meatpacking facility at nearby Thoroughfare Gap, where two million pounds of salted beef and bacon had accumulated.

Wet winter weather rendered the roads useless, and the Orange and Alexandria Railroad was used exclusively to remove excess supplies. Because of its single track and lack of sidings, a train required thirty-six hours to travel from Manassas to Gordonsville, sixty miles south.

Johnston complained often and bitterly of railroad management and surplus stockpiled supplies, but still Davis remained ignorant of his general's intentions. Johnston accepted McClellan's aborted operations on the Potomac River as evidence that the Federals knew Manassas was being abandoned and were threatening both his flanks. While these events hurried the evacuation, Davis, planning for the future, urged Johnston to save all possible materials if Manassas was required to be evacuated, particularly the heavy fortress guns.

On March 7, Johnston started withdrawing forty-five thousand Confederate soldiers stationed east of the Bull Run Mountains to a position behind the Rappahannock River, which he had belatedly discovered was the next natural obstacle on the road to Richmond. Stonewall Jackson remained in the Shenandoah Valley with fifty-four hundred troops to threaten the Union left.

The withdrawal was completed in two days, but nearly all the big artillery pieces had been left behind, most of them unspiked. Mountains of supplies were torched by Confederate cavalry. Smoke and the smell of one million pounds of burning salted meat alerted Federal pickets of Johnston's maneuver, which caught both McClellan and the Confederate president by surprise.

On March 10, Davis wired Johnston to expect additional troops and recommended an attack against McClellan when the skies cleared. Davis remained ignorant of Johnston's redeployment until the general informed him three days later.

Meanwhile, McClellan was taking his own lumps. Lincoln summoned his general to a severe scolding for the poorly organized Potomac River escapade. McClellan was shocked and dismayed because Stanton, still playing both sides of the street, had assured the general that Lincoln was "fully satisfied" about that matter.

Lincoln then voiced second thoughts about the Urbanna amphibious operation, although he had approved it nine days earlier. According to McClellan, Lincoln said that he had been told it was a plot to allow Washington to be captured by the Confederates. Enraged, McClellan demanded an apology, and the president hastily explained that he placed no credence in the rumors. Hardly placated, the general returned immediately to his headquarters and put the campaign to the vote of his twelve divisional commanders. Satisfied by the eight-to-four vote in his favor, McClellan paraded all of them to the White House to demonstrate the soundness of his plan.

The Scapegoat for Ball's Bluff ■ Charles Pomeroy Stone

Charles Pomeroy Stone, whose Puritan ancestors had supported every war involving America, was born in Greenfield, Massachusetts, on September 30, 1824. He graduated from West Point in 1845 and won two brevets in Mexico. After serving in ordnance, Stone resigned his commission in 1856 and surveyed Sonora, Mexico. On January 1, 1861, General in Chief Winfield Scott appointed him a colonel, the first of several million volunteers who would serve during the war, and gave him the responsibility for the safety of the president and the capital. He

became a brigadier of volunteers on August 6, sixth on the list of seniority maintained by the War Department.

During the First Manassas campaign, Stone led three brigades in the Army of the Shenandoah with Robert Patterson, who ineffectually opposed Joseph E. Johnston. He next commanded a corps of observation on the upper Potomac River when Edward Baker, an old friend from California, exceeded orders and got himself killed and his unit slaughtered at Ball's Bluff.

Radical Republicans in the Congress and the Cabinet conspired to blame Stone for the embarrassment at Ball's

Bluff. Arrested on February 8, 1862, he was held for 189 days without charges. In 1863 Stone joined Nathaniel Banks at Port Hudson and on the Red River campaign of 1864. Resigning on September 13, 1864, Stone served as chief of staff for the khedive of Egypt for thirteen years. He engineered the foundation for the Statue of Liberty in New York Harbor, where he had been imprisoned, and died on January 24, 1887. He is buried in New York City.

LIBRARY OF CONGRESS

Another bombshell exploded on March 8 when the War Department placed four conditions on the Urbanna operation. First, Washington had to be entirely secure and the number of men to be left for its defense had to be approved by McClellan's senior commanders. Second, he could not shift over half his army until the Confederate batteries below Washington had been captured. Third, he had to start the advance in the next ten days. Last, and most galling, Washington had reorganized his twelve divisions into four corps, and three of the four commanders chosen to lead them had opposed the Urbanna operation. The four were Irwin McDowell, Edwin V. Sumner, Samuel P. Heintzelman, and Erasmus D. Keyes.

McClellan thoroughly resented this civilian intrusion into his authority. The general was convinced that only he should choose the commanders who suited his style, preferably after they had proven themselves in combat, and he alone should determine the proper conditions for conducting the campaign.

The following day brought word of Johnston's evacuation of Manassas Junction to McClellan, Lincoln, and Stanton. The general's reaction was "incredulity which at last gave way to stupefaction," wrote one of the president's secretaries. McClellan left immediately to organize a pursuit, hoping to catch the Confederate rear guard before it reached the Rappa-

The Ordeal of General Stone

The U.S. Army believed Col. Edward Baker was entirely responsible for the disaster at Ball's Bluff, but powerful politicians, particularly Sen. Charles Sumner and Massachusetts Gov. John Andrew, carried a vendetta against Charles P. Stone that was not related to Ball's Bluff but to army doctrine concerning escaped slaves. Sen. Benjamin F. Wade gave McClellan an order for Stone's arrest on January 28, 1862. Before the joint committee on January 31, Wade informed Stone that they believed he had initiated the battle at Ball's Bluff without being able to withdraw or reinforce his troops. They felt he had "undue communication with the enemy" via letters he passed through the lines, and further that he had allowed the Confederates to fortify the south bank of the Potomac River when his artillery could have prevented it.

Stone explained that he had carefully monitored letters exchanged

between the lines and had gained valuable intelligence by the practice. He stated that he would not waste valuable artillery ammunition on unmanned earthworks "simply to amuse the soldiers." Stone declared his innocence, expressed hurt and outrage at his patriotism's being questioned, and chided the committee of military amateurs who presumed to sit in judgment of professional soldiers. At no time did the committee reveal the names of Stone's accusers.

The committee met for "some hours" on February 4 with Secretary of War Edwin Stanton, who was attacking McClellan and all West Pointers through Stone. The next night Stone attended a White House reception at the invitation of President Lincoln. Stone spent time with McClellan on February 7 at the general's request and met with Stanton on February 8,

when he asked if an official investigation into his actions would be held.

"There is no occasion for your inquiry; go back to your command," he was assured.

Around midnight Stone was arrested by a squad of soldiers led by Brig. Gen. George Sykes, an old friend who was baffled by his assignment. Stone was sent to Fort Lafayette in New York Harbor, where he was allowed no visitors and his mail was censored.

Legally, soldiers could only be held for 8 days without cause; Stone was imprisoned for 189 days. The military never announced his arrest, but when word leaked out the public approved, blaming him for Ball's Bluff. Stanton and the War Department refused all requests by Stone and his supporters for a copy of the charges. Stanton had the audacity to turn away senators, leading Sen. James A. McDougall to claim, "Strange times have come

upon the land when the Secretaries of the president deny the right of Senators to official intercourse." McDougall added, "In this country, which is called free, these are strange things. Strange things to be done in the name of constitutional liberty."

The question of Stone's treatment was debated for three days in the Senate. Stone was a victim of "the tyrant's law," one speaker declared, "the law of power, which one man may possess and exercise without limitation and without authority." He further charged Stanton with hiding his crimes out of "fear, coward fear."

Lincoln, distracted by the death of his son Willie on February 20, claimed ignorance of Stone's arrest for some time but told Stanton, "I suppose you have good reason." To the Senate, he said that charges "will be furnished in due season," and a trial was promised "without unnecessary delay." No

hannock. Federal troops occupied the abandoned trenches around Centreville and Manassas, marveling at the great cannon, Quaker guns, and charred ruins of supplies. Newspapermen embarrassed McClellan by reporting that the Confederate camps could only have housed half the 150,000 soldiers McClellan had claimed for months were there, preventing his attack. One wit dubbed the scene "Camp Disappointment."

While McClellan was in the field, Lincoln gave in to pressure by several Radical Republicans, led by Stanton, and relieved McClellan of his general-in-chief position. The pretense was that he could not coordinate the other theaters of war while operating in the field. However warranted or necessary the change might have been, it could have been handled better. First news of the move appeared in Washington papers. Friends wired the revelation to McClellan at Fairfax Court House. Only weeks later was McClellan officially notified. Remarkably, the general was magnanimous. "I shall work just as cheerfully as before," he assured Lincoln.

The pursuit, however, was called off. Johnston had burned six bridges on his retreat, and recent rains had rendered the streams unfordable and the roads impassable. The operation was recalled only halfway to the Rappahannock.

---

charges were ever filed, and no trial was ever held. Appropriately enough, on July 4, Stone wrote Lincoln personally, but received no reply.

Stone was finally released after an act of Congress passed on July 17 required officers to be released in thirty days if no trial was held. Stanton followed the letter of the law, waiting until August 17 to release Stone.

Stone immediately reported for duty, but even with a personal request by McClellan for his services, Stanton refused a reply. On September 29, Stone asked General in Chief Henry Halleck for a copy of the charges against him, emphasizing that 228 days had passed since his arrest. In December, Stone asked McClellan, who had been the official arresting officer, for the list of charges. McClellan described Stanton's order of arrest and stated that the joint committee had requested it,

based on the testimony of a Leesburg refugee. McClellan had forgotten the refugee's name, explaining that he had forwarded the report to the War Department. Stanton refused to produce it, and its contents, even its existence, remain a mystery today. Stone wrote Lincoln again, inquiring why he had been arrested. The president stated his ignorance and referred Stone to Halleck, who claimed that McClellan had recommended the arrest. Halleck complained that McClellan "now seemed to be pushing the whole thing on my shoulders."

Stone requested the return of his papers and private property, which had been seized when he was arrested, but they had apparently disappeared in the morass that was official Washington.

It was not until February 27, 1863, when Stone appeared before the committee for the third time that

he was given a transcript of the testimony against him. Stone gave thorough rebuttals to every charge, leading a somewhat contrite Senator Wade to ask, "Why did you not give us these explanations when you were here before?" Stone pointed out that he never received a list of charges to rebut.

Lincoln agreed with Stanton's position on this matter, writing, "to hold one commander in prison untried is less harmful in times of great national distress than to withdraw several good officers from active battle-fields to give him a trial."

"No reparation to him for the protracted defamation of his character," wrote Congressmen James G. Blaine twenty years later, "no order was published acknowledging that he was found guiltless, no communication was ever made to him by National Authority giving even a hint of the

grounds on which for half a year he was pilloried before the nation as a malefactor. The wound which General Stone received was deep."

Stone retired on April 14, 1864. He operated a Virginia coal mine from 1865 until 1869, then, deeply in debt in 1870, Stone left the country to serve as an officer for the khedive of Egypt. There he joined fifty other Americans, Federal and former Confederate alike, including Walter Jenifer, who served the Confederacy at Ball's Bluff. When Great Britain conquered Egypt in 1882, Stone returned to the United States. One wonders what Stone thought of his last job, engineering the conversion of the brick fort in New York Harbor, where he had been imprisoned, into a pedestal for the Statue of Liberty. He died on January 24, 1887, sickened after attending the dedication ceremony the previous October bareheaded.

Johnston had unknowingly frustrated McClellan's Urbanna plan. There was no need for the Federals to flank the Confederates out of the Centreville-Manassas line since they had done it themselves. The new Southern position on the Rappahannock placed them so close to Urbanna that Johnston could speedily contest a landing. Still McClellan resisted a campaign to attack Johnston directly in his new position.

McClellan revised the Urbanna plan, incorporating an earlier plan to land one peninsula below Urbanna. This one, bordered by the York and James Rivers, had the considerable advantage of a base already held by Federal forces at Fort Monroe. Richmond was seventy land miles away via roads that, McClellan was informed, were passable in any weather. The powerful U.S. Navy, which promised unstinting cooperation, could escort troop transports far up the York River, and the James River led directly to Richmond itself.

McClellan's personal board of directors, the four corps commanders, approved the plan if sufficient troops were left to guarantee the security of Washington. Lincoln concurred, and for a while at least McClellan would call the president "my strongest friend."

There remained only one pesky problem to be resolved—the mighty ironclad CSS *Virginia*.

TOUR NOTE: The Antietam campaign tour passes the site of Ball's Bluff, where only a tiny cemetery marks this often-neglected battle.

3

The Battles of the Ironclads

H AMPTON ROADS WAS ONE of the most important positions in the Confederacy. An eighty-mile-long body of water formed where the James, Elizabeth, and Nansemond Rivers flow into Chesapeake Bay, the Roads controlled access to the James, York, Rappahannock, and Potomac Rivers. The Potomac led directly to Washington, and the James was navigable to Richmond. Four other cities had developed around the Roads: Norfolk and Portsmouth to the south and Hampton and Newport News to the north across Chesapeake Bay.

When Virginia seceded from the Union, possession of the Gosport Navy Yard, one of the most vital military installations in the country, was contested. The facility was situated along the Elizabeth River at Portsmouth, and there were naval shops in the larger city of Norfolk, across the river. At the time the navy yard hosted twelve ships, including the *Merrimack,* a big steam-screw frigate that displaced thirty-two hundred tons and mounted forty guns. Because of persistent engine problems, she had been decommissioned on February 16, 1860, at Gosport for a major overhaul. After a year her machinery was still dismantled.

On April 11, 1861, Como. C. S. McCauley, commanding at Gosport, informed Secretary of the Navy Gideon Welles that the *Merrimack* would require a month to move. Branding McCauley "feeble and incompetent," Welles sent his chief engineer, Benjamin Isherwood, to prepare the ship for towing. McCauley, allegedly drunk, continually interfered with the work. Welles then dispatched Comdr. James Alden with a shipload of explosives to destroy the facility and to take the *Merrimack* to Philadelphia.

Mere hours before Alden arrived on April 20, eight days after the Confederates fired on Fort Sumter, McCauley panicked. Only three ships escaped, including the *Cumberland;* the remainder were scuttled. Union

On August 3, 1861, the U.S. Congress appropriated $1.5 million for construction of three different types of ironclads, a bill endorsed by Kentucky Sen. John C. Breckinridge, who would soon lead Confederate troops as a general and later become Jefferson Davis's secretary of war.

On June 19, 1861, Lt. H. A. Wise, who had destroyed the *Merrimack* at Gosport Navy Yard, wrote: "The reports relative to the raising of the *Merrimack* are and have to be all 'bosh,' for I had hardly time to push off from her side, as I touched a match to the train of turpentine waste hanging from a port, when flames sprouted out in volume. Flames were belching from her lower decks, with her upper works, masts and rigging burning at the same time. I have no doubt that she was consumed to a mere hull and that only below the water line; and even to raise what may be left of her would cost more time and money than were taken to build her."

reinforcements, led by Capt. Hiram Paulding, burned the ships to the waterline and destroyed tons of powder and shells, but he left many facilities untouched, others barely damaged. When Confederates under Maj. Gen. William B. Taliaferro occupied Gosport several hours later, they found foundries, forges, and dry docks intact and one thousand heavy cannon. This wealth moved a Richmond newspaper to crow two days later that "we have material enough to build a Navy of iron-plated ships."

Confederate Secretary of the Navy Stephen R. Mallory had a great interest in ironclad warships. "I regard the possession of an iron-armored ship as a matter of the first necessity," he wrote in mid-April. Mallory expected that a single such vessel could break the Union blockade of the South and cruise along the coast shattering wooden Federal vessels. It was useless to attempt the construction of wooden ships in the face of vast Union superiority, but "inequality of numbers may be compensated by invulnerability." He urged, "Not a moment should be lost."

Mallory certainly lost no time. He had been considering such ships since February. Soon Lt. John M. Brooke, a naval expert; John L. Porter, a constructor at Gosport under the Federals and now with the Confederates; and Confederate Chief Engineer William P. Williamson, working individually and as a group, formulated plans for the first Confederate ironclad.

It would be a shallow-draft, flatbottomed ship with a pointed bow and rounded stern. Atop the deck, which would be submerged or barely awash, would be an iron-plated casemate protecting a gun deck. The shield, slanted forty degrees to deflect an opponent's shot, would consist of two feet of solid wood with three inches or more of iron plate. The armor would extend several feet below the waterline to protect the wooden hull. Large cannon would be placed in broadside to fire out gun

The USS Merrimack

The *Merrimack* was named for the Merrimack River in New England, not for the Merrimac Valley through which the stream flows. There has been considerable confusion over the correct spelling for near a century and a half.

The keel of the frigate was laid September 23, 1854, at the Charlestown Navy Yard in Boston. She carried forty big guns, weighed 3,211 tons, and was 275 feet long, 26 feet wide, and drew 24 feet of water. Twenty thousand people watched her launch on June 14, 1855.

The main mast of the *Merrimack* was 242 feet long, and the canvas needed for her sails covered an acre. Her steam mechanism consisted of two boilers weighing 28 tons apiece and measuring 15 feet high, 14 feet wide, and 12 feet in depth. Each section of the *Merrimack*'s solid wrought-iron drive shaft was 30 feet long, 18 inches in diameter, and weighed 10 tons. The engines provided 869 horsepower to a propeller 17 feet in diameter and weighing 13 tons, which turned at 40 rpm. Her crew numbered 500 and she carried 620 tons of coal.

LIBRARY OF CONGRESS

After six months' work, the scuttled Merrimack *was converted into the first American ironclad at the drydock of the Gosport Navy Yard. An iron ram was installed on the prow, just below the waterline, and was more effective than the rest of the ship's weaponry.*

John Porter was the only U.S. Navy contractor to join the Confederacy, but not entirely for ideological reasons. Porter had required ten years to pass the examination for constructor, and then was tried, but acquitted, for faulty construction of a warship.

ports, and fore and aft would be larger guns mounted on pivots so they could be swiveled to fire forward or from the sides. Boilers and other machinery would be placed below the waterline for protection from enemy fire. The ship would be 150 feet long and 40 feet wide.

This general plan had been settled upon by June 23. When the Tredegar Iron Works in Richmond was requested to manufacture the engine, the company estimated it would require a year, which the Confederacy could ill afford. But there was an alternative.

The decision to raise the *Merrimack* was made on May 11. She was raised from the Elizabeth River on May 30 for five thousand dollars and moved to dry dock. The ironclad design was quickly modified to fit its hull, which retained most of its machinery. Besides the engines, which had never been reliable, the only other drawback was her draft, designed for an oceangoing vessel. But the Confederacy would have to work with what it had. The new plan, prepared by July 10, called for an ironclad mounting ten guns, four in each broadside, two on pivots.

On first inspection, acting chief engineer H. Ashton Ramsay described the ship as "nothing but a burned and blackened hulk. Mallory, however, valued her at $250,000. He informed Congress that it would require $450,000 to recreate her as a frigate that could never escape the Union blockade. When he announced that she could be converted into an ironclad for $172,000, Congress gave its approval.

The conversion chore was overseen by a triumvirate. Porter supervised construction, Brooke handled armor and guns, and Williamson

Catesby Jones and John Brooke tested the *Virginia's* armor on historic Jamestown Island. They replicated a twelve-foot-square section of the ironclad's casemate, first covering it with three layers of inch-thick iron bolted to two feet of wood, and inclined it to an angle of 36 degrees. An 8-inch Columbiad shattered the iron and penetrated the wood backing to a depth of several inches.

Next they used two layers of two-inch-thick iron plate and fired an 8-inch and a 9-inch Columbiad at it from 327 yards. The first layer of iron was shattered but the second layer only cracked.

A third trial involved two layers of railroad T-rails, which saw the rails broken and the wood penetrated.

To deceive the Federals, newspapers published leaked reports that the plating had been "almost worthless."

LIBRARY OF CONGRESS

The Confederate Secretary of the Navy ■ Stephen Russell Mallory

Stephen Russell Mallory, born in 1813 in Trinidad and raised in Florida, was a nineteen-year-old customs inspector at Key West before studying law and becoming a judge. He served in the militia, fought the Seminoles, and in 1851 reached the U.S. Senate, where he served for ten years on the Committee on Naval Affairs.

Mallory had little enthusiasm for secession, but he resigned his seat in the Senate in early 1861. He worked energetically to prevent war from sparking over the Union occupation of Fort Perkins at Pensacola, a crisis that occurred before the climactic confrontation at Fort Sumter. On February 21 Mallory was appointed secretary of the Confederate navy and was one of only two cabinet officers to hold the same post throughout the war. Considering what he had to work with, his accomplishments were respectable. He built a navy from scratch and was influential in the adoption of new technologies, including ironclad gunboats, torpedoes, and submersibles.

Mallory fled Richmond with Jefferson Davis on April 2, 1865, and was captured in LaGrange, Georgia. Paroled in March 1866, he practiced law in Pensacola until his death in 1873.

dealt with the engine and machinery. Disputes over authority and credit for the ironclad plan caused numerous arguments during construction and continued for decades following the war.

At times fifteen hundred men, the entire navy yard, worked on the project, frequently day and night and on Sundays. The upper decks of the *Merrimack* were cut down to within three feet of the waterline, and the gun deck was built atop that. The work was completed by the end of July. Her engines were still flawed, but the Confederates could not wait for a new powerplant to be manufactured.

"The government is constructing a monster at Norfolk," wrote a clerk in the War Department. Tredegar was contracted to supply the iron plate, one inch thick, eight inches wide, of various lengths. Three hundred tons of iron were scavenged at Gosport. The remainder was removed from the Baltimore and Ohio Railroad to the north, which also annoyed the Federal war effort, and Virginia railroads that lay close to Union territory. Tredegar had no problem producing one-inch iron plate, but then Brooke decided to use two layers of two-inch plate instead of three layers of one inch. Tredegar geared up for that production, but drilling holes in the thicker iron was difficult, particularly with the frequent design changes made by Porter and Brooke. Some plates had four different sets of holes.

For six months, from September 1861 until February 1862, Tredegar did nothing but roll iron plate for the *Merrimack,* a total of 723 tons at a cost of $123,015. Transporting the armor to Norfolk proved to be the most difficult chore. In October 100 tons of iron sat idly in Richmond. The last plate reached Gosport on February 12, 1862, delivered via the railroad from Weldon, North Carolina.

Brooke selected six 9-inch smoothbore guns for the broadsides, but Mallory wanted rifles for the other ordnance, firing long wrought-iron bolts for attacking other ironclads. Brooke designed the rifles, reinforced with several iron rings around the powder chamber to allow larger charges. Two 6.4-inch Brooke rifles completed the broadside, while the cannon forward and aft were 7-inch Brooke rifles.

The weapons were also manufactured by Tredegar, which supplied shells but no bolts, since the North at that point lacked ironclads. Both armor and weapons were tested on Jamestown Island by Lt. Catesby ap Roger Jones.

The Confederacy's few sailors had joined the army, making the task of assembling a three-hundred-man crew into a major problem. Lt. John Taylor Wood accepted that job. He secured eighty men from John Magruder's force on the peninsula, then recruited in Richmond and Petersburg.

The ironclad was scheduled for completion in November 1861, but with the extensive changes and alterations suggested by Brooke to Mallory, who then ordered Porter to execute them, construction time crept toward March 1862. "Somebody ought to be hanged," was Jones's com-

HARPER'S

The Virginia's *armament consisted of two 7-inch rifles, two 6-inch rifles, six 9-inch Dahlgren smoothbores, and two 12-inch howitzers. The bow and stern guns were designed to pivot, but the other guns were stationary.*

A Naval Innovator ■ John Mercer Brooke

Born in Florida in 1826, John Mercer Brooke joined the U.S. Navy at age fifteen, gaining entrance to the U.S. Naval Academy in 1845. After graduation in 1847, he served in the Coastal Survey and at the Naval Observatory. Among his accomplishments was plotting a route to China. In April 1861 Brooke resigned to join the Confederacy and served as naval adviser to Robert E. Lee.

After the Confederates seized the Gosport Navy Yard in 1861, Brooke proposed to Confederate Secretary of the Navy Stephen Mallory that the hulk of the *Merrimack* be converted to an ironclad warship. His suggestion for a submerged bow ram was also adopted.

Brooke designed heavy artillery for the Confederacy, became a commander in 1863, and directed the Office of Ordnance and Hydrography from the Richmond Navy Yard. He died in 1904.

ment on the delays. The ironclad was finished in late January and launched on February 7. Water was let into the dry dock and the ship floated, to considerable surprise, into the Elizabeth, where she was commissioned the CSS *Virginia.*

The Confederacy's first ironclad was 262 feet long. The casemate was 178 feet long, sloped 36 degrees and shielded by 2 feet of solid pine and oak backing and two layers of two-inch-thick iron plate, the first layer secured horizontally, the second vertically. Large bolts secured the iron to the shield with giant nuts fastened inside the casemate. The top of the casemate, 14 feet across, was an iron grate made of two-inch-square bars. Three hatches provided access to the gun deck. On the top was a conical pilothouse with four sight holes set in the thick iron bars. Four gun ports pierced each side, and three ports were located forward and aft for the two pivot rifles. The gun ports would be covered with heavy iron shutters, which had not arrived by the time the vessel was launched. Attached to the bow just below the waterline was a poorly installed fifteen-hundred-pound cast-iron ram. The main deck, which extended 30 feet toward the bow and 55 feet to the stern, was covered with one-inch iron, as were the sides to 3 feet below the waterline.

The *Virginia,* like every other Confederate ironclad, leaked badly. Pumps worked constantly to keep her afloat, and the damp, poorly ventilated ship kept a third of her crew on sick call.

The most serious deficiency was revealed after launching when Porter realized he had badly miscalculated the weight. The ship was much lighter than anticipated, which left her vulnerable hull visible. "We are least protected where we need it most," Jones noted. To partially remedy this deficiency, hundreds of tons of pig iron and 150 tons of coal were added, but the *Virginia* still floated higher than was deemed safe.

On February 24, Mallory gave command of the ironclad to Capt. Franklin Buchanan, who controlled all naval defenses along the James River. Buchanan had served in the U.S. Navy since 1815 and had been the first superintendent of the Naval Academy at Annapolis. "Action," his

John Porter undeniably designed the *Virginia,* but in years to come others claimed credit for the ironclad, including John Brooke, who had developed an earlier plan for a casemate ship. Other claimants were E. C. Murray, William P. Williamson, and Virginia Gov. Henry Wise.

Of the *Virginia,* John Porter recorded: "Hundreds—I may say thousands—asserted she would never float."

Even Capt. Sidney S. Lee, Robert E. Lee's brother and executive officer of the navy yard, asked, "Mr. Porter, do you really think she will float?"

An ordnance man, Capt. Archibald Fairfax, claimed Jones had "a want of faith in her ability to float."

When the *Virginia* was floated out of dry dock and into the Elizabeth River, only four privates and a corporal would stand on the ship. Others thought the ironclad would capsize. When the *Virginia* started to battle, one spectator shouted: "Go on with your old metallic coffin! She will never amount to anything else!"

Of construction delays Catesby Jones told John Brooke, "Somebody ought to be hung," probably John Porter.

orders read, "prompt and successful action—now would be of serious importance to our cause."

The North lagged considerably in development of its own ironclad. Receiving news of the Confederate activity at Norfolk, Welles initiated his own project. He requested a $1.5 million appropriation from Congress to construct three prototype ironclads and established a board to examine designs for the vessels. Congress approved on August 3, 1861, as did Lincoln.

Welles advertised for designs on August 7 and appointed a board of review the following day. Of seventeen plans submitted, two were chosen. First to be developed was the *Galena,* which figured in early actions on the James River. It was 180 feet long and armored with interlocking plates. The second design produced an ironclad famous for its involvement at Charleston, *New Ironsides.* Both ships resembled the *Virginia* in structure.

C. S. Bushnell, designer of the *Galena,* sought the counsel of a brilliant but eccentric inventor, John Ericsson, for a technical problem. Ericsson quickly disposed of Bushnell's business, then "asked if I had time just then to examine the plan of a floating battery absolutely impregnable to the heaviest shot or shell," Bushnell recalled.

The design had been originally made during the Crimean War in 1854 for the French, who ignored it. Ericsson had refined the plan since. His ship was 172 feet long and 41 feet wide, with an overhung hull to reduce its vulnerability to ramming. Important machinery, propellers, rudder, and anchor were well protected. In the center of the deck was a round iron turret mounting two powerful guns. The cannon would fire out two

A Reluctant Confederate ■ Franklin Buchanan

Franklin Buchanan, a Marylander born in 1800, joined the U.S. Navy at age fourteen and saw his first action against pirates in the Caribbean. After helping to establish the Naval Academy at Annapolis, he served as its first superintendent. Buchanan was afloat during the war with Mexico, then accompanied Matthew Perry's famed expedition to Japan, and commanded the Washington Navy Yard.

Believing Maryland would secede following the riots in Baltimore in April 1861, Franklin resigned from the navy. When Maryland remained in the Union, the navy refused to disregard his resignation. Buchanan waited until September to join the Confederacy, when he was made a captain and given the Bureau of Orders and Details. In that capacity he faced a chronic shortage of officers, sailors, and vessels.

In February 1862 Buchanan escaped the desk job for command of the Chesapeake Bay Squadron. Within two weeks he steamed forth in his flagship, the ironclad *Virginia,* to sink the *Cumberland* and *Congress.* Infuriated over being fired upon while under a flag of truce, Buchanan foolishly grabbed a rifle and stepped on deck to return fire. A painful thigh wound forced him to miss the following day's combat with the *Monitor.*

In September Buchanan, now an admiral, was placed in charge of the defenses protecting Mobile, Alabama. Two years later, when Union Adm. David Farragut took a large fleet into

LIBRARY OF CONGRESS

the bay, Buchanan met him aboard another ironclad, the *Tennessee.* His reckless bravery threw the Federals into confusion, but soon the *Tennessee* was surrounded by three monitors and wooden ships mounting hundreds of big guns. After an iron splinter broke Buchanan's leg, his successor surrendered the vessel.

Buchanan was exchanged in March 1865 and recaptured with Mobile in April. A postwar college president and insurance businessman, he died in 1874.

portholes in one section of the turret, protected by heavy iron shutters. The truly revolutionary aspect of this ship was that the turret revolved. It rested upon a brass ring set in the deck and was moved by a steam engine on ball bearings ten inches in diameter. The turret "is composed of eight thicknesses of wrought-iron plates, each one inch thick, firmly riveted together," Ericsson specified.

At the front of the ship was a pilothouse, projecting four feet above the deck and composed of wrought-iron blocks a foot long and nine inches high, with narrow vision slits all around.

Ericsson believed the ship could be built cheaply and quickly, in three months. It would be able to operate in shallow water like Chesapeake Bay and the inland rivers of the South. The ironclad could easily train its guns in narrow streams by simply moving the turret instead of turning the entire vessel as required with traditional ships.

Two engines provided 320 horsepower to the four-bladed screw propeller, which was nine feet in diameter. One hundred tons of coal provided eight days of continuous steaming. The confines of the nine-foot-high turret, twenty feet in diameter, made swabbing out the cannon and loading them difficult for the gun crew.

Every part of the ship except the turret and pilothouse would be below the surface, and the deck, three feet above the waterline, was also armored. An extensive ventilation system drew seven thousand cubic feet of air per minute from the deck.

Bushnell immediately introduced Ericsson's design and model to Welles. The secretary of the navy found it "extraordinary and valuable." Bushnell secured a letter of introduction from Secretary of State William Seward to Lincoln, an inventor himself, who pronounced himself "greatly pleased" by the project on September 12. On the following day Bushnell and Lincoln met with Assistant Secretary of the Navy Gustavus Fox and the board. On September 14 Welles met with the board, which rejected the plan because of a spectacular failure Ericsson had experienced with a previous ship. One board member advised Bushnell, "Take the little thing [the model] home and worship it."

Bushnell, knowing Ericsson to be eloquently persuasive, traveled to New York and lied to the inventor, inducing him to come to Washington and address the board personally. "He thrilled every person present in your room with his vivid description of what the little boat would be and what she could do," Bushnell later told Welles.

The board conferred, then asked Ericsson to leave and return twice during the day before approving $275,000 for development of the prototype.

Ericsson went to work immediately. To speed up construction he divided the job. The hull was made by one company, the turret by another, and the iron plate by a third. He demanded that the best workers and tools be used and that construction proceed as quickly as possible, around the clock and on Sundays, like their Confederate counterpart to the south.

LIBRARY OF CONGRESS

The Federal Secretary of the Navy ■ Gideon Welles

Born in Connecticut in 1802, Gideon Welles was a renowned journalist and state legislator and had served as chief of the Navy Bureau in the 1840s. When Abraham Lincoln was elected, he chose Welles to be his secretary of the navy, one of only two cabinet officers who served throughout the Civil War. Politically moderate, Welles was able to assist Lincoln in keeping his fragile coalition together, a task that grew increasingly difficult as the war progressed. He successfully administered the U.S. Navy as it grew rapidly in vessels, manpower, and facilities. Welles coordinated the blockade that eventually strangled the Confederacy economically and militarily by capturing Southern ports one after another, and he organized the successful campaign for the Mississippi River. Welles served Andrew Johnson to the end of his turbulent presidency, then retired and wrote about his wartime experiences before his death in 1878.

Franklin Buchanan could be an ogre in command. Before the war, he had verbally disciplined a Chinese pilot so severely that the man jumped overboard.

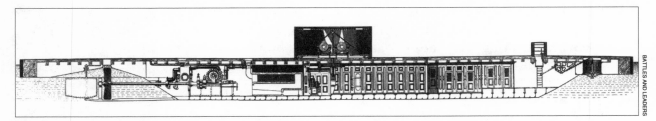

The Monitor *surpassed the* Virginia *in terms of odd appearance. Most observers believed the floating gun platform—whose austere design lacked the graceful lines of traditional naval vessels—would sink as soon as it was launched.*

Upon seeing Ericsson's plans for the *Monitor,* Lincoln stated, "All I have to say is what the girl said when she stuck her foot into the stocking. It strikes me there's something in it."

John Ericsson's ego knew no bounds. When invited to visit Niagara Falls, Ericsson asked, "Is anything the matter with them?"

Ericsson faced the same problems Union shipbuilders faced along the Mississippi River. Government contracts were slow to be issued, and payment was even slower. Welles required that the ship be delivered completed in ninety days and be capable of nine knots. Payment came in installments, and 25 percent of the money would be withheld until the ship's performance was proven. A total refund was expected if Ericsson's vessel was a failure in combat.

On that same day Comdr. Louis Goldsborough, commanding the Union naval forces in Hampton Roads, initiated a long season of "ram fever" by declaring that the *Merrimack* would soon attack. Welles decided that Ericsson's trial would be to destroy the Southern ironclad in dry dock. Final payment would be delayed until that occurred.

From the moment the keel was laid on Long Island, New York, on October 25, Ericsson supervised all aspects of his ironclad's construction. Parts of the ship soon flowed in from across the Northeast.

Welles selected Lt. John L. Worden to command the ship. He arrived January 16, just two weeks before the ship, which Ericsson named the *Monitor,* was launched. As at Gosport, many were surprised that she

Captain of the *Monitor* ■ John Lorimer Worden

John Lorimer Worden, born in 1818, joined the U.S. Navy in 1835. As a lieutenant in 1861 he was dispatched to Fort Pickens, dangerously isolated on an island opposite Pensacola, Florida, and threatened by Secessionists; Worden was ordered not to surrender. The mission ended ignominiously when Worden was arrested while returning tto Washington, traveling across the South by train. After a seven-month imprisonment, he was released in October 1861 and almost immediately given command of the warship *Monitor.* He put the revolutionary

vessel through its shakedown and was then towed to Hampton Roads in early March 1862. Finding the *Congress* and *Cumberland* sunk by the Confederate ironclad *Virginia,* Worden placed his unproven ship between it and the Federal wooden vessels. For four hours the *Monitor* shielded the fleet, fighting its larger adversary to a draw. Near the end of the fight, Worden was temporarily blinded by an exploding shell.

He received a Thanks of Congress citation and was quickly promoted to commander and then captain. He skippered a second monitor, the

Montauk at Charleston and Savannah, where it attacked Fort McAllister on the Ogeechee River and destroyed the raider *Nashville.* From June 1863, he oversaw ironclad construction in New York. Worden was promoted to rear admiral before his retirement in 1886, and he died in 1897.

floated. The craft weighed 776 tons and drew eleven feet of water. The launch was witnessed by a Confederate spy who soon reported his observations to Mallory.

The *Monitor*'s crew consisted of fifty-seven sailors, including ten officers. The guns would be served by nineteen men. Welles armed the ship with two 11-inch Dahlgren smoothbores, bottle-shaped guns with thick breeches to accept heavy 15-pound power charges that fired 175-pound solid iron balls. If concentrated against one area of an ironclad, the armor should be penetrated. The *Monitor* also had long wrought-iron bolts like the ones ordered by Mallory to specifically pierce ironclads, but Welles feared the force of firing them would burst a gun and wipe out the gun crews.

The ship was commissioned on February 25, and on March 6, towed by a tugboat and escorted by two other ships, the *Monitor* started south. Union sympathizers in Norfolk had regularly forwarded reports of the *Virginia*'s progress to Maj. Gen. John Wool at Fort Monroe, leaving the authorities in Washington anxious to have their ironclad on its way.

The *Monitor*'s freeboard was so low that she could be swamped in moderate seas. If she took on two feet of water she would sink. Less than that would drown the fires and fill the ship with deadly fumes.

The *Monitor* rode well that first night on calm seas, but rough weather soon sent waves crashing across the deck like "a regular Niagara Falls!" one officer noted. The warship's deficiencies as a seagoing vessel were quickly made evident. Every hatch leaked and no one could find a dry place to sleep. Many of the crew grew seasick as the waves rolled higher, crashing over the six-foot-tall smokestacks and almost extinguishing the boilers. Wet belts stopped the air blower, stilling the engines and filling the engine compartment with carbon dioxide, which overcame half a dozen men, then started to spread throughout the ship. The slipped belts also stopped the pumps from operating as the ship took on more water.

Men overcome by the fumes were laid atop the turret while others started a bucket brigade to bail out the ship. The accompanying vessels could offer little help, but the *Monitor* was saved when the tug pulled her close to shore, where repairs were made in calmer waters. "I think I lived ten good years," wrote Lt. Samuel Greene of the experience.

Back at sea, the *Monitor* had a repeat of this episode on the following night, with the added misadventure that the tow rope nearly parted.

Officers and crew alike were relieved to enter Chesapeake Bay on the early afternoon of March 8, but then they "heard heavy firing in the distance," a crewman wrote. Nearing Fort Monroe "clouds of smoke could be seen hanging . . . in the direction of the Fortress," and the explosion of shells in the air was visible. Late in the evening artillery fire lit up the horizon. The pilot who arrived to guide the ship informed Worden that the *Virginia* was attacking the Federal fleet in Hampton Roads.

BATTLES AND LEADERS

The Inventor of the Monitor ■ John Ericsson

The inventive mind of John Ericsson, born in 1803, was first noted while he was serving in the Swedish military. He took a leave of absence to demonstrate his caloric engine in Great Britain and never returned home. Sweden allowed Ericsson to resign honorably and he remained in England until 1839, earning thirty patents. When the British Admiralty failed to adopt his screw propeller, Ericsson went bankrupt and was thrown into debtor's prison.

Immigrating to America, Ericsson won a contract to design the USS *Princeton,* the U.S. Navy's first steam-powered warship. The ship was a marvel, but in 1844 Ericsson was blamed when a cannon (named the Peacemaker), which he had not designed, exploded on a trial run, killing several people, including the secretaries of state and the navy.

Hard times returned for Ericsson until the Civil War started and the U.S. Navy solicited designs for ironclads. Ericsson's proposal was accepted, and twenty-two monitors of four different classes were constructed. After the war he sold ironclad designs to a number of countries and continued research in ordnance and torpedoes. He died in 1889 in New York.

Robert E. Lee at Fort Monroe

On May 7, 1831, two years after graduating from West Point, Lt. Robert E. Lee arrived at Fort Monroe, Virginia, which was substantially complete except for some outworks. He soon took leave to marry Mary Anna Randolph Custis on June 30. The couple lived in the top western portion of Building No. 17. The young lieutenant had a good rapport with his commander and enjoyed the work. His social life was stimulated by the presence of prominent visitors to the Hygeia Hotel, a resort also located at Old Point Comfort. On post with Lee were future Confederate notables Joseph E. Johnston and Benjamin Huger.

At Fort Monroe, Lee excavated the moat, completed the water battery, and designed various buildings and fortifications. He ended his stint here by working on Fort Calhoun (Wool), which was delayed several times by the steady sinking of the stone that composed the man-made island. Ordered to live on the island in August 1834, Lee was unhappy with the hot, humid conditions as he super-vised the unloading of additional stone. In November he accepted a despised desk job in Washington to escape the ripraps.

The *Monitor*'s complement were frustrated by the slow pace as the battle raged before them. "Oh how we longed to be there," wrote acting assistant paymaster William Keeler. Dozens of ships raced past the *Monitor* "like a covey of frightened quail," he continued. As darkness fell they sighted a red glow on the horizon—fire dancing above a warship.

A year earlier two capital ships had escaped Gosport, the *Cumberland* and the *Minnesota.* They took up station to protect Hampton Roads in what would eventually become the North Atlantic Blockading Squadron under its second commander, Goldsborough, in service since age seven, who arrived aboard the *Congress.* When the *Roanoke* joined them, Goldsborough had 188 guns and two thousand sailors to control one of the world's most important waterways.

The *Cumberland,* nine years old and once a forty-four-gun frigate, had been cut down a deck to a sloop of war mounting twenty-four guns—twenty-two 9-inch smoothbores, one 10-inch smoothbore, and a single 70-pounder rifle. She was commanded by her executive officer, Lt. George Morris.

The frigate *Minnesota,* a sister ship of the *Merrimack* and the *Roanoke,* mounted twenty-eight 9-inch Dahlgren smoothbores, fourteen 8-inch guns, two 24-pounders, two 12-pounders, and one 10-inch gun. The flagship of Goldsborough, her captain was Gershom J. Van Brunt. Worden had recently served aboard the ship.

The *Roanoke* mounted forty-six guns similar to the *Minnesota*'s, but her engine had been inoperable for four months and no work had been done to repair it. Her captain, John Marston, was also short 180 crewmen on what was little more than a floating battery.

Comdr. William Smith aboard the frigate *Congress* had forty 32-pounder guns and two 8-inch smoothbores. The enlistment of virtually her entire crew had recently expired, leaving her manned with an odd assortment of sailors, including eighty-eight infantrymen from Fort Monroe. Her paymaster, McKean Buchanan, was the brother of the Confederate officer.

There were two main approaches to Fort Monroe: Slaves seeking their freedom arrived at the sally port, or main entrance (below left), and reinforcements disembarked at the port office (below right).

BATTLES AND LEADERS

Crewmen volunteering for service aboard the *Monitor* followed an age-old naval tradition by signing up under assumed names. Samuel Lewis, who came aboard as Peter Truscott, said it was done "on account of danger of running afoul of bad captains or bad ships, when we might have to decamp at the first port."

Impregnable Fort Monroe gave the Federals a foothold on the Virginia peninsula. The fort is in the background, and the Hygeia Hotel occupies the foreground.

The Elizabeth River flows south into Hampton Roads, whose mouth was protected on the western bank by earthworks erected on Craney Island. Five miles to the northeast, Sewell's Point defended the eastern approach. West of the Elizabeth River is the Nansemond, flowing to the southwest, whose entrance was controlled by batteries at Pig Point.

To the north the James River flowed southeast from Richmond. Across the peninsula to the east was the York River. The western bank of the peninsula was controlled by the Confederates, but the southern tip of the eastern bank was in Federal hands from Newport News east to Hampton and the original Union foothold at Old Point Comfort, where Fort Monroe was isolated on a sandspit.

The channel between Hampton Roads and Chesapeake Bay ran between Fort Monroe and the ripraps, shoals where engineers had begun building what is now called Fort Wool on an artificial stone island. At Fort Monroe and at Camp Butler in Newport News, seventy-two-year-old Maj. Gen. John Wool, who had served during the War of 1812, commanded the

The Early Truce at Fort Monroe and the Burning of Hampton

In the spring of 1861, Confederate Lt. Col. Benjamin S. Ewell, president of the College of William and Mary in Williamsburg, was placed in command of the lower peninsula. Robert E. Lee instructed him to erect defenses and recruit volunteers.

On May 14, Ewell visited Union Col. Justin Dimick, commander of Fort Monroe, near Hampton. They agreed to keep their pickets apart to avoid bloodshed. When the Federals advanced on Hampton on May 23,

Confederates set the bridge on fire, but when the Yankees explained they meant no harm, the fire was extinguished. The Union troops entered Hampton then returned to Fort Monroe.

After Benjamin Butler arrived, he explained to Maj. John B. Cary, Ewell's officer in Hampton and former principal of Hampton Military Institute, that he needed to establish a military camp but would not harm anyone if his forces were unmolested.

Upon entering the Union lines, Ewell was captured, but at Cary's protest Dimick released him. Displeased, Ewell had the bridge burned.

On May 30, Butler occupied Fort Calhoun (Wool) and later Newport News to establish Camp Butler. He seized Hampton on July 3 with two regiments, but withdrew them on July 26 after Washington transferred some of his garrison following the disaster at First Manassas. Confederate Gen. John Magruder, now command-

ing on the peninsula, believed some false newspaper reports that Butler would establish camps for soldiers and contrabands in Hampton. On the night of August 7, Magruder sent Capt. Jefferson C. Phillips and four companies to destroy Hampton. Each company fired a quarter of the town, and the community was soon in flames, destroying one hundred homes and thirty businesses. Saint John's Church, although gutted, was the only structure remaining standing.

Union Department of Virginia with seventeen regiments of infantry and five artillery batteries under Brig. Gen. Joseph K. F. Mansfield.

Confederates controlled the James, Nansemond, and Elizabeth Rivers and the entrance to Norfolk, Portsmouth, and the Gosport Navy Yard, but the Federals controlled access to the York River, Chesapeake Bay, and the Atlantic Ocean, which was the northern border of Hampton Roads.

The *Virginia* could upset this year-long balance in the Roads, dispersing or destroying the Union fleet and breaking the blockade. The Federals had to keep the Confederate ship bottled up. Goldsborough planned to meet the *Virginia* near Sewell's Point with the *Cumberland, Congress,* and *Minnesota,* cutting off its avenue of retreat and punishing her with a deadly

Beast Butler at Fort Monroe

There were no Federal generals more controversial than Benjamin Franklin Butler, a critical, opinionated political general who always seemed to rile regular army officers. Butler's first misstep was the unauthorized seizure of Baltimore early in the war. Rather than dismiss him for this popular action, Butler was exiled to Fort Monroe. General in Chief Winfield Scott is reported to have said, "General, you are very fortunate to be assigned to duty at Fortress Monroe. It is just the season for soft-shell crabs, and hog fish have just come in, and they are the most delicious pan fish you ever ate."

Before Butler's arrival, the Confederates and Federals on the peninsula had arrived at a gentlemen's agreement to avoid conflict. That changed with Butler. After three slaves reached Fort Monroe on May 23, 1861, their owner invoked the Fugitive Slave Law and demanded their return. After Butler refused, contending that the slaves had been confiscated as "contraband of war," Fort Monroe was swarmed by large numbers of slaves. Washington supported Butler, instructing him to protect, feed, shelter, and employ them. This policy was adopted for all Union forces.

Reinforcements soon swelled the Federal ranks at Fort Monroe to six thousand troops, who were housed in

Camp Hamilton (today's town of Phoebus). Butler seized Newport News, at the mouth of the James River, and constructed Camp Butler for another six thousand men. A battery containing four 8-inch guns was erected to control the James. As a counterpart to these successes, Butler organized a poorly planned and executed attack against Big Bethel, which was soundly repulsed. The Federals also occupied Hampton but abandoned it in late July, enabling Confederate forces to enter on August 7 and torch the town to deny its use to the Northerners. Butler brought an observation balloon to Fort Monroe for aerial reconnaissance of nearby Confederate activities. During his second term here in 1863, Butler purchased a number of Gatling guns for use by his troops.

Command of Forts Monroe and Wool, Camps Hamilton and Butler, and Hampton and Newport News, then known as the Department of Virginia, was transferred to a regular army officer and an elderly Mexican War hero, Gen. John W. Wool. Butler retained command of volunteer troops outside Fort Monroe before leaving with an expedition that seized a portion of the North Carolina coast. He then returned to Fort Monroe to head a force that

steamed for the Gulf of Mexico to conquer and occupy New Orleans in February 1862. There Butler hanged a man who tore down a U.S. flag and imposed repressive measures upon the civilian population, resulting in the nickname "Beast." After a few chamber pots had been emptied on his officers and other acts of disrespect directed toward his soldiers, Butler ordered that future acts by the women of the city would lead to their being treated as prostitutes. Due to his rancorous relationship with European consuls and persistent rumors of theft and corruption, particularly concerning his brother Andrew, Butler was relieved of command in New Orleans in December 1862.

Returning to Washington, an infuriated Butler demanded that Lincoln tell him who had ordered his removal. Lincoln passed him to the secretary of war who sent him to the secretary of state who referred him to General in Chief Henry Halleck, who sent him back to the secretary of state. Butler never received an answer and chose to blame Halleck.

After a year of inactivity, Butler returned to Fort Monroe to command the much larger Department of Virginia and North Carolina, which included everything north to Williamsburg and south to the sounds of North Carolina. Fort Monroe had become a primary prisoner exchange point, but Confederate authorities refused to deal with Beast

Butler's troops fortifying Camp Butler at Newport News.

crossfire by dozens of heavy guns. Goldsborough's crew practiced constantly and kept a vigilant watch.

In September 1861 Goldsborough had advised the government that a fleet of thirty Federal ironclads "will have the enemy thrown upon his knees." Since they were not forthcoming, he forwarded an almost daily recounting of *Virginia* developments to Welles. She was "exceedingly formidable" and was reported to be coming out at any time. Most observers expected the *Virginia* to appear in early March, but the constant threats ultimately lulled the Federals into complacency.

Two developments should have caught the attention of the watching Federals. On March 1, Confederate ships began ferrying civilians who

The cramped quarters worked on everyone's nerves, and even the officers found privacy at a premium. Any talking in officers country was heard in every other cabin. Paymaster William Keeler found himself unconsciously recording nearby conversations while writing letters home.

Butler. When Butler cleverly sent five hundred Confederate prisoners to City Point, however, the Southerners were forced to respond.

Next Butler assembled a fleet of army gunboats and fought Confederate guerrillas on the rivers and inlets of southern Virginia. His notoriety spread as he raided the great James River plantations, carrying off slaves and food. Always the Massachusetts abolitionist, Butler organized black infantry, cavalry, and artillery units and used them extensively in his operational area.

To satisfy his taste for cloak-and-dagger operations, Butler was in contact with a Federal spy in Richmond, Elizabeth Van Lew. Acting on her intelligence, he ordered a raid on Richmond

The site of the June 10, 1861, battle of Big Bethel.

by the Union garrison in Williamsburg. Butler blamed its failure on the escape from the Williamsburg guardhouse of a Union soldier who alerted the Confederates. The man, sentenced to die for killing an officer, had been granted a reprieve by Lincoln. Butler insolently wrote the president: "You may see how your clemency has been misplaced. I desire that you will revoke your order suspending executions in this Department. Please answer by telegraph." The unfortunate guard who allowed the prisoner to escape was court-martialed and shot at Yorktown on March 7, 1864.

When Ulysses S. Grant took the offensive in Virginia in the spring of 1864, he met with Butler at Fort Monroe in April. The political general

was ordered to seize City Point on the James River and march on Richmond from the south as Grant battled from the north. Butler allowed P. G. T. Beauregard to drive him back and seal the Union army up on a peninsula called Bermuda Hundred. There it remained until Grant arrived to besiege Petersburg.

Butler's last opportunity for glory or shame occurred late in 1864 when he was ordered to capture Fort Fisher, the primary position defending the port of Wilmington, North Carolina. He sent a ship loaded with three hundred tons of gunpowder close to the fort and exploded it, expecting the installation to be demolished. The fort, however, was unscathed and Grant demanded Butler's removal.

Butler returned to Washington and promptly complained to the Committee on the Conduct of the War that Fort Fisher would be captured only after a long siege. As he spoke, those present heard a newsboy outside shouting, "Fort Fisher done took!"

Although Butler was gone by the time Jefferson Davis was imprisoned at Fort Monroe, it would have been interesting had the Beast been his jailer. At the rancorous Democratic presidential convention in 1860, Butler had nominated Davis for president fifty times.

Returning to politics as a Massachusetts congressman, Butler stoutly supported the impeachment of President Andrew Johnson. By authorizing twenty-five thousand dollars for the purchase by the Federal government of Mathew Brady's photographs, Butler helped preserve priceless images of the Civil War. He became governor of Massachusetts and ran unsuccessfully for president in 1884. While speaking in Cleveland, hecklers threw tin and wooden spoons on the stage, a reference to prevalent rumors that Butler had stolen family silver in New Orleans and elsewhere.

At Fort Monroe during his second incarnation, Butler spent government money to build a school for black children at Hampton, which developed into the notable Hampton Institute. As president and treasurer of the National Asylum for Disabled Volunteer Soldiers and Seamen, Butler established a system of soldiers homes (for Union veterans only) across the north. In 1870 Butler suggested a southern soldiers home, which offered a good climate for sufferers of tuberculosis and was convenient for black veterans. He suggested Hampton as the site, where he happened to have purchased a suitable building while serving at Fort Monroe. It was sold to the government for fifty thousand dollars.

The fifty-seven crewmen slept on hammocks slung in the crowded spaces of the *Monitor*. Privacy was not possible. During the day the ship was a furnace; at night it grew as cold as the surrounding water.

Worden's cabin and adjacent stateroom were ten feet square. The officers' rooms were six by eight, with short bunks, tapestry rugs, polished black-walnut woodwork, brass fixtures, a skylight for light and air, closets and drawers for storage, and a desktop that dropped down from a wall. They dined together in the wardroom, served only the best food on fine china and fine liquors in exquisite glassware, all of which was paid for by the officers, who could bring aboard one personal servant each.

desired transportation north to Union ships in Hampton Roads. Foreign observers daily left their ships at Fort Monroe to observe Confederate activity in Gosport, but on the morning of March 8 the French ships abruptly got up steam, apparently ready to move.

The *Virginia*'s crew boarded her on February 17 and obstructions protecting the Elizabeth River were removed, but Buchanan was delayed while scarce powder was gathered from every source in the region. Buchanan had convinced Magruder to attack Newport News when the *Virginia* sallied, but boggy winter roads and Federal reinforcements convinced the general to cancel the infantry's role.

Only four Confederates knew of the pending attack: Buchanan, Magruder, Mallory, and Comdr. John R. Tucker, who led the Confederate flotilla on the James River that would accompany the *Virginia*. Mallory had suggested that, after the destruction of the Union fleet in Hampton Roads, the *Virginia* should steam into Chesapeake Bay and turn north up the Potomac River to the Union capital, where it would destroy bridges and the Washington Navy Yard. The secretary of the navy now suggested an attack against New York City, where the ironclad would "shell and burn the city and the shipping. Such an event would eclipse all the glories of the combats of the sea." Mallory believed that "peace would inevitably follow . . . such an event, by a single ship, [and] would do more to achieve our immediate independence than would the results of many campaigns."

Heavy weather delayed the *Virginia*'s attack until March 8. After the casemate was covered with a thick coating of tallow, which was hoped to deflect enemy projectiles, the *Virginia* cast off at 11 A.M. Workers labored at assorted tasks until the ship cleared the dock, jumping off at the last second as she steamed away. The banks of the river were crowded with thousands of cheering civilians from Norfolk and Portsmouth. The great

A luncheon was scheduled to be served to the officers while the *Monitor* took its maiden trial cruise. The steward, Daniel Moore, took courses away before anyone could eat them and ruined the meal. Paymaster William Keeler wrote that the steward, "upon whom it all depended, was drunk."

Moore was slapped in irons until the ship docked. Given a chance to retrieve his honor, Moore was drunk again the following morning and ironed once more.

In the early afternoon of March 8, 1862, the Virginia *entered Hampton Roads and engaged four vessels of the Union blockading fleet. The first victim of the new ironclad was the USS* Cumberland, *a sloop of war mounting twenty-four cannon rumored to be of the latest design and considered to be the greatest threat to the armored Confederate ship.*

LESLIE'S

U.S. NAVAL HISTORY CENTER

Although its gunners did good work against the Cumberland, *the most damage was done by the* Virginia's *prow-mounted ram. Buchanan drove it deep into the Union vessel, causing it to sink immediately and threatening to take the ironclad with it to the bottom. The ram broke off as the Southern craft extricated itself from the foundering ship, and the Union gunners manned their stations until the deck was awash.*

ship was accompanied by seemingly every vessel that floated, loaded to the water's edge with spectators. The "whole city was in an uproar," wrote a Georgia private, "women, children, men on horseback and on foot running down towards the river from every conceivable direction." It was estimated that every Confederate soldier for twelve miles around had come to bid the *Virginia* farewell.

Buchanan planned to attack the *Cumberland* first, having heard that she had received rifled guns, "the only ones in their whole fleet we have cause to fear," he wrote. "I'm going to make right for her and ram her." He would then destroy the *Cumberland* before the *Minnesota* and *Roanoke* could steam up in support.

The *Virginia*'s maiden voyage was into combat. She was slow, making only five knots, and required half an hour to turn. The crews of both the *Virginia* and the *Monitor* had been allowed little time to familiarize themselves with their weapons and ships.

Rounding the point, Buchanan could plainly see everything in Hampton Roads. The Federals had spotted a column of smoke and watched anxiously

As the *Virginia* chugged to combat, officers ate a hurried meal of tongue and biscuit, but the sight of the surgeon preparing his tools "took away my appetite," H. Ashton Ramsay found.

Franklin Buchanan introduced a new flag signal for his ships: "Sink before you surrender."

"Sailors," Franklin Buchanan told the crew, "in a few minutes you will have the long-expected opportunity to show your devotion to your country and our cause. Remember that you are about to strike for your country and your homes, your wives and your children."

Arriving on the scene in somewhat timely fashion, the Monitor *steamed into Hampton Roads just hours after the* Virginia *had wreaked havoc among the Federal fleet. The stumpy vessel moored near the* Minnesota, *which had run aground trying to escape the Confederate craft after Buchanan had destroyed two Union ships—the* Cumberland *and the* Congress.

for what would come out of the Elizabeth River. The Confederates saw a score of small vessels flee "to the far shore like chickens on the approach of a hovering hawk," noted acting chief engineer H. Ashton Ramsey. Signal flags were hoisted on the big frigates as smoke billowed from the stacks of the *Minnesota, Cumberland,* and *Congress,* and tugs raced to assist the *Roanoke.* The sounds of fife and drums drifted across the water while Confederates in the batteries at Craney Island and Sewell's Point sent up great cheers.

At noon the Federals had been alerted to unknown activity on the Elizabeth, and the *Virginia* was first spotted at 1:08. Signal 551, "Enemy Approaching," was raised. The *Roanoke*'s Marston ordered his ship towed to attack the *Virginia,* which one sailor called a "great black thing, different from any vessel ever seen before."

The *Minnesota* was steaming in eight minutes. The *Roanoke* grounded first, then the *Minnesota,* closer to the *Cumberland* and *Congress,* stuck in the shallow middle ground that divided Hampton Roads into two channels, north and south. A new arrival, the fifty-two-gun frigate *Saint Lawrence* ran aground near the *Minnesota.* The *Cumberland* and the *Congress,* lying three hundred yards off Newport News and two hundred yards apart, were trapped and would receive no help.

Federal soldiers at Newport News saw the *Virginia* emerge at 12:40, the same time that sailors aboard the *Cumberland* spotted black smoke near Craney Island. From a distance of seven miles, one saw "the hull of a large vessel shaped like the roof of a house" with one smokestack. "I believe *that thing* is a-comin down at last," the quartermaster of the *Congress* told an officer.

Drums ashore sounded the "long roll" and those afloat "beat to quarters." Guns were charged with double the normal powder load and saw-

When Union shore batteries opened on the *Virginia* as she accepted the surrender of the *Congress,* one of the cannon was manned by fifteen gunners from the sunken *Cumberland.*

dust was spread across the decks to absorb the blood and gore that naval battles produce in abundance.

The *Virginia* was soon under fire from batteries at Newport News and the artillery aboard the *Cumberland* and *Congress,* but her guns remained silent until Buchanan signaled "Close Action." The ironclad's first shot, from the 7-inch Brooke rifle in the bow, wounded several marines aboard the *Congress.* The second decimated a gun crew, leaving two alive, and one of them lost both arms at the shoulders from the exploding shells and splintered timbers. The *Virginia* and *Cumberland* fired rapidly, and casualties mounted aboard the Federal vessel. The dead were tossed out of the way, the wounded sent below.

"No one flinched," Lt. Thomas O. Selfridge Jr. recalled, "but went on loading and firing, taking the place of some comrade, killed or wounded, as they had been told to do."

In approaching the *Cumberland,* the *Virginia* passed the *Congress* abreast. A tremendous broadside from the Federal frigate left little impression on the Confederate, which replied with a volley from her four broadside guns, including two glowing solid rounds from the hot shot furnace. Two fires started aboard the *Congress,* one near a magazine, and the shells dismounted a gun, felling the entire crew.

"Now she nears the *Cumberland,*" wrote a Northern newspaper reporter, "silent and still, weird and mysterious, like some devilish and superhuman monster, or the horrid creation of a nightmare . . . and from the sides of both pour out a living tide of fire and smoke, of solid shot and heavy shell." Federal shot glanced off the ironclad's slanted casemate,

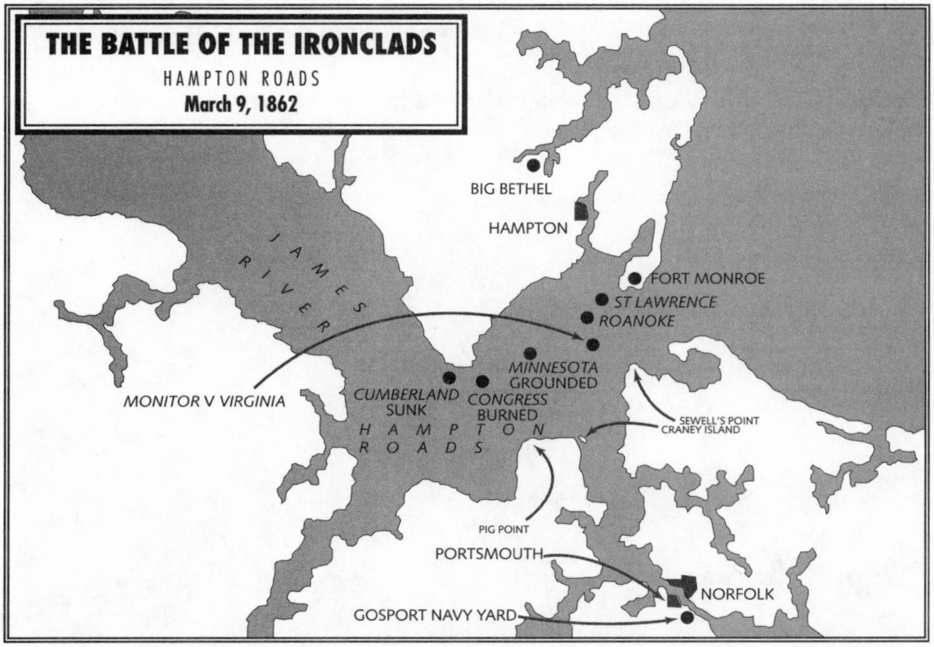

A young powder boy gave his purse to Midshipman Henry H. Marmaduke, whose father had been governor of Missouri, telling him, "I'm likely to be killed in this fight. If I am, will you send my money to my father?"

During the fight a shell from the *Cumberland* entered a porthole of the *Virginia* and exploded, knocking off two feet of a gun muzzle, killing a man, and wounding the rest of the gun crew, including Marmaduke.

"Oh, Mr. Marmaduke," the powder monkey cried, "you're going to die. Give me back my money."

THE BATTLE OF THE IRONCLADS
HAMPTON ROADS
March 9, 1862

BIG BETHEL
HAMPTON
JAMES RIVER
FORT MONROE
ST LAWRENCE
ROANOKE
MINNESOTA GROUNDED
MONITOR V VIRGINIA
CUMBERLAND SUNK
CONGRESS BURNED
HAMPTON ROADS
SEWELL'S POINT
CRANEY ISLAND
PIG POINT
PORTSMOUTH
NORFOLK
GOSPORT NAVY YARD

William H. Parker of the CSS *Raleigh* accepted the surrender of the *Congress* and discovered that his old friend and Annapolis classmate Lt. Joseph Smith had been killed.

When news of the ship's demise reached Washington, the secretary of the navy went to notify personally Smith's father, Como. Joseph Smith.

"Then Joe is dead," the commodore replied.

Welles argued that there was no indication of that.

"You don't know Joe as well as I do," Smith stated. "He would not survive his ship."

U.S. NAVAL HISTORICAL CENTER

He Fought the Monitor ■ Catesby ap Roger Jones

Catesby ap Roger Jones was born in 1821 and became a midshipman in the U.S. Navy at age fifteen. He saw sea duty until the 1850s, when he became an assistant to John A. Dahlgren in ordnance development. Resigning in 1861, Jones saw extensive duty with the Confederate navy. His most celebrated service involved the ironclad CSS *Virginia*. Jones selected the artillery for the ship, drawing on his experience with Dahlgren, and was the vessel's executive officer, second in command, when she sank the *Congress* and the *Cumberland*. After the *Virginia*'s skipper, Franklin Buchanan, was wounded, Jones took control of the ship. It was Jones who steamed out the following day and battled the *Monitor* to a draw.

Jones commanded his own ship, the CSS *Chattahoochee*, then directed operations at the vital naval foundry at Selma, Alabama, which produced cannon and armor plate for ironclads. He left the military in 1864 and became a businessman after the war. In 1877 Jones was murdered by J. S. Harral.

"having no more effect than peas from a pop-gun," but from the *Congress*'s scuppers were "running streams of crimson gore."

"They struck our sloping sides," Ramsey remembered, "were deflected upward to burst harmlessly in the air, or rolled down and fell hissing into the water, dashing the spray up into our ports."

Buchanan drove the *Virginia* straight for the *Cumberland*'s bow at six knots. The ironclad's crew barely felt the impact that drove the ram deep into the Federal, opening a hole seven feet wide. The rush of water immediately started flooding the frigate, which listed and trapped the *Virginia*'s ram inside her. Buchanan had backed the engines when the collision occurred, but the *Cumberland* seemed determined to take her tormentor down with her.

"The engines labored," Ramsey wrote, "the vessel was shaking in every fiber." The *Virginia*'s bow was dipping further and further forward as the *Cumberland* sank, but the current and a wave pivoted the ironclad until the ships were parallel and the ironclad slipped free, leaving the ram broken off inside her opponent.

Taking up position twenty feet from the doomed Federal, the *Virginia* slammed round after round into the *Cumberland*. "The shot and shell from the *Merrimack* crashed through the wooden sides of the *Cumberland* as if they had been made of paper," acting master's mate Charles O'Neil wrote, "carrying huge splinters with them and dealing death and destruction on every hand."

There were no cowards aboard the *Cumberland*. Her crew stood and fought amid "a scene of carnage and destruction never to be recalled without horror," one Federal wrote. O'Neil described the deck as "slippery with blood, blackened with powder and looked like a slaughter house."

The Virginia *reentered Hampton Roads early on the morning of March 9 to finish off the* Minnesota *and prey on the other Federal warships in the area. The* Monitor, *however, thwarted those plans, and the two ironclads engaged at close quarters.*

LESLIE'S

CONFEDERATE BATTERY, SEWELL'S POINT CONFEDERATE BATTERY, CRANEY ISLAND   JAMES RIVER
CONFEDERATE STEAMERS YORKTOWN AND JAMESTOWN   CONFEDERATE BATTERIES AT PIG POINT AND BARREL POINT

BATTLES AND LEADERS

GOSPORT   UNION BATTERY RIPRAPS   FRENCH MAN-OF-WAR   MONITOR AND VIRGINIA   MINNESOTA   WRECKS OF CONGRESS AND CUMBERLAND
PORTSMOUTH   UNION FRIGATE ROANOKE AND TRANSPORTS AND STORE SHIPS   FORT MONROE   UNION BATTERIES AND CAMP AT
NORFOLK   NEWPORT NEWS AND HAMPTON

The battle between the ironclads went on for four hours. The hulls occasionally scraped against each other as the two captains maneuvered their vessels. This view offers the approximate position of other ships in Hampton Roads as well as the relative placement of Confederate and Union shore batteries.

Below decks the wounded drowned and the magazines were submerged, but Union gunners worked their guns until they sank beneath the water. One Confederate declared that "no ship was ever fought more gallantly."

When the ship was ordered abandoned at 3:35, men swam for Newport News or clung to the rigging that protruded above the surface of the Roads. "She went down bravely," wrote a Confederate, "with her colors flying."

During the exchange two Confederate gunners were killed and half a dozen wounded as a Union shot exploded against a gun, knocking two feet off the muzzle. Gun flashes ignited the tallow covering the *Virginia*'s sides. "It seemed that she was literally frying from one end to the other," one sailor thought. The crew could barely breathe and one shouted to a comrade, "Jack, don't this smell like hell?"

Finished with the *Cumberland,* the *Virginia* started a wide slow turn, which at first took her away from the Federal ships, whose crews cheered, believing the Confederate was withdrawing. Turning back, the *Virginia* was joined by two gunboats from the James River, the *Patrick Henry* and the *Teaser.* The *Raleigh* and the *Beaufort* had accompanied the ironclad from Portsmouth.

The *Congress,* alone and still on fire from the *Virginia*'s passing, set sails as a tug labored to tow her into water too shallow for the ironclad to follow. The *Virginia* fired three shots, dismounting two guns and decimating a line of cooks and boys passing powder. At 4 P.M. she took station off the *Cumberland*'s stern and unleashed terrible volleys. An exploding shell decapitated Lt. Joseph Smith Jr., the *Cumberland*'s commander, and blood from her deck poured onto the tug "like water," one remembered.

Lt. Austin Pendergrast took command of the *Cumberland.* Her stern was soon demolished by the *Virginia* and all the guns that could bear on the ironclad were dismounted. Fires were blazing out of control when the *Congress* grounded again. Pendergrast ordered the wounded evacuated to small boats bound for the shore, but the Confederate gunboats added their fire and the carnage rapidly escalated. At 4:45 Pendergrast struck his colors and raised a white flag of surrender. The crew spiked their guns as the tug cut her line and fled.

Curious atmospheric conditions during several Civil War battles prevented the sound of battle from being heard even at close range. Three miles across open water from the naval battle between the *Virginia* and the *Monitor,* Raleigh Colston heard no sound of the battle. He watched "every flash of the guns and the clouds of white smoke, but not a single report was audible."

Lt. Catesby ap Roger Jones was of Welsh descent. The *ap* stood for "son of." His uncle, Thomas ap Catesby Jones, had led the American flotilla at the mouth of the Mississippi River in 1814 that, along with two forts, prevented the British from sailing up the river to New Orleans while Andrew Jackson defeated the British army.

Jones was the gunnery officer for the first voyage of the USS *Merrimack.* In 1858 her chief engineer was Allan C. Stimers, who later served in the same capacity on the *Monitor.* The *Merrimack*'s second assistant engineer in 1859, H. Ashton Ramsay, was engineer in chief on the *Virginia.*

Edwin Stanton's conduct while waiting for news from Hampton Roads was "inexpressibly ludicrous," Gideon Welles remembered. "The wild, frantic talk, action and rage of Stanton as he ran from room to room, sat down and jumped up after writing a few words, swung his arms, scolded, and raved."

Stanton ordered canal boats filled with ballast and sunk in the Potomac River below Washington to obstruct the channel. The barges were prepared but sat on the river for some time. Later, when a party that included Lincoln, Stanton, and others steamed downriver, Lincoln remarked: "That is Stanton's navy. Stanton's navy is as useless as the paps of a man to a sucking child. There may be some show to amuse the child, but they are good for nothing for service."

Buchanan stepped out onto the casemate and ordered Lt. William H. Parker on the *Beaufort,* accompanied by the *Raleigh,* to accept the *Congress*'s surrender, take off her officers, and let the crew go ashore. He would then burn the ship.

"My God, this is terrible," said Parker after he boarded the *Congress.* "I wish this war was over." He sent his men to help evacuate the Federal wounded, assisted by the *Beaufort*'s crew.

The Federals ashore had only received an occasional shell from the *Virginia,* but one of them smashed Mansfield's headquarters and failed to explode. The general, covered with splinters but alive, was livid. He had earlier ordered his sharpshooters to fire on the Confederate ships, but they had lacked a decent target until the *Congress* surrendered and the Southern ships stopped to board prisoners and help the wounded. "I know the damned ship has surrendered," Mansfield shouted at a captain who dared to point that fact out to him, "but we haven't!"

The marksmen and three rifled cannon inflicted casualties to the Confederates and surrendered Federals alike. When Parker was forced to abandon the *Congress,* Pendergrast disappeared to avoid capture and the Federals still aboard the *Congress* fired on the *Raleigh.*

Parker steamed off to unload prisoners and casualties at Sewell's Point without informing Buchanan of the circumstances. Angry, Buchanan sent eight men in his only undamaged boat, covered by the *Teaser,* to burn the

The Real Inventor of the Monitor's Turret

While studying Castle William, a circular fort in New York Harbor, in 1841, Theodore R. Timby conceived the notion of a rotating circular iron fort that would keep targets under a continuous heavy fire as every cannon could be rapidly brought to bear. The nineteen-year-old inventor sketched plans for the device and had a model prepared that so impressed influential Sen. John C. Calhoun that Timby was introduced to several navy officials. Five thousand dollars was raised to craft a working model, measuring fifteen feet in diameter, which President John Tyler admired.

Nothing came of Timby's invention, however, until the *Monitor* was constructed in 1861–62. Although John Ericsson always claimed credit for the revolving armored turret, one of his financial associates, John A. Griswold, and a witness to their contract, William L. Barnes, recognized Timby's claims. In 1862 Griswold suggested that Timby receive eleven thousand dollars for his patent, five thousand dollars for each ironclad the partners constructed, and royalties from other contractors who built similar ships. (The navy had commissioned thirty-three ironclads with revolving turrets.) Barnes took the five-thousand-dollar-per-monitor idea to Secretary of the Navy Gideon Welles, who referred the matter to Ericsson, who later told Barnes that he had advised Welles to disregard Timby's claims. Timby's only compensation was twenty thousand dollars paid by the partners.

Efforts were made over the following decades to gain recognition for Timby's invention. To that end, the New York state legislature sent two resolutions to Congress, but when the navy reported that there was no evidence to substantiate the claim, the matter was dropped in the Senate.

In 1902, when Timby was eighty-two, a Senate bill was sent to the Court of Claims for action. In 1907 the government decreed that there were no contracts that granted Timby money or credit for the clever device, only Ericsson. Timby died on November 9, 1909, the true inventor of the famous gun turret that was the basis for all future warships, including modern missile-armed vessels.

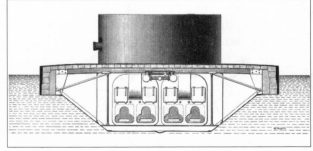

BATTLES AND LEADERS

NATIONAL ARCHIVES

The Monitor *lost its captain during the engagement. The* Virginia's *gunners struck the Federal ironclad's pilothouse, wounding and temporarily blinding Worden. Command passed to executive officer Samuel D. Greene, who had been directing the ship's turret and guns. Worden charged him to protect the* Minnesota, *and Greene pulled back to do so. The two ironclads disengaged, each believing it had won the day.*

Directing one of the *Virginia's* guns was Lt. Walter R. Butts. While he attended the U.S. Naval Academy, his roommate had been Lt. Samuel D. Greene, then commanding the *Monitor's* guns.

Congress. Three men in the boat were wounded and the party required rescue by the *Teaser.*

Enraged by the attack, Buchanan shouted to his crew, "Destroy that damned ship!" The *Virginia* steamed in close and raked the *Cumberland* with hot shot and explosive shells, which started many fires on the splintered vessel. "Dearly did they pay for their unparalleled treachery," Lt. John R. Eggleston remembered.

Buchanan's anger overcame his common sense, and he took a rifle and stood atop the *Virginia's* casemate to fire on the marksmen. The Federals, numbering about fifty, fired back and disabled Buchanan with a bullet in the thigh. He passed command to Catesby Jones with orders to fight until dark.

While all this transpired, the *Saint Lawrence* and *Roanoke* had been freed and towed to the safety offered by Fort Monroe. All available tugboats were now attempting to budge the *Minnesota,* which was being effectively shelled by the gunboats *Jamestown* and *Patrick Henry.* One Yankee crewman saw two comrades killed several yards away, the shot "strewing the brains, even the head of one, all over the deck."

To approach the *Minnesota* safely, the *Virginia* needed to travel by the south channel around the middle ground and up the North Channel, but the light was failing. "We fought until it was so dark that we could not see to point the guns with accuracy," Jones reported. He returned to Sewell's Point, firing his last shot at 6:30.

Samuel D. Greene was an 1859 graduate of the Naval Academy. He served under five different commanders aboard the *Monitor* and was aboard the vessel when it foundered off Cape Hatteras in December 1862.

BATTLES AND LEADERS

After the battle between the ironclads broke off, the Monitor *remained with the blockading fleet but never engaged the* Virginia *again. The Southern vessel steamed out to challenge the Federal ship again but never threatened another Union ship. Thus the crew (above left) and officers (above right) of the turreted vessel adapted to the boredom of blockading and posed for photographers.*

Observers watching the *Monitor's* guns being reloaded were treated to a strange sight. With the port shutters closed after a shot, the long-handled sponges and rammer could not be used. Two small holes had been cut in the shutters, and gunners ran the handles out those to swab out the barrels.

While Worden pulled out of the fight to replenish ammunition in the turret, a gill of whiskey (one-eighth of a pint) was distributed to the men. Keeler normally did not drink but thought that "if liquor ever does good to any one & is ever useful it must be on some such occasion."

In the growing darkness the burning *Congress* lit the Roads, her cannon discharging as the fire reached them. Confederate and Federal fire lighted the horizon like streaks of lightning. One Northerner described "red-tongued flames running up shrouds, masts, and stays" of the *Congress*. "About midnight came the grand finale. The magazines exploded, shooting up a huge column of firebrands hundreds of feet in the air, and then the burning hulk burst asunder and melted into the waters." Another witness described it as "the eruption of a volcano." Debris rained down on Fort Monroe, seven miles distant. The mighty Federal fleet was stunned by this destruction caused by a technological revolution in naval warfare.

The *Virginia* had lost 2 killed and 8 wounded, with 17 additional casualties in the accompanying flotilla. Of the *Congress*'s complement of 376, 121 were dead and 30 were wounded. The *Cumberland* counted 110 dead and 26 wounded of her 434-man crew. Close naval combat does not leave many wounded.

The Southern ironclad anchored at 8 P.M., but the men did not receive their second meal of the day until midnight. Many were still blackened by powder when they sat on the deck to eat and watch the *Congress* burn.

Jones's inspection of the *Virginia* found a leak in the bow, but he failed to notice the ram was missing. Two guns had their muzzles broken off by shot, and every feature outside the casemate had been swept away. The armor was dented in eighty places. Although her machinery had proven adequate, Buchanan thought "a gale, or a very heavy swell" would sink the ironclad. Another officer suggested, "She never should have been found more than three hours' sail from a machine shop." Attacking New York City or even Washington was out of the question.

Wool telegraphed the loss of the *Cumberland* and the *Congress* to Washington and predicted that the *Minnesota* and the *Saint Lawrence* would be destroyed the next day. An engineer aboard the *Minnesota* wrote that "none cared to look forward to the morrow." A newsman in Newport News observed, "The night was not half so heavy as our hearts, nor so dark as our prospects."

In Hampton Roads, Worden boarded the *Roanoke* to find repeated orders from Welles to steam immediately up the Potomac River and defend Washington. Considering the devastation wreaked by the *Virginia* that day, Manston and Worden agreed that the *Monitor* should remain and protect the *Minnesota,* which Worden reached as the *Congress* exploded. The sound "went straight to the marrow of our bones," wrote Lt. Samuel D. Green on the *Monitor.*

The *Minnesota*'s crew was dejected and dispirited. A sailor reported that he was not encouraged by the appearance of the *Monitor,* calling it "but a speck on the dark blue sea at night, almost a laughable object by day." Others remembered that the crew "gave a cheer that might have been heard in Richmond." One described the diminutive ship as a "little black 'Pill Box' on a 'shingle.'"

Thinking the battle over, the *Monitor's* crew opened her hatches and emerged for some fresh air. As William Keeler filled a box with shattered pieces of shells that littered the deck, a parting shot from the *Virginia* exploded twenty feet overhead, startling the men and flinging shrapnel to the deck. "Paymaster," said a gunner quietly, "here's some more pieces."

Capt. Franklin Buchanan's brother McKean was paymaster aboard the *Congress* but managed to escape her destruction. Lying wounded aboard the *Virginia,* Buchanan sobbed, certain he had killed his brother.

Lincoln Captures Norfolk and Destroys the *Virginia*

Following the *Virginia-Monitor* battle, the *Virginia* underwent extensive repairs from March 11 until April 4, 1862, causing a lull in Hampton Roads that allowed George McClellan to land the Army of the Potomac at Fort Monroe and advance toward Yorktown. When the *Virginia* reappeared, she stuck close to the batteries at Sewell's Point while the *Monitor* and the Union fleet remained near the protection of Fort Monroe. Neither was willing to fight on the opponent's chosen ground, and a stalemate resulted. While this situation continued, Como. Louis M. Goldsborough refused to send ships up the York River to support McClellan, whose advance had stalled at Yorktown.

On May 5, the situation was so serious that Lincoln, Secretary of War Edwin Stanton, Secretary of the Treasury Samuel Chase, and Brig. Gen. Egbert L. Viele cruised down the Potomac River on the armed revenue steamer *Miami.* Their purpose was

"to ascertain by personal observation whether some personal vigilance and vigor might not be infused into the operations of the army and navy," Lincoln reported. The party arrived late the next day, met with Maj. Gen. John E. Wool, and continued immediately to confer with Goldsborough aboard the *Minnesota.*

On May 7, Lincoln and his party toured the *Monitor* and the powerful luxury yacht *Vanderbilt,* outfitted to ram the *Virginia.* A salute of twenty-one guns met the president at Fort Monroe, where he reviewed the troops then visited Wool. Later in the day the regiment at Camp Hamilton was reviewed, and Lincoln was saddened by the charred ruins of Hampton, torched a year earlier.

The president settled into Quarters No. 1 at Fort Monroe then convened a conference to deal with the *Virginia.* It was determined that Norfolk would have to be captured to deny the ironclad a base. At that point the

Virginia would have three options. She would be forced to run up the James River to Richmond, run past Forts Monroe and Wool to Chesapeake Bay, where she would have no support, or be destroyed.

The initial plan was to bombard the extensive batteries at Sewell's Point to cover a landing there by four regiments. On May 8, six warships, including the *Monitor,* attacked Sewell's Point while Lincoln watched from Fort Wool. The abrupt appearance of the *Virginia* chased the president's party back to Fort Monroe and forced cancellation of the landing.

A second plan was soon adopted. Troops would be landed from Chesapeake Bay, east of Norfolk, and march on the city. To intervene, the *Virginia,* anchored at Sewell's Point, would have to pass between Forts Monroe and Wool, where she would probably be destroyed by the big guns there or by the ram *Vanderbilt.* On May 9, Chase and Wool steamed

off to reconnoiter and found a good spot at Ocean View. They returned to find the president studying a map and questioning a local pilot. Lincoln, believing a landing could be made closer to Fort Monroe, took Stanton and twenty soldiers and set out to locate his own site. It was to no avail, as Wool chose to land his troops at a spot he had personally seen.

On May 10, four regiments went ashore at Ocean View, forcing the Confederates to fire Gosport Navy Yard and abandon Norfolk. Mayor William W. Lamb met Wool to surrender the city. Lincoln received the welcomed news at midnight in Quarters No. 1.

While the president prepared to return to Washington the following morning, Goldsborough arrived to announce the destruction of the *Virginia* several hours earlier. Lincoln insisted on visiting the site himself, after which he returned to the capital, mission accomplished.

The Remains of the *Virginia*

The *Virginia*'s magazine contained eight tons of gunpowder when she exploded. Union Rear Adm. Charles H. Davis reported that a thirty-ton piece of the armored casemate was blown two hundred yards by the tremendous blast, and a seventy-ton section of the armor was found fifty yards from the hull. These and other pieces of the *Virginia* posed serious obstructions to navigation.

A salvager was hired in 1866 to remove the *Virginia* from the channel. He raised part of the hull and the boilers before the contract was canceled. In 1868 the iron prow, some plate, the drive shaft, and additional machinery was salvaged. Work on the *Virginia* continued until 1871, when another wrecker removed all the armor. During 1874–75 Baker Brothers of Norfolk, who had raised the *Merrimack* to facilitate its redesign as the *Virginia*, removed the cannon and several tons of assorted iron and towed the hull back to the ship's original dry dock in Portsmouth.

Most of the iron portions of the *Virginia* were sent to a foundry as scrap and were melted down, but a few pieces of dented armor, part of the drive shaft, the bell, and the anchor were preserved. The *Virginia*'s bell, some armor, a model built by a crewman, and uniforms may be viewed inside the Museum of the Confederacy in Richmond. The anchor and drive shaft are displayed just outside the entrance to the museum. The thirteen-thousand-pound iron ram is in the Smithsonian, and one ship's bell is in the Chrysler Museum.

A number of canes were carved from the *Virginia*'s oak hull, including one presented to Jefferson Davis in prison.

BATTLES AND LEADERS

To prevent the Federals from wringing any advantage from the occupation of Hampton, Virginia, the Confederates torched the town.

Despite their exhaustion from the terrifying trip from New York, "no one slept" aboard the *Monitor,* reported one officer. He found the crew anxious for battle.

Wool's report of the unequal fight and word of Worden's arrival failed to reach Washington until the following morning, March 9, a Sunday. Welles and Stanton were summoned to an emergency meeting with Lincoln at the White House. John J. Hay, Lincoln's secretary, remembered Stanton as being "fearfully stampeded. He said [Confederates] would capture our fleet, take Ft. Monroe, be in Washington before night."

Welles agreed with Hay, finding Stanton "inexpressibly ludicrous." Stanton stalked the room, expressing fear that the Union navy and every city on the East Coast would be destroyed. "Not unlikely we shall have a shell or cannon-ball from her guns in the White House before we leave this room," the secretary of war said. Stanton and Lincoln peered out the window repeatedly, apparently anticipating the arrival of the *Virginia* at any moment.

Welles patiently explained that the *Virginia*'s draft would prevent her reaching Washington. Unfortunately, his description of the *Monitor*'s two guns drew derision and further apprehension from Stanton.

Stanton telegraphed the governors of New York, Massachusetts, and Maine, urging them to obstruct their harbors with timber rafts and to erect batteries. He next ordered that canal barges be filled with debris and sunk in the Potomac River.

Q.M. Gen. Montgomery Meigs urged every steamship at Annapolis to attack the *Virginia* at once. They would board and toss shells down her smokestacks. "Sacrifice the steamers in order to retake the *Merrimack*," Meigs prompted. "Promotion, ample reward awaits whoever takes or destroys her."

"It seemed as though we had scarcely been asleep" when fife and drum awakened the crew of the *Virginia*, a sailor remembered. They ate a good breakfast, accompanied by two jiggers of whiskey, and steamed away before 7 A.M., accompanied again by a score of small boats packed with spectators. Thousands more crowded the shore.

The *Minnesota* stirred with activity too, as tugs continued their attempt to move the big frigate. Sailors disembarked for transfer to shore, and guns and other materiel were thrown overboard to lighten the warship.

"I will stand by you to the last if I can help you," Worden promised Van Brunt, but some thought his help would not amount to much. Keeler considered "the idea of assistance or protection being offered to the huge thing by the little pigmy at her side seemed absolutely ridiculous."

The sight of the *Monitor* surprised and mystified the *Virginia*'s crew. At first they thought it was a raft evacuating the *Minnesota*, and another officer believed the Union ship was sending a boiler ashore for service. Eggleston considered her "the strangest looking craft we had ever seen before." An officer aboard the *Patrick Henry* called it "an immense shingle

Millionaire patriot Cornelius Vanderbilt donated his yacht, the *Vanderbilt*, to the Union navy. The seventeen-hundred-ton side-wheeler had a speed of fifteen knots, and after her engines and boilers were overhauled and her bow and stern were strengthened with iron plate and timbers, naval officials believed the *Vanderbilt* could cut the *Virginia* in half by ramming.

Taking the *Virginia* out to battle, Josiah Tattnall sat in an armchair placed on the open casemate deck. "Now you go to your stations," he ordered the crew, "and I'll go to mine." He was court-martialed for the loss of the *Virginia*, but he was exonerated and resolved of blame.

Successors of the *Virginia*

The Confederacy never stopped building casemate ironclads similar to the *Virginia*. Nearly thirty were constructed for harbor and river defense. They were built at Richmond; on rivers that led to the sounds of North Carolina; in Wilmington, Charleston, and Savannah; up the Chattahoochee River at Columbus, Georgia; at Selma, Alabama, for the defense of Mobile; at New Orleans and Memphis on the Mississippi River; and on the Yazoo, Tennessee, and Red Rivers.

Built in Richmond were the *Virginia II*—which was 197 feet long, mounted four guns, and had three inches of armor on the sides and six inches forward; the *Fredericksburg*—188 feet long and armed with four guns; the uncompleted *Texas*—launched in January 1865,

which was 217 feet long and was to have had six guns and six inches of armor; and the *Richmond*.

The *Richmond* had five sister ships. These six were built according

to the primary Confederate ironclad design that was not based on an existing hull. They were much smaller than the *Virginia*, 172 feet in length, mounted four guns and

Like the Virginia, *the CSS* Atlanta *(below) was a modified version of a seagoing vessel. Unlike the* Virginia, *she was damaged in her first action and taken into Federal service.*

U.S. ARMY MILITARY HISTORY INSTITUTE

rifles, and were protected by four inches of iron and twenty-two inches of wood. Designed by John Porter, the original *Richmond* was started at Norfolk and towed up the James River at the start of McClellan's Peninsula campaign.

The James River Squadron defended the river from Federal advances by water and land and made two aborted attacks against the Union navy that were repulsed at Trent's Reach on June 21, 1864, and January 29–30, 1865. When Lee abandoned Petersburg and Richmond was evacuated on April 3, 1865, the ironclads were destroyed. Underwater archaeologists have recently begun exploring their remains.

The *Congress* was raised and taken to the same dry dock where the *Virginia* had been built.

floating in the water, with a gigantic cheese box rising from its center; no sails, no wheels, no smokestack, no guns."

"She could not possibly have made her appearance at a more inopportune time," recalled Lieutenant Wood. "No words can express the surprise with which we beheld this strange craft."

A surgeon from the *Congress* "feared she would only constitute additional prey for the leviathan." Another survivor added, "To tell the truth, we did not have much faith in the *Monitor.*"

The Union ironclad was readied for action and started for the *Virginia.* As one of the 175-pound solid shots was loaded in a gun, Worden said, "Send them that with our compliments, my lads." Worden, his pilot, and another officer were in the pilothouse while Greene commanded the two officers in the turret who directed the guns. "The suspense was awful," one Federal remembered, fearing that "the enemy's first fire might make it a coffin for all."

At 8:45 Worden stopped the *Monitor,* then its turret slowly rotated. A port opened, and a gun was run out and fired. The Union quartermaster swore "there was surprise all over the *Merrimack.*" Greene noted that "after the first gun was fired, we forgot all fatigue, hard work, and everything else—& went to work fighting as hard as men ever fought."

The Demise of the *Monitor*

The crew of the *Monitor* spent a miserable summer in 1862, lying in Hampton Roads plagued by mosquitoes, flies, and the summer sun. They also awaited the appearance of the *Richmond,* often called *Merrimack II.* "Some of us will die off one of these days with *Merrimack*-on-the brain," Keeler noted. "The disease is raging furiously."

On September 30, the *Monitor* was towed up Chesapeake Bay to the Potomac River and on to the navy yard at Washington for much-needed repairs and maintenance work.

At 2 P.M. on Christmas Day 1862, the *Monitor* was taken under tow by the *Rhode Island* and entered the Atlantic Ocean. Her destination was Beaufort, South Carolina, a staging area for operations against Charleston, where Federal sea and land forces operated futilely against what they considered the heart of secession.

The first day on the open water was pleasant, but during the evening of December 26 a storm struck, sending towering waves across the *Monitor*'s low deck and dashing against the turret. No one dared venture onto the deck. The waves were so high that the *Monitor*'s wooden hull broke the surface repeatedly, slamming down with great force.

Water entered the ship from every opening, and the battering the *Monitor* received increased the flow. All of her pumps, including one that poured three thousand gallons a minute out of the vessel, could not keep up with the leaks. Bucket brigades supplemented the pumps as a foot of water filled the engine rooms. At 10:30 P.M. Comdr. John P. Bankhead, captain of the distressed vessel, signaled the *Rhode Island* for assistance. Before the steamer could help, the

hawser connecting the two ships had to be cut. As a team from the *Monitor* cut the thirteen-inch line, two men were washed overboard. Water snuffed out the furnace and with it the pumps. When the anchor was dropped for stability, the shock started additional leaks.

The *Rhode Island* seemingly could not see signals from the *Monitor,* including the cry: "Send your boats immediately. We are sinking." Some

crewmen demanded that the *Monitor* open fire on the tow ship.

"Words cannot depict the agony of those moments as our little company gathered on the top of the turret," Keller wrote, "stood with a mass of sinking iron beneath them, gazing through the dim light, over the raging waters with an anxiety amounting almost to agony for some evidence of succor from the only source to which we could look for

Jones intended to ignore the *Monitor* and close to within half a mile of the *Minnesota* to destroy the stranded wooden ship. When his pilots failed to maneuver the ship close enough to the frigate, Jones decided to fight the *Monitor.*

For two hours the *Virginia* and *Monitor* circled, at times touching and scraping as their guns dueled. The *Monitor,* quick and maneuverable, darted about as she fired while the *Virginia* had difficulty bringing her guns to bear on the smaller target.

The *Virginia*'s crew were now veterans, but the Federals were only skittish until the first Confederate shot struck the turret. Looking at the big dent, the crew realized they were safe. In the turret Greene saw that "a look of confidence passed over the men's faces."

The heat in the enclosed iron turret was stifling. Men stripped off their shirts, "the perspiration falling from them like rain," Keeler wrote. After firing, the port shutters were closed and the turret rotated away from the *Virginia* to reload. Worden observed the effect of each shot and sent a messenger to relay the news to the gunners.

After the port stoppers proved difficult to move and the mechanism that stopped the turret was found to be rusted, Worden and Greene decided to leave the ports open and fire the guns as the turret turned, "on the fly."

The last captain of the *Monitor* was Comdr. John P. Bankhead, a loyalist from South Carolina. His first cousin was Brig. Gen. John B. Magruder, who defended the peninsula against McClellan's advance.

---

relief. Seconds lengthened into hours & minutes into years."

The *Monitor*'s crew could not see the *Rhode Island*'s boats as they crept across the terrible seas, but they were coming and at considerable risk. Below decks the water rose higher and crewmen made nightmare journeys while they struggled upward, wading through iron corridors as the water continued to rise and furniture and all manner of debris bobbed around.

The *Monitor*'s entire crew climbed atop the turret and watched the rescue boats, then the *Rhode Island* itself, come alongside. Each man was required to climb a ladder down the side of the turret then creep across the unprotected deck before leaping into a boat as the huge waves crashed down and tossed the ships around. Some sailors were washed away and others refused to peril the journey, choosing instead certain death on the *Monitor.* The captain begged them to leave, but to no avail.

"As we pulled away," wrote one survivor, "I saw in the darkness some black forms I knew to be men clinging to the top of the turret."

The transfer to the *Rhode Island* was almost as dangerous. Men climbed up on ropes or were hauled up the sheer sides of the ship. Some were crushed to death as the ships were tossed about on the heavy seas.

Once aboard they were fed hot food and coffee and given dry clothes and blankets. Most lined the rail to watch the light cast by lanterns hung on the *Monitor*'s turret. At 1 A.M., December 31, 1862, the *Monitor* sank sixteen miles south-southwest of Cape Hatteras, North Carolina, in 220 feet of water. "The *Monitor* is no more," Keeler wrote. Sixteen of her sixty-man crew perished with the ship.

In 1973 marine scientists from the National Geographic Society and Duke University discovered the wreck of the *Monitor.* In 1977 a submersible recovered the first artifacts spilled from the vessel, including its fifteen-hundred-pound, four-and-a-half-foot-long anchor. An effort to retrieve the propeller in 1995 failed. Apparently as the top-heavy *Monitor* sank, the turret was torn from the hull, which came to rest atop the turret. Half the hull is now covered with silt and sand, and much of

the iron plate has collapsed into the wooden hull. The boiler and other machinery are in good shape. Over twenty years of study have followed, marked by periodic debates over whether the vessel should be raised. Scientists believe the hull would never survive such an attempt, but many think the turret might one day become a fascinating museum artifact.

Recent research indicates that the *Monitor* is deteriorating at an alarming rate and must be stabilized and rescued. The problem, as is frequently the case with historic properties, is the cost. Stabilizing the ship and raising vital parts will cost at least twenty million dollars. Recovering the 120-ton turret, composed of eight layers of inch-thick iron plates bolted together, would be a massive undertaking. Within are the two 11-inch smoothbore Dahlgrens, each weighing thirty tons, that battled the *Virginia* to a draw.

When the *Monitor* was repaired at the Washington Navy Yard, the words *Monitor & Merrimack Worden* were engraved on one cannon, and *Monitor & Merrimack Ericsson* were carved on the second. Iron patches covered every dent, engraved with the source of the wound, *Merrimack*'s shell, *Minnesota*'s misdirected shells, etc.

These refinements enabled the cannon to fire every seven minutes, but with diminished accuracy.

The *Virginia* was staggering around the Roads. Water leaked from the bow, she moved slowly and sluggishly, and the perforated smokestack barely drew enough air to keep the engines operating. A number of plates on the casemate had been broken. Had the *Monitor* been able to concentrate her fire on one area of the armor the casemate might have been breached, with disastrous results. Two days' steaming had consumed tons of coal ballast, leaving the poorly armored areas below the casemate dangerously exposed. A few shots there might have sunk the *Virginia*. Fortunately for the Confederates, the *Monitor* had difficulty aiming and was not using the wrought-iron bolts.

By 10:30 continued maneuvering across the channel had confused the Confederate pilots, who ran the *Virginia* hard aground. "Our situation was critical," wrote Ramsey. "In she [the *Monitor*] came and began to sound every chink in our armor."

In the next fifteen minutes Worden slapped six 11-inch shots into the *Virginia*'s armor from point-blank range, cracking the iron plate and driving back the pine and oak backing. The Federal position was so well chosen that no Confederate gun could bear on its adversary.

Below the *Virginia*'s gun deck Ramsey tied down the steam safety values and stuffed wood, oiled cotton waste, and turpentine into the boilers to build up pressure. "It seemed impossible the boilers could long stand the pressure," he wrote, which quickly increased to a dangerous level. The propeller spun furiously until suddenly the *Virginia* lurched free, accompanied by cheers and cries of relief from the crew.

Successors of the Monitor

Sixty iron-turreted warships similar to the *Monitor* were produced during the Civil War, each generally an improvement based on experience with the original and later models. The Passaic class, with ten ships, followed the original *Monitor*. They included the *Weehawken*, which devastated the Confederate ironclad CSS *Atlanta*. The four monitors of the Miantonomoh class mounted two turrets. The Canonicus class had nine ships, counting the *Tecumseh*, which sank in Mobile Bay on August 5, 1864, and remains there. The twenty Casio-class monitors were designed to have light drafts to serve on rivers. They were so poorly

designed that they barely rode above the water even before their turrets were mounted. A few served as turretless gunboats. The four Kalamazoo-class vessels were 345-foot-long giants, but none were ever launched because they were constructed with poorly seasoned wood. The Milwaukee class also mounted two turrets, one Ericsson turret and one designed by James B. Eads, who constructed a number of ironclads for the Union that served on the Mississippi River and its tributaries. The *Roanoke*, a converted frigate, had three turrets.

After the *Virginia-Monitor* affair, Confederate and Federal ironclads only

clashed three other times. In each instance the Southern ship was badly outclassed. In 1863 the CSS *Atlanta*,

converted from a merchant ship trapped by the blockade, ventured from Savannah into Wassau Sound,

A direct descendant of the Monitor, *the twin-turreted* Onondaga *patroled the James River throughout the war.*

One gun captain, Eggleston, ordered his men to cease firing.

"Why are you not firing, sir?" Jones asked.

"It is quite a waste of ammunition to fire at her," Eggleston replied. "Our powder is precious, sir, and I find I can do the *Monitor* as much damage by snapping my finger at her every five minutes."

Jones had apparently arrived at the same conclusion. "Never mind," he told Eggleston. "We are getting ready to ram her."

Jones maneuvered the sluggish vessel toward the *Monitor,* then ordered, "Go ahead, full speed," as it started a half-mile run.

"Look out now," Worden warned Keeler, "They're going to run us down, give them both guns." The *Monitor* turned away, hoping to escape with a glancing blow.

Keeler recalled a "moment of terrible suspense, a heavy jar nearly throwing us from our feet."

The *Virginia* needed twice the distance she had to reach full speed, and Jones, apparently fearing getting stuck inside the *Monitor* as had occurred with the *Cumberland,* started backing the engines before impact. No damage resulted to the Federal ship save a small dent, but the *Virginia,* ramming an iron-plated ship with a wooden bow, sprang a worse leak and took on additional water. Worse yet were the two shots Keeler had fired as the ironclad rammed. The casemate was hammered back three inches where they struck, and the concussion knocked down several gun crews, who bled from nose and ear. "Another shot at the same place would have penetrated," Wood believed.

"The sounds of the conflict at this time were terrible," Keeler wrote. "The din inside the turret was something terrific," echoed Peter Truscott.

The *Monitor* was credited with saving the Union. While certainly an exaggeration, the Northern public clamored to tour the ship while it was in Washington. "Our decks were covered & our ward room filled with ladies," Keeler remembered, "& on going into my state room I found a party of the 'dear delightful creatures' making their toilet before my glass, using my combs & brushes. We couldn't go to any part of the vessel without coming in contact with petticoats. There appeared to be a general turn out of the sex in the city, there were women with children & women without children, & women—hem—expecting, an extensive display of lower extremities was made going up & down our steep ladders."

The ladies not only toured the warship, but they pillaged it for souvenirs, acting master Louis N. Stodder noted. "When we came up to clean that night, there was not a key, doorknob, escutcheon—there wasn't a thing that hadn't been carried away."

---

where two monitors—the *Weehawken* and the *Nahunt*—were waiting. The big ironclad grounded on a sandbar and was unable to return effective fire. The *Weehawken* fired only four shots from her big 15-inch guns, 440-pound wrought-iron bolts powered by 60 pounds of gunpowder. Concussion and flying splinters from the wooden backing incapacitated half the *Atlanta*'s crew. She quickly surrendered. The *Atlanta* was repaired and towed to the James River, where she joined the blockading fleet.

In August 1864 four monitors accompanied Adm. David Farragut's fleet past the forts at the entrance to Mobile Bay. The aforementioned *Tecumseh* was sunk by a torpedo. She also suffered depth charging during World War II and is in poor shape, although iron plates have been salvaged and displayed in local museums. The other three monitors pounded the ironclad CSS *Tennessee* into submission later that day. The *Tennessee* was commanded by Franklin Buchanan, who was wounded for a second time while directing an ironclad.

Federal monitors penned up three Confederate ironclads at Richmond for the last years of the war. On January 29, 1865, when most of the Union monitors were attempting to capture the entrance to Wilmington, North Carolina, the Richmond ironclads started down the river to attack Grant's massive supply base at City Point, which supported the siege of Petersburg. The double-turreted Yankee monitor *Onondaga* fired only one shot at the ironclads before they withdrew, but from a mile away the 15-inch bolt shattered the six inches of iron on the *Virginia II* and crushed the two-foot-thick wooden backing.

The monitors saw considerable duty in capturing Mobile Bay and attempting to seize the city, in blockading Savannah, during numerous fruitless operations over a two-year span to capture Charleston, in efforts to seize the entrance to Wilmington, and in bottling up the Confederate ironclads at Richmond.

After the war, several monitors crossed the Atlantic to show the flag or were sold to European governments. A number saw service during the Spanish-American War as harbor defense ships, but they were broken up afterward. The ships commanded by George Dewey that destroyed the Spanish fleets in the Philippines and Cuba were equipped with the latest generation of movable turrets, direct descendants of the *Monitor*.

Frantically bailing water out of the *Monitor*'s turret shortly before it sank, Francis Butts was distracted by the mewing of the ship's feline mascot. Scooping it up, he stuffed the animal in a cannon and plugged it with a wad. Presumably it remains there.

"The noise of every solid ball that hit fell upon our ears with a crash that deafened us." Added to the noise was the roar of the *Monitor*'s guns.

The turret was filled with smoke, but the only injuries had been inflicted by the nuts that held the layers of iron together. Snapped off by impacting shells, they flew across the turret and caused great bruises. One shell hit when three men were leaning against the wall, conversing. "I was flung by the concussion clean over both guns in the turret," one testified. He remained unconscious for an hour. "I dropped over like a dead man," recalled a second, whose head had been inches from the turret wall, but he too recovered.

Shot and powder had been stockpiled in the turret, but three hours of constant combat had exhausted it. Because only one hatch led from the turret into the *Monitor* and the turret had to be stopped directly over it, Warden steered for shallow water to replenish ammunition.

Jones used the lull at 11 A.M. to resume his attack against the *Minnesota*, which had fired at the *Virginia* over the *Monitor* throughout the

The Siege of Suffolk

The siege of Suffolk is one of the most neglected episodes of the Civil War. While Robert E. Lee dazzled Joseph Hooker at Chancellorsville, a large portion of the Army of Northern Virginia was in southern Virginia fighting a controversial campaign.

After Ambrose Burnside's failures at Fredericksburg and in the infamous "Mud March," the Federal Ninth Corps was shipped to Fort Monroe, a move that forced the Confederacy to face an array of disturbing scenarios. The Federals could continue to North Carolina, Charleston, or Tennessee, or drive up the James River to Richmond while Lee was on the Rappahannock, one hundred miles to the north. Five thousand Union soldiers wound up in Suffolk, which had been occupied by Federal forces a year earlier when Norfolk and Portsmouth were abandoned.

Suffolk, at the head of the Nansemond River, was served by two important railroads, the Norfolk and Petersburg—which connected those cities—and the Seaboard and Roanoke—which ran southwest to Weldon, North Carolina. Union occupation also denied Confederate access to the mouth of the James River and Lake Drummond, from which a system of canals ran through Jericho and Dismal Swamp to the hotly contested sounds of North Carolina.

On February 8, 1862, Burnside seized Roanoke Island and Albemarle Sound, on coastal North Carolina, which was a back route to Suffolk. In early May, when Norfolk and Portsmouth were abandoned by the Confederates, railroad iron, ammunition, and troops were sent through Suffolk to Richmond via the Petersburg and Richmond. Federal forces entered Suffolk on May 12 and ringed the position with a network of fourteen mutually supporting earthen forts and batteries commanding every approach: roads, bridges, canals, and railroads. The works, eight miles in circumference and three miles across, were flanked by impenetrable swamps and gunboats operating on the two branches of the Nansemond. The strongpoints, eight feet high and twelve to fifteen feet thick at the top, were connected by covered ways and log-reinforced rifle pits five to six feet thick. Ten miles of new roads, bridges, and corduroyed swampy areas provided quick communications between threatened sectors. The Yankee soldiers constructed small log huts and dugouts roofed with brush, where they spent most of their time. Water continually pooled in the works, making the task a miserable experience. Many houses were destroyed to clear fields of fire, and trees were felled to form dense abatis. Signal stations ringed the perimeter.

On February 15, 1863, Lee sent George Pickett's division to Richmond, and John Bell Hood's division and two artillery batteries quickly followed. On February 25, James Longstreet replaced Gustavus Smith, exiled since his poor showing at Fair Oaks the previous June, as commander of the Department of Virginia and North Carolina, which was an unwieldy collection of three departments. A third division, commanded by Brig. Gen. Robert Ransom, gave Longstreet a total of forty-five thousand men. At Suffolk, Federal Maj. Gen. John J. Peck had fifty-one thousand troops in various locations.

Lee ordered Longstreet to defend Richmond against attack and to forage in the region, little disturbed by the war. He was also instructed to be ready to rejoin Lee if Hooker crossed the Rappahannock.

Longstreet first ordered D. H. Hill, one of the displaced department commanders, to capture Union-held New Bern, North Carolina, but the plan fell apart when William H. C. Whiting, commanding at Wilmington, North Carolina, as a result of his lackluster performance during the Seven Days, refused to cooperate.

In mid-March, Longstreet convinced Lee to authorize him to forage extensively along the fertile Blackwater and Chowan Rivers, protected by his

morning. Confederate shots did damage and exploded a tug, but the *Virginia* still could not close on the vessel.

The *Monitor* was soon back in the battle, inserting itself between the *Virginia* and *Minnesota* once again. The fighting quickly resumed its earlier intensity as the ships closed. One Federal claimed the ironclads touched five times.

Finding the *Monitor* invulnerable to his shells, Jones briefly considered boarding the little ship. Wood sent men for hammers and wedges to stop the turret from turning. Another planned to throw his jacket over the pilothouse to blind the pilot, and one excited sailor stepped through a port.

"They're going to board us," Worden shouted, calling for canister to be loaded. Crew members stood ready in the turret to throw grenades out onto the barren deck.

The boarding scare over, Worden decided to ram the *Virginia* at 11:30. A thrust at the stern could destroy the *Virginia*'s rudder and propeller, leaving the behemoth dead in the water. As the Federal raced for

The Federals had surrounded Suffolk with signal stations, platforms built atop trimmed pine trees. A Confederate who scrambled up one for a view of the Federal works made an undignified descent when Union artillery shells began bursting all around him.

His ego wounded, the soldier spent the night constructing a lifelike dummy, which he named Julius Caesar and lashed to the platform. After daybreak revealed the figure, the distant Federals again peppered the platform, but they grew frustrated when it showed no fear. After the laughing Confederates shouted "Three cheers for Julius Caesar," the Yankees got the joke.

---

full force. If he saw "an opportunity of dealing a damaging blow," Lee wrote, "act promptly."

While Hill besieged Federal forces at Washington, North Carolina, Longstreet crossed the Blackwater River at Franklin, Virginia, on April 9 to invest Suffolk. With Union troops bottled up, the Confederate commissary was free to pack entire wagon trains with food.

Peck put up little resistance as he withdrew behind his defenses. He had twenty-five thousand troops within his lines, outnumbering the besiegers by five thousand.

Longstreet's seven-and-a-half-mile-long line, constructed two to three miles from the Federals, stretched from the Dismal Swamp on the right to the Nansemond's western branch on the left, where Hood was vulnerable to an amphibious assault supported by Union gunboats. To remedy this weakness, Longstreet expanded an old Confederate work called Fort Huger, which was only

fifty yards from the channel, near the confluence of the western and northern branches. The channel was further narrowed by three lines of pilings. By April 13 Fort Huger contained five cannon and two infantry companies, with supporting guns and troops stationed nearby. Other batteries were established at Pig Point at the mouth of the Nansemond and at other points along the river.

Federal naval forces on the Nansemond consisted of the converted ferryboat *Stepping Stones,* mounting four cannon, and two small tugs. They were reinforced by the *Commodore Barnes,* a converted side-wheel ferryboat, the four-gun river steamer *Mount Washington,* and the tugs *Cohasset* and *Alert,* each mounting two guns. The Nansemond, a narrow, shallow, twisting channel, was a nightmare to navigate. When the *Mount Washington, Stepping Stones,* and *West End* attempted to pass to Suffolk on April 14, the *Mount Washington* was disabled by a shot through the

boiler, and the *West End* grounded. *Stepping Stones* freed the other ships but took a pounding from Confederate gunners, losing six killed and fourteen wounded. The Northerners prudently withdrew.

Two aborted attempts to assault Fort Huger followed, but late on April 19, while Federal land batteries and gunboats opened a concentrated fire on the position, Lt. Roswell H. Lamson of the *Mount Washington* landed 300 men downriver. With their batteries firing canister into the rear of the fort, the Federals poured into the work, capturing 160 men and four cannon while suffering only 14 casualties. This foothold was rapidly expanded into a line of works manned by 1,000 Federals. For no discernible reason, Peck ordered his troops back across the river and the Confederates reoccupied Fort Huger and again closed the Nansemond to shipping.

On April 24, Federal Brig. Gen. Michael Corcoran led five thousand troops, five hundred cavalry, and ten

guns out of the Union works to probe the Confederate lines, but they withdrew after a brief skirmish with Confederate pickets. Five days later Longstreet was informed that Hooker's army had crossed the Rappahannock River, and he was ordered to rejoin Lee immediately. D. H. Hill held the siege lines while the scattered foraging parties were concentrated and Longstreet pulled back. The Confederates crossed the Blackwater River on May 4 and joined Lee too late for Chancellorsville but just in time to invade Pennsylvania.

As a result of the siege, Federal troops leveled both Confederate and Union works and abandoned Suffolk on July 3, 1863, at the height of the Gettysburg campaign, and manned the trenches surrounding Portsmouth. The navy was relieved that it was no longer required to operate on the troublesome Nansemond.

BATTLES AND LEADERS

After the Virginia *had been destroyed, the only obstacle on the James River between the Union fleet and Richmond was a battery of guns at Drewry's Bluff. The fort was erected hurriedly, and the guns were manned by the crew of the erstwhile ironclad.*

After a month of siege work at Suffolk, the Federals had become quite gamy in the filthy trenches. Lt. Col. T. J. Thorp of the 130th New York ordered his men to take up soap and towels and marched them to the Nansemond River. At water's edge he playfully shouted: "Battalion, attention! Undress feet! Undress head! Unbutton coats! Lay off coats! Unbutton breeches! Jerk breeches! Strip off shirts! Right face! Front! Column forward, guide center, double-quick, dive!" then led them through undress parade and other military maneuvers before all collapsed with laughter.

At the conclusion of the siege of Suffolk, every farmhouse within seven miles of the town had been burned.

her adversary, the *Monitor*'s steering suddenly malfunctioned and she sheered off, completely missing the Confederate.

Jones had ordered his fire concentrated on the *Monitor*'s pilothouse, and as the ironclad slid past, a shell fired from twenty yards away exploded on it, breaking one of the iron logs.

"A flash of light & a cloud of smoke filled the house," recorded Keeler, who was standing beside Worden. When he offered to help, Worden said, "My eyes. I am blind." Two men helped Worden out of the pilothouse as Greene, second in command, came from the turret. He found Worden's face "perfectly black with powder & iron & he was apparently perfectly blind," and bleeding profusely from the face.

Quartermaster Peter Williams, who had been with Worden in the pilothouse since the engagement started, turned the ironclad away from the *Virginia* and into shallow water, and the turret ceased firing. "Save the *Minnesota* if you can," Worden instructed as he was led to his cabin.

Thinking the *Monitor* had withdrawn from the battle, Jones returned his attention to the *Minnesota,* but the pilots still could not maneuver within a mile of the stranded ship. Worse yet, they informed Jones that the tide was running out. If they did not enter the Elizabeth River now, they would be unable to cross the sandbar there until the following morning.

Jones explained the situation to his officers, adding: "This ship is leaking from the loss of her prow; the men are exhausted by being so long at their guns; . . . I propose to return to Norfolk for repairs. What is your opinion?"

All but one concurred and the *Virginia* started for home. "Had there been any sign of the *Monitor*'s willingness to renew the contest," Jones later stated, "we would have remained to fight her."

"We had evidently finished the *Merrimack,*" Greene boasted. So both ships claimed victory in what clearly had been a draw.

130

A Federal soldier considered the conflict "one of the greatest Naval Engagements that has ever occurred," noting that the adversaries "fought like tigers for four hours." A sailor who had little faith in the *Monitor* and expected it to be destroyed thought the battle "one of the grandest fights between two war vessels that the world has ever seen."

The *Virginia* returned home to a tumultuous reception. Thousands ashore and afloat cheered and waved flags. "The whole city was alive with joy and excitement," Parker remembered. Three cheers were raised for the crew, which replied in kind, then the crew cheered Jones as batteries fired salutes.

Buchanan sent Wood to Richmond with his official report, which was received by Davis, Mallory, and Secretary of War Judah Benjamin. Although Wood admitted "we had met our match" in the *Monitor,* Mallory, who called this "the most remarkable victory which naval annals record," immediately promoted Buchanan to admiral. The Confederate Congress officially thanked the crew for their valor.

Jones was discouraged by the outcome. "I feel as if we had done nothing," he said. If he was given command of the *Monitor,* Jones continued, he would sink the *Virginia* "in twenty minutes."

WORDEN AND his crew were received similarly by joyful shouts from Union sailors. Assistant Secretary of the Navy Gustavus Fox had arrived from Washington in time to witness the historic battle.

At Suffolk, sharpshooters were a deadly annoyance on both sides of the lines. One day a Confederate trooper watched a cat stretch out on a meat block in a farmyard. Within seconds a Federal sniper fired and "ruthlessly cut off 'Tommy's' entire caudal appendage." Calling the incident a "cat-astrophe," he believed the cat ran forever. The cavalryman retrieved the tail and used it as a plume on his hat.

The Hampton Roads Peace Conference

Northern statesman Francis P. Blair held hopes throughout the Civil War that a peaceful resolution of the conflict could be achieved. As the war's last year started, he persuaded Lincoln to issue him a pass to visit Confederate President Davis in Richmond. Davis promised to send a party of peace commissioners "with a view to secure peace to the two countries." Lincoln consented only to meet them "with the view of securing peace to the people of our one common country." Not an auspicious start.

Davis chose Vice President Alexander Stephens; S. H. Douglas, a good friend of Lincoln from earlier years when both had served in Congress; Robert M. T. Hunter, also a former congressman and presiding officer of the Confederate Senate; and Assistant Secretary of War John A. Campbell, a former associate justice of the U.S. Supreme Court.

The four men passed through the Confederate lines at besieged Petersburg and met Grant at his headquarters in City Point, on the James River. Lincoln proposed to meet them at Fort Monroe, immediately setting out with Secretary of State William H. Seward.

The men assembled aboard the *River Queen,* Lincoln's steamer, anchored off Fort Monroe, on February 3, 1865. They negotiated for four straight hours, but unfortunately no notes were kept of the discussions.

When Lincoln refused to negotiate with the Confederacy under arms, Hunter reminded Lincoln that England's Charles I had done so. Lincoln dryly commented that although he was not so familiar with history, he did know that Charles I was beheaded.

In the end, Hunter said he understood that Lincoln considered the Confederate authorities to be traitors. "That's about the size of it," the president concurred, to which Hunter responded, "Well, Mr. Lincoln, we have about concluded that we shall not be hanged as long as you are President—if we behave ourselves." On that the conference ended.

By this point in the war the emancipation of Southern slaves was a certainty, but Lincoln, believing North and South were both responsible for the institution, favored compensating slave owners to the tune of $400 million. When Lincoln presented the proposal to his cabinet three days later, they unanimously opposed it, and he put it aside.

Lincoln was assassinated two months later, and Stephens was arrested in Georgia and imprisoned at Fort Warren in Boston Harbor until October. Hunter and Campbell were confined for several months in Fort Pulaski, near Savannah, Georgia. The *River Queen* burned at Washington on July 8, 1911.

As the *Virginia* was abandoned on May 11, Midshipman Hardin B. Littlepage stuffed the ship's flags into his knapsack. On May 15 he ran them up over Drewry's Bluff when the *Monitor* approached. The *Virginia*'s crew, if not the *Virginia* itself, repulsed the attack.

"Well, gentlemen," Fox announced when the *Monitor* arrived, "you don't look as though you were just through one of the greatest naval conflicts on record."

"No, sir," Greene responded, "we haven't done much fighting, merely drilling the men at the guns a little."

Fox informed a relieved Washington that "the *Monitor* is more than a match for the *Merrimack.*"

"Have I saved that fine ship, the *Minnesota?*" Worden anxiously asked Lt. Henry A. Wise after the battle.

"Yes," he was reassured, "and whipped the *Merrimack* to boot."

"Then I don't care what happens to me."

At 2 A.M. on March 10 the *Minnesota* was freed after two days of continuous effort.

The *Monitor* had taken twenty-two hits from the *Virginia* and sustained no appreciable damage besides the pilothouse. In return she fired forty-one solid shots.

Worden was taken to Washington for medical care. After Lincoln had been briefed on the battle, he said to his cabinet, "Gentlemen, I am going to shake hands with that man." He then walked to the house where Worden was being treated.

"You do me great honor, Mr. President," said the wounded Worden, "and I am only sorry that I can't see you."

Submarines and a Semisubmersible in Hampton Roads

On November 1, 1861, the U.S. government let a contract for a fully submersible submarine designed by Frenchman Burtus Villeroi and constructed by Neafie and Levy. Named the *Alligator,* it was forty-six feet long, six feet deep, and four and a half feet wide. The ship was powered by sixteen oars, eight to a side, which were connected to a rod. The rod was attached to a crank that turned a propeller, enabling the sub to go forward and backward. The crew consisted of sixteen men and a commander. Like the Confederate submarine *Hunley,* the *Alligator* had no air purification system, which severely hampered its operation.

Completed early in 1862, the *Alligator* arrived in Hampton Roads on June 23, 1862, after the region was under Federal control. Old-fashioned Como. Louis Goldsborough had no use for the new contraption and sent it up the James River to Comdr. John Rodgers, supporting McClellan's army on the peninsula. Rodgers kept the experimental machine only four days before returning it, as Goldsborough expected. With no Confederate ships operating nearby, the submarine had no practical use.

The *Alligator* was shipped to the Washington Navy Yard but returned to Hampton Roads in March 1863 under Acting Master Samuel Eakins. On April 1, it was towed by the USS *Sumpter* toward Port Royal, South Carolina, for use with the South Atlantic Blockading Squadron. As with the *Monitor* four months earlier, a storm off Camp Hatteras, North Carolina, parted one hawser, and the *Sumpter*'s officers agreed to cut the other. The *Alligator* joined the first Union ironclad on the ocean floor.

Federal authorities believed reports that a Confederate submarine was being developed in Hampton Roads for use against the Union blockading ships. On the night of October 9, 1861, Southerners unleashed floating torpedoes into the Roads, hoping the current would carry them against the USS *Minnesota,* anchored near Fort Monroe. The torpedoes came close enough to throw the crew into a panic, and the ship took emergency measures to get away from the threat. In Union reports this was portrayed as an attack by a Rebel submarine, but no such machine ever operated in Hampton Roads.

Three years later, on April 9, 1864, the small torpedo boat *Squib* steamed one hundred miles down the James River from Richmond and entered the Roads at night. Attached to a long pole at the end of the prow was a torpedo loaded with fifty-three pounds of gunpowder. The *Squib* also attacked the *Minnesota,* lying at anchor off Newport News. The explosion started fires in the rigging and planking, set off ammunition, destroyed three gun carriages, and blew the *Squib* back a number of yards. The single-cylinder engine on the torpedo boat stalled, but under rifle fire Lt. Hunter Davidson repaired it and the *Squib* escaped, having thrown another fright into the Federal blockading fleet.

Cornelius Bushnell's iron-sheathed Galena *was one of the nearly twenty designs submitted to the Naval Review Board for consideration as the first Federal ironclad. It joined the fleet at Hampton Roads and on May 15, 1862, was dispatched up the James River with three other ships and the* Monitor. *At Drewry's Bluff, the small fleet encountered the Confederate battery then known as Fort Darling. Only the* Galena's *guns could elevate to engage the Southern gunners, and so the other ships held back while the* Galena *ventured forth. After a three-hour duel, the Federals withdrew with the* Galena *badly damaged. The Southern gunners had struck the vessel twenty-eight times and perforated the ship eighteen and caused twenty-eight casualties.*

An emotional Lincoln held his hand and replied, "You have done me more honor, sir, then I can ever do to you."

On February 3, 1863, at Lincoln's request, Congress voted Worden its thanks.

As the *Monitor, Galena,* and other Federal gunboats retreated from Drewry's Bluff, a Confederate sharpshooter shouted, "Tell the Captain that is *not* the way to Richmond!"

JUDAH BENJAMIN, appointed secretary of state on March 18, ordered Confederate diplomats in England and France to emphasize that this naval victory had almost broken the Union blockade. He hoped the affair would gain foreign recognition for the Confederacy. A Southerner in London reported that "the success of the *Virginia* has caused great excitement here." The British Admiralty soon announced that it would build no more wooden warships.

Buchanan informed Mallory that the *Virginia* was "by no means invulnerable" and could never attack New York. The big guns at Fort Monroe might destroy her, any rough sea would sink her, and he felt the *Virginia* drew too much water to cross the bar into New York Harbor.

Capt. Sidney S. Lee, Robert E. Lee's less-accomplished brother, oversaw repairs of the *Virginia* as commander of Confederate forces at Norfolk. Porter found one hundred dents in the armor, twenty of them inflicted by the *Monitor.* Six cracked iron plates were replaced and the timber backing repaired where needed. A better-designed iron prow was added, the damaged guns replaced, and armor extended below the casemate. Solid wrought-iron bolts were produced by Tredegar, and the iron

John Rogers commanded the *Galena* in the failed assault on Drewry's Bluff.

shutters were finally installed to protect the gun ports before the *Virginia* left dry dock on April 4. Sixty-seven-year-old Josiah Tattnall was considered by many too old physically and mentally for such a position, but he nevertheless received command of the ironclad.

With the immediate crisis over, Stanton abandoned his plan to block the Potomac River, but Welles ordered the channel between Fort Monroe and the ripraps obstructed. Stanton persuaded millionaire Cornelius Vanderbilt to donate his fast seventeen-hundred-ton steamer *Vanderbilt* to the U.S. Navy, specifically for the task of sinking the *Virginia*. The bow was reinforced and a strong iron prow added for ramming.

Worden informed Lincoln that the *Monitor* could easily be boarded, the turret immobilized with wedges, and the engines drowned with water poured into vents. Considering that weakness, Lincoln ordered the *Monitor* to remain on the defensive in Hampton Roads. Small arms and grenades were prepared to repel boarders, and the pilothouse was sloped and covered with tallow.

McClellan's plan to attack Richmond via the peninsula had been threatened on March 8 and saved the following day. He had "such a lively faith in the gallant little *Monitor*" that his campaign remained unchanged. Throughout April the Confederates believed that McClellan would move up the James River rather than the York, and the Federals endured successive rumors that the *Virginia* was coming down again.

Learning that McClellan would use the York River, Tattnall realized he would have to defeat the *Monitor* to defend the peninsula. On April 6 he took the *Virginia* down the Elizabeth River. He planned to engage the

The Imprisonment of Jefferson Davis

After the assassination of Abraham Lincoln, President Andrew Johnson received false information that implicated Jefferson Davis in the killing. Johnson offered a rich reward for the capture of Davis, who was apprehended by Union cavalry in southeastern Georgia on May 10, 1865. Taken to Augusta, Davis boarded the USS *William B. Clyde*.

To prevent the escape or rescue of Davis, Federal authorities decided to incarcerate him at Fort Monroe, the strongest installation in the Union. The Confederate president arrived on May 19 but was kept aboard ship while a cell was constructed in Casemate No. 1. The gun port was equipped with strong iron bars, and

the moat beyond was eight feet deep and one hundred feet wide.

When Davis was escorted from the ship on May 22, Chief of Staff Henry Halleck and Assistant Secretary of War Charles Dana were present. Halleck prevented Dana from shackling Davis, but Dana left written orders to that purpose. Seventy armed soldiers guarded Davis, with two in a locked outer room, two in the corridor, and lines of sentries across the moat, on the ramparts above, and lining the inner road of the fort. Casemates on either side of the president contained off-duty guards. Davis was not going anywhere.

Officer of the Day Capt. Jerome Titlow, reporting to Maj. Gen. Nelson

A. Miles for orders on May 23, was instructed to place iron leg shackles on Davis. Late in the day, Titlow, the blacksmith and his assistant, and two soldiers armed with bayoneted muskets entered Davis's cell, where the former president was sitting on his cot reading an Episcopal prayer book. Noting their purpose, Davis assured Titlow that the shackles were unnecessary. Titlow replied, "Mr. Davis, you are an old soldier and you know what orders are . . . an officer is bound to execute an order given him."

Davis began to walk around his cell in great agitation, then stopped and put a foot on a chair. Thinking he had acquiesced, the blacksmith knelt to rivet a shackle. Davis smashed the

man to the floor, but the blacksmith sprang up with his hammer raised. Titlow stepped between the men, then called in four beefy, unarmed men and instructed them to, "with as little force as possible," place Davis on his cot and hold him while the shackles were secured. Davis was old and gray haired, but the wiry man put up a furious struggle before the restraints were applied. As Titlow left the cell, he saw tears streaking Davis's face.

Lt. Col. John J. Craven, chief medical officer of the Department of Virginia and North Carolina, visited Davis the next morning. Concerned by the prisoner's appearance, he immediately confronted Miles and demanded

Monitor while the *Raleigh, Patrick Henry, Beaufort,* and *Jamestown* came alongside the Federal with boarding parties. Hawsers from the four gunboats would be run around the turret to prevent its escape. Blankets would blind the pilot while the turret was immobilized with wedges and flaming bottles of turpentine were thrown down her stacks.

The commanders of both vessels, however, had become cautious. The *Monitor,* now commanded by Lt. William N. Jeffers, refused to leave the security of Fort Monroe's guns, and the *Virginia* ventured no farther than the batteries at Sewell's Point and Craney Island.

An aborted attempt to steam into Hampton Roads occurred before McClellan's campaign made the evacuation of Norfolk necessary. In the background was a disagreement between Confederate officials. Mallory and Robert E. Lee wanted the *Virginia* to fight past Fort Monroe to attack McClellan's transports in the York River, but Sidney S. Lee believed the ironclad was essential to Norfolk's defense.

On May 1 the Confederates began removing munitions, stores, and machinery from Norfolk. Any materials that could not be moved were prepared for destruction. To divert Federal attention, the *Virginia* steamed into Hampton Roads every day.

On May 6, Lincoln, Stanton, and Chase arrived at Fort Monroe to observe and ascertain "whether some further vigilance and vigor might not be infused into the operations," Lincoln's secretary wrote. The president was concerned by reports that the *Virginia* was repaired and out of dry dock. It might venture again into Hampton Roads and disrupt McClellan's campaign. Stanton was impatient to capture Norfolk, across Hampton

A Lincoln Conspirator at Fort Monroe

Samuel Arnold had conspired with John Wilkes Booth to kidnap Abraham Lincoln, a scheme that failed in March 1865 when the president was not in the carriage they expected to waylay. When talk turned to assassination, Arnold left Washington and on April 1, 1865, found work in a sutler's store at Old Point Comfort Wharf.

After Lincoln was killed on April 14, authorities found a letter in Booth's trunk implicating Arnold, who was arrested on April 17. The letter proved Arnold guilty of conspiracy to kidnap but cleared him of the assassination charge. Tried with the Lincoln conspirators, he escaped the noose but was imprisoned until 1869 in Fort Jefferson in Florida's brutal Dry Tortugas.

---

that Davis be unshackled for reasons of health. When news of Davis's shackling appeared in prominent newspapers, many Americans, including ardent supporters of the Union, were outraged. On May 28, Miles relented and the irons were removed.

Craven conversed extensively with Davis and kept a diary of their talks. His continued intervention on Davis's behalf led to the president's removal from the casemate, where he had spent four and a half months, to Carroll Hall, a two-story brick building no longer standing. Superiors who found Craven too sympathetic to Davis had him removed in December 1865, and the doctor left military service a month later. At home in

New Jersey, Craven wrote *Prison Life of Jefferson Davis,* published to great sales in America, Britain, and France. In addition to creating widespread sympathy for Davis, Craven also stated that if Davis were charged with the murder of Lincoln and the condition of Federal prisoners during the war, then he should be tried. Otherwise, a noble nation should forgive Davis the crime of rebellion and free him.

In May 1866, President Johnson allowed Davis's wife, Varina, to live in one of Fort Monroe's casemates, which were often used for family housing during peacetime. Miles's replacement, Gen. Henry S. Burton, allowed Varina, her daughter Winnie,

and Varina's sister Margaret Howell to join Davis in Carroll Hall. Mrs. Davis traveled frequently to seek support for her husband's release.

Perhaps surprisingly, vocal opponents of secession supported Davis, including famed newspaper editor Horace Greeley of the *New York Tribune* and Gerrit Smith, a supporter of John Brown. Davis was finally freed on May 13, 1867, his one-hundred-thousand-dollar bail signed by Greeley, Smith, and Commodore Vanderbilt. All charges were dropped in 1869.

A freed Davis traveled abroad, engaged in the insurance business in Memphis, and retired to the Mississippi Gulf Coast to write his memoirs,

The Rise and Fall of the Confederate Government. After his death at age eighty-one in 1889, Davis was buried for four years in New Orleans, then exhumed in 1893 and reinterred with great ceremony at Richmond's Hollywood Cemetery.

Craven went on to make a fortune inventing processes and machinery for the meat industry. He died on February 19, 1893, in Patchoque, New York, at the age of seventy.

Titlow settled in Hampton, where he was sheriff of Elizabeth City County for eleven years, then traveled west. He died in 1912 at the Minnesota State Soldiers Home.

A Confederate picket at the Nanse-mond River shouted to his Federal counterpart, "Say, Yank, you 'uns bring Abe down heah to the river, we 'unse will bring Jeff; then we drown 'um both 'n go home!"

Roads from Fort Monroe, which would result in the capture or destruction of the *Virginia* and open the James River, which led directly to Richmond. He was certain that the ten thousand men at Fort Monroe, under seventy-two-year-old General Wool, and the navy could accomplish the goal.

Lincoln ordered Goldsborough, aboard the *Minnesota,* to open the James River with the *Monitor* and the newly arrived *Galena.* Hearing that Norfolk was being evacuated, Lincoln further instructed Goldsborough to attack Sewell's Point to determine if any Confederates remained and to draw out the *Virginia.*

The *Monitor* and five ships steamed across Hampton Roads while Lincoln and his cabinet officers observed from a tug at the ripraps. Although the Confederates remained, Federal fire soon silenced the batteries. When the *Virginia* reached Craney Island at 2:45 P.M., Goldsborough withdrew to Fort Monroe.

Two nights earlier the *Jamestown* and *Patrick Henry* had towed an unfinished ironclad, later commissioned the *Richmond,* up the James River to the Confederate capital. The *Virginia* would have to follow or be destroyed. In order to prevent the Federals from steaming up the Elizabeth River, she anchored at Sewell's Point until Norfolk was abandoned.

The next Federal effort, scheduled for May 8, was an amphibious landing of troops at Sewell's Point, seven and a half miles north of Norfolk, under cover of a naval bombardment led by the *Monitor.* The appearance of the *Virginia* canceled that operation.

Attention now turned east to a landing from Chesapeake Bay. If the *Virginia* dared interfere she would be caught in a crossfire between Forts Monroe and Wool. On the night of May 9, five thousand men, four regiments under General Wool, landed, the action monitored from Fort

Raise the *Monitor!*

In 1973 John G. Newton of Duke University's Marine Laboratory studied the logs of the USS *Rhode Island,* which was towing the *Monitor* when the ironclad sank off stormy Cape Hatteras, North Carolina, known as the "Graveyard of the Atlantic" because fierce storms have sunk many ships there. His research narrowed the location of the ironclad's wreck to an area six by sixteen miles.

The *Eastwind,* Duke's 117-foot-long research ship, then set forth to locate the *Monitor.* She was equipped with sonar, a depth sounder, underwater television cameras, a navigational positioning system, and a side-scanning radar operated by Harold E. Edgeton of the Massachusetts Institute of Technology. Two military ships joined the *Eastwind* to conduct a submarine geological survey. The expedition was supported by the National Geographic Society, MIT, the National Science Foundation, and the U.S. Army Reserve.

Within a week twenty-one wrecks had been identified and dismissed. The twenty-second contact was detected on sonar by Fred Kelly, an oceanographic expert. A second run with the side-scanning radar confirmed that it was the *Monitor.* Cameras discovered that the turret had apparently torn away from the hull as the ship capsized and hit the ocean floor first. The hull landed upside down on top of the turret and is filled with sand. The massive turret was thought to be in good shape, but the hull was severely damaged, with plates of iron scattered all around. It is believed that the wreck of the *Monitor* was depth charged during the early months of World War II, when the area was a prime hunting ground for German submarines and every sonar target was bombarded.

To preserve this historic site, in July 1974 the U.S. Department of the Interior placed the *Monitor* on the National Register of Historic Places. One year later the National Oceanic and Atmospheric Administration (NOAA) established the *Monitor* National Marine Sanctuary. In 1985 NOAA joined with the National Trust for Historic Preservation to form the USS *Monitor* Project. It will study the historic vessel through underwater archaeology and determine if any part of the *Monitor* can be safely raised and displayed.

Monroe by Lincoln and Chase. Norfolk Mayor William W. Land met the column on the outskirts of town and made a show of surrendering the city. He bought a little extra time for Maj. Gen. Benjamin Huger to evacuate his nine thousand Confederates from the area and to destroy Gosport Navy Yard.

Tattnall was not informed of the Confederate withdrawal and remained ignorant until 10 A.M. on May 10, when messages to the batteries at Sewell's Point were unanswered. Jones was sent to Norfolk for orders from Huger or Lee, but they had left the city. Confederate property was afire and Federal troops were approaching when Jones departed at 7 P.M. The *Virginia* had to get up the James River by dawn or she would be trapped.

Pilots assured Tattnall that the *Virginia* could get over the sandbar at the mouth of the James River if they could reduce her draft from twenty-two feet to eighteen. Tattnall, however, was ill in bed, so Jones started work at 1:30 A.M. on May 11. Throwing all the ballast overboard brought the draft to twenty feet, then everything except cannon, powder, and shot was removed. In the midst of this work the pilots brought bad news. The wind, blowing hard from the west, was driving water from the bar to the Roads. The ironclad would never be able to cross. But neither could she stay and fight with two feet of unarmored hull, the propeller, and rudder exposed. As Ramsay noted, she was "no longer an ironclad."

Jones ran the *Virginia* aground off Craney Island. Several hours were spent ferrying her three hundred crewmen to shore, where they started a twenty-two-mile hike to Suffolk to join Huger. Jones and Woods remained to set the ship afire. Through the night the sailors heard her guns discharge, then around 5 A.M. the magazine exploded with a force felt for miles around. "The *Virginia* no longer exists," Tattnall sent to Mallory.

From Suffolk the *Virginia*'s former crew entrained for Petersburg, where they ate, and continued on to Richmond on May 12. Their journey ended on the James River at Drewry's Bluff, where the *Jamestown* and other ships were sunk in the channel.

Word that Norfolk was in Union hands provoked cheers aboard the Union fleet in Hampton Roads. During the early morning hours of May 11 Keeler saw the glow cast by the *Virginia*'s burning, then "a sudden flash & a dull heavy report brought us all on deck to conjecture & surmise."

At dawn the *Monitor* steamed up the Elizabeth River, followed by ships bearing Stanton, Chase, and Lincoln, who saluted the *Monitor.* All hands marveled at the ruins of the *Virginia*.

The first and only James River defense of the Confederate capital was established five miles south of Richmond atop Drewry's Bluff, which rose two hundred feet above the river on the south bank. It was a good position, where the river was only two hundred yards wide and made a sharp curve, the final bend before a straight run to Richmond. A previous set of defensive works was quickly, desperately expanded during the night of May 14 under the supervision of Col. Custis Lee, Robert E. Lee's eldest

Grant at Fort Monroe

After becoming a lieutenant general and general in chief in early March 1864, Ulysses S. Grant made his headquarters with the Army of the Potomac in the field near Culpeper. He left late in the month to confer with Benjamin Butler at Fort Monroe, arriving on April 1. Grant ordered Butler to seize City Point and advance on Richmond from the south, then he discussed a second matter with Butler, who was commander of exchange of prisoners.

Confederate captives accumulated at Point Lookout, Maryland, and were transferred to a stockade at Camp Hamilton and to Fort Monroe's casemates, then exchanged for Federal prisoners arriving down the James River. Butler had just convinced Confederate authorities to deal with him in exchanging prisoners, but Grant was convinced that strategically it was more important to deny the Confederates their captive soldiers than it was for the North to get theirs back.

"It is hard on our men held in Southern prisons not to exchange them, but it is humanity to those left in the ranks to fight our battle," Grant wrote. "If we commence a system of exchange which liberates all prisoners taken, we will have to fight on until the entire South is exterminated." Inadvertently, this led to the tragic situation at the Confederate prison located at Andersonville, Georgia, and other camps across the South.

After Grant's departure on April 3, Butler left to land on Bermuda Hundred, a peninsula between the James and Appomattox Rivers. Butler did not attack until May 13, when P. G. T. Beauregard drove him back and bottled up the Federal Army of the James.

The Elderly Naval Man
■ Josiah Tattnall

Born in 1795 in Georgia and educated in England, Josiah Tattnall saw service in the War of 1812, against the Barbary pirates, and in the Mexican War. Although opposed to secession, he resigned from the U.S. Navy in February 1861 and was assigned the defense of coastal Georgia and South Carolina. Despite his age, Tattnall attacked Federal warships in the Savannah River and futilely assaulted the Union fleet that captured Port Royal in November.

Called to Norfolk in March 1862, Tattnall was Buchanan's replacement in commanding Chesapeake Bay's defenses. He never found another opportunity to attack the *Monitor* and destroyed the *Virginia* after the Confederates evacuated the region. When a court of inquiry censured his actions, Tattnall demanded a court-martial, which subsequently absolved him of blame.

Tattnall resumed his previous job in Savannah but was given shore command in April 1863. Thought too old for sea duty, he supervised the construction of ironclads and the procurement of supplies.

After surrendering with Joseph E. Johnston in North Carolina in 1865, Tattnall moved to Canada, then returned to Savannah in 1870. The city created a job for the elderly man, who died a year later and was buried in Bonaventure Cemetery.

son. The sailors emplaced additional naval guns, two 8-inch and one 10-inch Columbiad, atop the bluff, where Jones commanded. Rifle pits were dug and sandbags filled to protect the artillery.

Three hundred yards downstream, old ships were scuttled and wooden cribs filled with stone were sunk in two rows across the channel. The *Patrick Henry* was anchored between the bluff and the obstructions. On the opposite side of the river and at the foot of the bluff a number of sharpshooters were placed to worry Federal gunners.

The *Monitor* led a fleet of five warships up the river on May 15. At 7:35 they rounded a curve with the *Galena* in the lead. The Confederates opened at seven hundred yards, but the ironclad, despite taking repeated hits, advanced another six hundred yards before replying with a broadside.

The slow-firing *Monitor* quickly learned that its turreted guns could not be raised sufficiently to hit the bluff. She was forced to withdraw downstream to fire effectively. The *Galena* took an advanced position and gamely traded shots with the Confederates. The *Naugatuck,* a one-gun ironclad, and two vulnerable wooden gunboats, *Aroostock* and *Port Royal,* backed down the river to safer positions, but sharpshooters firing from trees plagued them throughout the attack. Keeler described "a perfect tempest of iron raining upon & around us" for four hours.

The *Galena* did good work exploding her one-hundred-pound shells over the Confederate trenches and showering them with shrapnel, which killed seven. One of the big Confederates guns recoiled off its firing platform after being loaded with a double charge of gunpowder. A log casemate collapsed on another cannon, and the surviving guns were forced to fire slowly to conserve ammunition.

By 11:05 the *Galena* had been hit fifty times, each a plunging shot from the bluff. Many penetrated the thin iron plating on the deck. Comdr. John Rodgers had suffered thirteen killed and eleven wounded before fleet Comdr. John Rodgers ordered the flotilla to withdraw. Keeler boarded the *Galena* and found "a slaughter house . . . of human beings."

The retreat caused great cheering from the Confederates. Upriver in Richmond, civilians had cowered at the booming of the great cannon that rattled windows. But the city was safe, at least from a waterborne threat.

A Tour of Hampton Roads and
Virginia-Monitor Sites

INCLUDED IN this tour are a number of museums, monuments, and sites associated with the construction of the CSS *Virginia* and its monumental battles during two days in March 1862 in Portsmouth, Norfolk, Hampton, and Newport News. We also include the Suffolk campaign (spring 1863) and Smithfield because of their proximity. No tours in subsequent books will approach this region of southern Virginia. The area was a vital shipbuilding, transportation, and agricultural region that maintained communication with the North Carolina sounds through a system of canals. The tour begins at the Portsmouth Naval Shipyard Museum at 2 High Street in Portsmouth, but we will first examine sites to the west.

After evacuating Norfolk, twenty miles to the southwest, Confederates passed through Suffolk, then abandoned it also as they continued to Richmond. A large Union garrison of seven thousand men occupied the strategic city on the navigable Nansemond River, which flows into the James River, and was served by two vital railroads, the Norfolk and Petersburg and the Seaboard and Roanoke. Suffolk was connected with the North Carolina sounds by the Jericho Canal, Lake Drummond, and Dismal Swamp Canal. A strong ring of fortifications was soon erected around Suffolk, and harassing raids into the surrounding country were mounted.

Besides George McClellan's 1862 effort, there were other scares during the war concerning Federal advances up the peninsula. In February 1863 the Federal Ninth Corps was sent to Newport News in an attempt to convince the Confederates that Richmond would be attacked from the south by Maj. Gen. John J. Peck's 25,000 men. The successful ruse led Robert E. Lee to send James Longstreet's 20,000-man corps to counter the supposed threat, with the secondary chore of foraging the region, which was largely untouched by war. On May 4, after a twenty-four-day siege of Suffolk, Longstreet rejoined Lee for the trek to Gettysburg, having missed the battle of Chancellorsville. Confederate casualties totaled 900; Federal losses were 250.

A bizarre incident occurred in the predawn hours of April 12, 1863, when Federal Brig. Gen. Michael Corcoran, returning to his camp, was challenged by Lt. Col. Edgar A. Kimball. "General Corcoran and staff," came the reply, but the password was omitted. Kimball angrily refused to let them pass and drew his sword, prompting Corcoran to draw his pistol and shoot the colonel dead.

Peck's headquarters were established at Riddick's Folly (1839, 510 North Main Street). It is open to the public and features a room furnished as a Civil War hospital, which it was. On the walls are scrawled signatures and messages left by wounded and sick soldiers. The Old Nansemond County Courthouse (524 North Main Street) was a Union headquarters and barracks for much of the war. First Baptist Church (1839, 237 North Main Street) was used as a hospital by Federals who destroyed the benches and pulpit. It was not restored until 1869. Main Street Methodist Church (1861, 202 North Main Street) was also a Federal hospital. The Godwin House (1830, 504 West Washington Street) was a Union hospital during the siege. A monument to local Confederates, a stone soldier at parade rest atop a tall base, was dedicated on November 14, 1889, in Cedar Hill Cemetery (Main Street and Constance Road).

The only remaining earthworks from the siege are just west of Lake Meade Bridge on Pitchkettle

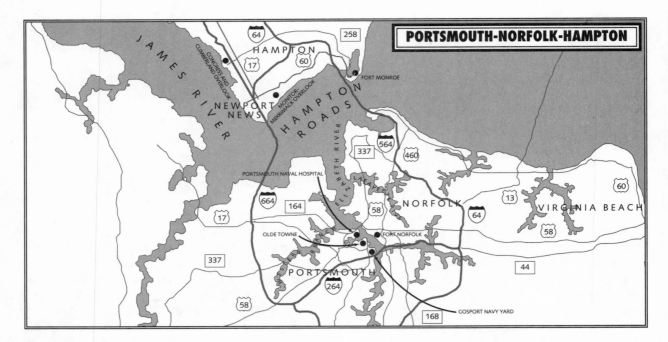

PORTSMOUTH-NORFOLK-HAMPTON

Road. Longstreet crossed the Nansemond River to reach Suffolk in Isle of Wight County at Route 640, six miles northwest of Windsor. A skirmish occurred at Chuckatuck Church, on Route 10 nine miles northwest of Suffolk, on May 3, 1863. A historical marker indicates the Confederate line on Route 10 a mile and a half northwest of Suffolk.

Fort Boykin, named for Revolutionary War figure Maj. Francis Boykin, is on the south bank of the James River north of Smithfield. The high bluff, commanding two bends in the river, has been fortified since 1623 when Englishman Roger Smith constructed a work to defend against hostile Indians.

Other forts followed, including one from the War of 1812. By 1862 this extensive, two-acre, seven-pointed-star earthwork anchored the Confederate defenses on the south bank of the James opposite defenses around Lee's Mill on the north bank.

In May 1862, isolated on the southern bank and outgunned by Federal naval cannon, the garrison fled at the approach of the USS *Susquehanna*. The Federals fired on the fort and landed a party when there was no response. The artillery was removed or spiked, two magazines exploded, and wooden structures burned. Later in the war Georgia poet Sidney Lanier, a cavalry scout, was stationed here, where he wrote "Hoe Cakes" and "Beautiful Ladies" and

started a novel, *Tigerlillies*. Historically minded citizens have restored the earthworks and grounds and installed interpretive markers.

Fort Boykin, open 9 A.M. to dusk Wednesday through Sunday, is north of Smithfield off Route 10 (Church Street in Smithfield). Turn right off Route 10 onto Route 673–Blount's Corners Road then left onto Fort Boykin Trail–Route 673 to the fort parking lot.

The Isle of Wight County Museum (103 Main Street) in Smithfield has a Civil War gallery that displays many area artifacts, including materiel recovered from Fort Boykin. The 1913 bank building preserves and exhibits other local historical and archaeological displays. The courthouse (1750, 130 Main Street) is a visitors center. The bell of Christ Episcopal Church (1830) was offered but apparently refused by the Confederate Ordnance Department in 1862. A small stone monument honoring Southern dead, dedicated May 30, 1916, is in Ivy Hill Cemetery. The churchyard of historic Saint Luke's Church (1632, two miles south of Smithfield) was a Confederate campground. On the green in Isle of Wight, a stone soldier at parade rest stands atop a tall shaft to honor local Confederates. It was dedicated May 30, 1905.

On January 31 and February 1, 1864, a Union expedition left Fort Monroe for Smithfield, where it was surprised by a large body of Confederates. A pitched battle in the streets left all ninety Federals killed, wounded, or captured, and Confederate artillery destroyed the gunboat *Smith Briggs* that attempted to extract the Federals. Another skirmish was fought at Cherry Grove Landing on April 13–15, 1864, and in a daring December raid Confederates captured a ship here.

To the south of Portsmouth is Chesapeake, which was important in connecting Chesapeake Bay with the North Carolina sounds. Dismal Swamp Canal, south of Interstate 64 on Route 17 is the oldest operating artificial waterway in the United States. The village of Great Bridge, off Route 168 north of Route 165, is the crossing point of the Albemarle and Chesapeake Canals. All three canals were seized by the Federals in May 1862. A monument to the Jackson Grays, a Confederate unit, is at Pleasant Grove Baptist Church, just off Route 165.

Pig Point, located off Route 480 eight miles west of Portsmouth and eight miles north of the mouth of the Nansemond River, was the site of Confederate batteries defending the Nansemond against Federal naval incursions aimed against Suffolk. On June 5, 1861, the Union gunboat *Harriet Lane* was engaged and driven off.

Projecting north from Portsmouth into Hampton Roads is Craney Island, at the mouth of the Elizabeth River. During the War of 1812, a British attack there was repulsed on June 27, 1813. After Norfolk was abandoned on April 10, 1862, it was discovered that the *Virginia* was unable to cross the bar into the James River. In the early morning of May 11 the ironclad was run ashore at Craney Island and destroyed. Until recent decades fishermen complained that their nets were often entangled by portions of the wreck. Iron and other usable parts were salvaged soon after the war. Craney Island is now restricted U.S. Navy property, and the island can be viewed only on harbor tours.

The Portsmouth Naval Shipyard Museum (No. 2 High Street, 757-393-8591) is an excellent facility that tells the history of the Gosport Navy Yard (now the Norfolk Naval Shipyard) and the extensive naval history of the area. The development, battles, and destruction of the *Virginia* are a special emphasis, with a diorama depicting the ironclad's conversion in dry dock and large models of the *Virginia* and *Monitor* in full fighting trim. A hull plate of the *Monitor* and sections of armor and a carriage for a 9-inch Dahlgren from the *Virginia* are also displayed. A large model of the *Cumberland* accompanies artifacts recovered from the wreck, and preserved here is a flag from the *Congress*. Other models include the *Minnesota,* a Federal balloon carrier, a cutaway model of the Confederate ironclad *Richmond* that shows interior details, and the double-turreted monitor *Onondaga,* which fought on the upper James River in 1865. Other displays explain the burning of the navy yard by the Federals, development of the blockade, the North Atlantic Blockading Squadron, the closing of the Confederate coast, efforts to maintain the

Erected near Smithfield, Fort Boykin anchored Confederate defenses on the south side of the James River.

This monument on the grounds of the Portsmouth Naval Hospital honors the dead of the Congress *and* Cumberland.

blockade, and the defense of Richmond from the Peninsula campaign to the final Union operations on the James River. A light map pinpoints significant historical sites in the region. There is a large diorama of early Portsmouth, and extensive collections of fine large-scale ship models, including aircraft carriers, uniforms, weapons, flags, maps, prints, and other artifacts. Local naval history continues through the operations of NATO. The research library (by appointment) preserves records of naval history, the Portsmouth area, and the Norfolk Naval Shipyard.

The Gosport Navy Yard, established in 1767, was American's first and largest facility. It constructed our first warship, the *Chesapeake,* in 1799. Dry Dock No. 1, again the nation's first (1833), is a granite cradle that could be flooded with water from the Elizabeth River. There the hull of the *Merrimack* was cut down and the ironclad *Virginia* constructed during 1861–62, then repaired after its battering in Hampton Roads. When the Confederates captured the shipyard they seized 1,195 guns, including 64-pounders and 11-inch guns. The first U.S. battleship, the *Texas,* was

built here in the 1890s, as was our first aircraft carrier, the *Langley.* Giant battleships and aircraft carriers were constructed here during World War II. The yard no longer produces ships, but it remains our primary repair and maintenance facility and hosts the world's largest naval base, supporting 120 ships and 51 aircraft squadrons. Unfortunately, national security concerns prevent regular tours of the facilities, although special group tours can be arranged (757-396-9550) and several companies provide harbor tours.

A trip on Hampton's Olde Town Trolley Tour (Portsmouth Visitors Information Center, 6 Crawford Parkway, 757-393-5111) is the only way to reach Trophy Park inside the Norfolk Naval Yard. Created in 1870 on the grounds of the old Gosport Navy Yard, a number of naval artifacts are displayed. Of particular interest are the slabs of iron from the *Virginia* and a 32-pounder gun, one of 744 produced for frigates and ships of the line, which served aboard the *Congress* at the time of its sinking. It was recovered in 1864. A broken 32-pounder was produced in 1846 at Richmond's Tredegar Iron Works and is from the USS *Pennsylvania,* a receiving ship that was burned in the Union evacuation of Gosport in 1861. One 9-inch Dahlgren shell gun from the USS *Richmond* was fired more than 250 times, mostly during the Civil War. A 20-pounder Parrott rifle (1861) is from the USS *Sumter,* which sank after a collision off North Carolina on June 24, 1863, and was salvaged in 1866. A 12-pounder bronze Dahlgren boat howitzer saw war service aboard the USS *Constellation,* and a 12-pounder Dahlgren rifled bronze howitzer was produced at the Washington Navy Yard in 1863 and used aboard the USS *William G. Anderson* during the war and aboard the monitor *Mahopac* later. One 6.4-inch 100-pounder Parrott rifle was installed aboard the USS *Florida* in 1862. Long after the Civil War, a 5.3-inch 50-pound Parrott rifle, produced in 1865, was mounted on the USS *Kearsarge,* which had sunk the Confederate raider *Alabama.* There are many other Civil War–era artillery pieces here, but they saw no active service.

Adjacent to Trophy Park is Tar House (1834), which was constructed of granite blocks left over from the construction of Dry Dock No. 1. Benjamin Latrobe designed the eight-sided structure. Unfortunately, the famous dry dock where the *Virginia* was built is not available for viewing. During the Civil War, one of Gosport's commanders was Sidney S. Lee.

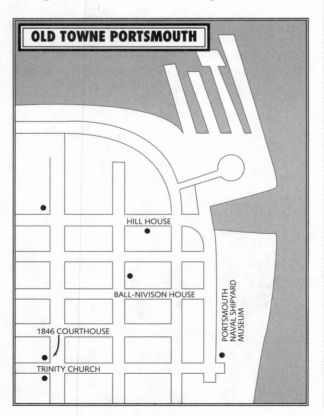

OLD TOWNE PORTSMOUTH

HILL HOUSE

BALL-NIVISON HOUSE

PORTSMOUTH NAVAL SHIPYARD MUSEUM

1846 COURTHOUSE

TRINITY CHURCH

Other Civil War sites in Portsmouth can be seen on the trolley tour.

The Portsmouth Naval Hospital (1830, foot of Effingham Street at the end of Green Street, 757-398-5205) is America's oldest such facility. The historic building, complete with great granite pillars, overlooks the Elizabeth River opposite Fort Norfolk. A modern sixteen-story building serves naval personnel in Hampton Roads and the southeastern United States, military vessels, and the Caribbean. On the grounds is a cemetery containing the graves of both Federals and Confederates, and a stone cairn commemorating the three hundred dead from the *Congress* and *Cumberland.* Stop at the gate for a pass.

Trinity Episcopal Church (1762, corner of Court and High Streets, 757-396-0431, call for a tour) conducted a communion service for the officers of the *Virginia* on March 8, before the ship steamed into battle. On several occasions planks were laid across the pews and the sanctuary used as a hospital. After refusing to take the oath of allegiance, assistant rector John Wingfield was jailed for "spreading trai-

Portsmouth's impressive Confederate monument has figures representing the infantry, cavalry, artillery, and navy.

torous dogma" and raising his head during a prayer for Lincoln. The church also irritated Reconstruction government officials in 1868 by dedicating a memorial window to Confederates who were killed opposing the "invasion" of Virginia. Authorities threatened to close the church if the offensive wording was not removed. It was then but was later restored.

The William Peter House (1859, 315 Court Street), designed by Pierre L'Enfant, was the home of John L. Porter, who made the plans for the conversion of the *Merrimack* into the ironclad *Virginia.* He supposedly hid the blueprints in the walls during Union occupation. The home became Benjamin F. Butler's headquarters during the occupation, and a story told locally wherever Butler served has a woman stopping him on the stairs and finding silverware spilling out of his pockets, hence his nickname "Spoons." The house at 23 Court Street is also listed as a residence of Porter, a relative of noted Federal officers David Dixon Porter and Fitz John Porter.

The Pass House (412 London, corner of London Boulevard and Crawford Street) was headquarters of the Federal adjutant general who issued passes allowing civilians to enter and leave Union territory.

Underneath the hearthstone of 408 Washington Street, Federals found smuggled medicines intended for the Confederate army. Frank M. Ironmonger lived at the northeast corner of Crawford and High Streets. Thought to be the Confederacy's youngest soldier, he was a courier at age ten and in 1864 was captured and reportedly sentenced to be shot as a spy, but he managed to escape. A hospital was established at 420 London Boulevard (1846), and the Butt House (327 Crawford Street) was the Federal commissary headquarters.

Cedar Grove Cemetery (London Boulevard, between Effingham Street and Fort Lane) in Portsmouth contains the graves of 257 Confederates, including chief naval contractor John L. Porter, who supervised the construction of the *Virginia.* Others buried here were naval officers and crew and Gosport workers. Recently unveiled in the Confederate section is a large piece of Massachusetts granite erected to the "Men Who Built and Manned the CSS *Virginia.*" The granite was taken from Dry Dock No. 1, where the *Virginia* was converted.

The Portsmouth Confederate Memorial, dedicated on June 15, 1893, at the intersection of High

Within Nauticus is the Hampton Road Naval Museum, which explores the naval history of Hampton Roads, including the first clash between ironclads.

and Court Streets, is one of the few monuments that represents all four branches of military service—infantry, artillery, cavalry, and navy. The tall obelisk and four figures are surrounded by an iron fence in the center of the street. In City Park is an obelisk erected in 1906 to the memory of the Grimes Battery, and a monument to the Confederate dead is found in Cedar Grove Cemetery.

From the waterfront at the Portsmouth Naval Museum drive west on High Street. The Confederate Monument will appear at the intersection to your right at Court Street, followed by the 1846 courthouse. Turn left onto Effingham, then left onto Route East 264 and pass through the tunnel. At exit 9 and the sign for Nauticus, turn left to leave the highway. At the sign indicating Waterside Drive–Nauticus to the right, turn right. Go straight on Waterside Drive, and Nauticus is to the left. A convenient parking garage is on the right.

The Hampton Roads Naval Museum was once on the grounds of the Norfolk Naval Base, which occupies the site of Sewell's Point and is the largest such facility in the world. The Confederate batteries there, which dueled with Union shore installations and ships, were eradicated by the construction of the base. By October 1861, twenty-nine cannon, including 32-pounders, 9-inch guns, and 42-pounder carronades, were emplaced. When Norfolk was abandoned in May 1862, the works had been expanded to

three batteries and a large earthen fort that mounted forty-five guns, including 80-pounder rifles. The guns harassed Federal shipping for nearly a year. On December 29, 1861, Confederate gunboats captured a Federal schooner under cover of Sewell's Point. During the *Virginia*'s first day in Hampton Roads, these guns shelled the Union ships *Minnesota, Saint Lawrence,* and *Roanoke.* Lincoln's initial plan for capturing Norfolk was a concentrated naval attack of Sewell's Point to cover a Union landing. On May 8, the *Monitor* and five gunboats bombarded the batteries but withdrew when the *Virginia* appeared.

On July 5, 1861, Confederates operating from Sewell's Point set adrift two pairs of torpedoes connected by thirty fathoms of lanyard into Hampton Roads, hoping the tide would carry them into the Union warships *Minnesota* and *Roanoke.* At the same time a similar attempt was made to sink the *Pawnee* in the Potomac River. On October 9, a series of torpedoes containing a total of four hundred pounds of gunpowder were again released into the Roads. Although this attempt also failed, the weapons got close enough to frighten Federal crews who maintained they were attacked by a submarine, a myth that persists in some historical accounts today.

The museum now occupies the second floor of Nauticus, the National Maritime Center, on the Norfolk waterfront. Topics explored include the burning of Gosport, the Federal blockade of Southern ports, Confederate defenses around Hampton Roads, the construction of the *Virginia* and her battles in the Roads, McClellan's Peninsula campaign, operations on the James River in 1862 and 1864, and amphibious operations against the North Carolina coast. The turret of the *Monitor* has been recreated and a fiber-optic map points out important Civil War sites in the area. There are models of the *Virginia, Cumberland, Minnesota, Monitor,* the Confederate ironclad *Richmond,* and the double-turreted monitor *Onondaga.* One gallery explores underwater archaeology, particularly the *Cumberland* and the Confederate raider *Florida,* which sank here.

The wreck of the *Congress* was raised in January 1865 and towed to Gosport, where the vessel was broken up and sold. The wreck sites of the *Cumberland* and the Confederate raider *Florida,* which sank nearby, were opposite Newport News but lost until 1982 when an expedition led by novelist Clive Cussler discovered the hulks of both. The *Cumberland*'s bronze bell was recovered, but the *Virginia*'s first ram remains elusive. Large sections of the *Florida* remain—one hull section measures 121 feet long. The artifacts of the discovery are displayed in various Hampton Roads museums, but particularly the Hampton Roads Naval Museum.

The impressive Norfolk Confederate Monument (Main Street and Commerce Place, unveiled on May 16, 1907) features a soldier atop a tall column holding a Confederate flag. It was designed by Norfolk native William Cooper. Across the street from it rises the fifty-foot cupola of old Norfolk city hall (1850), now the impressive MacArthur Monument on MacArthur Square. Although Gen. Douglas MacArthur's Medal of Honor is on display, that of his father, Arthur MacArthur, who won his for charging up Missionary Ridge near Chattanooga in November 1863, has dis-

One of the most impressive Confederate monuments in the country is in the center of Norfolk.

appeared. They are the only father and son to both win the medal.

In 1860, five thousand people gathered at city hall to hear Democratic presidential candidate Stephen A. Douglas. The crowd was described as attentive but unenthusiastic. After Mayor William Lamb met Union Gen. John E. Wool to surrender Norfolk on May 10, they and Secretary of the Treasury Salmon P. Chase returned here. Lamb told the Federals that had the decision been left to him, he would have defended the city to the last. He then led a crowd in three cheers for Jefferson Davis and three groans for Abraham Lincoln. For the remainder of the war, Norfolk and Portsmouth were under Federal rule, which went fairly peacefully. At first merchants were not allowed to trade within Union lines, which caused considerable hardship for the residents. Wool's successor at Fort Monroe, Maj. Gen. John A. Dix, relaxed the rules but had to convince the new naval commander, Rear Adm. Samuel P. Lee, that the cities were no longer Confederate territory and he should allow traffic to them. To prevent profiteering, merchants could only charge prices found in Baltimore. The Customs House (101 East Main) was used as a prison during the Union occupation.

The first Confederate flag in Norfolk was displayed near the corner of Market Street and Monticello Avenue on April 2, 1861. West of the corner of Oak Grove Road and Granby Street was Confederate Camp Talbot, which housed Virginia and Georgia troops from April 1861 until May 10, 1862. On May 9, Federal Gen. John E. Wool had landed six hundred men at Ocean View, on the Chesapeake Bay side of Norfolk. The landing site is on West Ocean View Avenue near Mason Creek Road. The bridge across Lafayette River (then Tanner's Creek) on New Granby Street at Indian Pool Point was torched by retreating Confederates on May 10 to slow the Union advance.

The city of Norfolk (established 1680) grew up around a natural harbor and thrived until 1776 when a British fleet bombarded the city and destroyed the waterfront. Retreating Americans burned the rest of town. Among the few surviving structures was Saint Paul's Episcopal Church (1739), where a cannonball remains embedded in the southeastern wall, and Trinity Church (1762, 500 Court Street), which has a Confederate memorial window.

Father Ryan, the Confederate poet-priest, lived at the corner of Lafayette Boulevard and Cottage Road; the house is marked by a historical marker. The Selden house (1807, southwest corner of Freemason and Botetourt Streets) was the home of Dr. William B. Selden, Confederate surgeon and friend of Robert E. Lee, who visited here in April 1870. Federals appropriated the home for use as a headquarters. Col. Walter H. Taylor, a member of Lee's staff, was born in the house at the southeastern corner of North Duke and West Freemason Streets (227 West Freemason).

Norfolk's Elmwood Cemetery (Princess Anne Road) contains a tall obelisk dedicated to the Confederate dead who are buried all around it. Another memorial, an anchor and capstan unveiled in 1900, honors the unknown Southern dead. A stone cross, dedicated on May 22, 1900, stands at the grave of Father Ryan.

Also buried in Elmwood Cemetery is Walter H. Taylor, who served throughout the Civil War as Robert E. Lee's aide-de-camp, assistant adjutant general, and chief of staff, rising in rank from lieutenant to lieutenant colonel. Born June 13, 1838, in Norfolk, he left the Virginia Military Academy at sixteen to support his mother and nine siblings. Taylor wrote most of Lee's orders and determined who gained access to the general. Because Lee left no memoirs, Taylor's book *Four Years with General Lee,* published in 1877, is considered the final arbiter of many post–Civil War disputes. After a stormy

fifteen-year love affair, which began when he was twelve, Taylor received Lee's permission to leave the army and marry Bettie Saunders in Richmond's Saint Paul's Episcopal Church on April 2, 1865, just as Petersburg fell. He rejoined Lee in the retreat to Appomattox but refused to stand by his general's side at the surrender. Taylor made out paroles for all of Lee's staff except himself, which was the only one Lee wrote. In the famous post-Appomattox Mathew Brady photos taken of Lee at his home in Richmond, Taylor can be seen beside him. Taylor raised eight children in Norfolk and started a number of successful business enterprises. When he died on March 1, 1916, at age seventy-seven, the Virginia General Assembly ordered every state flag lowered to half-staff. In the West Point section is the Black Soldiers Monument, a rare tribute to African-American veterans of the Civil War.

Continue past Nauticus on Waterside Drive, which becomes Boush, then turn left onto Brambleton. At the sign for Fort Norfolk Headquarters turn left onto Colley Avenue, and at the next corner, at the sign for Fort Norfolk USA Engineers, turn right on Front Street to Fort Norfolk.

Opposite Portsmouth on the Elizabeth River is Fort Norfolk, the oldest defensive work in Hampton Roads. Constructed by 1810, it was used during the War of 1812. At Virginia's secession on April 19, 1861, state authorities seized the fort with its eleven

This Civil War–era image shows the main entrance, or sally port, of Fort Monroe. Note the railroad tracks.

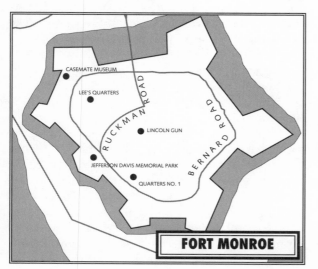

big guns and a large quantity of munitions. The low, single story, semicircular fort became a prison in 1864. Confederate prisoners, probably captured aboard the blockade-runner *Mary Summers,* spent March 3–24 in the damp casemates. Graffiti scrawled on the walls claim that "the dam guard officer" had stolen "everything in our possession." A caricature of the Federal, with a chamber pot on his head, was apparently used for target practice, as evidenced by numerous nicks in the wood, suggesting a knife.

Fort Norfolk has been preserved virtually unchanged since 1865 and is little known to Civil War enthusiasts. The Norfolk Historical Society is currently restoring the four-acre fort, long the property of the Norfolk district of the Corps of Engineer. They hope to preserve the original double oak doors in the arched gateway, the powder magazine and dungeon, the guardhouse, and a two-story brick building that will house museum exhibits, a visitors center, a gift shop, a library, and offices of the society.

Fort Norfolk may be seen on a harbor cruise or Sunday afternoons, when guided tours are offered (Norfolk Historical Society, P.O. Box 6367, Norfolk, VA 23508-0367, 804-652-1720). Because the casemate gunports have been bricked in, little can be seen of the fort from the outside.

The Norfolk Historical Society hosts a reenactment each March with one-fifth replicas of the *Virginia* and *Monitor.* The *Virginia,* big enough to be manned, has eight 100-pound guns, and can make ten knots, considerably better than the real one. The *Monitor* can make twelve knots and has two functioning guns in its revolving turret.

Return to Brambleton and turn left. Turn right at the sign for Hampton Boulevard East, which is also Route 337. Turn right onto Thirty-eighth Street. Turn left on Granby, which becomes Route 460 East and runs into Interstate 64. Take the second left onto Interstate 64 to follow the signs for West 64–Hampton-Richmond. Brave the inevitable heavy traffic, and after emerging from the bridge-tunnel, turn off Interstate 64 at exit 26B onto Mallory Street in Hampton. Signs at each intersection point the way to the Casemate Museum in Fort Monroe. After the exit, turn left onto South Mallory Street. Turn right onto East 143–East

CASEMATE MUSEUM

This aerial view of Fort Monroe highlights the isolation of the installation on the sandspit known as Old Point Comfort. The Hotel Chamberlain is to the lower left.

Mellen Street (which becomes Ingalls on the base). Pass through the gate straight into modern Fort Monroe on Ingalls; do not bear right on McNair but turn left to cross over the moat into the fort. After passing through the narrow gate, turn right and park on the left in front of the museum. Headquarters of the U.S. Army Training and Doctrine Command, Fort Monroe is the only moat-encircled fort still in active use today.

There were no fortifications in Chesapeake Bay when the American Revolution started. As a result British naval forces entered Hampton Roads at will, bombarding Norfolk and Hampton, and capturing Portsmouth. During the War of 1812 the British attacked Norfolk, landed at Hampton, then ascended the Potomac River to torch Washington, D.C., and besiege Baltimore. British forces also attacked, besieged, and captured numerous other coastal cities. Obviously the United States needed a system of coastal defenses.

In 1816 the task was given to Brig. Gen. Simon Bernard, a former French military engineer given a commission by the U.S. Army. To defend Hampton Roads, a strong fort was planned for Old Point Comfort, a two-and-a-half-mile-long sandspit that extends into Chesapeake Bay, where the channel narrows to one mile. The isolated position made the fort difficult to storm by infantry. Named for Pres. James Monroe, the fort was started in 1819, occupied in 1823, and completed in 1834. The brickwork was a six-sided hexagon with seven projecting bastions to provide flank and crossfires and direct fire from the main walls. The stout walls, which enclose sixty-five acres, run 2,304 feet, have a circumference of one and a half miles, and are surrounded by a wet moat measuring 8 feet deep and 60–150 feet wide. Fort Monroe had two tiers of guns—the first was contained in interior chambers called casemates and fired through embrasures, and the second tier was on top of the wall. The water battery added another forty guns to the strength of the fort, and a redan and large redoubt defended the land approaches. A full garrison required 2,625 men to serve the 412 guns.

Fort Monroe was the strongest fortification in the United States when the Civil War began. It had to be, as it controlled the vital entrance from Chesapeake Bay into Hampton Roads, the largest and most important anchorage for naval and merchant fleets in the country with access to three major rivers, including the James, and the cities of Richmond, Norfolk, Portsmouth, Hampton, Newport News, and Suffolk. In addition, the navy yard at Portsmouth was one of the navy's most important installations.

Secure on the long spit known as Old Point Comfort, Fort Monroe was never threatened by the Southerners, making it one of only three facilities in the South to remain in Federal hands. Half its guns had been mounted and seven companies of artillerists, four hundred soldiers, manned them. After Fort Sumter fell in Charleston, five regiments were rushed

by boat to secure Monroe, and by the end of 1861 the facility had been reinforced to six thousand men. This force severely hampered Confederate operations in Hampton Roads and threatened Richmond, which could be reached via the James River or overland via the peninsula. The garrison was first housed at Camp Hamilton at present Phoebus, then Camp Butler at Newport News, where a battery commanding the mouth of the James River was constructed.

To counter this buildup Confederates constructed batteries on Sewell's Point (Norfolk Naval Base) opposite Fort Monroe; on Craney Island at the mouth of the Elizabeth River, leading to Portsmouth and Norfolk; and at Pig Point at the mouth of the Nansemond River, gateway to Suffolk.

Fort Monroe served as a base for extensive operations against the Atlantic and Gulf Coasts of the Confederacy. On August 26, 1861, an expedition left from here to capture Hatteras, the first of several campaigns for the sounds of North Carolina. On October 29 another force steamed off to secure Port Royal, South Carolina, and on November 11 Benjamin Butler departed to seize the mouth of the Mississippi River and New Orleans. In December 1864, Butler led an unsuccessful campaign to capture Wilmington, North Carolina, which was the last Confederate port open to blockade-runners. On January 15, 1865, a second expedition captured the primary fort protecting the city by direct assault.

Hampton Roads was headquarters for the North Atlantic Blockading Squadron, which helped close

A guncrew of cutouts mans a 32-pounder in one of the outer casemates at Fort Monroe.

Fort Monroe mounted hundreds of cannon, many within a casemate like this and others on a gun platform atop a wall.

one Confederate port after another. Other naval forces kept the Confederates bottled up on the James River and assisted Grant in operations against Petersburg and Richmond in the final year of the war.

Confederate prisoners awaiting exchange were housed at Camp Hamilton, with smaller numbers in Fort Monroe, whose most famous inmate was Brig. Gen. William H. F. "Rooney" Lee, Robert E. Lee's son. While convalescing near Richmond in the summer of 1863, Lee was captured in a Union raid and held in Fort Monroe to ensure that two Federal officers in Richmond's Libby Prison, Capts. Henry W. Sawyer and John L. Flinn, were not killed in retaliation for the execution of two Confederate officers held in Kentucky. There were no more executions, and Lee was allowed to roam the fort freely. It was reported that Butler was startled upon his return to command here by the sight of a Confederate general watching the garrison drill. Lee was transferred to Fort Lafayette in New York Harbor and exchanged early in 1864.

After the famous Confederate raider *Florida* was illegally seized on October 4, 1864, in a Brazilian port, it was brought to Newport News. The 700-ton vessel, 192 feet long and capable of ten knots, was armed with nine cannon, including a 7-inch Blakely rifle. In nearly two years of operation it had destroyed fifty-two ships. Amid the resulting international controversy, the end of the *Florida* came on November 28 when it was rammed and sunk by a transport under somewhat suspicious circumstances.

The excellent *Guide to Historic Points, Fort Monroe, Virginia,* has fourteen tour stops. The Casemate Museum, opened in 1951, is contained in a series of casemates, which are double-roomed chambers within the brick fort. The outer room held cannon and the inner served as housing. Two casemates have been restored to their Civil War appearance, and two original 32-pounders have been authentically mounted and are manned by crews of large cutouts. Jefferson Davis's prison has been faithfully recreated in Casemate No. 1. Exhibits describe Davis's imprisonment and other notable visitors to Fort Monroe, including Edgar Allan Poe, a sergeant major during 1828–29. One casemate is dedicated to the *Virginia* and *Monitor.* Other casemates are presented as housing. One exhibit illustrates the escape of slaves to freedom in the fort. The first black men were enlisted in the U.S. Navy here in 1861. Because Fort Monroe was the army's coastal artillery school, this is also the army's coastal artillery museum, displaying impressively detailed models of the artillery used here through World War II, plus uniforms, drawings, and dioramas. There is also an excellent gift shop.

Atop the fort, the flagstaff bastion offers an excellent view of Hampton Roads, Fort Wool, and ships passing through Hampton Roads.

Contained on the grounds within the fort are Lee's Quarters, where he lived for three years, from 1831 to 1834, and Quarters No. 1, where Lincoln stayed several days in May 1862. Carroll Hall, where

This 1864 image shows two huge 15-inch Rodmans mounted on barbettes on one of Fort Monroe's outer walls.

Inner casemates were used for officers quarters. In 1864 post commander, Col. Joseph Roberts, posed with his family below.

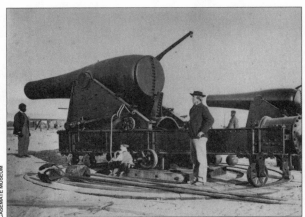

CASEMATE MUSEUM

CASEMATE MUSEUM

The cell of Confederate president Jefferson Davis has been recreated in Casement No. 1 at Fort Monroe.

Quarters No. 1 was occupied by Abraham Lincoln for several days in May 1862.

Davis and his wife, Varina, lived for some months, has been demolished. On the parade ground is the Lincoln Gun, Fort Monroe's largest cannon. The 25-inch Rodman, manufactured in 1860 and named by Secretary of War Edwin Stanton, weighs 49,000 pounds and fired a 330-pound cannonball 5,700 yards. The gun arrived at Fort Monroe in March 1862 and a month later fired several shots at Confederate fortifications at Sewell's Point, across Hampton Road. Outside the walls are Engineers Wharf (1818), where McClellan's army embarked on the Peninsula campaign and where Jefferson Davis arrived on May 22, 1865, and a half-dozen reinforced-concrete forts from the Spanish-American War.

Because of the limited range of artillery at that time, the decision was made to construct a fort (to be named for Secretary of War John C. Calhoun) on the other side of the channel from Chesapeake Bay, opposite Fort Monroe at shoals called the ripraps. Starting in 1819, granite was brought down the Potomac River and piled here for seven years before construction could be initiated. Only after twenty-four years of work was the island considered stable. Building Fort Calhoun was thought to be one of the worst duties in the U.S. Army. There were no trees for shade, and food and water had to be imported. The original design of a three-story castle was scrapped because the island would have sunk beneath the weight. Eventually one row of casemates with a parapet atop it was constructed. Andrew Jackson visited the ripraps for vacations in 1829, 1831, 1833, and 1835, and Pres. John Tyler came here three times after the death of his wife. In May 1861, Butler sent the Naval Brigade, supported by a gunboat, and one rifled cannon, the Sawyer Gun, the only piece that could reach Sewell's Point, to Fort Calhoun. Designed originally for 232 guns, no more than 12 were ever mounted, including 7 8-inch Columbiads and 2 rifled 42-pounders. These guns fired on the *Virginia* on March 8–9, 1862, and the ironclad responded, with no damage resulting on either side. Lincoln visited Fort Calhoun twice in May, attempting to locate a site at which troops could be landed to capture Norfolk and to observe the bombardment of Sewell's Point. Secretary of War Edwin Stanton changed the name of the facility to Fort Wool to honor seventy-seven-year-old Gen. John E. Wool, the elderly officer who had served since the War of 1812 and was coaxed out of retirement to command Chesapeake Bay. For a time Confederate POWs, political prisoners arrested after the Union occupation of Norfolk, and Federal criminals were housed here. The guns were removed in June 1864. Only the first tier of casemates was ever completed at Fort Wool; further work was abandoned because cracks developed in the stonework.

Wool's successor, Maj. Gen. John A. Dix, released the political prisoners. He had no doubt they were Southern sympathizers, but he believed they had committed no acts against the United States. If all such persons were arrested, he said, Northern prisons "would not contain a tithe of them."

The Lincoln Gun, a 15-inch Rodman, fired a 330-pound cannonball with a range of 5,700 yards.

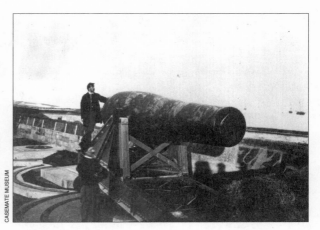

The Lincoln Gun was the first 15-inch Rodman cast in the United States and was mounted on Rampart No. 4.

By the 1870s Fort Wool had fifty-four stone casemates armed with 8-inch Columbiads protected by iron shutters. At the turn of the century, most of the casemates were demolished and replaced with concrete emplacements for six 6-inch disappearing guns and six 3-inch rapid-fire cannon. The fort was manned during both world wars, and an antisubmarine net stretched between Fort Monroe and Fort Wool to prevent German U-boats from devastating the shipping in Hampton Roads. Abandoned in 1967, Fort Wool suffered vandalism and destruction by growing trees before ownership was transferred to the city of Hampton, which cleaned the fifteen-acre site and opened the remaining sixteen casemates for tours in 1985. A World War II–era observation tower offers good views of Chesapeake Bay. Fort Wool can only be reached by boat. In season, tours leave Hampton for the fort twice daily.

Following the Civil War, Federal authorities concentrated a large number of artillery pieces at Fort Monroe on the parade ground and in the Ordnance Yard. "Trophy" guns included many captured from the Army of Northern Virginia and others seized from Lord Cornwallis during the Revolution and in various other American conflicts. The Ordnance Yard was surrounded by a fence composed of muskets, with bayonets attached, captured from Robert E. Lee and sent by the Washington Arsenal in 1866.

The collection has been broken up over the years as pieces were transferred to Civil War and Revolutionary War battlefields or melted down during World Wars I and II. A number of these guns are mounted in front of the museum, and others are scattered across the post. The collection consists of smoothbore and rifled seacoast guns, field artillery, mortars, and stacked cannonballs and shells.

For seventy-five years the primary guns at Fort Monroe were muzzle-loading smoothbore seacoast guns. In 1843, 374 32-pounders and 24 42-pounders were mounted, primarily for defense against enemy ships. Two of these guns, both 32-pounders, are mounted in the Casemate Museum. Large-caliber Columbiads, which fired heavy solid shot and shell at high angles of elevation, were developed next. During the Civil War, 15 8-inch and 9 10-inch Columbiads were mounted here, but none remain. The next step in big-gun technology was taken by Thomas Rodman, whose guns burst less frequently. He also developed a better gunpowder. One 10-inch Rodman remains here today, a survivor from the long-demolished water battery. At the entrance to Fort Monroe are 2 8-inch rifled Rodmans.

Other Civil War guns at Fort Monroe are Austrian 6-pounders used by the Confederacy, two Confederate 3-inch rifles, two 12-pounder Confederate howitzers (cast at Tredegar in Richmond), a 14-pounder James Rifle, an 8-inch siege mortar, and two bronze Coehorn mortars used in trench warfare to drop shells on troops behind fortifications.

Harbor cruises leave downtown Hampton (Hampton Visitors Center, 710 Settlers Landing

Road, 804-800-2202) twice daily for Norfolk Naval Base (with its hundreds of vessels, including aircraft carriers and battleships), a seaside view of Fort Monroe, and an hour-long stop at Fort Wool.

Return to Ingalls and turn right. Outside the base gate, bear left on West 143–Mellen. Turn right onto Libby, then left at the first intersection onto Route 143 West–County Road and not to U.S. 258. At the light turn left to get on Woodland Road, which becomes U.S. 60 and Settler's Landing. Ignore the national cemetery on your left, which is the new section. Just beyond the interstate exchange, turn left onto Tyler to enter Hampton University (1868). Turn left at the first light onto poorly marked Cemetery Road–East Queen. Drive through the brick gates to the Hampton National Cemetery straight ahead.

The location and climate of Hampton, at the southern tip of the peninsula, made it an important Federal hospital center. The huge Hygeia Hotel, immediately adjacent to Fort Monroe, became the first hospital—followed by the Chesapeake Female College, whose students had fled—on Hampton Roads. A Confederate agent was found using the cupola as an observation post. Tent wards and two temporary buildings gave these hospitals a twelve-hundred-bed capacity. The Hampton Military Hospital, a large pavilion-like structure with eighteen hundred beds, was also built on the shore of Hampton Roads. Four hundred hospital tents and sixty wall tents brought hospital capacity in the area to four thousand beds. In addition to Federal soldiers, many wounded Confederate prisoners were also treated.

Most of the buildings were demolished after the war, but former Union Gen. Samuel C. Armstrong, who had commanded black troops, salvaged the lumber from three hospital buildings to open a school for freedmen on the site of the Hampton Military Hospital. It became Hampton Institute, a famed black college.

At the entrance to the Hampton Institute (established in 1868 as the Hampton Normal and Agricultural Institute) is the old gnarled Emancipation Oak. Legend holds that beneath its young branches Lincoln's Emancipation Proclamation was first read to local blacks, primarily Butler's "contrabands" who had established a school and church here.

The same conditions that made Hampton a desirable hospital center led to the establishment after the war of the Hampton Veterans Administration Center, which started in the Chesapeake Female College, previously purchased by Butler. The last Civil War veteran here, Charles Woodcock, died in 1946 at age 112.

Between these two institutions born in the wake of the Civil War is the Hampton National Cemetery, which originated as the burial ground for the local

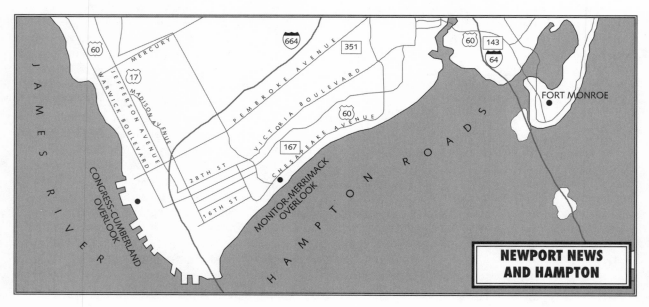

NEWPORT NEWS AND HAMPTON

Union and Confederate soldiers are buried in the National Cemetery on the campus of historic Hampton Institute.

Civil War hospitals and contains a number of Confederate graves.

"Shall [Confederates] be allowed the use of this property [slaves] against the United States and we not be allowed its use in advantage of the United States?" Butler wrote early in the war. He considered the escaped slaves seeking askylum as "contraband of war" and refused to return them to their owners around Hampton. Instead, Butler enlisted all able-bodied freedmen into U.S. service, a policy that freed slaves eighteen months before the Emancipation Proclamation was issued. These freedmen became laborers, carpenters, teamsters, stevedores, cooks, and servants, paid with rations and a small wage. They also fished, oystered, peddled goods, and acted as local guides for military expeditions. While the men worked for the military, the women tended gardens, took in washing, baked goods for sale, and worked in hospitals. Missionaries soon arrived to teach the children by day and the adults by night. In 1863 Butler spent government money to construct a school for blacks that continued to function for twenty-five years. In July 1865 Harriet Tubman arrived to nurse at Fort Monroe's Colored Hospital.

There were two primary contraband camps on the southern peninsula: Slabtown—near Camp Hamilton, constructed with the rough exterior pieces of sawn logs—and the Grand Contraband Camp, parallel to West Queen Street in Hampton. The first has disappeared, while the second was incorporated into reconstructed Hampton with streets named Lincoln, Union, and Grant. The site of Camp Hamilton became the community of Phoebus.

At what became the Hampton National Cemetery, names, companies, and dates of death were written on both sides of the coffin lids and on wooden headboards, an efficient system that resulted in fewer unknowns than in other Civil War cemeteries. Most of the 638 unidentified here came from battlefields, camps, and hospitals at Fort Monroe, Big Bethel, Newport News, Jamestown, Craney Island, Deep Creek, Norfolk, Portsmouth, Blackwater, Smithfield, Suffolk, and Cherry Stone. The national cemetery was established in 1866 and expanded to eleven acres in 1868. Later that year the number of dead totaled 5,122, including 475 unknowns, 25 officers, 66 sailors, and 985 black soldiers. The two Medal of Honor recipients here—Pvt. Charles Veale and Sgt. A. B. Hilton—were both black. An extension of the national cemetery at Phoebus is a post–Civil War addition.

A large, rough-hewn granite obelisk honors Federal veterans with the inscription, "Died to Maintain the Laws." It cost twelve thousand dollars. In sections D and E are 272 Confederate soldiers, marked by two granite monuments. Also buried here are 31 German and Italian POWs who died during World War II, and 29 crewmen from a German U-boat sunk off the coast in April 1942.

In Hampton's Greenlawn Memorial Park is a mass grave containing 163 known Confederates and 110 unidentified ones. In the center of the cemetery is

In addition to historic air and space craft, the Virginia Air and Space Museum has displays illustrating Civil War history in Hampton Roads.

an obelisk and large stone tablet engraved with the names, ranks, divisions, and home states of the dead. Oakland Cemetery has a monument to the Southern dead, a Confederate soldier on guard duty atop a high granite base, which was unveiled on October 29, 1901.

Return to Settlers Landing Road–U.S. 60 and turn left. After .8 miles the Virginia Air and Space Museum is on the left, with parking on the right.

The *Virginia* and *Monitor* seem to have renewed their titanic battle inside the Hampton Roads History Center, part of the Virginia Air and Space Center, which is the official visitors center for NASA's Langley Research Center. Seven feet above the floor are scale models of the *Monitor*'s turret and the forward casemate of the *Virginia,* cannon ready for action. The reproductions are supported on eight cubes that contain information about the ironclads' clash, Butler's administration of the area from Fort Monroe, and the Confederate burning of Hampton.

This fantastic facility also has aircraft suspended from the ceilings, ranging from the Wright Brothers' to modern jets and an Apollo spacecraft. Other features are moon rocks and an IMAX theater.

Nearby is Saint John's Church (1728). Among its stained-glass windows is one depicting the baptism of Pocahontas. A Confederate statue stands in the churchyard. The church was one of the few structures spared during Hampton's destruction by the British during the American Revolution and again by the Confederates in 1861. Butler had occupied the town on July 1, but following the battle of First Manassas, the War Department reinforced the garrison at Washington with three regiments from Fort Monroe, forcing Butler to abandon Hampton. Seeing an opportunity to deny future use of the city to Butler, Brig. Gen. John B. Magruder ordered his men, led by Col. Jefferson Phillips, to torch the town. Lincoln visited the blackened ruins in May 1862.

From the museum parking, turn right onto Settlers Landing Road–U.S. 60. Turn left onto South Armisted. Turn right onto Victoria Boulevard, then left onto Kecoughtan Road (it has become West U.S. 60). Turn left onto LaSalle Avenue (West 167, which becomes Chesapeake), and turn left into the Merrimac-Monitor Overlook. *(Yes, southerners and even northern Civil War enthusiasts know it should be the* Virginia *and that the real warship* Merrimack *had a k at the end.)*

Soldiers from Camp Butler and civilians from Hampton and Newport News gathered here on March 8, 1862, when the *Virginia* destroyed the *Cumberland* and *Congress* by ramming and shelling within rifle shot of this spot. Spectators returned the next morning to observe the four-hour slugfest between the *Virginia* and *Monitor.* There is a monument to the two ships and their commanders and a large painting of the titanic battle between the ships as it would have been seen from this location. Near this spot was Camp Butler, a Union installation with a battery

The bow gun of this model of the Virginia's *gundeck seems ready for action at the Virginia Air and Space Museum.*

A replica of the Monitor's *turret is displayed with the gun shutters open and ready for action.*

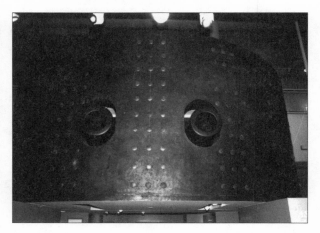

The Virginia-Monitor *Overlook at Newport News marks the spot where civilians gathered to watch the ironclads do battle on March 9, 1862.*

that fired on the *Virginia,* where a new monument honors Confederates who died in a prisoner-of-war camp established from April to August 1865. On the western edge of Newport News off U.S. 60 is a new attraction, the *Congress-Cumberland* Overlook, near the site where the Federal warships were sunk.

From the overlook parking, turn left onto West 167–Chesapeake, which shortly becomes Sixteenth Street. Turn left onto Jefferson Avenue to enter the Monitor-Merrimack *Center on the right.*

The prime attraction here is a huge diorama depicting the battle between the ironclads and the surrounding area of Hampton Roads. There are plans to build quarter-scale replicas of the ironclads. From time to time area organizations propose projects to construct full-scale models of the ironclads, either floating for tours or land bound in museums. Visitors may take harbor cruises from here at Waterman's Wharf. Included are views of the Norfolk Naval Base, the world's largest shipbuilding facilities at Newport News, and Civil War sites, particularly the area where the ironclads fought. At the courthouse in Newport News is a Confederate monument, a stone soldier at parade rest atop a tall column, dedicated May 27, 1909.

From the parking lot turn left onto Jefferson, which also becomes Route 143 and U.S. 17. Turn left on West Mer-

cury–U.S. 258, turn right onto U.S. 60–Warwick Boulevard toward Fort Eustis, and almost immediately turn left (be very careful here) into the entrance to Huntington Park. Take the first right inside the park, then turn left to circle around the Virginia War Museum to the parking area in front. Note the large collection of military vehicles and artillery on the grounds.

The War Memorial Museum of Virginia is one of the best military museums in the country. With an extensive collection of more than six thousand artifacts, it illustrates America's military history—battles, leaders, economic, social, and political influences—from 1775 to the present. It has detailed Civil War displays containing Confederate and Union uniforms, rifles, pistols, swords, cannon, and camp equipment. There are special collections of weapons produced in Virginia, Virginia militia uniforms, and artwork concerning the Peninsula campaign and naval combat. There is a blockade-runner's uniform, a flag from the CSS *Florida,* and a Butler Medal, awarded by Butler to African-American soldiers for heroism during the war.

Return to West U.S. 60–Warwick Boulevard and turn left. Turn left onto Museum Drive, and the Mariners' Museum will soon appear on the left.

The Mariners' Museum explores three thousand years of maritime history with an impressive series of thirteen interpretive galleries featuring real and miniature ships, figureheads, paintings, navigational instruments, steam engines, and much more. Its 35,000 maritime artifacts are displayed in 77,000 square feet of exhibit space. The research library contains 75,000 volumes, including 5,000 maps and charts, 500 ship's logs (including that of the *Florida*), 350,000 photos, and considerable material on the Civil War navies. The National Oceanic and Atmospheric Administration chose the Mariners' Museum to serve as the repository of the 160 *Monitor* artifacts recovered from the bottom of the ocean off Camp Hatteras. The exhibit explains the nearby naval battle and features *Monitor* artifacts, including the 1,450-pound anchor, a navigational lantern (which a rescue vessel watched wink out as the ship went down), and domestic objects—a wine bottle, relish jar, mustard container, and hair restorative. Other materials recovered are two dozen bottles, ironstone dinnerware, a thimble, cuff buttons, and even leather, clothing, rope, and wooden objects. Large photos of the *Monitor* and her crew, and their uniforms, weapons, letters and documents, and a bust of Ericsson complete the display. The *Virginia's* steering wheel, two dented armor plates, a shaving-toilet box, money, horseshoes, and a wooden cane made from *Virginia* wood are displayed. There are models of the *Merrimack, Virginia,* and *Monitor,* and one of the *Monitor's* wreck as it appears today. A twenty-minute video shot in 1991–92 guides visitors on an underwater tour of the *Monitor,* partially collapsed and half-hidden by silt. Blueprints, photos, and a statistical chart compare the two ships. The deck and turret of the *Monitor* had been recreated.

In January 1998 an expedition retrieved the Monitor's cast-iron four-bladed propeller—nine feet in diameter and weighing two tons—and eleven feet of wrought-iron driveshaft, which weighed two and a half tons. Also recovered were half-inch deck plates with oak wood backing, the anchor hatch, and giant bolts that held the turret plates together. The material was transported to the Mariner's Museum and is on display in a conservation tank, in which it will remain for several years.

Marine archaeological experts have recently declared that the *Monitor* has "reached a critical state of decomposition" which will result in "catastrophic collapse" if drastic action is not taken soon. NOAA is proposing a twenty-two-million-dollar program to shore up major structural components so the propeller, cannons, engine, and 120-ton turret can be salvaged in 2002 and eventually displayed here.

Also exhibited are the giant billet-head of Adm. David G. Farragut's legendary flagship the *Hartfort* and a model of the Confederate raider *Alabama*. A five-mile nature trail encircles Lake Maury, named for the great Confederate naval scientist Matthew Maury, whose statue stands on Richmond's Monument Avenue.

A side trip from the Mariners' Museum leads to Big Bethel, where the first battle of the Civil War was fought. Return on Museum Drive and go straight across Warwick Boulevard–U.S. 60 onto North Route 312–North U.S. 17, then turn right on Harpersville Road. Go straight when the first road goes off to the right and you will now be on Saunders Road.

Turn left onto Big Bethel Road and on the left, behind a fence near the corner of Saunders Road and Big Bethel Road, is a Confederate cemetery and a monument to the first soldier from North Carolina to be killed in the Civil War. It is open weekends from 6 A.M. to 8 P.M. (804-766-3017). Big Bethel Reservoir is to the right. Most of the battle area lies beneath the reservoir. In 1861 the direct route from Hampton to Yorktown passed through this marshy area. Confederates erected fortifications on both sides of the Back River here in early June, anchored by five artillery pieces. On June 10, a badly organized assault by green Union troops was easily repulsed. The Federals suffered seventy-six casualties, including Lt. John T. Greble, the first West Pointer killed in the war; Confederate losses totaled seven.

Recently completed is the third in the outstanding Virginia Civil War Trails publications, *1862 Peninsula Campaign: Civil War in the Tidewater* (for a copy call 888-CIVIL WAR), a large full-color brochure that provides a good orientation to the military activity of the Peninsula campaign, the leaders, and area geography, with a list of museums. A large map illustrates the theater from Chesapeake to the south through Hampton Roads and up the peninsula to Richmond and between the James and York Rivers. Three inset maps provide additional details and lists of thirty-six sites described on the self-guided driving tours. Each site is marked by the symbol of the Trails: stars and a bugle.

4

The Peninsula Campaign to the Battle of Seven Pines

A FTER SEVEN MONTHS OF relatively inactive command and intense scrutiny, George B. McClellan was finally taking an opportunity to prove himself. Following extensive logistical work, he embarked his first troops at Alexandria on March 17, 1862. Over the next three weeks, four hundred assorted vessels repeated the two-hundred-mile journey from Alexandria's docks to Fort Monroe. They ferried 121,500 men, 44 batteries of artillery, 1,150 supply wagons, 74 ambulances, 14,6000 animals, pontoon bridges, and equipment and supplies of every description. It was undeniably the largest military endeavor the world had ever seen, leading an impressed British observer to call it "the stride of a giant."

At the last minute President Lincoln appropriated the ten-thousand-man division of Brig. Gen. Louis Blenker and dispatched it to Harpers Ferry in western Virginia to join the army of Maj. Gen. John C. Frémont, a Radical Republican favorite whom Lincoln had recently removed from command of all forces in the West. Lincoln professed "great pain" at the taking of McClellan's troops, but he promised they would be the last to be siphoned from the general's army. Surprisingly, McClellan accepted it gracefully. The general was simply relieved to depart "that sink of iniquity," the capital, he told his wife, leaving aboard the *Commodore* on April 1 and reaching Fort Monroe the following day.

The historic Virginia peninsula is fifty miles long, fifteen miles or less wide, and covered with dense forest. Many streams flowed sluggishly through the low, flat, sandy landscape, creating extensive areas of marsh and swamp. McClellan hoped to move rapidly across this difficult terrain to West Point. He believed that a "decisive battle" would be fought between

In 1846 George B. McClellan graduated second in his class at the U.S. Military Academy. Of fifty-one surviving members, forty-four participated in the Civil War, including six who served under McClellan and a number of Confederates who fought against him. Virginian A. P. Hill was his roommate at the academy.

Winfield Scott thought highly of Joseph E. Johnston's performance in Mexico, excepting his "unfortunate knack of getting himself shot in nearly every engagement," five times all told, by Mexicans and Indians. Sending Johnston off to the peninsula, Robert E. Lee had "held his hand a long time," a witness observed, "and admonished him to take care of his life." Ironically, it was Johnston's wounding at Seven Pines that catapulted Lee to military fame.

At times McClellan sounded like a true Southerner. In his writings he declared that "I was fighting for my country & the Union, not for abolition and the Republican party." It was a theme he returned to throughout the war years. "The Radicals had only the negro in view, & not the Union," he maintained after the war. On another occasion he revealed, "I confess to a prejudice in favor of my own race."

McClellan proclaimed so many general orders and addresses to his troops that his field headquarters was equipped with a portable printing press. An early pronouncement included a promise to watch over them "as a parent over his children; and you know that your General loves you from the depths of his heart."

On March 17, 1862, the first contingent of McClellan's one hundred thousand troops departed from the Alexandria docks for Fort Monroe.

West Point and Richmond. The first objective, however, was Yorktown, which McClellan confidently expected to seize by April 5.

The general immediately encountered two major disappointments. Arriving in Hampton Roads, he sought out Flag Officer Louis M. Goldsborough to coordinate the combined operations on the tributaries of Chesapeake Bay. McClellan was unpleasantly surprised that the navy had few resources available to him—all the warships in Hampton Roads were being used to bottle up the *Virginia,* which had been reported repaired in dry dock and ready for action. Further, as would soon become evident at Drewry's Bluff, naval guns could not elevate sufficiently to bombard the Confederate forts on the high riverbanks.

McClellan next learned that the ten-thousand-man garrison at Fort Monroe, previously promised to him by the War Department, had been assigned duties elsewhere.

Meanwhile intelligence reports indicated that the Southerners had fortified the historic village of Yorktown, twenty miles up the York River from Fort Monroe. Many of the earthworks were adapted from the British fortifications from the Revolutionary War siege in 1783 at Yorktown and across the narrow, one-thousand-yard channel at Gloucester Point. The Southern positions were equipped with several heavy naval guns that had been seized at the Gosport Navy Yard in Norfolk and covered all approaches from the land and river. Maj. Gen. John B. Magruder had fifteen thousand men to man the guns and provide infantry support.

Early on the morning of April 4 McClellan started up the peninsula in two columns. Brig. Gen. Samuel Heintzelman's Third Corps followed the direct road to Yorktown. Paralleling him was Brig. Gen. Erasmus Keyes's Fourth Corps, which marched on the Lee's Mill road to outflank Yorktown at Halfway House, four and a half miles northwest of Yorktown and halfway between Yorktown and Williamsburg, McClellan's second objective. In reserve on the Yorktown road was Brig. Gen. Edwin Sumner's Second Corps.

Confederate pickets fell back before the Federal juggernaut as McClellan made ten miles that first day under perfect weather conditions. They passed through Big Bethel, scene of the embarrassing Union rout nearly a year earlier.

The Federals' problems began the next day as heavy rainstorms overflowed the innumerable streams and turned the "all-weather" roads into quagmires. Still, by noon Heintzelman had reached Yorktown to find earthworks fifteen feet thick behind ditches ten feet deep and fifteen feet wide. The defenders started throwing large-caliber artillery fire at the Federals from long range.

McClellan's hopes rested on a flanking maneuver to the left, but at noon Keyes encountered the swampy Warwick River. His maps indicated that the stream paralleled the road, but he found it blocking the route. Dams had backed the narrow river up to form an extensive barrier, and the tops of the dams were the only avenues across. Of course, those were protected by redoubts studded with cannon and manned by infantry.

The strongest point on the Warwick line was in the center of the peninsula, six miles east of Yorktown at Lee's Dam. Keyes gloomily informed McClellan that the Confederate position could not be taken "by assault without an enormous waste of human life."

The position was strong but Confederate troop strength was weak. McClellan's fifty-eight thousand men at Lee's Mill and fifty thousand at Yorktown vastly outnumbered Magruder's paltry force. A bold move would have carried the line quickly, but McClellan grew cautious and elected to await the arrival of Irwin McDowell's thirty-eight-thousand-strong First Corps, which contained most of the Army of the Potomac's veterans. But they never boarded ship in Alexandria.

At the last minute, Lincoln's paranoia raged again, and he retained McDowell for the defense of Washington. He contended that the loss of the capital would win foreign recognition and support for the Confederates.

A week earlier McClellan had informed the War Department that he was leaving seventy-three thousand men to defend Washington, thirty-three thousand more than recommended by his corps commanders. Lincoln

At West Point Erasmus P. Keyes had taught artillery tactics to George McClellan, his future commander, and wrote that "a pleasenter pupil was never called to the blackboard."

A Harper's Weekly *artist sketched the arrival of Union troops at Hampton. In all, within three weeks, 400 vessels shuttled more than 120,000 men, 14,500 animals, 1,100 wagons, 44 batteries of artillery, and 74 ambulances over a 200-mile route to the Virginia Peninsula.*

LIBRARY OF CONGRESS

In Kansas before the war, Joseph E. Johnston had been second in command to Edwin D. Sumner, a future opponent on the peninsula. At the time Johnston had written his friend George McClellan that to get along with Sumner one had to act as if "he is utterly ignorant professionally, and that his Colonel is not."

Brig. Gen. John Bankhead "Prince John" Magruder had long cultivated a theatrical reputation. At a formal ball in Washington he once appeared as the king of Prussia, his costume authentic to the last detail. While posted to the Canadian border, he staged a fancy dinner for his British counterparts, borrowing or renting fine china, glassware, and silver to dazzle his guests. When one discreetly inquired how much money an American officer earned, Magruder replied casually, "Damned if I know."

Of Magruder's demonstration before Yorktown that froze McClellan's army, diarist Mary Chesnut wrote, "It was a wonderful thing, how he played his ten thousand before McClellan like fireflies and utterly deluded him."

rejected this figure, which counted some units twice and included the ten thousand marching to Harpers Ferry. Half the troops were in the Shenandoah Valley, fifty miles distant, which McClellan believed would be the starting point for any threat against the capital. In that he was correct, for Stonewall Jackson was growing more active, but Lincoln did not appreciate this position.

Washington's military governor, a political general, Brig. Gen. James S. Wadsworth of New York, informed Stanton that fewer than twenty thousand men, none of them elite troops, defended the city. He thought a Confederate attack "very improbable," but Radical Republicans suggested to Lincoln that McClellan had left the city poorly defended.

Informed of the president's decision while observing Yorktown's defenders firing on his army, McClellan denounced it as "the most infamous thing that history has recorded." His own paranoia regarding the danger of the Radical Republicans to his career was justly confirmed. He had lost, arguably to politics, one-third of his projected force for the Peninsula campaign. Stanton had even closed Federal recruiting offices, thus preventing any further increase in troop strength. "McClellan is in danger," John Hay, Lincoln's secretary, remarked, "not in front but in rear."

The reduction in strength did not lessen the pressure from Washington. From the War Department, where he was monitoring a battle raging at Shiloh, Tennessee, Lincoln urged McClellan "to break the enemy's line from Yorktown to Warwick River at once."

McClellan rejected this order. He had already decided against assault. The disgruntled general demanded additional troops and reported that Joseph E. Johnston's army was massing in front of him. A siege, "tedious, but sure," he said, was the correct course at Yorktown.

In truth Johnston was not yet present. Confronting McClellan was Magruder, a flamboyant man who marched his men in view of the Federals

The Great Pretender ■ John Bankhead Magruder

John Bankhead Magruder's Civil War career was a series of ups and downs. Born May 1, 1807, at Port Royal, Virginia, "Prince John" was a member of the West Point class of 1830. An artillery officer in Mexico, he was thrice breveted for gallantry. After resigning his commission on April 20, 1861, he received a Confederate brigadier's rank, then made major general by October 7, 1862.

Assigned command of the vital peninsula, Magruder strongly fortified all approaches to Yorktown and Williams-

burg. Applying the theatrics of which he was so fond, he brought George B. McClellan's massive advance to a halt with a small force. Magruder's star was tarnished when he, like Stonewall Jackson, neglected to follow orders and bungled opportunities to help destroy the Army of the Potomac during the Seven Days' battles.

Magruder redeemed himself while commanding the District of Texas, New Mexico, and Arizona by cleverly recapturing Galveston and dispersing Federal blockading ships.

When the Civil War ended, Magruder went to Mexico rather than surrender and apply for a parole. Emperor Maximilian made him a major general in the imperial army, but the Virginian reentered the United States when Mexico overthrew the French puppet government. Magruder died in poverty on February 18, 1871, in Houston, where he was initially buried, but he was later reinterred in Galveston.

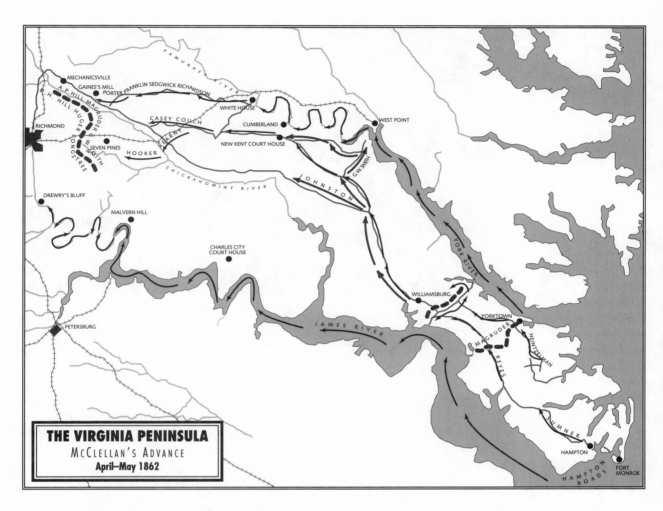

THE VIRGINIA PENINSULA
McClellan's Advance
April–May 1862

across the Warwick River then had them double back through the forest and repeat the performance again and again. Bands played loudly after dark and his artillery opened vigorously on every target. In fact, there were only five thousand men deployed on the ten-mile-long river line.

One impressed witness of this charade was McClellan, who personally scouted the Confederate positions. That information was bolstered by a new reconnaissance tool, hydrogen-filled observation balloons flown by Thaddeus Lowe.

By April 7 McClellan was in full panic, informing Lincoln, "I shall have the whole of the enemy on my hands," more than one hundred thousand he believed. The situation "grows worse the more you look at it," he groaned.

While studying military science in Europe, McClellan had witnessed the classic siege of Sevastopol during the Crimean War. Siege appealed to his conservative inclination to save lives and move cautiously. Of course, the longer he dallied the greater the opportunity Johnston had to transport his army to the peninsula.

In camp, Confederate soldiers elected a number of their officers, who campaigned with whiskey. On election day an Alabama private wrote, "A great many of the men got gloriously *tight.*"

So much rain fell during the first day of McClellan's march to Yorktown that one officer swore a mule sank into mud to its ears. He did admit that it was a small mule.

Union Brig. Gen. William F. "Baldy" Smith had a full head of hair for an adult, but it had been judged thin when he entered West Point. Twenty years later the nickname still stuck.

On the eve of the campaign, McClellan was photographed at Upton Hill, Virginia, with members of his staff and two foreign observers, the Prince de Joinville (in civilian clothes) and his cousin, the Comte de Paris.

Lincoln responded to McClellan's inactivity with word that the general was receiving widespread criticism in Washington. He stated that an attack by McClellan was "indispensable . . . I am powerless to stop this."

On April 16 McClellan ordered the Second Division of the Fourth Corps, under Brig. Gen. William F. Smith, to conduct a reconnaissance in force of Dam No. 1 at Burnt Chimneys, in the center of the Warwick defenses a mile north of Lee's Mill. After two batteries of Federal artillery knocked out two of the three Confederate guns covering the dam, two companies from the Third Vermont, Brig. Gen. William T. H. Brooks's brigade, forded the Warwick River and drove off the Confederate pickets. Three companies of the Fourth Vermont then raced across the mill dam as another four companies of the Sixth Vermont also forded.

The Warwick line had been quickly pierced and McClellan could have rolled it up, isolated Yorktown, and advanced directly on Richmond, but he fumbled the opportunity and did nothing. An hour later Confederate Brig. Gen. Howell Cobb counterattacked and drove the Vermonters back across the river.

Meanwhile, despite McClellan's hesitation, Johnston's Army of the Potomac (at that time McClellan's and Johnston's armies were sharing the name) dallied in position between the Rappahannock and Rapidan Rivers, fifty miles north of Richmond. Earlier in the month Johnston had thought McClellan might attack Norfolk, across Hampton Roads from Fort Monroe. If indeed the peninsula was his objective, the general believed that the terrain was indefensible. Any line he erected would be

As the first organized campaign of the Civil War, European observers flocked to the peninsula. In June, McClellan thought his camp infested with "a large dose of Spaniards."

blasted by powerful naval guns on the James and York Rivers. Johnston determined to remain where he was and protect Richmond.

Jefferson Davis repeatedly urged Johnston to defend the peninsula. He was supported in this by his new military adviser, Robert E. Lee, whose duties were the "conduct of military operations under the direction of the president." Lee had performed in a number of capacities for the Confederacy, most recently inspecting coastal defenses in Georgia. He was brilliant, tactful, and polite, often smoothing relations between Davis and Johnston, who were ever alert for any perceived slight. Davis's position had improved after the appointment of a new secretary of war, George W. Randolph, who was easier to work with than Judah Benjamin, who found his niche as secretary of state. Randolph was experienced and generally did not meddle in matters of military strategy.

Lee ultimately convinced Johnston to defend the peninsula, which to Lee, being an engineer, offered excellent defensive positions. On April 10 Johnston started his move. Within a week five of his divisions had arrived on the peninsula, bolstering Confederate strength to fifty thousand against McClellan's one hundred thousand. This alone presented the Federals with longer odds against assaulting strong prepared defenses.

McClellan's constant requests for additional forces were rewarded on April 22 when the War Department sent a twelve-thousand-man division from McDowell's corps under Brig. Gen. William B. Franklin. McClellan considered using them for an amphibious landing at Gloucester Point below Yorktown, but he decided to keep them aboard transports. When Yorktown was taken, they could rapidly be steamed up the York River and landed to cut off Johnston's retreat to Richmond.

McClellan appointed Brig. Gen. Fitz John Porter, an old friend, to supervise the siege operations. His was the only experienced and regular

The British observer who described the start of McClellan's Peninsula campaign as "the stride of a giant," found its concluding step as "that of a dwarf."

A Confederate wounded in the hip at Yorktown complained that it "was very painful but he could not show it to any of the fair ones."

Federal planners had been told that the roads on the peninsula were passable all year round. Heavy spring rains, however, turned most roads into quagmires, which slowed the army's advance (lower left). McClellan's headquarters was established at Camp Winfield Scott (lower right), below Yorktown.

A Federal seemingly out of danger at Yorktown was killed by a random shot. "Some men seem born to be shot," an observer commented.

army division under McClellan's command. After studying the Confederate defenses from both ground and balloon, Porter set his men working at night to erect a line of fortifications parallel to the Confederate positions and a mile distant. Behind the earthworks they prepared ramps and log platforms to support the siege weapons. Extensive works were built for supporting infantry, who were protected from frontal assault by chevaux-de-frise, logs studded with wooden spikes. Defense against Confederate shells was provided by gabions (long baskets of woven branches filled with dirt) and fascines (large bundles of branches).

This physical labor was easy compared to the task of bringing up and emplacing the siege guns. Transported from the York River and up a creek by boat, the guns were placed in large carts and moved across long stretches of roads corduroyed with tree trunks laid crosswise across bottomland where mud lay three feet deep. The largest pieces of artillery, 10-ton Parrott guns removed from coastal defenses, were pulled by one hundred horses. The 13-inch seacoast mortars weighed eight and a half tons each and fired 220-pound shells a distance of forty-three hundred yards. Each gun in the fourteen batteries was mounted on its firing platform with heavy block-and-tackle rigs.

Informed that "an awful thing had just happened!" a Confederate colonel feared Federals were overrunning his regiment. The officer was then told that it was worse than that—an artillery shell had struck his tent and destroyed a barrel of whiskey.

The difficulties did not end there. Heavy rains fell most days, mosquitoes and fleas infested the lowlands, and Southern artillery regularly dropped shells on the work parties. Despite these problems, on May 3, 114 heavy cannon, supported by 300 field guns, were ready for action,

The Balloon Corps

The Union balloon corps was created by Thaddeus S. C. Lowe of New Hampshire, whose title "Professor" was self-generated. He arrived with two large yellow balloons named *Intrepid* and *Constitution* and a hydrogen generator that enabled his balloons to be used anywhere.

As America's first aeronaut, Lowe made his first military ascent on April 6, 1862, at Yorktown, where he and ground observers were entertained by John B. Magruder's performance. Generals frequently accompanied Lowe, at least until April 11 when the *Intrepid* broke its tether and started drifting toward Confederate territory with Fitz John Porter aboard. A fortunate gust of wind blew the balloon back across the Federal lines, where

the general immediately grounded himself. Lowe noted that for some time afterward, officers were wary of accompanying him.

The effectiveness of balloon observation was questionable. The wooded terrain of the peninsula prevented much military activity from being observed, and Confederate artillery fire required Lowe to maintain a discreet distance.

At dawn on May 4, Lowe and Samuel Heintzelman ascended to find at Yorktown no "guns on the rebel works or a man," the latter reported. "Their tents were still standing & all quiet as the grave."

Joseph E. Johnston's intricate troop movements on May 31 as he prepared to attack Seven Pines went

BATTLES AND LEADERS

In their first aggressive action against the defenders of Yorktown, Union troops attacked at Lee's Mill on April 16. After gaining the position, no one knew what to do, and the Federals fell back under the force of a counterattack, suffering more than 40 percent casualties.

At Yorktown the Second Rhode Island was embarrassed to find the Confederates opposite them equipped with canteens and haversacks stenciled "2nd RI," part of the equipment captured at Bull Run. When asked what unit they were, the Federals called back "150th Rhode Island."

most of them concentrated on Yorktown and a gap in the works at the head of the Warwick River where an infantry assault was prepared.

"No one but McClellan could have hesitated to attack," a grateful Johnston said as he prepared to evacuate that same day before the big guns opened. Late in the evening a heavy Confederate artillery bombardment of

At Yorktown four machine guns saw action for the first time. Dubbed "Coffee-mill guns" by Lincoln, himself an inventor, they were crank operated and fed from hoppers of cartridges. Its builder called them "an Army in six feet square." One Federal said they fired one hundred rounds a minute but were prone to breakdowns.

---

unobserved because high winds grounded both balloons on the Chickahominy. They finally rose in the afternoon, but the forested ground revealed little of the battlefield.

The situation was repeated as Lee concentrated to attack Mechanicsville on June 26, although Lowe later claimed to have ascended at noon and contributed greatly to the Federal defense. At the time Lowe stated he had gone up at noon and returned at two, a fact supported by the Comte de Paris, who remembered Lowe's ascension was "too late to boast of his exploits."

Lacking a portable source of hydrogen, the Confederates had stitched together a simple hot-air balloon filled over a fire of pine knots doused with

turpentine. Capt. John Bryan could not remain aloft for more than thirty minutes at a time, and his mooring rope generally untwined and spun the balloon. On his third and final ascent, the rope broke. Bryan was blown into Union territory then returned by the whim of the breeze. "This was indeed luck of the greatest kind," he wrote.

A second balloon arose behind the lines on June 27, this one a brilliantly colored affair composed of silk dresses donated by the ladies of Charleston and Savannah. Created by Capt. Langdon Cheves, it was filled with gas from a works in Richmond and sent east tethered to a boxcar on the York River Railroad. The replacement aeronaut was Edward Porter Alexander. Federal

troop movements were observed, and the balloon's appearance reinforced McClellan's belief that Magruder and Huger were preparing to attack while Lee was actually massing at Mechanicsville.

Lee wanted the balloon aloft on June 28 to determine whether McClellan was retreating or defending Gaines's Mill, but high winds kept the craft grounded.

By June 30 Alexander had Cheeve's balloon tied on the steamer *Teaser,* an armed tug, which headed down the James River to Drewry's Bluff, where he observed McClellan's dispositions at Malvern Hill. He reported the information to Lee personally.

The Confederate air force flew its final mission near Malvern Hill on

July 4, again suspended above the *Teaser.* Wind forced Alexander to cut the observation short, and the balloon was deflated and stored. Unfortunately, the *Teaser* grounded, and before she could be refloated, the Union gunboat *Maratanza* appeared. The Confederates fired one round then slogged to shore, leaving the world's first aircraft carrier in Union hands. A Federal who knew Alexander claimed he "wept on reaching shore & exclaimed 'What will the ladies say?'"

Johnston withdrew so suddenly that fourteen of the fifteen heavy batteries McClellan had prepared to destroy the Confederate works at Yorktown never fired a shot. Prince de Joinville, a member of French royalty exiled in 1848, commented, "We had spent a whole month constructing gigantic works that have now become useless."

BATTLES AND LEADERS

Frustrated by Magruder's tenacious defense of Yorktown, McClellan decided to lay siege to the town. Fifteen batteries were prepared for no fewer than seventy guns. Battery No. 4 (above) mounted the heaviest artillery, 13-inch seacoast mortars. None were ever fired.

the Union lines covered the withdrawal as Southern infantry fell back on Williamsburg, twelve miles to the west, along two parallel routes, the Yorktown and Lee's Mill roads.

At midnight McClellan noted a "perfect quietness which reigns now." Dawn of May 4 confirmed his suspicion that Johnston had abandoned Yorktown and the Warwick line. Pickets crept into the vacated works to find fifty-six old smoothbore coastal guns seized at Norfolk, too massive to move over the boggy roads.

For the first time, soldiers encountered a new defensive weapon, torpedoes. These rudimentary mines were artillery shells buried in the ground with fuses triggered by passing men, horses, or vehicles. McClellan's response, typical throughout the Civil War, was to force Confederate prisoners to excavate the "infernal devices," which the general called "murderous and barbarous."

Johnston's escape caught McClellan by surprise. Pursuit was delayed until afternoon, when Brig. Gen. George Stoneman's cavalry encountered a two-brigade Confederate rear guard several miles east of Williamsburg. The Confederates occupied an extensive, four-mile-long line of thirteen redoubts that had been prepared months earlier by Magruder to block a narrow neck of the peninsula fifty miles from Richmond. The center of the line was dominated by Fort Magruder, where artillery dominated the intersection of the Yorktown and Lee's Mill roads a mile away. The intervening flatland was covered with rifle pits, logs, stumps, branches, and abatis of trees felled to clear fields of fire. The flanks rested securely on

"My system of obtaining knowledge was so thorough and complete," Allan Pinkerton boasted, "my sources of information were so varied, that there could be no serious mistake in the estimates."

creeks and marshes. The Union horsemen were easily repulsed with artillery fire.

In the meantime Johnston was marching rapidly in an effort to pass beyond West Point on the York River, thirty miles above Yorktown. He feared what McClellan actually did, sending four divisions upriver on transports to cut off the Confederate retreat at that very point. The rear guard would have to fight stubbornly to buy time for the wagon trains to get clear of the Union pursuit.

A heavy downpour marked the night. On May 5 Smith's division of Fourth Corps deployed at dawn on the Yorktown road to the right of Fort Magruder, awaiting instructions from Sumner, whom McClellan had placed in charge of the pursuit. Smith was soon joined by aggressive Brig. Gen. Joseph Hooker, who decided to attack without orders at 7:30 A.M. to the left of Smith's division. He opened with an artillery bombardment, but Confederate counterfire inflicted many casualties among the six Union gun crews, causing them to panic and flee.

Hooker's chief of artillery, Maj. Charles H. Wainwright, attempted to rally the men at the point of his sword, to little avail. "Drive two or three to a gun," he remembered, "and by the time you got some more up, the first had hid again." Wainwright deployed another group of artillerists to work the original battery. The Federals and Confederates exchanged serious fire. One Union gunner remembered, "The air perfectly whistled, shrieked, and hummed with the leaden storm."

Hooker advanced steadily across the tangled terrain for two hours. Johnston, needing additional time for the slow wagons to reach safety, dispatched Maj. Gen. James Longstreet's division to reinforce the defense at Fort

A Southern woman whose farm was pillaged informed the Federals that Magruder "kin drink more whiskey nor enemy generals you'uns got."

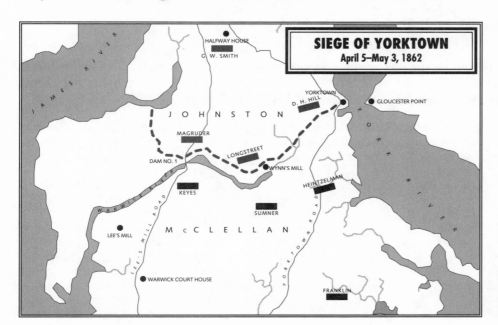

SIEGE OF YORKTOWN
April 5–May 3, 1862

On a tent in abandoned Yorktown a Confederate had written in charcoal, "He that fights and runs away will live to fight another day."

Land mines, called "torpedoes," developed for the Confederacy by Brig. Gen. Gabriel J. Rains, had been used in America as far back as the Seminole War in Florida in 1840, but the weapons were still not accepted as tools of war. To impede the Federal pursuit, Rains had buried artillery shells, triggered by pressure on percussion fuses, in the road. Reportedly, some were placed in houses, around wells, and even in flour barrels. McClellan considered the practice "murderous & barbarous," and forced Confederate prisoners to disarm them. Rains would next manufacture underwater torpedoes to impede Federal shipping on the James River.

Magruder. By noon he had committed six brigades, driving Hooker back and capturing twelve cannon, although deep mud prevented their removal.

Hooker's men fought valiantly, the general himself rallying the troops while Sumner stood by, seemingly paralyzed into inactivity. The elderly general allowed Smith and two other divisions that had arrived from Yorktown to do little but observe. Only one brigade was sent to reinforce Hooker by 4 P.M., and by then the Federals had been driven back over a mile and a half from Fort Magruder in hand-to-hand fighting. Jeb Stuart's cavalry was poised to pursue if a Union rout developed.

The situation finally grew desperate enough for Sumner to take action, but instead of sending in the twenty-eight thousand troops that stood ready, he called up Brig. Gen. Philip Kearny's Third Corps division, which had been the last to leave Yorktown. The fiery, one-armed Kearny, a Mexican War veteran, fought his way through idle Federal units, threatening to burn wagons if they were not cleared from his path. His men threw off their knapsacks in the rush forward.

Kearny reached the front about 4 P.M. and attacked after personally reconnoitering the situation. "Don't flinch, boys!" he shouted as two staff officers fell to Confederate fire. "They're shooting at me, not at you!" With sword in hand and reins in his teeth, Kearny led the Second Michigan to recapture Hooker's cannon, shouting, "That's it, boys! Go in gaily!" Longstreet's men were forced back into Fort Magruder.

At length Sumner again stirred himself into motion. Noticing two undefended redoubts at the northern end of Magruder's line, he dispatched twenty-five hundred men, a brigade of Smith's command under Brig. Gen. Winfield Scott Hancock, to flank Longstreet's position. They marched two miles to the right, crossed a creek near the York River by a dam, and entered the works. Noticing other barely occupied redoubts, Hancock continued on, gaining the rear of Longstreet while the Confederate

An Ineffective General ■ Samuel Peter Heintzelman

LIBRARY OF CONGRESS

Born on September 30, 1805, at Manheim, Pennsylvania, Samuel Peter Heintzelman graduated from West Point in 1826 with Albert Sidney Johnston. His peacetime activities were spent in garrison duty, recruiting, and the quartermaster office. Heintzelman was breveted for gallantry in Mexico and again later in the Southwest while fighting Indians.

Heintzelman was made a colonel on May 14, 1861, and a brigadier of volunteers three days later.

Despite his brave example at First Manassas, his division fled and he was wounded. At Yorktown in the spring of 1862, where Heintzelman's command of the Third Corps was forced on McClellan by the rule of seniority, he discouraged his superior from attacking John Magruder's thinly held line. A major general by Seven Pines, he again performed gallantly, though ineffectually, in rallying Union troops. His attacks against the Confederate left at Groveton were no more effective

than other Union efforts at Second Manassas. Heintzelman's field service ended there, and he afterward served in the defense of Washington and on court-martial duty. The competent performance at Williamsburg earned him the rank of major general in the regular army in 1865.

Heintzelman remained in the army until 1869, posted in Texas and to various boards. He died in Washington on May 1, 1888, and is buried in Forest Lawn Cemetery, Buffalo, New York.

LESLIE'S

Confederate commander Joseph E. Johnston decided to retreat to the old Virginia capital of Williamsburg rather than defend Yorktown. The evacuation, carried out stealthfully on the night of May 3, surprised McClellan, and his army cautiously advanced into the town.

On McClellan's overestimation of Confederate strength, one Federal wrote that the general was "realizing hallucinations."

was occupied with the renewed attack by Hooker and Kearny. Placing his brigade and ten 3-inch ordnance rifles in line, Hancock thought it prudent to wait for additional troops to cover his rear and right flank. His requests were twice refused by Smith, who at 2 P.M. ordered Hancock's recall. Hancock dallied as long as he dared, still hoping for reinforcements. When he started to withdraw at 5 P.M., Longstreet, attracted by artillery fire, finally noticed the Federal threat on his left flank.

Longstreet's first inclination was to withdraw. He had accomplished his mission admirably, checking McClellan for an entire day. The trains were well out of reach of Federal pursuit, but Maj. Gen. Daniel Harvey Hill, who commanded the Confederate reserves, and Brig. Gen. Jubal A. Early wanted to put their twenty-seven hundred men into action. Johnston was on the scene now, and either he or Longstreet deployed four regiments for an attack. Unfortunately, the regiments on the flanks advanced before the two center units. The troops charged in disorder, screaming Rebel yells and shouting "Bull Run" and "Ball's Bluff." Hill's men drove into the Federal skirmishers as Hancock skillfully withdrew his division behind the top of a hill. As the quickly pursuing Confederates crested the ridge, Hancock's men fired a volley into their ranks from thirty yards away. Additional volleys wounded Early and caused 189 casualties in the Twenty-fourth Virginia alone. When the Confederate advance shuttered to a stop, Hancock rode to the front of his line shouting, "Forward! Charge!" The Southerners retreated before the inspired Union assault, leaving 150 of their number prisoners.

On the Confederate retreat an artillery piece bogged down in deep mud as Union cavalry approached. An English observer urged that the "damned thing" be abandoned.

"We can't afford to lose it," a Confederate captain replied.

"Pardon me," the Englishman ventured, "if I may ask how much it is worth?"

The Confederate estimated a thousand dollars.

Watching the rapidly advancing Federals who had now opened fire, the observer stated, "Well, then, Captain, let's move on. I'll give you my check for it at once."

The Confederates left behind more than seventy artillery pieces, but most were antiquated naval smoothbore guns

LIBRARY OF CONGRESS

McClellan, like Johnston, made a belated battlefield appearance and threw in massed reinforcements, but the fighting was over. As dusk enveloped the field, McClellan wired Washington, "Hancock was superb," giving life to yet another battlefield legend. The clash had caused 1,603 Southern casualties and 2,239 Union losses, included 456 killed.

The Federal commander was prepared to storm Fort Magruder at dawn on May 6 but found the position abandoned. The retreating Confederates had resumed their first forced march. Wet, cold, exhausted, and hungry, "many seemed indifferent alike to life or capture," Hill remembered.

On May 7 Brig. Gen. William B. Franklin landed at West Point, at the head of the York River thirty-five miles from Richmond, with hopes of isolating Johnston from the Confederate capital. That effort failed, due largely

Jamestown During the Civil War

At the beginning of the Civil War, Jamestown Island was owned by thirty-three-year-old William Allen, the richest man in Virginia, who in 1850 had inherited twenty-three thousand acres in five counties. His fiancée, Sally Minge, broke off their engagement to marry future Confederate Gen. George E. Pickett on January 28, 1861. She died in childbirth ten months later. In 1861 Allen joined the Confederate army and helped fortify his own property. Before the war ended he had lost half his wealth.

The Confederates chose to fortify Jamestown for the same reasons the first English settlers had in 1607. Just below Jamestown the broad James River is over three miles wide, nearly impossible to defend even with batteries positioned on both banks. Jamestown Island, over two miles long, juts into the river and narrows it to just over one mile, and the deep 250-yard-wide channel required

ships to venture very close to the island. The island was also located on a bend that provided a commanding view down the river. Four colonial forts were constructed on a ridge at the northern end of the island, one mounting twenty guns, where the community of Jamestown was also situated. The colonial capital of Virginia was moved to Williamsburg in 1699 and by 1750 the island was substantially abandoned.

On May 4, 1861, students from the College of William and Mary and prominent local citizens marched to Jamestown with a servant each and carriages piled high with food, clothing, and other possessions. The first regular officer to arrive was Maj. John Mercer Patton Jr., descendant of Hugh Mercer, a Revolutionary War general, and great-uncle of World War II general George S. Patton. The volunteers immediately started to work on the primary defensive position, Fort Pocahontas, adjacent to

the ruins of the famous church tower at Jamestown. Excavations uncovered sections of armor and timber butts from the original fort. Later Civil War works included Point of Island Battery at Black Point on the eastern end of the island, Sand Battery downstream of Fort Pocahontas—which defended against Federal landings intended to outflank Pocahontas, the Square Redoubt—protecting the road that bisected the island, and a lunette and redan covering a bridge across Back River to the mainland. These were substantial earthworks. For example, the Square Redoubt had walls six feet high and a ditch fifteen feet wide and eight feet deep.

The forts contained more than twenty guns, including 9-inch Dahlgrens, 8-inch Columbiads, rifled 32-pounders, and 12-pounders. Fort Pocahontas contained thirteen of the pieces: the Sand Battery 4, the Square Redoubt 4, Point of Island

Battery 2, and the Bridge Redoubt 1. The Jamestown garrison never numbered more than twelve hundred, and often there were not enough soldiers to man the guns, which were never fired in anger.

The fever that killed most of the original English settlers occasionally flared up among the Confederates, presenting "a more fearful enemy than our Northern foe & more dreaded by the men," an officer noted.

When Magruder took command of the peninsula he obtained canal boats, filled them with granite and sand, and sank them to block the entrances to the Warwick and Back Rivers. Although he tried, Magruder never gained permission to block the James River to any significant degree.

Before his assignment to the *Virginia*, Lt. Catesby ap Roger Jones was in charge of Jamestown's defenses. He tested the guns and armor used on the ironclad at this remote location to avoid spying eyes in Richmond,

The Southern army was not alone on the roads leading up the peninsula. Virginia families also fled from the invaders.

BATTLES AND LEADERS

to lack of effort. By May 11 McClellan had concentrated his army around the town.

The city of Richmond was in an uproar. Crowded with refugees from the peninsula and more than a few army deserters, many of the panicked residents fled the Confederate capital, including Jefferson Davis's wife and their four children, who were bound for North Carolina. Government archives and the Confederate treasury were prepared for shipment south. The Virginia legislature vowed to burn the city before allowing it to be occupied by McClellan.

On May 14 Davis asked Lee to select a new line of defense should Richmond fall. The general chose the Staunton River, one hundred miles to the southwest, but implored Davis: "Richmond must not be given up! It shall not be given up!"

where newspapers published every fact they managed to ferret out.

Jones prepared three twelve-by-twelve-foot sections of armor, inclined to an angle of 36 degrees. All had two-foot backings of oak and pine, and one had three layers of one-inch-thick iron plates, another two two-inch layers of iron plate, and the last consisted of railroad T-iron. The armor was tested by firing the 8-inch and 9-inch guns of Jamestown's defenses from a distance of three hundred yards with ten pounds of powder. Shots penetrated deeply into the T-iron, penetrated the three-inch armor and entered the wood, but only broke the top layer of the two-inch iron plates, cracking the second and leaving the wood untouched.

The garrison hurriedly evacuated the island on May 10, 1862, abandoning most of the cannon. Later that day the Union ironclad *Galena* approached and carefully inspected

the batteries before continuing upstream with other ships to attack Drewry's Bluff. The *Galena* returned on May 16 to bury its thirteen dead from that action, which led one Williamsburg resident to write, "Heard a little cheering news this morning." In June the guns were spiked and carriages and fort buildings burned.

When the island was reoccupied, many Union soldiers were ignorant of the historical importance of Jamestown. "George," a sergeant asked a man, "didn't you ever hear of Powhatan?" The bored response was negative. "George," the noncom continued, "didn't you ever hear of Pocahontas?"

"Yes," the soldier replied, "of course I've heard of her, but I never seen her trot. But I've seen Flora Temple go a mile in two forty."

Jamestown was only periodically occupied until spring 1864 when Grant operated against Petersburg

and Butler was penned up on Bermuda Hundred on the James River south of Richmond. At that time Jamestown became an important telegraph station, although guerrillas frequently cut the lines and harassed the garrison. Union regiments whose enlistments had expired camped here until transportation arrived to take them home. Jamestown was visited by Secretary of State William Seward and by George McClellan, and from June until August 1862 the Federal transport fleet anchored here. In June 1864 the USS *Mayflower* visited Jamestown, which had been settled thirteen years before the original *Mayflower* reached Plymouth Rock.

When the Confederates withdrew from Jamestown, the thirty slaves who worked the island, augmented by contrabands from surrounding areas, armed themselves with rifles and took control of the property. On October 20, 1862, an incident

occurred that chilled the blood of a slave-holding culture. That day Jacob M. Shriver, Joseph A. Graves and his young nephew George, and Gilbert Wooten, a free black, landed on the island to recover some tools. They were seized by seven armed blacks and taken to the bridge, where they were surrounded by one hundred escaped slaves led by a man named Windsor whom they called "the judge." Shriver and both Groves were shot to death, but Wooten, seriously wounded in the stomach, leaped into the swamp and escaped into the darkness. Confederate cavalry failed to round up the murderers.

Predictably, Southern newspapers claimed that these actions would become commonplace if the slaves were emancipated. However, it was an isolated occurrence and several Union soldiers were also killed by runaway slaves in the area.

Williamsburg, the first combat for most of its participants, was a confused nightmare fought in mud and rain. Much of the fighting occurred in the forest of abatis that in places reached ten feet in height. Soldiers moved slowly through the branches and trunks, which were splintered by heavy artillery and rifle fire.

Hundreds of dead and wounded lay in the tangle for several days. Before most could be recovered, the drying wood caught fire. The Comte de Paris recorded that "the conflagration spread rapidly, [and] swept away the last traces of the victims of the struggle."

While McClellan remained in Williamsburg to organize his further advance, Confederate and Federal casualties were gathered at makeshift hospitals. There were so many wounded that McClellan sent a message under a flag of truce to request the assistance of Confederate surgeons. A number hastened to help Union doctors and local citizens care for soldiers of both armies.

On May 10 McClellan began advancing from West Point. Part of the army marched overland, but another section, accompanied by the commander, steamed fifteen miles up the Pamunkey River to White House, the ancestral plantation home of Martha Dandridge Custis, George Washington's wife, and presently the property of Confederate Gen. William Henry Fitzhugh "Rooney" Lee, whose mother, Robert E. Lee's wife, Mary, was a granddaughter of Martha Washington.

The Richmond and York River Railroad originated on the Pamunkey River at White House Landing, which McClellan intended to use as a supply base for his push against Richmond. The five hundred tons of supplies the army needed daily were unloaded there. Barges, kept loaded for a month in Baltimore Harbor, soon delivered five locomotives and eighty railcars to White House. Trains on the Richmond and York would supply the army as it advanced and deliver the great siege guns that McClellan so loved.

By May 15 the Union Army of the Potomac had established a vast camp between White House Landing and Cumberland Landing farther up the Pamunkey. There McClellan received the welcome news that the War Department had decided to send him the remainder of McDowell's corps, forty thousand strong. They were in Fredericksburg, halfway between Washington and Richmond, in order to screen the Northern capital. McClellan preferred that the troops be shipped to White House Landing, but Lincoln insisted they march directly to McClellan, which would save time and provide a buffer between Washington and the Confederate army. This development forced the general to alter his plans to approach Richmond.

Yorktown remained in Union possession for the rest of the war. As soon as the army occupied the town it became an enormous artillery depot in anticipation of the siege of Richmond.

LESLIE'S

From Yorktown, Magruder had fortified the area near Williamsburg with a line of defensive works about two miles east of the colonial capital. Johnston's rear guard utilized these to stymie the Federal pursuit, but the left flank was vulnerable.

McClellan had reorganized his army into five corps that would advance along the railroad on the south bank of the Chickahominy River. To join McDowell and cover White House Landing, the general was required to extend his right. As a result, Sumner's Second Corps, Franklin's Sixth Corps, and Porter's Fifth Corps extended for ten miles from the north bank of the Chickahominy to Mechanicsville, six miles northeast of Richmond, where Porter held the extreme right, which would be joined by McDowell, advancing from the northwest. The other two corps occupied the south bank of the Chickahominy. Keyes's Fourth Corps marched west on the Williamsburg road and entrenched near the crossroads of Seven Pines, with Heintzelman's Third Corps following five miles behind.

This deployment was completed by May 24, the day before McDowell was expected to arrive, but Washington was struck again by a case of the dithers. Jackson's activity in the Shenandoah Valley had prompted the War Department to send armies under Maj. Gen. Nathaniel Banks and John C. Frémont to counter the perceived invasion threat to Washington. McDowell was to be rerouted to join them, a plan that was opposed by both McClellan and McDowell. At Richmond "will be settled" the real issue of the war, McClellan protested to Stanton, which prompted a sharp rebuke from Lincoln: "I think the time is near when you must either attack Richmond or else give up the job and come to the defense of Washington."

Newspapers reported that Winfield Scott Hancock sent his men in shouting, "Charge, gentlemen, charge," but Maj. Thomas W. Hyde said the general "was more emphatic than that, the air was blue all around him."

Federal Maj. Gen. Samuel Heintzelman found several regimental band members standing around uselessly during the battle of Williamsburg. "Play!" he shouted. "Play! It's all you're good for. Play, damn it! Play some marching tune! Play 'Yankee Doodle,' or any doodle you can think of, only play something!" Union troops were soon fighting to "Yankee Doodle" and "Three Cheers for the Red, White, and Blue." One of the soldiers wrote, "It saved the battle," believing the boost to morale was worth a thousand extra soldiers.

At Williamsburg, Philip Kearny found a New Jersey unit leaderless. "Well, I am a one-armed Jersey son-of-a-gun. Follow me!" Kearny ordered a Michigan regiment to "drive those blackguards to hell at once."

A wealthy man, Kearny had traveled the globe in search of military adventure. In France he studied at the Saumur Cavalry School and practiced those skills in Mexico, where he lost an arm at Churubusco. While fighting with Napoleon III's Imperial Guard in Italy in 1859, he was awarded the Legion of Honor.

Neither commander anticipated the battle of Williamsburg, and a torrential rain did nothing to dampen the resolve of either army. One-armed Union Gen. Philip Kearny led his division in the attack with the reins of his horse clenched in his teeth and brandished his saber with his good arm. "Don't flinch, boys!" he shouted to his men. "They're shooting at me, not at you!"

McClellan found himself in a precarious position. His army was split by the Chickahominy, a narrow stream, but it was surrounded by a mile of swamp. With the recent rain the river was the highest it had been in twenty years. To protect communications between the two wings of his army, McClellan ordered his engineers to build eleven bridges along a twelve-mile stretch of the river between Mechanicsville and Bottom's Bridge. The most demanding chore was corduroying the miles of roads leading to the spans.

Still hoping for reinforcements from McDowell—after all, Washington often changed its mind—McClellan extended his right farther, sending Porter's division to occupy Hanover Court House and destroy the Virginia Central Railroad, twelve miles northwest of Mechanicsburg.

Porter advanced behind Brig. Gen. George W. Morell's brigade, which included three artillery batteries and Col. Hiram Berdan's sharpshooters. At Hanover they encountered Brig. Gen. Lawrence O. Branch's North Carolinians which, to the consternation of all, promptly attacked, overrunning one battery and breaking the Twenty-fifth New York. The day was saved by the men of the Fourteenth New York, who fired so rapidly that they had to pour water over their rifles to cool them. A counterattack by the Ninth Massachusetts and Sixty-second Pennsylvania put the brash Confederates to rout. They left 500 casualties behind, including 200 prisoners, to Porter's 335 losses.

John Charles, eleven years old in 1862, remembered that a Confederate soldier died after being carried to a house for care by a woman and her daughter. A Federal who arrived later to remove the body wept to learn that the Rebel was his brother. The two attending women were also moved to tears.

To the concern and mystification of his superiors, Johnston continued to exercise his preeminent skill—retreating—without notifying Davis or Lee of his plans. After Yorktown he had established a line on the south bank of the Chickahominy, the last natural barrier before Richmond, which lay only twelve miles distant. Johnston then abandoned this river line and withdrew to the outskirts of the city itself, causing even greater alarm among the populace.

But now even Johnston realized that the climactic moment had arrived. The Hanover expedition, in addition to reports that McDowell was marching south from Fredericksburg, twenty-five miles from Hanover, led Johnston to believe that McClellan and McDowell would soon join forces. A juncture by the two Union armies raised the odds against him to more than two to one, with the Federal horde numbering 150,000. Nor could Johnston ask for a better opportunity to strike McClellan, whose army was now split by the raging Chickahominy. Accordingly, a plan of attack was drawn up, again without the knowledge of the president or Lee.

To prevent the union of the two Federal armies, Johnston planned to attack McClellan's stronger right wing at Mechanicsville. The assault was planned for May 29, but that night, as he met with his commanders, the general learned that McDowell had returned to Fredericksburg after executing a feint designed to deceive the Confederates. It had succeeded.

Johnston was relieved. The change allowed him to revise his plan of attack to one he had initially favored. He would destroy the two corps of Keyes and Heintzelman on the Union left wing before McClellan could cross troops from the north bank of the Chickahominy to save them.

Along the road between Yorktown and Richmond, Maj. Thomas Hyde found an old signpost indicating to the west, "Richmond 21 Miles" and a new one beneath it, pointing north, "Gorham, Maine 647 Miles."

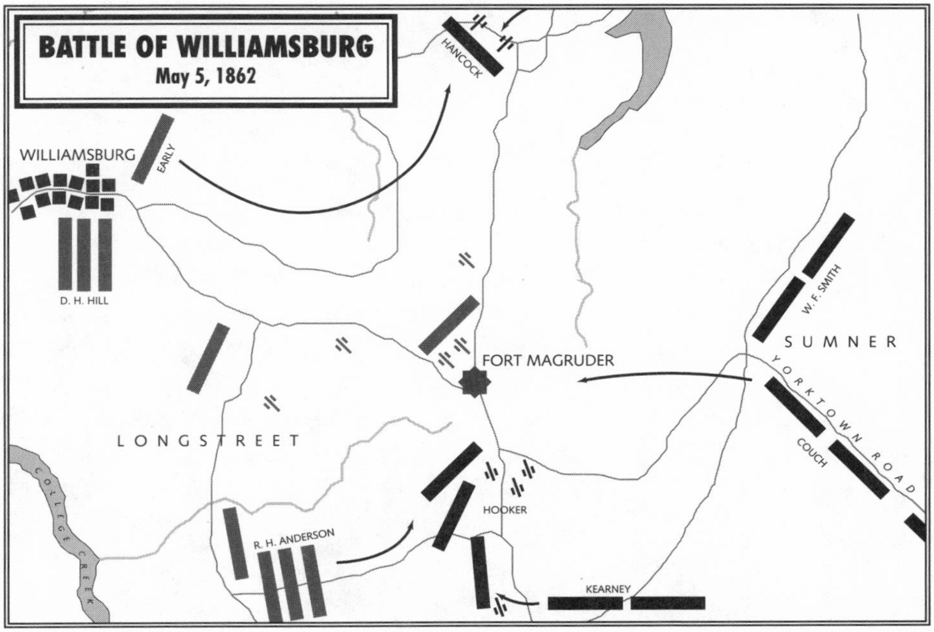

BATTLE OF WILLIAMSBURG
May 5, 1862

WILLIAMSBURG
EARLY
D. H. HILL
HANCOCK
FORT MAGRUDER
W. F. SMITH
SUMNER
YORKTOWN ROAD
COUCH
LONGSTREET
COLLEGE CREEK
R. H. ANDERSON
HOOKER
KEARNEY

On May 30 scouts reported that the Union left was unbalanced. In the forefront was the division of Brig. Gen. Silas Casey, who commanded McClellan's greenest unit, which was also understrength and poorly equipped. The brigade certainly did not belong on the front lines. Casey's position was on the Williamsburg road, half a mile west of Seven Pines. His strong left was anchored on White Oak Swamp, and three divisions of reinforcements waited in his rear, where Brig. Gens. Darius Couch and Philip Kearny occupied six miles of the Williamsburg road between Seven Pines and Bottom's Bridge to the east. To their left was Hooker's division. The right flank to the north was considerably weaker, stretching from the Williamsburg road to Fair Oaks on the Richmond and York Railroad. From that point to the northeast were three miles of impenetrable wilderness woods and swamps, which led to the Chickahominy River. Immediately north of the river was Sumner's corps, thirteen thousand strong.

Johnston scheduled the attack for early on May 31. He split his army into two wings consisting of three divisions each. Longstreet held the right and Maj. Gen. Gustavus W. Smith the left. Longstreet's forty thousand would launch the primary attack east to Seven Pines along three roads. Maj. Gen. Benjamin Huger would advance on the Charles City road, which ran from Richmond to the southeast, where a side road

No Man's Land

Throughout the war the country between Williamsburg and Richmond was a no man's land, patrolled by the cavalry of both armies and the target of frequent raids. Skirmishes broke out on numerous occasions.

Federal garrisons on the peninsula, Williamsburg being the closest to Richmond, were ports of refuge to Union raiding parties that attacked the Rebel capital from the north, then fled for safety, pursued by Confederate horsemen. In May 1863, during the Chancellorsville campaign, a large Union cavalry force under Maj. Gen. George Stoneman splashed across the Rapidan and Rappahannock Rivers to destroy railroad track, bridges, stations, and water tanks and cut telegraph lines. From Louisa Court House, northwest of Richmond, Col. Judson Kilpatrick and Lt. Col. Hasbrouck Davis raided toward the Confederate capital, then dodged

southeast with angry Confederates close behind. After a five-day ride covering two hundred miles, the Federals reached Union lines at Gloucester Point, opposite Yorktown.

Information received from Union spy Elizabeth Van Lew early in 1864 convinced Benjamin Butler at Fort Monroe that Richmond was vulnerable to a cavalry raid. He dispatched Brig. Gen. Isaac J. Wistan from Yorktown, who reached Bottom's Bridge on the

Chickahominy, twelve miles from Richmond, on February 7, where they were jumped by a Confederate force tipped off by a Union deserter from Williamsburg, William Boyle.

Butler, angry that Lincoln had postponed Boyle's execution for killing an officer, went over the head of his superior, General in Chief Henry Halleck, and sent a letter criticizing Lincoln to Secretary of War Edwin Stanton. The jailer who allowed

Boyle to escape was executed on March 7. His regiment formed a hollow square about the condemned man while the jailer knelt calmly to pray with a chaplain before being killed by a firing squad.

Weeks later, Brig. Gen. Judson Kilpatrick crossed the Rapidan River at Ely's Ford on February 28, his purpose to liberate Federal prisoners at Richmond, interrupt Confederate communications, and

branched off north to Seven Pines. Daniel Harvey Hill would use the Williamsburg road, which extended directly east from Richmond to Seven Pines. Longstreet, supported by Smith's southernmost division, that of Brig. Gen. W. H. C. Whiting, would support his attack from the north on the Nine Mile Road, which paralleled the Williamsburg road for six miles then turned southeast to cross the railroad at Fair Oaks and intersected the Williamsburg road a mile beyond at Seven Pines. This would place the Union left wing under attack from left, right, and front simultaneously. Two of Smith's divisions, those of Magruder and A. P. Hill, were held in reserve upstream of the Chickahominy River northeast of Richmond to prevent McClellan from crossing his two corps concentrated there.

The battle would be set in motion when Huger reached a position one and a half miles south of Seven Pines and signaled A. P. Hill to attack. The sounds of Hill's assault would be Longstreet's cue to attack. Huger would first ensure that the Confederate right flank was clear then drive north to help D. H. Hill at Seven Pines.

During the night thunderous storms dumped more than four inches of rain on the area, which helped isolate the Federal left wing by flooding streams and bottomlands and swamping several of McClellan's new bridges.

Federal Gen. William Franklin landed at Eltham's Landing to cut off the Confederate retreat. Ordered "to feel the enemy gently and fall back," John Bell Hood drove the Federals back to the river, which prompted Joseph E. Johnston to inquire, "What would your Texans have done, sir, if I had ordered them to charge and drive back the enemy?"

"I suppose, General," Hood answered, "they would have driven them into the Pamunkey River, and tried to swim out and capture the gunboats."

Hood's Texas Brigade, consisting of the First, Fourth, and Fifth Texas, also included the Eighteenth Georgia, affectionately dubbed the "Third Texas" by their comrades.

---

distribute a presidential proclamation of amnesty. The expedition split into two columns, one led by Kilpatrick and the other by his twenty-two-year-old protégé, Col. Ulric Dahlgren, son of Rear Adm. John A. Dahlgren.

Repulsed before Richmond on March 1, the Federals fled for the Pamunkey, pursued as usual by infuriated Confederate horsemen. Kilpatrick met friendly troops at New Kent Court House and was escorted to Williamsburg. Dahlgren, seeking sanctuary at Gloucester Point, was ambushed and killed on March 2. A hot controversy erupted when papers found on his body revealed a plot to kill Jefferson Davis and his cabinet and burn Richmond. Federal authorities claimed the documents were falsified. Davis agreed to send Dahlgren's body to his father through Fort Monroe, but the grave was

found to be empty. Agents of Elizabeth Van Lew had spirited the body away to a farm, where it remained until war's end.

Not just Federal cavalry sought sanctuary on the peninsula. Union prisoners who managed to escape from Libby Prison and Belle Isle in Richmond made their way southeast. Traveling at night, sleeping by day, and relying on slaves and Union sympathizers for food and directions, they were found by cavalry patrols or welcomed into the Union lines at Williamsburg, then sent to Fort Monroe.

On December 13, 1863, Federals surprised a Confederate unit camped at Charles City Court House, twenty miles north of Williamsburg. Trapped in two buildings, the Confederates were forced to surrender 90 men and 158 horses and mules. One of the Rebels was found to be a woman masquerading as a man.

LIBRARY OF CONGRESS

New Kent Court House (facing page) witnessed the passage of both armies on the peninsula in 1862 and was in no man's land for most of the war. Saint Peter's Episcopal Church (above) was the scene of Martha Custis's marriage to George Washington. In 1862 Edwin V. Sumner's corps camped on the site.

On May 10 the Federal army occupied White House Landing, the plantation on which George Washington had courted Martha Custis. The property now belonged to Mary Lee, the wife of Robert E. Lee. She had fled just prior to the army's arrival. McClellan established a massive supply depot on the grounds—and forbade anyone to go near the house.

Robert E. Lee's wife, Mary Custis Lee, was the great-granddaughter of Martha Dandridge Custis, whom George Washington courted at White House, where Martha had inherited a four-thousand-acre plantation on the Pamunkey River. White House became the home of the Lees' son Rooney before McClellan established his vast supply depot there. After being forced to leave Arlington at the advance of Union forces, Mary Lee had retired here. She departed shortly before McClellan arrived, leaving this note on the front door: "Northern soldiers who profess to reverence Washington, forbear to desecrate the home of his first married life,—the property of his wife, now owned by her descendants.—A Grand-daughter of Mrs. Washington." It was a slight lie; the original structure had burned a few decades earlier. To prevent damage to the historic property McClellan placed guards around the house and exempted it from military use. The general ordered it spared when the depot was abandoned, but Federal soldiers burned it to the ground on June 28.

At dawn the Confederates started their march to initiate the battle at 8 A.M., but confusion reigned as Johnston undertook his first offensive. He had revealed the complete battle plan only to Longstreet, and then only verbally. The confused Georgian marched south on the wrong route—the Williamsburg road—quickly eliminating one of Johnston's three directions of attack. The assault was also delayed as Longstreet's six brigades blocked Huger, who was to signal the start of the battle.

A. P. Hill followed his instructions to the letter and hid his eighty-five hundred men in the woods only one thousand yards from the Union line. Although impatient, he waited for Huger's signal from the Charles City road. When it arrived, four hours late, Hill attacked, catching the 103d Pennsylvania by surprise and scattering them. Beyond this picket regiment Hill found the Federals dug in behind an extensive abatis. A quarter-mile-long Union earthwork featured an incomplete star-shaped fort mounting six cannon.

Casey stood the storm for a while, but soon Brig. Gen. Robert Rodes attacked the artillery redoubt from the front as Brig. Gen. Gabriel Rains lapped around the right and into the rear. Hill placed Capt. Thomas H. Carter's battery to fire into the work, and gunners and horses began to fall. When the Confederates renewed the attack, the Union artillery commander was hit, and Casey's division broke and fled for the rear. Despite being nearly surrounded and suffering 40 percent casualties, Casey was seen "raging" at his men to rally. One witness considered him "brave as a lion," but his panicked force continued to race for Seven Pines.

Alerted by the firing and encountering streams of terrified soldiers, Keyes, commander of the Fourth Corps, dispatched two of Couch's regiments forward. The Fifty-fifth New York was hurled back and the Tenth Massachusetts, almost encircled, joined the retreat. "It really seemed as

With Richmond in his sights, McClellan divided his army. He sent two corps south of the Chickahominy and three north of the river. Reinforcements were expected to join the northern wing but were diverted by action in the Shenandoah. Heavy rain swelled the river and complicated the Federal situation. Seizing the moment, Johnston attacked.

though a man could not live there one moment," wrote a Massachusetts officer of the hurricane of shot, shell, and canister that hissed around him.

At Seven Pines, Keyes managed to establish a strong line with the remnants of Casey's and Couch's divisions and two of Kearny's brigades, which arrived after a three-mile forced march.

Hill had fought alone without reinforcements for two hours and was now outnumbered. A fierce counterattack by Kearny drove the Confederates back to Casey's redoubt. Kearny was described as the very god of war, commanding fearlessly at the front and glorying in the combat. Directing a regiment into line, Kearny said: "Oh, anywhere! T'is all the same, Colonel, you'll find lovely fighting along the whole line." Kearny later boasted that once again, "I was sent for to redeem the blundering and shortcomings of others.

Since they had served together in Mexico, John B. Magruder had little regard for Joseph Hooker, writing, "Hooker was a mean man and a liar."

"Fighting Joe" ■ Joseph Hooker

Born November 13, 1814, in Hadley, Massachusetts, Joseph Hooker, grandson of a Revolutionary War officer, graduated in the middle of the West Point class of 1837. After a commendable peacetime career, he served as staff officer to three generals in Mexico, including two future Civil War leaders, Federal Benjamin F. Butler and Confederate Gideon J. Pillow. Hooker participated in both of the major campaigns in Mexico, where, for gallantry and meritorious service, he was breveted from lieutenant to lieutenant colonel, a feat accomplished by few others.

Hooker took a leave of absence from the army after Mexico, then resigned his commission in February 1853 to farm in California. Finding no success in civilian life, Hooker asked for a commission in early 1858. It did not materialize until August 6, 1861,

when he was made a brigadier of volunteers. Hooker's division bore the brunt of hard fighting at Williamsburg, where he won the title "Fighting Joe Hooker" from mangled newspaper headlines. He fought well in the Seven Days', Second Manassas, Antietam, and Fredericksburg campaigns, leading the First Corps. After commanding the Central Grand Division on Ambrose E. Burnside's Mud March, Hooker criticized his superior. Burnside wanted Hooker removed, but it was he who was replaced—with Hooker, in part due to his connections with presidential aspirant Salmon P. Chase and other Radical Republicans.

Commanding the Army of the Potomac in the spring of 1863, Hooker skillfully led 135,000 men across the Rappahannock River and into Virginia's Wilderness. But at Chancellorsville Hooker lost his nerve and the advance stalled. With James

Longstreet in North Carolina, Lee divided his scanty force and sent Stonewall Jackson on a sweeping march around the Federal right flank. With a large portion of his army rolled up, Hooker retreated. He quickly pursued Lee into Pennsylvania, however, which earned him the Thanks of Congress, but denied the use of the Federal garrison stationed at Harpers Ferry, he quarreled with Washington and was replaced by George Gordon Meade.

In the fall of 1863, after William Rosecrans's defeat at Chickamauga, Hooker led two corps to relieve Chattanooga. Under Ulysses S. Grant in November, Hooker seized Lookout Mountain in the fabled "Battle Above the Clouds." In the spring of 1864 Hooker directed a corps in the Atlanta campaign under William T. Sherman. When Army of the Tennessee commander James B. McPherson was

killed at Atlanta in July, Sherman replaced him with Oliver O. Howard, Hooker's subordinate, which induced Hooker to resign.

Hooker commanded departments until his retirement in 1868 with the rank of major general. He died on October 31, 1879, in Garden City, New Jersey, and is buried in Cincinnati.

Mary Lee left White House for Marlbourne, the home of radical Secessionist Edmund Ruffin, on the Pamunkey River. After it was also overrun, McClellan arranged to send her across the Chickahominy at Meadow Bridge, escorted by Union cavalry. Her arrival was cheered by Confederate troops.

Rodes bore the brunt of the bruising counterattack while his support, Rains, struggled through White Oak Swamp. Men fought in three feet of water, pausing to lean wounded comrades against trees to prevent their drowning. When wounds forced Rodes out of action, his place was taken by Col. John B. Gordon, who admirably demonstrated his leadership. Gordon's lieutenant colonel, major, and nineteen-year-old brother were killed around him and his horse was shot from under him as he directed the Sixth Alabama. Their valor was proven by the 59 percent casualties they suffered—the most of any Confederate regiment in the entire Civil War.

The beleaguered Hill begged Longstreet for support, but his commander had managed to blunder further, sending three brigades to the Charles City road where Huger's three brigades sat unengaged. A fourth brigade was dispatched to guard the railroad, and Longstreet's remaining two brigades hurried to the front. Col. James L. Kemper, deployed on the Confederate right, encountered fierce resistance and a punishing crossfire from artillery and Kearny's rifles. Kemper's men went to ground behind Casey's earthworks, unable to advance or retreat.

Longstreet's last brigade, under Brig. Gen. Richard H. Anderson, fought northeast from the Williamsburg road on a primitive trail and almost struck the Nine Mile Road, a move that cleaved the Federal line in half between Seven Pines and Fair Oaks. Two Confederate regiments under Col. Micah Jenkins, turning east, approached Seven Pines around 4 P.M., cutting off Couch, four regiments, and an artillery battery from the remainder of his division. Couch was forced to retreat north toward Fair Oaks.

"Pouring in my volleys at close range as I advanced," Jenkins recorded, "I drove them back, losing heavily myself, but killing numbers of the enemy, leaving the ground carpeted with dead and wounded." By dusk Jenkins was half a mile east of Seven Pines, which required Kearny to retreat a mile in order to cover his left flank.

The highest-ranking generals on both sides of this confused battle had little idea how the fight was proceeding or whether a battle was even being fought. Johnston was at the Nine Mile Road, prevented by a freak

Great Expectations ■ Benjamin Huger

Benjamin Huger, born on November 22, 1805, in Charleston, South Carolina, graduated from West Point in 1825. His twenty-six-year career before the Civil War saw him command a number of army installations. In Mexico, as chief of ordnance under Winfield Scott, he received three brevets for bravery—to major, lieutenant colonel, and colonel. He resigned his commission after Fort Sumter and became a Confederate brigadier general on June 17, 1861, and a major general on October 7.

Much was expected of Huger, but he proved unsuited for high command. After destroying the navy yard in Norfolk in 1862, he held his only field command, a division at Seven Pines and the Seven Days, where he performed poorly. An investigation of his actions resulted in his transfer on July 12, 1862, to inspector of artillery and ordnance. In that capacity he served well until the war's end, primarily in the Trans-Mississippi Department.

Huger farmed in Virginia following the war and died in his native Charleston on December 7, 1877. He is buried in Baltimore's Green Mount Cemetery.

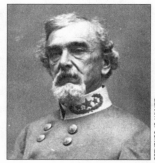

LIBRARY OF CONGRESS

By May 16 most of McClellan's army was camped between White House Landing and Cumberland Landing along the Pamunkey River.

McClellan's Pamunkey River camp extended two and a half miles from White House Landing to Cumberland Landing. Among the staples stockpiled at White House were crude wooden coffins. Setting up shop were a number of undertakers who charged twenty-five dollars for embalming privates and fifty dollars for officers. "The scene as we disembarked at the landing was neither cheerful nor encouraging," Federal Capt. Robert Taggat wrote.

acoustical phenomenon from hearing any sounds of the battle. The general knew his troops had been misdirected and could not locate Longstreet until 10 A.M., when he was heard to say, "I wish all the troops were back in camp."

At noon, as Hill's assault began on the Williamsburg road, Johnston led Longstreet's support, the three brigades of Whiting's division, to Old Tavern on the Nine Mile Road, two miles short of Fair Oaks and two miles from a raging battle that he could not hear. There he waited with Smith.

Robert E. Lee reached the front in the afternoon. Although he and the president had been uninformed about the attack, every civilian in the city seemed to have heard about it. While citizens crowded hilltops to watch the battle, Lee and Davis rode to the battlefield.

Lee thought he had heard the sounds of a battle but Johnston replied that it was just an artillery exchange. Johnston received his first definite word that the battle had begun at 4 P.M. when Longstreet requested reinforcements. Although it was certainly by chance, Johnston rode off with Whiting's ten-thousand-man force just as Davis arrived.

Every battle has a turning point, and it arrived here. If Jenkins were reinforced, McClellan's left would be destroyed. Johnston and Whiting reached Fair Oaks at 5 P.M. to find it abandoned. Johnston expected to press on toward Seven Pines, but Whiting cautiously thought there must be Federal forces to their left and rear, hidden in the Chickahominy wilderness. Johnston admonished Whiting for his caution seconds before a concealed battery opened on them from eight hundred yards—from the left and rear.

Federal soldiers were appalled by the appearance of Confederate prisoners. "They were horrible looking devils, lank, long haired, clad in a nasty brick colored stuff that a beggar in the North would be ashamed to wear."

The Confederate assault forced the Federals to fall back on May 31. One of the Union bulwarks near Fair Oaks was Fort Sumner, which was photographed a few days after the battle.

Union Col. Samuel H. Starr loved his horse despite a peculiar habit it developed in battle. Under fire it turned its hind end to the enemy. It never ran away, as some horses did, so Starr simply turned around in the saddle to face the enemy.

On the evening of the battle of Seven Pines a tremendous thunderstorm struck both armies. A bolt of lightning killed four Alabamians, and another strike in the Federal camp killed one and stunned twenty others.

Couch and his isolated command had attempted several times to fight through the Confederate lines and link up with the corps east of Fair Oaks. Couch had lost two regimental commanders in the efforts and had picked this moment for another try.

Whiting immediately attacked with four regiments and was twice repulsed by six Union cannon firing canister at close range. A third charge almost overran the battery, which had exhausted its supply of the deadly ammunition. Explosive shells with fuses set as short as possible exploded twenty yards downrange and shredded the assault. As the Confederates formed once again, they and Couch were both shocked by the sight of Union reinforcements racing out of the flooded Chickahominy swamps.

At 1 P.M. McClellan, ill with malaria at Gaines's Mill, was roused from bed by the sounds of battle. He immediately alerted Sumner to prepare to cross the flooded river to relieve Keyes at Seven Pines. Sumner, embarrassed by his laggard performance at Fort Magruder, smartly marched the troops to two of the temporary bridges. When McClellan ordered them to march at 2:30 P.M. both spans were underwater. A single brigade managed to cross one bridge before it collapsed. Sumner then shifted the entire corps one and a half miles downstream to Grapevine Bridge, which looked as if the raging floodwaters would consume it shortly. To an engineer who swore it would be impossible for him to use the bridge, Sumner replied: "Impossible! Sir, I tell you I *can* cross! I am ordered!"

When Sumner's Second Division, led by Brig. Gen. John Sedgwick, started across, the span settled into place, but two hundred yards of corduroy beyond had been swept away. Soldiers manhandled artillery pieces across the marsh and struggled for two hours to reach Couch. Many arrived without shoes, which had been lost in the morass. "God was with us," Couch believed, "and victory ours."

Sedgwick's three brigades of eight thousand men reinforced Couch and deployed a second line perpendicular to the first and extending into

Twin frame houses mark the center of Union Gen. Silas Casey's position on the battlefield of Seven Pines. A central building was supposed to connect the two wings but was never built.

182

the woods. Confederates attacking into the resulting angle were slaughtered by a deadly crossfire.

Not realizing that Couch had been reinforced, Johnston ordered another attack by Whiting's three brigades, then rode off to untangle Longstreet's mess at Seven Pines. Whiting encountered eleven pieces of artillery, which crushed his command with five hundred rounds of canister, case, shell, and solid shot during the following two hours of combat. Confederates fell fifteen yards from the cannon muzzles, and hundreds of others were cut down by the infantry crossfire. One of Whiting's brigadiers, Robert H. Hatton, was killed; another, James J. Pettigrew, left the field gravely wounded; and the third, Wade Hampton, ordered a surgeon to cut a bullet out of his foot while he commanded from horseback.

Learning the true situation as dusk enveloped the field, Johnston disengaged, intending to reorganize during the night and renew the contest at dawn. The general was two hundred yards north of Fair Oaks and riding toward the front lines when an artillery shell passed overhead. "Colonel," Johnston laughed at a staff officer who had instinctively ducked, "there is no use of dodging; when you hear them, they have passed." It was one of those seemingly prophetic remarks. Seconds later a bullet hit Johnston's left shoulder and almost simultaneously a shell fragment struck his chest, breaking ribs and knocking him unconscious from his horse.

Lee and Davis arrived shortly to watch Johnston being carried off on a stretcher. Johnston, wounded numerous times in previous wars with Mexico and Indians, would require six months to recover.

Gustavus Smith assumed command of the fluid situation. To the south Longstreet and D. H. Hill had gained nearly three miles, pushing the Federals

Pvt. Alexander Hunter of Virginia was appalled by what he saw while approaching the battle lines at Seven Pines, particularly the wounded soldiers "in every species of mutilation. Some were borne on stretchers, others swung in blankets from whose folds blood and gore dropped in horrible exudations, staining the ground and crimsoning the budding grass."

Continuing on, Hunter encountered a Confederate battery where every man and horse had been killed except one powder boy who "cowered behind a wheel of one of the guns, with eyes protruding, hands clasped, teeth clenched and a face wearing a look of horrified fright—face so white, so startling in its terror, that it haunted me for days after."

A Federal colonel sent his regiment into battle by shouting, "Charge them like hell, boys! Show 'em you *are* damned Yankees!"

The Other Hill ■ Daniel Harvey Hill

Daniel Harvey Hill, born in South Carolina on July 12, 1821, graduated from West Point in the class of 1842. He won two brevets for bravery in Mexico, then left the military in 1849 to teach math at Washington College in Lexington, Virginia, and Davidson College in North Carolina, before serving as superintendent of the North Carolina Military Institute.

Hill joined the Confederate army as colonel of a regiment, and a month after achieving victory in the first battle of the war, at Big Bethel on the peninsula, he was promoted to brigadier general on July 10, 1861. A

major general by March 1862, he led a division at Yorktown, Williamsburg, Seven Pines, the Seven Days, Second Manassas, South Mountain, and Antietam. Commanding the Department of North Carolina in 1863, he defended Richmond while the Army of Northern Virginia was in Pennsylvania.

Hill's problems started after his promotion to lieutenant general on July 11, 1863. Sent to reinforce Braxton Bragg and the Army of Tennessee, he commanded a corps at Chickamauga and during the Chattanooga campaign. He was soon relieved because of his vocal condemnation of Bragg,

and Jefferson Davis refused to nominate Hill's last rank to the Senate. In the final year of the war, he served at Petersburg then led a division under Joseph E. Johnston at Bentonville.

Hill edited a southern magazine and served as president of several colleges before his death on September 24, 1889. He is buried in the Davidson College Cemetery in Davidson, North Carolina. Hill's brothers-in-law included two Confederate generals—Stonewall Jackson and Rufus Barringer.

BATTLES AND LEADERS

BATTLE OF SEVEN PINES
May 31, 1862

a mile east of Seven Pines to their third defensive position. Whiting was stalemated at Fair Oaks.

Smith was not one to inspire confidence. Responding to Davis's query as to his plans for the next day, he honestly replied that he had no idea what he should do. He might hold the present positions; he might retreat. At some point during the night he decided to attack and summoned Longstreet. Whiting would hold in front of Fair Oaks while Longstreet's three divisions wheeled north from the Williamsburg road and attacked east of Fair Oaks toward the railroad.

Longstreet hated the concept, pointing out that his left flank would be invitingly open to a strong Federal counterattack west along the Williamsburg road. Smith confidently declared that Union troops there had been routed, but he would have A. P. Hill and Magruder cover the flank at the Chickahominy. Longstreet's obstinate objections forced Smith to order him to attack.

Longstreet rode away at three in the morning unmollified and secretly planning to ignore the attack orders. He had no confidence in the plan, no respect for Smith as a commander, and no trust that he would have any support once the battle was joined. "It was evident," he declared,

"Old Prayer Book" ■ Oliver Otis Howard

Oliver Otis Howard, born November 8, 1830, in Leeds, Maine, taught school to put himself through Bowdoin College, then he graduated from West Point in 1854 and taught math there before rising rapidly in rank during the Civil War. Although his brigade was routed at First Manassas, Howard was made a brigadier. A wound suffered at Fair Oaks forced the amputation of an arm. After John Sedgwick's wounding at Antietam, Howard led the division through Fredericksburg, when he was given command of the Eleventh Corps, which was surprised and routed by Stonewall Jackson at Chancellorsville because he failed to properly anchor his flank. After the death of John F. Reynolds on the first day of Gettys-

burg, Howard led the retreat of the First and Eleventh Corps and occupied the important position on Cemetery Hill, for which he received the Thanks of Congress.

Howard was sent west late in 1863 and assigned to the Army of the Tennessee, which helped relieve the Confederate siege of Chattanooga. He led the Fourth Corps until the death of James B. McPherson at Atlanta, then took command of the Army of the Tennessee, leading it as the right wing on William T. Sherman's march through Georgia and into the Carolinas. Howard was difficult for Sherman to accept on a personal basis, for he had no vices. The pious Howard did not smoke, drink, or swear, and he was a staunch New England abolitionist.

Howard did not fight just to end slavery. When the war was over, he became a vocal advocate of education for blacks. He helped establish a number of schools for former slaves, including Howard University in Washington, D.C. He also led the work of the Freedmen's Bureau in helping blacks adjust to life as free citizens. Although he personally was honest, corruption was rampant in the organization. Howard saw service in the West in the 1870s and 1880s, then became superintendent of West Point and held other positions before retiring in 1894 to speak and write. He also helped organize Lincoln Memorial University, near Cumberland Gap, at Harrogate, Tennessee, for the education of mountain youth. In

1893 Howard was given the Medal of Honor for his actions at Seven Pines. He died in Burlington, Vermont, on October 26, 1909, and is buried there in Lake View Cemetery.

LIBRARY OF CONGRESS

The Seventy-first New York, part of the Excelsior Brigade commanded by Gen. Daniel E. Sickles, charged and routed Confederates in the woods east of Seven Pines.

Joseph E. Johnston's secrecy was legendary. "It is scarcely necessary to add," Jefferson Davis wrote later of his visit to the front with Robert E. Lee the day the battle of Seven Pines was fought, "that neither of us had been advised of a design to attack the enemy that day."

"that our new commander would do nothing and we must look to accident for such aid as might be drawn to us during the battle." After conferring with D. H. Hill in Casey's tent, Longstreet ordered a probe by several brigades to determine the enemy's strength, which was considerable.

McClellan reinforced the threatened points of his left wing. Sedgwick defended from the Chickahominy to Fair Oaks. The division of Brig. Gen. Israel B. Richardson followed Sedgwick across the river and took a position along the railroad from Fair Oaks to a mile farther east. Turning south, perpendicular to the Williamsburg road, the line was held by Kearny and Hooker. The savaged remnants of Couch and Casey were held in reserve.

Soldiers slept on their arms as a light rain fell on the swampy land, for the first time resting amid the dead and wounded felled by a major battle. "You could not move without falling over them," a Massachusetts soldier recalled. "The air was filled with shrieks and groans."

At dawn Hill relieved Jenkins with two fresh brigades from Longstreet— men from Brig. Gens. Roger E. Pryor and Cadmus M. Wilcox, who would stand against any counterattack. One of Longstreet's brigades, under Brig. Gen. George E. Pickett, and two of Huger's, commanded by Brig. Gens. Lewis A. Armistead and William Mahone, were sent north through the woods toward the railroad. Incredibly, each brigade was unaware that other Confederate units were also being sent forward. As a result, their movements were uncoordinated and their flanks unsupported.

At 6:30 A.M. Mahone, with Armistead on his right, encountered the brigade of Union Brig. Gen. William H. French, which had been sent on

On the second day at Seven Pines, Union Brig. Gen. Oliver O. Howard was hit twice in the right arm. His brother, Lt. Charles Howard, was wounded in the thigh as he helped Oliver off the field.

When Philip Kearny, who had lost his left arm in Mexico, saw Howard he said with a smile, "I am sorry, General, but you must not mind it; the ladies will not think the less of you."

Howard laughed and responded, "There is one thing we can do, General—we can buy our gloves together!"

Sumner's Corps was moved to reinforce the endangered right side of the Federal line. Artillery was dragged through the swamp to rescue the battered Union forces at Seven Pines, and soldiers marched over the inundated Grapevine bridge to aid Darius Couch's division at Fair Oaks.

As darkness fell, soldiers were ordered to sleep on their arms. "Some dark forms lay around which might have been the dead," one New Hampshire soldier said, "but I chose to lie down and not search."

an identical mission. A sudden volley from the dense woods sent the three Federal regiments fleeing back to a railroad cut and embankment that sheltered the remainder of Richardson's division. There they rallied, and French called for assistance from Brig. Gen. Oliver O. Howard, deployed behind him. Howard sent Col. James Miller's Eighty-first Pennsylvania to protect French's left flank in the woods. While they took position Miller spotted a line of battle forward. He ordered his troops to shoulder arms and aim before one of his officers shouted, "They are our men."

"Recover arms!" Miller yelled hastily, then called, "Who are you?" his last words.

An Undistinguished General ■ Erasmus Darwin Keyes

Born in Brimfield, Massachusetts, on May 29, 1810, Erasmus Darwin Keyes was a member of the U.S. Military Academy class of 1832. He taught at West Point and was Winfield Scott's aide and military secretary on three separate occasions while serving in the infantry, cavalry, and artillery, but he never saw combat. As a colonel Keyes led a routed brigade at First Manassas before becoming the third brigadier general of volunteers in August. Lincoln personally selected Keyes to

command the Fourth Corps on the peninsula, where he failed to distinguish himself. He did, however, receive the brunt of the Confederate attack at Seven Pines, which won him a brevet promotion to regular army brigadier.

Commanding around Washington afterward, Keyes withdrew from what he thought to be a larger force when his superior, Gen. John A. Dix, demonstrated against Richmond during the Gettysburg campaign. In the aftermath, Keyes

resigned and moved to California, where he grew wealthy in mining, wine making, and banking. He died on a European trip in Nice, France, on October 14, 1895, and is buried at West Point.

"Virginians!" came the massive reply, and Armistead's men fired a volley that killed many, including Miller. As the survivors fled toward the railroad, Howard dispatched Lt. Nelson A. Miles to rally them, which he did with such conspicuous valor that he was immediately jumped two ranks to lieutenant colonel. Howard personally led the Sixty-first and Sixty-fourth New York through French and toward the Virginians. Two horses were shot out from under him and two bullets shattered his right arm. Howard was brought off the field by his brother Charles, a lieutenant, who was soon shot in the thigh.

The Sixty-fourth New York halted after Howard was wounded, but the Sixty-first forged into fierce Confederate resistance led by Col. Francis C. Barlow. "Men were dying and groaning and running about with faces shot and arms shot," Barlow remembered, "and it was an awful sight."

Mahone committed his three regiments one at a time instead of launching a coordinated strike against Richardson's strong position. Thrown back successively, Mahone soon withdrew to the Williamsburg road, where D. H. Hill attempted to blame him for the morning's collective bungling.

The reinforced Union line held at Seven Pines and maintained its position, preserving a tactical victory for McClellan. One of the most fateful shots of the war had been fired, however, wounding Joseph E. Johnston and elevating Robert E. Lee to field command.

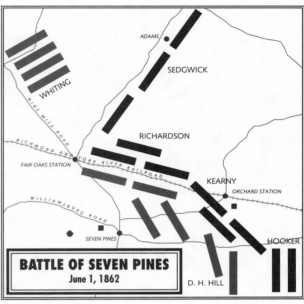

BATTLE OF SEVEN PINES
June 1, 1862

Joseph E. Johnston entered the battle of Seven Pines with the sword his father had carried in the American Revolution. Davis and Lee had ridden up just as Johnston was seriously wounded, and Davis knelt beside Johnston and asked if he could help. Johnston shook his head no, then remembered the sword. "I would not lose it for $10,000," he said. "Will not someone please go back and get it for me?" The sword was recovered.

Sgt. Charles A. Fuller of the Sixty-first New York watched a dead man who didn't realize that fact immediately. "Sanford Brooks, a stalwart man of my company," he wrote, "and from my town, was shot through the head. The bullet entered at the side and just behind the eyes. The blow did not fell him to the ground—he stood upright with his gun clenched in one hand, his sightless eyes bulged out of his head and he staggered about, bereft of reason."

Wounded Southerners were taken to Richmond for care and treatment (above left). The sight led many to evacuate the city, and the relocation of the capital was considered prudent. The Union line was strengthened at Seven Pines, but the high rate of casualties also unnerved McClellan.

The 4,749 Confederate wounded were taken by wagon directly to Richmond, where they were housed in hospitals, homes, churches, and public buildings and largely tended by local women.

To Mahone's right was Armistead, who found that the dense woods that had allowed him to surprise the Eighty-first Pennsylvania also brought confusion to his own men. The Fourteenth Virginia fired on the Fifty-third Virginia. Pickett, right of Armistead, fell behind and a gap developed between the two brigades, leaving Armistead's right flank and Pickett's left flank vulnerable to attack.

Union Col. J. H. Ward noticed this situation when he came into line along the railroad to the left of Richardson with one of Kearny's brigades. He charged Armistead's right flank, shouting "Fire, charge, and give them the bayonet." The Virginians were quickly routed.

The Confederate Commissioner ■ Gustavus Woodson Smith

Gustavus Woodson Smith, born in Georgetown, Kentucky, on December 1, 1821, graduated from West Point in 1842, won three brevets in Mexico, taught at West Point, and constructed coastal fortifications. After resigning his commission in 1854 to work as a civil engineer, he became the New York City street commissioner. Commissioned a senior Confederate major general from September 19, 1861, Smith led a wing of the Southern army on the peninsula and received command after Joseph E. Johnston was

wounded at Seven Pines on May 31, 1862. He served only hours, inspiring little confidence from his subordinates and making only a tentative attack at Fair Oaks on June 1. Falling ill, or suffering a nervous breakdown, Smith was soon replaced by Robert E. Lee. After brief service as acting head of the War Department, in November he resigned in protest after junior officers were appointed lieutenant general over him. Georgia Gov. Joseph E. Brown made Smith a major general of Georgia militia,

which he led first in the trenches around Atlanta in the summer of 1864 under Johnston again, and that fall in the works before Savannah under William Joseph Hardee. Smith surrendered in Macon, Georgia, on April 20, 1865. He managed an iron works in Tennessee, worked in insurance in Kentucky, and wrote about the Civil War. Smith retired to New York City where he died June 24, 1896. He is buried in New London, Connecticut.

Pickett, yet to be engaged, was startled to hear the rattle of battle on his left. The general rode out to survey the scene and located Armistead. They agreed to ask D. H. Hill for support, but when none was forthcoming they prudently withdrew.

Several hours earlier Longstreet had requested that Smith send Whiting in, but Smith had done nothing, which is what Longstreet now did for Hill. Hill took it upon himself to withdraw all his brigades. On the Williamsburg road to the east, Pryor and Wilcox, who had repulsed Hooker's attacks through the day, were surprised by the orders to disengage, but they complied, pursued by two of Hooker's brigades. At the railroad one of Ward's regiments charged and drove the Confederates there back to the Williamsburg road.

The confused two-day combat sputtered to a halt around 2 P.M. Excepting the recently concluded struggle at Shiloh, this had been the largest battle in America history, called Seven Pines for the Confederate victory of May 31 and Fair Oaks by the Federals, where they fared better the following day. The Confederates lost 980 killed with a total of 6,134 casualties. The Federal loss was 5,031, including 790 killed.

Johnston, Smith, Longstreet, D. H. Hill, et al. had failed to destroy McClellan's left wing through a combination of confused orders and poor leadership. Smith was unsuited for high command and resigned two days later, proving Longstreet correct.

George McClellan was appalled by what he saw on the battlefield of Seven Pines. "I am tired of the sickening sight of the battlefield, with its mangled corpses & poor suffering wounded! Victory has no charms for me when purchased at such cost."

D. H. Hill was equally repulsed, informing his wife: "I would to God it could be the last & our country saved. The dying and the dead, the rebel & the federal side by side. The groans of the wounded, & the lifeless corpse of the prostrate on the field, half covered with water."

Kearny at Seven Pines ■ Edmund C. Stedman

NATIONAL ARCHIVES

So that soldierly legend is still on its
    journey,—
That story of Kearny who knew not
    to yield!

'Twas the day when Jameson, fierce
    Berry, and Birney,
Against twenty thousand they rallied
    the field.
Where the red volleys poured, where
    the clamor rose highest,
Where the dead lay in clumps
    through the dwarf oak and pine,
Where the aim from the thicket was
    surest and nighest,—
No charge like Phil Kearny's along
    the whole line.

When the battle went ill, and the
    bravest were solemn,
Near the dark Seven Pines, where
    we still held our ground,
He rode down the length of the
    withering column,
And his heart at our war-cry leapt up
    with a bound;

He snuffed, like his charger, the wind
    of the powder,—
His sword waved us on and we
    answered the sign;
Loud our cheer as we rushed, but his
    laugh rang the louder.
"There's the devil's own fun, boys,
    along the whole line!"

How he strode his brown steed! How
    we saw his blade brighten
In the one hand still left,—and the
    reins in his teeth!
He laughed like a boy when the
    holidays heighten,
But a soldier's glance shot from his
    visor beneath.
Up came the reserves to the melay
    infernal,
Asking where to go in,—through
    the clearing or pine?

"O, anywhere! Forward! 'Tis all the
    same, Colonel:
You'll find lovely fighting along the
    whole line!"

Oh, evil the black shroud of night at
    Chantilly,
That hid him from sight of his brave
    men and tried!
Foul, foul sped the bullet that clipped
    the white lily,
The flower of our knighthood, the
    whole army's pride!
Yet we dream that he still,—in that
    shadowy region
Where the dead form their ranks at
    the wan drummer's sign,—
Rides on, as of old, down the length
    of his legion,
And the word still is "Forward!"
    along the whole line.

The large number of dead at Seven Pines were poorly buried. After rains "here and there a leg or hand or head could be seen protruding in all its ghastliness," a Federal observed.

McClellan, who barely left his bed until the firing had ceased, contributed little to the battle. One Federal bitterly noted that the commander was "received with as hearty cheers as if he had done the fighting. He did nothing." The action, however, made McClellan even more cautious than before. He ordered his troops to prepare extensive defenses while he initiated his second siege of the campaign.

The Confederates withdrew to their original positions during the night of June 1, the same day that Davis replaced the wounded Johnston. He decided to appoint his military adviser, Lee, to command.

A Tour of the Peninsula Campaign to Seven Pines

HAVING INCLUDED Fort Monroe with the *Virginia-Monitor* tour takes a large chunk out of the list of sites related to the Peninsula campaign. An ambitious local initiative, however, has preserved a chain of important sites that are actively being developed. They are along the Confederate Warwick River line that stopped McClellan's flanking move beyond Yorktown. Extensive earthworks remain from John Magruder's cleverly designed defenses. They once extended across the peninsula from the James River to Yorktown, which despite its emphasis on the famous Revolutionary War siege, has preserved a number of Confederate defensive fortifications and Federal siege works.

We then continue east to follow the Confederate retreat toward Richmond. Portions of Fort Magruder, where one of the earliest Civil War battles occurred, and other Williamsburg works remain, and heavy Confederate river defenses still exist at historic Jamestown. The remainder of the peninsula tour, which crosses the storied Chickahominy, is fairly short because little remains of the Seven Pines–Fair Oaks battlefield.

McClellan advanced from Fort Monroe on two routes. He sent two divisions by the Yorktown road to threaten Yorktown. Advancing parallel to these divisions, the Union commander dispatched two more divisions via the Hampton–Lee's Mill road, which passed through Warwick Court House and Lee's Mill toward Williamsburg. The twin-pronged advance was intended to flank the Confederates out of stoutly defended Yorktown.

The city of Newport News has issued a valuable tour brochure titled *Civil War Sites of Newport News, Virginia.* Unfortunately for our direction of travel, six of the eleven areas (three are part of the Hampton Roads–*Virginia-Monitor* tour) are on the left side of the highway, across the very busy Warwick Boulevard–U.S. 60. I suggest driving north from this spot and doubling back to visit the Skiffes Creek redoubt, Lee's Mill, the 1810 Warwick Courthouse, and Young's Mill in reverse order.

This is just the beginning of an ambitious, expensive, and long-term project by the city of Newport News and the Virginia War Museum to create a complex of Civil War sites. In 1994 the museum started acquiring property, particularly the three important Peninsula campaign sites at Lee's Mill, Lee Hall, and Endview. In 1996 it purchased a total of four hundred acres. Civil War Trails intepretive markers have been erected for the Peninsula campaign at Warwick Courthouse, Lee's Mill, Skiffes Redoubt, Lee's Hall, Endview, Gloucester Point, Redoubt No. 12, Fort Magruder, Bloody Ravine, New Kent Courthouse, and Seven Pines.

From the Mariners' Museum on Warwick Boulevard–U.S. 60, turn left. Just beyond Route 105–Fort Eustis Road turn left onto Enterprise Drive to Oakland Industrial park. Park in the second parking lot on the right (AAFES) and walk across the road into the tree line, where thirty acres containing extensive redoubts and trenches will be encountered.

Skiffes Creek Redoubt supported Lee's Mill and prevented Federal access to Skiffes Creek and Mulberry Island, which defended the James River. It is part of Magruder's second defensive line, which helped slow McClellan on the peninsula.

Return to Warwick Boulevard–U.S. 60 and turn right onto the highway to Lee's Mill, marked by a historical marker at a traffic light.

The actual site is to the right in the residential development and is accessible by a trail. Lee's Mill stands

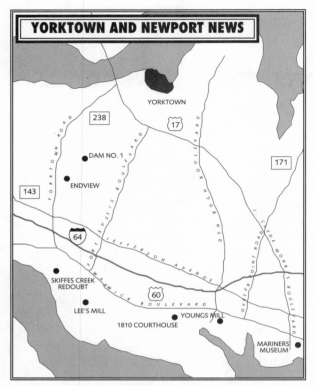

YORKTOWN AND NEWPORT NEWS

the peninsula to Yorktown. The Union offensive was halted until May 4, ending McClellan's plan to flank Yorktown. The Auger coffee-mill gun, a prototype machine gun, was first used here. Nearby was the Miles Curtis farm where Union observation balloons operated in April and May 1862.

Continue south and turn right onto Old Courthouse Way to two historic courthouses on the right.

The 1810 Warwick Courthouse (14421 Old Courthouse Way) served as headquarters of the Fourth Corps from April 6 until May 3. It was looted and the grounds used as Camp Winfield Scott. The gas observation balloon *Constitution* was deployed here. On the green is the local Confederate monument, erected in 1909 to honor the Warwick Beauregards. Adjacent is the "new" courthouse (1884).

Return to Warwick Boulevard–U.S. 60 and turn right to Young's Mill (1820) on the right.

This historic structure marks the western flank of Magruder's first defense line across the peninsula, which continued through Harwood's Mill to Ship's Point on the Poquoson River. The Confederates withdrew from this line on April 5 and occupied Lee's Mill six miles west. A large Confederate camp was here during 1861–62, and earthworks remain.

Continue south on Warwick Boulevard–U.S. 60 to Oyster Point Road and double back north on Warwick Boulevard–U.S. 60. Pass Skiffes Creek Redoubt and turn right onto Route 238–Yorktown Road to Lee Hall on the left.

The city of Newport News purchased this antebellum home and twelve acres for the establishment of the Peninsula Campaign Museum, which features historical exhibits and the Donald Tharpe Peninsula Campaign Gallery. Artifacts include part of a Federal observation balloon, a monogrammed tablecloth from the *Monitor,* and a wooden model of the *Virginia.*

where the old road crossed the Warwick River. It was a landmark on the Hampton road near the point where the Warwick empties into the James. On April 5, 1862, as part of Magruder's second line of defense, four companies and two batteries under Brig. Gen. Lafayette McLaws halted the tentative advance of two Union divisions and six batteries of the Fourth Corps. For 130 years two great redoubts, each thirty feet high, remained intact on a wooded bluff sixty feet above the Warwick River. After one of them was bulldozed in 1995, the resulting media attention led to the preservation of the other, near River Ridge Circle in the development.

On April 4 a division of Brig. Gen. Erasmus D. Keyes's Fourth Corps arrived here to find the Warwick River flooded from recent rains and impressive Confederate fortifications defending against a crossing. Keyes wrote that he had encountered a "torrent of rain" and "sheets of flame." John G. Barnard, chief engineer of the Army of the Potomac, called the work "the most massive fortification known to modern times." The strength of the position induced McClellan to halt his advance and besiege the Warwick line, which started here and extended across

Richard D. Lee built Lee Hall in the 1840s as the center of his seven-thousand-acre plantation. He was placed in charge of local civilian forces early in the war. Magruder arrived and established his headquarters here on April 5, 1862, and remained until Joseph E. Johnston took command in the field. Lee showed Magruder how the Warwick River could be easily defended by damming the stream and erecting works at the crossing points. A small work was erected on the front lawn. The war and his strong support for the Confederacy, however, ruined Lee financially, forcing him to sell Lee Hall in 1866. Confederate observation balloons were launched here and at Wynne's Mill to observe Federal movements.

From Lee Hall turn left onto Route 238–Yorktown Road. Just past the intersection with Route 143–Jefferson Avenue turn right to Endview (1720), currently being developed into a house museum.

Although this area will probably be dramatically changed by construction of a shopping complex (a two-story, million-square-foot mall), substantial historic properties have been preserved. The city of Newport News purchased three hundred acres for industrial and commercial development, but the War Memorial Museum plans to build a Civil War

Union troops occupied Warwick Courthouse, which stands near Confederate defenses on the Warwick River.

"campus" on thirty-two acres of Endview. An eighteen-thousand-square-foot museum, with exhibit space, classrooms, and a large theater, will focus on the Civil War. Trams are planned to take visitors past ten miles of pristine earthworks. Much of the land has never been farmed and is in excellent condition. It is estimated that 160 Confederates who died at hospitals here lie somewhere on the grounds. Living history programs are sponsored, including reenactments in replica earthworks behind Endview. Tours of the house are arranged by appointment (757-247-8523).

Endview, situated midway between the James and York Rivers and on one of two roads to Yorktown, witnessed a great deal of history. In 1781 three thousand Virginia militiamen on their way to Yorktown bivouacked here, and George Washington may have visited the house. American soldiers camped here during the War of 1812, as did Confederates during the Peninsula campaign. After they withdrew on May 5, McClellan briefly visited the house.

Endview was owned by Humphrey H. Curtis, who enlisted local men for the Warwick Beauregards, which fought on the peninsula. His wife, Maria, who helped nurse members of the Mecklenberg Grays, was given a silver cup and an honorary commission in the Thirty-second Virginia for her service.

Turn left onto Route 238–Yorktown Road a short distance, then turn left onto Route East 143–Jefferson Avenue to the main entrance (Constitution Way) into Newport News Park, which is near the intersection with Route 105–Fort Eustis Road. At 8,065 acres, this is considered the largest municipal park in the world.

Obtain a park map at the welcome station and continue into the park. Turn right into the interpretive center, which features displays of artillery projectiles and other artifacts recovered from the nearby battlefield and photographs of the dam. Outside is a well-appointed 10-pounder James rifle and limber.

Across the road from the interpretive center is the Warwick River, crossed by a long footbridge near the site of submerged Dam No. 1. The site is marked on this side by a bronze marker set on concrete and a large map board with a painting of the battle that occurred here.

On April 16, 1862, McClellan's troops successfully assaulted the Confederate works on the other side by fording and racing across the dam, but the Federals failed to reinforce the effort and a Confederate counterattack drove them back. Union drummer boy Julian Scott of Vermont won the first Medal of Honor here. Five and a half miles of well-preserved continuous earthworks are maintained on the opposite bank, weaving through campgrounds and across park roads. The .7-mile Twin Forts Trail leads to well-preserved works and descriptive signs, while Wynn's Mill Historical Trail, 1.1 miles long, ends at some of the largest Confederate fortifications in Virginia. The water-powered gristmill no longer exists. Encampments and reenactments are held regularly.

To the west on Route 105–Fort Eustis Road is Fort Eustis, headquarters of the U.S. Army Transportation Center. The Transportation Museum explores that theme with wagons, trucks, armored vehicles, air-cushioned vehicles, cybernetic walking machines, flying jeeps, a giant "Flying Crane" helicopter, models, and dioramas. Part of a transportation diorama and a portion of an exhibit on rail transportation relate to the Civil War. On Mulberry Island in the James River is Fort Crafford, a pentagonal earthwork enclosing eight acres that anchored the extreme right flank of the Warwick River line. The walls are eight to twenty feet high. The fort was armed with eight heavy cannon and eight smaller guns, including 8- and 10-inch Columbiads, 7-inch guns, 32- and 42-pounder carronades, and field guns, with additional support provided by the ships of the Confederate James River Squadron. On the opposite shore, at Hardy's Bluff, was another fort. During the war Fort Crafford had three magazines, two bombproofs, a number of buildings, and supporting earthworks. Started in February 1862, it was completed by the first week in April and was connected with Lee Hall on the mainland by telegraph. It is well preserved but isolated at a remote location on the base. Check with the museum to see if it is open.

Return to the entrance of the interpretive center and turn left. Turn left to follow the sign to Fort Eustis Boulevard. (If this route is blocked, return to the main entrance, turn left briefly on Route 143–Jefferson and then left onto Route 105–East Fort Eustis Boulevard.) Turn left to get on U.S. 17 North, then turn right onto Colonial Parkway at the brown sign for Yorktown Battlefield. Bear right at the first intersection. Con-

Miles of substantial earthworks are protected in Newport News Park. These are near Dam No. 1, where Union troops briefly pierced the Warwick Line.

tinue to the first stop sign and the Yorktown visitors center is straight ahead, on the right.

The center has an orientation film, a museum interpreting the Revolutionary War siege, and the realistically recreated gun deck of a British warship. A rooftop overlook provides a good view of impressive British earthworks around the visitors center. While still at war with Great Britain in 1781, George Washington ordered the British defenses at Yorktown destroyed so they could not be used against the French, who remained in Yorktown. During the 1930s many of the earthworks were reconstructed by the National Park Service to their Revolutionary War configurations. A self-guided driving and walking tour leads to every significant place on the battlefield, ending at the site of the British surrender, which occurred on October 19, 1781. Living history camps are hosted during the summer.

Confederates fortified this position for the same reasons that led Lord Charles Cornwallis to hole up here in 1781. The wide York River narrows at Gloucester Point, opposite Yorktown, to only half a mile. Since the James River was controlled by the Confederates, only a few vital points, such as Jamestown, had been fortified, but Federal occupation of Fort Monroe left the York River in Union hands. For the Confederates to hold any position on the peninsula, Federal access to the upper reaches of the York River had to be denied at Yorktown. Construction of earthworks started in the spring of 1861. Work continued into the fall under Magruder, who extended them across the York River to Gloucester Point and west along the Warwick River to the James River. By late October Magruder had a large battery at Yorktown mounting six to eight 32-pounders and 64-pounders, and Gloucester Point was defended by twelve such cannon. These batteries, constructed on high ground to cover all river and land approaches, were surrounded by extensive infantry works. Furthermore, thirteen ships were sunk in the channel between Yorktown and Gloucester Point to obstruct Union access.

Other batteries contained 8-inch Columbiads, 9- and 10-inch Dahlgren rifles, and 42-pounder carronades. All told, the works mounted ninety-four guns facing the York River or sweeping the land approaches. The retreating Confederates did a poor job bursting or otherwise damaging their cannon, leaving fifty-three to be captured in good shape. McClellan's engineers estimated it would require two thousand men thirty days to level the earthworks, which measured seven to twenty feet high, twenty feet thick, with exterior ditches seven to fifteen feet deep.

In 1864 Benjamin Butler gathered forty thousand troops here for his new command, the Army of the James. They invaded the south bank of the James River at Bermuda Hundred, where P. G. T. Beauregard bottled them up. During the siege of

This 10-pounder Parrott rifle and limber are preserved on the Federal side of Dam No. 1.

Petersburg several months later, Ulysses S. Grant ordered Yorktown abandoned.

The historians at Yorktown emphasize that while they preserve Civil War fortifications, their primary mission is preserving and interpreting the American Revolutionary War siege. Many of the Civil War works are in heavily wooded areas with no established trail system.

Recognizing the interest in Yorktown's Civil War history, the park has recently printed two brochures. One describes the park's Civil War significance, and the other features a driving tour of surviving Civil War sites. The guide is titled *Yorktown: A Civil War Auto Tour Companion,* which supplements the NPS tour of Revolutionary Yorktown. Secure a copy of both tours and an auto tour tape, if you desire. Rangers also provide occasional guided tours of Civil War sites. Each Memorial Day weekend Confederate and Union encampments, tactical demonstrations, and field hospitals are recreated, and in March tours of Williamsburg's Civil War earthworks are conducted.

The Hornwork, on the left after leaving the visitors center, was a British work greatly enlarged by the Confederates. The Grand French Battery lay between the Confederate and Federal lines during the 1862 siege. To the east and west, extensive earthworks from the numerous Federal heavy siege batteries survive in the woods. Several hundred yards to the south was the line of Confederate works that extended to the James River.

Yorktown National Cemetery (established 1863, at the corner of Routes 634 and 637) contains the graves of Union soldiers who died here or at Williamsburg, West Point, Warwick Court House, and White House and Cumberland Landings, a total of twenty-eight sites within a radius of fifty miles. Of 2,183 burials, 1,596 are marked but only 747 are identified. Ten Confederates are also buried here, and several hundred yards to the east is a small granite stone that marks a Confederate cemetery containing an unknown number of graves.

Redoubts Nos. 9 and 10 mark a no man's land between the Confederate and Federal lines, occupied only by scattered Union rifle pits. Three batteries of siege guns were located behind a double line of fortifications to the east. Opposite Redoubts Nos. 11 and 10 was the Federal line, with pickets and sharpshooters stationed in the woods during the siege. Some earthworks on Gosley Road are marked as Confederate.

One park road crosses Wormley Creek, which the Federals used to transport their huge siege guns, which were then manhandled through the swamps. The tour route then descends a ravine along a branch of Wormley Pond. Union soldiers used the cover of these depressions to construct four large siege batteries at the heads of the ravines. A network of roads and bridges was constructed around the pond to transport the big Union guns and their ammunition. Confederate rifle pits dug on a bluff overlooking this area had been abandoned.

The Moore house, which lay between two rows of batteries, was a Federal signal station severely damaged during the siege by soldiers who used all the woodwork for firewood. Cannonball holes have been patched.

Walking from the parking lot at the Surrender Field to the pavilion, Union Battery No. 6, a field-work erected for mortars, is on the right. To the left are earthworks that protected soldiers moving to and from the battery. From the pavilion additional Federal earthworks can be seen across the field, just inside the tree line.

Gen. Andrew Porter camped at the site of Lafayette's headquarters. Washington's First Parallel marks the most advanced battery of McClellan's Third Corps.

The impressive Yorktown Victory Monument on the bluffs overlooking the river is the third to occupy the site. The first, consisting of a stone cairn and four poplar trees, was replaced in 1860 by a thirteen-foot-high white marble shaft on a granite base, dedicated by the Twenty-first Virginia Militia Regiment. By the end of the occupation, Federal troops had destroyed it for souvenirs. Confederate earthworks were leveled in 1881 for construction of the present monument.

Grace Episcopal Church (1697) was used by Cornwallis as a powder magazine. During the Civil War its belfry served as a lookout post and the interior as a hospital. The bell, inscribed "Yorktown, Virginia, 1725," was broken when the British burned Yorktown during the War of 1812. Union troops removed the bell, but it was later found in Philadelphia, recast, and returned in 1889. The courthouse (original 1818) across the square was used as a Fed-

The Yorktown Victory Monument replaces one that was hacked to pieces by Union soldiers for souvenirs.

eral powder magazine and arsenal. When it blew up in December 1863, the Swan Hotel (original 1719, rebuilt in 1934), across the street and used by the Federals, was severely damaged. Much of the town was destroyed.

The Customs House (1721), Magruder's headquarters, remains on Main Street and is identified by a marker. Reenactments are held at the Nelson house, a Confederate field hospital. The Thomas Sessions house (1692) was the headquarters of Federal Gen. T. S. Negley of McClellan's staff. The Somerwell house was a Civil War hotel. At the base of the bluff on Water Street is Cornwallis's Cave, a British powder magazine, carved out of the marl, where Cornwallis held staff meetings. Confederates also made use of it.

Some earthworks remain from both the Revolutionary and Civil Wars at Gloucester Point. Cross the high bridge over the York River on Route 17, then turn left and park on the left. The Virginia Institute of

Marine Science Aquarium is across the highway. This small four-acre preserve is Tindall's Point Park (Gloucester County Parks and Recreation, P.O. Box 157, Gloucester, VA 23061, 804-693-2355). The half-mile-long Tindall's Point Trail leads to a scenic overlook of the York River and a display station with information concerning the fortifications erected here. The first colonial works were constructed in 1667. The British arrived in October 1781, the Confederates in 1861, and the Federals the following year.

Farther east on Route 17 is Gloucester Courthouse (1766). The adjacent jail (1873) replaces one burned by the Federals. Debtors Prison (1810), used as a Civil War arsenal, now houses the Gloucester Historical Commission. A skirmish was fought here on January 29, 1864. On the green is an obelisk on a high stone base dedicated in 1889 to 132 local Confederate veterans, and a monument at Abington Episcopal Church (1937) salutes veterans of the Abington District.

From Gloucester, three miles east on Virginia Route 14 is Ware Episcopal Church (early seventeenth century). During the Peninsula campaign, Union and Confederate troops camped around the church. In the cemetery is the grave of Confederate Gen. William B. Taliaferro, who served unhappily under Stonewall Jackson and fought in Georgia and the Carolinas.

Fifteen miles farther on Virginia 14 to Matthews and a right on Route 614 leads to Christ Episcopal Church, where Sally R. Tompkins is buried. She founded a private hospital for soldiers in Richmond that maintained one of the lowest mortality rates in the South. When the Confederate government took control of all hospitals, President Davis appointed Tompkins as a captain and allowed her facility to continue operation. She was the only woman with an officer's commission in the Southern army.

The Jamestown-Yorktown Foundation, a separate entity from the federally sponsored historical parks at the two sites, operates the Yorktown Victory Center, which celebrates the Revolutionary War siege, and the Jamestown Settlement, a reconstruction of the first English settlement in America in 1607. A combo ticket can be purchased for entry to both attractions.

From the stop sign at the end of the visitors center entrance road, the historic community of Yorktown is located down the road to the right. We go straight, and at the sign for Colonial Parkway–Williamsburg–Jamestown go straight onto it. Turn left into the parking area at Jones Mill Pond to read the historical marker and examine the area.

On the bluff across the pond and overlooking it is one of fourteen redoubts, this one fifty yards square, in the Confederate defense system known as the Williamsburg line. Although it is labeled Redoubt No. 14, it is west of Redoubt No. 12 and Redoubt No. 13 and was positioned to defend a prominent Civil War battlefield feature, a dam that spanned Jones Mill Pond. This roadway now covers the dam. It was here that Union Gen. Winfield S. Hancock crossed unopposed to seize Redoubt No. 11, a short distance to the west. The first Federals across Cub Dam Creek were cavalry led by Lt. George Armstrong Custer.

Continue toward Williamsburg on Colonial Parkway, then exit to the right at Parkway Drive and turn left onto Parkway. Turn right onto Second Street, then left onto U.S. 60 East–Page Street. At the traffic signal turn left onto U.S. 60 East–York Street. To the right will appear Quarterpath Park, then Fort Magruder Inn.

The Confederate fallback position called the Williamsburg Line extended across the peninsula just east of Williamsburg from Queens Creek on the York River to College Creek on the James. Fort Magruder was at the center of the line, where the roads from Yorktown and Lee's Mill converged. Johnston retreated via those two roads, uniting the army at this point, where Fort Magruder protected the crossroads. Fighting occurred here on May 4–6, with the primary combat on May 5. Little remembered today, the battle caused thirty-nine hundred casualties.

The Williamsburg line consisted of fourteen redoubts, actually redans of various sizes and shapes. At Fort Magruder Inn and Conference Center is Redoubt No. 3, not Fort Magruder as is implied. Most of the earthwork was destroyed by construction of the facility, leaving only one sixty-yard-long wall and ditch surrounded by the hotel. Several historical markers are at the preserved site and a painting, map, text, and artifacts in the lobby interpret the battle of Williamsburg.

This may not be Fort Magruder, but artillery here and at Redoubts Nos. 4 and 5 did effective work against Federal soldiers struggling through an abatis. Combat in this area occurred on May 4 and May 5 in the present area of James York Terrace. A roadside marker on U.S. 60 West indicates the location of Redoubt No. 4, but it and Redoubt No. 5 have been destroyed.

Fort Magruder, or Redoubt No. 6, the focus of the battle on May 5, has only about 160 yards of walls remaining. They are enclosed in a UDC-maintained park at the intersection of Queens Creek Road and Penniman Road, two miles east of Williamsburg. The works—nine feet high, twenty feet wide at the base, and twelve feet wide at the top—are heavily wooded and choked with undergrowth. A large stone monument commemorating the one-hundredth anniversary of the battle was dedicated in 1962.

The most intense combat at Williamsburg occurred in that area, largely between Confederate Col. George B. Anderson and Union Gens. Joseph Hooker and Philip Kearny. It is bordered by U.S. 60 East, Route 199 South, and Quarterpath Road. The property, privately owned and heavily wooded, offers little access and no markers. The center of the heaviest fighting on May 5 took place in a large ravine, eighty yards wide, twenty feet deep, and a half-mile long, between U.S. 60 East and Tutters Neck Pond. The area was known as the "Bloody Ravine."

To the north, Redoubt No. 7, on Wilkins Drive, has been destroyed, and Redoubt No. 8 exists on private property near Interstate 64. Both were small, chevron-shaped redans oriented to face east. Federal and Confederate cavalry inflicted heavy casualties on each other there on May 4. Redoubt No. 9, at Queens Creek Road and Interstate 64, has been destroyed, and a tiny eroded portion of Redoubt No. 10 survives on private property at Queens Creek Road and Springfield Drive. Confederates in Redoubts No. 9 and No. 10 helped stop Hancock's assault on May 5, and Jubal Early was taken to No. 10 after being wounded.

Redoubt No. 11, a square with sixty-yard-long sides, survives on wooded private property near Allendale Drive and Colonial Parkway. Hancock seized this fortification without opposition and decimated Early's attempt to dislodge him. The combat between Hancock and Early took place along Queens Creek Road between Penniman Road and Colonial Parkway.

Redoubt Nos. 12 and 13, which anchored the extreme left of the Confederate line near the York River, survive in New Quarterpath Park. Like the others, Redoubt No. 12 is eroded and covered with woods and brush. It is behind a baseball park on Lakeshead Drive. Redoubt No. 13, a half-mile south, guarded a road over Cub Dam Creek, which flows into Queens Creek and then into the York. It is pre-

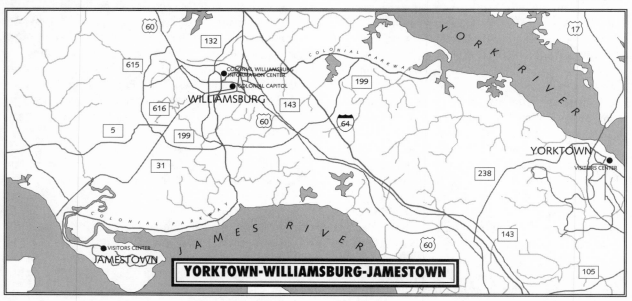

YORKTOWN-WILLIAMSBURG-JAMESTOWN

served in good condition, with a ditch eight feet deep and twenty-five feet wide and walls seven feet high, but the fort is inaccessible.

To the south of Fort Magruder Inn and Conference Center are two redoubts on the Confederate right. Redoubt No. 1, a rectangle roughly eighty yards to a side, exists a mile south of U.S. 60 at Tutters Neck Pond on Quarterpath Road, but it is overgrown and inaccessible. On May 5 Confederate infantry there fended off Union cavalry under George Stoneman and Philip St. George Cooke.

The eroded remains of Redoubt No. 2 are also inaccessible, but a seven-foot bronze marker erected in Quarterpath Park, on Quarterpath Road, half a mile south off U.S. 60, describes the battle and contains a detailed map of the Williamsburg fortifications. Anderson's division organized a counterattack from this area on May 5.

At the extreme western end of the Confederate line on the James River were earthworks and a wharf. They are now occupied by the Busch developments of Kingsmill on the James and Kingsmill Golf Club, but several historical features have been preserved.

Tours of surviving earthworks are offered yearly by the Williamsburg Civil War Round Table.

On U.S. 60 at the southeastern outskirts of Williamsburg is the Whitaker house, headquarters of Gen. W. F. Smith during the battle of Williamsburg.

A brick office at the Cock-Garrett house (1812, east end of Nicholas Street) was used by Dr. Robert Garrett to treat both Confederate and Federal wounded after the battle. Wounded soldiers were tended on the lawn, in college buildings, the Baptist church, and the courthouse. The Brafferton (1723), used to school Indians, was stripped of interior woodwork by Union soldiers who used it for firewood. The Bowden-Armistead house (1858, Duke of Gloucester Street) was owned by Lemeul J. Bowden, one of the town's few Union sympathizers (called "Virginia Yankees"). The Palmer house (then the W. W. Vest house, end of Duke of Gloucester Street) was temporary headquarters for Magruder and then Johnston during the battle, and for their opponent McClellan and other Federals over the next three years. Before the battle Early camped at the Wren Building (now an administration building), and Confederate reserves lounged

on the campus of the College of William and Mary. Benjamin Ewell, who served as president of the college, helped build the peninsula defenses as a Confederate engineer. The school suspended classes one month after the war started when 90 percent of its students joined the Confederate army. A minor skirmish occurred on September 9, 1862, when Confederates raided the community, charging down Duke of Gloucester Street and capturing thirty-three Federals camping at the school. Other Union troops were forced into the safety of Fort Magruder. Hours later the Wren Building, used as a Union headquarters and quarters, burned to the ground, perhaps in retaliation. It was rebuilt in 1900 for sixty-four thousand dollars. Confederate Capt. John Lea was wounded at Williamsburg and cared for in Basset Hall–Durfey house on Francis Street. Lea fell in love with and married Margaret Durfey. The best man at their wedding was Union Capt. George Armstrong Custer, a West Point classmate of the groom.

One of the oldest original structures in Williamsburg is the Magazine (1715), which in colonial times contained several thousand muskets, ammunition, swords, pikes, tents, and all the equipment necessary to equip an army. Confederates used it to store gunpowder. Williamsburg remained under Federal occupation and martial law until the end of the war.

A tall obelisk in Bicentennial Park in Williamsburg, unveiled May 5, 1908, honors local Confederate veterans. An obelisk in Cedar Grove Cemetery, dedicated May 5, 1935, memorializes Confederate dead, including 250 buried in a mass grave after the battle of Williamsburg. Southern dead are also memorialized by a small obelisk (1887) in the Bruton Parish Churchyard, where 50 Confederate casualties lie.

Colonial Williamsburg consists of 173 acres and five hundred buildings; eighty-eight of these are original eighteenth-century structures. Situated between Jamestown and Yorktown, which are connected by the Colonial Parkway, this area is known as Virginia's Historic Triangle.

To reach Jamestown you may retrace your route and get on Colonial National Parkway, which takes a looping route to Jamestown with no traffic snarls. A more direct route is to continue east on U.S. 60 toward Newport News and turn right onto Route 199, then turn left onto Route 31–Jamestown Road. Jamestown Festival Park appears to the right, and past it is the Jamestown portion of Colonial National Historical Park. At the end of Route 31 is the Jamestown-Scotland Wharf Ferry.

The palisaded fort, village, and full-scale reproductions of the three ships on which John Smith and company sailed to America, plus a recreated Powhatan Indian village, have been placed immediately outside the historic site at Jamestown Settlement. Seventeenth-century life is recreated daily in the park, which also houses numerous indoor galleries of historic exhibits and a twenty-minute orientation film.

At Jamestown, the national park, walk through the visitors center, which has a film and historical exhibits, and follow the path to the beautiful church ruins, the statue of Pocahontas, and the monument to John Smith. Prominent are the earthworks of a substantial Confederate fort, constructed here because the island projects far into the James. Confederate guns here controlled a long stretch of the river. The latest archaeological information suggests that the original Jamestown fort lies beneath an extensive Confederate fortification erected in 1861 and 1862 on the James River. The guns and armor for the *Virginia* were tested on the island by Catesby ap Roger Jones, who fired the guns at various compositions and thicknesses of iron plate and wood backing.

There are two other Confederate forts on the island that may be seen on a three- to five-mile loop road around James Island, but there is little to be seen on the long and featureless drive save for marsh. Other Southern works remain along the river, including one at Windmill Point, an observation point.

The ferry connects Jamestown with the mainland across the James River. A trip across leads to Bacon's Castle (1665), the largest and oldest brick house in English America, built in the shape of a cross. Famed for its use by Nathaniel Bacon during his rebellion against colonial rule, it is also the scene of a moving Civil War love story. While noted Georgia poet Sidney Lanier was stationed around Fort Boykin, he met lovely Ginna Hankins, daughter of the owner of Bacon Castle. They fell in love, took long rides across the beautiful countryside and romantic walks through the extensive gardens, recited poetry to each other, and Sidney played his flute. Lanier was later captured on a blockade-runner and contracted tuberculosis at Point Lookout Prison. At war's end he asked Ginna to marry

Jamestown Island has more surviving Civil War fortifications than structures associated with the first English settlement in America.

him, but her mother had died the day Lee surrendered and she felt obligated to care for her father and six younger siblings. Although Lanier married someone else, he and Ginna corresponded for the rest of their lives. There is reported to be a Civil War graveyard on the grounds. The house is open daily.

IF YOU made the trip to Jamestown, return the same way and follow the directional signs to U.S. 60 West or Interstate 64 West, both heading to Richmond. Assuming you are leaving Fort Magruder for the rest of the peninsula tour, you have three routes, depending upon your dedication to tracing history. I will explain the options and leave it to your discretion. U.S. 60 goes straight to Richmond but much of the route is not historic until Bottom's Bridge near Seven Pines. Interstate 64 is crowded but direct and definitely the fastest route. We will take Interstate 64 to exit onto Route 30 for Barhamsville, although you can stay on the interstate until Route 249–U.S. 60. If you take that easy route, from the exit turn left onto Route 249, then right onto U.S. 60 to cross the Chickahominy at Bottom's Bridge to reach Seven Pines. We will join you shortly.

Leaving Fort Magruder, turn left onto U.S. 60 West. Signs will direct you to U.S. 60 West or Interstate 64 West. At the split in Williamsburg you can choose to turn left to Colonial Williamsburg or go straight to Interstate 64 West.

Johnston marched along U.S. 60, the old Williamsburg stage road, through New Kent Court House and Baltimore Crossroads toward Richmond on May 4–6, with McClellan following on May 6–10, with his 100,000 men, 3,600 wagons, 700 ambulances, 300 artillery pieces, a herd of 2,500 cattle, and 25,000 horses and mules. McClellan needed 500 tons of food and forage daily to subsist his great army, a task difficult to accomplish over these primitive roads that turned into liquid mud in the spring rains. Considerable effort was spent hauling wagons, guns, and animals out of the swamps. The troops, on their first campaign march, were exhausted and miserable.

Exit Interstate 64 onto Route 30. We pass through Barhamsville but continue straight on Route 249 when Route 30–Route 33 goes right to Elthams and across the Pamunkey River to West Point, which is where the Pamunkey and Mattaponi Rivers meet to form the York River.

McClellan's original plan was to land his enormous army one peninsula to the north, at Urbanna on the Rappahannock River, and march across it to West Point on the Pamunkey River. Opposite West Point was Eltham's Landing. McClellan had kept Franklin's corps on transports during the siege at Yorktown, hoping to race it upriver to Eltham's when Johnston retreated and cut off the Confederate army from Richmond. One of Franklin's divisions landed on a four-hundred-foot-long floating dock, protected by five gunboats, and advanced toward the Williamsburg road at Barhamsville, five miles distant.

Federals occupied West Point in 1862 and destroyed Glass Island Shipyard then and in 1863.

Johnston was vulnerable, his men still marching past Eltham's toward Richmond. Two divisions were on the Williamsburg stage road, heading to Bottom's Bridge on the Chickahominy, where he intended to make a stand, and another division was marching toward Long Bridge. When the Federals advanced, Johnston unleashed Hood's men, whose fierce attack drove the Federals back to the cover of the gunboats. McClellan quickly reinforced Eltham's Landing and established supply bases farther upstream at White House Landing—where the Richmond and York River Railroad originated and continued twenty-three miles to Richmond—and at Cumberland Landing.

Urbanna was shelled by Union gunboats during the war, and Confederates were quartered in the Middlesex County Courthouse (1849). Of historic interest is a tobacco warehouse dating to 1680, a small brick structure now used as a library, and a former customs house (1680) across the street.

Continue on Route 249 to New Kent Courthouse, which is between Eltham's Landing–West Point and White House Landing.

On May 6, 1862, the part of Johnston's army commanded by Longstreet passed through here from Williamsburg on the present route of U.S. 60, bound for Bottom's Bridge. The tiny hilltop courthouse (1906, the original 1654 structure was destroyed during the Civil War) features a Confederate monument, an obelisk erected in 1934. Across the street is an ancient tavern that hosted McClellan's headquarters several days after Johnston passed through. Union cavalry commanded by Philip Sheridan met Judson Kilpatrick here on March 4, 1864. Skirmishes occurred on May 9 and June 30, 1862, and on February 6, June 12, 21, and 30, 1864, during Grant's Overland campaign. From here to Bottom's Bridge, Route 33, the main road to Williamsburg, was called the New Kent road, which Johnston traveled in May 1862. The New Kent Historical Society Museum in the old New Kent County Jail (1909) highlights local history, including the Civil War. It is open Mondays from 8:30 until noon.

The site of White House Landing is on the Pamunkey River, reached by turning right just after New Kent Courthouse at Cary's Corner onto Route 608 and then right on Route 614–White House Road to the railroad (now the Southern Railroad), but absolutely nothing remains to be seen and the site is posted No Trespassing.

George Washington courted the widow Martha Dandridge Custis in the original White House. It burned before the Civil War and a six-room, two-story house was constructed on its foundation. The property was left by Washington's adopted son, George Washington Parke Custis, to his daughter, Mary Custis Lee, Robert E. Lee's wife. She deeded the property to the Lees' second son, William Henry Fitzhugh "Rooney" Lee, who moved here in 1859 with his wife, Charlotte Wickham. After Mary Lee was evicted by the Federal occupation of Arlington, the home of the Lees across the Potomac River from Washington, she sought refuge at White House in 1861. Mary and her daughter-in-law lived there until the Union Army of the Potomac arrived on May 11, 1862. The women were forced to move again, leaving a note on the door: "Northern soldiers who profess to reverence Washington, forbear to desecrate the home of his married life, the property of his wife, now owned by her descendant." An addition to the note was soon added: "Lady, a Northern officer has protected your property in sight of the enemy." Possessions left behind were stored by Union Capt. T. H. Patterson aboard the Union gunboat *Charcora*. All the trees on the grounds of White House were cut to clear fields of fire in case of Confederate attack. On June 5 the Sisters of Charity arrived to establish a hospital and cared for sixty patients.

White House was vital to McClellan's Peninsula campaign. It was an excellent landing on the Pamunkey River, navigable from the York River, and the Richmond and York River Railroad originated there. More than four hundred ships were unloaded, their cargo including twenty-five hundred head of cattle, which was driven along with the army. Also delivered were a number of locomotives and dozens of cars used to transfer supplies to the army near Richmond. McClellan ordered the property protected, but at 3 P.M. on June 28, as White House Landing was being abandoned, a member of the Ninety-third New York torched the house, which burned along with barges and mountains of supplies. It is said that the hulls of abandoned Federal transports are still visible when the river is low.

When Lee invaded Maryland and Pennsylvania in the summer of 1863, the U.S. War Department ordered Maj. Gen. John A. Dix to threaten Richmond from the south with eighteen thousand men. It was hoped that he could prevent Confederate troops in Richmond from joining Lee. From White House Landing he dispatched raiding parties that destroyed railroad bridges and track and captured prisoners, including Rooney Lee, recuperating from a wound. He was imprisoned in Fort Monroe.

Rooney Lee, a widower by war's end, built a small home here and farmed before marrying Mary Tabb Tolling in 1867. He inherited the Ravensworth estate in Fairfax from his mother and spent the rest of his life there, serving in Congress and the Virginia state legislature.

Several miles upstream on the Pamunkey is Garlick's Landing, now a boat landing at the end of a dirt road off Route 607–Steel Trap Road. It supplied Fitz John Porter's corps when two regiments of Virginia cavalry appeared at 6 P.M. on June 13 during Stuart's ride around McClellan. The horsemen burned two schooners and a loaded wagon train and captured three hundred horses and mules.

If you have seen enough of nothing here, return on 614 and turn right onto 608, then turn left onto 606 to see more of nothing at Tunstall (formerly Tunstall's Station), following the line of the Richmond and York River Railroad.

On June 13, 1862, Jeb Stuart, on his famous ride around McClellan, surprised and was surprised by a Federal train running back to White House Landing. His men fired on it with carbines but were unable to stop it. Continue on 606 and turn right onto 612 to regain Route 249.

You doubtless skipped this side trip to White House. If you stayed on Route 249, you passed through Talleysville, known as Baltimore's Crossroads when Stuart rested his command here on June 13, before continuing to the Chickahominy River.

Three miles east of Talleysville on 606 is Saint Peters Church (1701–3), site of George Washington's marriage to Martha Dandridge Custis on January 6, 1759. Names of Federal soldiers and their units are carved into the brick. Legend claims that Lee attended church here after the Civil War, presumably while visiting his son.

Return to Route 249 and turn right to pass through Quinton, where the side tour on Route 612 returns to the main tour. Pass under Interstate 64 to intersect U.S. 60. Turn right onto it to Bottom's Bridge over the Chickahominy.

Johnston briefly considered establishing a defensive line between the Chickahominy and Pamunkey Rivers but instead retreated behind the Chickahominy and gave up that last natural defensive line to retire even closer to Richmond.

McClellan crossed the Chickahominy here on the Williamsburg stage road–New Kent road, the primary route between the Chickahominy and Pamunkey Rivers, on May 23, 1862, just days behind Johnston. Half a mile south is Sloane's Bridge, where Stuart crossed on June 14, 1862, to end his sweep around McClellan. On June 13–14, 1864, Grant crossed his Ninth and Sixth Corps there as he marched to the James River to invest Petersburg. Five miles southeast of Bottom's Bridge and one mile south, on Route 106, is Long Bridge, where Longstreet crossed in May 1862 on pontoon bridges, and Grant's Second and Fifth Corps passed in June 1864 to the James River.

Turn right into Seven Pines National Cemetery.

U.S. 60–Route 33 was traveled numerous times by Confederate and Union armies as they attacked, retreated, and maneuvered for possession of Richmond, the Confederacy's capital city. Johnston's army marched east in the spring of 1862 to challenge McClellan on the peninsula. A month later Johnston retreated along this road with McClellan in pursuit. By late May, McClellan had established a defensive line across the road when D. H. Hill and Longstreet attacked along it to start the two-day battle of Seven Pines here and at Fair Oaks, a short distance to the right and reached from Richmond on the Nine Mile Road.

A month later, while Lee attacked to the east at Mechanicsville and Gaines's Mill, Magruder advanced down U.S. 60 to Savage's Station, on the railroad about two miles east of Seven Pines, to assault the strongly held Union rear guard. After repulsing the attack, the Army of the Potomac retreated along this route toward White Oak Swamp, pursued a day later by Stonewall Jackson. Farther to the east is Grapevine Bridge on the Chickahominy, where Heintzelman crossed the dangerously flooded river to save the Union army at Seven Pines.

McClellan's headquarters were in the Trent house on Grapevine Road to the north. He intended to capture Old Tavern and force a decisive battle on the Williamsburg road, but typically moved too slowly.

Johnston attacked McClellan's left wing, isolated south of the Chickahominy, along three parallel roads. Closest to the river was Whiting (Longstreet's assignment, although he wound up on the Williamsburg road), who was to take the Nine Mile Road (Route 33) out of Richmond to Old Tavern (today's Highland Springs), where the New Bridge road intercepted from the north, to strike the railroad at Fair Oaks. This route was frequently used during the spring and summer of 1862 by both armies. On the night of May 30, 1862, on the Nine Mile Road, Davis informed Lee that he would succeed Johnston as the next Confederate commander. In the center, D. H. Hill and one of Longstreet's divisions attacked along the Williamsburg stage road (U.S. 60) to Seven Pines. A third assault, by Huger on the Charles City road from the south, miscarried. The objective was to split the Union army and isolate it from the railroad supply line at Fair Oaks.

When the Civil War started, Federal dead were buried on the battlefield, at hospital sites, near private homes and churches, and along the road. To deal with mounting casualties, on July 17, 1862, Lincoln signed into law an act creating fourteen military cemeteries "for the soldiers who shall die in the service of the country." At the end of the war recovery teams labored five years to recover the remains of more than 250,000 Federal soldiers, and fifty additional cemeteries were authorized.

There are six burial grounds in the Richmond National Cemetery complex, three involving the Peninsula–Seven Days' battles and three from Grant's 1864 campaign. All were established by an act of Congress on April 13, 1866, to take "immediate measures to preserve from desecration" and to be "kept sacred forever." Seven Pines National Cemetery contains the graves of 1,407 Union dead. Measuring two acres, it was established on June 27, 1866, for casualties exhumed from a four-mile area, principally the battlefields of Seven Pines, Fair Oaks, and Savage Station. A cast-iron plaque contains the text of Lincoln's Gettysburg Address, and relevant facts concerning the cemetery are engraved on a cast-iron seacoast mortar.

The parking area at the national cemetery is tiny, and exiting it can be difficult at certain times. Explore the cemetery and continue toward Richmond. Note the historical marker to the right and turn left into the Sandston Library where a Civil War Trails marker describes the initial Confederate attack at Seven Pines on May 31.

Near here was the left flank of McClellan's initial defensive line, which stretched across the Chickahominy River to Mechanicsville. The Federal position was split by the river and Johnston determined to destroy McClellan's weaker left before it could be reinforced from across the swampy stream. D. H. Hill's determined attack overran Federal earthworks and destroyed Couch's and Casey's divisions, driving the Federals back to a second line, which is marked by a historical marker erected between here and at Seven Pines. The arrival of Kearny shored up the line until Longstreet reinforced the Confederate attack to break this position. The Federals were forced back to a third line near the national cemetery, which held. After the battle McClellan retreated several miles to a more secure location.

To connect the two halves of the army, McClellan had several bridges constructed across the Chickahominy, including Grapevine Bridge on Route 156 that Sumner used to save the day with Sedgwick's division, which stopped Whiting's attack late in the day at Fair Oaks.

The uncoordinated and halfhearted Confederate assault by D. H. Hill against Kearny on June 1 was directed at Fair Oaks, a short distance east of Seven Pines and U.S. 60. To reach Fair Oaks, from U.S. 60 at Seven Pines turn right onto Route 33 to the railroad at the intersection of Route 33 and Route 156 (Nine Mile Road). This was Fair Oaks Station, a stop on the Richmond and York River Railroad and the center of fighting on the second day of Seven Pines. Johnston was wounded near the railroad at Route 33–Route 156.

Continue on U.S. 60 West–Route 33 toward Richmond and turn left onto Airport Drive. After a mile turn left. Across the road to the right are earthworks, a cannon, and a historical marker. Another artillery position is to the left. This is part of the extensive Confederate works that surrounded Richmond by the end of the Civil War.

Earthworks from Richmond's extensive defensive lines survive piecemeal at many places around the city. These are at the Richmond International Airport.

Return to the entrance of the airport (note the second cannon on the right) and turn left onto U.S. 60–Route 33. Turn left into Richmond National Cemetery.

Of the 5,706 Union dead in the thirteen-acre cemetery, only 838, from Hollywood and Oakwood cemeteries in Richmond, are identified. The remainder died on the battlefields of Seven Pines and Cold Harbor and a total of seventy different locations scattered across a twenty-five-mile area. In addition to the Gettysburg Address plaque there are four seacoast mortars. One unidentified Confederate, found along Beaverdam Creek in 1978, was buried with full military honors. He had apparently been killed by the four bullets found among his bones.

Return to the entrance of the cemetery and turn left onto U.S. 60. Turn right to follow U.S. 60 as it maneuvers violently up and around. Turn left into the Chimborazo portion of the Richmond National Battlefield Park visitor center.

A Tour of Civil War Richmond

RICHMOND WAS not only the capital of the Confederacy and its operational and industrial center, it became the heart and soul of the fledgling nation. To Southerners, Richmond became the impregnable fortress, the most important target in the country, which, despite furious Federal efforts, remained free and defiant. Entire regions of the Confederacy might fall, but so long as Richmond stood and Lee's Army of Northern Virginia survived to defend it, there was still hope.

Richmond was the city of Confederate President Jefferson Davis, revered in the beginning, despised at the end, and worshiped again in the decades following the Civil War. It was Lee's city. It was the place where Confederate heroes Stonewall Jackson, Jeb Stuart, and so many others were eulogized. It was the city where sons, brothers, and fathers were hospitalized and too often buried. It was the Confederacy's "shining city on a hill," where hopes and dreams slowly crumbled. Southerners a century ago could tell you where they were and what they were doing when they heard that Richmond had fallen.

For more than one hundred years Richmond has been the city of museums, monuments, and graves, a fabled place to which every true Southerner who could afford the trip made at least one pilgrimage. Today Richmond attracts Americans from every part of the country and a growing number of Civil War enthusiasts from around the world.

There are several book-length guides to Civil War Richmond, and a number of guided tour services are provided. A comprehensive tour of the Confederate city could require days to complete. This tour touches the most significant sites, the White House of the Confederacy and its incomparable museum, the Virginia State Capitol—home for four years of the Confederate government, Lee's home, the graves of Davis and Stuart, cemeteries containing dozens of celebrated Southern leaders and tens of thousands of fallen soldiers, the churches where they worshiped and prayed for victory, the remains of the great arms factories, a number of museums, and the many monuments a defeated people erected to preserve their memories. Unfortunately, much of the historic city was destroyed by fire in the final hours of the war.

The tour begins at the Chimborazo portion of the Richmond National Battlefield Park Visitors Center. On the grounds is a 12-pounder Confederate Napoleon. It has recently been joined by a mammoth and rare double-banded 6.4-inch Brooke rifle, over five tons of cast iron. Discovered in a military landfill on Governor's Island, New York, in 1981, it had been displayed at a Coast Guard station for fifteen years before being transferred here. The cannon has a strictly Richmond pedigree. Designed by John M. Brooke, the naval ordnance expert who developed the *Virginia*'s armor, it was cast on July 26, 1862, at Tredegar and shipped a few miles down the James River to serve in the defenses at Drewry's and Chaffin's Bluffs. Only nine others are known to exist, seven cast at Tredegar and two at Alabama's Selma works. The big siege gun is mounted on a stout wooden carriage.

Brooke developed Lee's suggestion of mounting a 32-pounder Columbiad on an armored railcar to shell McClellan's army during the Seven Days' battles. It was first used at Savage's Station.

This is the starting point for a series of small parks that illustrate the battles of the Seven Days and several sites associated with Grant's Overland campaign in 1864. Three national cemeteries are also included in the park. A brochure, with optional audiotape guide for purchase, leads visitors on a hundred-mile loop to five separate battlefields and ends at Drewry's Bluff. From 1864 are Cold Harbor, a long series of fortifications along the north bank of the James River, and several sites on the south side. Those last two will be saved for *The Killing Time*.

Until recently this was the visitors center for the Richmond National Battlefield Park. That has been moved to the Tredegar Iron Works, which will be visited later in this tour. The Chimborazo center exhibits now focus on medical care during the war.

Chimborazo Hospital, named for a South American volcano, occupied this broad plain on a high bluff overlooking the James River in southern Richmond. The site had natural springs and wells, and the proximity of the James River and Kanawha Canal facilitated the transportation of supplies. Opened on October 17, 1861, it covered forty acres and consisted of 150 pinewood, whitewashed frame buildings (each 150 feet long and 30 feet wide and capable of treating eighty patients), and 150 Sibley tents. The wards were divided into five divisions, and each had a separate kitchen and laundry. A central bakery produced 7,000 to 10,000 loaves of bread daily, although shortages closed it during the war's last terrible winter. The hospital kept a herd of 500 cattle and goats. Chimborazo, which had a capacity of 3,000 patients, cared for 76,000 men during the war. The surgeon in chief was Dr. James B. McCow, a professor at Richmond's Medical College of Virginia. As the war continued, McCow had difficulty obtaining food and supplies because of the ravaged countryside and the decaying Confederate transportation system, so he rented land to grow vegetables and bought two canal boats to transport the goods he found. Soap was made with grease supplied by the hospital's kitchens. Despite these efforts, Chimborazo was filthy and almost uninhabitable during summer, when the stench drew hoards of flies. There was never enough staff to tend the men properly and clean the wards.

Although Chimborazo was one of the best hospitals in the Confederacy, antibiotics and antiseptic surgery had yet to be invented. More than 20 percent of its patients died, which was nevertheless an excellent mortality rate for the period.

The manpower shortage forced the Confederate government to authorize the use of women, whose service proved invaluable. The most famous matron was the renowned Phoebe Yates Pember of Savannah, who described her experiences in the book *A Southern Woman's Story*. When male guards and attendants abandoned the complex on the horrible night of April 2, 1865, Pember noted that the "lame, the halt, and the blind had been cured" and left the hospital without assistance. Pember remained with the truly sick, guarding them with a pistol in her lap until a Federal officer arrived to take command.

Richmond became a vast hospital center. Of the five military hospitals created here, Winder could treat four thousand men at one time in ninety-eight buildings, and others could handle twenty-five hundred and eighteen hundred patients. The city also had twenty-eight general hospitals during the war. Several were established following First Manassas, but the number grew rapidly during the spring and summer of 1862 to handle the flood of casualties from Fair Oaks and the Seven Days. Most of the hospitals occupied Richmond's numerous large tobacco warehouses, but they also utilized factories, schools, stores, hotels, churches, and Masonic halls. In addition, each state of the Confederacy created special hospitals in the city for its soldiers, although some were also general hospitals. Georgia and Alabama both had four hospitals.

Finally, there were five church hospitals and seven private hospitals, all of them militarized by the government except for one established in the Robertson Hospital by Sally Tompkins Jefferson Davis commissioned Tompkins a captain on September 9, 1861, to enable her to continue running the hospital. She was the only woman to receive a commission in the Confederate army.

Portions of seven general hospitals remain. A good example is the Second Alabama Hospital, established in the Yarborough and Turpin Tobacco Factory, which is now Pohlig's Paper Box Factory on the southwest corner of Twenty-fifth and Franklin Streets, established by Mrs. "Judge" Hopkins, who spent her husband's estate of two hundred thousand dollars on the hospital. Mrs. Hopkins was twice wounded while tending soldiers in the field. Another is General Hospital No. 12

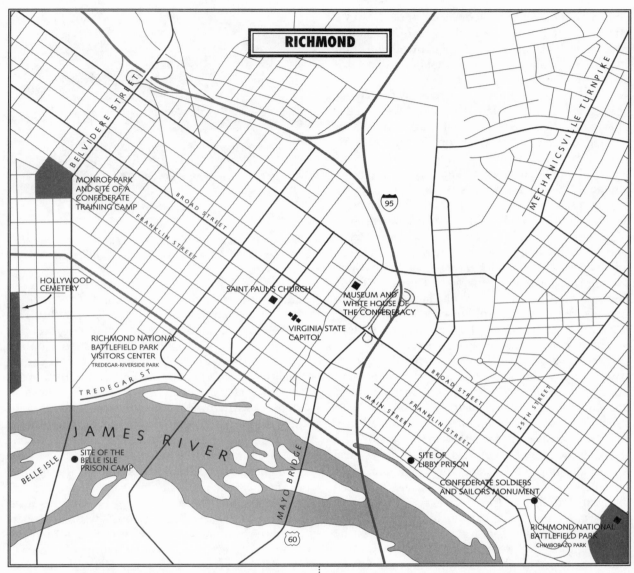

(1835, presently the William H. Grant Tobacco Factory, northeastern corner of Nineteenth and Franklin), used as a Confederate barracks then a military hospital and as a barracks again following the Union occupation.

A wonderful, frequently told story concerns the young angels of mercy who inundated Richmond's hospitals early in the war. One casualty assured a girl that he did not need anything, but she persisted, asking if she could wash his face. "Yes ma'am," he sighed, "but it's been washed fifteen times today already."

Walk to the edge of the bluff and examine the James River Valley. Rockett's Landing is on this side (northern) of the river, the Confederate Navy Yard was on both banks, the north-bank portion being twice as large as the southern one. Rockett's Landing, head of navigation on the James, was the farthest point ships could venture. Vessels drawing more than ten feet used a landing four miles downstream at Warwick. Soldiers and supplies were frequently shipped downriver, particularly in 1864 to counter a series of maneuvers by Grant that threatened Richmond. Until the very end of the war the steamer *Shultz* departed at 3 P.M. daily for Drewry's Bluff, a distance of seven miles, all of the James River that the Confederates still controlled. Union POWs were loaded here for exchange, and expatriated Confederates were returned.

During the war the Confederate navy's training ship *Patrick Henry* docked here. It also housed the short-lived Confederate Naval Academy, which opened in October 1863 under Comdr. John M. Brooke, who had earlier been chief of the Confederate navy's bureau of Ordnance and Hydrography. Its students included twelve-year-old Raphael Semmes Jr., a son of former U.S. vice president and Confederate Gen. John C. Breckinridge, and a brother-in-law of Jefferson Davis. The training ship had been the first Confederate ironclad, but the railroad iron was later removed. The *Patrick Henry,* armed with 8-inch guns, also steamed regularly to Drewry's Bluff. High-ranking military and civilian Confederate officials frequently visited. The cadets were trained on ironclads and shore batteries at Drewry's Bluff, where they were living in huts when the end came.

The most famous visitor to Rockett's Landing was Abraham Lincoln. "Thank God I have lived to see this," he said when informed that Richmond had surrendered. "It seems to me that I have been dreaming a horrid dream for four years, and now the nightmare is gone. I want to see Richmond." The day after Richmond fell, April 4, 1865, three Federal ships struggled upstream through numerable obstructions of pilings, sunken ships, and torpedoes (mines). All three—the *Bat, River Queen,* and *Malvern*—ran aground. Lincoln, his twelve-year-old son Tad, and David Dixon Porter were rowed by barge to Rockett's, protected by a nervous guard of twelve sailors. The president was immediately recognized by a slave who knelt before him and cried, "Bless the Lord! The Great Messiah."

"Don't kneel to me," Lincoln kindly told the man. "You must kneel to God only, and thank him for your freedom."

When Norfolk and Portsmouth fell in May 1862, an unfinished ironclad was towed up the James River to the Confederate Navy Yard. Christened the *Virginia II,* it was joined by the ironclads *Fredericksburg* and *Richmond.* A fourth vessel, the giant *Texas,* was nearing completion when it was burned on April 3, 1865, along with the navy yard,

Lincoln visited Richmond and toured the White House of the Confederacy shortly after the city had fallen into Union control in April 1865.

during the evacuation of Richmond. The facilities had been supervised by Comdr. R. G. Robb. The James River Squadron, headquartered here, primarily supported the vital Confederate position at Drewry's Bluff. The magazines of the three ironclads, filled with gunpowder and ammunition, were exploded at 2 A.M. near Drewry's Bluff. The blasts shattered windows in Richmond and shook buildings; hundreds of shells were ejected into the air and exploded all around the countryside.

Adm. Raphael Semmes, recently arrived after his famed raider *Alabama* was sunk off Cherbourg, France, commanded Confederate naval assets on the James River. After Semmes blew up his ironclads and the *Patrick Henry* downstream, he supervised the torching of the navy yard then loaded five hundred sailors and cadets on five small gunboats and landed at Mayo's Bridge. The last train had departed hours earlier, but a search turned up an engine. Several old cars were coupled, and handy fences were demolished for fuel. The group reached Danville, where they joined Jefferson Davis and guarded the remaining six million dollars in the Confederate treasury. The cadets were dismissed on May 2, 1865, in Abbeville, South Carolina.

By June 1861 Matthew Maury had developed an electrically detonated torpedo, an oak cask filled with gunpowder, which he tested off Rockett's wharf. When it exploded in midstream, a column of water shot twenty feet into the air and Confederate officials applauded wildly. These experiments sparked rumors that the Confederates were testing a submarine built at Tredegar for use as a delivery vehicle for mines, which led to a fantasy still believed in some quarters. The story claimed that Union spymaster Allan Pinkerton sent Mrs. E. H. Baker, a former Richmond socialite, to observe these tests at Rockett's. Mrs. Baker allegedly wrangled permission to attend the trials and saw a submarine submerge and sink a scow with a mine. The story has no basis in fact.

From the Richmond National Battlefield Park, turn left onto East Broad Street and left onto North Twenty-ninth, to the monument in Libby Hill Park.

The house at 1 North Twenty-ninth Street was owned by Luther Libby, a New England Yankee who became a successful businessman in Richmond. Confederate provost marshal John H. Winder seized his warehouse so quickly that Libby was unable to remove his sign—L. Libby and Sons, Ship Chandlers—from the entrance to the structure. As a result his name became forever linked to the prison, although Libby had no association with the Confederacy. Libby, his wife, and an infant daughter were living south of Richmond when they were captured during a Federal cavalry raid. Because of his infamous name, he was imprisoned in Fort Monroe, then Boston's cold, damp Fort Warren, where he contracted the tuberculosis that killed him on August 28, 1871, in Richmond. The Civil War also cost Libby six ships. The Confederates seized three, sinking one as an obstruction below Drewry's Bluff, and the Federal government captured the other three.

You are at the Confederate Soldiers and Sailors Monument in Libby Hill Park, at the edge of the bluff overlooking the James River, which affords great views of the valley and the site of the Confederate Navy Yard. Black Union occupation troops camped here during the summer of 1865. One might think this magnificent seventy-three-foot monument that replicates the famous Pompey's Pillar in Alexandria, Egypt, would be the first entry on Monument Avenue, but that was reserved for generals and other "important" heroes of the Confederacy. This memorial to the common Confederate soldier and sailor stands alone. Each of the thirteen cylinders of local James River granite represents a Southern state. Funds were raised across the South for the monument, dedicated on May 30, 1894. The bronze soldier standing guard atop the column was sculpted by local resident William R. Sheppard.

Circle the monument and return to Broad Street, where you turn left.

On the southeastern corner of Broad and Twenty-eighth Streets (2619 East Broad Street) stood the Crenshaw house, where Joseph E. Johnston was taken to convalesce from his Seven Pines wounds on May 31, 1862.

To the left is Saint John's Church (1740) where Patrick Henry gave his stirring "Liberty or Death" speech. It has little Civil War significance, but the night that Stuart died in Richmond a severe storm blew its steeple off.

To the left, down Twentieth Street, is the Old Stone house (1737, 1916 East Main Street), Richmond's oldest structure. After a brief stint in city hall, the Federal provost marshal's office was moved here near Libby Prison and Castle Thunder, which the Federals filled with escaped criminals, looters, and deserters caught in their dragnet.

On the right just before the turn for the Confederate White House is the Monumental Church. On the block behind it is the Egyptian Building (southwestern corner of Marshall and College Streets), originally the Medical College of Virginia, built in 1845 by Thomas Stewart, who also designed Saint Paul's Church. After John Brown's raid in October 1859, 144 southern medical students at the University of Pennsylvania's Jefferson School of Medicine transferred here to study. They were led by Dr. Hunter H. McGuire, who became chief surgeon of Stonewall Jackson's corps. Through 1865 the school graduated 333 doctors from the Confederacy's only medical school. It is the oldest medical college building in the South.

Turn right onto North Eleventh Street at the sign for the Confederate White House. Turn right onto East Clay. The Confederate White House is across Twelfth Street on your right, and the Museum of the Confederacy is behind it. Park in the Medical College of Virginia, Commonwealth University garage beyond the White House.

The White House of the Confederacy was constructed in 1818 by Robert Mills, who also designed the Washington Monument. In 1844 the house was sold to Sally Bruce, who married Confederate Secretary of War James A. Seddon. When the Confederate government relocated to Richmond from Montgomery in May 1861, the city of Richmond purchased this house for use as the executive mansion. The cost was $42,800 for house, land, and furnishings. Jefferson Davis, believing the city should not bear the entire expense, had it leased by the Confederate government. On August 1 the Davis family moved here from the Spotswood Hotel.

Davis held regular receptions, or levees, in the White House, where he met the public. Informal cabinet meetings became common there also. The house, which became the political and social center of Richmond, was occupied by Davis, his wife, Varina, and their three children: Margaret, Jefferson Jr., and Joseph, who died tragically after a fall from the south portico. The Davises had two additional children, William and Varina Anne, while living here.

Davis sent his family away to North Carolina in the spring of 1862 when McClellan's army drew near. On January 9, 1864, Jefferson's manservant and Varina's maid ran away. Ten days later, at a nighttime reception, an arsonist attempted to destroy the White House by starting a fire in a basement woodpile. Fortunately, the smoke was detected early, and the blaze was extinguished before the structure was damaged. That same night two additional servants departed, and the mansion was burglarized. The people of Richmond thought a Federal plot was responsible for the incident.

In March 1865 as the military situation deteriorated at Petersburg, the president again sent his family away. Before leaving, Varina sold her silver, china, and other belongings to raise money for her journey with the children to a more secure location in North Carolina. On April 2, as Davis himself prepared to leave, he instructed his housekeeper to surrender the house to the Federal authorities. He packed a large valise and a small case, including four pistols, a box of ammunition, and photos of Varina and Robert E. Lee. He left as Lee evacuated Petersburg.

After Federal occupation on April 3, Maj. Gen. Godfrey Weitzel moved into the house, which became headquarters for Military District No. 1 for the next five years. On the following day Lincoln and son Tad walked hand-in-hand to the Confederate White House from Rockett's Landing. The president sat at Davis's desk and after a pensive moment sprang up and said, "Let's go! Let's have a look at the house." In the afternoon he took a carriage tour of Richmond.

After the city reacquired the house, the furnishings were auctioned and the building turned into a school for six hundred students. The school board nearly demolished the structure in 1889 to construct a new school on the site, but prominent citizens organized the Confederate Memorial Literary Society and saved the historic house, purchasing it in 1894. The house was restored, fireproofed, and opened to the public on February 22, 1896, the thirty-fourth anniversary of Davis's inauguration at Richmond's Capitol Square. Important Confederate material had been donated from across the South for a museum.

In the early 1970s the Museum of the Confederacy was constructed adjacent to the White House. When it opened in 1976, the extensive collections of artifacts from the White House were transferred and the executive mansion closed for a twelve-year renovation. Considerable research allowed the house to be restored to its Civil War appearance. Seventy percent of the furnishings are the originals used by the Davis family, much of it donated by Varina Davis. The remainder is from the period of the house, early Victorian. Only the textiles are reproductions. Featured on the tour is a horsehair rocker, where tradition has Lincoln resting during his brief visit. Note the 1863 portrait of Davis, which was painted here.

The White House exhibit gallery on the ground floor of the White House contains the permanent exhibit called Victory in Defeat: Jefferson Davis and the Lost Cause, which interprets the life of the Confederacy's first and last family. In Service to the President: The Staff of the Confederate Executive Mansion explores the lives of office staff, servants, and slaves who worked for the Davis family, through portraits, photos, and biographical sketches. The White House of the Confederacy hosts many lectures, film showings, and other special events.

In the parlor on the first floor, the Davises held formal receptions on holidays and other special occasions. The dining room saw numerous formal and informal dinners, luncheons, and meetings. Varina Davis entertained in the drawing room, and close friends were received in the library.

On the second floor were Davis's office, the master bedroom, and four other rooms, including a guest room and a nursery for the children. During his illnesses late in the war, Davis conducted much of his work and held informal cabinet meetings here. When healthy, Davis walked or rode to his official office on Capitol Square. Five bedrooms occupied the third floor, one for Davis's secretary, Barton Harrison, and the remainder usually occupied by relatives who often visited. In the White House, Davis was baptized on May 10, 1863, and confirmed the same day at Saint Paul's; Varina's sister, Jennie K. Howell, married Lt. William Waller on November 12, 1863; Joseph Howell Davis was killed in a fall on April 30, 1864; and Winnie was born on June 27, 1864.

An important part of the Confederate Memorial Literary Society's purpose was collecting, preserving, and displaying relics of the Confederacy. Before 1976 each Confederate and Border State had a separate room devoted to it in the White House. Generous donations over the years included valuable possessions of such Civil War notables as Lee, Jackson, Stuart, and many others. Artifacts, documents, and artwork expanded the museum's holdings, including a number of battle flags returned by the U.S. government in 1905. Five hundred flags are preserved here.

The White House was not only running out of display space, but the artifacts were being threatened by insects and humidity. In 1970 the Confederate Museum became the Museum of the Confederacy and a new three-story museum opened in October 1976. Permanent and themed exhibits examine the history of the Civil War and many related topics, including people and issues. The museum has the most comprehensive collection of Confederate artifacts in the world, numbering more than fifteen thousand. Its archives include twenty thousand books, manuscripts, photographs, and other material.

Possibly the most prized object in the collection is the large painting *The Last Meeting of Lee and Jackson,* which depicts the pair plotting strategy just hours before Jackson's mortal wounding at Chancellorsville. It was the work of Everett B. D.

Julio, an immigrant with no personal experience with either the Civil War or its leaders. Julio offered the painting to Lee in 1869, but it was declined. The image soon became a southern icon, reproduced on countless prints, postcards, china plates, and all manner of souvenirs. After decades of display in Louisiana, the museum acquired it in 1992. It is displayed in its original monumental frame.

Another favorite is *The Burial of Latane* by William D. Washington, depicting a plantation family burying the only casualty of Stuart's ride around McClellan. Prints of it once adorned the walls of many southern homes. Another collection of thirty-one oil paintings by Conrad Wise Chapman illustrates Confederate defenses and other wartime scenes of Charleston.

Near the entrance of the museum and on the first floor is the largest permanent exhibit, The Confederate Years, which is a history of the Confederate military effort. Artifacts, art, documents, and manuscripts tell the story of Southern army and navy activities from the beginning of the Confederacy to Appomattox, including the surrender of other Confederate armies, the capture of Jefferson Davis, and the last acts of Southern resistance by the commerce raider CSS *Shenandoah,* which docked at Liverpool, England, on November 5, 1865.

On the ground floor is another permanent exhibit, The Hope of Eight Million—The Confederate Soldier, which illustrates the daily lives of soldiers through displays of weapons, uniforms, personal possessions, diaries, and letters home. The second floor is devoted to special, changing programs that explore the military, political, economic, and social history of the Confederacy and all those who lived within it, including civilians, women, and African Americans, through domestic artifacts, locally manufactured products, documents, photos, music, and narratives. These exhibits highlight the museum's extensive collections of flags, weapons, paintings, prints, portraits, busts, and other materials.

Many artifacts belonged to noted Confederate generals and important civilian officials, such as cabinet member Judah P. Benjamin and Vice President Alexander Stephens. Lee's field tent has been recreated with his original cot, tables, mess kit, boots, and headquarters flag. Included are the dress coat and sword he wore at Appomattox and the pen with which he signed the surrender document. The collections also include Stonewall Jackson's Bible, sword, spurs, haversack, a copy of Napoleon's *Maxims of War,* and the saw used to amputate his left arm; the Great Seal of the Confederacy, made in Great Britain in 1863; the Confederacy's Provisional Constitution; Jeb Stuart's black plumed hat, boots, saddle, revolver, carbine, headquarters flag, and the last dispatch he wrote the morning he was killed, May 11, 1864, and the pencil he wrote it with; the coat Jefferson Davis was wearing when captured; the sword A. P. Hill wore at the time of his death; P. G. T. Beauregard's field glasses; Joseph E. Johnston's pistol and sword (worn by his father during the Revolutionary War); the flag of the Cherokee regiment led by Stand Watie; and Raphael Semmes's telescope and pistol. Also featured are possessions of John Bell Hood, Simon B. Buckner, Joseph Wheeler, and John Hunt Morgan.

Too many artifacts memorialize generals killed in battle. John Adams's shattered pocket watch stopped at the moment of his death in November 30, 1864, in Franklin, Tennessee. From Pickett's Charge are the sword of Lewis Armistead, the telescope of Richard Garnett, and the coat of James Kemper (who survived the battle). Also on display is the sketchbook of Capt. Keith Boswell, one of Jackson's mapmakers, which was penetrated by the bullet that killed Boswell at Chancellorsville.

At 1105 East Clay Street, between Eleventh and Twelfth Streets, is the Robert H. Maury house.

The remains of the CSS Virginia *were salvaged for iron following the war. Outside the Museum of the Confederacy are preserved its drive shaft (below) and anchor (facing page).*

During the spring and summer of 1861 Matthew Maury, a cousin, lived in a third-story front room. Servants lugged tubs of water to his room to fill a water tank provided by Tredegar. Maury borrowed batteries from the Richmond Medical College and electrically exploded small quantities of gunpowder in underwater containers. Reportedly the house was drenched and the residents terrified, but the experiments worked. Soon full-scale torpedoes (mines) helped protect Richmond and many other Southern port cities and rivers.

The Wickham-Valentine house (1812) housed members of the Confederate Congress during the Civil War. It was purchased by Mann S. Valentine, brother of sculptor Edward Valentine, whose studio was in the back of the house. In April 1870 Edward Valentine traveled to Lexington, Virginia, where Robert E. Lee sat for a bust. The Valentine Museum was established in 1892 with the bequest of Mann Valentine, who left his home, collections, and an endowment for a museum dedicated to the preservation of Richmond's history, people, and culture. Since the development of Valentine Riverside, this original museum has emphasized the Valentine family. Valentine's studio contains the plaster cast of the recumbent statue of Lee, which is in the Lee Chapel at Washington and Lee University in Lexington. Also on display are the death masks of Jackson and Stuart, both by Frederick Udek, taken as they lay in state in the governor's mansion, and busts of Jefferson Davis, Albert Sidney Johnston, and George E. Pickett.

From the intersection of East Clay and Twelfth Streets at the Confederate White House, turn right onto Twelfth, then right onto Broad. Turn left onto Fifth Street, then left on Byrd Street. Turn right onto Tredegar Street to descend to Tredegar Iron Works–Valentine Riverside.

To the right coming down Tredegar Street was the Confederate Armory, operated by chief of ordnance Gen. Josiah Gorgas. This facility, in connection with Tredegar, helped manufacture 341 big Columbiads and other heavy siege pieces, 1,306 field guns, 23,000 rifles (made with machinery seized at Harpers Ferry), 34,000 carbines for cavalry use, 6,000 pistols, and 920,000 rounds of artillery ammunition. By war's end Gorgas was raiding North Carolina whiskey

the army, the navy yard, railroads, and other private companies. Operated by Brig. Gen. Joseph R. Anderson, the plant developed the 7-inch Brooke rifled cannon and the world's first mines. Canal boats and railroads delivered raw material and transported manufactured arms and other materiel throughout the Confederacy. When Richmond was evacuated, Anderson wisely armed his workers to prevent Confederate soldiers from torching Tredegar.

Spared destruction during the evacuation fire, the foundry was functioning again by August 1865, producing rails to restore the South's ravaged railroads. It did not close until the 1950s, having manufactured munitions for every American war up to and including the Korea War. The property was neglected for years, and the buildings were condemned following a devastating flood in 1972. A flood wall has been constructed to prevent further damage.

The eight-acre site is owned by the Ethyl Corporation, a petroleum company that has stabilized and restored the surviving buildings. In cooperation with the Valentine Museum, a twenty-four-million-dollar historical interpretation of the site is being developed. The primary exhibit space, including ten thousand feet of permanent exhibit space dedicated to city history and changing exhibits, is in the renovated three-story Pattern Storage Building, which houses a visitors center, displays, and an auditorium. One floor is the map room, where large maps illustrate the Union campaigns in 1862 and 1864 to capture Richmond and the many Civil War sites preserved in the city. Another floor features a twenty-five-minute film describing the Confederate capital during the war. Also displayed here are a replica pontoon boat (used for building temporary bridges) and two rare artillery pieces manufactured at Tredegar. A 6-pounder Napoleon was cast in 1841; it is rare because most 6-pounders were melted down in 1862 to make new weapons. This gun was stamped "# 1," indicating that it was the first to be manufactured here. The second piece is a 42-pounder 7-inch siege rifle cast here in 1859. It was inspected by U.S. ordnance inspector Benjamin Huger, who was a Confederate general. Until 1996 the gun stood in Cedar Hill Cemetery in Lebanon, Pennsylvania, and was sold for thirty-three thousand dollars, making it the largest historic iron cannon ever purchased. The Ethyl Corporation purchased

stills for the precious copper used in the 3,000 percussion caps he produced daily. Over 100,000 artillery shells remained in the facility when fire reached it at 8 A.M. on April 3. Explosions continued for four hours as many shells were propelled into the city, spreading fire and destruction.

Valentine Riverside is a fantastic new museum at the site of the Tredegar Iron Works, the most important manufacturing facility in the Confederacy. It turned out 1,160 cannon (half the number produced by the Confederacy), rolled armor for several ironclad warships (part of the *Virginia*'s armor was made from a streetcar line finished just prior to the Civil War), and fashioned all manner of war materiel (often using church bells and salvaged train rails). Established in 1836, this "Arsenal of the Confederacy" employed thousands of workers on a vast forty-acre site that featured an iron foundry with forty forges, two rolling mills, and dozens of other buildings. Despite a fire in 1863, the complex continued to expand during the war. Tredegar had contracts with

the piece and mounted it at Tredegar. The final floor is a traditional museum display area with artifacts illustrating the issues, weapons, and tactics of the Civil War, the defense of Richmond, and the lives of the city's people: women and children, refugees and spies, slaves and Union African-American troops (who initially occupied the city when it fell in April 1865). Audiovisual displays feature letters, diaries, and newspaper accounts of the home and battle fronts.

In addition to the Pattern Storage Building, other surviving structures include parts of the gun foundry, an eighty-six-foot tall chimney, a commissary building, and a carpentry shop. Replicas of workers' housing, a shoemaking shop, a hospital, a pork packing plant, and a farm will be recreated.

Also featured are canal boat journeys, tram rides to historic sites throughout the multilevel park, and guided and self-guided tours of Civil War sites. An industrial history walking tour features a locomotive and caboose, gun foundry, crane, waterwheel, cupola furnace, bulldozer press, and hydraulic turbine. Some of the historical machines are operational and can be activated by visitors. There are numerous outdoor displays, structures for children to play on, restaurants, and living history programs. Motor tours also transport visitors to historic sites outside Tredegar, including Hollywood Cemetery, where many Confederate notables are buried. The African American Monument tells the story of black troops in the Civil War. They were used extensively in operations around Richmond and were among the first Union soldiers to occupy Richmond.

Tredegar–Valentine Riverside, situated on the north bank of the James River near downtown Richmond, promises to be one of the finest such facilities in the country, a standard by which other museums will judge themselves, and a symbol of the city as a focus for its numerous historic sites. It will also be a fantastic educational opportunity for students in the region.

A series of murals have been developed on the floodwall, three of them with Civil War themes. One represents Lee, another Richmond in flames during the evacuation fire, and the last depicts Sgt. Powhaten Beaty, a black Union soldier who took command of his brigade after all the white officers had been killed in an attack on New Market Heights on September 29, 1864. Beaty's action won him the Medal of Honor.

A pedestrian footbridge from Tredegar Street brings visitors to Belle Isle, under the U.S. 1–Lee Bridge in the middle of the James River. The large numbers of prisoners captured during the Seven Days' battles in 1862 inundated existing facilities and led Confederate authorities to herd ten thousand "live Yankees," as they were called, to this natural corral. By the end of the war a total of twenty thousand Federal enlisted prisoners were confined here. This "temporary" prison was initially well organized, a tent camp with orderly streets and adequate sanitation facilities, but the prison became permanent and increasingly crowded. Epidemics of typhoid, pneumonia, diarrhea, and dysentery broke out, and there was little food, clothing, or shelter. About thirty men died each day. Wagons that brought bread to the prisoners in the morning departed with cargoes of corpses, men killed by disease, malnutrition, and exposure. The dead were originally buried in Hollywood Cemetery, then transferred to the Richmond National Cemetery. In 1864 a doctor found that 90 percent of the men weighed less than one hundred pounds. During winters the prisoners slept on the bare ground without shelter. They dug pits to escape the chill winds that swept off the river, and they slept in rows, spoon fashion to preserve body heat, or in groups standing up, everyone leaning toward the center.

The Association for the Preservation of Virginia Antiquities has hired an archaeologist to determine

The rapids of the James River mark the end of navigable water at Richmond. Visible from Hollywood Cemetery, the falls are just above the site of the Belle Isle prison and Tredegar's industrial works.

the boundaries of the site. There was no stockade usually associated with Confederate prisons, but an earthen berm ten feet wide and several feet high, constructed between three-foot-deep trenches, surrounded the five-and-a-half-acre camp. A dead line was marked fifteen feet inside the berms, and guards were posted every twenty yards. To discourage escape attempts after Ulric Dahlgren's aborted raid on Richmond (which had as one goal the liberation of Union prisoners in the city), artillery loaded with canister was emplaced on the shore and surrounding hills. Plans are to recreate the berms, develop interpretive signs, and mark significant features with wildflowers. Until recent years the fifty-six-acre island was heavily industrialized with iron and power works and a quarry.

On Cary Street (between Twentieth and Twenty-first Streets) was Libby Prison, a three-story tobacco warehouse converted for officers. A complex was ultimately established with the addition of three neighboring buildings. Conditions were filthy and overcrowded, with from six hundred to one thousand prisoners. There was generally little food or clothing and no heat in the winter. Libby had become a fertilizer plant when a group of Chicago businessmen purchased it in 1889 for $11,600. They dismantled the structure and shipped its six hundred thousand bricks in 132 freight cars for reassembly at the 1893 Chicago World's Fair. Named the Libby Prison War Museum, it housed Civil War artifacts for ten years before it was demolished. The walls of the Chicago Coliseum contain Libby Prison bricks, and the remainder, with woodwork containing the carved names of prisoners, became a large barn in Hamlet, Indiana.

The site of Libby, now crossed by a massive flood wall constructed by the Corps of Engineers, is a park with two bronze historical plaques, one dedicated by the Confederate Memorial Literary Society in 1911, and the second placed by the Sons of Confederate Veterans in 1980.

During the war, the officer inmates discovered that they could slide down the inside of a chimney to the basement of the warehouse. Led by Col. Thomas Rose, the men dug a sixty-foot-long tunnel to another building using only a knife, a chisel, and an auger. They carried off the excavated dirt in a spittoon. A mass escape was made by 109 prisoners during the night of February 9, 1864. They divided into a number of small groups and headed east, down the peninsula, for the safety of the Federal lines around Williamsburg. Some went to Union spy Elizabeth Van Lew's house, but she was not there. Half the officers escaped, stumbling cold and hungry into Union patrols.

The stories of inhuman conditions at Libby and other Richmond prisons, which the escapees told Northern newspapers, inflamed the Union. Weeks later Dahlgren's attempt was launched to free the prisoners, allegedly to help burn Richmond and kill Jefferson Davis and other high-ranking Confederate officials. In response the Confederates buried a large quantity of gunpowder in the basement and threatened to blow up the prison and kill every man before they could be liberated by Federal cavalry.

Lincoln visited Libby during his April 4 inspection tour. When slaves offered to destroy the hated structure, Lincoln replied, "No. Leave it as a monument."

Not far away from Libby on Camp Street were two large brick factories named Castle Thunder and Castle Lightning, used during the war to house criminals, spies, and deserters. Castle Thunder hosted three women found disguised as men in the Confederate army. One of these was Lieutenant Buford, also known as Loreta Janeta Valesquez, but there is little to support her story. She allegedly raised a company in Arkansas after her Louisiana planter husband had been killed early in the war. Supposedly she served as a Confederate courier in the West, where she was twice wounded. There is more to substantiate the story of sisters Mary and Molly Bell. They fought in Virginia for two years and had risen to the rank of noncommissioned officers before they were discovered and sent home to southeastern Virginia.

Just upstream of Belle Isle is Brown's Island, close to the James River rapids. At the Confederate laboratory there, women and children packed individual rifle cartridges with gunpowder. They prepared a staggering total of seventy million during the war. On Friday, March 13, 1863, an explosion there shook the city and killed forty workers and seriously injured twenty more. Gorgas called it "a fearful accident."

The powder magazine, near Fifth and Hospital Streets, exploded at dawn on April 3, 1865, destroying several buildings and killing eleven. Thousands of windows were blown out as buildings swayed, and the Federals outside Richmond were alerted to the city's evacuation.

Downstream at the foot of Fourteenth Street, Mayo's Bridge occupies the same location as the Civil War span that was immortalized in a Currier and Ives print depicting the evacuation as Richmond burns in the background. The span, like today's bridge for U.S. 1–U.S. 310–Jefferson Davis Highway, led to Manchester and points south. Confederate forces were marching to join Lee on his retreat from Petersburg. Throughout April 2 columns of troops, artillery, supply wagons, prisoners, and frightened refugees crowded across the wooden bridge. At 4:30 A.M. on April 3, Lt. Gen. Richard Ewell ordered Col. Clement Sulivane to prepare the bridge for burning. Barrels of tar and bundles of kindling were rapidly procured and placed. The rear guard marched across Mayo's Bridge about 8 A.M., when Brig. Gen. Martin W. Gary tipped his hat and tersely said, "All over! Good-bye! Blow her to hell!" Consumed by a hot fire, the span fell into the James River.

Two railroad bridges just upstream had been destroyed before dawn. The previous evening Davis had gone to the Richmond and Danville depot, where a special train awaited him and the cabinet. Davis delayed his departure until 11 P.M., hoping for good news from Lee, which never came. The train, with thirty passengers and sixty naval cadets guarding the Confederacy's gold reserves, slowly pulled away from the station.

The Confederates destroyed all five James River bridges leading into Richmond, and Union General Weitzel's first action was to open an avenue of communication. Within two days the Federals had constructed a pontoon bridge at the foot of Seventeenth Street. It was constructed of anchored wooden boats, chained together, with heavy wooden timbers secured across them to form a lane. Lee reentered Richmond over it after the surrender at Appomattox, and two weeks later, May 1, fifty thousand members of the Army of the Potomac crossed to march through the devastated capital of the Confederacy, where many caught a glimpse of the capitol and Lee's home. Union Gen. George Gordon Meade and General in Chief Henry Halleck reviewed them from city hall. They were followed later by nine thousand of Philip H. Sheridan's troopers and William Tecumseh

On the observance of George Washington's birthday, February 22, 1862, Jefferson Davis was inaugurated as the Confederacy's only president at the base of Richmond's magnificent Washington Monument.

Sherman's troops. Both armies continued out of the city on the Brock turnpike and marched triumphantly in review through Washington, D.C. Southern troops were required to cut off Confederate buttons before entering the city.

Because Manchester was at the southern approach to Richmond, five of seventeen star forts constructed to defend the city were built here to defend the Richmond and Danville Railroad and the Richmond-Petersburg turnpike. One fort is marked by a UDC granite monument at the intersection of Harwood Street and Ingram Avenue at Jeff Davis Highway.

From Tredegar retrace your route on Tredegar Street, which becomes Seventh Street. Turn right onto Franklin Street, and the Lee house will be on your right.

Mary Lee, Robert E. Lee's wife, had a hectic time during the war. Forced in 1861 to abandon her family mansion, Arlington, which was soon occupied by Federal forces who converted the grounds into a cemetery in 1863, she fled to her son Rooney's home at White House Landing on the Pamunkey River, east of Richmond. In 1862 Federals rousted her from that shelter, which they burned soon afterward. She escaped into the Confederate lines across the Chickahominy at Meadow Bridge near Richmond, seeing her husband for the first time in fifteen months. Mary

Thomas Jefferson helped to design the Virginia State Capitol, which served as the Confederate Congressional Building from 1861 until 1865.

Lee and her daughters spent a year as guests in the James Caskie house (southeastern corner of Eleventh and Clay, near the Confederate White House), then in the fall of 1863 they moved to 210 East Leigh Street, remaining until January 1864, when they moved here to 707 East Franklin Street. This building, the Stuart house (1844), had been rented to Custis Lee, another son, who lived here with other Confederate officers. Lee managed to visit his wife and daughters here several times during the fighting around Richmond and Petersburg. The ladies always seemed to be knitting socks for the troops (Lee remarked once that the house looked like an industrial school). Mary, crippled by rheumatism, did little socializing. The evacuation fire came close to the house, burning the United Presbyterian Church only a half block away, but Mrs. Lee stubbornly remained in her parlor, her calm a rebuke to those who begged her to flee.

General Lee returned here after the surrender at Appomattox and remained until he accepted the presidency of Washington College in September 1865. The famous post-Appomattox photos of Lee by Mathew Brady's men were taken on the back porch. Confederate Secretary of War George W. Randolph lived next door, but that house has been destroyed.

One block over is Main Street. On April 20, 1862, the Army of Northern Virginia marched down it from west to east, heading for Yorktown. Crowds filled the sidewalks all day and into the night as the procession of gray-clad soldiers passed. The men were met with cheers, tears, kisses, and food. Most men sported flowers in their rifle barrels and a loaf of bread impaled on their bayonets. While bands played "Dixie," "The Bonnie Blue Flag," and "Maryland, My Maryland," soldiers darted out of formation briefly to hug loved ones then resumed their positions in the ranks.

A frequently told story has the soldiers passing a window where a young man stood with a beautiful woman. The Confederates jeered, shouting, "Come along, boy, the lady'll spare you. Here's a musket for you." The young man, a veteran, placed the stump of a leg on the windowsill and shouted, "Have you got one of these for me, too?" The marching soldiers then loudly cheered one of their own.

That same day eight thousand cavalry and all the Confederate artillery clattered down Franklin street, which was also filled with cheering residents.

Continue on Franklin, then turn left onto Ninth. The capitol is to the right and Saint Paul's Church is on the left.

Virginia initially opposed secession and joined her Southern sisters only after Lincoln called for seventy-five thousand volunteers to subdue the Confederacy—Virginia's contribution was to be eight thousand. The Secession Convention, which had been in session for months, voted to leave the Union; an earlier vote had rejected such an action. Virginians approved the action by a four-to-one popular vote. Only four voters in Richmond opposed secession.

Virginia soon became the front line of the Civil War and saw more military activity than any other state. She contributed more general officers than any Southern state and raised sixty-three infantry and twenty-three cavalry regiments. Virginia proudly hosted the Confederate government from May 29, 1861, until the end, April 3, 1865.

If you enter the capitol grounds from the entrance at Ninth and Grace Streets, the Washington Monument and the capitol are straight ahead, the Bell Tower to the right, and the governor's mansion beyond the capitol at the northeastern corner.

The first Confederate flag was raised at Capitol Square on April 17, 1861. During the battles around

217

Richmond in the spring of 1862, Gov. John Letcher and others watched anxiously from the roof of the capitol while thousands of residents crowded the hills and rooftops for a glimpse of the powder smoke–shrouded battlefields. The square was the gathering place of Richmond's residents on many happy and sad occasions. One of these occurred in late 1864. For its role in the victory at New Market in 1864, the Virginia Military Institute in Lexington was destroyed by Federals. When the cadets arrived in Richmond, Davis reviewed them here and praised their heroism.

The magnificent equestrian statue of George Washington, surrounded by six nine-foot-tall statues of other prominent Virginians, was made in England and hauled from Rockett's Landing. Dedicated in 1858, the monument had existed for only four years when on Washington's birthday, February 22, 1862, Judge John D. Halyburton administered the oaths of office to Jefferson Davis and Alexander Stephens, the only president and vice president of the Confederacy, on a platform erected at the base of the statue. Despite a cold, pelting rain, Davis delivered his inaugural address. Washington's statue is featured on the Great Seal of the Confederacy.

Three Civil War–related statues stand on the square. On the north side is a standing figure of Stonewall Jackson, hands on hip and sword hilt, funded by English admirers and dedicated on October 26, 1875. Executed by Irish sculptor J. H. Foley, it was presented by A. J. B. Beresford. The statue of William "Extra Billy" Smith—twice governor, a U.S. Congressman, a state legislator, and a Confederate officer—also stands on the north side of the square. Created by W. L. Sheppard and dedicated on May 30, 1906, it depicts the colorful governor in a dignified stance. The final statue depicts Dr. Hunter H. McGuire, surgeon for Stonewall Jackson and a prominent physician following the war. This work of William Cooper, with McGuire seated on a chair atop a stone base, was dedicated on January 1, 1904.

The brick Bell Tower (1824) is on the southwestern corner of the square. On "Pawnee Sunday," April 21, 1861, the bell rang for the first of many times during the Civil War to warn residents that a Federal warship was ascending the James River to shell Richmond. Citizens rushed out of church and took what weapons they had to the heights overlooking Rockett's Landing to defend their city against a threat that never materialized. On the previous day the *Pawnee* had entered the Elizabeth River to destroy the Portsmouth Naval Shipyard and tow off the *Cumberland,* but it never entered the James.

The signal warning of a military threat to the city—three peals of the bell, a pause, and three more peals—rang with increasing frequency as the war progressed. It summoned a military reserve named the City Battalion, which consisted largely of government and factory workers and convalescent soldiers, to form on the square. In 1864 the militia was often called upon to meet Grant's threats along the James. These reserves would hold until Lee rushed in regular Confederate soldiers. The City Battalion was called out on March 1, 1864, at the approach of Dahlgren's aborted raid.

When Union Gen. Godfrey Weitzel reached the capitol at 8 A.M. on April 3, 1865, he found the square jammed with refugees seeking shelter from the firestorm consuming the city. Weitzel had the fire bell rung, but only five men of the Richmond Fire Department responded, and their hoses had been slashed. Without hesitation Weitzel deployed forty-five hundred Federal soldiers to save the city. The men stacked arms and went to work with wagonloads of gunpowder, shovels, and picks, which the general had hurriedly ordered up. The only chance to stop the conflagration was to create a firebreak. Buildings were exploded and walls knocked down while bucket brigades saved many structures from stray sparks. The Court Building on Capitol Square was lost, but the capitol, mansion, and the remainder of the city were saved by its conquerors. In all, nine hundred buildings were destroyed, including nearly every structure between Main, Fourth, First, and the James River. Damages were estimated at thirty million dollars.

Lt. Johnston L. DePeyster claimed the honor of raising the Stars and Stripes above the roof of the capitol while a regimental band below played "The Star-Spangled Banner."

Not all of Richmond despaired when the Federals arrived. A young girl named Nellie clapped her hands and shouted, "The Yankees have come! Now I have something to eat!" She declared that she would eat delicacies "until I have a fit and die!"

The Virginia State Capitol is a true American architectural gem. Thomas Jefferson designed it after the Maison Carrée, a late Roman temple in Nimes, France. A twelve-acre site in the center of Richmond, atop Shockee Hill, was prepared before construction started on August 18, 1785; it was completed three years later. The stuccoed brick walls are four to five feet thick, and eight large columns adorn the front. Two wings were added early in the twentieth century.

The treason trial of former Vice President Aaron Burr, who was acquitted of those charges, was held here in 1807. Virginia's Secession Convention met here part of the fifty-four days it was in session. Robert E. Lee was commissioned as commander in chief of all Virginia military forces in the House of Delegates on April 23, 1861. The Confederate Congress met here from May 8, 1861, until its final adjournment on March 18, 1865. The chair used by Vice President Alexander Stephens remains in the old Senate Chamber, where he rarely presided over the Confederate Senate.

On May 12, 1863, a large funeral procession led from Main Street to the capitol, where the body of Stonewall Jackson was laid on a catafalque in front of the speaker's chair. Jackson was wrapped in the new Confederate flag, the stars atop his chest. Thousands passed by to pay their respects. A number of other Confederate notables, including Jeb Stuart, were also laid in state here.

In the House of Delegates Chamber is a life-sized bronze statue of Robert E. Lee, clad in full uniform with one hand on the hilt of his sword and the other holding his hat. It stands on the exact spot where he accepted command of Virginia's military forces. In reality, Lee was dressed in civilian clothing. In attendance were Gov. John Letcher and Vice President Stephens.

The capitol became the command post for the Federals fighting the fire on April 3, and occupation forces set up in the House of Delegates on April 4. When Lincoln visited, he advised Weitzel, "I'd let 'em up easy." A later occupation commander was Gen. F. M. Dent, Grant's brother-in-law.

The capitol contains busts of John Tyler, Jefferson Davis, Thomas J. Jackson, Joseph E. Johnston, Fitzhugh Lee, Matthew Maury, Alexander Stephens, and Jeb Stuart. In the rotunda is a life-sized statue of George Washington, sculptured by Jean Antoine Houdon with Washington as a live model. It is considered the finest and most valuable marble statue in the United States.

At the northeastern end of Capitol Square is the governor's mansion (1814), home to two Civil War governors, John Letcher and William "Extra Billy" Smith. Many official events were held here during the war. On May 11, 1863, Jackson lay in state in a coffin covered with the national flag. Constance Cary described the scene: "Two sentries paced to and fro in the moonlight streaming through the windows. A lamp burned dimly at the end of the hall, but we saw distinctly the regular white outline of the quiet face in its dreamless slumber." On the following day the body was viewed in the capitol. Following the Civil War eight of ten Virginia governors had served in the Confederate army, their ranks ranging from private to major general.

South of Capitol Square on Main Street, between Tenth and Eleventh Streets, is the three-story U.S. Post Office (1858, originally the U.S. Customs House). Although most Confederate offices and bureaus—concentrated in a complex among Eighth, Twelfth, Grace, and Cary Streets—were destroyed in the evacuation fire, this stout structure was the primary Confederate government building and survived the conflagration. Davis's office was on the second floor, and the first floor contained the Treasury Department. The last regular meeting of the Confederate cabinet was held here April 2, 1865, which included Davis, Secretary of State Judah Benjamin, Secretary of War John C. Breckinridge, Secretary of the Navy Stephen Mallory, Secretary of the Treasury George A. Trenholm, Postmaster General John T. Reagan, Gov. William Smith, and Mayor Joseph Mayo. The fire destroyed the War Department at Mechanic's Hall (Ninth and Bank Streets), where on April 17, 1861, the Virginia Secession Convention had passed the Ordinance of Secession.

Ironically, on May 15, 1867, Davis was brought here from Fort Monroe to be arraigned on charges of treason. When the judge called the case "bailable," Horace Greeley immediately raised the amount from Cornelius Vanderbilt and others. Davis was free and took the same suite in the Spotswood Hotel that he had occupied on his arrival in Richmond in 1861. All charges against him were dropped two years later.

On April 2, 1865, the headquarters of Richard Ewell, commanding the Department of Richmond, were at Franklin and Seventh (since destroyed). At 10 A.M. he received orders to evacuate the city at 8 P.M. and immediately went to work. Dispatches were sent to the government and military leaders and orders were written to coordinate the evacuation of records, supplies, and personnel. Manufacturing facilities and supplies that could not be moved were to be destroyed. After Ewell departed the city over Mayo's Bridge and joined Lee, he was captured on April 6 in the disaster at Sayler's Creek.

Saint Paul's Episcopal Church (1845, 815 East Grace Street, at the southwest corner of Ninth and Grace Streets) is often called the "Church of the Confederacy." Davis and his family occupied pew no. 63, and Lee's family worshiped from pew no. 111, with the general in attendance when he was not in the field. Both pews are marked with plaques, and there is a Lee memorial window. Here Davis was confirmed; Winnie Davis, the "Daughter of the Confederacy," was baptized; and the funeral of her brother "Little Joe" was held May 1, 1864. Other prominent members were W. H. F. Lee, Josiah Gorgas, Samuel Cooper, and George W. Randolph. The Confederate diarist Mary Chesnut noted fourteen Confederate generals in attendance on March 3, 1864, including Lee and Longstreet. Here Confederate Secretary of War James A. Seddon married Sallie Bruce, and Gen. Richard S. Ewell married the Widow Brown (his cousin, Mrs. Lizinka C. Brown) on May 26, 1863; he afterward would introduce her as "My wife, Mrs. Brown." On January 19, 1865, Maj. Gen. John Pegram married Hetty Cary, daughter of a prominent Richmond family. Pegram was killed February 6, 1865, at Hatcher's Run near Petersburg, and his funeral was held here three weeks after his wedding. Many members watched sexton William Irving enter during Sunday morning services on April 2, 1865, and hand Davis an envelope. Inside was a message from Lee reporting that he was evacuating Petersburg and Richmond would have to be abandoned immediately. Witnesses saw Davis turn gray before he rose and hurried out. More envelopes were brought in and delivered to other prominent men, who quickly left as the congregation whispered speculations. On the ground floor of the church, women gathered to sew uniforms and sandbags. On several occasions Lee stopped by to personally deliver his thanks for their work.

Saint Peter's Catholic Church (1834, northeastern corner of Grace and Eighth Streets) counted among its Civil War worshipers P. G. T. Beauregard, Stephen R. Mallory, and Postmaster General John Reagan. On April 21, 1861, four days after Virginia seceded, Father Teeling dropped his customary prayer for the president of the United States and substituted one for Governor Letcher, but he soon changed it for Jefferson Davis, a practice which continued through April 2, 1865. Secretary of War Edwin Stanton was so angry that an order requiring prayers for Lincoln and then Andrew Johnson was not enforced that he relieved General Weitzel of command in occupied Richmond. The church blessed its own rifle company and sent it off to Manassas on May 26, 1861, with Father Feeling as its chaplain. The company fought until Appomattox.

The Reverend Dr. Moses D. Hoge of Second Presbyterian Church (1847, near the northeastern corner of Main and Fifth Streets) served from 1847 until 1889. The church had 10,000 Bibles and 250,000 religious tracts run through the blockade from England to meet the spiritual needs of Confederate soldiers. The sanctuary became a hospital after Seven Pines. In July 1862 Stonewall Jackson and his staff slipped quietly into worship services but were soon recognized and mobbed by the congregation. The Confederate officers executed a skillful withdrawal. The evacuation fire destroyed all the windows in the church.

A hospital was set up in the basement of Centenary Methodist Church (1843, 411 East Grace Street) in 1862. Its Sunday school superintendent, Maj. John Walker, was killed at Malvern Hill.

Matthew F. Maury worshiped at Monumental Episcopal Church (Broad Street, between Twelfth and College Streets). Before the war Leonidas Polk, a Confederate general in the West, was associate rector.

Broad Street Methodist Church (Tenth and Broad Streets, destroyed in 1968) was pastored by Dr. James A. Duncan, a friend of Davis and Lee, who occasionally attended services. Beauregard was here when he learned of Richmond's imminent evacuation. Duncan accepted a seat Davis offered on the evacuation train, but he returned to his parishioners after Appomattox. The new church at 1205 West Franklin Street has a stained-glass memorial window dedicated to Sally Tompkins.

The funeral of Jeb Stuart on May 14, 1864, at Saint James Episcopal Church, was attended by Davis and other leading Confederate officials while crowds filled the streets. The building has also been destroyed.

From Ninth Street at Capitol Square and Saint Paul's Church, continue straight to Broad and turn left onto it. Turn left onto Monroe, then right onto Main and angle across Belvidere to remain on Main. Turn left onto Laurel, then right onto Albemarle at the sign for Hollywood Cemetery. Cross Cherry to the entrance to the cemetery on the left.

Hollywood Cemetery is one of the South's most sacred sites. Established in 1848, it contains the graves of three American presidents (two U.S. and one Confederate—Arlington National Cemetery has only two), twenty-five Confederate generals, the Con-

James Madison is one of three American presidents buried at Richmond's Hollywood Cemetery.

federate secretary of war, and over eighteen thousand Southern soldiers. There are more than sixty thousand burials on its 135 landscaped acres that occupy high bluffs above the James River and offer wonderful views of Richmond and the river below.

During the spring and summer of 1862 gravediggers could not work fast enough to bury the dead from the battlefields of the Peninsula and Seven Days, which created a disturbing stench and threatened public health. The city council directed that long trenches be dug and casualties buried side by side. The flood of dead continued from the dozens of military hospitals established in Richmond. Grieving family members from across the South descended on the city to care for sons, brothers, and husbands and too often to take bodies home for burial.

Richmond and many other Southern communities claim the honor of holding the first Confederate Memorial Day. Here it occurred on May 31, 1866, when twenty thousand people gathered to mourn the Confederate and Federal soldiers buried here. The national government had paid to have Federal casualties buried here in 1865, but they were moved to the Richmond National Cemetery in 1868.

Once past the Victorian caretaker house and Gothic chapel, turn right onto Confederate Avenue to the large stone pyramid marking the Confederate Soldier Section. Most of Hollywood's eighteen thousand Confederate dead rest here, with the ninety-foot-high pyramid of Richmond granite as their memorial. Immediately after the war the Hollywood Memorial Association raised twenty-six thousand dollars through bazaars and lectures to construct the rough-hewn monument. It was dedicated on November 8, 1869, while Virginia was still under Reconstruction rule. The massive structure was the first Confederate monument in the city. No mortar was used to erect the pyramid, and the crane used was not tall enough to place the metal cap on top. The only person brave enough to scale the monument for this purpose was an inmate from the nearby state prison, who was freed for the deed.

Most of the Confederates killed on the battlefield at Gettysburg were buried in a mass grave in Pennsylvania. In the 1870s the remains were disinterred and sent to several southern states, including three thousand who were reburied in this section. Gen. Richard B. Garnett, who died leading his men over the stone wall at Gettysburg, is believed to have been buried in the mass grave and probably rests here today. He has no monument, just a modern headstone. Near the pyramid is a marker for James F. Ames, one of John S. Mosby's famed raiders.

Continue to the loop for the grave of George E. Pickett (1828–75), who wanted to be buried near the men who had sacrificed themselves in his legendary charge. The granite twenty-five-foot-high Pickett Monument, unveiled on October 5, 1888, has an octagonal stone base with a pillared temple structure on top and contains bronze plaques detailing the exploits of the general and his three brigadiers at Gettysburg. In March 1998 the restored monument was rededicated, and the ashes of Pickett's devoted third wife and child bride, LaSalle "Sallie" Corbett, who outlived him by thirty years, were interred beside the general. When she died in 1931, Hollywood would not allow a woman to be buried in the soldiers section. Her cremated remains were placed in a mausoleum near Arlington National Cemetery. Sallie spent most of her life writing and lecturing extensively in defense of her husband.

Return to Confederate Avenue and turn right, then turn left on Western and left again onto Ellis Avenue to Jeb Stuart's grave on the right, which is flanked by two 10-pounder cannon. An inscription reads, "He saved Richmond but gave his life." Stuart (1833–64) was one of the Confederacy's most flamboyant generals, one of its best cavalry leaders, and a perennial favorite among Civil War enthusiasts. After three years of nearly constant operations, Stuart was mortally wounded defending Richmond at Yellow Tavern. He died the following day at the home of his brother-in-law, Confederate Gen. John R. Cooke, who is also buried in Hollywood. During the first ride around McClellan, Stuart was pursued by his father-in-law, Union Gen. Philip St. George Cooke, a native Virginian. Prior to the war, the Stuarts had named their son for him, but when Cooke remained with the Union, they renamed the boy for his father.

Continue down Ellis and turn left onto Freeman Road to the grave of Douglas Southall Freeman (1886–1953), a renowned Confederate historian whose series *Lee's Lieutenants* remains a classic. Freeman, who won a Pulitzer Prize for his biography of Lee and another for a biography of George Washington, was editor of the *Richmond News-Leader*

for thirty-four years. He guided Winston Churchill across Virginia's Civil War battlefields, and during World War II Gens. George S. Patton Jr. and Omar Bradley studied *Lee's Lieutenants*.

On Circular Avenue not far from Freeman's grave is the Valentine plot. Edward Valentine was a skilled sculptor who produced the magnificent *Recumbent Lee* in the chapel of Washington and Lee University in Lexington.

Turn right at Westvale Avenue, then left onto Waterview Avenue and right on Riverside to President's Avenue.

Here are the graves of two Virginia presidents: James Monroe (1758–1831), originally buried in New York City and reinterred here in 1858, and John Tyler (1790–1862). Tyler is the only U.S. president who participated in a war against his own

Confederate President Jefferson Davis was laid to rest in Hollywood Cemetery in 1892, three years after his death and brief interment in New Orleans. His wife, Varina, chose Richmond over proffered sites in every former Confederate state.

A stone angel guards the grave of Winnie Davis, the beloved "Daughter of the Confederacy," born to Jefferson and Varina in the Confederate White House.

country. In 1861 he tried without success to resolve the problems between the North and South as president of the Washington Peace Conference, whose only delegates came from Southern states. Because he believed the North would use military force against the South, Tyler urged Virginia and other states to join the Confederacy. He died as a member of the Confederate Congress in January 1862. Because of these actions, the Federal government refused to honor Tyler with a monument for half a century, erecting this one in October 1915. Legend claims that the family had him buried here because they feared desecration if he were buried on his plantation.

Also buried here is the "Pathfinder of the Seas," Matthew Fontaine Maury (1806–73). He joined the navy at age eighteen and dedicated his life to ocean research. He invented the science of oceanography, charted ocean currents and depths (which revolutionized sea routes), and proposed the establishment of the U.S. Naval Academy and the laying of a transatlantic telegraph cable.

Maury left Annapolis in 1861 to develop electrically detonated mines, which greatly contributed to the defense of the Confederacy's rivers and harbors

and resulted in the destruction of a number of Union ships. After the Civil War, Maury worked in Mexico, refused a number of commands in European navies, and taught at the Virginia Military Institute in Lexington. He also authored many books about oceanography.

Joseph Reid Anderson (1813–92), an 1836 graduate of the U.S. Military Academy, resigned his commission after a year to enter civil engineering. He built the Valley turnpike, so often traveled by Stonewall Jackson's troops, and purchased the Tredegar Iron Company in Richmond in the early 1840s. By the Civil War it was not only the largest foundry in the South but one of the finest in the United States. Anderson employed twenty-five hundred men during the war to produce most of the Confederacy's artillery plus armor for four Confederate ironclads. He earned the loyalty of his workers with good pay, health care, housing, and food and clothing allowances during Richmond's war years, and he refused to have his factory destroyed when the city was evacuated. Saved by Anderson and his employees, by August 1865 Tredegar was again manufacturing products invaluable to the devastated South.

Continue on Monroe Avenue, then take the first left and the next right onto Davis Avenue to Davis Circle. Jefferson Davis (1808–89) fled Richmond on April 3, 1865, and was captured in southern Georgia in May. After being imprisoned at Fort Monroe for two years, Davis traveled in Europe, engaged in an insurance business in Memphis, and retired to the Mississippi Gulf Coast to write his memoirs, *The Rise and Fall of the Confederate Government*. Following his death, he was buried in New Orleans. Every Confederate state offered his wife, Varina, a prominent burial site for the president of the Confederacy. She chose to have him interred in Richmond, the Confederate capital. The train bearing Davis's remains was stopped by crowds at every station, ceremonies were held at each state line, and the body lay in state in several state capitols. When Davis was reinterred in 1893, more than twenty thousand people mobbed Hollywood Cemetery. A simple statue of Davis, standing nobly, hat in hand, was dedicated on November 9, 1899. Varina rests beside Jefferson, and nearby is daughter Winnie, the "Daughter of the Confederacy," who had been born in the Confederate White

House. A stone angel watches over her. Her brother, "Little Joe," who died after a fall at the Confederate White House, is also buried here.

Across the drive is the grave of Fitzhugh Lee (1835–1905), a nephew of Robert E. Lee, who was almost suspended while his uncle was superintendent of West Point. Fitzhugh Lee commanded the Army of Northern Virginia's cavalry from January 1865 to the end. He served as Virginia's governor and promoted construction of the Lee statue on Monument Avenue, insisting that it be as grand as Washington's statue on Capitol Square. With former Confederate Gen. Joseph Wheeler, Lee reentered the U.S. Army in 1898 to lead the force that invaded Cuba. The elderly three-hundred-pound cavalier, however, directed the campaign from Tampa.

Fitzhugh Lee, nephew of Robert E. Lee and commander of the Army of Northern Virginia's cavalry after the death of Jeb Stuart, became Virginia's governor after the war. He is one of twenty-five Confederate generals buried at Hollywood.

Return toward the cemetery entrance on Waterview Avenue to East Vale Road and the Confederate Officers Section, marked by the entrance arch on the right. Across the lane is the grave of William "Extra Billy" Smith (1796–1887), a colorful Virginia personality. His nickname originated when he started a postal route from Richmond to Petersburg. Every time he extended the service he earned additional payments from the government. Smith was governor during the Mexican War and led a regiment during the Civil War at age sixty-five, earning the rank of brigadier general. He charged into battle beneath an umbrella that shaded him from the sun. Smith was again elected governor during the war and then served in the state legislature at age eighty-seven.

Five Confederate generals are buried in the Confederate Officers Section, and many more rest throughout the cemetery: Henry Heth, John D. Imboden, brothers David and Samuel Jones, and John Pegram. Pegram, killed February 2, 1865, while rallying his troops at Hatcher's Run near Petersburg, was buried here by Hetty Cary, his wife of three weeks. His brother, William, was killed two months later and also was buried here. Military engineer Charles Dimmock, who laid out Richmond's defenses, is also here. Two other Confederate notables buried in Hollywood Cemetery are Confederate Secretary of War James A. Seddon and Hunter H. McGuire, Jackson's surgeon.

Some of the fiercest fighters in the Confederate army were the First Special Battalion, colorful Zouaves known as the "Louisiana Tigers." They were led by Maj. Chatham Roberdeau Wheat, who survived grievous wounds at First Manassas and returned to his men for the Seven Days, during which he was killed at Gaines's Mill, crying: "Bury me not on the field, boys." He is buried at Hollywood, where a granite slab monument was dedicated to his memory in 1993. Also buried here is the first Confederate to be killed in the war, Pvt. Henry Wyatt of North Carolina, who fell at Big Bethel on June 10, 1861.

Three of James Longstreet's children died of typhoid fever during the war's first winter and are buried here. Pickett supervised the funeral for his grief-striken friend.

Take advantage of the overlook for a magnificent view of Richmond and the James River.

Other memorials in Hollywood include the Confederate Women's Monument, a small rectangular stone honoring the contributions of Southern ladies, dedicated on November 8, 1869; the Confederate Monument, a large rectangular stone slab with bronze medallions unveiled on October 25, 1902; and the Otey Battery Monument, an obelisk dedicated on November 11, 1887.

A thirty-page booklet, *Hollywood Cemetery, A Tour,* by James E. DePriest Jr. is a must for touring Hollywood. The foldout map is invaluable. It is widely sold in the Richmond area.

Atop Shockoe Hill on Hospital Street, between Second and Fourth Streets northwest of Capitol Square, is Shockoe Cemetery, which contains the graves of Revolutionary War soldiers and Chief Justice John Marshall. Most of the 91 known and 582 unknown Federal soldiers and 220 Confederates interred here died directly across the street at General Hospital No. 1 (originally the city hospital and poor house, 1820), a large four-story brick structure. The building housed Union prisoners captured at First Manassas in 1861, then became a Confederate hospital through December 1864, although Federal sick and wounded also received care. In December 1864 the refugee VMI cadets were housed here, having occupied tents at Camp Lee since their arrival in May, when Union Gen. David Hunter torched the campus in retaliation for the cadets' participation in the battle of New Market. Hundreds of other Civil War dead lie in unmarked graves—records of them either never existed or were destroyed. The premier Confederate notable interred here is Civil War Mayor Joseph Mayo, who surrendered the city.

Across Hospital Street from Shockoe Cemetery is Hebrew Cemetery (1816), which has a section reserved for Jewish Confederates, surrounded by a cast-iron fence shaped like stacked rifles and crossed swords. Richmond's foremost Unionist resident, Elizabeth Van Lew rests here. She ran a network of spies in the city and was ostracized from Richmond society for the next forty years. When she died on August 25, 1900, not one person attended her funeral. The grave lacked a headstone until an admirer in Massachusetts sent one. The inscription reads, "She risked everything that was dear to her—friends, fortune, comfort, health, even life itself—all for one absorbing desire of her heart—that slavery might be abolished and the Union preserved." Also buried in Hebrew Cemetery is Nicholas Mills, the last Richmond citizen to fly the Stars and Stripes in 1861. He died in 1864. During the war seven spies were executed on a scaffold erected on Shockoe Hill.

Oakland Cemetery, in East End off East Broad Street near Richmond Battlefield Park, can be entered from Hospital Street or from Nine Mile Road on Oakland Avenue. Near the entrance is the Confederate Soldier's Monument (1871), erected by the Oakland Memorial Association. The granite obelisk stands atop a seven-tiered pyramid and honors the eighteen thousand dead buried here. They were gathered from surrounding battlefields and hospital burial grounds. Oakland was designated a Confederate burial ground in 1861 and received many casualties from the Seven Days' battles and

President John Tyler was interred at Hollywood Cemetery. He was shunned by the U.S. government for serving in the Confederate Congress.

Chimborazo Hospital. An unknown number of Federals from Richmond's prisons and hospitals are also found here. After Federal Col. Ulric Dahlgren was ambushed and killed on an aborted cavalry raid against Richmond, he was secretly buried in a pine coffin here on March 7, 1864. A tree was planted on top of the grave to disguise it. Because documents found on Dahlgren's body indicated the Federals planned to burn Richmond and assassinate Davis and his cabinet, Dahlgren was considered a war criminal.

To safeguard Dahlgren's body, Elizabeth Van Lew's network went to work. She discovered the grave's location from Martin Lipscomb, Oakland Cemetery's director. F. W. E. Lohman led a party to disinter the body on the night of April 6, carefully replacing the sapling. Van Lew viewed the remains, which were hidden in a wagon beneath a load of young fruit trees. It barely escaped a search by Confederate sentries. Dahlgren was reburied on the farm of Robert Orrick, a German immigrant, beneath one of the fruit trees.

Davis agreed to send Dahlgren's body to his father, Rear Adm. John A. Dahlgren, who sent one hundred dollars in gold for that purpose. There was great consternation when the corpse was reported missing. A reward of five hundred dollars went unclaimed. Van Lew's people exhumed the body in October 1865 after Richmond was occupied. It lay in state in Washington, then at Independence Hall in Philadelphia before final burial on November 11 in Laurel Hill Cemetery there.

Maury Cemetery, at 2700 Maury Street, contains many Confederate graves and those transferred from the Masonic and Old Plank Church cemeteries.

From the entrance to Hollywood Cemetery turn left onto Cherry. Turn right onto Idlewood, then left onto Belvidere, and left onto Broad. Turn left onto Allen and left onto West Grace. Turn right onto Lombardy. The Stuart statue is in front as you turn right onto Monument Avenue.

The fifteen-foot-high bronze equestrian statue of Jeb Stuart, perched on a seven-and-a-half-foot-high granite pedestal, is the first memorial on Monument Avenue. The statue was executed by sculptor Frederick Moynihan. Stuart holds a sword in his right hand and reins in his left, and his hat is graced with its distinctive plume. Stuart rides the spirited General, the horse he was riding when he was mortally wounded defending the northern outskirts of Richmond at Yellow Tavern. He died a day later, May 12, 1864, aged thirty-one, at his brother-in-law's house, which stood at 210 West Grace Street. The decorative iron fence surrounding the monument at Stuart Circle suggests crossed swords and cannon. The statue was unveiled on May 30, 1907, part of a frantic week when seventeen thousand Confederate veterans descended on the city for a great reunion. The Jefferson Davis statue was also dedicated that week.

Stuart (1833–64) was one of the most beloved figures in the Confederacy. A colorful, energetic figure, he performed brilliantly as the eyes and ears of the Army of Northern Virginia and fought furiously at Brandy Station, Yellow Tavern, and many other battles. Note that the statues of Stuart and Jackson both face north, their faces to the enemy, symbolizing their deaths in combat.

To the right, on Lombardy Street at the corner of West Grace Street (1142 West Grace), is the American Historical Foundation, which has exhibits of artifacts, uniforms, and photos about Monument Avenue, Jeb Stuart, and John Mosby. It also tells the history of the U.S. military through the Vietnam War.

Drive straight on Monument, keeping the series of monuments on your left.

The beloved Confederate cavalier Jeb Stuart rides an appropriately spirited steed on Monument Avenue.

The statue of Jefferson Davis on Monument Avenue is dwarfed by columns representing the Confederate states and a tall column supporting a figure of Vindicatrix, representing the South.

In order they are Lee, Davis, Jackson, and Maury. Immediately after Lee's death on October 12, 1870, two organizations were formed to memorialize him. First was the Ladies Lee Memorial Association, which began soliciting funds from across the South. It was soon followed by the Soldiers' Lee Association, founded after Gen. Jubal A. Early made a newspaper appeal for Confederate officers and soldiers to meet in Richmond on November 3, 1870, to honor Lee and plan a monument. By the time Virginia's General Assembly consolidated the groups, the women had received models of proposed memorials from the finest artists in America and Europe. Two were chosen for further consideration, but Charles H. Niehaus was an Ohio Yankee and Richmond resident Moses Ezekiel seemed too much of a favorite son. From Paris, French sculptor Mercie had sent an excellent horse, but his Lee was rejected. A plaster cast of Lee's death mask, photos of the general, and his uniform were dispatched to France, where one of Lee's daughters, Mary, visited the studio regularly. Mercie's third model was commissioned.

The location of the statue was given careful consideration. Many sites were examined, but it was decided to accept a gift lot from Ottway S. Allen, which was outside the city limits on an extension of Franklin Street. Allen hoped the statue would spur growth for other properties he owned. Despite a heavy rain, when the cornerstone was laid on October 27, 1887, nearly twenty thousand people attended the procession led by Gov. Fitzhugh Lee and Wade Hampton.

When the massive statue was completed in February 1890, Richmond engineer Col. C. P. E. Burgwyn inspected it and wired home, "Nothing in Paris superior to it." The statue reached the Richmond, Fredericksburg, and Potomac Railroad Depot on Broad Street on May 7, where it was met by ten thousand people who helped unload four large crates onto four wagons festooned with Confederate flags. Thousands of Confederate veterans, schoolchildren, and ordinary citizens pulled the wagons along Broad Street, First, and Franklin, and out to the site.

Three weeks later the twelve-ton monument had been erected atop a high stone pedestal. The dedication on May 29, 1890, lasted two and a half hours and was watched by a massive crowd of 140,000 people. Leading the procession was Lee's nephew Fitzhugh Lee, a governor and Confederate general, with Joseph E. Johnston, James Longstreet, Wade Hampton, Jubal Early, John Gordon, Joseph Wheeler, many other Confederate generals, and an estimated 18,000 veterans. Marching bands played "Dixie" and numberless drums and fifes kept the pace lively. Dozens of battle flags, bloodstained and shot riddled, were carried by veteran campaigners. The cheering of the crowd was said to be deafening.

When Johnston unveiled the monumental statue, one hundred cannon were fired and the throngs cheered and shouted uninterrupted for ten minutes. They hugged each other and cried unashamedly, all the time waving thousands of flags, banners, handkerchiefs, umbrellas, and scarfs. For a few minutes one could believe that the Confederacy had triumphed.

The monument is still impressive today. Standing atop a forty-foot-high white granite pedestal is Lee astride a mighty steed. The general is depicted in full uniform with sword, a wide-brimmed felt hat clutched in his right hand, reins in the left, and he faces south. The figure is a dignified, commanding pose, at ease astride a graceful but powerful horse. The sculptor thought Lee's head "too noble" to be covered, making this the first equestrian figure depicted without a hat. To the disappointment of many, Lee does not ride the renowned Traveller, who was thought too slender for the powerful memorial. Instead, the general rides a French hunter, its great head bowed. The only inscription on the monument are two large bronze plaques which read simply "Lee" and "1807–1870."

Two of Lee's daughters, Mary and Mildred, were present at the unveiling of the seventy-seven-thousand-dollar monument. They felt it a "very striking resemblance" to their father, but the greatest tribute came from Confederate veterans who assured each other, "Yep, that's Marse Robert."

The statue immediately became a revered Richmond landmark. Noted historian and Lee biographer Douglas Southall Freeman tipped his hat whenever he passed the statue.

Continue down Monument to the Davis Monument. The seven-and-a-half-foot-tall bronze figure of Jefferson Davis (1808–89), with one arm outstretched in a speaker's pose, stands atop a nine-and-a-half-foot-high granite pedestal. The statue, by local artist Edward Valentine, is dwarfed by a sixty-seven-foot-tall stone column topped by a bronze figure of Vindicatrix, produced by William Sievers, which represents the South. The monument, which was designed by William C. Noland, has thirteen Doric columns to represent the eleven seceded states that formed the Confederacy and the two states that sent delegates to the Confederate Congress in Richmond.

Fund-raising for the memorial was started in 1893 by the UDC, which held a series of bazaars. The cornerstone was originally laid in Monroe Park,

Stonewall Jackson rides Little Sorrel forever on Richmond's Monument Avenue.

a site selected by Varina Davis, then moved here. On April 18, 1907, the monument was drawn to this spot by three thousand students and dedicated on June 3, during a Confederate Veterans Reunion.

Continue to the Jackson Monument. This is Richmond's second statue of Thomas Jonathan Jackson (1824–63). The first, by English sculptor John Foley, was donated by English admirers and dedicated at Capitol Square in 1875. This equestrian statue depicts the general sitting stiffly atop his horse, Little Sorrel, at the battle of First Manassas, where he won the nickname Stonewall. Designed by F. William Sievers, who also produced the Lee monument at Gettysburg, the bronze figures are seventeen and a half feet high and stand atop a twenty-foot-high granite pedestal. The stuffed remains of Little Sorrel at the Virginia Military Institute in Lexington served as the model for the horse. When it was dedicated on October 11, 1919, only one hundred Confederate veterans managed to attend.

A right on Boulevard from the Jackson statue leads to the Richmond Visitors Center at Interstate 69–95 and on to the A. P. Hill Monument at Laburnum Avenue.

This memorial was sponsored by Pegram's Battalion. William L. Sheppard created the nine-and-a-half-foot-tall figure, which stands atop a twenty-four-and-a-half-foot-high pedestal, itself elevated on a mound. A long parade wound through the city to this spot, donated by Maj. Lewis Ginter, on May 30, 1892. Later Hill's body was disinterred from Hollywood Cemetery and buried beneath the monument.

Hill was killed at Petersburg only days before the Civil War ended and was buried at three different locations. At 2 A.M. on April 3 his body reached Richmond in an ambulance driven by a nephew, Henry Hill. Despite the chaos in the city, he found a coffin in an abandoned furniture store, crossed Mayo Bridge, and buried his uncle on the Winston farm on the south side of the James.

A left turn onto Boulevard from the Jackson Monument leads to the Virginia Historical Society–Battle Abbey, one block away at the corner of Kensington.

The great neoclassical structure was dedicated in 1913 by the Confederate Memorial Association as a shrine to the Confederate war dead and as an archives for records of the Southern military and government. In 1914 Charles Hoffbauer, a French mural artist and later a Walt Disney animator, was commissioned to paint a series of monumental works depicting the history of the Confederacy. Unveiled in 1921 and titled *Four Seasons of the Confederacy,* they are displayed in the Cheek Mural Gallery.

The Spring mural shows Stonewall Jackson reviewing his army in the Shenandoah Valley. Two panels depict the naval battle between the *Virginia* and the *Cumberland* and the *Congress* and the arrival of a hospital train.

The Summer mural depicts a fantasy meeting of Confederate generals, the greater ones on horses, lesser luminaries standing. Included are Robert E. Lee, Joseph E. Johnston, P. G. T. Beauregard, Stonewall Jackson, James Longstreet, Jeb Stuart, John Bell Hood, A. P. Hill, Richard S. Ewell, Wade Hampton, John B. Gordon, Fitzhugh Lee, and George E. Pickett.

Portrayed in the Autumn mural is Jeb Stuart leading his troopers on a raid, with a panel showing Confederate raider John S. Mosby, "the Gray Ghost," on a night foray. Another panel has Confederate marines manning coastal artillery.

The Winter mural depicts the desperate condition of an artillery battery retreating through the snow, the crews exhausted, their equipment shattered.

In front of the murals is displayed an excellent collection of weapons manufactured by the Confederacy. The exhibit, called Arming the Confederacy, draws upon the three-hundred-piece collection of firearms and equipment from the Maryland-Steuart Collection to demonstrate the success of a rural, agricultural society that was forced to develop its own weapons factories.

The Casten Gallery presents Making the Confederate Murals. After Hoffbauer started the projects, he returned to France during World War I. On his return from the trenches, Hoffbauer destroyed his earlier work as unrealistic and started over. Here are clay models, oils, pastel watercolors, pencil sketches, and photos of the developing work.

The collection of the Virginia Historical Society, founded in 1831, barely escaped destruction during the evacuation fire in 1865. In the 1890s its extensive holdings were displayed in the Lee house on Franklin Street. In 1946 the Virginia Historical Association merged with the Confederate Memorial Society, and the collection was moved to Battle Abbey in 1959.

The Story of Virginia: An American Experience, a permanent exhibit, explores the storied history of the Old Dominion from prehistory to the present. Considerable attention is given to the Civil War era. Topics explored are slavery, the outbreak of war, the roles of various groups including women and African Americans, Reconstruction, and the legacy of the South's fascination with the Civil War. Included are a carving of Lee's head beside the figure of a crucified Jesus, Lee's prayer book, the orders to evacuate Richmond written by Col. Walter Taylor on a scrap of paper in Petersburg and telegraphed to Richmond, Stonewall Jackson's watch, the sash Jeb Stuart wore at Yellow Tavern, John Brown's Bowie knife, a window from Libby Prison, a crucifix belonging to George E. Pickett, and the bullet that killed Capt. John Q. Marr, the first Confederate to die in combat on June 1, 1861, at Fairfax Court House.

Another permanent exhibit is Sculpture from the Permanent Collection, which includes the plaster model of the nearby equestrian statue of Stonewall Jackson, a bronze of physician Dr. Hunter H. McGuire, and a bust of John S. Mosby.

The Virginia Historical Society houses the largest and most comprehensive collection of Virginia material in the state and the most extensive portrait collection in the South, much of it donated by the Robert E. Lee Camp No. 1, Confederate Veterans, in

Battle Abbey, the Virginia Historical Society, displays inspiring paintings that depict the Confederacy and numerous important artifacts from the Civil War.

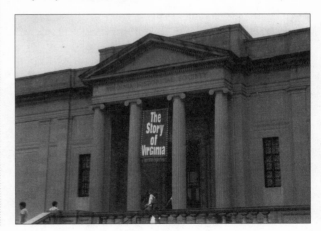

the early 1900s. The archives contain 7 million manuscripts and 125,000 books.

A unique new sculpture welcomes visitors to the Virginia Historical Society. Standing atop a six-foot-high stone platform is an emaciated, riderless horse, suggesting a Southern mount late in the war whose rider has been killed in battle. *The War Horse,* by Tessa Pullan, a noted British equestrian sculptor, was commissioned by philanthropist Paul Mellon, who served at the U.S. Army's cavalry school at Fort Riley, Kansas, during World War II. He was inspired by the fierce cavalry battles at Aldie, Middleburg, and Upperville, Virginia, which occurred as Lee marched to Pennsylvania in 1863. The monument honors the estimated one and a half million horses and mules that were killed, wounded, or died of disease during the war. Despite the advent of railroads, these animals were the backbone of the transportation system of the time, pulling artillery, supply wagons, and ambulances and carrying cavalry, officers and couriers. One of the two copies of *The War Horse* stands at the National Sporting Library at Middleburg; the other was placed at the U.S. Cavalry Museum at Fort Riley.

Beside Battle Abbey is the United Daughters of the Confederacy Headquarters Memorial Building (8 Stuart Avenue), a repository of rare books, diaries, and letters concerning Confederate history. The UDC was established in 1894 for historical, educational, benevolent, and patriotic purposes. A major responsibility is preserving historic sites and collecting and preserving the records and efforts of men and women during the Civil War. The UDC has a heavy iron safe used by the Confederate government in the treasurer's office.

The next major institution on Boulevard is the Virginia Museum of Fine Arts, and behind it (2900 Grove Road) is the Confederate Memorial Chapel (also known as Pelham Chapel), a tiny building that is one of two buildings remaining from the Confederate Soldier's Home. The home opened in 1883 to care for aged veterans who were suffering in the alms house. Ulysses S. Grant contributed one hundred dollars of the twenty-five thousand dollars needed to purchase the thirty-six-acre farm. It opened on January 1, 1885, and included a large three-story house, a chapel-museum, cottages, a hospital-mess, and a meeting hall. The complex

housed up to three hundred veterans. The facility closed in 1947. The restored chapel, the site of seventeen hundred funerals for soldiers and their relatives, was once filled with Confederate memorabilia, including Jackson's stuffed mount, Little Sorrel, now displayed at VMI in Lexington. The Robinson house, on the north side of Grove Avenue between Boulevard and Sheppard Street, is also part of the home. It is marked by a cannon that served in the defenses of Charleston. At 301 Sheppard Street is the Confederate Home for Ladies, which resembles the White House in Washington, D.C.

On the southeastern corner of Boulevard and Monument is the present location of First Baptist Church. The original Greek Revival church (1841)—designed by Thomas U. Walter, who was also responsible for the dome and wings of the Capitol in Washington, D.C.—still stands at the northwest corner of Broad and Twelfth Streets. It was used as a hospital on May 31, 1862, during the battle of Seven Pines, when pew cushions were sacrificed for the wounded. Two months earlier, on April 6, the

Matthew Maury, immortalized on Monument Avenue, was the first oceanographer and developed "torpedoes" (mines) to defend Southern harbors and rivers.

congregation had approved a resolution to donate their bronze bell to the Confederate war effort. A parishioner, John Thomas, visited the secretary of war and paid gold for the bell's redemption. It is now in a loggia on the grounds of the new church.

The Virginia State Archives, on Broad Street opposite First Baptist Church, has a vast collection of Civil War books and manuscripts.

Continue on Monument to the final memorial, an eight-foot-high seated bronze of Matthew F. Maury (1806–73), designed by F. William Sievers and dedicated in 1929. Rising behind Maury on a granite pedestal is a nine-foot-wide globe with figures in the waves at its base representing his study of winds and currents. "The Pathfinder of the Seas" was a pioneer in oceanography who developed contact and electrically detonated mines for use by the Confederacy. After the Civil War, Maury taught meteorology at VMI. He is buried in Hollywood Cemetery at President's Circle.

In 1965 a monument to Confederate nurse Sally Tompkins, commissioned a captain in the Confederate army, was proposed for Monument Avenue. Artist Salvador Dali proposed a memorial consisting of one thousand pounds of pink aluminum in the shape of a mushroom, with a figure of Tompkins atop it armed with a sword and dueling a giant germ. The base would be a twenty-foot-tall model of Dali's little finger. To the relief of all, the idea was rejected.

Other notable Richmond monuments include the Howitzer Monument (1892), honoring a renowned Confederate battery. The memorial by W. L. Shephard was dedicated on December 13, 1892. Erected at Park Avenue and Harrison Street on the western edge of Virginia Commonwealth University, it portrays Number One, a gunner holding his sponge staff. The William C. Wickham statue, given to the city by men of his Civil War company and employees of the Chesapeake and Ohio Railroad, stands in Monroe Park surrounded by Franklin, Belvidere, Main, and Laurel Streets. Also in Monroe Park is a statue of Joseph Bryan, a member of John Mosby's Rangers, unveiled with Mosby present on June 10, 1911.

The area of Monroe Park was formerly the fairgrounds, where in 1861 Jackson's VMI cadets drilled the raw Confederate recruits who poured into Richmond. Civilians flocked to watch the drills, mock combat, and parades. The area became the camp-grounds for the city guard before sixteen buildings were constructed in 1864 for Stuart Hospital, which had a capacity of five hundred men.

In 1861–62 Vice President Alexander H. Stephens boarded in the Bruce house at the northwestern corner of Twelfth and Clay. He soon returned to Georgia and sniped verbally at Davis from long distance. Gen. Samuel Cooper, the oldest and highest-ranking Southern general, who served as the Confederate adjutant and inspector general, lived near the northwest corner of Third and Grace Streets. Secretary of the Treasury Christopher G. Memminger lived in the John Wickham house at the southwest corner of Eleventh and Clay, now the Valentine Museum.

Jeb Stuart's headquarters from before the battle of Seven Pines through the end of the Seven Days was at Montebello, at 5102 Montebello Circle.

In 1896 the Sons of Confederate Veterans was formed in the auditorium at Cary and Linden Streets. Jeb Stuart Jr. was its first commander in chief.

On the morning of April 3, 1865, the convicts in the Virginia State Penitentiary (on Second Street between the Tredegar Iron Works and Hollywood Cemetery) awoke to learn that their guards had vanished. They donned civilian clothes from the storehouse, started fires, and set out to plunder the ruined city. Most were soon captured by a dragnet of Federal troops that the Union provost marshal sent out. They were then incarcerated in Libby Prison or Castle Thunder while the penitentiary was repaired.

After the Civil War, George E. Pickett lived at the southwestern corner of Sixth and Leigh with his bride, LaSalle Corbel, whom he married just after Gettysburg in September 1863, when she was but fifteen years old. The Barret house (1844), 13 South Fifth Street, was later purchased by Maj. David N. Walker, who commanded a Confederate battery. During the Civil War he gave his family pew, No. 111, at Saint Paul's Church, to the Lee family.

Many historic structures were destroyed in the evacuation fire or during the intervening 130 years. Lee wrote General Order No. 1 at the General Court Building, where many counties sent records for safekeeping during the war. Erected at the southeastern corner of Capitol Square, it burned on April 3, 1865.

The Spotswood Hotel, southeastern corner of Eighth and Main, hosted Davis and his family for two

BATTLES AND LEADERS

Much of Richmond was destroyed in a fire that swept through the city during the evacuation of April 1865.

months. Lee and Beauregard and virtually every renowned personality in the Confederacy stayed there. A number of Confederate officers' wives were here on July 21, 1861, when some, including Francis Bartow's wife, were informed of their husbands' deaths. "God help us," one said. "Is this what we prayed for?" Following Appomattox many Union generals—including Grant, Sherman, Sheridan, and Meade—and President Andrew Johnson spent time in the hotel. After the surrender at Appomattox, Grant returned to Washington from City Point without visiting Richmond, although his wife toured the Confederate capital. Grant visited Richmond only once in his life, on May 18, 1867, five days after Davis was released from prison. The Spotswood burned on Christmas Day 1870.

Gen. John Hunt Morgan was feted at the Ballard house, northeastern corner of Fourteenth and Franklin, after his legendary escape from an Ohio prison. Former U.S. President John Tyler, turned Confederate congressman, died there on January 8, 1862, as did his wife, Julie, in 1889.

On May 11, 1864, mortally wounded Jeb Stuart was taken to the house of his brother-in-law, Dr. Charles Brewer, at 210 West Grace Street. Davis stopped by several times, but Jeb's beloved wife, Flora, whom he repeatedly asked for, did not arrive until five hours after he died. Stuart expressed joy at rejoining his daughter Flora, who had died in late 1862. He asked those attending him to sing "The Old Rugged Cross," his favorite hymn, and he struggled to sing along. He died at 7:30 P.M. on May

12. Just over two weeks later, on May 29, Federal Pvt. John A. Huff, who had shot Stuart, was killed in combat at Haw's Shop.

On the evening of April 2, 1865, eighty-year-old Mayor Mayo and the city council gathered at city hall to discuss surrendering the city to the Federals. They drafted a note and at 3 A.M. of April 3 started out in two carriages for the city's southeastern outskirts. At 6:30, near the intersection of New Market and Osborn Roads, they encountered a Federal officer. City hall was demolished in 1874.

The Van Lew house stood a block east of Broad on Grace Street, now the site of Belle Vue School. "Miss Lizzy," who converted to abolitionism while being schooled in Philadelphia, freed the family slaves when her father died in 1860. She refused to disguise her Unionist beliefs and carried food to Union prisoners held in the city. As the Federal army approached in May 1862, she prepared a "McClellan Room" so the general would be comfortable after he captured Richmond. When Davis declared "days of fast," Lew feasted openly.

Although Confederate authorities kept Van Lew under surveillance, she managed to organize a network of spies who gathered intelligence about Southern strength and activities and passed it on to the Union lines at Fort Monroe. A black servant (and possibly others) whom she is thought to have infiltrated into the Confederate White House may have set the arson fire in January 1864. Van Lew is thought to have aided the Union prisoners who escaped from Libby Prison on February 9, 1864, although other accounts have her absent from home that night. Nonetheless, prisoners who fled Libby on April 3, 1865, may have taken shelter in her home. Her most famous exploit, however, was engineering the body-napping of Ulric Dahlgren.

Recognizing Van Lew's dangerous position, Grant posted guards at her home after the Federal occupation of the city. Later, as president, Grant appointed her postmaster of Richmond, which really riled the locals. In her old age, lonely and poor, "Crazy Bet" kept forty cats for company.

The Virginia Central Railroad Depot, a modest wooden shed, stood on the southwestern corner of Broad and Sixteenth. Armies arrived and departed here for fields throughout northern and eastern Virginia. Lee arrived for wartime service on April 22, 1861, and left May 26, 1870, for the final time.

The Richmond and York River Railroad depot stood just off Cary Street on Canal Street between

Most of Richmond's residents fled to Capitol Square during the conflagration of April 1865.

BATTLES AND LEADERS

Twenty-third and Twenty-fourth Streets. The line, which McClellan advanced along in 1862, was used to tow the Confederacy's first observation balloon to the front along the Chickahominy. Col. Josiah Gorgas, Confederate chief of ordnance, acting on Lee's suggestion in June 1862, designed a flatcar armored with bolted iron plates and mounting a cannon. An engine pushed it out on the York Railroad to shell the Federals at Savage Station on June 30. Dahlgren's body arrived there on March 6, 1864, where it was reviled by a furious public and mourned only by Van Lew.

When the city was occupied, the Federals seized 42 locomotives and 419 assorted types of railcars.

Confederate observation balloons were filled from Richmond's gas storage tank near Seventeenth and Cary. The first balloon, commanded by Maj. Edward Porter Alexander, was launched on June 27, 1862. His silk-dress balloon was filled with seventy-five-hundred cubic feet of gas (at a cost of $22.50), then hauled by wagon to the Richmond and York River Depot.

Richmond College, which stood at Grace and Lombardy, was a Confederate school for artillery instruction and a hospital, then a Federal barracks. The unique Confederate Coffee Factory was located on Cary between Seventeenth and Eighteenth. There artificial coffee was manufactured until a fire consumed one hundred thousand dollars' worth of ersatz coffee.

The infamous Bread Riot started at Capitol Square on April 2, 1863. A crowd of women, children, and a few disreputable men, estimated to number thirty-five hundred and wielding knives and hatchets, marched to the southwestern corner of Main and Eighteenth Streets where they demanded food and broke into stores. There they were confronted by armed militia, who seemed unlikely to fire on local civilians. The mob paid little heed to pleas made by Mayor Mayo and Governor Letcher, but Davis made a pacifying speech, then gave the crowd five minutes to disperse. If they did not, he promised, he would order the soldiers to fire. Realizing they had pushed their luck, the mob scattered. Authorities then placed canister-loaded cannon at intersections and patrolled the streets with soldiers. The incident motivated the city council to initiate a program to procure food and sell it at cost to the poor. As time passed and conditions deteriorated, the food was offered to all classes.

The defenses of Richmond will be studied in detail in the third Virginia book in the Civil War Explorer Series, *The Killing Time,* so we will only present an overview here. The Confederacy's capital was ringed by three sets of earthworks. The outer set was seven to nine miles from Capitol Square and ultimately totaled sixty-five miles of works. Chickahominy Bluffs marks the northern extent of this line, the 6600 Block of West Broad Street denotes the western boundary, and Fort Harrison was at the eastern boundary.

The intermediate line extended five miles from central Richmond, a nearly continuous line manned in emergencies. Its limits are defined by a cannon on the 3400 block of Monument Avenue and a stone at Laburum Avenue and Brook Road.

The inner defenses consisted of twenty-five star forts at important entry points, extending from the James River on the east to the James River on the west. Each was permanently occupied by ten men and an officer. One is marked by a cannon in the 2300 block of Monument Avenue.

Richmond's defenses were first commanded by provost marshal John H. Winder, then Gustavus W. Smith, Arnold Elzy, Robert Ransom, and sickly Richard Ewell, who accepted the position on May 29, 1864, and held it to the end. The works were manned by four battalions of heavy artillery, the Louisiana Guard Artillery, and the Engineer Company, plus, from 1864 on, three thousand government employees organized into a Local Defense Special Service. The works were manned on a number of occasions in 1864 when Grant threatened the city and several other times when Union cavalry approached. Most of these defenses were never attacked, the exceptions being largely to the southeast.

Since the end of the Civil War, Richmond has been the most prominent landmark of the former Confederacy. Dozens of generals and thousands of veteran soldiers regularly visited the city, singly and in great conventions. More than twenty thousand men and a dozen generals gathered in 1896, but of course the numbers declined over time. The last convention was held in 1932. Virginia's last surviving Confederate, John Salling, died at age 112 on March 16, 1959. Only one Confederate remained, Walter Williams of Texas, who died on December 19, 1959, aged 117, the last of three hundred thousand revered figures who had fought for their principles.

Richmond may be toured at your leisure. Besides this modest overview, I recommend two guides: *Moore's Complete Civil War Guide to Richmond* by Samuel J. T. Moore Jr. and *General Lee's City: An Illustrated Guide to the Historic Sites of Confederate Richmond* by Richard M. Lee.

Many different tours of Richmond are available, including aerial views of the battlefields, cruises on the James River, and traditional bus tours. Most notable are the Historic Richmond Tours (804-780-0107), which offer four-hour guided tours to Richmond-area battlefields, a shorter excursion around the city, and walking tours of Hollywood Cemetery for both groups and individuals.

At the end of your Richmond tour you can turn right from the Maury Monument onto Belmont and turn right onto West Broad, which leads back to the Richmond National Battlefield Park Headquarters. An alternative is to follow the signs northeast on U.S. 360 to start the Seven Days' Tour, or follow signs for U.S. 1 North to begin the tour of the Second Manassas campaign.

5

The Seven Days' Battles

OR ALL JOSEPH E. JOHNSTON'S shortcomings, the most prominent being his tendencies to be overly cautious and prone to abandon good defensive positions, he was an adored Confederate hero when he fell at the battle of Seven Pines. The appointment of his successor, Robert E. Lee, however, was widely regarded with suspicion and apprehension. Southern newspapers emphasized that he had never held a field command, which was a reservation shared by the staff of the army he had been appointed to command. Lee's ascension was regarded universally as a blunder.

Making matters worse, Lee had faced George B. McClellan before, in western Virginia. He had been pilloried afterward as "Evacuating Lee" and "Granny Lee" when he retreated following the minor battle of Cheat Mountain, leaving western Virginia open to Federal occupation and elevating McClellan to the national stage.

Thus the Federal commander was delighted by the news and said: "I prefer Lee over Johnston. The former is too cautious and weak under grave responsibility—personally brave and energetic to a fault, he yet is wanting in moral firmness when pressed by heavy responsibility and is likely to be timid and irresolute in action." McClellan rarely succeeded in evaluating his opponents—but this was a trait at which Lee excelled.

Johnston recognized Lee's ability, telling a friend: "The shot that struck me down is the very best that has been fired for the Southern cause yet. For I possess in no degree the confidence of our government, and now there is in my place one who does possess it, and who can accomplish what I never could have done—the concentration of our armies for the defense of the capital of the Confederacy."

Robert E. Lee inherited an officer corps influenced by Joseph E. Johnston's philosophy of withdrawal over battle. Many of his generals advocated retreating even closer to Richmond. At Lee's initial meeting with his generals, Brig. Gen. William H. C. Whiting started lecturing and drawing diagrams, which to the engineer proved that, scientifically and mathematically, McClellan could not be beaten. "Stop! Stop!" Lee shouted. "If we go to ciphering we shall be whipped beforehand."

Friendly relations prevailed during lulls in the fighting as soldiers exchanged newspapers and Southern tobacco for Northern coffee. On June 23 a Union captain on picket duty was cordially invited to Richmond for a party held in honor of Stonewall Jackson's victory in the Shenandoah Valley. The would-be host "promised to be civil to him & bring him back in the morning," the official report read.

Jefferson Davis trusted Lee, having worked closely with him for months and realizing the value of Lee's counsel to Johnston on the peninsula and to Stonewall Jackson in the Shenandoah Valley.

Col. Joseph Ives, who was well acquainted with Lee's qualities, was asked by Maj. Edward Porter Alexander whether the new commander possessed "the audacity that is going to be required for our inferior force to meet the enemy's superior force—to take the aggressive and to run risks and stand changes?" Ives declared Lee "heads and shoulders above every man in service," Confederate or Federal. "His name might be Audacity," Ives continued. "He will take more desperate chances, and take them quicker, than any other general in this country."

McClellan had one hundred thousand well-trained, well-equipped soldiers on the outskirts of Richmond. Lee's command consisted of fifty thousand badly fed and ill-clothed troops in conditions highly detrimental to a disciplined defense.

The Union army, however, was paralyzed by two weeks of rain that prevented repair of the Chickahominy bridges and rendered the roads too sloppy to support its siege guns. McClellan persisted in his requests for McDowell's thirty-thousand-man Army of the Rappahannock, but Jack-

The Confederate Capital

In 1861 Richmond had a population of 38,000, a third of them slaves, making the city the third largest in the South. At its height during the Civil War, the city's population reached 135,000 to 150,000. Richmond had the most industries in the Confederacy, with several iron works capable of producing weapons, twelve substantial mills, and fifty tobacco warehouses.

Virginia had the second largest population in the South and was first in industrial capacity. Most citizens rejected secession and membership in the Confederacy until after Fort Sumter surrendered and Lincoln called for seventy-five thousand soldiers to subdue the rebellious states. A convention passed an Ordinance of Secession on April 19, and the voters approved it on May 24.

The Confederate government soon moved from Montgomery, Alabama, to Richmond, which was quickly flooded with amateur soldiers who were then housed in camps, warehouses, and factories. Richmond's population increased dramatically, not just from the soldiers and a newly created governmental bureaucracy, but from war speculators and even less desirable people—gamblers, prostitutes, criminals, and spies. They crowded hotels, rooming houses, and the streets.

First Manassas brought casualties to Richmond, the first of more than two hundred thousand. The city became an extensive hospital center for the remainder of the war.

Inflation drove prices ever higher, and soon shortages of luxuries and then basic necessities were noticed. Prices continued to soar and supplies shrunk as the war proceeded.

The exhilaration of Jefferson Davis's inauguration on February 22, 1862, had hardly faded when Richmond was threatened from the east, down the peninsula at Hampton Roads. With the destruction of the ironclad *Virginia,* a great Union army pressed to the outskirts of Richmond, where siege batteries of big guns were being prepared to batter the city and its defenses. Many residents, including the president's wife, fled the city.

Frantic work prevented the Federals from approaching via the James River. Fighting raged within sight of Richmond, the cannon fire resounding through the streets as residents took to roofs and hilltops in a vain effort to divine events on the gunsmoke-shrouded horizon. Savage fighting delivered Richmond at Seven Pines and the Seven Days, but countless casualties flooded into the city—twenty thousand Southern soldiers had fallen at Richmond's doorstep.

When provost marshal John H. Winder enforced price ceilings, farmers withheld their produce. Winder and the people lost the battle.

Five countries—Great Britain, France, Brazil, Austria, and Belgium—established consulates in the Confederate capital.

While the residents had cheered in relief as the defenders passed through the city in April, they cheered in joy as their soldiers marched through to take the war north to the enemy.

In 1863 the war never got closer to Richmond than Fredericksburg, but privation and shortages continued and casualties and Union prisoners accumulated. Residents made their own clothes and put up their own food while making soap and medicine and started selling off silver and family heirlooms to survive. Refugees from the fighting farther north crowded the city, joining the legions of the dispossessed.

This cluster of earthworks on the Mechanisville road formed part of Richmond's early defenses.

son's activities in the Shenandoah prevented all but one division from being sent to reinforce the army on the peninsula.

Lee renamed his force the Army of Northern Virginia. Most of them were veterans of Manassas, the Peninsula, and Seven Pines, but raw recruits were flooding in from across the Deep South. Lee trained them constantly and worked to secure better food and uniforms. He promoted accomplished officers and sacked others. Rejecting the advice of many generals who advocated further retreat, Lee ordered extensive fortifications to be erected. Eight miles of trenches and redoubts soon stretched from White Oak Swamp to the Chickahominy at New Bridge and continued along the riverbank to beyond Mechanicsville. His grumbling soldiers, working with picks, shovels, and axes for the first time, revived an old disparaging nickname for Lee from a growing list—"King of Spades."

McClellan was engaged in similar activity, and this was centered at Fair Oaks. He was preparing for a classic European siege. "I will bring up my heavy guns," McClellan stated, "shell the city, and carry it by assault."

In anticipation of seizing Richmond, George B. McClellan and members of his staff reviewed the approach to the Confederate capital from the Chickahominy River near Mechanicsville. To his army, the Federal commander announced, "The final and decisive battle is at hand."

The York River Railroad delivered six hundred tons of supplies and forage, which the Army of the Potomac needed to survive every day, and transported the giant siege guns that McClellan planned to use to conquer Richmond.

237

BATTLES AND LEADERS

Confidently McClellan waited for the swollen rivers to shrink and the soggy roads to dry out so that he could bring up his siege guns. In the meantime, artillery dueled across the Chickahominy River, and a new Confederate commander presented his strategy to Jefferson Davis and his generals.

Most of McClellan's force, three corps, was now south of the Chickahominy and facing Richmond. Lee's plan was to hold that area with a small force behind earthworks while the largest portion of his army swung north, crossed the Chickahominy, and hit the depleted Union right wing, which consisted of two corps at Mechanicsville. He would then threaten McClellan's vital supply line, the Richmond and York River Railroad, which extended to White House Landing on the Pamunkey River. McClellan would be forced to abandon his works and fight in the open, where the Confederates would have a better chance of victory. This plan would relieve the siege of Richmond and possibly "change the character of the war," Lee proposed to Davis.

Before any movement occurred, Lee needed information on the location of Federal positions north of the river. Jeb Stuart was quickly dispatched to conduct a reconnaissance in force with twelve hundred men. The dashing cavalryman left on June 12 and circled completely the vast Union Army of the Potomac, riding one hundred miles in three days and reaching Richmond on June 15. Stuart gave Lee the welcome news that Porter's right flank was unprotected, "up in the air," and vulnerable to attack.

The embarrassing episode made McClellan realize how vulnerable his supply line was. He resolved to shift the two corps now north of the Chickahominy to the southern bank of the troublesome stream, and his supply base would be transferred completely across his rear from the Pamunkey to the James River. On June 18 the first supplies were moved, and Franklin's Sixth Corps crossed the Chickahominy. Porter's Fifth Corps remained to protect the movement of material.

Lee ordered Jackson, who had recently defeated and confused three Union armies in the Shenandoah Valley, to march east with 18,500 men to strike Porter's exposed right flank. Lee had dispatched Whiting's division and a brigade under Brig. Gen. Alexander Lawton to assist Jackson in leaving the Valley. When Jackson struck Porter, three of Lee's divisions—Longstreet's, Ambrose Powell Hill's, and Daniel Harvey Hill's—would advance east to the north bank of the Chickahominy and threaten McClellan's rail link with White House Landing.

On June 16 Jackson started his worn men on the 120-mile march to Richmond. He rode ahead to meet with Lee and the other commanders and learned that the operation would not begin until his force arrived. Jackson promised to attack on the morning of June 26.

The failure of his offensive to take shape at Mechanicsville irritated Robert E. Lee. Spotting Jefferson Davis, cabinet members, congressmen, and military advisers on the battlefield, Lee angrily said, "Mr. President, who is all this army and what is it doing here?"

"It is not my army, General," Davis responded.

"It is certainly not *my* army, Mr. President, and this is no place for it," Lee snapped.

Another version of this story has Lee approaching the president and bowing formally before asking, "Mr. President, am I in command here?"

After an affirmative answer, Lee continued, "Then I forbid you to stand here under the enemy's guns. Any exposure of a life like yours is wrong. And this is useless exposure. You must go back."

The latter account has the sound of revisionism.

McClellan meanwhile was planning his own offensive, although on a smaller scale. He was satisfied with recent affairs. The ninety-five-hundred-man division of Brig. Gen. George McCall arrived from McDowell and was added to Porter's corps, and seven regiments had been gleaned from the defenses of Washington and other Northern cities. The torrential rain had finally ceased, the roads were drying out, and his bridges were repaired.

On June 26 McClellan hoped to seize Old Tavern, a mile west of his current position and occupying the important intersection of the Nine Mile Road and the New Bridge Road. It would also bring Richmond that much closer to his siege guns. To prepare for that attack, he opened an artillery bombardment on June 25 of Confederate positions in front of Samuel P. Heintzelman's Second Corps. At 8 A.M. Joseph Hooker's division struggled through difficult bogs and forest to gain ground from Benjamin Huger. Inexplicably, at 11 A.M. Heintzelman recalled Hooker, only to have McClellan order the advance continued. McClellan gained half a mile of ground, losing 626 men to Huger's 441 in an action remembered as the battle of Oak Grove. The Federals were now less than five miles from the Confederate capital.

The Confederate General ■ Robert Edward Lee

Robert Edward Lee, born on January 19, 1807, at Stratford, the family estate in Westmoreland County, Virginia, was the fifth son of famed Revolutionary War general Richard Henry "Lighthorse Harry" Lee by his second wife, Ann Hill Carter. After losing his fortune in land speculation, Henry Lee moved the family to Alexandria, where it survived on a trust fund established by Ann's father. Henry Lee died aboard a ship returning from the West Indies when Robert was eleven.

After an early education in Alexandria schools, Lee entered the U.S. Military Academy and graduated second in the class of 1829. Until the Mexican War, he served as an engineer during the construction of Forts Pulaski, Monroe, and Hamilton. In 1831 Lee married Mary Anna Randolph Custis, a great-granddaughter of Martha Washington. They had seven children, and each of the sons served the Confederacy—William Henry Fitzhugh and George

Washington Custis as major generals and Robert Jr. as a captain. In 1859 Lee's wife came into possession of Arlington, the Custis property overlooking the Potomac River just outside Washington, D.C.

Lee was sent west in 1846 as a captain, where he served first under Gen. John E. Wool in San Antonio, then campaigned into Mexico with Winfield Scott. Marching from Vera Cruz to Mexico City, Lee exhibited such gallantry and skill that he won three brevets to full colonel.

After Mexico, Lee continued his engineering duties at Fort Carroll in Baltimore and in 1852 became superintendent of West Point. After three years there Lee, with Secretary of War Jefferson Davis's approval, returned to field command as a lieutenant colonel of the Second Cavalry in Texas.

Home on leave at Arlington in October 1859, Lee was given command of the marines who stormed Harpers Ferry and captured John

Brown. With southern states seceding, Winfield Scott brought Lee to Washington from Texas and on April 18, 1861, with Lincoln's approval, offered Lee command of all U.S. armies. Lee revered the Union and the Constitution, but like many others he could not fight against his home state. On April 20, after Virginia's secession, Lee resigned and traveled to Richmond, where Gov. John Letcher immediately placed him in charge of all Virginia military forces. Lee became a Confederate brigadier on May 14 and full general on June 14.

Lee saw varied early service. After training and equipping Virginia troops, he attempted unsuccessfully to keep Union troops out of mountainous western Virginia. Lee inspected and recommended improvements of Confederate defenses in Georgia and the Carolinas, then returned to Richmond in March 1862 to act as Davis's military adviser. He initiated Stonewall Jack-

son's brilliant Valley campaign, which tied up Federal troops and prevented them from reinforcing George B. McClellan on the peninsula, and managed to convince Joseph E. Johnston to counter the Federals there. Johnston's serious wounds on May 31 at Seven Pines led Davis to place Lee in command of the Army of Northern Virginia, where his legend began.

For generations a common painting in Southern homes was *The Burial of Latane,* by William D. Washington. Capt. William Latane was the only casualty of Stuart's famous raid around McClellan. He died in the arms of his brother John, who sent the body to the nearest plantation. The sole inhabitants of the estate, two women, buried Latane in the family plot.

Lee left twenty-five thousand men under Magruder to face McClellan's seventy-five thousand along a line that stretched for four miles. The flashy general was to renew the tactics that had frozen the Federals east of the Warwick River: heavy artillery fire, marching his troops back and forth in view of the enemy, and making noise as if preparing for a heavy attack. If he failed to hold McClellan in a defensive posture, a Union attack could easily capture Richmond.

McClellan was aware that Jackson had left the Valley and knew where he was marching and to what purpose. As a result, the general canceled his Old Tavern attack and instructed Porter to send out probes to find Jackson and slow his progress. It was almost too late.

On the morning of June 26 Lee stood on a bluff peering across the Chickahominy at Mechanicsville, anticipating Jackson's attack. D. H. Hill and Longstreet were waiting at two bridges leading to Mechanicsville, and A. P. Hill was two miles upstream at Meadow Bridge. The dawn assault never materialized, and at 9 A.M. Lee received a message from Jackson that promised an attack in six hours.

A. P. Hill was closest to Jackson's anticipated position. As the day progressed, he strained to hear the sounds of combat that would be his signal to cross the Chickahominy, pass through Mechanicsville, and attack the primary Union defenses at Beaver Dam Creek, with support from D. H. Hill and Longstreet to his right. A. P. Hill was young, impatient, new to command, and eager to prove himself. When no word from Jackson had been received by 4 P.M., he attacked, expecting Jackson to join in at any moment. Across the river he routed a regiment of pickets and deployed five brigades on the plain beyond, facing Porter, who was entrenched on a ridge behind Beaver Dam Creek. At 5 P.M. D. H. Hill sent in his first brigade. He knew it was suicidal but hoped Jackson would flank Porter out of the strong works. His division would then be in position to pursue the fleeing Federals.

Jackson's men, however, were exhausted, hungry, and demoralized. They had fought five battles in forty days and had marched four hundred miles. On June 26 they made only thirteen miles in fourteen hours because Federal cavalry had burned every bridge, felled trees across the roads, and skirmished constantly in an effective attempt to slow their advance.

Jackson had reached Hundley's Corner, just two miles from A. P. Hill, when he heard firing to his right. For reasons frequently speculated upon but never explained by Jackson, he bivouacked

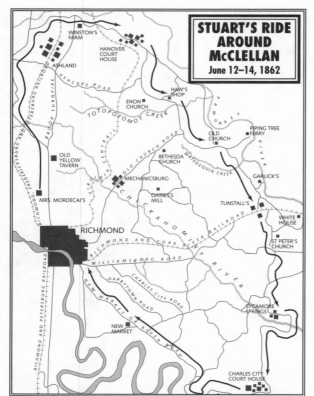

STUART'S RIDE AROUND McCLELLAN
June 12–14, 1862

To gather sufficient information for Robert E. Lee's audacious offensive, Jeb Stuart led twelve hundred men on a one-hundred-mile circuit around the Union army. The Southerners occasionally clashed with Federal troopers and returned with news of a vulnerability in the Northerners' lines.

his troops and went to sleep, neglecting to send any word to Lee. One officer said that Jackson was not himself but "under a spell." He had slept only ten hours in the previous four days, and apparently his mind and will failed him.

D. H. Hill meanwhile was attacking the recently arrived McCall, who possessed an impregnable position. From the creek the land rose up to a ridge where thirty-six pieces of artillery in six batteries were aligned. Hill's men were slaughtered. Lee, who had ridden up to observe, sent an order to end the attack, but apparently Hill never received it.

Lee crossed D. H. Hill and Longstreet and sent the lead brigade, that of Brig. Gen. Roswell S. Ripley, to relieve A. P. Hill. They struck the strongest portion of Porter's line, at Ellerson's Mill. One regiment, the Forty-fourth Georgia, quickly lost 335 of its 514 men. The battle of

Birth of a Legend: Stuart Circles McClellan

Before Robert E. Lee could attack George B. McClellan along the Chickahominy River, he had to know the disposition of the Federal forces. To gather this intelligence, Lee turned to Brig. Gen. James Ewell Brown "Jeb" Stuart, his chief of cavalry. With twelve hundred men and two light guns, Stuart left the Confederate lines at 2 A.M. on June 12. On the mission was William Henry Fitzhugh Lee, Lee's second-oldest son, and the general's nephew Fitzhugh Lee.

Riding to the northeast, they crossed the Chickahominy and early the following day rode through Hanover Court House. Their first skirmish occurred on June 13 when Capt. William Latane charged part of the Fifth U.S. Cavalry. Latane wounded Union Capt. William Royall with his saber, but the Federal responded with two pistol shots that

killed the Confederate, Stuart's only fatality. The Union party was vanquished in a pistol-and-saber duel.

Later that afternoon the expedition arrived at Old Church, having sacked a nearby Federal cavalry camp. Stuart had scouted the area of Lee's concern, Fitz John Porter's Fifth Corps, and was deep in McClellan's rear. Believing that masses of Northern troops would be waiting if he retraced his steps, Stuart opted to make a complete circuit around McClellan, just the thing to create a legend for a dashing cavalier.

Stuart's brother-in-law, Lt. John R. Cooke, would say that this was "the gayest portion of the ride. It was neck or nothing." He figured the odds of success at one in ten.

Many of Stuart's men lived in the area. Women brought food to the roadside and briefly spoke to hus-

bands, brothers, and sons for the first time since the war began.

Inspired by their daring mission, the troopers continued southeast to seize Tunstall's Station on the Richmond and York River Railroad. They captured guards, fired supply wagons, and riddled a passing supply train heading for White House Landing. Stuart's next stop was a hospital at Talleysville, where his command raided a sutler's store.

The Chickahominy was now only seven miles away, but the Confederates had to contend with 165 prisoners, and they had not stopped for sleep in two days. The troops dozed in the saddle. The horsemen rode through the night, expecting an attack by Federal cavalry at any moment. Union troopers were only four miles behind them, led by Brig. Gen. Philip St. George Cooke, Stuart's father-in-law.

The Confederates reached the Chickahominy at dawn on June 14, but heavy rains had rendered the river unfordable. Stuart located a skiff, which was anchored in the middle of the forty-foot-wide river. This makeshift pontoon was bridged with planks from a warehouse, enabling the Confederates to cross at 2 P.M. The span had just been fired when Cooke arrived on the northern bank.

Stuart started for Richmond, thirty-five miles distant, but stopped for a full night's sleep. They rode into Richmond on June 15, their deed heralded throughout the Confederacy. They had ridden one hundred miles in three days, circling a massive Federal army and embarrassing McClellan. Stuart bragged that he had left one general behind—"General Consternation."

While John Magruder occupied McClellan's attention in front of Richmond, Lee launched an attack on the Federal camps near Mechanicsville. The Confederate attack stalled at Beaver Dam Creek, where Union Gen. Fitz John Porter's men dug in and held. A. P. Hill continued the attack in anticipation of Stonewall Jackson's imminent arrival from the Shenandoah Valley.

Mechanicsville, also known as Ellerson's Mill and Beaver Dam Creek, petered out as darkness fell about 9 P.M. "The result was, as might have been forseen," said D. H. Hill, "a bloody and disastrous repulse."

Lee's plan had called for an advance of four miles, which would have ended by uniting with Magruder at the Chickahominy. His gain was negligible. He had lost 1,484 men and had only managed to use a fourth of his army. One Federal observed that casualties lined Beaver Dam Creek "like flies in a bowl of sugar."

McClellan, who lost only 361, informed Washington of a victory "complete and against great odds. I almost begin to think we are invincible," he bragged.

At the same time McClellan recognized Porter's precarious position against Lee's concentrated strength and withdrew the Fifth Corps four miles during the night to a better defensive line at Boatswain's Creek. The slopes of the valley and banks of the creek were steep, and the stream was bordered by marsh and tangled woods. Porter's entire corps was arrayed on the crest of the opposite ridge. Brig. Gen. George Sykes's regular army division held the right, Brig. Gen. George W. Morell's division the left, with McCall in reserve. A powerful line of eighty pieces of artillery, placed wheel to wheel, were positioned to fire over the infantry. Federal soldiers spent the night digging trenches and piling up trees and fence rails for breastworks.

In response Lee split his four divisions on three parallel roads to hit Porter in the front and on both flanks. Jackson and D. H. Hill swung north through Old Cold Harbor to get behind the Federal right flank. A. P. Hill was in the center to pursue when Porter was flanked, and Longstreet marched along the north bank of the Chickahominy on the Confederate right to support A. P. Hill.

At noon the five regiments of Brig. Gen. Maxey Gregg, A. P. Hill's lead brigade, found the Union rear guard at Gaines's Mill, a five-story gristmill.

Soldiers knew to accept their own newspaper accounts with a great deal of skepticism. After Stuart swept around McClellan's army, newsboys slipped into Federal lines and quickly sold out their copies of the Richmond papers to troops eager to hear the true story.

The Federals withdrew after a brief contest, and Hill pressed on a mile to New Cold Harbor, a crossroads where one road led southeast and the other due south. Skirmishers discovered that both roads led six hundred yards to Boatswain's Creek and Porter's bristling defenses.

With a dreadful sense of déjà vu, at 2:30 P.M. A. P. Hill sent six brigades across the open fields leading to the creek and up the long slope into the teeth of fierce Federal opposition. Lee accompanied A. P. Hill and promised the support of Longstreet on the right. D. H. Hill and Jackson were expected soon on the left at Old Cold Harbor, a mile away.

Gregg led the attack into the heavy artillery fire, then the Federal infantry opened with what one Confederate cannoneer called "one living sheet of flame." The situation worsened as the Southerners advanced across a three-quarter-mile front, their lines disarrayed in the struggle through the woods and creek. Three of Gregg's regiments started up the far slope, and Sykes's regular army troops counterattacked, inflicting 60 percent casualties on the Confederates, who were forced to fall back.

Other Rebels continued up the slopes and cut down Sykes's Fifth New York Zouaves. A third of the Federals fell and the line wavered, but two flag bearers marched thirty yards in front of the regiment to stand alone and defiant. Emboldened, the Zouaves raised a "demonic and horrid"

Reflecting upon his suicidal charge at Mechanicsville after the war, D. H. Hill wrote, "We were lavish of blood in those days, and it was thought to be a great thing to charge a battery of artillery or an earth-work lined with infantry."

The arrival of Jackson's corps did not contribute to the outcome of the battle, mostly because Jackson failed to engage the enemy and instead bivouacked his men. The Federals, however, were well entrenched. From the slopes overlooking Beaver Dam Creek, thirty-six Union guns poured a deadly fire on Hill's men. Lee attempted to compensate by enlarging the assault and assailing the Northerners across the creek at Ellison's Mill, but his losses were too great to maintain the attack. Darkness ended the fighting.

BATTLES AND LEADERS

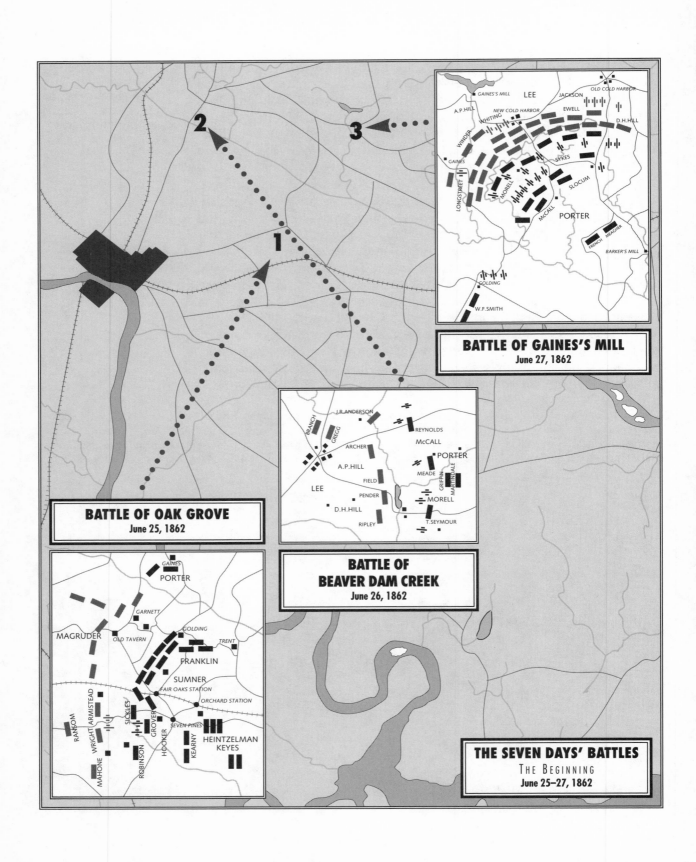

BATTLE OF GAINES'S MILL
June 27, 1862

LEE
GAINES'S MILL
JACKSON
OLD COLD HARBOR
A.P.HILL
NEW COLD HARBOR
EWELL
WHITING
D.H.HILL
WINDER
GAINES
SYKES
LONGSTREET
MORELL
SLOCUM
McCALL
PORTER
FRENCH
MEAGHER
BARKER'S MILL
GOLDING
W.F.SMITH

2

1

3

BATTLE OF OAK GROVE
June 25, 1862

BATTLE OF BEAVER DAM CREEK
June 26, 1862

J.R.ANDERSON
BRANCH
GREGG
REYNOLDS
McCALL
ARCHER
PORTER
A.P.HILL
MEADE
FIELD
GRIFFIN
MARTINDALE
LEE
PENDER
MORELL
D.H.HILL
RIPLEY
T.SEYMOUR

GAINES
PORTER
GARNETT
MAGRUDER
GOLDING
OLD TAVERN
TRENT
FRANKLIN
SUMNER
FAIR OAKS STATION
ORCHARD STATION
RANSOM
ARMISTEAD
SICKLES
SEVEN PINES
WRIGHT
GROVER
HEINTZELMAN
MAHONE
ROBINSON
HOOKER
KEARNY
KEYES

THE SEVEN DAYS' BATTLES
THE BEGINNING
June 25–27, 1862

and defiant. Emboldened, the Zouaves raised a "demonic and horrid" shout and with bayonets drove the Confederates into the creek.

After fighting ninety minutes without reinforcement, Hill ordered his brigades to withdraw, saying his "brave men had done all that any soldiers could do."

Jackson had been misdirected and did not reach Old Cold Harbor until 2 P.M. Longstreet, however, was on the right, and Lee was determined to wait until Jackson arrived before committing his division. It was 4:30 when Jackson sent D. H. Hill, under his command for this operation, from Old Cold Harbor to Erasmus Keyes's right through bogs and fields swept by the guns of three regular army batteries. Ordered to capture the guns, the Confederates' precise parade-ground maneuvers impressed one Federal. "Not a gun did they fire until within less than fifty yards," he said, "when after a volley they gave a yell, and charged, five lines deep."

The Twentieth North Carolina drove back the Union infantry and seized two guns, felling the gunners who fought bravely for their weapons. The Confederates were in turn driven back by the Sixteenth New York, which led a division of reinforcements from Brig. Gen. Henry W. Slocum's Fourth Corps.

In the center of the line at 4:30, Lee directed one of Jackson's divisions, three brigades of Shenandoah Valley veterans under Maj. Gen.

Alabama Pvt. W. A. McClendon saw his friend Tom Burk shot. "A minie ball had hit him in the pit of the stomach, and with each pulsation his life's blood would gush from the hole. In his delirium he made an unsuccessful attempt to stop the hole with his canteen stopper."

The Ultimate Horse Soldier ■ James Ewell Brown Stuart

The dashing cavalier James Ewell Brown "Jeb" Stuart was born on February 6, 1833, in Patrick County, Virginia. After graduating from West Point in 1854, he served with the First Cavalry in Kansas. In October 1859, Lieutenant Stuart served as Robert E. Lee's aide at Harpers Ferry, personally delivering a final surrender demand to John Brown.

Resigning from the U.S. Army in 1861, Stuart was made a colonel and led Joseph E. Johnston's cavalry in the Shenandoah. In July his men rode to First Manassas, where they fought well. Promoted to brigadier, Stuart's legend began in June 1862, when Lee sent him to scout George B. McClellan's lines before the Seven Days' battles. He swept completely around the Union army, embarrassing the Federals and delighting the Confederacy.

This feat earned him the rank of major general and command of the Army of Northern Virginia's cavalry.

Stuart's exploits were bold and colorful. He raided John Pope's headquarters before Second Manassas, garnering important dispatches. Stuart effectively screened Lee's invasion of Maryland, keeping McClellan ignorant of Confederate whereabouts, and after Antietam he looped the Union army again, an incident that hastened McClellan's final downfall.

Stuart participated in every major Virginia campaign. His artillery under young John Pelham slowed the Federal attack at Fredericksburg, and his force screened Stonewall Jackson's flank attack at Chancellorsville, where Stuart took command of the Second Corps after Jackson and A. P.

Hill fell wounded. Weeks later Stuart participated in the largest cavalry battle ever fought in America, Brandy Station. Initially caught by surprise, he fought tenaciously and drove the Federals from the field.

Stuart held off determined Union cavalry attempts to locate Lee on the road to Pennsylvania, but following that fine action came the single blot on Stuart's career. Choosing to circle the Army of the Potomac for a third time, he left Lee stumbling blindly through Pennsylvania. With little information, which Stuart had always gathered skillfully, Lee fought the great battle poorly.

As Ulysses S. Grant started for Richmond after the battle of Spotsylvania in the spring of 1864, Stuart intercepted a massive Union cavalry raid aimed at the Confederate capi-

tal. He was mortally wounded there, at Yellow Tavern, on May 11, and died the next day. Stuart is buried at Richmond's Hollywood Cemetery. His father-in-law was Union Brig. Gen. Philip St. George Cooke, whose son was Confederate Brig. Gen. John Rogers Cooke.

BATTLES AND LEADERS

McClellan realized that his right flank was vulnerable. He ordered Porter to withdraw to the east, to a defensive line erected near Boatswain's Swamp, a sluggish stream, and a gristmill belonging to the area's largest landholder, Dr. William G. Gaines.

One Federal swore the air at Gaines's Mill was too full of bullets for standing men. A Louisiana lieutenant had a strange "desire to see how many I could catch with my open hand stretched out."

Richard Ewell, to attack on A. P. Hill's left. The Fifteenth Alabama went up against a triple line of Zouaves in combat so fierce that Confederate Pvt. W. A. McClendon could not hear his rifle discharge. He only knew he had fired by the weapon's recoil against his shoulder.

Ewell lost two brigade commanders quickly. Col. Isaac G. Seymour was killed leading his Louisianans, and the brigade soon lost Maj. Chatham Roberdeau Wheat, who had been pronounced all but dead a year earlier at Manassas. Brig. Gen. Arnold Elzey was shot in the face, and his staff was decimated as they carried him off.

The Alabamians and Louisianans both broke and ran, shouting, "We are whipped!" which frightened fresh units just arriving on the field. A Maryland officer failed to rally them "with my sword and the rifles of my men."

Ewell roamed the length of his line, bareheaded and waving a sword, encouraging and cajoling. When Alexander Lawton's Georgians paused

Sleeping Beauty

"When he went to sleep he was the most difficult man to arouse I ever saw," remembered Dr. Hunter Maguire of Stonewall Jackson's sleeping habits. "If his rest was broken for one night, he was almost certain to go to sleep upon his horse if riding the following day."

This might explain Lee's problems with Jackson during the Seven Days'

battles. On June 26, when Jackson was supposed to strike the Federal right flank at Mechanicsville, Jackson halted his column at 5 P.M. and—without informing Lee and ignoring the sounds of battle a mile away—went to sleep.

In the previous forty days Jackson had fought five major battles and marched over four hundred miles. In

the last four days Jackson had only managed ten hours of sleep. One witness said Jackson at Mechanicsville "was not really Jackson. He was under a spell."

Facing the Federal rear guard at White Oak Swamp on June 30, Jackson went to sleep at 3 P.M. beneath a tree, taking no more offensive action that day. His chief of staff, Rev. Maj.

Robert C. Dabney, believed physical and mental fatigue "had sunk the elasticity of his will and the quickness of his invention for the nonce below their wonted tension."

In the evening Jackson fell asleep while eating supper. Jerking awake, he told his staff, "Now, gentlemen, let us at once to bed, and see if tomorrow we cannot do something."

under what an officer called "a perfect sheet of fire," Ewell renewed the advance by yelling, "Hurrah for Georgia!" Through the murderous fire the Confederates advanced farther up the ridge.

Longstreet's interpretation of Lee's instructions for a diversion sent three brigades against Morell's Union division, but to no avail.

Sometime after 5 P.M. Jackson rode up to Lee, who never seemed capable of harshly criticizing his recalcitrant lieutenants.

"Ah, General," Lee said, "I am very glad to see you. I had hoped to be with you before." He then turned toward the battle. "The fire is very heavy. Do you think your men can stand it?"

"They can stand anything," Jackson replied. "They can stand that."

Atop the ridge at the Watt house, Porter suddenly noticed an "ominous silence" at 6 P.M. Lee was organizing his entire army for the first coordinated assault of the day. After a long afternoon of desperate, short-range combat, Porter was low on ammunition. So many rounds had been fired that his troops' rifles were fouled. No reserves remained, and casualties had been heavy. An hour earlier he had asked McClellan for reinforcements, but only two brigades had been dispatched. McClellan retained nearly sixty thousand men to meet the assault still expected by Magruder's twenty-five thousand, whose antics continued to hold the Federals in place.

At 6:30 the sounds of battle steadily increased to a roar as fifty-six thousand Confederates advanced all along the Federal line, sorely pressing Porter's thirty-five thousand effectives. As the attack moved forward, Lee called over the commander of the last brigade in line, John Bell Hood. Explaining that Porter's line had to be pierced by dark, only an hour or so

The attack on Porter's entrenched Federals began in earnest in the early afternoon of June 27, but the Southerners again failed to coordinate their assault. Lee halted the action late in the day, and Porter received much-needed reinforcements to bolster his line. McClellan, however, refused to commit the bulk of his army, then south of the Chickahominy River, to the battle because he feared an assault from Richmond.

A Maryland regiment was rallied by shame when one officer shouted at them, "Are you going to remain here like cowards while the Stonewall Brigade is charging past?" One soldier nearly shot the officer.

LIBRARY OF CONGRESS

The Confederate attack sounded to a Rebel "like forty thousand wild cats." A Federal spoke of "that fiendish yell."

Enraged by the sight of a captain cowering behind a tree, A. P. Hill took the man's sword and attempted to break it over his knee. The cheap sword merely bent, prompting Hill to fling it away. "The sword was of as bad metal as the man," one observer noted.

away, Lee asked, "Can you do it?" Following Hood's assurances, Lee saluted and said, "May God be with you."

Moving forward, Hood spotted a gap in the Confederate line. He directed the Eighteenth Georgia and Fourth Texas into the opening between Lawton and Longstreet. Instructing them to hold their fire, he dismounted to lead them on foot. They topped the ridge and passed through A. P. Hill's men, who had taken refuge along Boatswain's Creek, and plunged into a cauldron of fire erupting from the ridge ahead. Bullets and shells felled hundreds of Confederates, but their places were filled as the ranks continued on, hunched over as if walking into a terrible storm.

Hood halted 150 yards from Porter's main defenses and aligned his troops. He gave the order to fix bayonets then to advance at the double quick as they trotted up the slope on the run. Gun smoke limited visibility to less than twenty yards, leaving the Federals no time to react. Hood's

Old Pete ■ James Longstreet

James Longstreet, one of the Civil War's most criticized and controversial generals, was born in South Carolina on January 8, 1821, but grew up in Georgia and entered West Point from Alabama. After graduating in 1842, "Old Pete" fought Indians in the West and in Mexico won two brevets for gallantry. He was a major in the quartermaster department at the time of his resignation on June 1, 1861.

Longstreet was appointed a brigadier on June 17, fought at First Manassas in July, and became a major general in October. He served with distinction on the peninsula, directing the battle at Williamsburg and fighting at Seven Pines and in the Seven Days. At Second Manassas, Longstreet launched the attack that crushed John Pope's army. He fought well at Antietam, holding the thin right side of the Confederate line, and in December 1862 he repulsed Ambrose E. Burnside's suicidal assault at Fredericksburg. In early 1863 he became the Confederacy's senior lieutenant general.

Dispatched to collect food and occupy Federal forces around Suffolk

in southern Virginia (where he was successful or not, depending upon your prejudices), Longstreet was absent from Chancellorsville. Although he urged Lee to fight on the defensive in Pennsylvania, Longstreet fought the last two days at Gettysburg, failing to capture Little Round Top and Cemetery Ridge. Sent west to reinforce Braxton Bragg in September, Longstreet exploited a gap in William Rosecrans's line at Chickamauga and routed the Army of the Cumberland. His attempt to recapture Knoxville ended in ignoble failure.

Longstreet rejoined Lee in time to repulse Ulysses S. Grant and counterattack at the Wilderness, but he was almost killed by "friendly fire," as Stonewall Jackson had been in the same area a year earlier. He was incapacitated for months and returned to the Army of Northern Virginia near the end, surrendering with Lee to his old friend Grant. Longstreet's considerable service, from the beginning to the end and in both theaters of war, demonstrated his brilliance as a corps commander, but he fared poorly in independent command.

After the war Longstreet's problems began when he urged Southerners to accept Reconstruction. After becoming a Republican, in New Orleans he led black troops in an unsuccessful attack against white rioters. Longstreet held four different government positions under three different presidents. Grant appointed him minister to Turkey in 1880; William McKinley and Theodore Roosevelt made him commissioner of Pacific railroads, and he retired to Gainesville, Georgia, as postmaster general.

Lee, who called Longstreet "my old war horse," never criticized his subordinate. But after Lee's death there was a conspiracy to place his failures on Longstreet, now a hated figure across the South. False accusations, supported by several former Confederate generals, blamed Longstreet for not attacking sooner on the second day at Gettysburg. That charge shrouds his reputation to this day.

Longstreet refuted his critics in his memoirs, *From Manassas to Appomattox*. He died on January 2, 1904, the last high-ranking Confederate general, but even the governor

of Georgia, Gen. John B. Gordon, refused to attend Longstreet's funeral in Gainesville. Accolades poured in from former Union enemies, and elderly infantrymen came to pay their respects.

A statue of Longstreet, his first, has recently been raised at Gettysburg. The city of Gainesville has recently recognized the famed general. A tour of sites associated with Longstreet has been produced, and visitors to his grave in Alta Vista Cemetery will often find an empty whiskey bottle and cigars left by admirers.

U.S. ARMY MILITARY HISTORY INSTITUTE

BATTLES AND LEADERS

When Jackson's men arrived, Lee had more than forty thousand men to hurl against Porter's two-and-a-quarter-mile front. The attack was renewed and fierce until the Southerners broke through the center of the line, led by John Bell Hood's and Evander Law's brigades, despite a "perfect storm of lead." The Confederates' gains were again halted by nightfall and the timely arrival of reinforcements.

men fired ten yards from the Union line, decimating Brig. Gen. George W. Taylor's brigade. "The volley that fell upon the brigade was the most withering I ever saw delivered," said a Federal lieutenant. "The New Jersey Brigade broke all to pieces."

Porter's left was forced to give ground slowly, then it broke, leaving two regiments isolated and captured. The Confederates racing in pursuit suddenly came upon the massed Federal batteries that had caused such slaughter among their ranks throughout the day. Guns jammed hub to hub spewed out double rounds of canister, but the Southerners charged forward undeterred.

"There was dreadful carnage in their ranks," a Northern gunner remembered, horrified by the sight, "but each horrible gap was instantly closed up, and the column pressed forward. When within twenty paces of the battery, at a single round the whole front rank was carried away, yet still forward rushed the infuriated enemy to the very muzzles of the guns."

To cover the artillery while the gun crews hastened to limber up and escape, Gen. Philip St. George Cooke ordered a charge by the Fifth U.S. Cavalry. Bugles urged the horsemen on, and the Texans felt "the ground begin to tremble like an earthquake and heard a noise like the rumbling of distant thunder," one recorded.

Cavalry, however, no longer struck terror in the hearts of foot soldiers as they once did. The Southern infantry was prepared as the troopers emerged from the battle smoke with sabers raised. A rifle volley at forty yards shattered the old-fashioned charge. Saddles not emptied by bullets were dealt with by bayonets. Over 150 of the 250 horsemen and 6 of their 7 officers fell. The terrified remainder raced for safety through the cannon they were sent to save. Hood's men gleefully captured fourteen guns.

A man severely wounded in front of a Union battery was snatched up by a passing comrade who "unceremoniously snaked me along for a few yards and landed me behind a big apple tree. He handled me without gloves and hurt me fearful, and in return for that act of humanity I cursed him. He made no reply, but hurried on."

When the final Confederate assault broke the Federal line, several Union regiments were captured. Demanding to know where the Fourth New Jersey was, Brig. Gen. George W. Taylor was told, "Gone to Richmond, sir." He lost 1,072 men that day.

A Pennsylvania private had three different rifles destroyed by enemy fire as he held them, but he himself escaped with minor wounds.

LIBRARY OF CONGRESS

When the Union infantry fell back in the face of the Confederate breakthrough at Gaines's Mill, the Federal batteries were overrun in fierce hand-to-hand fighting. Less than half of one eighteen-gun battery was able to withdraw because most of its horses had been killed or injured.

Porter's corps was broken, but the remnants were saved by darkness, exhaustion, and two brigades of reinforcements. Throughout the night, Federal stragglers stumbled across the Chickahominy.

McClellan reported events to Washington in typical petulant fashion. "The Government has not sustained this army," his telegraph read. "If you do not do so now the game is lost. If I save this army now, I tell you plainly that I owe no thanks to you or to any other persons in Washington. You have done your best to sacrifice this army." Stanton's staff carefully edited the message for their volatile chief, but he and Lincoln later read the original text.

Lee took a different tact. He gave God credit for the battle's result in his dispatch to his president.

The fierce assaults at the battle of Gaines's Mill cost Lee 8,751 casualties. Porter lost 6,837 men, 2,836 of them captured. Davis had found a worthy replacement for Johnston, and Lee's critics were silenced.

As the savaged Fifth Corps struggled across the Chickahominy, McClellan convened a council of war with his five corps commanders. His announcement was more shocking than the battle loss earlier in the day. McClellan intended to abandon the siege of Richmond and concentrate the army at a new base of operations at Harrison's Landing on the James River. There, protected by the big guns of navy gunboats, they would be resupplied and reinforced. McClellan emphasized that this movement was not a retreat, merely a "change of base." He left open the possibility of resuming the campaign against Richmond from the new position.

His generals were taken by surprise. They understood the necessity of relocating their supply base, for the Confederates now controlled the area

A Northern correspondent saw a horse ride by "carrying a man's leg in the stirrup—the left leg, booted and spurred. It was a splendid horse, gayly caparisoned."

BATTLES AND LEADERS

Confederate Lt. Col. J. C. Upton entered battle carrying a frying pan instead of a sword for swatting malingerers. When one of his soldiers was rounding up Union prisoners, Upton roared, "Let them go, you infernal fool. We'd a damned sight rather fight 'em than feed 'em."

Porter's beaten corps retreated across the Chickahominy and destroyed the supplies the men could not carry. The troops wearing the distinctive straw hats are from the Sixteenth New York, which was known to have worn the unusual headgear during the Peninsula campaign.

north of the Chickahominy and White House Landing was theirs as soon as they could reach it. But the mass retreat of the army was incomprehensible.

Word of the plan soon leaked, attracting combative divisional commanders Philip Kearny and Joseph Hooker. So aggressively did they protest to their commanding general that some witnesses expected them, particularly Kearny, to be summarily fired. The two argued that the army was now united south of the Chickahominy, and Richmond was less than five miles away. Change the base to the James River, but advance on Richmond from their current strong position, they implored McClellan.

McClellan rejected all recommendations, citing Magruder's energetic actions as the final evidence that had convinced him that Lee had two hundred thousand or more troops. Lee's attack north of the Chickahominy was a mere preliminary to the primary attack south of the river, he claimed. McClellan believed the country could only be saved if the Army of the Potomac was saved, and that was possible only by a complete withdrawal to the James.

At first light two corps would move east along the Williamsburg road, then cross White Oak Swamp on two bridges to prepare defenses at Malvern Hill, eight miles above Harrison's Landing, while the other three corps remained to protect the withdrawal.

When the First Maryland wavered at Gaines's Mill, Col. Bradley Johnston stopped and drilled the regiment under Federal fire. They then charged bravely into the fight.

LIBRARY OF CONGRESS

The ruins of Gaines's gristmill were photographed in April 1865. The structure was torched during the June 1864 battle at Cold Harbor.

When Jeb Stuart arrived at White House Landing on June 28, he found the supply depot there had been abandoned and mountains of supplies destroyed. In addition to the smoldering depot, the house that had given its name to the landing and had been "entrusted" to McClellan's safekeeping by Mary Lee had also been torched (left), presumably by stragglers, and nothing remained of the structure except the chimneys (right). One of the horsemen described the scene as "an awful destruction," but added that Stuart's cavalry dined well on salvaged sutler's goods and "filled their haversacks with good things."

Gaines's Mill belonged to Dr. William G. Gaines, a prominent landowner. Angry that Federals killed by fever had been buried on his property, he threatened to dig them up and feed them to the hogs as soon as the enemy departed. One soldier remarked that "it is rather rough to be compelled to protect such a man's property."

Maj. Chatham Roberdeau Wheat, commander of the celebrated Louisiana Tigers, had nearly died of wounds suffered at First Manassas. Minutes before the assault at Gaines's Mill, Wheat took a drink from Moxley Sorrel. "Sorrel," he said, "something tells old Bob that this is the last drink he'll ever take in this world and he'll take it with you." He was soon dead.

Lee, thinking that McClellan had moved along the north bank of the Chickahominy to defend the railroad to White House Landing, sent Stuart and an infantry division to cut the tracks. Encountering no resistance and discovering that the Federals had torched the railroad bridge over the Chickahominy, Stuart continued to White House Landing, where an incredible sight greeted him. Two square miles of stored supplies were burning, including locomotives and railcars. The last Union steamers were disappearing far down the river.

McClellan, only a mile away from Lee, had slipped away as quietly as Johnston had at Manassas and Yorktown. His evacuation was further evidenced later in the day by huge explosions that echoed across the Chickahominy as stores of artillery ammunition were being destroyed. Then dust clouds from marching columns were spotted in the distance over the Williamsburg road. McClellan was clearly on the move, withdrawing from Richmond. Lee, understandably excited by the development, was still uncertain whether the Federals were returning east down the peninsula toward Fort Monroe or making south for the James River.

Reports the next morning showed no Federals in the trenches at Fair Oaks and no activity at Bottom's Bridge, two prominent locations on the route to the peninsula. McClellan had gained a day's head start, but now the Confederates would follow relentlessly and with every available soldier.

To attack McClellan immediately on June 29, Lee sent Magruder, who was in front of the Union trenches at Fair Oaks, to pursue east along the Richmond and York River Railroad. He would be supported by Jackson, who was directed to cross the Chickahominy over Grapevine Bridge.

Longstreet and A. P. Hill crossed the Chickahominy on New Bridge. With Huger, on Magruder's left at Fair Oaks, they marched south to strike McClellan below White Oak Swamp on the following day. With this movement Lee hoped to isolate portions of McClellan's rear guard and destroy them.

Magruder's eighteen thousand men passed through the abandoned Federal works at Fair Oaks and encountered McClellan's strong rear guard three miles east, along the railroad at Savage's Station. He had discovered half the Union army—Heintzelman's Third Corps, Edwin V. Sumner's Second Corps, and William Franklin's Sixth Corps—supported by forty pieces of artillery. They had been ordered to hold the position through the day, then withdraw during the night.

Magruder wisely waited for Jackson, who had another eighteen thousand men, but it developed into a long delay, this one without end. This time, however, Jackson sent a message. He had "other important duty to perform." The only explanation ever offered was that he spent the day rebuilding Grapevine Bridge, but a suitable ford lay near at hand.

During this intermission the Federals destroyed stacks of supplies two stories tall at Savage's Station. Artillery shells and barrels of whiskey exploded spectacularly for hours.

Atmospheric inversions or acoustical shadows struck again at Gaines's Mill when Lee failed to hear early fighting on June 27. McClellan, across the Chickahominy, also heard little of a heavy artillery exchange. Confederate Secretary of War George W. Randolph, watching the fighting from hills east of Richmond, heard no sound. Soldiers marching through thick vegetation in the hot, humid, still air heard only muffled noises.

Richard Ewell's horse was killed under him, and after the battle he found a spent bullet in his boot.

A Thankless Job ■ George Gordon Meade

Born in Cadiz, Spain, on December 31, 1815, George Gordon Meade graduated from West Point in 1835, ranked fifteenth of fifty-six members. He resigned the following year for a career as a civil engineer but rejoined the army in 1842. Meade spent the next twenty years in geodetic survey work and constructing lighthouses and breakwaters, but he saw action in Mexico and was breveted.

On August 31, 1861, Meade was promoted from a regular army captain to a brigadier of volunteers. He received command of a Pennsylvania brigade at the insistence of Gov. Andrew G. Curtin. Meade spent the winter improving Washington's defenses and was heavily engaged on the peninsula and during the Seven Days, fighting at Beaver Dam Creek and Gaines's Mill before being badly wounded at Glendale. He returned to participate in the battles of Second Manassas, South Mountain, and

Antietam, where he commanded a corps after Joseph Hooker was wounded. He scored the only success at Fredericksburg, breaking Stonewall Jackson's line, but Burnside failed to reinforce him. Meade had a corps at the Chancellorsville disaster.

As the Federals chased Lee into Pennsylvania, Hooker was removed and Meade placed in command of the Army of the Potomac. Meade marched rapidly and encountered Lee only three days later, at Gettysburg, where Union forces were driven out of town and onto Cemetery Ridge. For the next two days his troops repulsed numerous Confederate assaults all along the line despite horrendous casualties, as Meade skillfully shifted them to meet each threat. Although Lee was stopped and forced to retreat on July 5, Meade was severely criticized for his slow pursuit of Lee, allowing the Confederates to escape back into Virginia.

When Lincoln let his dissatisfaction with Meade be known, the general offered his resignation, which caused the government to relent and promote him to brigadier in the regular army. He received the Thanks of Congress in January 1864.

Meade and Lee maneuvered throughout the fall of 1863, but the tenuous and indecisive Bristoe and Mine Run campaigns gained Meade no confidence from higher authorities. Over the winter Ulysses S. Grant was commissioned lieutenant general and general in chief. Although he decided to accompany the Army of the Potomac into battle in the spring of 1864, Meade still commanded the army, but he followed Grant's orders. It was an awkward but successful arrangement from the Wilderness to Appomattox. After Meade, who was known for his temper, quarreled with newspaper correspondents who accompanied the army, they con-

spired to slight him. His name was never used in connection with successful operations (including Appomattox) but mentioned prominently in every defeat.

Meade was tardily promoted to major general and headed departments following the war. He died on November 6, 1872, in Philadelphia, Pennsylvania, and is buried in Laurel Hill Cemetery.

To counter George B. McClellan's siege guns if Richmond were invested, Robert E. Lee had mounted a big 32-pounder rifle on a flatcar. Iron plating protected the gun, which fired out a porthole, much like a ship. A locomotive pushed the car to a point near Savage's Station on June 29 to support John Magruder's attack. It was the first time railroad artillery was employed in war.

At length Magruder decided to carry out his orders, but he utilized only half his force and a single artillery battery. Union cannon easily repulsed the assault, killing Brig. Gen. Richard Griffith.

It was fortunate for the Federals that the Confederate plan failed. McClellan had left for White Oak Swamp to oversee the evacuation without specifying a general to command the rear guard. Heintzelman left without orders and failed to inform anyone of the fact as he joined the retreat. Sumner thought so little of the Confederate attack that he bragged, "I would crush this rebellion" with twenty thousand additional men. He pulled back at 10 P.M. Twelve hours later all of the Army of the Potomac had passed through White Oak Swamp unmolested, but it was now strung out in a vulnerable line ten miles long to Malvern Hill. Porter's mangled Fifth Corps and Keyes's Fourth Corps were already at the James, shielded by powerful naval guns.

McClellan needed another day to reach his impregnable base. He deployed two of Franklin's divisions at White Oak Swamp to slow direct pursuit from Savage's Station, and five divisions were stationed three miles to the south around Glendale to block pursuit from the swamp and from roads that led southeast from Richmond, paralleling the James River. Glendale was

On the evening of June 27 McClellan announced to his generals that the army would withdraw from its entrenchments near Richmond, abandon the Chickahominy line, and move toward a new base on the James River. Despite his labeling the movement a "change of base," it was a retreat. In addition to the torching of the White House Landing depot, war materiel, such as this ammunition train, was destroyed as quickly as possible.

Many Federal prisoners were taken in the confusion following Gaines's Mill and the nightmarish retreat from Savage's Station. Stonewall Jackson, scouting forward, a habit that would kill him in less than a year, captured over a dozen himself. Some claimed to be honored to be nabbed by the famous Confederate.

BATTLES AND LEADERS

While vast quantities of supplies were destroyed at Savage's Station, Federal troops repulsed an undermanned attack led by Magruder. The battle was ended by darkness, and then the Union troops retreated. Per McClellan's orders, more than three thousand sick and wounded were abandoned here.

a vital crossroads and a potential bottleneck where two roads through White Oak Swamp—from White Oak Bridge and Brackett's Ford—converged at the Frayser farm to form the Willis Church road.

Approaching from the northwest on the Darbytown road were Longstreet and A. P. Hill, nearing the end of their long sweep. Magruder was to their left on the Charles City road and would intercept the Darbytown road from a side route. Huger continued straight to Glendale on the Charles City road.

Jackson completed his leisurely rebuilding of the Grapevine Bridge and crossed the Chickahominy in the predawn hours, then met Lee at Savage's Station. A soldier watched Jackson scrawling plans in the dirt with the toe of his boot. Jackson then stomped the ground and exclaimed, "We've got him!"

Wounded soldiers from the battles of Gaines's Mill and Savage's Station fill this yard (right). Most are from the Sixteenth New York, who had worn straw hats because of the summer heat. Many of their wounded had head wounds, leading some to suggest that the Southerners had been aiming at the hats.

George B. McClellan ordered the mountains of supplies stockpiled at Savage's Station to be destroyed. Every observer was fascinated by the firing of a mountain of boxes and barrels, estimated to be the size of several barns or a city block of two-story buildings. A munitions train was destroyed on a siding; a second was sent roaring into the Chickahominy off a burning bridge. "Bomb after bomb sprang from the fierce mass," noted a chaplain, "hissing and screaming like fiends in agony." Windows were shattered nearly a mile away by the explosion.

Medicine was dumped in wells. Molasses was poured onto the ground in large ponds and pork and beef throw in. Hundreds of whiskey barrels were smashed and the liquor set ablaze, burning soldiers who frantically attempted to take a drink or fill a canteen. Rifles were smashed against trees.

"The flames roared and snapped," one Federal officer wrote, "and its vicinity was exceedingly hot." Another called it "unearthly and demonic."

The walking wounded marched, but three thousand seriously wounded men were left behind. "Their cries are yet ringing in my ears," wrote Maj. Thomas Hyde.

LIBRARY OF CONGRESS

255

Brig. Gen. William T. H. Brooks's Vermont Brigade formed the Union rear guard at White Oak Swamp and convinced Stonewall Jackson not to aggressively pursue the retreating Federals. Uncharacteristically, Jackson failed to seek other avenues of pursuit despite the initiative of some subordinates. The scene was captured by Alfred Waud at the time (below) and gloriously depicted in 1869 (above) by Julian Scott, a Federal drummer boy at the time of the incident.

After two sleepless days, Union Brig. Gen. John F. Reynolds lay on the ground and the retreat passed him by. Confederate soldiers woke him and escorted the general to see his old friend D. H. Hill.

It was a promising start to the new day, June 30, but Jackson soon reverted to recent form, slowing his march to gather one thousand Union stragglers. He reached White Oak Bridge only two hours after it was burned. Across the swamp he observed Federal artillery and wagons rattling away and Union infantry resting on the ground.

At 2 P.M. Jackson directed twenty-eight cannon into a clearing and opened a heavy bombardment. He personally led skirmishers and cavalry to scout across the swamp, where they were engaged by four batteries of artillery and two Union infantry divisions commanded by Brig. Gen. Israel B. Richardson. The reconnaissance was quickly driven off, and the artillery prevented repair of the bridge.

Jackson reacted to the setback by falling asleep beneath a tree. Later he refused to act on a cavalry report of a ford four hundred yards downstream or the account by one of his brigadiers who had constructed a bridge a mile downstream and beyond Richardson's right flank.

While Jackson failed to dislodge the Federals in White Oak Swamp, Lee had Huger, Longstreet, and A. P. Hill, with Magruder in reserve, converge on the crossroads at Glendale. On Jackson's right, to the southwest, was Huger on the Charles City road, and two miles right of Huger were Longstreet, A. P. Hill, and Magruder on the parallel Darbytown road. Huger would announce his arrival at Glendale by firing artillery, which would be Longstreet's signal to attack.

Near noon Huger encountered trees felled across the road by Federal skirmishers two miles northwest of Glendale. Rather than clear the road, the lead Confederate brigade, under Brig. Gen. William Mahone, sent men into the woods paralleling the road to cut a new path, a logic that escaped the comprehension of all. Seeing this, the Union skirmishers, part of Henry W. Slocum's division, proceeded to cut more trees. A senseless two-hour delay resulted. It was 2 P.M. when Mahone regained the road, having chopped a path one mile long. The road was at last unobstructed, but the delay had given Slocum time to deploy on a hill one mile west of Glendale. Huger outnumbered the Federals by three to two, but he limited his activity to a brief artillery exchange. Jackson and Huger had accomplished all they intended to do for the day.

Lee, with Longstreet and A. P. Hill, had departed the Darbytown road for the Long Bridge road and arrived a mile southwest of Glendale with eighteen thousand men. Huger's artillery fire caused Lee to fire in reply, which triggered a Union response. A shell dropped in the midst of a conversation between Lee, Longstreet, and Jefferson Davis, killing several horses. "Our little party speedily retired to safer quarters," Longstreet remembered.

Farther south, a fourth and new portion of the Army of Northern Virginia approached. Commanded by Maj. Gen. Theophilus H. Holmes, these

The Federal retreat through White Oak Swamp was necessarily slow. A single poor road was the only avenue open for the withdrawing artillery reserve—which numbered one hundred pieces, one-fourth of them two-ton siege guns—and three thousand wagons and ambulances, fifteen thousand horses and mules, and twenty-five hundred head of cattle.

Two unique items seized in the wake of the Union withdrawal were crude machine guns, whose feeding mechanism often failed in battle, and hundreds of "bullet-proof" steel breastplates sold to soldiers by Northern charlatans. Although they offered a degree of protection—one Confederate counted seven dents in one, although an eighth had penetrated and killed its owner—the devices were so heavy that they were jettisoned during the retreat.

The Fiercest Fighter in the Army ■ John Bell Hood

LIBRARY OF CONGRESS

If ever a soldier was promoted beyond his capabilities, it was John Bell Hood. What made his career a greater tragedy is the fact that he was one of the most ferocious fighters in the Confederate army. Had he remained in divisional command, history would have recorded him as an excellent subordinate officer.

Born in Owingsville, Kentucky, on June 1, 1831, Hood graduated near the bottom of his West Point class in 1853 and was sent to the western frontier, where Indians had the first opportunity to wound the unfortunate fellow. Hood soon began his Confederate service in the retreat from Yorktown and gallantly led the Texas Brigade during the savage Seven Days' battles, where he broke the Union line at Gaines's Mill. He fought well at Second Manassas and saw his brave brigade decimated in the bloody fighting at Antietam. His conspicuous heroism brought him command of a division, which he led at Fredericksburg and Gettysburg, where a severe wound cost him the use of his left arm.

Two months later Hood accompanied James Longstreet to Georgia. While leading his men into the carnage that was Chickamauga, Hood suffered a wound that required the amputation of his right leg. He remained in Georgia and received a corps under Joseph E. Johnston, but during the Atlanta campaign Hood undermined Johnston's position with poison-pen letters to Jefferson Davis. When the young general was appointed commander of the Army of Tennessee, he lost Atlanta by launching four determined but poorly conducted strikes against William T. Sherman's superior force. Abandoning Georgia, Hood nearly destroyed his army with a suicidal campaign into Middle Tennessee.

Following the war, Hood entered business in New Orleans, but ill fortune followed him even there. The business failed, and Hood and his wife died from yellow fever, leaving a large family of small children to be divided among various foster homes.

Thousands of knapsacks were captured and "the whole Confed. Army refitted itself with blankets, rubber clothes, tentflies, haversacks, and canteens," a South Carolinian wrote while they feasted on Federal provisions.

Confederate Gen. William Mahone, who attacked at Glendale, ensured his personal milk supply by hitching a cow to his headquarters wagon.

reinforcements from Drewry's Bluff had crossed the James River on a pontoon bridge and were marching on the river road. Lee hoped they would intercept the head of McClellan's columns. At 4 P.M. scouts informed Holmes that Union wagon trains were approaching Malvern Hill on the Willis Church road, three miles east of his position. Unaccountably, he rode off with six cannon, presumably to take the wagons under fire. Lee, checking out the same report, encountered Holmes, who was instructed to bring up his infantry for an attack. Lee then rode back to Longstreet.

By 4:30 Holmes had deployed his cannon eight hundred yards from the Federal trains on Malvern Hill and opened fire. From atop the rise, Porter had observed the approaching dust clouds stirred up by Holmes's force. He had McClellan's artillery reserve with him, thirty artillery pieces from the hill, which were joined by 100-pounder guns from the ships on the James and directed by signal officers assigned to Porter. The Federals opened fire on Holmes, who suffered terrible casualties before withdrawing.

The last of McClellan's wagon trains were safe, proceeding past Malvern Hill to Harrison's Landing, several miles farther south on the banks of the James. All that was left on the Willis Church road were seven Federal infantry divisions.

The Southerners perceived that McClellan was moving toward the James River and pursued the retreating Federals the next day. As they approached the area of Glendale, Jefferson Davis joined Lee in the front lines. In reply to a Confederate volley, Union batteries opened, firing blindly, but the effect was deadly in the rough clearing where a large part of the Confederate high command had gathered. A. P. Hill dutifully ordered Davis and Lee to the rear, and the two rode out of range of the guns.

LESLIE'S

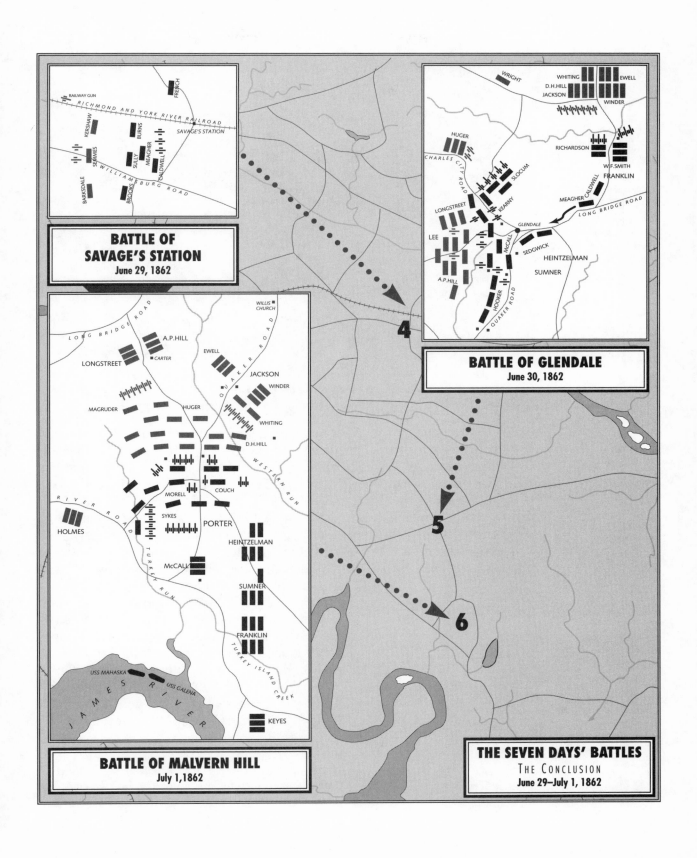

BATTLE OF SAVAGE'S STATION
June 29, 1862

RAILWAY GUN
RICHMOND AND YORK RIVER RAILROAD
FRENCH
KERSHAW
BURNS
SAVAGE'S STATION
SEMMES
SULLY
MEAGHER
CALDWELL
BARKSDALE
BROOKS
WILLIAMSBURG ROAD

BATTLE OF GLENDALE
June 30, 1862

WRIGHT
WHITING
EWELL
D.H.HILL
JACKSON
WINDER
HUGER
RICHARDSON
CHARLES CITY ROAD
SLOCUM
W.F.SMITH
FRANKLIN
LONGSTREET
KEARNY
MEAGHER CALDWELL
LONG BRIDGE ROAD
LEE
GLENDALE
McCALL
SEDGWICK
HEINTZELMAN
A.P.HILL
SUMNER
HOOKER
QUAKER ROAD

BATTLE OF MALVERN HILL
July 1, 1862

LONG BRIDGE ROAD
A.P.HILL
WILLIS CHURCH
CARTER
EWELL
QUAKER ROAD
JACKSON
LONGSTREET
WINDER
MAGRUDER
HUGER
WHITING
D.H.HILL
WESTERN RUN
MORELL
COUCH
RIVER ROAD
SYKES
PORTER
HOLMES
McCALL
HEINTZELMAN
TURKEY RUN
SUMNER
FRANKLIN
TURKEY ISLAND CREEK
USS MAHASKA
USS GALENA
J A M E S   R I V E R
KEYES

THE SEVEN DAYS' BATTLES
THE CONCLUSION
June 29–July 1, 1862

4

5

6

In the confusion of battle, Philip Kearny suddenly found himself in the midst of Confederate soldiers. One Rebel ran up and asked, "What shall I do next, Sir?"

Kearny reported that he answered, "'Do, damn you, why do what you have always been told to do,' and off I went."

George A. McCall was not as lucky. Attempting to assemble a line, he asked a gaggle of soldiers, "What command is this?"

"General Field's," they replied.

"General Field. I don't know him," McCall said, then realized his mistake and started to ride away.

"Not so fast," a Confederate said, taking his bridle.

Longstreet was happy to see an old messmate and sent McCall off to Richmond as a prisoner.

BATTLES AND LEADERS

Lee had hoped to cut McClellan's army in half, but only half of the Southern army arrived to attack. The combination of darkness and the timely arrival of Federal reinforcements from White Oak Bridge to fill the break in the line blunted Confederate fortunes.

"If there was one Ball Whistled past my devoted head that day there was thousands," declared one Federal at Glendale. "It appeared to me they flew in every Square inch of air around me except the little Space I stood in."

Lee, despairing of any action in a long and frustrating day, ordered Longstreet to attack Glendale via the Long Bridge road at 5 P.M. The situation certainly looked familiar as the Confederates advanced across the swampy terrain to charge a prepared enemy position on a ridge, this one at Frayser's farm. Longstreet struck the Federal center held by McCall's division. The Federals resisted for a while, then the Fourth Pennsylvania broke for the protection of a six-gun battery. The Confederates were so close behind the Federal infantry that the artillery officer hesitated to order his pieces to fire until the enemy was only thirty yards away, "but it was too late," he said afterward.

The Eleventh Alabama seized the guns in desperate hand-to-hand fighting. One Confederate officer was stabbed six times by bayonet; another drew six thrusts after killing two Federals with his sword. Rifle butts crashed into skulls.

A. P. Hill's Fifty-fifth and Sixtieth Virginia followed into Longstreet's breach, causing McCall's division to flee; McCall himself was captured.

BATTLES AND LEADERS

The fighting swirled around the Union batteries. Many were placed ahead of their infantry support and were lost and recaptured and lost again in the savage combat at Glendale.

As the two armies collided, the soldiers found little time to reload their weapons. Flush with the heat of combat, they resorted to bayonets, clubbing their opponents with rifle butts, knives, and fists. Hand-to-hand fighting was the distinctive memory of Glendale for both sides.

The Federals still lacked a commander, but two divisions of Second Corps, those of John Sedgwick and Richardson, freed by Jackson's inactivity at White Oak Swamp, added their weight to the defense. To McCall's left the redoubtable Kearny stopped A. P. Hill then counterattacked savagely. "It was muzzle to muzzle," Pennsylvania Col. Alexander Hays wrote, "and the powder actually burned the faces of the opposing men."

The Confederate units were about to break when Hill rode to the front and grabbed a regimental flag in an attempt to rally the men, at first unsuccessfully. But when Hill shouted, "Damn you, if you will not follow me, I'll die alone!" the men responded with vigor, again driving the Federals back.

Night soon fell and ended the fighting with little settled. Lee lost 3,300 men and captured a Federal battery. Union casualties totaled 2,853, including 1,130 captured or missing. "The unbroken, mournful wail of human suffering was all that we heard from Glendale during that long, dismal night," related Hooker, who had held the Federal right.

It was obvious to Lee that a significant victory would have been won at Frayser's farm had his subordinates obeyed their orders. McClellan was now safe at Malvern Hill. Jackson crossed White Oak Swamp early on July 1 and met Lee at Glendale, where the Confederates resumed their pursuit, Jackson leading on the Willis Church road.

Malvern Hill, rising one hundred feet above the surrounding land, measured a mile and a half in length and three quarters of a mile in width. The only approach was from the north along the road. The flanks were guarded by creeks and gullies.

Atop the hill McClellan had marshaled 250 cannon, including 14 of his pet siege guns. His artillery reserve, 100 pieces strong, was deployed in a massive line across the summit. The infantry was arrayed in a semicircle facing north, where the Willis Church road ascended the slope.

"If General McClellan is there in force," D. H. Hill said wisely to Lee and Longstreet, "we

Virginia Pvt. Robert A. Christian was attacked by four Federals. Although sustaining several wounds, Christian killed three of the soldiers with his bayonet. Knocked to the ground by the fourth, Christian was about to be bayonetted himself when his brother Eli killed the last Yankee.

Gen. Edwin V. "Bull" Sumner urged troops going into battle by shouting, "Go in, boys, for the honor of old Massachusetts! I have been hit twice this afternoon, but it is nothing when you get used to it."

During the night the Federal army pulled back to an open plateau, about three miles south of Glendale, known as Malvern Hill. It was an excellent defensive position.

A Confederate shot through both lungs wondered whether he would live. He was willing to sacrifice his life for the Confederacy, he stated, but "I'd a heap rather get well & see my mother & my folks again."

Maj. Gen. Theophilus H. Holmes, who probed Malvern Hill on June 30, was severely deaf. When 100-pound shells from gunboats in the James River started falling amongst his troops, he cupped a hand to his right ear and said, "I thought I heard firing."

BATTLES AND LEADERS

had better let him alone." Longstreet disagreed, saying, "Don't get scared, now that we have got him licked." Lee agreed.

When Longstreet marched up to the base of the elevation, Federal artillery fire forced him into the woods, "smashing everything in reach," a Confederate noted. Shells shattered ancient oaks, adding to the carnage in the forest.

Lee spent several hours placing the Army of Northern Virginia along a mile-long arc in the woods bordering Malvern Hill. D. H. Hill's five brigades were in the center on the road. To his left were Whiting's three brigades, to the right were two brigades belonging to Huger, and Magruder's six brigades formed the extreme right. A. P. Hill and Longstreet were in reserve to the right, Ewell and Jackson in reserve to the left. Holmes's shaken unit was to the west on the river road.

Lee's frustration with the whole campaign had been evident earlier in the day when he told a officer that McClellan "will get away because I cannot have my orders carried out." The strength of the Union position was evident, but Lee chose to believe that the Federal troops were demoralized. He desperately hoped that here was one last opportunity to crush the Army of the Potomac.

Longstreet conducted a reconnaissance of the Confederate right and brought the results to Lee. The Georgian suggested placing forty to sixty guns on a hill facing the Federal artillery concentration and twelve hundred yards distant, and one hundred cannon in a field a half mile east of the Willis Church road. He believed the resulting enfilading fire would decimate the Union artillery crews and allow a successful infantry attack up the north slope of Malvern Hill. Lee approved the plan and at 1:30 issued this order: "Batteries have been established to rake the enemy's line. If it is broken, as is probable, [Lewis] Armistead, who can witness the effect of the fire, has been ordered to charge with a yell. Do the same."

The order was imprecise and open to many interpretations. Perhaps Lee's wits had been addled by the recent performance of his generals.

Brig. Gen. William Pendleton, the Confederate chief of artillery, received no orders and spent the day searching for Lee and Longstreet's reported vantage points. Not that it would have done much good had he found them, for Lee's ninety-gun artillery reserve was stuck in the rear. D. H. Hill's cannon were being

Three divisions of infantry and several batteries were positioned at the top of Malvern Hill. To their rear the reserve artillery of McClellan's army was arrayed wheel to wheel. All in all, there were approximately 250 guns facing the approaching Confederates. In addition, the Federal gunboats on the James were poised to add their substantial firepower.

The fields around the plateau were planted with wheat, which had been partly harvested and gathered in shocks. Behind each shock was a sharpshooter from Hiram Berdan's regiment of accomplished marksmen, each of whom had a breech-loading .52-caliber Sharps rifle.

BATTLES AND LEADERS

refitted at Seven Pines, and other generals had difficulty deploying their assigned artillery because of woods, swamps, and Federal cannon fire. Only 20 guns of Longstreet's 140 to 160 proposed pieces were deployed, and most were quickly put out of action by McClellan's superior artillery.

Eventually Lee abandoned his assault plan, although the order was never rescinded. At 3 P.M. he started scouting for a way to flank McClellan from Malvern Hill. He found nothing, but one hour later Lee received two fateful and misleading reports.

When Sumner shifted position atop the hill, Whiting, on the left, interpreted it as the withdrawal of Fifth Corps. Then Magruder, on the right, informed Lee that Armistead had made a breakthrough. Actually Armistead chased off some pesky Federal skirmishers and was in turn driven into a ravine by the hilltop artillery. Lee, however, was elated by the news and ordered Magruder, "Press forward your whole line and follow up Armistead's success."

Although Magruder had just arrived on the field and was unprepared for an attack, he had been recently castigated by Lee for his inactivity at Savage's Station and decided to comply promptly. He ordered two brigades of Huger's command forward, Mahone's and Ambrose Wright's. As the twenty-five hundred men marched gleefully across the open ground, they were joined by Armistead.

The charge was decimated by a hail of artillery fire. In addition, the Federal infantry fire was so disciplined that it seemed "as if at a dress parade," a Confederate remembered.

The yells of Magruder's troops were clearly heard by D. H. Hill at the Willis Church road. Since Lee had never canceled his original orders, Hill sent his division forward around 5 P.M. in a one-half-mile-long line. They had eight hundred yards of clear, gradually rising ground to cover.

The power of the Federal artillery fire was unprecedented. One shell killed six men around Col. John B. Gordon, and six color-bearers fell as he lost half the regiment. At a spot two hundred yards from the Federal battle line, Gordon ordered the survivors to hug the ground.

Horrified Union gunners fired solid shot then shell then case and canister as the range closed. They watched Rebel soldiers explode in front of

The Confederate attack was so suicidally determined that one Federal thought they "had been rendered insensible to fear by whiskey drugged with gunpowder."

As the Federals bombarded the Confederate lines beneath Malvern Hill on July 1, D. H. Hill sat in the open in front of a large tree. "Don't worry about me. Look after the men," Hill told an officer who expressed concern for his safety. "I am not going to be killed until my time." When a Union shell exploded nearby, Hill was thrown to the ground. Calmly he tidied his uniform and quietly moved behind the tree.

Lee had hoped to emplace his own guns to rake the Federal position and issued orders based on that prospect. His batteries, however, were far from the front, bogged down with other elements of the army. Nevertheless, his commanders launched the attack according to a schedule that presupposed artillery support. The Confederates were mauled by the Union gunners.

A Confederate officer found a dozen men lined up hiding behind one tree. He noted "a shiver pass up the file when the hindmost was struck with the flat of a sword," but none moved.

With his horse killed and Confederates pressing in, Fitz John Porter, fearing capture, burned his dispatch book and diary. He then returned safely to the Union lines.

them, sending body parts and equipment raining down the hill. One battery fired fourteen hundred rounds. While McClellan's chief of artillery, Col. Henry J. Hunt, roamed the crest of the hill to organize resupply, three horses were shot from under him.

The Union infantry fought just as desperately, many men exhausting their 150 rounds. A New York sergeant remembered that "the gun barrels became heated to the point that they could not be grasped and men held their guns by the sling strap."

By 6 P.M. the brigades of D. H. Hill retreated and Huger's men huddled beneath a bluff, temporarily safe from Union fire. Some of Huger's troops approached within twenty yards of the Federal position when they encountered fire "beyond description," recalled Brig. Gen. Robert Ransom.

Despite this devastation, Magruder continued feeding his brigades into the attack one at a time. The commander of the Fifteenth Virginia, Col. Thomas P. August, was cut down, then each of his stretcher bearers was felled. August's replacement, Maj. John W. Walker, was soon hit, dying in the arms of his brother, Capt. Norman Walker.

Clouds of powder smoke brought an early dusk to the battlefield. Advancing Confederates walked across a carpet of dead, wounded, or cowering comrades, horrified by the sight of corpses missing heads and limbs.

Despite the slaughter, Porter felt hard pressed. He cadged a brigade each from Heintzelman and Sumner and led one in a counterattack. Encountering Confederates stumbling out of the smoke fifty yards away, Porter said that they "rose and opened with fearful volleys upon our advancing line. I turned to the brigade, which thus far had kept pace with my horse, and found it standing 'like a stonewall,' and returning a fire more destructive than it received and from which the enemy fled." He positioned batteries of artillery to fire double rounds of canister across the field "at the risk of firing upon friends."

Lee never ended the assault, but Longstreet, A. P. Hill, Jackson, and Ewell were never committed. As had become the custom, darkness signaled the end of the battle to the infantry. The awesome Federal artillery ceased firing an hour later.

Confederate casualties, 5,355 of them, carpeted the hillside. "Dead and wounded men were on the ground in every attitude of distress," related Federal Col. William Averell. "A third of them were dead or dying, but enough were alive and moving to give to the field a singular crawling effect." A Union lieutenant noted, "One in particular, we could hear for hours in the same strained, high-pitched key, alternately praying and cursing."

During the night McClellan withdrew his entire army to Harrison's Landing. He had suffered 3,214 casualties at Malvern Hill. During the week's worth of combat that would become known as the Seven Days' battles, McClellan had lost 15,849 men, 6,053 of them captured. He was satisfied with saving the army, an accomplishment "unparalleled in the annals of war," or so he claimed. He might have believed it, but his army, the Northern public, and Lincoln knew the truth. Panicked and deluded, McClellan had been decisively driven away from Richmond by an inferior force. His soldiers did not fail to notice that their commanding general made only a few brief visits to the field while the fighting raged. He had also failed to command the army during times of crisis.

Jefferson Davis issued a proclamation of thanksgiving, and the Confederacy celebrated Lee's victory over a superior foe and the deliverance of their capital. But the cost had been staggering. One-fourth of the Army of Northern

When Confederate Maj. Joseph L. Brent shinnied up a tree to observe Union dispositions on Malvern Hill, he saw cannon crowding the crest from one end to the other and hordes of Union infantry. After the officer descended from his perch, a picket expressed surprise that he was alive—Federal marksmen had been very active in the area. "I would have preferred his warning before I climbed," Brent recalled, "to his expression of surprise that I had escaped."

The bravest artillery officer in Lee's army was without question Capt. William J. Pegram, who resembled a young professor and had been a student at the University of Virginia when the war started. His battery had participated in all the major battles of the Seven Days' campaign, losing forty of its eighty crewmen. At Malvern Hill five of his six guns were knocked out of action by Union fire, and Pegram worked the final one alone.

With few exceptions, every man who charged the guns at Malvern Hill spoke in awe of the Union gunners. According to Confederate Gen. D. H. Hill, the Federal batteries possibly accounted for more than half of the Confederate casualties on the field that day.

Malvern Hill (1866)
■ Herman Melville

Ye elms that wave on Malvern Hill
In prime of morn and May,
Recall ye how McClellan's men
Here stood at bay?
While deep within yon forest dim
Our rigid comrades lay—
Some with the cartridge in their mouth,
Others with fixed arms lifted South—
Invoking so
The Cypress glades? Ah wilds of woe!

The spires of Richmond, late beheld
Through rifts in musket-haze,
Were closed from view in clouds of
    dust
On leaf-walled ways,
Where streamed our wagons in
    caravan;
And the Seven Nights and Days
Of march and fast, retreat and fight,
Pinched our grimed faces to ghastly
    plight—
Does the elm wood
Recall the haggard beards of blood?

The battle-smoked flag, with stars
    eclipsed,
We followed (it never fell!)—
In silence husbanded our strength—
Received their yell:
Till on this slope we patient turned
With cannon ordered well;
Reverse we proved was not defeat;
But ah, the sod what thousands
    meet!—
Does Malvern Wood
Bethink itself, and muse and brood?

We elms of Malvern Hill
Remember everything:
But sap the twig will fill:
Wag the world how it will,
Leaves must be green in Spring.

Virginia—20,614 men—had been lost. There was certainly evidence that Confederate officers led from the front: Lee lost 66 regimental and 10 brigade commanders killed or wounded.

It was not only a bloody victory, but an incomplete one, as Lee noted. "Under ordinary circumstances," his official report read, "the Federal Army should have been destroyed."

Half of D. H. Hill's casualties had been inflicted by artillery, "an unprecedented thing in warfare," he noted. His anger at the slaughter simmered years later. "It was not war," he wrote. "It was murder."

Both armies were exhausted by the Seven Days' battles. With McClellan's troops sprawled across Harrison's Landing, Lee was content to keep an eye on him. Little skirmishing occurred as the armies suffered from the terrible heat and humidity of a southern summer, made worse by the malarial swamps that surrounded the camp.

The results of the recent battles split the North along party lines. Republicans blamed McClellan for the defeats while Democrats suspected that Republicans would conspire to remove their general from command.

The South remained concerned about Richmond. The city was safe, but McClellan remained nearby, being resupplied and reinforced via the James River. The Union campaign could be renewed at any time. Some in the South urged Davis to abandon his reactive defensive policy and take the war to the North. Jackson advocated such and committed the unpar-

Of the five hundred wagons and ambulances lost during the Seven Days, approximately a third occurred during the eight-mile retreat from Malvern Hill to Harrison's Landing. One piece of carefully preserved "equipment" was McClellan's printing press. On July 4 he dispatched an address to the troops lauding their victory over "adversity," not their adversary.

BATTLES AND LEADERS

Two great plantation houses highlighted the Union line established on the James River around Harrison's Landing. Porter made his headquarters at Westover (above left). The Berkeley mansion (above right) was a mile upstream and overlooked the landing wharf. For the remainder of the summer of 1862 it was a safe but miserably hot and humid encampment for the Union army.

donable military sin of taking the proposal to Davis after his superior rebuffed the idea. Lee did hope, "We shall at least change the theater of war from the James to north of the Rappahannock."

Pronouncing Harrison's Landing as impregnable, Lee left cavalry to keep an eye on McClellan and marched to Richmond to rest and equip his army with McClellan's own ample stores, captured during the Seven Days.

To assist Lee in controlling his command, the Army of Northern Virginia was reorganized into two corps. One, under Longstreet, had five divisions belonging to Maj. Gens. Richard B. Anderson and David R. Jones and Brig. Gens. Cadmus M. Wilcox, James L. Kemper, and John Bell Hood. Despite Jackson's tepid performance, he led the second corps, although it was considerably smaller. His two divisions were led by Richard Ewell and Charles S. Winder. Lee retained personal control of A. P. Hill's division. He

"Men could be seen falling in every direction," wrote Georgian Thomas Ware, "the grape & bombs falling & bursting just above our heads, taking off a great many heads & cutting some half into."

George W. White recorded a popular story making the rounds that claimed the Federals had been repulsed because, "First, they had to climb two damned steep *Hills,* then came a *Longstreet,* and next a *Stonewall,* which was impregnable."

McClellan Congratulates the Army for Its Skillful Change of Base

Our achievements of the last ten days have illustrated the valor and endurance of the American soldier. Attacked by vastly superior forces, and without hope of reinforcements, you have succeeded in changing your base of operations by a flank movement, always regarded as the most hazardous of military expedients. You have saved all your material, all your trains, and all your guns, except a few lost in battle [he actually abandoned fifty-two guns], taking in

return guns and colors from the enemy. Upon your march you have been assailed day after day with desperate fury by men of the same race and nation skillfully massed and led; and under every disadvantage of numbers, and necessarily of position also, you have in every conflict beaten back your foes with enormous slaughter.

Your conduct ranks you among the celebrated armies of history. No one will now question that each of

you may always say with pride, "I belonged to the Army of the Potomac."

You have reached this new base complete in organization and unimpaired in spirit. The enemy may at any moment attack you. We are prepared to receive them. I have personally established your lines. Let them come, and we will convert their repulse into a final defeat. Your Government is strengthening you with the resources of a great people.

On this our nation's birthday [the order was issued July 4] we declare to our foes, who are rebels against the best interests of mankind, that this army shall enter the capital of their so-called Confederacy; that our national Constitution shall prevail, and that the Union, which can alone insure internal peace and external security to each state, must and shall be preserved, cost what it may in time, treasure, and blood.

Of George B. McClellan's "change of base," Maj. Gen. Joseph Hooker wrote, "We retreated like a parcel of sheep." One soldier wondered whether it had been "an inglorious skedaddle or a brilliant retreat." Another Federal questioned why the army would "deify a General whose greatest feat has been a *masterly* retreat." For some time to come, in the Confederate army any activity that involved moving was derisively labeled a "change of base."

gave command of his cavalry to Maj. Gen. Jeb Stuart, whose brigades were led by Brig. Gens. Wade Hampton, Fitzhugh Lee, and Beverly H. Robertson.

Having observed his officers in action, Lee rewarded those who had performed well. The others, notably John Magruder, Benjamin Huger, and Theophilus Holmes, were exiled to the West. The generals who remained were trouble enough. Richmond newspapers fueled a dispute between Longstreet and A. P. Hill regarding credit for the success at Glendale. Hill refused to communicate with Longstreet, who had Hill arrested for insubordination. Lee was forced to prevent the two from fighting a duel.

Lincoln and Stanton considered launching an attack against Richmond from the north while McClellan renewed his drive from the south, which

McClellan at Harrison's Landing

Harrison's Landing encompassed two great plantations on the northern bank of the James River: Berkeley and Westover. Berkeley was established in 1619, and the manor house was constructed in 1726. Declaration of Independence signer Benjamin Harrison V and Pres. William H. Harrison were born on the fourteen-hundred-acre estate.

George B. McClellan had chosen Hexall's Landing, adjacent to Malvern Hill, as his choice of refuge, but Como. John Rodgers pointed out that the channel hugged the southern bank, which was under Confederate control.

When the Federals arrived they found Berkeley and Westover planted with ripe wheat and corn, the mansion surrounded by ornamental trees, gardens, and orchards. The house was uninhabited and boarded up, but the soldiers broke in and transformed the great structure into a hospital. Throughout the night of July 1, four thousand wagons and ambulances arrived, followed shortly by artillery and one hundred thousand troops. Over the next several days four hundred supply ships and transports arrived from the Pamunkey River.

The house's exquisite carpets were soon covered with blood and mud, and

a signal station was established on the roof of the three-story structure. Trees were cut down to give signalers a clear view, fences and outbuildings were consumed for firewood, and the iron-fenced family cemetery was used as a corral and slaughter pen for cattle. Every day a reconnaissance balloon rose from the lawn to keep an eye on Confederate threats.

On July 3 Capt. John Pelham of Jeb Stuart's horse artillery scouted the Federal position and found a commanding ridge unoccupied, Evelington Heights. Stuart ordered the Union camp shelled, which caused great consternation in the Federal ranks. Substantial Confederate strength was en route, but James Longstreet took a wrong turn and Stonewall Jackson made poor time in the mud. Union Brig. Gen. Nathan B. Kimball shortly displaced Stuart and the Federals dug in furiously. The right and left flanks were anchored on marshy creeks—Herring to the east and Kimage to the west—and a large mill pond protected a mile of McClellan's four-mile line. Vulnerable areas were soon defended by substantial earthworks with felled timber abatis in front, and gunboats mounting huge cannon kept the Confederates at a distance.

While McClellan pitched his big headquarters tents around Berkeley and his regiments played patriotic airs for the Fourth of July, the Confederates withdrew to rest while Stuart kept a watchful eye on the tent city.

When Lincoln arrived to inspect McClellan's encampment on July 9, some soldiers laughed at the angular president perched on a horse ("a pair of tongs on a chair back," one private thought). The president and the general were nonetheless met with great cheers, although McClellan would claim he "had to order the men to cheer" and they did so "very feebly." Interviews with the general and his five corps commanders revealed a consensus that the army was safe and healthy at Harrison's Landing. The lone dissenter was Erasmus D. Keyes, who thought that in two months "heat and sickness" would destroy the force.

McClellan demanded substantial reinforcements, thirty thousand to one hundred thousand, before he believed he could resume the offensive against Richmond. He also gave Lincoln an insulting letter explaining his interpretation of the proper purpose of the war. It should be fought to reunite the country, he wrote, not the "forcible abolition of slavery."

Six wharfs at Berkeley and Westover could handle one hundred of the six hundred ships that clogged the James River. Hundreds of contrabands unloaded cargo and loaded sick and wounded soldiers for evacuation to Northern hospitals.

The waving fields of grain that covered the plain when the army arrived were soon trampled or cut for forage and beds, replaced within days by a vast muddy field soaked by days of heavy rain. The tents of the Army of the Potomac's camp covered several square miles. The men enjoyed the rest but the heat—over 100 degrees during the day—was normal. Humidity, rain, poor water, and unsanitary conditions brought on considerable illness that killed hundreds. Swarms of stinging flies plagued all, including McClellan, whose inkwell was filled with them. When the general arrived he already had twenty thousand soldiers sick with fever and dysentery, and those were shipped north as soon as possible. Men constructed arbors of pine boughs to shelter the tents from the sun and built bed platforms to escape the mud and heat.

Supply ships brought new issues of uniforms, boots, tents, and blan-

could crush the Confederates between two forces. This plan was obstructed by McClellan's refusal to move without massive reinforcements.

On July 1 McClellan informed Washington that with fifty thousand more men "I will retrieve our fortune," a number he upped just two days later to one hundred thousand. He believed that Lincoln did not truly appreciate "the magnitude of the crisis."

Lincoln did, and patiently attempted to deal with McClellan. "Allow me to reason with you," the president responded. The reinforcements did not exist. Lincoln assured McClellan that he did not blame the general "for not doing more than you can." In turn Lincoln asked that McClellan "not ask impossibilities of me." If McClellan felt he could not capture

Unsanitary conditions bred clouds of flies that plagued everyone. "Here we have flies in regiments," wrote the Reverend A. M. Stewart, "in brigades, in divisions, and in corps, great armies of flies—big flies and little flies, biting flies and sucking flies—wood, field and tent flies—night flies and day flies—rising up or lying down, going out or coming in,—in all places and conditions—*flies.*"

---

kets and the first fresh vegetables and fruits that the soldiers had seen since the campaign had started. Fresh beef was slaughtered daily. Tens of thousands of soldiers bathed in the James River and other streams, ridding themselves of the ubiquitous lice. "The whole Army is lousy," a surgeon informed a brigadier. "You are lousy, I am lousy, McClellan is lousy."

Once the army was rested and nourished, boredom and low morale became the chief enemy. McClellan was forced to admit that 50,000 of his 125,000-man force were either sick or on leave—with or without orders. Many feigned illness or smuggled themselves aboard transport ships. One deserter had the letter D branded into his forehead. Men wrote letters, gambled against orders, picketed the perimeter, and drilled as squads, companies, battalions, brigades, and divisions. All that kept an entire corps from drilling together, one Federal noted, was lack of space. Many of the wounded McClellan had abandoned during the Seven Days were exchanged at City Point.

The Confederates did what they could to annoy the Northerners. On June 6–7 seven guns of the

Washington Artillery fired seventy-two rounds at Federal ships from Weyanoke Point and Willcox Wharf. On the night of July 26 five Confederates rowed across the James to burn a schooner. These harassments forced the navy to assign twenty-three gunboats to patrol the James. They frequently shelled the woods along the shore that might shelter snipers and waited anxiously for the arrival of a new Confederate ironclad reported nearing completion in Richmond.

At Lee's suggestion, on the night of August 1, D. H. Hill, commanding the region south of the James, placed forty-one cannon around Coggin's Point opposite Harrison's Landing and fired a thousand rounds into the camp before the Yankee gunboats and new batteries of 30-pound Parrott guns and Whitworth rifles could respond. Few casualties resulted—twenty-two Federal, six Confederate—but Union soldiers were required to do some fancy dodging. McClellan, who was writing his wife during the bombardment ("Queer times these!" he commented) had every tree on Coggin's Point chopped down the next day and for good measure burned the Maycocks estate.

McClellan refused to advance from Harrison's Landing without

reinforcements, although when he sensed trouble with his superiors he offered to cross the James and march on Petersburg, a move Grant would execute from a nearby position two years later. An order on August 8 directed McClellan to determine if Lee was leaving Richmond to confront John Pope in northern Virginia. In response, McClellan sent two divisions under Hooker to Malvern Hill. Their arrival on August 6 induced Lee to wonder if this was the beginning of a new offensive. He dispatched two divisions to Malvern Hill and a third around the Federal flank, which led Hooker to withdraw without a fight.

McClellan had received orders on August 3 to march to Fort Monroe as soon as possible. On August 9–10 thirty steamships and one hundred sailing vessels removed the sick and supplies. The grand retreat started on August 15. One division was fortunate to travel by ship, but the remainder marched. Heintzelman's corps crossed the Chickahominy River at Forge Bridge and continued to Williamsburg. The wagons, ambulances, and artillery started east to Charles City Court House, followed by the remainder of the Army of the Potomac. They

bridged the Chickahominy near its confluence with the James River and marched through Williamsburg to Fort Monroe. The army used one of Joseph E. Johnston's tricks and left Quaker guns and straw dummies wearing uniforms in their works, then felled trees across the road in their wake.

The Berkeley and Westover plantations were devastated. The owner of Westover estimated his loss at seventy-five thousand dollars; neighboring Buckland suffered sixty thousand dollars in damages. Many farms belonging to whites and free blacks in the area were also destroyed. So many contrabands decamped with the Federals that Charles City County could not feed itself for the remainder of the war.

Two years of relative peace descended on the great James River plantations until June 1864, when the Army of the Potomac returned under Grant. The Federals camped east of Berkeley and Westover and between June 16 and 19 crossed over a pontoon bridge anchored at Weyanoke Point and on transports from James Willcox's wharf, whose Buckland mansion was destroyed.

BATTLES AND LEADERS

BATTLES AND LEADERS

On July 8 Abraham Lincoln visited the Union encampment at Harrison's Landing (above left) to urge McClellan to renew the offensive. The general insisted that he needed at least one hundred thousand additional men to do so. An assault on Petersburg was discussed, but in the end McClellan did nothing. On July 30 orders were issued that the army be withdrawn. The last units withdrew on August 16, leaving behind straw soldiers and Quaker guns (above right). McClellan claimed that he was the last man to leave and that his final act was to stand on the parapet and shake his fist at the enemy.

Summer rains turned the giant Harrison's Landing encampment into a sea of mud. So miserable were the men that when Col. Hiram Berdan's First U.S. Sharpshooters spotted the carcass of a dead horse sticking out of the knee-deep mud, they crowded on top of it despite a horrendous smell. One man was so inspired by the sight that he penned a little ditty:

Old Horse! Old Horse! We find you
    here,
That plunged in battle fully a year,
You neighed for glory, you reared in
    fame,
To die in the mud on this vast plain.

Richmond, "I do not ask you to try just now," he said. Conserve the army and equipment, "and I will strengthen it for the offensive as fast as I can."

After relieving McClellan of the duties of general in chief of all armies, Lincoln and Stanton had assumed the job, albeit ineffectually. Now the president appointed a successor, Maj. Gen. Henry W. Halleck, who had previously commanded all Union forces in the West.

The day before Lee left for Richmond, Lincoln arrived to visit McClellan at Harrison's Landing. He reviewed the troops and conferred with McClellan's corps commanders. Erasmus Keyes advised withdrawal, but the others—Porter, Heintzelman, and Sumner—urged an advance against Richmond. McClellan claimed to side with the latter, but he lacked a plan of operations and continued to demand large numbers of reinforcements.

After Halleck arrived from the West two weeks later, Lincoln sent him to Harrison's Landing to issue an ultimatum. The administration had exhausted its patience. McClellan would receive twenty thousand reinforcements, and he would move against Richmond. If the general would not accept these conditions, his army would be ordered to join a force assembling north of the Rappahannock.

McClellan immediately started negotiating the order, then accepted it when he realized his precarious position, but the general had pushed his luck too far. On August 3 he was directed to withdraw his army. McClellan complied but wired Washington: "The order will prove disastrous to our cause. Here, directly in front of this army is the heart of the rebellion. Here is the true defense of Washington; it is here on the banks of the James."

A Tour of the Seven Days' Battles

RICHMOND WAS besieged many times during the Civil War, but the spring of 1862 was the first, the closest, and the most frightening for the people of the city and for the Confederacy. With very little opposition, George B. McClellan's 120,000 man force was able to approach within sight of the city's church spires. They had been stopped temporarily at Fair Oaks, but the South had been rattled by the loss of Joseph E. Johnston, and there were serious reservations concerning the competence of Robert E. Lee. The Confederates seemingly did nothing for a month as the Federal army remained at Richmond's door. The onslaught Lee unleashed, however, stunned McClellan, silenced the critics, and served notice that the war had entered a savagely aggressive phase that would end only when one opponent was destroyed.

If ever a Civil War campaign was made for an auto tour, the Seven Days' battles is it. Most of the Army of Northern Virginia left their trenches facing Seven Pines and marched north on the Mechanicsville turnpike to fight at Beaver Dam Creek, then turned southeast to pursue and fight McClellan at Gaines's Mill, Savage Station, White Oak Swamp, Glendale, and Malvern Hill, which ended the titanic campaign on the banks of the James River sixty miles from its starting point. For convenience, this tour starts at the Chimborazo visitors center of the Richmond National Battlefield Park. (A series of exhibits at the visitors center at Tredegar illustrate the history of the Seven Days' battles.)

Before heading north, you might want to drive out Nine Mile Road–Route 33 to visit the East Henrico Government Complex, one mile east of Interstate 64 and four miles west of Fair Oaks. The central part of this structure was the High Mead-

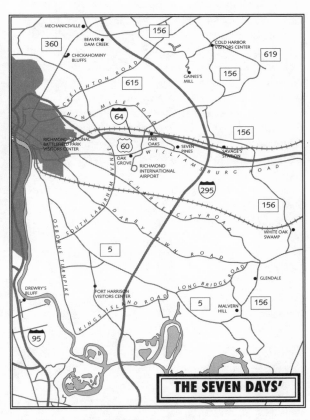

ows farmhouse (1840s), owned by widow Mary C. Dabbs. This was Lee's first headquarters as commander of the Army of Northern Virginia. On June 23 he met with James Longstreet, Stonewall Jackson, A. P. Hill, and D. H. Hill to plan what became the Seven Days' battles. Jeb Stuart received his instructions to scout McClellan's flank here, which turned into his ride around the Army of the Potomac. Lee returned here after the Seven Days and organized the Second Manassas campaign. On June 29 Longstreet and A. P. Hill marched toward Glendale on the Nine Mile Road to Old Tavern (modern Highland Springs).

Although portions of the major battlefields of the Seven Days have been preserved in a string of parks, which are part of the Richmond National Battlefield, they are small parcels. Additional properties are currently being added, but Richmond's suburban growth is inexorable. Still, this tour is worthwhile to facilitate an understanding of the Seven Days. Pick up a map brochure and purchase an audiotape at the visitors center and set out on the eighty-mile route. When the NPS tour stops at Malvern Hill, ours continues to Berkeley Plantation at Harrison's Landing and explores several of the other great James River plantations that have Civil War significance. Finally, we cross the James on a long sweep that takes us back toward Richmond to stop at Drewry's Bluff, where intrepid Confederate artillery crews drove off the *Monitor* and other Union gunboats to save Richmond from attack via this vital water route, a site that became important again in 1864.

From the exit of the Richmond National Battlefield Visitors Center, turn left onto U.S. 60–East Broad Street. Turn right onto North Twenty-fifth, and turn left onto Fairmont–Route 33 West. Turn right onto Mosby, which becomes Mechanicsville Turnpike–U.S. 360 East. Turn right into Chickahominy Bluff.

The Dabbs House was Robert E. Lee's headquarters prior to the Seven Days' battles. Here he met with his generals and planned the campaign.

At Chickahominy Bluffs, Lee anxiously but futilely waited for Stonewall Jackson's attack to begin at Mechanicsburg.

In the early hours of June 26, A. P. Hill marched out on the Meadow Bridge road to cross the Chickahominy River at Meadow Bridge, a mile and a half upstream. At this point Longstreet and D. H. Hill, with Lee in attendance, waited for A. P. Hill to cross the river and clear the Federals out of Mechanicsville, across the Chickahominy, which would allow them to cross unopposed on the Mechanicsville Bridge. A. P. Hill would advance when Stonewall Jackson, marching east from the Shenandoah Valley, hit Federal Gen. Fitz John Porter's right flank and rear. The three-pronged offensive, utilizing four divisions, was planned to drive Porter down the Chickahominy, perhaps trapping and destroying the Union Fifth Corps and cutting McClellan off from his supply base at White House Landing on the Pamunkey River. Lee could then turn on McClellan's forces south of the Chickahominy.

Stuart's famed raid around McClellan revealed that Porter was strongly entrenched on his left, which lay on the Chickahominy, but his right was vulnerable to attack.

The Seven Days had begun the previous day when McClellan assaulted down the Williamsburg road to Oak Grove, from where he intended to besiege Richmond. He bogged down after encountering fierce resistance from Benjamin Huger and John Magruder, who, with one-third of Lee's forces, were tasked with preventing the Federals from capturing Richmond before Lee was in position. If McClellan withdrew, Magruder and Huger were to attack his rear.

Lee's initial and subsequent plans failed to gel. Jackson and his men were exhausted from the march from the Shenandoah and failed to attack at all on June 26. McClellan had also learned of Jackson's approach, and Porter's men slowed him by skirmishing, destroying bridges, and felling trees across the road.

The attack at Mechanicsville was scheduled for 9 A.M. As the day continued, A. P. Hill became anxious. Expecting Jackson to immediately join the attack, Hill crossed the Meadow Bridge and cleared Mechanicsville, but the bridge there was destroyed. After rebuilding the span, Longstreet and D. H. Hill pitched in. Lee, Longstreet, and the Hills were not aware that Jackson had bivouacked early and intended to do nothing that day.

Walk to the interpretive shelter and climb the overlook platform at the earthworks. This was the outer line of Richmond's defenses, a substantial defensive belt consisting of artillery forts, connecting trenches, and rifle pits started when McClellan threatened the city in 1862. The line ultimately began at the James River to the north and ended at the James River to the south. Designed to hold heavy artillery and portable field guns, the works were considerably enlarged during the war. The fortifications were reinforced with timbers, surrounded by deep ditches, and protected in front by felled trees arranged to form abatis.

Lee's headquarters on June 26 was in a house across the road. He, his generals, and tens of thousands of infantry waited impatiently for the attack to begin. When the fighting began, Lee watched the opening of the battle from this area. Later that day Davis, some cabinet members, and assorted politicians reached the battlefield via the Mechanicsville Turnpike, and Lee strongly suggested that they leave.

Return to the entrance of the park and turn right. The village of Mechanicsville consisted of twelve buildings in 1862. Today a small earthwork guards an office building. Turn right onto Route 156 West (the old Mechanicsville road). At the stop sign turn right onto Route 156 South. Turn right at the sign for Beaver Dam Park, and at the end of the road is a parking lot.

When his pickets were driven out of Mechanicsville, Union Gen. George McCall's division settled into a two-mile-long line of works established on a ridge beyond swampy Beaver Dam Creek. The Federals were securely dug in on a brush-obstructed slope with artillery commanding every approach. This line extended from the Chickahominy River across to the Old Church road (U.S. 360) to the north. The dam at Ellerson's Mill backed up the stream, creating an open, swampy area covered with felled trees. John Reynolds's brigade held the right, where Jackson was to attack; Truman Seymour the left; with George Gordon Meade in reserve.

The overlook of swampy Beaver Dam Creek (with interpretive markers) faces the Union line east of the creek. Ellerson's Mill was one hundred feet in front.

The Confederates marched to Beaver Dam Creek on the Cold Harbor road (Route 156) and the Old Church road. A half mile to the left A. P. Hill attacked with three brigades and two batteries across open fields to the creek. The Confederate guns were driven off and Federal artillery decimated the infantry. A single regiment crossed the creek but was repulsed by Federal musket and canister fire. Hill next dispatched a brigade to attack here, from the ridge behind you, at a point near the mouth of the creek. Fierce cannon fire diverted one regiment to the left and another to the right, leaving a sole Confederate regiment that broke only one hundred yards from the Union line.

The National Park Service preserves a portion of the Beaver Dam battlefield where Confederates launched fruitless assaults against a strong Federal line.

When he arrived on the scene, Lee directed one of D. H. Hill's brigades to attack farther to the right, but it emerged at this same spot and suffered severe casualties before darkness closed the battle, the first major fight of the Seven Days. Lee lost fifteen hundred men; the Federals four hundred.

In 1993 fourteen acres, across the marsh on the Federal ridge where artillery and infantry were emplaced, were added to the twelve acres the National Park Service holds here. A pedestrian bridge takes visitors across the creek, where the landscape has been restored to its 1862 appearance and four interpretive wayside stations have been established. For the first time, visitors can envision the situation the Confederates faced as they attacked.

Threatened by the tardy arrival of Jackson, Porter withdrew four miles during the night to an equally impregnable position behind Boatswain's Creek near Gaines's Mill. The Confederates crossed Beaver Dam Creek at Ellerson's Mill here and pursued on the Cold Harbor road (Route 156).

Most of Lee's army was now isolated on the north side of the Chickahominy, and the battle had alerted McClellan to his intentions. Because McClellan could easily have captured Richmond before Lee arrived to defend it, Lee intended to seize the New Bridge, four miles downstream of Mechanicsville, so he could aid Magruder and Huger if necessary. Fortunately, McClellan thought he faced twice the number of troops Lee could actually muster, and believing that his supply base was threatened, he started to shift it across the peninsula from White House on the Pamunkey River to Harrison's Landing on the James River. McClellan ordered Porter to hold his "position at any cost until night."

Several miles north, at Rural Point, where Route 651 meets Rural Point Road, is the Dr. Edwin Shelton home where Lee and Jackson planned the Seven Days' campaign.

Return to Route 156 and turn right. Note Walnut Grove Baptist Church (1846), where Lee and Jackson met on June 27. Turn right onto the Cold Harbor road (Route 156 South). A small tablet marks the site of Gaines's Mill on Powhite Creek, and Boatswain's Creek will soon be crossed. Drive straight to the Gaines's Mill Park down the old farm road to the parking lot at the Watt house.

Gaines's Mill, where A. P. Hill drove off the Federal rear guard on June 27, 1862, was a five-story structure considered one of the finest in Virginia. It survived the battle named for it but was destroyed, along with the Gaines house, by Philip H. Sheridan in May 1864. This is the preserved 1830s home of Sarah Watt, a seventy-eight-year-old invalid whose grandson fought on the southern bank of the Chickahominy. Just before the battle her bed was loaded onto a wagon, and she was taken to her daughter's house nearby. Mrs. Watt died several months later, never returning home. While it was being used as Porter's headquarters, an artillery shell knocked down the chimney. The house was later utilized as a Confederate hospital. Porter positioned his reserve artillery near the house. When the Confederates broke through, Philip St. George Cooke led his cavalry brigade in a futile attempt to save the guns. Confident Rebel infantry broke the charge and captured fourteen guns.

Confederate Maj. Edward Porter Alexander watched the battle of Gaines's Mill from the gondola of an observation balloon made of silk dresses, the first combat use of such a device. From a height of five hundred feet he saw Porter being reinforced.

Examine the exterior of the house, the cannon, and the interpretive markers, then walk the Breakthrough Trail, a loop that follows the Union battle line to the point where John Bell Hood's brigade broke through. Shallow rifle pits, a painting of the breakthrough, and a plaque mounted on a concrete base mark the site. The trail has been expanded a mile so that the left of the Federal line, scene of heavy fighting, can be seen. Ten new interpretive stations and a monument to Cadmus Wilcox's Alabama brigade, which lost 1,050 of 1,800 men, mark the route. The five-foot-high granite stone has a bas-relief of Wilcox. The Chickahominy River can be seen from an overlook, where a map indicates Civil War bridge sites. On summer weekends rangers conduct guided tours of the trail. This is usually one of the quietest battlefields of the Civil War, evoking eerie feelings as one contemplates the savage fighting that occurred here.

Porter's line formed a semicircle on the ridge behind Boatswain's Creek, both flanks resting on the Chickahominy. His men dug rifle pits and piled up earth and felled trees to strengthen the natural defenses of the slope and deployed in three lines. Attackers would be forced to advance across open fields, descend into a gully to cross the creek, and climb uphill before reaching their opponents. George Morell's division held the left, George Sykes the right, with McCall in reserve, and Philip St. George Cooke's cavalry in the lowlands near the Chickahominy. When Howard Slocum's division joined the battle, Porter had thirty-five thousand men to face Lee's sixty thousand.

Longstreet was on the Confederate right, A. P. Hill in the center, and Jackson and D. H. Hill the left. Lee expected McClellan to defend White House Landing and ordered Longstreet to feint while A. P. Hill attacked. When Jackson and D. H. Hill attacked, Lee anticipated that Porter would shift troops from left to right to protect White House Landing, at which point Longstreet would strike.

A. P. Hill's men again did most of the fighting, starting at 2:30 P.M. At 5:30 Longstreet attacked the Federal left as D. H. Hill attacked the Federal right and A. P. Hill made another attempt on the center. For the second time Jackson was hours late. As night fell four hours after the battle started, Hood advanced across the open plains to the creek bottom, which was littered with Confederate casualties. Holding their fire as they advanced through the blinding gun smoke, Hood found a gap in the Union position and took two regiments of Georgians and Texans in a bayonet charge that broke through the Federal line. After five hours of brave resistance, the Northern units fled the field, searching desperately for ways across the swampy Chickahominy as the breach rapidly widened. Porter lost sixty-eight hundred men; Lee's losses in this bloodiest of the Seven Days' battles were eighty-eight hundred. Although McClellan had gained a day to shift his base to the James River, Lee had cleared the Federals from the north bank of the Chickahominy.

McClellan's plans after Gaines's Mill baffled Lee for another day. Rather than retreat to White House Landing, which Stuart found abandoned and ablaze, the Federals had destroyed their bridges across the Chickahominy, leading Lee to think McClellan was withdrawing down the peninsula, but he could not pursue because the river crossings were controlled by the Federals.

McClellan summoned his generals after the disaster at Gaines's Mill and announced the "change of base." Erasmus Keyes's Fourth Corps would escort the five thousand wagons, loaded with ammunition and supplies, and twenty-five hundred head of beef to Harrison's Landing. Porter's savaged Fifth Corps would protect a vital crossroads at Glendale and the Federal flank, and McCall's division guarded the reserve artillery. The remainder of the Army of the Potomac—First, Second, and Sixth Corps—would withdraw a mile and defend Savage's Station, where

When darkness ended the battle of Savage's Station, both sides held approximately the same ground as when the fighting began. Union casualties were significantly higher than Confederate losses.

LESLIE'S

supplies from the Richmond and York River Railroad were being shifted to wagons. After dark on June 29 they would destroy any remaining stores and withdraw.

While the Federals prepared to abandon their positions on June 28, Lee gathered information and determined McClellan's move. He set the entire Army of Northern Virginia in pursuit with hopes of catching and destroying McClellan as he emerged from White Oak Swamp near the crossroads at Glendale.

Jackson and D. H. Hill would rebuild Grapevine Bridge, destroyed by the retreating Federals, and attack the rear of the Federal column. Magruder and Huger were already on the southern bank of the river. Magruder, north of White Oak Swamp, would advance on the Williamsburg road and, with Jackson and D. H. Hill, attack the Federals crossing White Oak Swamp. Huger, south of the swamp, would pursue on the Charles City road and assault McClellan as he emerged from the swamp. Longstreet and A. P. Hill would cross the Chickahominy at New Bridge, captured during the fighting at Gaines's Mill, and march on the Darbytown road to the Long Bridge road, which met the Charles City road at Glendale, south of White Oak Swamp. If all went well the Confederates would split McClellan into two parts there. While Jackson, D. H. Hill, and Magruder chewed up the Union rear, Longstreet, A. P. Hill, and Huger would attack the head.

Return to Route 156 and turn right. Exercise a little self-discipline and resist the temptation to visit the Cold Harbor battlefield, national cemetery, and the Gathright house. These will be examined in the third book of this series, The Killing Time. *Turn right to follow 156 South, immediately crossing the Chickahominy River on Grapevine Road.*

This was one of a number of bridges McClellan's engineers constructed in May 1862 to enable his army to support units on either side of the swampy river. On May 31 Sumner heroically crossed the swamped bridge to stop the Confederate advance at Seven Pines. On the night of June 27–28 Porter's beaten corps crossed in confusion after the battle at Gaines's Mill, burning the span in their wake. Jackson stalled here a day, June 29, while rebuilding the bridge. He did not cross until early on June 30, which

probably cost the Confederates victories at Savage's Station, White Oak Swamp, and Glendale and might have prevented the slaughter at Malvern Hill. Jackson and D. H. Hill took this route as they leisurely pursued McClellan. The Trent house, one and a half miles southeast of the bridge, was McClellan's headquarters in May and June 1862.

Almost immediately after crossing Grapevine Bridge turn left onto Grapevine Road. After a left turn onto Meadow Road, pull over and park near the three historical markers describing the battle of Savage's Station.

The Confederate army was in motion at daybreak of June 29. Magruder reached the area of Seven Pines around noon and paused, correctly convinced that large Federal forces remained to his front. His request for reinforcements brought two of Huger's divisions, but still Magruder waited for Jackson to appear in the Federal rear. Unfortunately, Jackson required thirty-six hours to construct a bridge that should not have taken more than twelve hours. At Lee's insistence, Magruder attacked at Savage's Station, seven miles east of Richmond, with two and a half of the six brigades he had on hand. The 5 P.M. assault was half-hearted and uncoordinated, although one brigade reached the Union line and engaged in hand-to-hand combat. Unsupported, they were repulsed. During the night the Federals withdrew across White Oak Swamp, leaving tons of supplies on fire and abandoning twenty-five hundred severely wounded soldiers.

Jackson finally started across the Chickahominy at 3 A.M. on June 30, a move completed by dawn. He was now ordered to vigorously pursue the Union rear guard as Longstreet and A. P. Hill continued toward Glendale.

The battle of Savage's Station, the fourth of the Seven Days' battles, occurred beyond the historical markers and railroad, a half mile south of the Williamsburg road. The Federals were on the left, facing west in a line one and a half miles long that stretched from the Williamsburg road (U.S. 60) to this point. Because McClellan had left no orders for the three Federal corps, Heintzelman took it upon himself to withdraw across the swamp, leaving Sumner's Second Corps and Franklin's Sixth Corps deployed here. The Federal field hospital was pitched along the railroad. Down the tracks toward Richmond was the

Shortly after the battle of Fair Oaks (Seven Pines), McClellan crossed the Chickahominy and made his headquarters at the Trent house (above left). He directed the army from there until shortly before the battle of Gaines's Mill. The house was on the Grapevine Bridge road, and the general made sure that the bridge was repaired (above right) quickly after Sumner's men had been rushed over its submerged span to reinforce the line at Fair Oaks. He also ordered eight more bridges built to facilitate faster dispersal.

big Confederate gun mounted on an armored railroad car, which threw shells along the road in the Federal rear, causing additional confusion to the retreat.

Earlier on the morning of June 29, Magruder's men were distracted from chasing Sumner to Savage's Station and fought a skirmish at Allen's farm, also called the Peach Orchard, on Route 156 a half mile north of Seven Pines. The farmhouse, which still stands, has blood-stained floors and the names of Federal soldiers penciled and carved into the walls. Sumner withdrew to Savage's Station, four miles east of Seven Pines.

Another small battle had been fought just south of these historical markers, at Goulding's farm on June 27. Darkness ended the inconclusive battle.

Continue straight on Meadow Road to cross White Oak Swamp.

McClellan's entire army, with all its wagons and artillery, was forced to cross through White Oak Swamp over this one causeway, a situation that created a nightmare bottleneck, which Lee repeatedly attempted to exploit. Unfortunately, Jackson failed Lee twice during McClellan's retreat. When he tardily repaired the Grapevine bridge and crossed the Chickahominy, he reached the northern bank of White Oak Swamp here to find this bridge also destroyed and Franklin's artillery poised on a hill opposite the stream.

Jackson brought up his artillery and a spirited exchange developed, then Jackson went to sleep again. Scouts reported several usable crossing sites upstream and downstream, but Jackson ignored them. His inaction allowed McClellan's rear guard to hurry toward safety while Longstreet and A. P. Hill attacked Glendale four miles to the southwest. Had Jackson crossed in a timely manner and struck the flank and rear of the Federals at Glendale, a decisive victory might have resulted and the losses at Malvern Hill might have been prevented. Jackson finally crossed on July 1.

Continue on Meadow Road to the stop sign at U.S. 60–Williamsburg Road, which Longstreet and A. P. Hill had followed to attack McClellan at Seven Pines. Drive straight and the route becomes Elko Road and is once again Route 156. Turn left to follow 156–Willis Church Road. At the turn was Riddle's Shop, a blacksmith shop near the center of the battle of Glendale. The Glendale National Cemetery appears on the left, and Willis Church is farther down the road to the right.

This cemetery, established on July 14, 1866, contains the remains of 1,200 Federals—234 known, 920 unidentified—who died at Glendale, Malvern Hill, and other battles in the area. It was closed to burials on January 19, 1970. A cast-iron plaque, placed October 15, 1942, contains the Gettysburg Address. Although the National Park Service owns only three acres here, 208 acres have been purchased at Glendale (or Frayser's farm or Riddell's shop) by the Association for the Preservation of Civil War sites and donated to the Richmond National Battlefield. A peculiar feature of the legislation creating the park was a prohibition against using federal funds to purchase additional property. Land could be accepted as donations, however. The APCWS had added 705 acres (purchased for $2.2 million) to the park's original 765 acres. At certain times during the summer, exhibits interpreting Glendale and Malvern Hill can be seen in a small visitors center established in the caretaker's lodge. Featured are a five-minute fiber-optic map that makes the battles here at the end of the Seven Days more comprehensible, and ranger-led tours (call ahead for hours, 804-226-1981).

Willis Methodist Church is largely a reproduction of the 1803 building, rebuilt following a severe fire on December 31, 1946. Lee and A. P. Hill conferred here while the building served as a Confederate hospital. The parsonage, two miles to the south, was also a Confederate hospital after the fighting at Glendale.

Willis Church, near the battlefields of Glendale and Malvern Hill, was a Confederate hospital.

By June 30 McClellan's army was strung out for five miles, from Harrison's Landing to near White Oak Bridge, with wagons, ambulances, and walking wounded in the fore and infantry bringing up the rear. Longstreet and A. P. Hill were nearing Glendale on the Darbytown road. Huger was approaching on the Charles City road, Magruder was supposed to be following Longstreet and Hill, and a division of troops crossed from Drewry's Bluff, under Theophilus Holmes, and was marching on the New Market road (Route 5) to get between McClellan and the James River. Holmes was intercepted by Sykes's Fifth Corps and quickly halted by heavy Union land and naval artillery. Jackson did little in the swamp; Magruder was confused by road names and failed to show; and most ludicrous, Huger engaged in an infamous "battle of axes" (see page 253), which he lost.

Late in the day Longstreet and Hill attacked four Federal divisions near Glendale. The fierce attack broke the Union line but massive Federal reinforcements closed the gap. By the time darkness closed the battle, the combat had become a bloody hand-to-hand struggle.

The intersection at Glendale was the point where the Federals from White Oak Swamp on the Charles City road should have met Huger coming from the opposite direction. Today the Darbytown road intercepts the Charles City road at Glendale. In 1862 Longstreet and A. P. Hill left the Darbytown road a short distance to the west for the Long Bridge road, on which they approached Glendale. From Glendale Jackson was stymied two miles to the northeast.

Although there is little to be seen at Glendale, the battlefield is two hundred yards to the west of Willis Church and can be better appreciated a short distance to the west along Carters Mill Road. In the area where Long Bridge Road today intersects Carters Mill Road, the Confederates deployed to attack. The Federal line extended for a half mile north and south of Willis Church between Willis Church Road and Carters Mill Road. In the dark McClellan escaped to Malvern Hill, his army barely saved from being cut in two and destroyed in detail.

Continue straight (west) from the national cemetery and Willis Church on Route 156–Willis Church

The cannon at the National Park Service exhibit shelter at Malvern Hill represent the concentration of Union guns here that devastated heroic but foolish Confederate attacks that ended the Seven Days' battles.

Road. To the right, at the intersection with Carters Mill Road, is the spot where the most Confederate casualties were inflicted at Malvern Hill, where a Federal observing the wounded thought the land had "a singular crawling effect." Two ineffective artillery positions were placed on elevations left and right of the intersection. Continue west on Route 156. Turn right to the Malvern Hill display shelter.

The National Park Service interpretive kiosk at the top of Malvern Hill faces north, the direction from which the Confederates advanced. The Union line spread across this slight elevation, a mile-wide, one-hundred-foot-high plateau, which seems to barely deserve the term "hill." It was a good position, however, commanding open fields. Across from the NPS site is the West house, headquarters of Federal Brig. Gen. Darius N. Couch during the battle. Several hundred yards to the south, on the west side of the road, is the Crew house, where the Confederate brigades of William Mahone and Ambrose R. Wright concentrated. They were unsuccessful in rooting out Federal sharpshooters who hid in wheat shocks in fields west of the house. During the Revolutionary War, Lafayette camped here in the late summer of 1781.

To allow time for his wagons to reach the safety of the Union gunboats at Harrison's Landing, McClellan selected this site for a stand. The artillery here represent the hundreds of Federal cannon placed nearly hub to hub facing north. Seven full divisions of infantry supported the guns between Turkey Run on the left and Western Run to the right. Steep bluffs carved by the streams allowed only a northern approach, up gently sloping wheat fields. The reserve artillery was placed on bluffs a half mile to the rear, facing the New Market road. The road to Harrison's Landing passed directly across Malvern Hill, through these strong defenses. Infantry occupied the lower slopes, artillery the summit, and substantial reserves waited to the south.

Lee and his generals appreciated the strength of McClellan's position, but they thought that a massed crossfire of artillery would suppress the Union cannon and allow a successful assault. Only D. H. Hill demurred. The least decimated Confederate units, those of Jackson, Magruder, and Huger, were detailed to make the advance. Brig. Gen. Lewis Armistead, who had the best view, would launch the attack when he believed the Union batteries were silenced, and the others would follow. Few Confederate guns ever got into position, and those were quickly silenced by Union Parrott rifles, which far outranged those of the Rebels, and by fourteen siege guns positioned at the Malvern house, a mile to the rear.

Jackson was on the Confederate left, D. H. Hill in the center, with Huger and Magruder on the right. The Federal line had Porter on the left, with Keys and Heintzelman extended to the right. The attack started at 5 P.M. on the right with Huger when Armistead's charge to clear pesky Federal sharpshooters was mistaken as the signal to advance. Magruder sent his division in support, then D. H. Hill joined the attack, with Jackson late and last. The Confederates charged south toward the NPS shelter on Malvern Hill in a long arc with Willis Church Road in the center. No Confederate came closer than two hundred yards of the cannon on the hill.

The Seven Days' battles were over. It had cost 20,600 Confederate casualties to a Union loss of 15,850.

Until recently it was impossible to appreciate fully the battlefield at Malvern Hill. Open country in 1862, it had been heavily forested since the 1920s. More than 100 acres of the APCWS and NPS land

(APCWS added 540 acres to the park's 130 acres at Malvern Hill) have been cleared. For the first time, visitors can see a mile to the ruins of the Willis Church parsonage, a landmark where Confederate troops assembled for the assault against Malvern Hill. The parsonage burned several years ago and was part of the APCWS purchase. Preserved and interpreted, it has been added to the driving tour. An UDC monument marks the site. The clearing of the new property allows the Confederate line, marked by four cannon, to be seen clearly, as well as the two knolls where Southern artillery was positioned and folds in the terrain that protected the attacking Confederates from the awesome artillery fire. A new two-and-a-half-mile loop trail between the parsonage and the shelter features seven new interpretive signs and allows visitors to follow the route of the Southerners' advance. Landscape plans—showing wood lots, fields, pastures, fences, and orchards—have been prepared to restore Malvern Hill and Gaines's Mill to their 1862 appearance.

Return to Route 156 and turn right. Turn left onto 156 South–Route 5 East. At Route 608 you may turn right to Shirley Plantation at Harrison Point.

Shirley Plantation, one of the oldest in America, was established in 1613, just six years after Jamestown was settled. The present house dates to 1730. During the American Revolution, Shirley twice found itself between the lines, with the British across the James River at Hopewell (City Point) and Lafayette at Malvern Hill. Each side maintained pickets at Shirley. Anne Hill Carter, Robert E. Lee's mother, was born here and married Richard Henry "Lighthorse Harry" Lee in 1793 in the formal living room. Young Lee spent several years here, receiving his early education at a plantation school, today a converted laundry room. Known for its hospitality, Shirley hosted George Washington, Thomas Jefferson, John Tyler, Theodore Roosevelt, John D. Rockefeller, and many other notables.

By late June 1862 thousands of wounded Federal soldiers filled the mansion and lawn as the plantation was transformed into a large field hospital. Hill Carter, a cousin of Robert E. Lee, and his family fed soup and water to the soldiers, bandaged their wounds, and cared for them as best they could until Union ships

arrived to evacuate them to hospitals at Hampton Roads. The dead were buried on the plantation. McClellan personally thanked the Carters for the care they gave his soldiers and issued them a safe conduct pass. According to legend, during this period several Confederates were hidden in the pigeon house.

On July 7, 1862, Col. T. R. R. Cobb assured Lee that with additional troops he could cut off the retreat of McClellan's wagon train in this area. Lee dispatched the troops, but Cobb could not fulfill his boast. That night Lee sent out soldiers to recover the weapons abandoned by the Federals.

Shirley Plantation suffered some damage in 1862 and again in 1864 when Grant passed through to cross the James River and attack Richmond from the rear, through the vital rail center of Petersburg. This region had been famous for its enormous plantations and fine mansions since colonial times, but many residents twice fled the path of war or simply decamped for the duration, returning to find their lands devastated and their homes burned-out shells.

Shirley's eight hundred acres is a working farm still operated by the original family. The National Historic Landmark mansion and its outbuildings, only eighteen miles from Richmond, are open to the public.

From Shirley Plantation return to Route 156 South–Route 5 East and turn right. When Route 156 turns right continue straight on Route 5 East. Turn right onto 633 at the sign for Berkeley Plantation. Bear right, toward Berkeley, at several junctions on Harrison Landing Road. Turn right at the sign and the parking lot is to the left.

Contrary to popular conception, Harrison's Landing included not one but two of the great James River plantations: Berkeley at Harrison's Landing proper and Westover, downriver where the primary wharfs were located. Historic Westover Church was also within the Union lines, and Evelynton Plantation was nearby.

Berkeley Plantation is the site of the first thanksgiving celebration in America, held when thirty-nine people landed on December 4, 1619, and gave thanks for their safe voyage. The three-story brick Georgian mansion, constructed in 1726, was home to Declaration of Independence signer Benjamin Harrison, his son Pres. William Henry Harrison, and his grandson

Pres. Benjamin Harrison (a Union officer). After only a month in office William Henry Harrison died of pneumonia, making John Tyler, a neighbor from Sherwood Forest Plantation, the first vice president to succeed to the presidency. After Benedict Arnold defected to the British during the American Revolution, he led a force of redcoats that plundered Berkeley in 1781.

The advance element of the Army of the Potomac reached Harrison's Landing on June 30 with the supply wagons, ambulances, and beef herd following. After the battle of Malvern Hill, nine miles away on July 1, the main body of troops arrived on July 2 to start a forty-five-day, seven-week stay. Although McClellan was ordered to withdraw on August 4, he deliberately delayed his final departure until August 16, burning the docks behind him.

Confederate Capt. John Pelham, an enterprising artillery commander under Jeb Stuart, soon discovered that Evelynton Heights, which commanded all of Harrison's Landing, was unoccupied. Stuart inspected the location and prematurely ordered a bombardment of the host below. Alerted to the danger, Union Gen. William F. "Baldy" Smith ordered Gen. Nathan B. Kimball's division to dislodge the Confederate horse artillery, which was easily accomplished. The campaign might have ended differently had Stuart waited for infantry reinforcements, but Jackson was continuing the plodding pace he used throughout the Seven Days and Longstreet's corps had taken a wrong turn. The Federals soon threw up a four-mile-long, horseshoe-shaped line of earthworks that stretched from the James River at Herring Creek on the right to Kimages Creek on the James to the left, the perimeter defended by the Third and Sixth Corps. Two to three miles of the works survive in pristine shape in the woods around Harrison's Landing.

Military activity closed until the night of August 1, when Confederate batteries massed on the south bank and unleashed a heavy bombardment before scurrying away to escape the Union gunboats. McClellan was chagrined but hardly hurt.

The fields of the plantation, planted in wheat, were quickly reduced to mud as more than one hundred thousand men, thousands of animals, and thousands of wagons and artillery pieces occupied the two-square-mile area. Heavy rains rendered the broad riverbank into a vast swamp as hordes of biting flies, lice, and mosquitoes made soldiers and officers miserable. Virtually every tree was felled for firewood, docks, fortifications, cook houses, blacksmith shops, and latrines.

A forest of masts obscured the riverfront when a fleet of more than six hundred gunboats, transports, and supply ships arrived from Newport News in Hampton Roads and crowded six makeshift wharfs. The *Monitor* and other warships prowled constantly to protect the encampment from Confederate attack.

For a month and a half McClellan camped on this unsanitary flood plain, two square miles filled with tens of thousands of tents. His men drilled, amused themselves as best they could, and many succumbed to sickness and disease in the extreme heat and humidity of the Virginia summer.

The great mansion at Berkeley Plantation had been abandoned for some years when McClellan arrived. Soldiers broke through boarded doors and windows and lit roaring fires to dry the interior. Blood soaked once fine carpets while eighteen hundred wounded soldiers received treatment here and in tent complexes nearby. Gardens were destroyed and mahogany furniture broken up for firewood. McClellan's headquarters tents were set up around the mansion, and an observation balloon based on the grounds rose daily to keep an eye on Confederate activity. From July 2 until August 16, this was the headquarters of the Army of the Potomac.

Lincoln traveled to Harrison's Landing to confer with McClellan and reviewed the army on July 8. McClellan was his usual difficult self and issued the president an insulting diatribe that attempted to intrude into civil affairs.

During July, Union Gen. Daniel Butterfield composed a new bugle signal to mark the end of day and taught it to bugler Oliver W. Norton. For the first time the haunting notes of "Taps" was heard. It quickly became an official army bugle call and is recognized around the world.

By 1907 the mansion was a wreck and the land unproductive when John Jamieson purchased the property for twenty-eight thousand dollars. Ironically Jamieson, a Union drummer boy, had been here in 1862, summoned by his older brother Walter

Jamieson, who would win the Medal of Honor at Petersburg. The son and grandson of drummer boy Jamieson restored the mansion to its eighteenth-century appearance and developed the fourteen-hundred-acre plantation into a fertile working farm. Berkeley was opened to the public in 1935, and the mansion, grounds, and restored gardens can be toured daily.

A museum in the cellar displays artifacts found on the grounds, including lead bullets with teeth marks in them, suggesting surgery without anesthetics, and a cannon that apparently burst when fired. A tavern offers lunch and dinner. The campgrounds of different units are being plotted as researchers locate buttons, belt buckles, and other artifacts bearing unit insignia. They have already determined that Butterfield's camp was near the river, and a pavilion and memorial to the composition of "Taps" has been erected. The enclosed family cemetery, used as a Federal slaughter pen, survives, with the addition of a stone for Walter Jamieson, who is buried elsewhere. One outbuilding features a Confederate cannonball lodged in a wall, courtesy of John Pelham.

Arrayed off Route 5 to the east are Westover Plantation, Westover Church, Evelynton Plantation, North Bend Plantation, Charles City Court House, and Sherwood Forest, all visitable to some extent.

Westover Plantation, established in 1619, suffered losses during a coordinated Indian attack in 1666. The home had been constructed in 1730. On January 17, 1781, Lord Charles Cornwallis crossed the James River here in pursuit of Lafayette. Federal forces occupied the mansion and camped on the grounds when Westover Landing became the principal wharf for unloading supplies. That home was destroyed during the war but was rebuilt in 1900. Owner John A. Seddon, who fled before the Federals arrived, estimated his losses at seventy-five thousand dollars and sold the estate the day after he returned to Maj. Augustus H. Drewry. The grounds are open daily, but the house can only be visited during a spring garden tour.

On Route 5 is Westover Church (1739), which served the occupants of the river plantations. Worshipers included George Washington, Thomas Jefferson, William Henry Harrison, and John Tyler. The steeple was used as a Federal observation post, and the building was badly vandalized in 1862. It did not reopen until 1867.

Adjacent to Westover is Evelynton, owned by the Ruffin family since 1847. It was purchased by Edmund R. Ruffin Jr., whose father was a rabid Secessionist credited with firing the first shot at Fort Sumter and who committed suicide rather than live in a defeated South. He was also a brilliant agricultural scientist who made significant advances in southern farming.

Evelynton's position on the outskirts of the Union lines east of Herring Creek left it vulnerable to destruction. After the skirmish fought between Federal troops and Jeb Stuart for possession of Evelynton Heights on July 3, 1862, the main house and outbuildings were plundered and burned and the land ruined. Reportedly the fields were salted and the trees girdled. Confederates and Federals placed observation posts on the plantation, and Union troops returned again in 1864.

The Ruffin family recreated the old plantation house in 1937 with the help of the experts who reconstructed nearby Colonial Williamsburg. The twenty-five hundred acres are under cultivation and the house, gardens, and grounds are open to visitors. Earthworks survive from the Harrison's Landing encampment.

Other plantations farther down the James River along Route 5 and Charles City Court House will be explored in the third book in this series, *The Killing Time*. The first is Edgewood, home of Edmund Ruffin

The earthworks of Fort Darling, more commonly called Drewry's Bluff, are preserved along the James River.

In May 1862 cannon such as this one (above left) repulsed a naval attack by a small Union flotilla, which included the Monitor *and the* Galena. *The fort commanded this bend of the James River (above right).*

Sr. Stuart's men established a lookout post in the third floor, and it was burned later in the war, probably because of its ownership by Ruffin. Philip H. Sheridan visited North Bend Plantation (1819) while a pontoon bridge was being constructed across the James River for the strike against Petersburg. On his ride around McClellan, Stuart rested at Charles City Court House, which was frequently visited by Confederate and Union forces. Sherwood Forest was owned by John Tyler, a U.S. president who served in the Confederate Congress. In 1864 an attempt was made by Union troops to burn the mansion (1730s). Portions of the house, outbuildings, and gardens were destroyed, and scars remain on floors, walls, woodwork, and furniture. Earthworks survive on the grounds.

A combination ticket is available for touring Berkeley, Shirley, Evelynton, and Sherwood Forest.

Return to Route 5 and turn left. At the intersection of Route 5 and 156 South turn left onto Route 156. Turn right onto Route 10 West and continue on 10 West. Turn right onto U.S. 1 North–U.S. 301 North. After four miles turn right onto East Bellwood Road–656 at the sign for Drewry's Bluff–Fort Darling. Just beyond the overpass, turn left onto 1435. Turn right at the sign for Drewry's Bluff. Parking is on the right. It is open during daylight hours.

Seven different campaigns aimed to capture Richmond with land attacks, but the James River, navi-

gable to the city, left it open to a naval offensive. To close this vulnerable avenue, on March 17, 1862, the Southside Heavy Artillery, led by Capt. Augustus H. Drewry, who owned the land, arrived to construct log-and-earthen emplacements for three heavy naval guns, a 10-inch Columbiad and two 8-inch Columbiads. They also surrounded the battery with earthworks and built a barracks.

The pace of activity increased after Norfolk fell on May 9 under the direction of Comdr. Ebeneezer Farrand. The crew from the exploded *Virginia* arrived on May 13 and helped emplace five additional guns, including an 8-inch rifle from the *Patrick Henry* and two 6-inch guns from the *Jamestown,* which along with the steamers *James Curtis Peck* and *Northampton* had been sunk below the bluff. The river was further obstructed by the addition of log cribs filled with stone, a log boom, pilings, and later, torpedoes. Marines and sharpshooters were positioned along the riverbank to snipe at Union gunners.

This ninety-foot-high steep-sided cliff commanded a wide bend in the James and was the perfect position to stop any Federal naval incursion. It was, however, only seven miles south of Richmond. If the Federals were able to fight past Drewry's, the Confederate capital could be destroyed by the large artillery mounted on gunboats.

Early on the morning of May 15, a five-ship Federal flotilla arrived, led by Comdr. John Rodgers and including the ironclads *Monitor* and *Galena.* Soon after the battle opened at 7:15 the accurate fire of the Confederates' big cannon drove three wooden gunboats to a position three-quarters of a mile downstream of Drewry's Bluff. The *Monitor* was also forced downriver because her guns, mounted to fire on other ships, could not be elevated to reach the high Confederate position. After a fierce four-hour fight, heard plainly by anxious civilians in Richmond, Union ammunition was exhausted and the thin-skinned *Galena* had been wrecked. The Federals retreated with thirteen dead and eleven wounded, never to threaten Fort Darling, as they called it, by water again. Early in the battle the 10-inch Columbiad, overloaded with gunpowder, recoiled so hard it broke its carriage. Heavy rains had weakened one log-and-earth casemate, which collapsed onto an 8-inch Columbiad from the concussion of firing. Had McClellan been willing to spare a few thousand of the 120,000 soldiers he had at the gates of Richmond, Drewry's Bluff would have fallen easily to an attack from the rear.

Over the next three years the defenses here, commanded by Capt. Sidney S. Lee, Robert E. Lee's brother, were expanded and strengthened, making Drewry's Bluff, the first Confederate line of defense below Richmond, into a formidable defense line. A chapel, officers cabins, and additional barracks were constructed. Drewry's Bluff also became an important training center for the Confederate Naval Academy and the Marine Corps Camp of Instruction. The training ship *Patrick Henry* and Confederate ironclads often anchored here to bolster the defenses and drill cadets, sailors, and soldiers.

The next substantial threat materialized on May 5, 1864, when Maj. Gen. Benjamin F. Butler landed his Army of the James on Bermuda Hundred, eight miles downstream, and slowly started toward Drewry's Bluff. By May 9 his forces were only two miles away, and on May 14 two regiments captured an outer line of works. The Union general moved so slowly that Confederate Gen. P. G. T. Beauregard was able to bring up reinforcements and counterattack, driving Butler back and bottling him up at Bermuda Hundred. On May 16 Longstreet's corps crossed here to Petersburg. Beginning in 1862 Confederate troops frequently bridged the James here.

While Lee evacuated Petersburg on April 2, 1865, the artillery at Drewry's Bluff was spiked and the magazines exploded as the gunners, soldiers, sailors, and marines joined Lee on the long march that ended at Appomattox.

The Union navy immediately cleared the obstructions at Drewry's Bluff, and Abraham Lincoln passed the abandoned fortifications on his way to Richmond on April 4.

A self-guided walking tour of Drewry's Bluff is available at the Richmond National Battlefield Park Visitors Center. It leads through an impressive array of earthworks to an 8-inch Columbiad mounted at a site that still commands the broad James River. This is a beautiful, quiet, isolated place. Interpretive signs and a painting describe the history of the 1862 naval attack, Butler's 1864 land attack, and the training of Confederate naval cadets. A plaque honors Federal Cpl. John Mackie, the first marine to receive the Medal of Honor. With the Galena's gun crews decimated, Mackie directed the marines to serve the guns while under fire from Confederate marines.

From Drewry's Bluff return to U.S. 1 and turn left then right at the signs for Interstate 95 and head north, back to Richmond.

6

The Campaign and Battle of Second Manassas

G EORGE B. MCCLELLAN'S WITHDRAWAL from the peninsula was meant to reinforce a second army that was being formed to attack Richmond from the north. To command that force, Maj. Gen. John Pope was called east after his capture of the Confederate position at Island No. 10 along the Mississippi River.

Pope's Army of Virginia would incorporate three corps already operating between Washington and the Shenandoah Valley. Two of Irwin McDowell's divisions had arrived at Manassas Junction from Fredericksburg, where the third remained. Maj. Gens. Nathaniel Banks and John C. Frémont were summoned from the Shenandoah Valley, where Stonewall Jackson had buffaloed them in the spring. When Frémont resigned rather than serve under a junior officer, he was replaced with Maj. Gen. Franz Sigel.

Pope was a brash, indiscreet man. He loudly criticized McClellan's campaign on the peninsula, leading many to view him as self-serving. Then Pope bombastically criticized his own command in his first and soon infamous general order.

"I have come to you from the West," he wrote, "where we have always seen the backs of our enemies. Dismiss from your minds certain phrases which I am sorry to find much in vogue amongst you. I hear constantly of 'taking strong positions and holding them,' of 'lines of retreat and bases of supplies.' Let us discard such ideas. Let us look before and not behind. Success and glory are in the advance." Pope would soon be in a great deal of trouble for not looking behind him.

He was universally disliked. One of McDowell's brigadiers, Marseno Patrick, considered him "windy and insolent." At Banks's command, Brig. Gen. George H. Gordon said his men wondered whether Pope "were not a weak and silly man."

The Seven Days' campaign had been so forceful and well planned, if not well executed, that one soldier swore, "So great is my confidence in General Lee that I am willing to follow him blindfolded." An artilleryman who held Lee in awe wrote, "He is silent, inscrutable, strong, like a God."

Designed to allow state governors to have authority over troops raised within their borders, a Confederate law forbade any military unit larger than a division. To circumvent this restriction, Lee referred to his two new corps as "wings" or "commands."

When the focus of the war shifted away from the Virginia peninsula, it returned to the former area of activity around Manassas. A huge Federal supply depot was established near the old battlefield, and one of John Pope's first actions was to occupy Culpeper Court House. Above (left) a Union patrol encounters a group of children in March 1862 at Sudley Ford, site of the Northerners' retreat the previous July. A Federal supply wagon pauses on a Culpeper street (right).

Following the disastrous Seven Days' campaign, McClellan begged for additional troops, but none were immediately forthcoming. Encouraged by Federal successes in the West through the winter and spring, Secretary of War Edwin Stanton had closed recruiting stations. To reopen them would be seen as an admission of defeat, so Lincoln directed Secretary of State William Seward to persuade the sixteen governors of the states left in the Union to petition the president to raise an additional three hundred thousand volunteers to fight the war.

So that all would recognize him as an active field general, Pope signed his dispatches, "Headquarters in the Saddle," which led many men to quip, "General Pope doesn't know his headquarters from his hindquarters."

Pope also made himself the conflict's first war criminal by publicly announcing that his army would live off the land. Moreover, any citizen participating in guerrilla attacks against his vulnerable railroad would be shot without trial, and local civilians would suffer for partisan operations. Partly for this, Robert E. Lee considered Pope a "miscreant" who "ought to be suppressed." He would get his chance.

The new army began operating from a supply base at Manassas, which returned the war to its original theater. The Federals were gathering to the south along the vital Orange and Alexandria Railroad, between Warrenton to the north and Culpeper Court House to the south, and between the Blue Ridge and the Potomac River.

A standard objective of Union generals was to occupy Gordonsville, a vital railroad junction twenty-seven miles south of Culpeper. There the Orange and Alexandria met the Virginia Central that led to Richmond. The main line continued farther south to Charlottesville, where a branch ran west across the Blue Ridge Mountains to the Shenandoah Valley; the Orange and Alexandria continued on to Lynchburg and into the Carolinas.

Pope sent Banks to occupy Culpeper and threaten Gordonsville. Brig. Gen. John P. Hatch's cavalry led the way to destroy track on the Virginia Central east of Gordonsville, which would delay Confederate reinforcements rushing from Richmond. Hatch was slow to start and advance, then encountered heavy Confederate resistance. He withdrew and was promptly sacked, supplanted by Brig. Gen. John Buford.

Lee, informed of Banks's moves on July 12, set Jackson's small corps in motion. Three days were required to assemble the railroad stock, which consisted of eighteen trains of fifteen cars each, to haul his eighteen thousand men. They reached Gordonsville on July 19.

The Confederate commander gambled that McClellan would not stir from Harrison's Landing. Without Jackson, the Southern soldiers in Richmond amounted to less than half the Federal force on the James River. When Lee saw Pope gathering strength to the north around Culpeper, he threw the dice again, dispatching A. P. Hill's Light Division to Gordonsville with a letter encouraging Jackson to confide his plans to Hill, thus addressing two potential problems. Jackson's secretive ways and Hill's quick anger were both noteworthy.

In early August an exchange of prisoners brought Lt. John S. Mosby to Lee. While a prisoner he had overhead conversations discussing orders for Maj. Gen. Ambrose Burnside, arriving from North Carolina, who would continue up Chesapeake Bay on transports. Mosby believed, and Lee agreed, that Burnside would steam up the Potomac River to Aquia Landing and march the short distance east to Fredericksburg. This confirmed Lee's suspicion that Washington was not reinforcing McClellan but Pope. Thus McClellan was no longer a threat to Richmond; Pope was. Given the situation, Lee authorized Jackson to launch a preemptive

Southerners were appalled by Pope's orders concerning civilians, and Stonewall Jackson was no exception. When his aide Alexander S. "Sandie" Pendleton brought the order to him, a visiting preacher noted "a quiet smile and a frown" on Jackson's face. When the minister said, "Here is a new candidate for your favor," Jackson's response was, "Yes, and by God's blessing he shall receive my attention."

The Supremely Confident General ■ John Pope

Born in Louisville, Kentucky, on March 16, 1822, John Pope was a collateral descendant of George Washington. His father was a federal judge, an uncle was a U.S. senator, and he was related by marriage to Mary Todd Lincoln—in all, a remarkably connected man. Pope graduated in the West Point class of 1842, which provided seventeen generals to the Civil War. He was a surveyor for four years before being breveted first lieutenant and captain in Mexico. Pope then served as a topographical engineer and made regular army captain in 1856.

When the Civil War began, Pope's connections facilitated his jump to brigadier general on June 14, 1861, and he was sent west. In a brilliant campaign of the type Ulysses S. Grant would use against Vicksburg, Pope captured Island No. 10 and

New Madrid on the Mississippi River in March and April 1862. Promoted to major general on March 22, his troops assisted Grant at Shiloh and followed Henry W. Halleck to Corinth, Mississippi.

Because of these successes, Abraham Lincoln gave Pope command of all Union troops in the East except George B. McClellan's, which were invested on the Virginia peninsula. Pope's Army of Virginia was to defend Washington and open a second front against Richmond from the north, which would allow McClellan to renew his offensive from the peninsula.

Success apparently went to Pope's head. He alienated his new command with pompous proclamations that made him look foolish, and he aroused the hatred of Southerners with his harsh treatment of civilians. Pope, hopelessly baffled

by Confederate moves around and behind him, futilely searched for Stonewall Jackson and was goaded into attacks that left his force vulnerable to James Longstreet's devastating assault. Pope then had the ill manners to blame Fitz John Porter and Irwin McDowell for his own shortcomings.

Relieved of command by McClellan, Pope was exiled to Minnesota as head of the Department of the Northwest to deal with aggressive Sioux Indians. He commanded other departments before retiring in 1886. Pope was appointed brigadier in the regular army dating to July 14, 1862, and made major general in 1882. He died at the Ohio Soldier's and Sailor's Home at Sandusky, Ohio, on September 23, 1892, and is buried in Bellefontaine Cemetery in Saint Louis.

LIBRARY OF CONGRESS

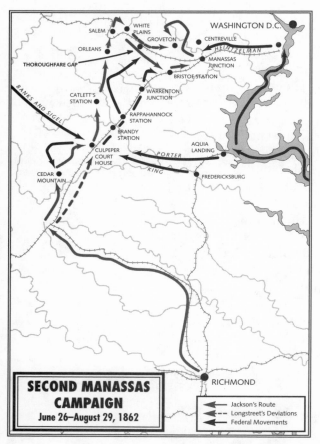

SECOND MANASSAS CAMPAIGN
June 26–August 29, 1862

→ Jackson's Route
--→ Longstreet's Deviations
➤ Federal Movements

strike against Pope, leaving operations "to your reflection and good judgement."

Jackson advanced through Orange Court House and on August 8 crossed the Rapidan River to attack. Lee's admonition that Jackson relax his legendary secrecy went unheeded. On the night of August 7 Jackson informed his generals that Richard Ewell would be the first division marching by the primary road north, followed by Hill and Winder, commanding Jackson's division. Later Jackson diverted Ewell to a side road but did not reveal this to Hill or Winder.

During the morning Hill watched as a division marched past, but it turned out to be Winder, not Ewell. Furious, Hill knew chaos would result if the two divisions were mixed. He waited until Winder passed, then joined the march late. He moved only two miles during the day to Winder's four, but Ewell had marched eight miles.

Ordered to return to Orange Court House for the night, Hill was further incensed, correctly blaming Jackson for the confusion. Jackson, however, laid the responsibility on Hill.

Pope departed Washington on July 29 to join his troops in the field. Only Banks's eleven thousand men were concentrated between Warrenton and Culpeper. Sigel's thirteen-thousand-man corps was crossing the Blue Ridge, and McDowell's thirty thousand were marching west from Fredericksburg.

General in Chief Henry W. Halleck, agonizing over the situation, warned Pope: "Do not advance so as to expose yourself to any disaster." He was urged to wait for reinforcements.

Order No. 2: Pope Insults His Own Command

Let us understand each other. I have come to you from the West, where we have always seen the backs of our enemies; from an army whose business it has been to seek the adversary and to beat him when he was found, whose policy has been attack and not defense. In but one instance has the enemy been able to place our Western armies in a defensive attitude. I presume I have been called here to pursue the same system and to lead you against the enemy. It is my purpose to do so, and that speedily. I am sure you long for an opportunity to win the distinction you are capable of achieving. That opportunity I shall endeavor to give you. Meantime I desire you to dismiss from your minds certain phrases, which I am sorry to find so much in vogue amongst you. I hear constantly of "taking strong positions and holding them," of "lines of retreat," and of "bases of supply." Let us discard such ideas. The strongest position a soldier should desire to occupy is one from which he can most easily advance against the enemy. Let us study the probable lines of retreat of our opponents, and leave our own to take care of themselves. Let us look before us, and not in the rear. Let us act on this understanding, and it is safe to predict that our banners shall be inscribed with many a glorious deed and that your names will be dear to your countrymen forever.

LIBRARY OF CONGRESS

Pope decided to base his army out of Culpeper. It was linked with Washington via the Orange and Alexandria line (the depot is pictured above), and to the new general it appeared to be a good point from which he could quickly target Richmond

Stonewall Jackson's pious nature was well known. "The General is a great man for praying at all times," remembered Jim Lewis, Jackson's civilian and military servant. "But when I see him get up a great many times in the night to pray, then I know there is going to be something to pay." Richard Ewell noted that Jackson tended to nod off during sermons and asked, "What is the use of General Jackson's going to church? He sleeps all of the time."

In an attempt to motivate McClellan, Halleck wired: "I must beg of you, general, to hurry along your movement. Your reputation as well as mine may be involved in its rapid execution. I cannot regard Pope and Burnside as safe until you reinforce him."

Pope required a considerable amount of time to consolidate his new command. By August 8 the elements of his army stretched from Aquia Landing to Sperryville, at the foot of the Blue Ridge Mountains east of the Shenandoah Valley. Union cavalry screening the line extended from Rapidan Station to Madison Court House.

The most advanced element of Banks's Army of the Valley corps was eight miles south of Culpeper. One of McDowell's divisions, under Brig. Gen. James B. Ricketts, was at Culpeper, while a second at Fredericksburg, commanded by Brig. Gen. Rufus King, protected the supply base at Aquia Landing, where Burnside would disembark. Sigel would have arrived earlier from Sperryville but had been misdirected.

On August 9 Jackson marched north again in a seven-mile-long column of more than twenty thousand soldiers and their trains of twelve hundred wagons. Ewell led, followed by Winder and Hill, as cavalry drove their Union counterparts back. At noon Ewell encountered a Federal force on the Culpeper road, which opened with artillery.

Jackson rode to the front and deployed artillery on the northern slopes of Cedar Mountain, then extended his line to the left with Ewell's brigades under Brig. Gen. Isaac Trimble and Col. Henry Forno. Then came Jubal Early, facing the Union center, which was concealed behind a ridge beyond Cedar Run. Winder moved in to the left of Ewell with the brigades of Col. Thomas Garnett and Brig. Gen. William Taliaferro. The line extended from Cedar Mountain to the Culpeper road. The Stonewall

On August 2 three Federal cavalry regiments crossed the Rapidan River and charged into Orange, driving out one Confederate regiment. Their colonel, William E. "Grumble" Jones, said that "half of his men charged and half discharged." As they retreated, a Southern woman told them, "Oh, I wish I was a man!" A trooper responded, "If you was, you would wish you were a gal again mighty soon!"

Stonewall Jackson's operational secrecy was legendary even before he joined Robert E. Lee. Jubal Early, who had served under Jackson in the Shenandoah Valley, stated in resignation: "I do not know whether we march north, south, east or west, or whether we march at all. General Jackson has simply ordered me to have the division ready to move at dawn." A staff officer noted, "It seems strange to see a large body of men moving in one direction and only one man in all the thousands knowing where they are going." Another general said of Jackson, "If silence be golden, he was a bonanza."

Jackson was poised to strike at Pope before the elements of the Federal commander's army could assemble at Culpeper. The summer heat, however, impeded his advance. Shortly after noon on August 8, Jackson encountered a large Federal force under Nathaniel P. Banks at Cedar Mountain, just south of Culpeper.

When Stonewall Jackson's doctor, Hunter McGuire, asked if a battle would soon occur, the general replied, "Banks is in our front and he is generally willing to fight, and he generally gets whipped."

Brigade, now led by Col. Charles Ronald, was in reserve, with Hill prepared to deploy where necessary.

Undetected in the dense woods to the Confederate left were two Union brigades. Not only were the Confederates ignorant of this threat, they faced southeast, away from the danger. The Federal line from left to right was composed of Maj. Gen. Christopher Auger's division of three brigades and the two-brigade division of Maj. Gen. Alpheus Williams. To the right, unseen in the woods, was Brig. Gen. Samuel Crawford with seventeen hundred men. Brig. Gen. George Gordon was to the right and rear of

A Union battery (below left) posed for a photographer while fording a stream en route to the fighting at Cedar Mountain. Artist Edwin Forbes sketched Capt. Joseph M. Knapp's battery in action (below right). Preoccupied with the safety of his artillery and fearful that Knapp's battery was about to be overrun, Banks ordered a cavalry charge. The oncoming Federal horseman provided a tempting target for Jackson's infantry, who viewed the charge as a desperate act of a beaten foe and counterattacked.

290

Crawford. Although Banks was outnumbered twenty-eight thousand to nine thousand, he had the superior position.

Earlier in the day in Culpeper, Banks had received orders from Pope that gave him control of all troops there. If the Confederates advanced, he was to "attack . . . immediately."

The afternoon saw a fierce artillery duel. Federal guns on the ridge gained the upper hand, mortally wounding Winder and his chief of artillery. At 4:30 Early sent word to Winder that the Federals were beyond his left. Taliaferro was now commanding the division, and he had no idea what Jackson's battle plan was.

At 5 P.M. Crawford attacked from the woods, falling upon an unprepared Taliaferro with three Union regiments—the Forty-sixth Pennsylvania, the Twenty-eighth New York, and the Fifth Connecticut. Crawford drove the Confederates from three successive lines, forcing three Southern brigades along the Culpeper road to retreat after hand-to-hand combat. Their artillery hastily limbered up and joined the withdrawal. Jackson's entire left wing was broken as Auger flanked Ewell.

Advised of the situation, Jackson raced to the front, grabbed a battle flag, and waved it overhead, shouting, "Rally, brave men, and press forward! Your

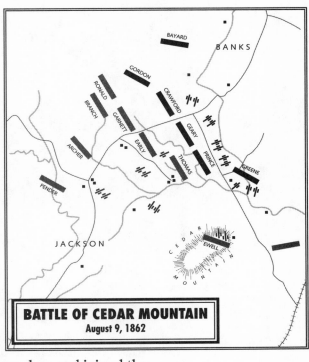

BATTLE OF CEDAR MOUNTAIN
August 9, 1862

"Old Brains" ■ Henry Wager Halleck

Henry Wager Halleck, born in New York in 1815, was third in his West Point class of 1839. His intelligence was recognized early, and he became an assistant professor at the academy before his graduation. Halleck supervised the building of U.S. coastal forts, traveled to France to inspect defenses there, and published his lectures on military engineering. After administrative duties in California during the war with Mexico, Halleck engineered forts and lighthouses on the West Coast. This talented man helped write California's state constitution, then studied law and left the army in 1854. Halleck declined to be a justice on the California supreme

court and the opportunity to serve in the U.S. Senate, choosing instead to enter business. He prospered by publishing a number of law books.

When the Civil War began, Gen. Winfield Scott advised Abraham Lincoln to appoint Halleck to the rank of major general. "Old Brains" arrived in Saint Louis in November 1861, to organize the Department of the Missouri. He basked in the reflected glow of victories achieved by his subordinates at Forts Henry and Donelson, Elkhorn Tavern, Island No. 10, and Shiloh. Following the battle of Shiloh, Halleck took to the field as commander of the Department of the Mississippi. After his deliberate occupation of Corinth, Lin-

coln called him to Washington to serve as general in chief.

There Halleck's star dimmed. He was soon committing serious blunders and attempting to shift the responsibility to others. He seemed to have lost sight of the war while concentrating on mundane matters. The nickname "Old Brains" was soon dropped for "Old Woodenhead." Lincoln called him a "first rate clerk." Secretary of War Edwin M. Stanton referred to Halleck as the "greatest scoundrel and most bare-faced villain in America." Gen. George B. McClellan thought him "hopelessly stupid," and Secretary of the Navy Gideon Welles believed he was "good for

nothing." Halleck, demoted to chief of staff in 1864, served in three insignificant commands before his death in 1872. He is buried in Brooklyn's Green-Wood Cemetery.

The battle had been going in favor of the outnumbered Federals. For the first time the vaunted Stonewall Brigade had been driven from the field. Jackson rallied his men by shouting, "Rally, brave men, and press forward! Your general will lead you. Jackson will lead you. Follow me!" and waving his sword's scabbard over his head—the sword had rusted in place. One of the soldiers recalled, "His face was lit with the inspiration of heroism."

general will lead you. Jackson will lead you. Follow me!" Handing the flag back to its bearer and drawing his sword to lead the assault, Jackson found that the rarely used blade had rusted into his scabbard. Undeterred, the general waved the scabbard over his head and rallied the men.

With the line stabilized, Jackson rode to the rear to hurry reinforcements from Hill. The lead troops, under Brig. Gen. Lawrence O. Branch, were enduring a speech from the former politician. "Push forward, general," Jackson interrupted. "Push forward!"

Hill stopped Crawford with Branch, then drove him back across the road into the fields and followed with the remainder of his division. Most of Crawford's commanders fell—one regiment lost 17 of 18 officers—and the brigade suffered 867 casualties, more than 50 percent. Crawford was overwhelmed, and his own reinforcements did not materialize. A charge by a squadron of the First Pennsylvania Cavalry caused casualties of 71 out of 164 troopers, but it gave Banks time to withdraw. Gordon's Federals advancing to protect the retreat were forced to withdraw, except for the Second Massachusetts, which fought alone against three-to-one odds.

"The roar of musketry was perfectly deafening," wrote a Union officer. "The noise of the bullets through the air was like a gale of wind; our poor men were dropping on every side."

A cavalryman watched superstitious Confederate soldiers running off the road to hide playing cards under leaves and in fence corners. Others quickly scribbled their names and regiments on pieces of paper and pinned them to their coats so their bodies could be identified if they were killed.

Infantry awaiting an advance can do little but endure artillery fire. As they attacked and encountered rifle fire, one green Confederate said, "I am awfully glad those shells have stopped coming. I don't mind these little things."

Pope's Infamous Orders No. 11

Head-quarters Army of Virginia, Washington, July 23, 1862.

General Orders No. 11

Commanders of army corps, divisions, brigades, and detached commands will proceed immediately to arrest all disloyal male citizens within their lines or within their reach in rear of their respective stations.

Such as are willing to take the oath of allegiance to the United States, and will furnish sufficient security for its observance, shall be permitted to remain at their homes and pursue in good faith their accustomed avocations. Those who refuse shall be conducted south beyond the extreme pickets of this army, and be notified that if found again anywhere within

our lines, or at any point in rear, they will be considered spies, and subjected to the extreme rigor of military law.

If any person, having taken the oath of allegiance as above specified, be found to have violated it, he shall be shot, and his property seized and applied to the public use.

All communication with any person whatever living within the lines of the

enemy is positively prohibited, except through the military authorities and in the manner specified by military law; any person concerned in writing or in carrying letters or messages in any other way will be considered and treated as a spy within the lines of the United States army.

By command of
Major-General Pope.

Darkness did not force Jackson to break off the battle. He ordered his artillery to shell the area to drive the Federals from the woods near Cedar Run Church. His gunners targeted the ill-conceived fires among the Union camp, but they were silenced by return fire from three batteries supporting James B. Ricketts's division.

Capt. William J. Pegram was one of the Confederacy's great artillery officers. When Federal troops threatened his guns, Pegram grabbed a battle flag and ran to each of his cannon, waving it at his crews and shouting, "Don't let the enemy have these guns or this flag; Jackson is looking at you. Go on, men, give it to them."

"We fired until the enemy were right at the guns," one Confederate artilleryman boasted. Only then did Pegram shout, "Limber to the road."

Three guns made a clean escape, but the team driver of the last was shot. Pegram drew his sword to strike down a soldier who refused to take his place, but another man jumped into the position and the cannon was removed.

"Men," Pegram said minutes later, "when the enemy takes a gun of my battery, look for my dead body in front of it."

Hill personally led the final assault, doffing his jacket to reveal the red battle shirt he always wore in combat. By 6:30, after an hour and a half of battle, the Federals were in full retreat.

Jackson ordered a pursuit, but exhaustion and darkness hindered the chase. It ended seven miles short of Culpeper, where Ricketts assembled a fresh Federal division. Jackson ordered a bivouac at 11 P.M., just before he nearly fell off his horse in exhaustion. Officers laid him on the ground, where he immediately went to sleep.

Jackson suffered 1,355 casualties. Banks's losses were 2,377, or 30 percent of his force. Jackson proclaimed victory and withdrew to Gordonsville, while Banks similarly claimed the win and retreated to Culpeper. The truth was that they had both directed the battle poorly. Jackson delayed his attack by one day because of poorly communicated orders, then allowed himself to be badly flanked. Banks had brought on a battle

Several days after the battle, these Union soldiers rest in the shade of some trees overlooking the wheat field where much of the battle of Cedar Mountain occurred. One of the officers detailed to bury the dead observed that the ground was "torn, trodden, cannon plowed, bloody; fences and corn fields obliterated; trees splintered and cut off by shot; dead men, dead horses, fragments of bodies, broken wagons, remnants of arms and equippage."

A captured Union sergeant was escorted to Stonewall Jackson's tent for questioning. While waiting for the general, an officer observed the soldier plucking hairs from the tail of Jackson's horse. As he was ordered to stop, Jackson arrived and inquired of the noncom, "My friend, why are you tearing the hair out of my horse's tail?"

"Ah, General," he replied, "each one of these hairs is worth a dollar in New York."

against overwhelming odds. He and Pope would argue over whose responsibility that had been.

On August 13 Lee learned that McClellan was withdrawing from the peninsula by water and overland march to Fort Monroe. The good news was that Richmond was saved, but the bad news was a possible junction between Pope and McClellan and the resumption of an offensive against the capital from the north. Lee, realizing he must deal with Pope before McClellan arrived, dispatched James Longstreet's thirty thousand men on the railroad to Gordonsville, leaving Richmond defended by only twenty-five thousand. His reinforcements would reach Jackson long before McClellan could join Pope.

That same day Washington rejected McClellan's last plea to allow him to march against Richmond. He had been given his chance and bungled it badly. It was now Pope's turn.

By August 15 Lee had concentrated fifty-five thousand troops on the Rapidan River. Pope was to the north at Culpeper.

Considerable activity occurred during the Civil War in the *V* formed by the Rappahannock River to the north and the Rapidan River to the south. At the end of the *V* the rivers joined and the larger Rappahannock flowed past Fredericksburg into Chesapeake Bay. Pope, with a matching force, was now in the angle between the rivers, along the Orange and

Confederates taken prisoner during the battle of Cedar Mountain were temporarily housed in the Culpeper County Courthouse. A photographer captured this image of some prisoners' laundry being hung out to dry on the balcony.

Stonewall Jackson's eccentric nature appeared again in mid-August. One night he ordered Capt. Charles Blackford to gather twenty horsemen for a scouting expedition. They were accompanied by Sandie Pendleton and Jackson, who led them "in by-paths and unused roads in places where neither friend nor foe would ever pass," Blackford wrote. "It was one of those freaks which sometimes seize him and which make many people think he is somewhat deranged."

Blackford and Pendleton rode together and alternately dozed and grumbled. At one point Blackford slept, then awakened and "said in an undertone, but very irreverently and somewhat petulantly, 'Sandy, where is the old fool taking us?'"

"What!" the figure on horseback beside him demanded. It was Jackson, and Blackford quickly fell back into the darkness.

To care for the wounded, hospitals were improvised wherever shelter could be found. This home near the Cedar Mountain battlefield was used by Confederate surgeons.

Alexandria Railroad on which flowed supplies from the massive Union stockpiles at Manassas Junction and reinforcements arriving in Alexandria via the Potomac River.

Before McClellan's troops could reinforce Pope, Lee planned to send his cavalry under Jeb Stuart to destroy the Orange and Alexandria Railroad bridge at the Rappahannock River in Pope's rear. The Confederate army would then move forward, screened behind Clark's Mountain, east of the railroad, to cross the Rapidan and attack Pope's left flank.

Unfortunately the move was delayed two days due to supply problems. During that time Federal cavalry turned the tables on Stuart by raiding his headquarters. Stuart barely escaped, but a member of his staff, Capt. Norman Fitzhugh, was captured with a copy of Lee's orders. Realizing his peril, Pope immediately withdrew north of the Rappahannock to the taunts of Southern civilians.

On August 20 Confederate cavalry nearly caught the end of Pope's retreating columns, but Brig. Gen. George Bayard bought the Federals enough time and was mauled for the effort.

Pope entrenched on the north side of the Rappahannock, where the bank was higher than on the southern shore, making it a perfect defensive position. Lee probed, but Federal artillery commanded all crossings of the stream. A good plan had been foiled by bad luck.

In another attempt to cut the railroad behind Pope, Lee sent Stuart circling to the west on August 22 with fifteen hundred men and two guns.

Three days after Cedar Mountain, Federal officer David H. Strother saw an entire company of men energetically digging up a large area where something had recently been buried. They were convinced it was treasure, and the exhumation of a decaying horse did not discourage them, Strother noted, but "only raised their hopes afresh. The horse must have been buried to conceal the treasure," they said. "When I left them they could hear a hollow sound at every stroke of their mattocks."

The Surgeon General ■ Samuel Wylie Crawford

Born on November 8, 1829, in Franklin County, Pennsylvania, Samuel Wylie Crawford graduated from the University of Pennsylvania Medical School in 1850. He became an army surgeon, serving in the West, and in 1861 found himself within Fort Sumter, where he commanded a battery during the Confederate bombardment.

Crawford led a regiment then a brigade in the Shenandoah Valley, where his service was praised by Nathaniel P. Banks. He was promoted to brigadier of volunteers in April and fought well at Cedar Mountain, where half his brigade became casualties, and at Second Manassas. Severely wounded leading a division at Antietam, Crawford was assigned a corps in the defenses of Washington. This force served in the Army of the Potomac as a division,

fighting at Gettysburg, the Wilderness, Spotsylvania, Cold Harbor, Petersburg, Five Forks, and Appomattox. Crawford rose to the rank of major general of volunteers and in the regular army. He supervised troops in the occupied South before retiring in 1873. Crawford died on November 3, 1892, in Philadelphia, and is buried in Laurel Hill Cemetery.

Stonewall Jackson and A. P. Hill clashed on a number of occasions. After the battle of Cedar Mountain, Hill wrote to Jeb Stuart: "I suppose I am to vegetate here all the winter under that crazy old Presbyterian fool—I am like the porcupine all bristles, and all sticking out too, so I know we shall have a smash up before long. . . . The Almighty will get tired of helping Jackson after a while, and then he'll get the d**ndest thrashing—and the shoe pinches, for I shall get my share and probably all of the blame, for the people will never blame Stonewall for any disaster."

They crossed the Rappahannock upstream at Waterloo Bridge and passed around Pope's right flank to strike the Orange and Alexandria at Catlett's Station, ten miles in the Federal rear and near an important bridge spanning Cedar Run. The bridge was too stout to cut down and rain prevented destruction by fire, but Stuart stumbled across Pope's headquarters. The general was not home, but his dispatch case was.

Stuart hastily returned to Lee with Pope's orders. From them Lee learned that on August 22 the first of McClellan's troops, Fitz John Porter's Fifth Corps, would arrive from the peninsula at Aquia Landing on the Potomac, then rapidly march east to join Pope. The news grew worse. Samuel Heintzelman's Third Corps was landing at Alexandria, to be followed by William Franklin's Sixth Corps. When they moved forward via the railroad, Pope's force would swell to seventy thousand and more.

Lee faced a dilemma. There was no possibility of dislodging Pope from his Rappahannock line, and waiting for him to be reinforced would prove disastrous. As he often would, Lee chose audacity. He split his army, sending twenty-five thousand under Jackson and led by Stuart's cavalry on a wide arc to the northwest, around Pope's right on the Rappahannock. Meanwhile, Longstreet's thirty thousand would keep Pope in check with a demonstration. Lincoln would certainly require Pope to withdraw and defend Washington. Longstreet would follow Jackson a day later, unite with him, and attack Pope while the Federal was retreating in confusion and before McClellan's troops could reach him. This maneuver would serve to relieve the pressure on Richmond and flank Pope out of a strong position. The plan demonstrated great daring, with Richmond the stake in this dangerous gamble.

The Revenge of Jeb's Hat

Robert E. Lee's orders may have been the most strategic loss from the Union raid on Jeb Stuart's headquarters at Verdiersville, but the morale loss was Stuart's plumed hat, which he had only recently acquired from Federal Brig. Gen. Samuel W. Crawford, an old friend. During a truce following Cedar Mountain, Stuart had bet Crawford a hat that Northern newspapers would claim the battle as a Federal victory. Of course they had, and Crawford promptly sent the colorful hat through the lines.

After losing his hat, Stuart covered his head with a handkerchief, which provoked catcalls from the troops. Even Stuart's stoutest supporter, Heros Von Borcke, admitted that the staff "could not look at each other without laughing."

"I intend to make the Yankees pay for that hat," Stuart swore.

When Stuart raided Catlett Station he had no idea that it was John Pope's headquarters. He netted several hundred prisoners, five hundred mounts, a full payroll chest, and the general's orders, but the finest booty was Pope's dress uniform. The cavalier gleefully sent this message to Pope: "General:

You have my hat and plume. I have your best coat. I have the honor to propose a cartel for the fair exchange of prisoners."

Pope did not reply, so Stuart sent the uniform to Virginia Gov. John Letcher, who displayed it in the capitol.

Another interesting story came out of the Catlett raid. When Stuart rode through Warrenton, he encountered a young woman who told him that she had befriended Federal Maj. Charles N. Goulding. He had bet her a bottle of wine that he would reach Richmond within thirty days. She knew him to be at Catlett Station and thought it would be great sport if Stuart could capture him and allow her to lose the bet in a way the Yankee never intended. Stuart accepted the challenge and noted the officer's name.

Goulding was nabbed at Catlett Station. When Stuart returned through Warrenton, he presented the major to the young woman, who greeted him with a smile and the bottle of wine. He entered Richmond as a prisoner of war.

LIBRARY OF CONGRESS

When Pope learned of Lee's plans to isolate him below the Rappahannock, he quickly pulled back to the river's northern bank. This bridge accommodated Franz Sigel's corps on August 19. In the image above, the main roadway accommodates cavalry and a herd of cattle while a man on foot navigates the plank walkway.

Gen. James Longstreet was inspecting his artillery during a duel with Union guns and found a soldier weeping over his dead brother. Just then another shell exploded nearby and the soldier growled, "Dad drat those Yankees! If I had known that they were going to throw such things as that at a fellow, I would have stayed in Texas."

On the afternoon of August 24, Lee, Jackson, Longstreet, and Stuart met to hear Lee's orders. Jackson marched before dawn, his men carrying three days' rations. There were no supply trains with him, just artillery, ammunition wagons, and ambulances.

At 8 A.M. on August 25 Federal observers posted on hills across the Rappahannock counted the marchers' flags and soon gave Pope an approximate number of enemy troops on the move. Pope thought that Jackson was returning to the Shenandoah Valley; he could not believe that the Confederate army was boldly marching for his rear.

Jackson followed the Rappahannock and crossed the stream at Amissville, then passed through Orlean and Salem before turning east to follow the Manassas Gap Railroad. It was a grueling march, even for men who had raced up and down the Shenandoah Valley with Jackson a few months earlier. Many men had no chance to cook their rations, which were soon eaten anyway. Soldiers broke ranks to pick green apples and green corn, which usually added to their woes. Civilians along the route brought water and food to the roadside for the troops. Like Pope, soldiers and civilians alike figured the corps was returning to the Valley. As usual, Jackson trusted no one with his plans.

Many barefooted soldiers left bloody footprints on the rough roads, their route marked by thick, choking clouds of dust. Exhausted and thirsty, they made little conversation. The only sound they made was the tromp of

One of Pope's aides was Col. Louis Marshall, whose uncle was the Confederate commander, Robert E. Lee.

Stonewall Jackson immediately called for religious celebrations to "render thanks to God for the victory at Cedar Run and other past victories and to implore His continued favor in the future." Returning from one such observance, Jackson stopped at another to listen to Rev. Daniel B. Ewing, a fellow Presbyterian, who was "in the midst of a splendid curl," one noted, while addressing William B. Taliaferro's brigade. At Jackson's appearance "the men all broke and marched to the road-side to cheer the Gen. as he passed, leaving Mr. Ewing in amazement at the height of his eloquence." Taliaferro announced that he would have Jackson "arrested for disturbing a religious meeting, and a Presbyterian one at that!"

marching feet, the chant of officers, and Jackson's occasional admonition, "Close up men. Close up."

The advance continued until late in the night, when the Southerners stacked muskets and fell to the ground, asleep instantly. It was dark still when they were rousted with great difficulty and started on the march again. Men fell out of line with heatstroke and exhaustion.

By midmorning of August 26 Jackson's corps was crossing the Bull Run Mountains via narrow Thoroughfare Gap, uncontested by a single picket. At Gainesville they turned to the southeast to gain the Orange and Alexandria Railroad bridge at Broad Run near Bristoe Station. In two days they had marched fifty-six miles and were twenty miles in Pope's rear.

In the late afternoon the Confederates surprised and captured two companies guarding the railroad at Bristoe and cut Pope's telegraphic link with Washington. Moments later an empty train raced north from Pope for another load of supplies. Jackson's men hurriedly placed railroad ties on the track but they failed to derail the locomotive and it sped on, riddled with bullets, to spread the alarm.

Prisoners revealed that more trains from the south were expected. To greet them Jackson ordered a rail removed and burned the span over Broad Run, to the north. The next train left the track in spectacular fashion. "Down the embankment rushed the engine, screaming and hissing," remembered a Confederate captain, "and down upon it rushed the cars, piling up one upon another until the pile reached higher than the embankment."

During a heavy thunderstorm on the evening of August 22, Jeb Stuart's cavalry attacked a Federal camp at Catlett's Station (below), ten miles behind the Union lines. Stuart's goal was to cut the railroad; only after he had taken possession of the depot did he learn that it was Pope's headquarters. The papers seized in the raid revealed the imminent arrival of three corps from McClellan's army, which would swell Pope's command to seventy thousand men.

At Catlett's Station Jeb Stuart seized $350,000 in cash.

Lee sent Jackson on a wide flanking march that most believed was a return to the Shenandoah. For his part, Jackson was close-lipped about his destination, but when the column turned east and passed unhindered through unguarded Thoroughfare Gap—Pope too assumed that Jackson was en route to the Valley—the army saw that Manassas and the Federal supply depot lay ahead of them.

BATTLES AND LEADERS

A third train plowed into the ruin of the second. "The locomotive plowed under the first three boxcars, setting them crossways on its bank and on the back of the tender," the officer continued. "The cars telescoped each other and many were forced out upon the pile over the locomotive."

A fourth train spotted the destruction on the track and managed to stop, then reversed to temporary safety.

Jackson was definitely getting Pope's attention, but additional work remained to be done. He sent Brig. Gen. Isaac Trimble's brigade, with the Twenty-first Georgia and Twenty-first South Carolina, four miles up the rails to Manassas Junction which, as it had served Johnston, was Pope's supply depot. The small garrison was surprised and managed to fire only one round before they were overrun.

Three brigades under Ewell remained at Bristoe Station while the rest of Jackson's worn command, "gaunt-cheeked and hollow-eyed, hair, beard, clothing covered with dust," described one Confederate, pushed on into the night, reaching Manassas at dawn to find themselves in soldier heaven. They encountered "vast storehouses filled with all the delicacies,

Near Salem, Stonewall Jackson dismounted and climbed atop a large rock to watch his corps pass. When the troops began to cheer their respected leader, Jackson feared the Federals would hear. After motioning for the men to stop cheering, the men took off their caps and waved them in the air. "Who could not conquer with troops such as these?" Jackson said.

The Soldier of Fortune ■ Philip Kearny

Born into a wealthy family on June 2, 1816, Philip Kearny was a nephew of Mexican War hero Gen. Stephen W. Kearny. Philip attended private schools and graduated from Columbia University in 1833. He read law and traveled until 1837, when he "retired" to a military life on a million-dollar inheritance from his grandfather. Kearny, a natural rider, became a second lieutenant in the First Dragoons. In 1838 he studied at the French cavalry school at Saumur before fighting with the Chasseurs d'Afrique in Algiers in 1840.

Returning home for the war with Mexico, Kearny became aide de camp to two generals in chief of the army, Alexander Macomb and Winfield Scott. While his company escorted Scott, Kearny's left arm was shattered at Churubusco and amputated. Kearny left the military in 1851 and circled the globe, then spent several years on his New Jersey estate. Wanderlust overcame him again, and in 1859 he returned to Europe and fought at Magenta and Solferino in the Italian campaign with Napoleon III, charging into combat with reins held in his teeth and a sword in his hand.

When the Civil War began, Kearny returned immediately to the United States and became the first brigadier general of volunteers on August 7, 1861. He commanded a brigade in the Peninsula campaign during the spring of 1862, then commanded a division, making major general on July 4, 1862. Leading recalcitrant troops into combat at the confused battle of Chantilly, Kearny was killed on September 1, 1862.

Winfield Scott thought Kearny the "bravest man I ever knew, and a perfect soldier." Kearny was buried at Trinity Churchyard in New York City, then reinterred in 1912 at Arlington National Cemetery, not far from where he fell. An equestrian statue marks his grave.

U.S. ARMY MILITARY HISTORY INSTITUTE

After Stonewall Jackson captured Catlett's Station, a civilian lying with a broken leg desired to see the famous general. Raised up, he stared at Jackson, then groaned and said, "Oh, my God! Lay me down." The remark became a catch phrase in Jackson's corps. For months any hardship or setback was met by a chorus of, "Oh, my God! Lay me down!"

BATTLES AND LEADERS

Jackson's exhausted men fell ravenously upon the Manassas supply depot at dawn on August 27. In addition to foodstuffs, they found clothing, shoes, weapons, ammunition, and luxuries like cigars. What they couldn't eat or wear they torched.

potted ham, lobster, tongue, candy, cakes, nuts, oranges, lemons, canned goods, etc," a private wrote.

The depot covered a square mile. Great warehouses were filled with food and supplies, so much bounty that it overflowed into piles stacked on the ground. Two parallel rail sidings, each extending for half a mile, were packed with loaded boxcars.

"To see a starving man eating lobster salad and drinking Rhine wine," wrote John Worsham of the spectacle at Manassas, "barefoot and in tatters, was curious, the whole thing was indescribable."

Rebels, half-starved, shoeless, attired in ragged uniforms, fell upon this bacchanalia. The men grabbed underwear, shoes, shirts, pants, and blankets. Gray rags littered the depot. With equal delight Confederates filled haversacks with coffee, sugar, bacon, and hardtack, and stuffed their bellies to bursting.

Stonewall Executes an Object Lesson

When Stonewall Jackson decided that desertion had become a serious problem in his command, he quickly tried, convicted, and executed three men who had left their units without orders. When the commander of two of the men requested leniency, Jack-son growled, "Sir! Men who desert their comrades in war deserve to be shot! And officers who intercede for them deserve to be hanged!"

Jackson's three divisions were formed around the execution site as the men marched past their compa-nies, which also served as the firing squads. After being blindfolded and tied to stakes, the chaplain led what was described as a prayer "of great earnest."

After the execution, each division filed by the bodies while bands, which had entered playing dirges, switched to a "lively air." Famed artilleryman Willie Pegram found the incident "cold blooded" but "neces-sary to keep the army together."

Jackson, a teetotaler himself, saw the danger to his command presented by hundreds of barrels filled with whiskey, brandy, and wine. "I fear that whiskey more than I do Pope's army," he announced. The barrels were opened and overturned.

"I shall never forget the scene," noted Maj. Roy Mason. "Streams of spirits ran like water through the sands of Manassas and the soldiers on hands and knees drank it greedily from the ground."

Later in the morning Brig. Gen. George W. Taylor marched his New Jersey Brigade, part of Franklin's corps then arriving at the docks of Alexandria, from the Bull Run railroad bridge in response to reports of a "cavalry raid" at Manassas Junction. The satiated Confederates were caught by surprise, but the Federals, believing the napping troops, newly attired in blue uniforms, were Union guards, marched straight into the depot. When the Rebels raised their rifles the Yankees were in a bad situation, caught in a crossfire. The brigade was routed after their commander was fatally wounded. Many Federals were captured in a pursuit by Hill's troops, who also torched the Bull Run bridge.

At the other end of the Federal supply line, Pope had stirred himself to action. Alerted by telegraph of the loss of Manassas Junction at his headquarters at Warrenton Junction, he sent a regiment up the tracks to disperse the expected cavalry raiding force. Encountering the Confederates at Broad Run, they quickly steamed back and gave Pope the bad news. Strong reinforcements were immediately dispatched toward Bristoe Station, and Ewell was soon pressed by an ever-growing force of Union troops. Skirmishing, he withdrew to Manassas Junction to rejoin Jackson.

Jackson now had to survive until Lee arrived with Longstreet's larger corps, hopefully on the following day via Jackson's route.

The Confederates set the vast Federal supply depot at Manassas Junction on fire, then marched off into the darkness. The night sky blazed as the bonfire of Union supplies burned.

Jackson was heading for a site close to the old Manassas battlefield from a year earlier. Wooded Stoney Ridge paralleled the Warrenton turnpike, which ran between Gainesville and Centreville, and the Manassas Gap Railroad. The cut of an unfinished railroad line formed a perfect breastwork.

To confuse Pope's pursuit, Jackson sent his force to Stoney Ridge by three different routes. Taliaferro marched straight to the position; Ewell approached the ridge from the north; and Hill crossed Bull Run and reached Centreville by mistake before doubling back.

Meanwhile, Pope's army had continued to grow. Numbering seventy thousand, it was bereft of unity. Sigel was mistrusted by Pope and placed under the command of Banks, whose corps was shaken from their mauling at Cedar Mountain. Porter's Fifth Corps and Heintzelman's Third Corps had arrived, adding their twenty-three thousand troops to the Army of Virginia, but Pope found Porter listless and indifferent, a McClellan worshiper who often disparaged his new commander. Pope admired the

When four Union regiments approached Manassas Junction, Stonewall Jackson asked the men around him if they were Confederate or Federal. Their weapons were too well polished for the advancing troops to be Confederate, one reasoned, and Jackson agreed.

Union Brig. Gen. George W. Taylor, thinking the lounging men were the depot guard, led his brigade into a deadly crossfire. To stop the unnecessary slaughter, Jackson waved a handkerchief and asked the Federals to surrender. In response, a bullet whistled past Jackson's head, and the Federals were decimated.

As John Pope marched his army across the Virginia countryside, his soldiers grew bored and restive. "I tell you, this damned war will be over and we will never get in a battle," groused a soldier in John Gibbon's Black Hat Brigade just before Jackson's corps marched off Stony Ridge and initiated a vicious battle at Brawner's farm.

The fighting there was the first combat many of the Federals had seen. They welcomed the battle, but it "eradicated our yearning for a fight," wrote one officer. "In our future history we will always be found ready, but never again anxious."

The Rebel yells emanating from the Confederates unnerved the Federals as much as their blazing guns. "That yell," said one Union soldier, "there is nothing like it this side of the infernal region, and the peculiar corkscrew sensation that it sends down your backbone under the circumstances can never be told."

fighting spirit of Joseph Hooker and Philip Kearny while judging their superior, Heintzelman, lacking in leadership. Pope's reserve division near Washington was led by Brig. Gen. Samuel Sturgis, who hated Pope. From Fredericksburg two of Burnside's divisions, under Maj. Gens. Jesse Reno and Isaac Stevens, managed to arrive free of rancor.

Even command of the newest Federal army was in question. Pope believed that when McClellan arrived, Halleck would lead both armies against Lee, as the general in chief had done with Grant at Corinth, Mississippi, during the spring. Pope thought that he and McClellan would direct their respective armies under Halleck's command.

Halleck did not intend this, perhaps being soured on field command by his incredibly slow campaign in the West, which had resulted in the Confederate army's escaping under his nose. McClellan's orders were to forward his units as quickly as possible, which he did slowly, even by his usual standards.

During the early morning of August 27 Pope sent McDowell and Sigel to march north from Warrenton to Gainesville. Later he dispatched Hooker directly from Warrenton Junction to Bristoe Station, which prompted Ewell to withdraw to Manassas. Pope arrived at Bristoe late in the afternoon, examined the remains of the camp, and finally understood that this was not a raid, but Jackson's entire corps. Rather than alarm him, the discovery excited the general. Destroying Jackson would cripple Lee.

A Man of Many Nicknames ■ Nathaniel Prentiss Banks

Born in Waltham, Massachusetts, on January 30, 1816, Nathaniel Prentiss Banks was labeled "the Bobbin Boy of Massachusetts" when he went to work at an early age in the cotton mill that his father supervised. He received little formal learning, but he educated himself in the law and entered the bar at age twenty-three. A persistent man, Banks was defeated for the Massachusetts house seven times before being elected, and he soon became speaker of that body. In 1853 he won the first of ten terms to the U.S. Congress, where he served as a member of five different political parties. After an incredible 133 ballots, Banks reached the pinnacle of his political career by being selected Speaker of

the U.S. House. In 1858 he became governor of Massachusetts.

Motivated purely by politics, Lincoln appointed Banks—a reliable source of votes, recruits, and money—a major general in January 1861. He was given a command in the Shenandoah Valley in the spring of 1862, and Stonewall Jackson taught him what war was about. The Confederates captured such enormous quantities of supplies that they labeled their opponent "Commissary Banks." After being defeated again by Jackson at Cedar Mountain in August, the political general was dispatched in December to clean up the mess left by Benjamin F. Butler on the lower Mississippi.

Extensive and poorly conducted campaigning led Banks to besiege Port

Hudson in May 1863. His two attacks against that bastion were badly executed, and Union soldiers began calling their commander "Napoleon P. Banks," or "Nothing Positive," for his initials. When Port Hudson fell because Ulysses S. Grant had taken Vicksburg, Banks received the official Thanks of Congress, a recognition that was also politically inspired.

During the spring of 1864, Banks commanded an expedition up the Red River to open an avenue of invasion into Texas. After a defeat by inferior Confederates forces, he decided to cancel the campaign, which turned into a disaster as David Dixon Porter's gunboat fleet was almost trapped on the tricky Red. Banks was relieved for his incompetent execution of the campaign.

Banks spent the remainder of his life in the U.S. House, the Massachusetts senate, and as a U.S. marshal. He died in 1894 and is buried in Waltham's Grove Hill Cemetery.

All that remained of the Federal rolling stock on the sidings near the Manassas depot were the wheels. Jackson's men destroyed hundreds of cars when they abandoned the area.

"Pope is a fool, McDowell is a rascal and Halleck has brains but not independence," wrote Fitz John Porter, an ally of George B. McClellan and opponent of McDowell.

To catch the elusive Jackson, Pope ordered Porter, from Warrenton Junction, and the divisions of Kearny, Reno, and Stevens, at Greenwich—a total of six divisions—to pursue Jackson along the railroad. He kept McDowell and Sigel at Gainesville, inadvertently blocking Longstreet's path. Through some wild mental calculation Pope decided this raid preceded Lee's movement to the Shenandoah Valley. He believed Jackson would attempt to escape on the same path he came.

On the morning of August 28 Pope announced a new strategy. He set all his forces in motion toward Manassas Junction, stating, "We shall bag the whole crowd." He called for McDowell and Sigel, from Gainesville, to help annihilate Jackson. He seemed unconcerned that Lee and Longstreet were unaccounted for.

The previous day in Thoroughfare Gap, John Buford's cavalry had skirmished with advancing Confederate troops. Buford perceptively informed McDowell that the second half of the Confederate army was approaching. As a result of this intelligence, McDowell mostly obeyed Pope's orders to concentrate at Manassas, sending Sigel and two of his three divisions. The third, under Ricketts, was used to block Thoroughfare Gap.

As night fell Pope saw Manassas Junction burning on the horizon. He believed Jackson would still be there at dawn. Pope was up before the sun "listening for the opening sounds of battle," reported Lt. Col. David H. Strother. It was noon of August 28 before the first Federals entered the vast, smoking ruins. They marveled at the sight.

The Fifteenth Alabama fired from behind a rotten rail fence at Brawner's farm. One private watched it torn to pieces by Federal fire as a friend stood at his side, "when at once I heard a thud and felt a jar and poor 'Lonzo began to relax and sink, exclaiming in a low tone, 'Oh, Lordy, I am a dead man.' These were his last words but I didn't move but kept loading and firing."

George B. McClellan relished this chance for personal redemption. On July 22 he had written his wife, Ellen, "I see that the Pope bubble is likely to be suddenly collapsed—Stonewall Jackson is after him, & the paltry young man who wanted to teach me the art of war will in less than a week either be in full retreat or badly whipped." McClellan continued in the same vein on August 10, "Pope will be badly thrashed within two days . . . they will be very glad to turn over the redemption of their affairs to me."

Jackson entrenched at the old Manassas battlefield to await the arrival of James Longstreet's corps and Lee, who were retracing his line of march through Thoroughfare Gap. This time the gap was guarded by James B. Ricketts's division, which arrived only minutes before the Confederates. Lee dispatched a brigade over the mountain to attack the Federals from behind.

Stonewall Jackson's nephew Willie Preston joined the Stonewall Brigade just before Second Manassas. It fell to Hunter McGuire to inform Jackson that Preston had been mortally wounded.

"The General's face was a study," he recalled. "The muscles were twitching convulsively and his eyes were all aglow. He gripped me by the shoulder till it hurt me, and in a savage, threatening manner, asked why I had left the boy. In a few seconds he recovered himself and walked off into the woods alone."

"As far as the eye could reach," wrote Strother, "the plain was covered with boxes, barrels, cans, cooking utensils, saddles, sabers, muskets and military equipment generally; hard-bread and cornpones, meat, salt and fresh, beans, blankets, clothes, shoes and hats, from brand new articles just from the original packages to the scarcely recognizable exuviae of the rebels, who had made use of the opportunity to refresh their toilets."

At Manassas Junction Pope was informed that A. P. Hill was in Centreville and apparently headed for Washington—the Confederates had seemingly imposed themselves between him and the nation's capital, whose defense was his highest responsibility. Pope immediately redirected the army to Centreville when, in fact, Hill had merely been misdirected on his way to Stony Ridge.

McDowell rode from Gainesville to Manassas Junction to confer with Pope, where he learned that the commanding general had started toward Centreville. Continuing his quest, McDowell was soon lost in the woods when a shortcut failed to materialize. He would not be heard from again until the following day.

The first half of McDowell's men reached Manassas Junction before detouring toward Centreville, but McDowell's last division to depart

Gainesville, led by King, marched directly to Centreville, a route that would take them past Stony Ridge.

Jackson's three-pronged march, including Hill's misadventure to Centreville, produced so many disparate reports that Pope was hopelessly confused concerning Jackson's objective. A few hours after noon of August 28, the entire Confederate force was resting on the slopes of Stony Ridge.

"The men were packed like herring in a barrel," Capt. Charles M. Blackford remembered. "There was scarce room enough to ride between the long rows of stacked arms, with the men stretched out on the ground between them, laughing and playing cards in all the careless merriment of troops confident in themselves, their cause and their leader. The woods sounded like the hum of a beehive in the warm sunshine of the August day."

Following a long afternoon nap, Jackson mounted and rode atop the ridge to observe the road below. A cavalry patrol had captured a Union courier and brought him out-of-date orders directing Pope's army to Manassas. Fearing the Federals would establish a strong defensive position north of Bull Run, where they would be easily reinforced from Alexandria, Jackson determined to provoke Pope into attacking him south of the stream.

After two Federal brigades passed below Stony Ridge, Jackson rode to his officers. "Here he comes, by God," one said, knowing what would happen next. Jackson saluted and said simply, "Bring up your men, gentlemen."

The troops had been watching their officers. When they rode toward them, "from the woods arose a hoarse roar like that from cages of wild beasts at the scent of blood," recalled Blackford.

Moments before the battle at Brawner's farm began, Virginia Pvt. Joseph Kauffman had written in his diary: "It is now sundown. They are fighting on our right. Oh, to God it would stop." He died within minutes.

When George B. McClellan was slow forwarding troops from Alexandria to Manassas, Henry W. Halleck was reduced to pleading. In a response as bold as any of McClellan's pronouncements, he informed Halleck: "I am not responsible for the past and cannot be for the future, unless I receive authority to dispose of the available troops according to my judgment."

War Criminal Pope

According to John Pope's Order No. 5, his army would "subsist upon the country," giving property owners vouchers redeemable after the war for those who could prove they had been loyal to the United States. Houses from which shots were fired would be burned, their civilian occupants imprisoned. If guerrilla activity developed, civilians within five miles of it "shall be turned out in mass to repair the damage," and would pay the soldiers overseeing their work.

Order No. 11 instructed officers to "arrest all disloyal male citizens within their lines or within their reach." Civilians willing to take an oath of allegiance could remain in their homes, but violation of the oath would result in their execution. Those unwilling to take the oath were to be expelled from Federal territory, and they would be hanged as spies if they returned.

Union troops took the measures as license to steal, particularly after Pope ordered military guards removed from civilian homes. Central Virginia was pillaged as food and possessions were ruthlessly stolen.

"The lawless acts of many of our soldiers are worthy of worse than death," one officer soon recorded. Many other officers agreed.

On July 7, 1862, George B. McClellan had declared that this was not "a war upon people," and such acts "should be treated as high crimes." On August 2 he wrote, "We are not engaged in a war of rapine, revenge, or subjugation." He emphasized the war was not "against population."

The South was outraged at Pope's stance. "They stop at no atrocity," a Charleston newspaper declared, and a Richmond paper declared Pope to be an "enemy of humanity." Protesting to Henry W. Halleck, Robert E. Lee claimed Pope and his associates were "robbers and murderers," and promised to execute a Federal officer for every civilian killed.

"We shall reluctantly be forced to the last resort of accepting the war on the terms chosen by our enemies until the voice of an outraged humanity shall compel a respect for the recognized usages of war," Lee concluded.

Finding Lee's message "exceedingly insulting," Halleck refused to receive it.

After darkness ended the battle, Confederates and Federals scoured the field for the wounded. A Confederate heard a young Federal soldier's cries for help answered by his father. "Charlie, my boy, is that you?" he said.

"Yes," the boy answered. "Father, my leg is broken, but I don't want you to think that is what I am crying for; I fell in a yellow-jackets' nest and they have been stinging me ever since. That is what makes me cry—please pull me out."

The boy soon died in his father's arms.

The Federals had recently gotten a taste of Confederate campaigning. They had marched rapidly across the countryside for days with little sleep, food, or reason. For them it was an unpleasant experience. "Up before dawn, a paltry ration of hard bread given each man, and again, on," wrote Capt. Charles Walcott of Massachusetts. The troops were "scorched by the noonday sun and almost stifled by dust, which lay ankle deep in the road, and sick at heart of General Pope and his strategy, which he had so bombastically told us was going to turn the tide of war in Virginia." The Union troops were exhausted, hungry, and disgusted, marching automatically without thought through the hot, dusty day.

Brig. Gen. John Gibbon first spotted motion in the woods, the disturbing sight of artillery pieces being deployed. Believing it was only the light guns of Stuart's cavalry, Gibbon ordered his own battery into action. He threw out a skirmish line with the Second Wisconsin and Nineteenth Indiana and advanced with them up the slope toward the farmhouse of John Brawner, near Groveton.

Confederate infantry moved forward to support the artillery "in as perfect order as if they had been on parade," Blackford wrote, "their bayonets sparkling in the light of the setting sun and their red battle flags dancing gaily in the breeze." Jackson outnumbered Gibbon sixty-two hundred to twenty-one hundred.

The Southerners emerged abruptly from the woods and fired from seventy-five yards away. Gibbon's raw troops stood their baptism of fire and returned volley after volley. Gibbon was quickly convinced that he had found the wandering Confederate army. He deployed his last two regi-

The Black Hatter ■ John Gibbon

Born April 20, 1827, in Philadelphia, John Gibbon grew up in North Carolina and entered West Point from that state. He was in the middle of the class of 1837 with A. P. Hill and Ambrose E. Burnside. Gibbon fought the Seminoles and the Mexicans, then taught at West Point. Confederate Gen. William Joseph Hardee is known for writing the standard drill manual used by Civil War armies, but in 1860 Gibbon wrote the standard artillery manual. Although three of his brothers chose to fight for the Confederacy, Gibbon remained with the Union.

Making brigadier general on May 2, 1862, Gibbon led the Iron Brigade,

also known as the "Black Hat Brigade" for its unusual felt headgear. The brigade's first battle was against Stonewall Jackson at Groveton, where it distinguished itself by fighting the veteran Confederates for two hours to a draw. Gibbon gained a division in November 1862 and was seriously wounded at Fredericksburg. Three months later he returned to lead a division and corps, displaying great heroism at Gettysburg, where he was again wounded. Resuming active command in the spring of 1864, he led a division at the Wilderness, Spotsylvania, Cold Harbor, and Petersburg, where he was commissioned a

major general. In January 1865 he received a corps in the Army of the James. Gibbon was one of the designated commissioners who received Lee's surrender at Appomattox.

Gibbon spent the next twenty years fighting Indians in the West, where he buried George Armstrong Custer's unfortunate command after the battle of Little Big Horn and defeated the Nez Perce Indians. He retired a regular army brigadier in 1891 and died at his Baltimore home on February 6, 1896. Gibbon is buried at Arlington National Cemetery.

BATTLES AND LEADERS

The frantic pace and confusion resulting from Pope's marches across northern Virginia prevented his tired troops from receiving regular rations. When a commissary officer informed Pope that a trainload of food had reached Bristoe Station, Pope barked at him, "Return to your post. When I want rations I will send for them." The soldiers remained unfed. "Their stomachs were as empty as their cartridge boxes," complained a Union general during the battle.

Very late in the afternoon of August 28, Jackson surprised Rufus King's division near Groveton on the Warrenton turnpike. Much of the fighting occurred on the property of the John Brawner farm, but the heavy woods that had concealed the Confederates also prevented them from exploiting their superior numbers against the Federals. Above, Union batteries fire over the turnpike and into the trees that defined the Southerners' line.

ments, the Sixth and Seventh Wisconsin, and requested help from King's other brigades.

Until dusk fell an hour and a half later, the two sides blazed away at each other from short range. "They stood as immovable as the painted heroes in a battle-piece," remembered Taliaferro, praising the conduct of both sides, "and although they could not advance, they would not retire. There was some discipline in this but there was much more of true valor." As dusk fell, Union Maj. Rufus Dawes "could see by the lurid light of the powder flashes the whole of both lines."

King, sick and suffering from an epileptic seizure the previous day, did nothing. Only one brigade responded to Gibbon's plea, that of Brig. Gen. Abner Doubleday. His Seventy-sixth Wisconsin, another green regiment, plugged a gap between the Sixth and Seventh Wisconsin and restored the line. In the darkness the Federals withdrew slowly, fighting well. The Confederates declined to pursue.

"The best blood of Wisconsin and Indiana was poured out like water, and it was spilled for

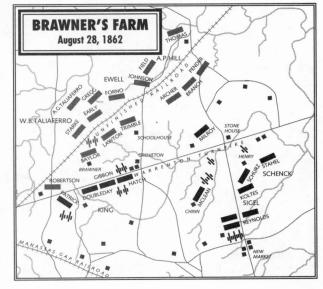

BRAWNER'S FARM
August 28, 1862

When the Twenty-ninth and Fifty-fourth New York stampeded after their first attack against Jackson's position, officers re-formed them with "bursts of lively language and an incidental slap with the flat of their blades," one recalled. "Never mind, boys!" he shouted. "Such things may happen to the best of soldiers. Now forward with a hurrah!" They returned to the fray and acquitted themselves.

John Reuhle of Michigan compared the artillery fire he encountered to a storm. "We had to pass through a perfect hail of grape and canister, which ripped the soil under our feet," he wrote. "In noticeable gusts the missiles swept through our ranks."

naught," Dawes wrote angrily. They had lost 900 men. Other Union casualties only totaled 400. The Second Wisconsin lost 298 of 500 men.

"The bodies lay in so straight a line that they looked like troops lying down to rest," Blackford noted the following day. "On each front the edge was sharply defined, while towards the rear of each it was less so, showing how men had staggered backward after receiving their death blow." Jackson counted thirteen hundred casualties, including Taliaferro, wounded three times, and Ewell, who lost a leg.

King and Gibbon faced a dilemma. Pope's orders were to continue to Centreville, but he could not be located. Their own corps commander, McDowell, had disappeared. The two agreed to withdraw to Manassas Junction, leaving their seriously wounded behind. The commander of McDowell's second division, Brig. Gen. John Reynolds, happened to hear of their decision and halted his advance to join them.

Lee had worried that Pope would block Thoroughfare Gap, but a courier from Jackson who reached him earlier in the day reported no enemy troops there. Longstreet drove Buford's cavalry before him but soon encountered Ricketts's division, which reached the pass minutes before the Confederates. Lee found four regiments with attendant artillery batteries jammed into the narrow gap. Longstreet later remarked that "this placed us in a desperate situation."

From a ridge Lee surveyed the scene with his field glasses. He sent one division through a rough pass five miles to the north, but the road proved too primitive to pass any number of troops to flank Thoroughfare Gap. Hood was instructed to have Col. Evander M. Law's brigade climb a pinnacle overlooking the gap and take the Federals from the rear. Hood also dispatched brigades to scale the other side of the steep pass, but they made little progress. Law's mission was nearly impossible. He lost his guide but continued on "through the tangled woods and huge rocks until the crest was reached," Law wrote, where he found the path blocked by a sheer rock wall. Locating a crevice eight feet off the ground, the brigade was boosted up and over one man at a time.

In the midst of this operation the sounds of battle started to the east and rapidly grew louder. "Each gun sounded like a call for help," Law remembered, a sentiment shared by an anxious Lee.

BATTLES AND LEADERS

Word of the fighting at Brawner's farm reached Pope, who redirected his army from Centreville to a position on the old Manassas battlefield. As his troops lined up for battle, he thought he was facing only Jackson; he had not yet heard that Lee and Longstreet had moved through Thoroughfare Gap.

Law's brigade formed on the down slope and advanced on the Federal rear. Outflanked, Ricketts's men withdrew. Unable to locate McDowell, Ricketts continued through Gainesville and marched southeast to Bristoe, informing no one of Longstreet's arrival.

In camp at Centreville that night, Pope also heard the guns, but he was satisfied that Jackson had been located and trapped. In the morning the force with him, twenty-five thousand strong, advancing from the east, and McDowell, with a similar number attacking from the west, would destroy Jackson between them. During the night Pope ordered Porter to march from his position at Bristoe Station to Centreville, setting up a three-way pincers movement. Drafting his own orders that night, Porter asked rhetorically, "How do you spell *chaos?*"

Learning that McDowell had disappeared, Pope cursed him, adding, "He's never where I want him." Unable to direct McDowell's crucial corps, Pope was forced to revise his plans. From their various positions across northern Virginia, Pope directed his army to find and attack Jackson.

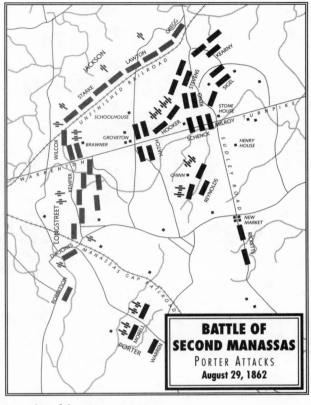

BATTLE OF SECOND MANASSAS
PORTER ATTACKS
August 29, 1862

The situation was indeed chaotic, and Pope remained ignorant not only of Longstreet's appearance but of the condition of his own tired and hungry men.

By daylight of August 29, Jackson was strongly positioned behind and along the railroad embankment atop Stony Ridge. His three-thousand-yard-long line extended from the Warrenton turnpike to Sudley Ford on

The Epileptic ■ Rufus King

Born into a noted family (his father was president of Columbia College) on January 26, 1814, in New York City, Rufus King graduated from West Point in 1833 but resigned in 1837. For twenty years he owned and edited a variety of newspapers while holding several public positions in New York and Wisconsin. Briefly appointed minister to the Papal States by Abraham Lincoln, King resigned his post after the fall of Fort Sumter and became a brigadier of volunteers. He raised the fabled Iron Brigade but did not lead it. King served in Washington's defenses during the war's first winter and led a division under Irwin McDowell in early 1862, missing the Peninsula and Seven Days' campaigns.

After Stonewall Jackson gained John Pope's rear in the Second Manassas campaign, McDowell posted James B. Ricketts in Thoroughfare Gap and King at Gainesville to prevent Lee from uniting his army. When King withdrew without orders, Ricketts was forced to do likewise, which allowed James Longstreet to join Jackson. King fought well at Groveton, primarily because of John Gibbon's leadership, but he was rumored to have been drunk during the battle. In fact, King suffered several epileptic episodes.

McDowell called a court of inquiry, and King was found guilty of willful disobedience of orders. Incredibly, King was then appointed to the court-martial of Fitz John Porter, accused of similar behavior in the same battle.

King resigned in 1863 and served six years in government posts before retiring in 1869. He died in New York on October 13, 1876, and is buried in Grace Churchyard, Jamaica, Long Island.

The first fighting of the second day of the battle of Second Manassas began on the morning of August 29 along a two-mile front. Elements of Pope's army tangled with Jackson's troops in piecemeal fashion, and the fighting escalated. Longstreet's corps and Lee appeared on the field around ten o'clock, and the number of Confederate troops swelled to fifty thousand. Pope did not reach the battlefield until one o'clock that afternoon, and he was unaware that Lee's army had reunited that morning. Federal assaults temporarily breached the left side of Jackson's line in the late afternoon but were thrown back.

To delay Fitz John Porter and Irwin McDowell until Confederate reinforcements could arrive, Jeb Stuart ordered his men to cut brush and limbs and drag them along the Manassas-Centreville road. They raised enough dust to convince the Federals that a large force was advancing toward them.

Bull Run. Pope attacked. His disjointed army hurled itself against Jackson as it arrived in a series of piecemeal assaults, primarily against Jackson's left, but all were repulsed.

After negotiating Thoroughfare Gap, Longstreet's corps slept several hours then continued east through Haymarket and Gainesville, where they gained the Warrenton turnpike and marched toward Stony Ridge. Lee was near the head of the column with Hood's division, which marched with grim determination to relieve Jackson. Several times they had gotten so far ahead of the other units that Longstreet ordered them to slow down.

Longstreet arrived at 10:30 A.M. and extended Jackson's right across the turnpike to the Manassas Gap Railroad. The four-mile-long line had four artillery batteries placed atop a ridge in the center.

Jackson reported his situation to Lee while Longstreet scouted the countryside. Fighting intensified as Stuart reported a Federal buildup on the Confederate right.

"Hadn't we better move our line forward?" Lee asked Longstreet, anxious to attack and relieve Jackson.

LESLIE'S

The largest attack of the day was launched at five o'clock by Philip Kearny's division. By nightfall Pope finally realized that Jackson was not alone. The next afternoon, from Henry Hill, formerly the site of Jackson's first fight more than a year previous, artist Alfred Waud sketched John Fitz Porter's assault against Jackson's corps. Pope's regiments are arrayed across the fields and into the distance, and on the left Robert H. Milroy's brigade is redeployed toward Chinn Ridge. Waud's original sketch is below.

"I think not," came the unexpected reply. Longstreet was dissatisfied with the terrain and wanted intelligence concerning the enemy on his right flank.

Stuart's men determined that the approaching troops were Porter's Fifth Corps and the division of the ailing King, who had relinquished command to Brig. Gen. John P. Hatch. Porter and Hatch had a world of problems.

Porter's lead division commander, Maj. Gen. George Morell, spotted Confederate cavalry ahead and advised Porter to halt until they knew what was ahead. At this time an order from Pope arrived urging Porter and McDowell to advance to Gainesville, which would have meant marching past Jackson and through Longstreet, although they did not know the latter was present.

McDowell also appeared, finally, from the wilderness, bearing an alarming dispatch from cavalry commander Buford. It reported that seventeen infantry regiments, one battery, and five hundred cavalry had passed through

Shot in the buttocks, one private tenaciously refused orders to go to the rear for treatment. When a sergeant persisted, the private swore and said he would not leave the firing line until he "received a more honorable wound."

LIBRARY OF CONGRESS

Col. Billy Wilson told his Georgians, "Boys we have come back to our old stomping ground. If any of you kill a Yankee, put on his shoes quick and if you get into a scuttler store, eat all the cheese and crackers you can possibly hold. And, if you get any good cigars, give old Billy two. Forward!"

Gainesville earlier that morning. McDowell now knew that Lee's entire army was united here, but he neglected to alert Pope.

Gainesville was straight ahead, and Porter expressed a fear that advancing would bring on a battle. "I thought that was why we were here," retorted McDowell, but he too decided not to continue in that direction. McDowell elected to take Hatch's division north to join Pope, who was riding from Centreville on the Warrenton turnpike.

Arriving at noon, Pope established his headquarters near the Stone House, where the Warrenton turnpike and Sudley road intersected. Throughout the morning Sigel, with heavy artillery support, had attacked Jackson's left piecemeal. Despite the arrival of twenty thousand reinforcements with Heintzelman's entire corps and the divisions of Reno and Stevens, the uncoordinated attacks continued to be repulsed.

Jackson's first crisis occurred at 3 P.M. when the brigade of Brig. Gen. Cuvier Grover attacked through heavy woods and up toward the railroad cut. Grover rode his line urging the troops to fire one volley and charge with the bayonet. The Confederates could only fire one round as the Federals emerged from the trees, then the enemy reached the embankment and leaped into the cut. Two Union regiments poured through an undefended length of the ridge and broke the Confederate line. "Many of the enemy were bayoneted in their tracks," Grover remembered, "and others struck down by the butts of pieces."

Grover broke a second Confederate line, but the third stood firm. The Federal attack faltered for lack of support, the result of continuing uncoordinated assaults. The Rebels hurled the weakened brigade back, inflicting 486 casualties on Grover's 1,500-man command.

Hooker and Reno made spirited but independent assaults, and Jackson's line remained intact until 5 P.M., when the fierce Kearny attacked

Kearny Throws a Fit

While Franz Sigel's men battled desperately against Stonewall Jackson, he waited in vain for a promised supporting attack by Philip Kearny's division, but those Federals engaged the Southerners in another part of the battlefield and created yet another combat controversy.

"The orders to Kearny were to attack immediately," remembered Gen. Samuel Heintzelman. "There was so long a delay that I sent him a second order to move at once. The message brought me was that he

was delaying to care for his division. Why it took so long I never learned, but I only know that the reply I got was very unsatisfactory."

Brig. Gen. Carl Schurz, whose division Kearny failed to support, believed "we might have succeeded in destroying the enemy's left wing, and thus gained decisive results before General Longstreet's arrival."

This was certainly not the aggressive Kearny history has lionized, and it seems that petty politics was the cause. Although Sigel and Kearny

had never met, Kearny had written a letter to the governor of New Jersey that included criticism of German-American soldiers. Sigel, a leader among German immigrants, had obtained a copy of the letter and had it widely published in newspapers. Kearny had obviously never meant the letter for public consumption and was enraged by Sigel's actions, believing his message had been misconstrued.

"I fancied General Sigel as extremely arrogant," Kearny would say.

Kearny ignored his orders to attack as he had Pope's order to march the night before. He had been so rude when the order arrived that Kearny later wrote a letter of apology to Brig. Gen. Adolph von Steinwehr "for what I said in reference to being commanded by an officer of a foreign country."

It was regrettable that his pique resulted in the wasted lives of Union soldiers. The reasons for Kearny's action, or inaction, will never be known. He was killed days later at Chantilly.

Jackson's extreme left near Sudley Ford. He advanced in typical fashion shouting, "Fall in here, you sons of bitches, and I'll make major generals of every one of you!"

They struck Maxey Gregg's South Carolina Brigade, which had repulsed six earlier attacks. Their ranks thinned and ammunition low, the Southerners retreated to a hill two hundred yards beyond the railroad embankment. When the Federal assault petered out, the Confederates pushed them back again.

"It was a fearfully long day," wrote Capt. Henry Kyd Douglas, Jackson's aide. "For the first time in my life I understood what was meant by 'Joshua's sun standing still on Gideon,' for it would not go down. No one knows how much time can be crowded into an hour unless he has been under the fire of a desperate battle waiting for a turning or praying that the great red sun, blazing and motionless overhead, would go down."

A. P. Hill asked Gregg if his men could stand another attack. Yes, he replied, according to an officer, although "his ammunition was about expended but he still had the bayonet." Confederates hurriedly stripped the dead and wounded of desperately needed cartridges. If this flank crumbled, the thin line on the ridge would be rolled up and the corps destroyed.

A Confederate counterattack captured three Union guns, but horses were unavailable to haul them back to their line. Quickly Southern soldiers found ropes and harnessed Federal prisoners. "The sight of some fifty Yankees hitched to a piece of artillery, with [Confederates] charging bayonets, coming across the battlefield at a double quick drew forth a burst of laughter from our Confederate boys," recalled Chaplain William Sheeran.

Despite the appearance of Lee's full army on the field in front of him, Pope interpreted every movement as a sign of retreat and viewed most of the fighting of the morning of August 30 as a rear-guard action. He hurled Fitz John Porter's corps against the right side of Jackson's line and ignored reports of a large Southern buildup on the left flank of his own line. When Porter's men entered the open fields west of Groveton, they were raked mercilessly by Confederate batteries and then encountered Southern infantry in force along the grade of an unfinished railroad.

As the Federals withdrew in disorder from the twilight fighting, Maj. Charles Livingston attempted unsuccessfully to stop the retreating troops. Finding one regiment marching back in order, he attempted to turn them back to the fight. When an officer demanded his name, he replied, "Major Livingston of the Seventy-sixth New York."

"Well, then, you are my prisoner," came the reply, "for you are attempting to rally the Second Mississippi."

Hill was realistic. He informed Jackson that while his men would fight to the last, he doubted whether they could hold out much longer. An aide noted that the statement "seemed to deepen the shadow on Jackson's face."

"General," Jackson told Hill calmly, "your men have done nobly; if you are attacked again you will beat the enemy back."

Jackson was interrupted by the sounds of renewed fighting on the left. "Here it comes," Hill said, riding off.

"I'll expect you to beat them," Jackson shouted at his back.

On the left, Gregg paced his position, exhorting his men to stand firm. "Let us die here, my men, let us die here," he chanted.

"We could hear the enemy advancing through brush," recalled Lt. Col. Edward McCrady, "and had not a round to greet them, but must meet the onslaught with only our bayonets. On they came."

As the Federal charge bore in, Jackson reinforced the line with regiments of Virginians and North Carolinians. They raced down the embankment with lowered bayonet and routed the Federals.

Hill sent the news to Jackson: "General Hill presents his compliments and says the attack of the enemy was repulsed." Smiling, Jackson replied, "Tell him I knew he would do it."

Two hours later an order from Pope reached Porter, still frozen five miles south at the opposite end of the line, just below the Manassas Gap Railroad.

"Your line of march brings you in on the enemy's right flank. I desire you to push into action at once."

For no accountable reason Porter still had little knowledge of what faced him. He hesitated to attack, using the late hour as an excuse, and made no move.

Thrice Lee advised Longstreet to attack, but the Georgian felt it was not yet time. He did send Hood to occupy Hatch, advanced by McDowell, and they battled until dusk astride the Warrenton turnpike at Groveton.

"Tardy George" ■ George Sykes

Born in Dover, Delaware, on October 9, 1822, George Sykes graduated from West Point in 1842, a class that provided twelve army and corps commanders in the Civil War. He campaigned against the Seminoles and Mexicans, winning one brevet, and Indians in the West. As a major leading a battalion of regular army soldiers, his troops fought better than any other Federals at First Manassas and covered the retreat.

Made a brigadier of volunteers on September 28, 1861, Sykes led a brigade and then a division, mostly regulars who fought on the Peninsula and during the Seven Days. At Second Manassas his men stopped the Confederate attack and again covered the Union withdrawal. Held in reserve during Antietam and Fredericksburg, Sykes was not routed at Chancellorsville. He took command of the Fifth Corps when George Gordon

Meade became army commander and defended the Federal left at Gettysburg. His forte was defense, but a failed offensive assignment at Mine Run caused Meade to relieve him in December 1863.

Sykes served in Kentucky for the remainder of the war then was stationed in various western posts until his death on February 8, 1880, at Fort Brown (Brownsville), Texas. He is buried at West Point.

LIBRARY OF CONGRESS

In the face of heavy fire, two Union regiments raced across the open field toward the unfinished railroad. Few shots were fired into the Southern ranks until the Federals found cover. Then they unleashed a volley that forced the Confederates to seek refuge, and both sides huddled against opposite sides of the excavation for protection.

Robert E. Lee was never seriously wounded in combat, but at Second Manassas he had his closest brush with death. After scouting forward, Lee told Maj. Charles S. Venable, "A Yankee sharpshooter came near killing me just now." Venable wrote, "We could see how near it was as his cheek had been grazed by the bullet."

Forward of the line held by Jackson and Longstreet, Hood withdrew in the night and Jackson's troops fell back for desperately needed ammunition.

At dawn on August 30 Pope was livid at Porter's refusal to attack the previous day. Pope entertained the notion that Porter's inaction was a deliberate act intended to bring about a defeat that might result in McClellan's return to command.

McClellan was not far away, at Alexandria with two full corps—Franklin's Sixth and Sumner's Second—and plentiful supplies that would certainly help Pope's soldiers at this point. McClellan informed Pope that he would dispatch a supply train if Pope sent a cavalry escort for it. "Such a letter," Pope would write, "when we were fighting the enemy and when Alexandria was full of troops, needs no comment."

Pope persisted in refusing to believe that Longstreet had reached the field, even though the Georgian had been present for an entire day. The Union commander also dismissed Buford's detailed report of a Confederate corps passing through Gainesville thirty hours earlier. Pope might have been justified in rejecting Porter's claim that a large Rebel force faced him considerably south of Jackson's position, but Hatch had been involved in a savage fight the previous evening with a concrete enemy on the turnpike.

Instead, Pope interpreted the movements of Hood and Jackson during the night as a general retreat to rejoin Lee. Accordingly, he ordered McDowell to pursue the beaten enemy. Pope directed Porter to move north

Stonewall Jackson's line bent but never broke. At one point a regiment of South Carolinians was retreating when a lieutenant spotted a normally reliable soldier making for the rear. "Benson, for God's sake, stop!" the officer shouted. Benson, finding "the appeal was irresistible," halted and helped re-form the line.

Three Union brigades and three Confederate brigades, only yards apart in places, slugged it out on the unfinished railroad. As the fighting progressed, the Southerners exhausted their ammunition. While some scavenged the dead and wounded, others waited for orders. Then one of the men shouted, "Boys, give 'em rocks," and those with empty rifles reached down and started lobbing rocks at their attackers. Some of the Federals returned "fire," and a rock-throwing melee broke out, but the attack was spent and Confederate reinforcements arrived.

As reinforcements arrived to push the Federals back down the embankment of the unfinished railroad, they were wildly cheered by the defenders. When gunners leaped atop their cannon to cheer, Col. Stephen D. Lee growled, "Less halloing and more firing!"

"Captain, the Yankees are running!" another soldier shouted. "Let us give thanks."

"Give them a few more shots first," Capt. W. W. Parker yelled. Thanks could wait for later.

So many shell explosions peppered the retreat that one Federal officer thought the "ground looked like a mill pond in a shower." Withdrawal seemed so deadly that many Federals slithered across the embankment and surrendered. "The slope was swept by a hurricane of death," wrote one Federal officer who attacked the railroad embankment, "and each minute seemed twenty hours long."

of his present position, which blocked Longstreet, to pursue Jackson west along the Warrenton turnpike. Ricketts's division, arriving from Bristoe Station after apparently fighting phantom Confederates at Thoroughfare Gap, would pursue west on the Sudley Springs–Haymarket road.

Ricketts's orders arrived while the general was enduring intense rifle fire. The orders "both surprised and annoyed" him, noted the messenger, Lt. Col. David H. Strother. "He told me that, far from retreating, the enemy was pressing him so heavily that he was not even sure of being able to maintain himself." The reply startled Pope, forcing him to reconsider the situation.

With Ricketts stalled and Pope, Reynolds, Porter, and Hatch advancing in the center, unknowingly directly toward Longstreet, resistance quickly thickened until Reynolds's lead troops stopped their advance around 1:30. "Impossible!" Reynolds replied to their claims that a heavy Confederate force was directly ahead. Then he saw the Rebels as they fired a volley that killed his orderly. Reynolds raced east to inform Pope.

"General Pope, the enemy is turning our left!" Reynolds shouted.

"Oh, I guess not," was Pope's calm reply.

At the same time Jackson's resupplied men let Porter's corps know they had not gone anywhere, opening fire with a vengeance from the ridge.

McDowell, commanding the advance, called Reynolds north to support Porter. All that remained opposite Longstreet on the Confederate right was Lt. Charles Hazlett's six-gun battery and a two regiment brigade of one thousand men under Col. Gouverneur K. Warren. As Porter assaulted Jackson on Stony Ridge, the Confederate artillery opened.

"The march had scarce begun," Confederate Captain Blackford remembered, "when little puffs of smoke appeared, dotting the field in rapid succession just over the heads of the men, and as the lines moved on, where each little puff had been lay a pile of bodies. But still the march continued with thinned but unshaken ranks until within pistol-shot of our lines."

Then the Confederate infantry opened fire. "Through a bursting cloud of light blue smoke gleamed a deadly flash of flame," Blackford continued. "The first line of the attacking column looked as if it had been struck by a blast from a tempest and had been blown away."

Federal dead covered the ground but the massed Union attack felled Confederates, who fired so quickly that ammunition ran short again. Grabbing stone ballast from the railroad cut, the Southerners let fly, felling a number of attackers who lapped closer and closer to the embankment. In moments the Twenty-first New York lost three color-bearers. Maj. Andrew Barnes rode atop the embankment urging his troops on until he was killed. The Stonewall Brigade's commander, Col. William Baylor, died leading a counterattack.

Jackson was desperate, asking Longstreet for a division of reinforcements. Longstreet cooly replied, "Certainly, but before the division can reach him, that attack will be broken by artillery."

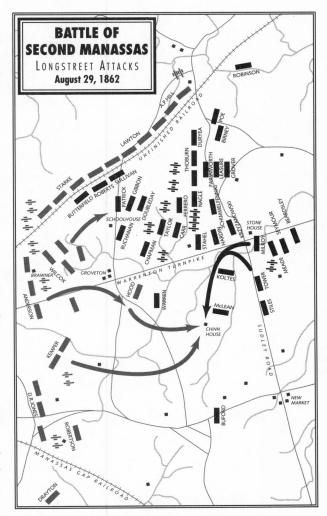

BATTLE OF SECOND MANASSAS
LONGSTREET ATTACKS
August 29, 1862

Pope's Generals at War—With Him

During the Second Manassas campaign, Federal generals fought more among themselves than they did with the Confederates. At the beginning of the battle, John Pope blamed Irwin McDowell for the confusion that he himself had generated. "God damn McDowell," Pope thundered. "He is never where he ought to be."

On the night of August 28 McDowell could not determine the best disposition of his corps. Gen. Franz Sigel told him "that as soon as he had come to an understanding with himself he should please notify me," and went to bed.

Receiving yet another marching order, Philip Kearny told the courier, "Tell General Pope to go to Hell. We won't march before morning."

Jesse Reno, believing an attack was suicidal, halted it and rode to Pope to personally protest the order. "We thanked God that General Reno stood between us and General Pope," a soldier remembered.

"Everything here is at sixes and seven," wrote Fitz John Porter on August 27, "and I find I am to take care of myself in every respect." On August 28 Porter continued in the same vein: "All that talk of bagging Jackson &c., was bosh." Further disgusted by events on August 29, Porter penned, "I hope Mac is at work, and we will soon get ordered out of this." Porter received another confusing order from Pope on August 29 that concluded with: "If any considerable advantages are to be gained by departing from this order it will not be strictly carried out"—a license to disobey if ever one was written.

When a part of the Confederate line in the railroad cut was temporarily overrun, rifle butts, bayonets, and knives were used freely. Lunging with a big knife at a Confederate, Sgt. Frank Wasley of New Hampshire heard the man shout, "Oh, for God's sake, *don't!*" For some reason Wasley stopped. "All right, Johnny!" he replied, and spared him.

Twenty-two guns opened on the fully exposed Federal left flank. Within fifteen minutes the Federals started to run for the rear, caught by surprise on the flank and finding an implacable foe above them on the ridge.

Only then, at 4 P.M., did Longstreet's thirty thousand troops advance into the open. The sight struck Pope dumb with astonishment. It was one of the greatest surprises of the Civil War.

Against this onslaught Hazlett and Warren's Fifth and Tenth New York briefly stood their ground. Hood's Texas Brigade felled many of the Tenth, driving the survivors into the Fifth as the Texans fired again, the passing bullets sounding like "an immense flock of partridges," recalled Federal Pvt. Andrew Coats. Another noted a "continual hiss and sluck, the last sound telling that the bullet had gone into some man's body."

The Fifth New York returned fire as the Confederates enveloped both flanks, felling nine of ten men in the regimental color guard. "Where the regiment stood that day was the very vortex of Hell," one member recalled. The din prevented anyone from hearing Warren's orders to withdraw. The Texans' fire from both flanks "virtually wiped them off the face of the earth," a Confederate said. "I never could understand why this fine regiment would make the stand they did until nearly every one was killed."

After one Federal volley the "Texans didn't give them time to reload," remembered one of Hood's men, "but with fixed bayonets moved upon

John Pope's Scapegoat ■ Fitz John Porter

Fitz John Porter, a native of Portsmouth, New Hampshire, was born August 31, 1822, into a family with a history of naval service. His father had been a captain; one uncle was Como. David Porter, and two cousins were Adm. David Dixon Porter and Como. William D. Porter. Fitz John chose West Point, from which he graduated in 1845, eighth in the class. He won two brevets for gallantry, to captain and major, while serving under Winfield Scott in Mexico. Six years of teaching artillery at West Point followed, then Porter served as Albert Sidney Johnston's adjutant on the Utah expedition.

Porter, a colonel when the war started, was commissioned a brigadier of volunteers on August 7, 1861, becoming the eighth-highest-ranking officer of volunteers. George B. McClellan persuaded Porter to join

the Army of the Potomac, where he led a division on the peninsula and the Fifth Corps during the Seven Days, fighting heroically and largely alone at Mechanicsville and Gaines's Mill. After a well-executed retreat, he fought again at Malvern Hill.

This distinguished service under McClellan won him promotion to major general of volunteers and brevet brigadier in the regular army. Blindly loyal to McClellan, Porter hated service under John Pope and was intemperate in his vocal remarks and written documents concerning his opinion of the new commander.

Porter performed as well as any Federal at Second Manassas and served through the Antietam campaign. Second Manassas had not ended before Pope decided to blame his failure on Porter. In November, Porter was relieved of command and

charged with disobedience and misconduct in the face of the enemy for failure to obey impossible orders issued by a confused superior.

The court-martial was stacked with officers under the influence of Secretary of War Edwin M. Stanton. Because McClellan was politically untouchable, Stanton chose to strike at the general through Porter. The trial was faulty from the start and shot through with dishonest testimony. Found guilty, Porter was dismissed from the service on January 21, 1863.

Porter spent the remainder of his life attempting to clear his name. Sixteen years later, in 1879, a military board completely exonerated him of all charges. The board declared that Porter had saved the Army of Virginia at Second Manassas and recommended that his rank be reinstated. That was delayed by the

political situation until 1886, when President Grover Cleveland restored Porter's name to the army's roll as a colonel dating to May 14, 1861.

Porter died at his home in Morristown, New Jersey, on May 21, 1901, and is buried at Green-Wood Cemetery in Brooklyn, New York.

LIBRARY OF CONGRESS

When Porter began to withdraw and other Federal units were repositioned to bolster the middle of the Union line, Lee and Longstreet, from their vantage point near the Confederate batteries (above), sensed the decisive moment of the battle had come. At four o'clock Longstreet's men fell on the left flank of the Union army, and a panic swept through the Federal ranks.

John Bell Hood's Texas Brigade slaughtered the Fifth New York Zouaves, which lost 297 of their 490-man complement. One Texan looked at the field where colorfully uniformed soldiers lay, giving "the appearance of a Texas hillside when carpeted in the spring by wild flowers of many hues and tints."

The Texans next fell upon the battery of Capt. Mark Kerns, whose gunners fled. Alone, Kerns loaded canister in one piece and prepared to fire. Charging Confederates ordered him to surrender, but Kerns yanked the lanyard, killing and maiming many Southerners at point-blank range. Kerns was mortally wounded by numerous bullets. As he died, Confederates heard him say, "I promised to drive you back or die under my guns, and I have kept my word."

them and getting within eight or ten paces emptied their guns at them— they couldn't stand but fled, we killing them at every step." For the second time in a year, Young's Branch "ran red," the Confederate continued, "completely damned . . . with their dead and dying bodies." Warren and 193 men survived; 297 were casualties, the largest percentage loss of any Union regiment during the entire war.

When the order was given, John Bell Hood's Texas Brigade smashed into the Fifth and Tenth New York on the weak Union left. Within a matter of minutes the two Federal units were destroyed. One of the Union privates in the fighting recalled, "Where the regiment stood that day was the very vortex of Hell. Not only were men wounded, or killed, they were riddled."

LIBRARY OF CONGRESS

Some enlisted men in the Fifth New York hated their commander, Cleveland Winslow, a notoriously sharp dresser. "You would think he was some foreign count to see him all rigged up for dress parade," wrote Pvt. Alfred Davenport. "He thinks he is the beau ideal of a man, but he looks to us more like a damned fool." Winslow was also overly fond of bugle calls. Davenport thought he had "calls for everything except the call of nature, which I suppose keeps him awake at night thinking how he will manage that."

BATTLE OF SECOND MANASSAS
The Federal Retreat
August 29, 1862

The hill beyond the creek was held by Capt. Mark Kerns's Pennsylvania Artillery. Many gunners fled from the terrifying sight of the Confederate masses surging up the slope. Kerns stood alone, refusing to surrender and firing a load of canister at point-blank range. He died beside his guns.

Greater Confederate success could have been realized but Longstreet attacked alone for two hours before Jackson's exhausted men joined the pursuit. Pope used the time to shift troops and reinforce the crumbled left flank. It was imperative that the Federals hold the Warrenton turnpike that crossed Bull Run at the Stone Bridge and led to safety. Two strong defensive positions remained—Chinn Ridge and farther east, across the Sudley road, at Henry Hill, scene of desperate fighting on July 21, 1861.

Chinn Ridge was defended by Col. Nathaniel McLean's brigade, which was reinforced by four additional brigades and a battery. The Federals

The fighting became focused on Chinn Ridge, and some commanders rushed as many men as possible to blunt the Confederate onslaught there. One of these units, the Forty-first New York (below), like many regiments under Franz Sigel, was comprised entirely of German immigrants. They were among the first to reach the ridge and reinforce the collapsing Union line. Impetuously, the Forty-first tried to recover an overrun Union battery; masked by powder smoke, they were caught in between and fired upon by both friend and foe. They retreated up the ridge in disarray.

On the morning of the battle of Second Manassas, Fletcher Webster, Sen. Daniel Webster's son, had written his wife: "This may be my last letter, dear love; for I shall not spare myself—God bless and protect you and the dear, darling children." He was wounded atop Chinn Ridge and died an hour later.

LIBRARY OF CONGRESS

By six o'clock Longstreet's legions had dislodged the defenders of Chinn Ridge, precipitating a panicked retreat. Pope formed a temporary line at Henry Hill and then fell back from there as darkness descended on the battlefield.

were attacked from the front and on their left by Brig. Gen. Nathan Evans's South Carolina Brigade and the division of Brig. Gen. James L. Kemper. Col. Montgomery Corse's Virginians led the assault. With Hood's Texans beside them, they charged the six guns of the Fifth Maine Battery.

The cannon fired, a "horrid roar, then a shock that seemed to shake the very Earth," remembered Virginia Pvt. Alexander Hunter. "Then the dull thud of the balls as they tore their way through the bodies of the men—

Pope Put Out to Pasture

On September 6, 1862, after only seventy-four days in command, John Pope was ordered to "proceed immediately" to put down a rebellion by Sioux Indians in Wisconsin. The gen-eral arrived in Chicago, in his home state, on September 12. That night five thousand people gathered outside his hotel, shouting for a speech as a band played "The Star-Spangled Banner" and, curiously, "Dixie." Pope walked out and spoke from his heart: "My Friends, I am glad to see you to-night. I am glad to be back to breathe again the pure air of the State of Illinois. It has been for many years my home, and I am glad to return to it. God Almighty only knows how sorry I am I ever left it."

John Pope informed Henry W. Halleck that the Confederates were "badly crippled" and "the army entitled to the gratitude of the country." But he wrote, "I should like to know whether you feel secure about Washington should this army be destroyed?"

then the hiss of the grape—and the mingled screams of agony and rage. I looked around me. The ground was filled with the mangled dead and dying." The survivors fell upon the battery, "some foaming at the mouth—they had run mad for the time," Hunter continued. Within moments most of the gunners lay dead among their artillery. Federal troops fled across a front of over a mile.

"The scene was terrible," remembered one Federal. "Pope's whole line, pressed in front and on our flanks, was breaking into fragments and dissolving into a multitude of fugitives."

A few scattered regiments withdrew in order, unable to stop and fight as Confederates now swarmed in from three directions. Officers attempted with little result to rally the panicked soldiers, threatening with pistol and sword and bayonet.

"We got within ten yards of them—and they broke—and in a second they were running for the rear," wrote Hunter. "Their guns were thrown away. They would unstrap their knapsacks as they ran—their hats would fly off—but nothing stopped them."

By 6 P.M. Chinn Ridge was controlled by the Confederates. The nearby turnpike was hopelessly clogged with thousands of soldiers—stragglers and intact regimental columns—artillery, wagons, and horses.

The McDowell Factor

Led by John Pope, many quarters of the Union command blamed Fitz John Porter for the embarrassing defeat at Second Manassas. Other accusations, however, were made regarding Irvin McDowell, who had been one of Pope's principal advisers on the battlefield and who may have been the only corps commander on the field whom Pope trusted. Therefore, McDowell was deeply involved in the decision-making behind Pope's failure on the battlefield, particularly in his concurrence with the false notion of a Confederate retreat on August 30.

Specifically, McDowell twice contributed significantly to the Union defeat. First, for several hours on August 29 he withheld John Buford's message reporting that Longstreet's corps had passed through Gainesville. Second, he committed one of the worst tactical decisions on the battlefield when he withdrew Reynolds's

division from Chinn Ridge immediately prior to Longstreet's attack. Only the timely efforts of other officers and their regiments prevented a greater disaster.

In contrast to the invective poured on Porter from the army and the government, the castigation of McDowell welled up from the ranks of the common soldier, making McDowell the most hated corps commander in any Union army.

A Michigan soldier wrote, "The men are very much exasperated against McDowell, saying that he is a traitor and threatening to shoot him." Another noted, "It is the universal opinion of all that [Second Manassas] was lost to us by the treachery of McD. The officers and men of his own corps in particular denounce him as a traitor."

McDowell's hat became a symbol of derision. Many suggested that its

appearance on the battlefield was a sign to the Southerners. Years later, one veteran observed, "Wherever it appeared on our front, it was a signal to the enemy to cease firing and reserve their ammunition for a more opportune moment. . . . On August 30, wherever the 'Hat' appeared, defeat and disaster followed in quick succession."

The general bore these criticisms well, but then a letter began to circulate in Washington purporting to be the last writings of Col. Thornton Brodhead of the First Michigan Cavalry. He had been mortally wounded at Lewis Ford during the final fighting. Brodhead asserted, "I have fought manfully and now die fearlessly. I am one of the victims of Pope's imbecility and McDowell's treason. Tell the president that to save our country he must not give our flag to such hands."

It was not long before the letter was published in newspapers across the North. None of them failed to portray it as the dying declaration of a hero of the republic.

With the scorn of the country upon him, McDowell demanded and received a court of inquiry. The review convened in November 1862. After the tedious testimony of numerous witnesses, examined by the general himself, the court ruled that the accusations were false. Not all of the testimony, however, had been flattering, and the press continued to examine McDowell for weeks.

In the end, McDowell was a ruined man. He held no command in the field for the remainder of the war. In 1864 he was assigned to the Department of the Pacific. McDowell retired in 1882 and died in San Francisco on May 4, 1885.

The confused resistance had slowed Longstreet, advancing south of the turnpike, but Jackson's men now joined in the attack with renewed energy, exulted to be on the offensive again.

Longstreet's aide, Col. Moxley Sorrel, remembered the infantry and artillery pouring over the ridges in pursuit. "The artillery would gallop furiously to the nearest ridge, limber to the front, deliver a few rounds until the enemy were out of range, and then gallop again to the next ridge." A Union soldier thought that the Rebels "came on like demons emerging from the earth."

Clouds and battle smoke brought dusk on early as a light rain began to fall. Pope finally mounted an organized defense in a sunken segment of the Sudley road at the foot of Henry Hill and atop the ridge itself. The divisions of Reynolds and Sykes, their artillery plus other brigades, took up a strong position on the hill. Confederate artillery, however, harried all movement, "the air shuddering with all the varied pandemoniac notes of shell, round shot, grape, rusty spikes and segments of railroad bars," a Union soldier recalled.

At Second Manassas a Confederate told a prisoner, "When we see General McDowell in command of your troops, we regard it as being better for us than 30,000 reinforcements."

Unlike the chaotic retreat that followed the battle of First Manassas, Pope's army withdrew in order across Bull Run Creek to take up new defensive positions around Centreville. A stubborn rear-guard action by a few Federal units along the Manassas-Sudley road and on Henry Hill held the Southerners at bay. Exhaustion and darkness finally stalled the Confederate pursuit. By midnight all but a few stragglers had crossed Bull Run, and the Federals destroyed the bridge.

A regimental history stated that during the Second Manassas campaign John Pope had been "kicked, cuffed, hustled about, knocked down, run over and trodden upon as rarely happens in the history of war. His communications had been cut; his headquarters pillaged; a corps had marched into his rear and had encamped at its ease upon the railroad by which he received his supplies; he had been beaten or foiled in every attempt he made to 'bag' those defiant intruders; and in the end he was glad to find a refuge in the entrenchments of Washington, from which he had sallied forth, six weeks before, breathing out threatenings and slaughter."

The Federals in the sunken road watched as their comrades emerged from the woods of Chinn Ridge "rushing, panic stricken," wrote Capt. Theodore Lang. The pursuing Confederates were driven back but, he continued, "being reinforced from the masses in their rear, came on again and again, pouring in their advance a perfect hurricane of balls." A Federal battery atop the ridge unloosed a fury of shells, but the Confederates redoubled their fire "and soon the battery gave way, followed by a general stampede on our left, and shortly after, our own line began to show distrust and started by twos and threes to leave the line," Lang concluded.

As they withdrew, Skyes's regular army brigade on Henry Hill "threw off their packs, pulled their cartridge boxes around to the front and knelt down in the grass to await the enemy." This display by cool professionals caused other units to fall in beside them. While the Confederates stopped to realign, the Federals atop Henry Hill grew stronger as Reno deployed a brigade and Sigel brought up another as a reserve.

With half an hour of sun left, the Confederates prepared for one final push. The batteries that had worked such devastation during the day opened with a terrible barrage. "The iron canister balls mowed the foliage from the branches and pelted against the trees and fences ominously," a Union soldier declared.

The Battle of Chantilly

John Pope's army had been decisively defeated, but it remained substantially intact. An effective rear-guard action had allowed the Federals to withdraw, mostly in order, and occupy strong fortifications at Centreville.

Robert E. Lee believed he could hand Pope another sharp reverse before the campaign ended. Centreville and Fairfax Court House farther east were too far from Washington, D.C., for Lee to feel secure about crossing the Potomac River and taking the war north. He wanted the Union army penned up behind the Yankee capital's defenses and fearful of ever leaving them to seek battle again.

After examining the extensive works at Centreville, Lee wisely rejected the idea of a frontal assault. He looked to Pope's right and found what he wanted. From the northwest the Little River turnpike intersected Pope's primary retreat route, the Warrenton turnpike, at Germantown, two miles northwest of Fairfax and seven miles east of Centreville. A successful attack would isolate whatever part of Pope's army remained at Centreveille, and simply threatening a move there would force Centreville's evacuation and perhaps Fairfax's as well.

Stonewall Jackson, on the Confederate left with A. P. Hill, Alexander Lawton, and William Starke, started north in a heavy rain on the afternoon of August 31, crossing Bull Run and turning right on the Gum Springs road, a rough, muddy, narrow road. His men were exhausted from a week of strenuous marching and intense combat, and Jackson, for once, went easy on the troops, even ordering Hill, in the lead, to slow down. The corps camped near Pleasant Valley Church on the Little River turnpike, having covered only eight miles in eight hours. Earlier in the month they had made fifty-four miles in thirty-six hours.

Longstreet, demonstrating against Centreville, was to follow a half day behind, and Stuart, with Fitzhugh Lee and Beverly Robertson, was to screen Jackson. The cavalry had reached Germantown several hours earlier, where they encountered a brigade of William Franklin's infantry. Alerted to a Confederate move on his right, Pope shifted forces in that direction.

Stuart reported the situation at Germantown to Jackson early on September 1. The Federals probed the Confederate right flank. Realizing his precarious position, Jackson slowed, deciding to wait on Longstreet and Lee before taking offensive action against what could be a large portion of Pope's army. At the crossroads of Chantilly, Jackson called a halt and found a promising tree for one of his long naps.

Reports of Jackson's advance provoked Pope into action. He started shifting large numbers of troops from

Isaac Stevens

Reno stalked his line, ordering his men to lie silently on the ground. "We had not long to wait," wrote Captain Walcott. "The sun had set and it was beginning to grow dark when we heard a confused hum and the rush of many feet in our front; stand up was the order and every man was on his feet; the open space in our front was now alive with the rebel masses, and General Reno gave the welcome order, 'Give them about ten rounds, boys. Fire!'"

The Confederates had three hundred yards of open ground to cross, but the devastating fire stopped them cold. As darkness fell with the rain, the Southern attack ended. The Federals remained on Henry Hill as the ruin of Pope's army stumbled past on the turnpike, retreating across Bull Run on the Stone Bridge for the second time in a year.

Kearny, who had fought well in yet another mismanaged campaign, complained bitterly to Gibbon, who commanded the rear guard: "I suppose you appreciate the condition of affairs here, sir? It's another Bull Run, sir, it's another Bull Run!"

"Oh, I hope not quite as bad as that, General," was the reply.

"Perhaps not," Kearny said. "Reno is keeping up the fight. He is not stampeded. I am not stampeded. You are not stampeded. That is about all, sir, my God, that's about all!"

Following Irwin McDowell's involvement in a second decisive defeat at Manassas, the entire army, from generals to privates, hated him. Gen. Alphesus Williams said, "It can with truth be said of him that he had not a friend in his command; from the smallest drummer boy to the highest general officer all *hated* him."

Union Capt. William Lusk was dispirited by the way the army had been led. "The battle comes—there is no head on the field—the men are handed over to be butchered—to die on inglorious fields," he wrote his mother. "Lying reports are written. Political Generals receive praises where they deserve execration. Old Abe makes a joke. . . . Alas, my poor country!"

Centreville to Germantown. To check Jackson until additional units arrived, Pope sent Isaac Stevens (the commander of the Ninth Corps while Jesse Reno was sick) cross-country from the Warrenton turnpike to the Little River turnpike at a point two miles west of Germantown. Stevens

Philip Kearny

BATTLES AND LEADERS

was to attack Jackson, stopping him if possible, but at least slowing the Confederates. Stevens energetically started on his mission with two divisions, followed by Samuel P. Heintzelman's Third Corps.

With Longstreet nearing around noon, Jackson continued his march, reaching the Ox Hill crossroads where the Little River turnpike intersected West Ox Road, the position where Stuart had earlier discovered a sizable body of Federal soldiers. When a probe was handily repulsed, Jackson prudently elected to wait for Longstreet, but the Federals refused to give him the time. A terrible storm was moving in at 5 P.M. when Stevens struck a heavy blow to Jackson's flank. Fierce fighting occurred as Stevens pushed his way to the front, passing his wounded son, Capt. Hazard Stevens, to personally lead

the attack. Taking the colors of the Seventy-ninth New York Highlanders, his first command, the general led his men forward until a bullet struck him in the head. Stevens's death stopped the drive as a thunderstorm, described by many participants as the most intense they had ever seen, broke over the battlefield. Thunder drowned out the sound of artillery firing and the sky was lit by apocalyptic streaks of lightning.

In response to a desperate plea for assistance from Stevens, a division of Heintzelman's under Philip Kearny arrived as a Confederate counter-attack was launched. Finding Stevens's men milling about in confusion and under heavy attack, Reno moved to relieve the pressure on them by sending Brig. Gen. David B. Birney's brigade against the Confederate right flank. When Birney

pointed out a gap in his line, Kearny chose the Twenty-first Massachusetts to make an assault, but its members were anxious about the strength of Confederates opposing them in a cornfield. His legendary wrath aroused, Kearny rode forward to see for himself. He found Confederates there in strength, and when he refused to surrender, Kearny was shot dead from his horse.

Desultory combat continued until 6:30 P.M., when the weather and darkness caused the inconclusive battle to sputter out. The Federals withdrew to Fairfax, and with Centreville abandoned, Pope continued to Washington. Casualties were 138 Federal soldiers killed and 472 wounded. For the Confederates there were 83 killed and 418 wounded. Lee had gained his opportunity to change the character of the war.

On September 2 John Pope and Irwin McDowell, retreating to Washington, encountered George B. McClellan, who was riding to the sounds of the guns. As Pope continued to the rear, John P. Hatch, a bitter enemy of Pope, was leading his division past the commanders and shouted to his men, "Boys, McClellan is in command of the Army again! Three cheers!" The soldiers cheered lustily as Pope rode to oblivion.

Even Jacob Cox, a strong supporter of McClellan, thought the display "an unnecessary affront to the unfortunate commanders of that army. But no word was spoken. Pope lifted his hat in a parting salute to McClellan and rode quietly on with his escort." Pope and McClellan never met again.

The orderly retreat continued over muddy roads through the dark night as officers attempted to re-form broken regiments. By midnight the Federal rear guard had crossed Bull Run and the bridge was destroyed to discourage pursuit. Pope established headquarters in Centreville and sat there dejectedly.

While Longstreet grumbled that Pope had not been annihilated, Lee wrote Jefferson Davis: "This Army today achieved on the plains of Manassas a signal victory." Lee still hoped to inflict further damage on Pope. On August 31 he dispatched Jackson across Bull Run north of Sudley Ford. Jackson swung north and around Centreville in an attempt to sever the Union line of retreat.

The Confederates, hindered by exhaustion and bad roads, moved slowly, allowing Pope to intercept them at Chantilly, twenty-five miles west of Washington, where a vicious battle fought in a heavy rain halted Jackson's advance. Pope's worst losses were division commanders Philip Kearny and Isaac Stevens, both killed. Pope was quickly relieved of command. Lincoln, ignoring the counsel of his cabinet, returned McClellan to lead the Army of the Potomac.

Lee's losses totaled 9,474; Federal casualties, including 4,000 captured, were 14,462. The Union army was again dazed, giving Lee an opportunity to abandon the offensive-defensive posture he had assumed three months earlier. He was now free to attack into the north.

The Death of Kearny

BATTLES AND LEADERS

On September 1, 1862, Stonewall Jackson encountered the Federal Ninth Corps at Chantilly. A Federal charge pierced Jackson's line, but a Confederate counterattack repaired the damage.

As Philip Kearny led a division to the front, he flew into "an ungovernable rage," an observer noted, by the reluctance of the Ninth Corps to resume their attack. He attempted to rally one regiment on the edge of a cornfield, but they refused, claiming two prisoners as proof that the Confederates were in strength in the field. "God damn you and your prisoners!" Kearny yelled and immediately rode into the field.

A heavy rain had darkened the field when Kearny encountered soldiers in the cornfield. "What troops are these?" he barked. They were

Georgians, who soon realized what he was. "That's a Yankee officer," one shouted. "Shoot him."

Kearny raced away, slipping to one side of the horse to reduce the Confederate's target, but the old Indian trick failed and he was killed instantly by a bullet that tore through his spine and chest.

"I was conscious of a feeling of deep respect and great admiration for the brave soldier," one Confederate officer remembered. The body was borne to the rear where an old friend of Kearny's, A. P. Hill, saw it and cried, "Poor Kearny! He deserved a better death than that!"

Robert E. Lee ordered the body delivered to the Federals under a flag of truce by Maj. Walter T. Taylor, who said, "There was no place for exultation at the death of so gallant a man."

The Return of McClellan

That George B. McClellan refused to forward his troops promptly was a major contributing cause to John Pope's defeat at Second Manassas. His behavior, which some considered tantamount to treason, was such that his greatest enemies, Secretary of War Edwin Stanton and Treasury Secretary Salmon Chase, started a petition in the cabinet calling for McClellan's removal from command. Most of the cabinet supported the move, but the petition was shelved in response to the crisis following Pope's defeat. Even Henry W. Halleck considered McClellan's actions to be not what "the national safety, in my opinion, required."

Stanton, as he was wont to do, panicked after Second Manassas. He ordered a steamboat prepared to evacuate Lincoln and the cabinet and prepared to ship the contents of the arsenal to New York City. Even McClellan concurred, writing his wife, Ellen, "I do not regard Washn. as safe against the rebels," and offered to quietly slip into the city to help her evacuate the family silver.

Halleck was most affected by the crisis. Four consecutive sleepless night, hemorrhoids, and the stress of dealing with the likes of Pope and McClellan nearly caused his breakdown. In desperation he wrote McClellan, "I beg of you to assist me in this crisis with your ability and experience. I am utterly worn out."

Lincoln concurred with Halleck's assessment. Early on September 2 he and Halleck traveled to McClellan's headquarters to place him in charge of the troops defending Washington. As McClellan would remember it, the president "asked me if I would, under the circumstances, and as a favor to him, resume command and do the best that could be done."

Back at the White House, Lincoln, "greatly distressed," according to Navy Secretary Gideon Welles, informed the cabinet of McClellan's return, which evoked a "disturbed and desponding feeling." Welles said the president's position was: "McClellan knows the whole ground; his specialty is to defend; he is a good engineer, all admit; there is no better organizer; he

can be trusted to act on the defense" and finally, "he had beyond any officer the confidence of the army."

Halleck ordered Pope to bring his men into Washington's fortifications where "General McClellan has charge . . . you will consider any directions . . . given by him as coming from me."

Despite his joy at Pope's problems (which he had helped cause and which had resulted in many Federal casualties), McClellan wrote that this was a "terrible and thankless task," which he assumed "reluctantly . . . I only consent to take it for my country's sake & with the humble hope that God has called me to it—how I pray that he may support me!"

On August 31 Porter wrote to McClellan: "I expect to hear hourly of our rear being cut and our supplies and train at Fairfax being destroyed." To his divisional commanders Porter wrote that there would be no more retreating until they were whipped again.

On the following day Pope sent Halleck: "I think it my duty to call to

your attention the unsoldierly and dangerous conduct of several Army of the Potomac officers," particularly Porter. There was dangerous talk from these officers "arising in all instances from personal feeling in relation to changes" in command from McClellan to Pope, which he felt was producing "disastrous results." They had indeed, and now McClellan had a second chance to prove, or disprove, himself.

LIBRARY OF CONGRESS

A Tour of the Second Manassas Campaign

THIS TOUR covers a considerable amount of territory, but then so did the campaign. We start with the Confederate advance out of Richmond north on the Virginia Central Railroad. At Hanover Junction the Virginia Central turned sharply west to Gordonsville, where it intercepted the Orange and Alexandria. A separate line—the Richmond, Fredericksburg, and Potomac—continued north to Fredericksburg and Aquia Creek on the Potomac River. This part of the tour skirts Grant's Overland campaign in 1864 and includes the sites of two important cavalry clashes from that time, Yellow Tavern and Trevilian Station.

Casual observers of the Civil War often assume that the most important Civil War route was directly between Richmond and Washington, but the geography of the Potomac River and other waterways prevented that. Before the Civil War, travelers from Richmond would ride the Richmond, Fredericksburg, and Potomac to Aquia Creek—a five-hour, seventy-five-mile trip—then continue north on the ships of the Potomac Steamboat Company—a three-hour journey—to the docks of Washington or Alexandria. A full railroad trip from Richmond to Hanover Junction, Gordonsville, Manassas, and Alexandria took much longer. The streams and wilderness between Richmond and Washington rendered the route impracticable for large armies. The roundabout all-rail route between the two capitals allowed both sides to supply and shift troops quickly by train. Every Federal offensive followed the rails at least as far as Warrenton (actually nearby Warrenton Junction) or Culpeper, but later efforts started for the Wilderness.

We continue north, past the battlefield of Cedar Mountain to Culpeper, then follow a network of minor roads to trace Jackson's famous flanking march around Pope's right flank through Manassas Gap and on to the battlefield of Second Manassas

This tour takes us through the Virginia piedmont, a region of beautiful rolling hills that lie between the Blue Ridge Mountains to the west and the flat coastal plain to the east. It was good terrain for marching and maneuvering armies and for swift cavalry actions. It became a supply corridor for both armies and a hospital center for scores of wounded and sick soldiers. Many skirmishes and near-battles occurred as troops advanced and retreated repeatedly over the same terrain, and great destruction was caused to civilian property and lives.

From Richmond National Battlefield Park headquarters turn left onto Broad Street through the city to U.S. 1–U.S. 301–Chamberlayne Parkway and turn right.

The intersection with Laburnum marks the intermediate line of the defensive works that surrounded Richmond. Brig. Gen. Judson Kilpatrick's Union cavalry penetrated near this point on March 1, 1864, but turned back before accomplishing their mission of freeing Union prisoners held in Richmond. On the following day part of his command under Col. Ulric Dahlgren was deflected to the west, resulting in Dahlgren's death.

The intersection of Chamberlayne and Azalea marks the closest advance on the Brook road of Philip H. Sheridan's cavalry on May 11, 1864, which had penetrated Richmond's outer defenses. From here he rode east to Mechanicsville.

Brook Run Shopping Center marks the outer layer of Richmond's extensive defenses from 1862 to 1865. Here Sheridan broke through after the great cavalry clash at Yellow Tavern to the north. In the shopping center parking lot to the left are preserved several artillery positions, remnants of the fortifications that once ringed Richmond. Lee visited the nearby Brook Hill Plantation (1719), and Stuart and A. P. Hill were entertained there. A number of skirmishes were fought around the property, and wounded Confederates were nursed in the main house. Several casualties rest in the family graveyard.

U.S. 1 was the Brook turnpike, the main road from Richmond to the north during the Civil War. This highway met the Telegraph road, which led from the east, and Old Mountain Road from the west, to become the Telegraph road, which led to Washington, D.C.

Preserved in the parking lot of Brook Run Shopping Center are earthworks that formed Richmond's outer defensive line.

On May 3, 1863, Union Brig. Gen. George Stoneman took ten thousand troopers and four batteries in an attempt to cut the railroad connecting Lee with Richmond during the Chancellorsville campaign. On May 4 Col. Judson Kilpatrick struck at Richmond's outskirts on the Brook road, where he was deflected. Kilpatrick's second effort at Meadow Bridge was also rebuffed, and he slid to the east to regain the Union lines at Gloucester Point on the peninsula. There he was joined by Lt. Col. Hasbrouck Davis, who had destroyed Hanover Station, was rejected at Richmond's defenses, and skirmished with Confederate cavalry at Tunstall Station. The raid destroyed 20 railroad bridges, 3 trains, and 122 wagons.

On February 28, 1864, Kilpatrick started south with four thousand men and a separate command under Dahlgren. Kilpatrick would attack from the north on the Brook turnpike while Dahlgren took advantage of the diversion to enter Richmond from the south. On March 1 Kilpatrick was repulsed by the intermediate defenses at Chamberlayne and Laburnum, and a second time at Meadow Bridge, before riding to Tunstall Station and again down the peninsula to safety.

Continue north to Virginia Center Parkway (or Old Francis Road–Route 677) and turn right then right again onto Telegraph Road, which leads to the battlefield of Yellow Tavern, where Stuart was mortally wounded on May 11, 1864, while attempting to defend Richmond from Sheridan.

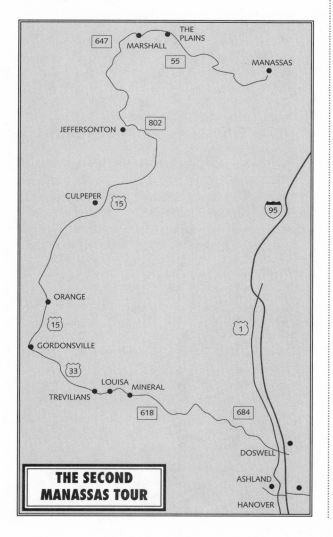

THE SECOND MANASSAS TOUR

On the right is the impressive monument erected to honor one of the South's greatest cavaliers.

Return to U.S. 1 and turn right.

Ashcake Road crosses U.S. 1 just south of Ashland. Jackson used this route as he traveled east from the Shenandoah Valley to attack the Federal right flank at Mechanicsville on June 26, 1862, just before he petered out and failed to participate in the battle.

Northeast of this route are two sites that will be covered in the third book of this series, *The Killing Time*. Marlbourne is the resting place of arch-Secessionist Edmund Ruffin, who reportedly fired the first shot at Fort Sumter and committed suicide rather than live in a defeated South. At Summer Hill Plantation rests Capt. William Latane, Stuart's only casualty during his famed first ride around McClellan. The captain became an early Southern martyr.

Four miles south of Ashland on Route 1 Lee maintained his headquarters on May 27, 1864, while retreating from the North Anna River to keep his army between Grant and Richmond. Near here Longstreet's and Hill's corps moved east to Cold Harbor. A short distance farther north on U.S. 1 occurred a skirmish on June 25, 1862, between the Fourth Virginia Cavalry and the Eighth Illinois Cavalry.

In Ashland turn left onto Route 54–Engbad Street to Railroad Avenue and turn right to the visitors center in the depot, across the tracks to your left.

One of the most poignant places in Civil War history—the site where Jeb Stuart was mortally wounded at Yellow Tavern.

A training center for recruits was established at Ashland soon after the war started and hundreds of wounded Confederates flooded the town after battles to the north. In May 1863 the train carrying Jackson's body stopped here. Stoneman's cavalry raided the town on May 3, 1863, followed by Kilpatrick on March 1, 1864, and Sheridan on May 11. The Yankee cavalry tore up track and destroyed supplies on all three occasions. Lee's Confederates passed through Ashland in 1864 on their way to fight at Totopontomoy Creek and Cold Harbor.

Ashland, a railroad town and prewar resort, was established in 1845. A self-guided walking tour available at the visitors center identifies two Civil War–related structures. The Hanover Arts and Activities Center on Railroad Street was the Ashland Baptist Church during the war. Used as a hospital, it has bloodstains still on the floor. On the corner of South Center and Macmurdo Streets is the Macmurdo house, used briefly by Jackson when he passed through the area.

Ten miles to the south is Scotchtown (1720), the home of Patrick Henry between 1771 and 1777 and briefly a childhood home of Dolley Madison. It is restored and open to the public.

To the east, on Route 54, is Hanover Courthouse (1735), the Old Gaol (1835, now housing a local museum), and Hanover Tavern (1733) across the street, where Patrick Henry married the proprietor's daughter and lived for three years. George Washington, Thomas Jefferson, and the marquis de

Jeb Stuart received command of the Army of Northern Virginia's cavalry at Historic Hanover Courthouse.

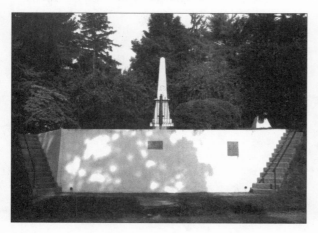

Lafayette stayed here. At one time the tavern served as a courthouse, and it was used as a stable for Lord Charles Cornwallis. During the Civil War it was a haven for refugees from northern Virginia. It is now a community theater and open by appointment (804-537-5050). Note the interpretive markers. Stuart was in Hanover on his famous ride around McClellan in 1862. While maintaining headquarters on the green, Stuart received his major general's commission and immediately organized the Army of Northern Virginia's cavalry. Note the monument to the 1,200 Confederate soldiers from Hanover County and the

"Noble women who loved them." The memorial lists 1,464 names. Like other counties, Hanover sent its court records to Richmond for safekeeping during the war and lost them in the evacuation fire.

The battle of Hanover Court House occurred on May 27, 1862, south of Hanover at the intersection of Ashcake Road and Pole Green Church Road, near Peake's Crossing, now known simply as Peakes.

Lee rested his left wing nearby along Little River on May 23–26, 1864. At Taylorsville to the west Lee maintained his headquarters on May 24–26. There Ewell's corps turned southeast toward Cold Harbor.

A Tour of the Battle of Yellow Tavern, Where Jeb Stuart Fell

Several excellent brochure guides to lesser-known and virtually unprotected Virginia battlefields are generally available from the nearest national battlefield park visitors center. You can also write ahead for copies.

The first we use is titled *The Battle of Yellow Tavern, May 11, 1864.* Although Yellow Tavern occurred two years after the period covered by this book, this is our closest approach to the battlefield, which is an emotionally charged visit for many Southerners.

Deciding to test Philip H. Sheridan's contention that he could defeat Jeb Stuart, Ulysses S. Grant sent him, with ten thousand troopers in two divisions, south from Spotsylvania on May 9, 1864. Stuart immediately dispatched Fitzhugh Lee's division to pursue, directed James Gordon's brigade to attack the Federal rear, and rode swiftly with two brigades, under Lunsford L. Lomax and William C. Wickham, to intercept the Federals.

Stuart's exhausted men reached Yellow Tavern, an important crossroads on Richmond's northern outskirts, on May 11, at 10 A.M., only an hour before Sheridan. Stuart placed Wickham on the right, west of the Telegraph road and facing south, while Lomax formed an angle on the left, facing west along the road. Sheridan's lead division, under

Wesley Merritt, immediately attacked Lomax. Although Merritt suffered terrible casualties from the front and flank fire, Lomax was flanked and withdrew to extend Wickham's position in a straight line at 2 P.M.

A two-hour lull developed while Sheridan fended off Gordon's attack on his rear and most of the Confederate troopers slept. Sheridan then elected to press the Confederate left again. George Armstrong Custer dismounted half his brigade to attack Lomax from the front while the other half swept around the Confederate flank, hoping to capture several cannon.

The Confederates fired furiously as Custer's horsemen leaped five fences, crossed Turner's Run over a narrow bridge, and drove steadily uphill. When Custer broke the Confederate line, Stuart rode into the melee to rally his men, and a counterattack by the First Virginia drove the Federals back. Before joining the retreat, Union Pvt. John A. Huff of the Fifth Michigan fired his pistol into the Confederates, mortally wounding Stuart in the side. "I am shot," the legendary general whispered calmly as his head fell forward and the famous plumed hat fell into the dust of the Telegraph road.

Fitzhugh Lee took command of a desperate situation as Stuart was led

away. Sheridan's continuing attacks with his superior numbers caused increasing numbers of Confederates to flee. Observing this from his ambulance, Stuart shouted, "Go back! Go back! Do your duty as I've done mine." Defiant to the end, he added, "I would rather die than be whipped."

The Confederates retreated across the north fork of the Chickahominy River, leaving the battlefield to the Federals. It was a double victory for Sheridan—he had proven the ability of Union cavalry and killed one of the South's greatest leaders.

Stuart had bought time for Richmond's defenses to be manned, forcing Sheridan to ride for Hexall's Landing on the James River. Stuart was taken to the Grace Street home of his brother-in-law, Dr. Charles Brewer. The people of Richmond crowded around the house, which was briefly visited by Jefferson Davis. When Stuart died on May 12, Robert E. Lee said, "I can scarcely think of him without weeping."

The tour of Yellow Tavern starts at a site we just left in Brook Run Shopping Center at the small remnant of the vast system of interconnected earthworks that surrounded Richmond. This area was threatened by George B. McClellan during the Peninsula campaign of 1862, by George

Stoneman's cavalry raid in 1863, and by Sheridan in May 1864. Braxton Bragg, exiled from the Army of Tennessee earlier, manned the inner defenses, and Stuart left these works unoccupied so he could maneuver. During the fighting at Yellow Tavern, part of a Federal brigade took the works and could hear church bells in Richmond pealing the alarm.

The Yellow Tavern (Stop No. 2) was deteriorating during the Civil War, but it stood near U.S. 1 just north of Interstate 73 on the Telegraph road, the main route from Richmond to the north. Interstate 95 cuts the Confederate lines in half (Stop No. 3). Lomax was to the south, and Wickham was at an angle to the northwest. Merritt's attack came up Maryland Avenue (Stop No. 4) from Yellow Tavern, forcing the Confederates to retreat behind Turner's Run. Stop No. 5 is a convenience store parking lot on Mountain Road, in the center of Sheridan's final attack. Stop No. 6, at the dead end of Battlefield Road, was Wickham's line, attacked while Custer assaulted Lomax again on the left. We are at Stop No. 7, the site preserved as a UDC shrine to Stuart. It was dedicated in 1888 by Gov. Fitzhugh Lee and stands only thirty feet from where Stuart fell.

On May 27, 1864, a mile north of Ashland, Lee's wagon train crossed the South Anna River. That same day Longstreet's and Hill's corps crossed on the railroad bridge to the east.

Return to U.S. 1 and turn left. In Doswell (wartime Hanover Junction), turn right on 688 to the railroad.

Behind a brick railroad building is the junction of the Virginia Central and the Richmond, Fredericksburg, and Potomac Railroads. Through this important junction passed food and supplies that kept the Army of Northern Virginia operating throughout the war, particularly in 1864 as Lee battled desperately with Grant. Lee crossed to the south bank of the North Anna nearby on May 22–23, 1864. It was also a hospital center.

In late May 1864 Lee and Grant battled along the banks of the North Anna River as the Federals attempted to capture this strategic railroad junction, which was protected by earthworks. The Confederates lured Grant into a trap, but the Federals escaped because Lee was ill and his best generals were dead or wounded. The battle, battlefield, and tour of this neglected campaign will be covered in *The Killing Time,* the third book of this series.

In June 1863 Union cavalry under Lt. Col. Hasbrouck Davis burned the depot and railroad property at Hanover.

Return to U.S. 1 and turn right briefly, then left onto Route 684 (Verdun Road) to follow the railroad west through Verdun, North Anna, Hewlett, and Holliday.

Historic Fork Church (1736) is on Route 738 (Gum Tree Road), which parallels Route 684 a few miles south. On the right is the entrance to Ox Ford Battlefield Park, part of the North Anna battlefield. It has well-preserved earthworks that can be examined on a trail with ten stops equipped with interpretive signs, but this site will be found in *The Killing Time.*

At the stop sign turn left onto Teman Road, then right onto Beaverdam School Road to Beaver Dam Station on the left.

The depot, constructed in 1840, was a strategic position along the Virginia Central Railroad. When a Fed-

Beaver Dam Station was torched repeatedly during Federal cavalry raids. In 1862 John S. Mosby, prior to his adventures as the Gray Ghost, was captured here.

eral cavalry raid under Judson Kilpatrick burned the depot on July 20, 1862, they destroyed one hundred barrels of flour and forty thousand cartridges and captured John S. Mosby, waiting on a train to transport him to Richmond. Mosby had secured permission from Jackson to see Stuart about an independent command that would operate behind enemy lines. Mosby spent ten days in the Old Capitol Prison in Washington. Upon his release he gave Lee important information about Federal concentrations before Second Manassas. Although rebuilt, the depot was torched twice more, on February 29, 1864, and May 9, 1864, on the latter occasion by George Armstrong Custer's First Michigan, part of Sheridan's raid that culminated at Yellow Tavern. They destroyed two locomotives, one hundred railcars, and 1.5 million rations of bread and meat and liberated four hundred prisoners and a large number of weapons the Confederates had gathered at the Wilderness and Spotsylvania. The Federals also tore up ten miles of track. The depot was rebuilt in 1866 and restoration continues on its worn and scorched brick walls.

From the depot bear right onto Route 715–Beaverdam Road. When Route 601 comes in, bear left and follow 601 to Bumpass, another railroad town. Cross the railroad tracks and bear right to stay on 601 to Route 618 and bear right onto 618 through Frederick's Hall, a rail station during the war, to Mineral.

In Mineral turn right onto Route 22–208 to the outskirts of Louisa, where you join U.S. 33 West through town. Turn left beside Louisa County Courthouse (1908) to the parking area on the right

The adjacent Old Jail (1818, rebuilt in 1868 after a fire) houses the Louisa County Historical Society Museum (open Saturdays and Sundays, 2 to 4 P.M., from May to September). Stoneman raided the town on May 2, 1863, and destroyed the railroad. Fitzhugh Lee camped nearby on June 10, 1864, before the battle of Trevilian Station. After the battle the courthouse, a tavern, the railroad station, and the Methodist church were used as field hospitals.

While Grant confronted Lee at Cold Harbor, he sent two cavalry divisions under Sheridan to destroy Lee's transportation and communications link at Gordonsville on the Virginia Central. Wade Hampton caught up with the Federals and on June 11–12, 1864, the battle of Trevilian Station occurred.

After driving off Fitzhugh LeeCuster took a farm road between Routes 669 and 693 to capture Hampton's trains at Trevilian. Farther north, near the intersection of Routes 669 and 613, Sheridan's camp, Clayton Store, is a short distance to the right. Just before Trevilian, Route 613 leads north to the location where Hampton defeated Torbert before returning south to recapture his wagons.

From the courthouse turn left onto U.S. 33 West and turn right onto Route 666 to Oakland Cemetery on

The Old Jail beside the Louisa County Courthouse has several historical displays.

the right, where one hundred dead from the battle, ninety-four of them unidentified, are buried.

Most of the graves are Confederates, but some are Federals. Monuments have been raised to Col. J. L. McAllister and a Captain Hines of Georgia. A stone column was erected by the Reverend John Cowles, who had lost two sons earlier in the war. A third was mortally wounded at Trevilian. All three were killed within a year. On June 12, 1983, a monument was dedicated by the United Daughters of the Confederacy to all those buried here.

Return to West 33 and turn right. Turn left into the small parking area with a historical marker and a UDC monument (1926) at the site of the battle of Trevilian Station.

The battle is being interpreted by Virginia Civil War Trails and the Trevilian Station Battlefield Foundation. A driving tour guide is available from area national parks. During the fighting of May 11 Hampton's wagon train was parked here. When Fitzhugh Lee retreated, Custer inserted his command between Lee and Hampton and seized the train. Hampton's sudden, savage attack recaptured all his wagons and Custer's headquarters wagon to boot, containing stolen silver spoons and what were termed "racy female items." On May 12 Sheridan attacked Hampton and Lee here along the road before being driven off to the east.

Turn left onto the highway then turn right immediately onto Route 33 to Gordonsville. Continuing straight on Route 22 leads to historic Boswells Tavern.

To the left in a mile (on Route 33) was Hampton's position on June 12, behind the railroad embankment. Sheridan attacked across the fields to the right. The combat climaxed when Lee assaulted Sheridan's right flank from left to right.

Continue on Route 33.

At Green Springs, between Trevilian and Gordonsville on U.S. 33, Stonewall Jackson camped before the battle of Cedar Mountain. Hampton's cavalry also camped here on June 10, 1864.

At the stop sign turn right to continue on West 33, joining U.S. 15 from Boswells Tavern, into Gordonsville. Take a sharp right onto the paved road at the sign for the Exchange Hotel. Cross the railroad tracks and enter on the left to park.

Federal forces attempted repeatedly but with little success to destroy this strategic railroad junction, although a cavalry battle once erupted in the streets. Here the Virginia Central and Orange and Alexandria met, making this a major supply depot and hospital center for the Confederacy, whose armies camped in the area on numerous occasions. Gordonsville was headquarters for A. P. Hill during the winter of 1863–64.

On September 19, 1864, Sheridan sent two cavalry brigades, five thousand men under Maj. Gen. Alfred Torbert, to disrupt Lee's rail supply route to the Shenandoah Valley. Two Confederate cavalry brigades, nineteen hundred men under Maj. Gen. L. L. Lomas, intercepted the Federals in Madison County, to the east. Fighting stubbornly, the Confederates were forced out of Madison Court House to the Rapidan, where the contest continued at Liberty

Many Virginia historical markers are mounted on concrete and stone bases. This one describes the great cavalry clash on June 11–12, 1864, at Trevilian Station.

Mills until Lomas was forced to burn the bridge and barricade the ford. The Federals flanked the position and fought to a gap in Southwest Mountain, on the outskirts of Gordonsville, where they were halted by three thousand infantrymen forwarded by Lee.

The three-story Greek Revival Exchange Hotel was constructed in the 1850s for passengers on the

The Battle of Trevilian Station

After the bloody battle of Cold Harbor in early June 1864, Ulysses S. Grant decided to cross the James River to capture Petersburg and sever the railroads that supplied Robert E. Lee's army and the city of Richmond. At the same time David Hunter was to cross the Blue Ridge Mountains and seize Charlottesville and destroy the railroad hub there. If these rail lines were cut, Lee would no longer have a supply route, and Richmond would have to be abandoned.

To prevent the skilled Confederate cavalry from discovering his perilous Potomac River crossing, Grant sent Philip H. Sheridan with two divisions of cavalry, 8,000 men, 24 guns, and 125 wagons, under generals Alfred Torbert and David M. Gregg, to support Hunter by destroying the Virginia Central Railroad. Sheridan left

on June 7 for Trevilian Station, a stop on the Virginia Central.

Two Confederate cavalry divisions, those of Wade Hampton and Fitzhugh Lee, set out in close pursuit on June 9. On the following day Hampton was at Trevilian, Lee a few miles east at Louisa Court House. Hampton devised an attack on the Federal camp, situated north of Louisa at Clayton's Store, via two roads, one from Trevilian Station, to be taken by Hampton, the other from Louisa, which would be used by Lee. One drawback to the plan was the heavy forest that separated the roads, making it difficult for the Confederates to support each other.

On June 11 Hampton drove Torbert back to Clayton's Store, but Lee withdrew toward Louisa after battling George Armstrong Custer's brigade.

Custer capitalized on the resulting gap by seizing Hampton's wagon train, eight hundred horses, and three caissons. Learning of this development, Hampton immediately sent Thomas Rosser's brigade after Custer. Other Confederate units joined in, and a spirited attack recaptured the Confederate property as Custer found himself surrounded by Hampton and Lee at Trevilian. Sheridan rescued Custer with a strong assault that forced Hampton to retreat west of Trevilian and drove Lee east back to Louisa. This ended the first day of heavy fighting, with Sheridan in possession of the field.

During the night Hampton formed an angled line, with his left flank protected by a railroad embankment, Lee reinforcing the right flank, and an open field in front. Sheridan

destroyed five miles of track on June 12, then rode to attack Hampton's position west of Trevilian. The Federals launched repeated attacks against the Southern line, but all were bloodily repulsed. The Confederates, however, were weakening. Hampton was running low on ammunition, a Union artillery battery was pummeling a portion of his line, and sharpshooters in a barn were systematically killing off officers.

The tide turned for Hampton when additional ammunition arrived, the barn was set ablaze, and Confederate guns silenced the Union battery. When Lee attacked Sheridan's right flank in the late afternoon, Sheridan withdrew to rejoin Grant, his mission a failure. The Federals lost 735 men, the Confederates about 1,000.

Virginia Central Railroad, which stopped at a platform in front of the establishment. When the Civil War began, the hotel became the center of the Gordonsville Receiving Hospital. The railroad delivered seventy thousand men for treatment here from the battlefields of Cedar Mountain, Chancellorsville, Brandy Station, Mine Run, Trevilian, the Wilderness, and dozens of smaller engagements. During one week of fighting in the Wilderness, six thousand casualties arrived. Seven hundred men died and were buried behind the hotel, including twenty-three Federals. The grounds were crowded with tents and sheds where the wounded were treated and housed.

The grand hotel, ruined by war's end, was restored and prospered until the 1940s when passenger rail traffic waned. The Exchange Hotel was restored and is now a notable Civil War museum that showcases weapons, uniforms, and personal effects of both Confederate and Federal soldiers in every branch of the service—infantry, artillery, and cavalry. Antique

The Exchange Hotel in Gordonsville was used extensively as a hospital during the Civil War and now houses an excellent Confederate museum.

medical instruments are displayed in a hospital room where they saw extensive service. Reenactments emphasizing Civil War medical practices are held here. Interpretive markers are found at the visitors center in the old depot.

Return to Main Street–Route 33–U.S. 15 and turn right.

The Gordonsville Presbyterian Church (1833) is on the right. The beautiful church has changed little since Jackson worshiped here several times in 1862.

Continue north to turn left at the traffic circle and follow West 33, then turn right into Maplewood Cemetery and bear right to the Confederate section.

The seven hundred Confederates who died at the Exchange Hotel were reinterred here following the war. All lie unidentified in a grassy area marked by a bronze plaque on a stone base. Federals who died in local hospitals were reinterred in the Culpeper National Cemetery.

Return to West 33, turn left, and return to the traffic circle. Go around the circle and turn left onto U.S. 15 North–James Madison Highway.

After the battle of Cedar Mountain, Jackson's force camped three miles south of Orange along this route

A monument with a classic image of a Confederate soldier stands guard before the Louisa County Courthouse.

on August 13–15, 1862. When U.S. 15 turns right, go straight into Orange on Carolina Street. On the right at 119 Caroline is Saint Thomas Episcopal Church (1833), influenced by Thomas Jefferson's architecture. Robert E. Lee, Jefferson Davis, A. P. Hill, and many other Confederate luminaries worshiped here. The pew used by Davis and Lee is marked. The church served as a hospital following Cedar Mountain, Fredericksburg, Chancellorsville, the Wilderness, and Spotsylvania. Tours are by appointment.

Next door to the church is the Madison Museum, which interprets the life of James Madison, fourth president of the United States and father of the Constitution. His home, Montpelier, is four miles southwest of Orange on Route 20. Across the street is the Orange County Historical Society, which contains extensive research materials.

A great deal of Civil War activity occurred to the east during the Civil War, including Mine Run, which almost developed into a major battle between Lee and Meade after Gettysburg; historic fords on the Rapidan; and the battlefields of the Wilderness, Chancellorsville, Spotsylvania, and Fredericksburg, which will be explored in the next two books of this series, *The Storm Tide* and *The Killing Time*.

Route 20 to the east is the old Orange plank road that leads through the Wilderness to Fredericksburg. One and a half miles east of Orange was the site where Lee maintained his headquarters from December 1863 until May 1864 when Grant started east. Four miles farther east and two miles north, near Pisgah Church, was the campsite of Jackson, A. P. Hill, and Richard Ewell on August 15–20, 1862, while they awaited the arrival of Longstreet from Richmond. Ten miles east of Orange on Route 20 is Verdiersville where Stuart, Von Borcke, and Mosby were almost captured and where Stuart's orders and famed plumed hat were nabbed at 4 A.M. on August 18, 1862, by a Union cavalry raid. The intelligence gathered induced Pope to withdraw behind the Rappahannock River. Meade assembled his army at Locust Grove in November 1863 during the Mine Run campaign. North of the road to Verdiersville, off Route 697 from a network of county roads, is Clark Mountain, on the southern bank of the Rapidan. Here Jackson built an observation and signaling tower in 1862. Around the peak Lee concentrated his army in 1862 before Second Manassas. From the

summit he, Jackson, and Longstreet studied Pope's movements and determined to attack him between the Rapidan and Rappahannock, but the Federals wisely retreated first. From the peak Lee studied Meade in 1863, and on May 2, 1864, he saw the start of the Wilderness campaign as Grant moved east. The view from the top, which is now a commercial orchard, is still worth a visit. The Rapidan River fords at Rapidan and Raccoon saw considerable activity.

Three miles north of Orange is the grave of Maj. Gen. James L. Kemper, who was badly wounded leading his brigade of Virginians during Pickett's Charge at Gettysburg. Just northwest of Orange is Willow Grove Plantation, now a bed and breakfast, which took cannonballs in its eaves and preserves trenches on the grounds.

Continue the short distance to the stop sign on Carolina and turn right onto West Main Street. At the light, turn left to follow U.S. 15.

The Orange County Courthouse (1859) on the left has changed little since 1861, when the basement was used as an arsenal. The statue of the Confederate soldier leaning on his rifle was dedicated on October 18, 1900. Rebel Hall on Mary Fray Avenue was a gathering place for Confederate officers.

U.S. 15 crosses the Rapidan River at Madison Mills in Madison County and passes through Locust Dale, where Jackson crossed the Robinson River on

Wounded and sick Confederates who died in the hospitals around Gordonsville are buried at Maplewood Cemetery on the outskirts of town.

the way to Cedar Mountain. Some Civil War activity occurred in Madison County. Near Criglersville Jackson camped on November 25, 1862, after Antietam, as he marched east from Winchester to join Lee at Fredericksburg. On September 22, 1863, at Jack's Shop (modern Rochelle) on Route 231, Stuart attacked Federal cavalry under John Buford only to be assaulted from the rear by Judson Kilpatrick. Stuart changed fronts and fought through Kilpatrick to safety. Buford pursued to the Rapidan River. A day-long cavalry battle between Stuart and Kilpatrick occurred on October 10, 1863, at James City, near the intersection of Routes 29 and 31. Historical markers are situated at the last two sites. At the courthouse (1829) in Madison is a memorial to local Confederate soldiers, a statue of an infantryman at rest, standing atop a tall column. It was unveiled October 31, 1901. In Cedar Hill Cemetery is a monument, dedicated April 26, 1910, to the unknown Confederate dead buried there.

Piedmont Presbyterian Church (1834) was used as a Civil War hospital. Kemper occupied the Kemper mansion in Madison. Tours are available by appointment (540-923-4469).

The Rapidan was one of the most important rivers during the Civil War. In August 1862 Pope on the north bank faced Lee on the south bank before orders captured from Stuart induced him to retreat. After Gettysburg Lee and Meade faced off twice along the Rapidan, and in November 1863 Meade crossed to confront Lee at Mine Run, which almost developed into a major battle before Meade withdrew to the north bank. During that winter Lee camped south of the river in Orange County, monitoring the many fords and watching the Federal camps in Culpeper County.

Upstream is Liberty Mills; downstream are the town of Rapidan and the fords at Raccoon and Germanna. Along the river, east of U.S. 15, is Horseshoe (1825, on Route 614 at the junction of the Rapidan and Robinson Rivers). A number of earthworks remain on private property. In 1862 Pope torched outbuildings, ransacked the house, and drove off livestock. Nearby Annandale (1835, on Route 614 at Rapidan), was home to Col. Alexander Taliaferro, called "the Fighting Cock of Northern Virginia." Federals searched the place repeatedly but never caught him at home. Confederates and Federals camped along the river in the area. Historic homes farther east will be detailed in *The Storm Tide*.

Between Orange and Culpeper, to the east on the Rapidan River, is the community of Rapidan, which changed hands fifteen times during the Civil War. It has the noteworthy Waddell Memorial Church, featuring Gothic spires, and an interesting train depot.

Turn left onto Route 691–Carver School Lane. On the right before turning is the Major house, which was Jackson's headquarters and a hospital during the battle. Turn right onto Route 657–General Winder Road, which is a remnant of the original wartime route between Orange and Culpeper.

A UDC monument commemorating the battle of Cedar Mountain is on the left where the road turns sharply right to rejoin U.S. 15. Straight ahead was Crittendane Lane, which led to the Crittendane farm and is blocked here by a gate. It led across U.S. 15 toward Cedar Mountain. This was the Confederate line of Ewell, which Federal forces paralleled. Confederate artillery was emplaced at the Gate, on the lower slopes of Cedar Mountain, and on a knoll between the two at the Cedars. During a terrific artillery duel here, Brig. Gen. Charles S. Winder was mortally wounded.

Banks attacked in two prongs, one directed here, at the Gate, and the second through a cornfield at the Cedars. The attack here, by Brig. Gen. Samuel W. Crawford, crumbled Jackson's line after a brutal hand-to-hand battle that forced Confederate cannon here and at the Cedars to withdraw hurriedly. Into this desperate situation Jackson charged, at one point carrying a flag then brandishing his sword encased in its rusted scabbard. Braving a fierce fire, Jackson rallied the men as A. P. Hill arrived to reinforce the line. The First Pennsylvania Cavalry sacrificed itself in a charge to buy time for the retreating Union infantry. Nearby is the Wiseman house, where the Confederates broke early in the battle. At the entrance drive is a monument to Winder. The APCWS has acquired 152 acres here, including the gate, the wheat field through which the Federals attacked, and the Winder Monument.

Drive up to U.S. 15 to view Cedar Mountain, then turn left. Turn right onto Route 649–Cedar Mountain

Drive, which follows the wartime Mitchell Station road that paralleled the Federal line.

Just before reaching Cedar Run is the site where Brig. Gen. Christopher C. Augur attacked toward the Cedars. Cedarcroft, on Route 649 at the foot of Cedar Mountain, witnessed the full spectrum of battle.

Return toward U.S. 15 but turn right onto Route 692–Old Orange Road, also part of the original Orange-Culpeper road, to the church.

Jackson drove the Federals past the church (only the foundation is original). The Confederates established a line just beyond, and Confederate and Federal artillery began another duel. Young Capt. William J. Pegram commanded the Southern cannon.

There are a number of historic homes around Cedar Mountain that have connections to the battle. The Civil War owner of the Guinn house (1860, three miles south of Culpeper on Route 522), Abiah Guinn, captured a Federal soldier and placed him in a well. He was, however, persuaded to release him. The soldier returned later with a Union squad, and Guinn was imprisoned until the war ended.

Federals used a room in Highland (1832, three miles west of Mitchell's on Route 649) as a chapel. The Yager family saved a window from Calvary Church, which survives today in All Saints Episcopal Church.

Forrest Grove (1846, three miles from Culpeper on Route 15) was a refuge for civilians during the battle and a Confederate hospital afterward. Green Valley (1835, four and a half miles south of Culpeper on Route 15) served as Pope's headquarters and as a hospital.

When Federal troops plundered Springfield (1865, off U.S. 15 South, a replacement for the house burned during the war), feathers covered the grounds from beds shredded in a futile search for booty. Wounded of both sides were cared for at Clover Dale (1805, four and a half miles south of Culpeper on U.S. 15), and Confederate officers were entertained there.

While Union troops were in the area, Mrs. John H. White of White House (1855, Route 603 off U.S. 15) sheltered two Confederates in her attic and reportedly drove off Federal searchers with a butcher knife.

Cedar Mountain looms over the fields where Stonewall Jackson's corps and Nathaniel P. Banks's army clashed in a desperate battle on August 9, 1862.

Turn around and return to U.S. 15, where you turn right. When U.S. 15 North goes right, continue straight onto Business U.S. 15–Orange.

The long peak to the right on the outskirts of town is Pony Mountain, which Pope used as a signal station in 1862. Ironically, Pony Mountain, which witnessed several Civil War cavalry battles and other skirmishes and maneuvers, was later engineered to survive the ultimate conflict—nuclear war. Located seventy miles southwest of Washington, it contains a secure Federal bunker to protect the people who would rebuild the country's financial structure after a nuclear war. It has been used by the Federal

This marker commemorates the battle of Cedar Mountain at the site of the fiercest fighting.

Reserve System to store gold and currency and a backup computer system. Congress has recently designated it the National Audiovisual Conservation Center, a climate-controlled repository for the preservation of more than 150,000 movies, because thousands of early films perished before preservation efforts were started.

Another signal station was atop Cole's Hill, an elevation to the northeast off Route 3.

Go straight on Orange Street when Business 15 turns off to the left. After .6 mile turn right onto Stevens Street at the sign for the national cemetery. Go straight at the stop sign, then turn right and enter the cemetery.

The seven-acre Culpeper National Cemetery, established in 1867, contains 473 known Union dead, 912 unknown Federals, and 23 Confederate unknowns from nearby battlefields, but particularly Cedar Mountain. During military occupation a large Union camp extended from here to the north. As the war progressed a Confederate cemetery was established on the southern edge of town. Each of the 357 dead was marked by a wooden headboard, which quickly deteriorated. In 1880 all were reburied in one mound at Fairview Cemetery on the western edge of town. A granite obelisk atop the mass grave, dedicated on July 21, 1881, notes the number of soldiers resting there from each state. Georgia has the most with 78; 82 are unknown.

Return to Orange and turn right. Turn right onto Davis, and the Culpeper Museum is on the left.

The museum has much Civil War material, including weapons, uniforms, flags, maps, ammunition, and exhibits explaining the considerable military activity that occurred in Culpeper and the rolling hills of Culpeper and Orange Counties. Culpeper County is bordered to the north by the Rappahannock River, which is midway between Washington and Richmond, the opposing capitals. The river was also the first defensible position south of Manassas, and there were few others to the south. The Wilderness to the east and mountains to the west naturally funneled armies through this area. For much of the war this was the real border between North and South as generals maneuvered, flanked, parried,

The Federal dead from the battles of central Virginia are gathered at Culpeper National Cemetery.

and struck across the Rappahannock River, the major axis of the war.

The border between Culpeper County and Orange County to the south is the Rapidan River, where Pope and Lee, Lee and Meade, and Lee and Grant faced off during 1862, 1863, and 1864. The Rapidan merges to the east with the Rappahannock, forming a *V* that offered opportunity and threat as the armies marched back and forth. Pope's cavalry forded the Rapidan to raid Stuart's headquarters at Verdiersville, and Stuart crossed the Rappahannock to capture Pope's headquarters at Catlett's Station. The first incident led Pope to abandon the Rapidan and retreat behind the Rappahannock, and the latter induced Lee to flank Pope's Rappahannock line to the west before the Federals were reinforced from Fredericksburg, on the Rappahannock River to the east. Lee and Burnside returned to opposite sides of the Rappahannock in November 1862, and Burnside raced along the north bank to Fredericksburg, with Lee tardily following. Delayed by the absence of pontoons, Burnside crossed the river in December and saw his men slaughtered in senseless assaults against Lee's strong position. In the spring of 1863, Joseph Hooker flanked Lee to the west and crossed the Rappahannock to fight at Chancellorsville. After that battle Lee shifted west through Culpeper to the Shenandoah and marched into Pennsylvania. He returned after Gettysburg, and Meade again placed the Army of the Potomac on the northern bank of the Rappahannock, with Lee to the south. Learning that

Longstreet had been called to Georgia, Meade crossed the Rappahannock and forced Lee to withdraw behind the Rapidan. After discovering that Meade had been weakened to reinforce Rosecrans at Chattanooga, Lee crossed the Rapidan to outflank Meade and chased him across the Rappahannock and beyond Bull Run. As 1863 ended Meade had pressed Lee across both the Rappahannock and the Rapidan and tried to initiate battle at Mine Run. Meade withdrew north of the Rapidan, and the two armies settled into a watchful winter in Culpeper and Orange Counties. Grant arrived during the winter, and in the spring he crossed the Rappahannock to the east, with Lee intercepting him in the Wilderness.

Culpeper was an important transportation center during the war. Situated on the Orange and Alexandria Railroad, which had arrived in 1852, it had four major roads converging here. Several skirmishes were fought in the streets, and the city was shelled at least twice by Federal forces. Both armies wintered here, and soldiers were treated in churches, homes, commercial buildings, and tent complexes. Most of the two thousand men who died here succumbed to disease and infection. The opposing armies marched through the area repeatedly, and a vast Union army occupied the county during the winter of 1863–64.

Confederates controlled the area until Pope's advance elements arrived in the summer of 1862. It was recaptured by Confederates as Pope fled north of the Rappahannock; Lee returned following Antietam and retained control until after the return from Gettysburg, when Longstreet camped around the town. Ewell was in Madison and Orange Counties, and the cavalry bivouacked to the north, around the Rappahannock River. Meade sent cavalry raiding parties into Culpeper County, and on September 13 substantial Federal forces shelled the town, killing several civilians, as they attempted to capture a Confederate train that hastily reversed to safety.

Confederate and Federal soldiers were quartered in the Old Virginia Hotel (1864, 202 North Main Street). The large, three-story brick structure on the northwest corner of Main and Davis was the boyhood home of noted Confederate general A. P. Hill, killed at Petersburg days before the war ended. The Hill mansion (1855, 501 South East Street) was owned by Edward B. Hill, brother of A. P. Hill. It was a natural gathering spot for Confederate officers during the Southern occupation and was a hospital where Lee visited his son Rooney, wounded at Brandy Station. While it was occupied by Federal officers, Mrs. Hill was about to hide a bag of silver when she heard soldiers approaching. Thinking fast, she placed the bag on the floor under her hoop skirts until the Yankees left.

The Episcopal rectory (1835, 702 South East Street), had a large, deep cellar where civilians huddled on several occasions when Culpeper was bombarded. The Rossom-Walters house (1860, 1001 South East Street) was a hospital following Brandy Station and housed Union officers during Grant's winter stay. The Broadus-Apperson house (1858, 121 Edmondson) has two interior walls sporting bullet holes from the war. Mrs. James G. Broadus was slightly wounded by a spent bullet.

Saint Stephen's Episcopal Church (1821, 115 North East Street) was used as a hospital following First and Second Manassas, Cedar Mountain, and Brandy Station. More than five hundred funerals were held there in 1863. Stuart worshiped here during the winter of 1863. It is said that the mistress of Bowie house (1830, 114 North East Street) feared the Federals would seize the bell at Saint Stephen's across the street. To disguise its existence she cut the rope and draped dark fabric over the hole so the bell would not be seen.

Culpeper Presbyterian Church (1820, which stood at North Main and West Streets) was so badly damaged during its use by Federal authorities as a hospital that church services were never held there again. The U.S. government finally made reparations in 1910.

Redwood (1830, U.S. 522 West) hosted Lee, Longstreet, Stuart, Robert Toombs, and Alexander Stephens. The great Confederate artillery officer Maj. John Pelham spent the night here before the battle of Kelly's Ford and ate breakfast with the family before he was killed hours later. William H. Seward, U.S. secretary of state, was a guest, and Federal Gen. James C. Rice and staff stayed several months, with troops camping on the grounds. Pelham died on March 17, 1863, at the Shackleford house (corner of Main and Cameron), where he had courted Lucy Shackleford. There is a commemorative plaque on the building that replaced the house.

The present post office occupies the site of the Smith Hotel, used from March 26 until May 3, 1864, as headquarters by Grant while he planned the Overland campaign. The building at 195 East Davis (1835) was used by both armies as a jail.

On the courthouse square is a Confederate monument dedicated on May 31, 1911, to honor Culpeper citizens who died in the Civil War. The green and old courthouse were frequently used as a hospital. Across the street (133 Davis Street) is the Culpeper County Chamber of Commerce. *Historic Culpeper,* available locally or from the Culpeper Historical Society, is an invaluable resource for exploring the area.

Circle the block, turning left at the light onto East, turn left onto Cameron, and right onto Main, which was Orange. On the outskirts of town, stay on Route 229 as U.S. 522 turns left and U.S. 15–29 turns right. To the right U.S. 15–U.S. 29 leads to Brandy Station, site of several cavalry battles, Kelly's Ford, other sites related to 1863 action, and Warrenton, often occupied by Federals and filled with Mosby sites. All will be covered in The Storm Tide.

A number of Civil War–related homes line both sides of Route 229. To the right is Afton (1840, Route 666 near Culpeper and Inlet), which was headquarters for Federal officers and for Stuart at Brandy Station.

The silver communion service from Little Fork Episcopal Church (1774, Route 624 just west of Route 229) was hidden during the Civil War while the colonial church was used as a stable. Holes in the floor held stanchions for tethering horses. All the interior wood was consumed as fuel. On the grounds is a Confederate monument to the Little Fork Rangers, who drilled here early in the war. The memorial, a tall column topped by a female figure, was unveiled on May 25, 1904.

Continue north on Route 229 to turn right on Route 802 to Jeffersonton. Turn right at the first stop sign onto Jeffersonton Road and right at the next stop sign beside the church, still following Route 802.

On October 11, 1863, during the Bristoe Station campaign, cavalry fought in the streets of Jeffersonton, particularly around this Baptist church, the surrounding stone walls and fences, and an academy. The Union horsemen retreated across the Rappahannock River at Fauquier White Sulphur Springs where, covered by artillery, they made a stand on the north bank, but a spirited Confederate charge forced them to continue the withdrawal.

In the 1800s Jeffersonton was an important community highlighted by the prominent Jeffersonton Academy. The walls of Jeffersonton Baptist Church are original (1848); the interior burned in 1877. The church was twice used as a Confederate hospital, and seventy-three Southern soldiers are buried in the churchyard. Federals used the Methodist church as a hospital. At the intersection in front of the Methodist church stood the Davisson house, where Lee, Jackson, and Longstreet met on August 24, 1862, to formulate their flanking of Pope's Rappahannock line before McClellan could arrive to reinforce him.

Continue on Route 802 to cross the Rappahannock and enter what was Fauquier White Sulphur Springs.

Old buildings are preserved at the Fauquier Springs Country Club. Freeman's and Beverly's Fords are downstream. In August 1862 Longstreet was on the right around Beverly's Ford, Jackson upstream at Jeffersonton, facing this community, with Stuart's cavalry farther upstream at Waterloo Bridge.

On August 18 Lee's forces held the Rapidan River from opposite Rapidan Station east to Raccoon Ford. He intended to send Stuart to destroy the railroad over the Rappahannock at Rappahannock Station in Pope's rear, but the Federals learned of the plan from orders captured from Stuart at Verdiersville and retreated behind the Rappahannock, establishing a line from Beverly's Ford to Kelly's Ford farther east. Lee's new line started opposite Rappahannock Station and extended west to this point, with Stuart at Waterloo Bridge. Longstreet shifted west to Sulphur Springs and Waterloo Bridge as Jackson started around the Federal flank. Pope guarded against a Confederate flank move at Kelly's Ford to the east but concentrated most of his forces near the Rappahannock south of Warrenton, facing Longstreet. When forced to withdraw, Pope took parallel routes along the railroad and the Warrenton turnpike toward Manassas.

On August 21 Jackson and Stuart crossed at Beverly's Ford, but the Federals reacted quickly and aggressively. In a tremendous artillery duel the Confederates were driven back. On August 22 Jackson passed Freeman's Ford en route upstream to Sulphur Springs, and the Federals crossed and attacked his train. The Northerners were driven back across the river. Later in the day Jackson crossed a brigade and a regiment at Sulphur Springs, where the bridge had been burned, but the troops were isolated by high water, which raised the water level six feet during the night. Jackson concentrated his artillery on the southern bank and had his engineers rebuild the bridge the next day.

On August 2, 1863, Buford's cavalry crossed at Beverly's Ford as others crossed the river at Kelly's Ford, which initiated a major battle around Brandy Station before the Federals were forced to withdraw. On August 5 Federal infantry under Brig. Gen. David M. Gregg crossed the Rappahannock at Waterloo and advanced toward Rixeyville.

Return to Jeffersonton and drive straight on Route 621 to Route 229. Turn right on Route 229 to U.S. 221.

From Jeffersonton Jackson and the rest of the army turned west to Amissville, then north to cross the Rappahannock at Hinson's Mill on August 25. All that remains of Civil War interest is found at Amissville United Methodist Church to the left from U.S. 211. In the middle rear of the cemetery lies John M. Marshall, the last survivor of Mosby's rangers, who died at age ninety-four. The road to Hinson's Mill becomes a private lane before dead-ending at the river.

We turn right briefly on U.S. 211 then immediately left onto Route 622 to narrow one-lane Waterloo Bridge.

Stuart crossed the Rappahannock on August 22, 1862, at Waterloo Bridge and turned southeast through Warrenton and Auburn Mills to Catlett Station, then returned here. After Jackson started his flanking move, Longstreet's corps concentrated here. Federal cavalry crossed several times in late 1863.

Waterloo Landing (1840, Route 622 north of Jeffersonton) retains cannonball holes in its walls from the Civil War. Reportedly Mosby's men captured a Federal payroll while the Federals were at Water-

loo, and each man received two thousand dollars, including a son of Pickett Withers, owner of Lakeview (1750, intersection of Routes 624 and 625, to the northwest of Route 229). The Glen (1734, off Route 613 on the Rappahannock River) contained Miller's Woolen Factory, which made uniforms for the Confederate army. It was burned by Federal soldiers, who spared the house because it was occupied by wounded Southern troops.

A Federal soldier caught looting an upstairs room of Pleasant Hill (1806, off Route 640 one mile west of Rixeyville on Route 229) was killed with a shovel wielded by owner James Temberlake. Spurs marked the stairs as the soldier was dragged out of the house. Rose Dale (1840, just east of Route 229 on Route 640) was home to Martha Fixey, who fed Union soldiers and pumped them for information, which she passed on to the Confederates. Near Butler's Store is the Crigler Place (1790, three miles from Rixeyville off Route 640). Nearby, where the Hazel and Thornton Rivers join, is Storke's Ford, often used by Civil War troops. Sunny Side (1707, Route 633 off Route 729) was occupied by Federal troops. El Dorado (1830, Route 729 east of Route 229) served as a campground for Union troops marching between Winchester and Richmond.

Across Waterloo Bridge turn left onto Route 688, which becomes Leeds Manor Road, to Orlean, through which Union and Confederate armies marched. At the courthouse a stone Confederate sol-

Waterloo Bridge spans the Rappahannock and was used by Stuart's cavalry on the raid of John Pope's headquarters at Catlett Station in August 1862.

dier rests atop a tall pedestal, dedicated on June 3, 1910. In Orlean turn right on Route 732–John Barton Payne Road. Turn left onto Route 733 to Route 647–Chest Hill (alternately known as Cresthill). At the stop sign turn left to cross Interstate 66 and turn right onto Route 55 East–West Main Street into Marshall, known during the Civil War as Salem. It was renamed for local resident John Marshall, generally considered the greatest chief justice of the U.S. Supreme Court.

These are narrow, twisting roads that skirted Pope's right flank, hidden from Federal view by ridges. Jackson's soldiers, ill shod, marched rapidly over the rocky lanes, suffering from the heat and diarrhea, brought on by a diet of green apples and corn.

On August 25, after a twenty-six-mile forced march, Jackson allowed his men a few hours' rest here. Two days later Lee and his staff, riding to join Jackson, were almost captured by the Ninth New York Cavalry two miles west of Marshall. The officers relied on bluff, forming a line of battle and apparently ready to charge, and the Federals withdrew. Here Lee and Longstreet learned that Union troops blocked Thoroughfare Gap. On October 5, 1864, Mosby placed two howitzers atop Stephenson's Hill, south of Marshall, and fired on the railroad station and workers repairing the railroad, destroyed by retreating Confederates. One shell penetrated the roof of the Frye house but failed to explode. The proprietor threw the shell out the back door into a Union camp, whose occupants quickly scattered. Mosby's goal, to delay the rebuilding of the railroad, was accomplished. Rather than surrender the Forty-third Virginia Cavalry, also known as the Partisan Rangers, Mosby disbanded the group here on April 21, 1865. Part of his message to the two hundred troops read: "The vision we have cherished of a free and independent country has vanished, and the country is now the spoil of a conqueror. I disband your organization in preference to surrendering it to our enemies."

Col. Henry Dixon was the only man in the county who had dared vote for Lincoln in 1860. It is said he carried his ballot in one hand and a pistol in the other. After the war he was killed in a gun battle in the streets of Alexandria.

A handy brochure titled *Historic Marshall, Virginia, 1797* (available from the Historic Marshall Planning Committee, P.O. Box 203, Marshall VA 22115) lists several historical sites, including the Frye house (1853), the Norfolk-Southern Railway Depot (1852, Salem Station during the war), and the Confederate Post Office (1805), all situated along Main Street. At the corner of the Marshall National Bank is a marker where Mosby disbanded his Rangers. Stephenson's Hill is just west of the marker, above a nursing home. In the city cemetery is a Confederate monument, unveiled in October 1928.

To the west is Delaplane, known as Piedmont Station during the Civil War. Jackson marched his soldiers from the Shenandoah Valley to Piedmont, where they boarded trains that took them to First Manassas.

Continue east on Route 55 to the Plains (White Plains during the war).

The Army of Northern Virginia passed through in August 1862 to turn southeast toward Manassas. This was part of Mosby's Confederacy. Twice Federal forces scoured the area trying to eradicate him. Frustrated by their failure to do so, they burned homes, smokehouses, barns, stables, and fields. Note the antebellum Grace Episcopal Church (1852).

Continue east on Route 55 to Thoroughfare Gap where rocky ridges rise two hundred feet to either side. Pass between Biscuit Mountain to the south and Mother Leathercoat Mountain to the north. In the gap note two historical markers and a Civil War Trails marker on the north side of Route 55. Turn right onto Turner Road to cross Interstate 66, then turn left on Beverly Mill Drive to the mill, which is not open to visitors. Above the impressive structure rises Mother Leathercoat Mountain.

The Manassas Gap Railroad was built through Thoroughfare Gap in 1852. Until early 1862 the Confederate Commissary Department stored large quantities of meat in the mill. As Joseph E. Johnston withdrew from Manassas in March, the interior of the mill was burned, along with a million pounds of salted meat and bacon, a smell that alerted the distant Federals to the evacuation. The mill was in the center of the Union lines during the battle at Thoroughfare Gap. Fighting raged on both sides of the gap as Confederate troops climbed over and through narrow crevices, one man at a time, to flank the Federal position. Southerners firing from Beverly's Mill were driven out but returned to resume their work. The impressive six-story Chapman's Mill (1740), on Broad Run, has stone walls six feet thick at the base and two feet thick at the top. It was renamed Beverly's Mill after its postwar reconstruction and operated until 1952. Jackson's troops passed through in July 1861 via rail, and Stuart followed on horse. In 1862 the Army of Northern Virginia marched near here en route to Second Manassas. Tragedy struck on October 22, 1998, when an incredibly fierce arson blaze consumed all the woodwork within the mill, as well as considerable and irreplaceable mill machinery. The incident led the owner to donate the eight acres of the site to preservationists who will stabilize the ruins and interpret the site in the old mill store. To help, contact Turn the Mill Around, P.O. Box 207 Broad Run VA 20137.

To the north is Hopewell Gap, where Antioch Church is found. It was a campsite for three brigades of Confederates under Cadmus Wilcox. To the south was Lambert's Gap, where an attempt to flank Union forces in Thoroughfare Gap was canceled.

Return to Route 55 and turn left. Continue east on Route 55 to Haymarket, then turn right on Fayette Street to Saint Paul's Episcopal Church.

Federal troops torched every structure in Haymarket except two homes and this church (1801), constructed as a district courthouse and used as a school in 1814 and a public meeting hall in 1833 before becoming a church in 1833. Here the Prince William Rifles, created in November 1859, drilled and became part of the Seventeenth Virginia. Religious services were suspended for six years after July 21, 1861, when the battle of Manassas was fought just a few miles to the east. Casualties filled the church during both battles at Manassas. Furniture was carried outside and straw placed along the outside walls to form beds. Local women brought food and linen to the church and tended the men. Eighty men who died were buried in a long trench on the south side of the churchyard. When Jackson passed through on August 26, 1862, the locals fed and watered his men. Fifteen Federal stragglers were captured. Union cavalry soon appeared, looking fruitlessly for Jackson. When Stuart arrived, skirmishing broke out. On

The Grace Episcopal Church in Marshall dates from 1852.

August 28 the Federal division of Brig. Gen. James B. Ricketts, supported by cavalry under Kilpatrick, arrived to block the path of Longstreet, marching to the relief of Jackson at Second Manassas. Stuart returned to open a path for Longstreet in the afternoon, then broke off the engagement to rejoin Jackson at Groveton. Some of Pope's troops retreated through Haymarket in the early morning of August 29. While Kilpatrick ate lunch in a local home, the community was shelled as Longstreet approached. Saint Paul's was used as a hospital for the Union wounded from Groveton, and their dead were buried in the west end of the churchyard. With the departure of the Federals, the church again became a Confederate hospital for the wounded from Manassas, and again in September when an epidemic swept through the Eleventh Alabama.

On October 16 a Federal wagon train escorted by cavalry was jumped here by the Second North Carolina cavalry, who inflicted fifty casualties. A week later heavy Union forces from the Eleventh Corps arrived to watch Lee in the Shenandoah. On November 4 Federals returned to loot the town. Then, as families huddled together in fear, the Northerners burned nearly every structure in town. Saint Paul's was used in the latter years of the war as a Federal barracks, stable, and slaughterhouse. Northern troops eventually burned the building, leaving only the brick walls for reconstruction, which was accomplished in 1867.

War returned to Haymarket on June 21, 1863, as Confederate and Federal cavalry skirmished on the way to Pennsylvania. When the Union First Corps marched through on June 25, Stuart shelled the column, forcing the Federals to stop and deploy to chase him away. After the battle of Gettysburg, Lee and Meade maneuvered across northern Virginia. On October 13, at Buckland, Stuart routed Custer's troopers, who fled to Haymarket where infantry support waited. Stuart and Fitzhugh Lee's two cavalry brigades encountered the Union infantry, artillery, and troopers a mile from town at the current intersection of Routes 15 and 55. Undeterred, Stuart attacked the Federals directly and with a flanking move that failed, resulting in sixty casualties on each side. Reportedly Lee, Jackson, and Longstreet met on Route 29 west of Route 234 during the Second Manassas campaign.

The massive stone Chapman's Mill is a landmark in Thoroughfare Gap, which was traveled by a number of Civil War armies. To reach the battle at Manassas in 1862, Longstreet's corps swept Union forces out of the gap.

Return to Route 55 and continue east to Gainesville, where Stuart joined Jackson on August 26.

Jackson followed the Manassas Gap Railroad to Gainesville. Instead of continuing to Bull Run on the Warrenton turnpike, however, he turned right to Bristoe Station on the Orange and Alexandria Railroad. Longstreet turned left here onto the Warrenton turnpike (U.S. 29) to Groveton and the battlefield of Second Manassas.

In Gainesville turn right onto U.S. 29 for a short distance, then left on Route 619–Linton Hall Road. Cross Route 28 and remain on Route 619–Bristow Road to Bristow (Bristoe during the Civil War).

On August 24, 1862, Jackson wrecked the rails and caused two trains to crash spectacularly. He also cut telegraph wires and destroyed the railroad trestle over Broad Run. His rear guard skirmished with Pope's probes. A year later, after Gettysburg, A. P. Hill suffered heavy casualties in a senseless attack along the track.

Bristoe is one of many Civil War battlefields where nothing is preserved or protected and development is steadily creeping east from Washington to Manassas. A hundred-acre golf course and giant church complex are due to be built, and the county plans only to erect historical signs. Adding the 143 Confederate dead from Bristoe and those who died during the summer and fall of 1861 (mainly from typhoid fever) when this was Confederate Camp Jones on the Orange and Alexandria Railroad, about five hundred soldiers lie in unidentified plots. Several miles to the south and along the railroad and Virginia Route 28 is Catlett, a rail station.

Brentsville, one of Prince William County's five county seats, is several miles farther south on Route 619–Bristow Road. The fourth courthouse (1822), a brick two-story structure, remains, preserved in a Historical Recreation Area by the Prince William County Park Authority. Capt. Joseph K. Newell of Massachusetts was detailed to collect brick during the Federal occupation of the area. At this courthouse he noted that the work party "commenced at the top to get bricks, beginning with the chimneys and working down, while with the clerk's office, they commenced at the bottom and worked up." Newell found four of the rooms filled "fully two feet deep with the papers and documents, some of great antiquity," and expressed a hope that the citizens would "appoint a county clerk who will take better care of his papers in the future." Units of both armies maintained headquarters here during the war.

Also in Brentsville is Saint James Episcopal Church (1847), a stone structure so damaged by use as a Federal stable that the congregation could barely pay for repairs. It is now Hatcher Memorial Baptist Church.

Return to Route 28–Nokesville Road and turn right onto it. The highway becomes Route 28–Center Street in Manassas. Turn right into Manassas Cemetery, which surrounds the Confederate Cemetery.

Established by local Confederate veteran W. S. Fewell in 1867, the one-acre plot contained 250 reinterments within a year. In 1889 the Virginia General Assembly voted funds for the tall red sandstone monument, dedicated by W. H. F. Lee. The stone Confederate standing at parade rest was added in 1909.

From the cemetery turn right onto Route 28–Center Street, then turn left onto Peabody and right onto Lee Avenue. The Peace Jubilee Monument will be on the left.

This is the fifth Prince William County courthouse (1894). For the fiftieth anniversary of First Manassas, local resident George Carr, a Union veteran, organized the Great National Peace Jubilee, held on July 21, 1911. Ten thousand attended, including one thousand Confederate and Federal veterans. After a battle reenactment, concluding services were held here. Speakers included Pres. William Howard Taft, whose speech brought tears to the eyes of all present, and Virginia Gov. William H. Mann. A pageant featuring forty-five maidens represented the reunited states. All present held hands, and peace was declared between North and South. Carr, who arrived in Manassas in 1868, served in the Virginia General Assembly and the local city council, helped found the first public school in 1869, and worked to establish the national park at the battlefield.

This monument, dedicated four years later, is a memorial to the jubilee. It includes a bronze tablet, two cannon, and three four-hundred-pound anchors, each with three fathoms of chain, presented by Assistant Secretary of the Navy Franklin D. Roosevelt.

A different series of battles was held at Manassas in 1904, military maneuvers involving five thousand soldiers and twelve thousand militia. The teams were Blue—led by Brig. Gen. Frederick D. Grant, son of Ulysses S. Grant—and Brown. In one exercise the Blue army had to drive the Browns back through Thoroughfare Gap before reinforcements arrived, then the Blue had to defend the Stone Bridge. Grant won the first exercise but lost the second.

Continue to the end of Lee and turn right onto Grant. Turn left onto Prince William, and the Manassas Museum is on the right.

The museum, opened in 1991, has twenty-five hundred feet of exhibit space. The history of the northern Virginia piedmont is explored, with an emphasis on the two battles of Manassas and the war's impact on the local population. An eight-minute video, *A Community at War,* facilitates an understanding of the region. Artifacts include uniforms, weapons, and flags. During Jackson's attack, the grounds contained fortifications and camps.

Pick up a copy of *Driving Tours of Old Town Manassas,* which lists five Civil War sites on its twelve-stop driving tour and five Civil War sites of the nine points on a walking tour. The community originated in 1852

The Peace Jubilee Monument in Manassas was dedicated in 1911 to symbolize the united country and to commemorate a large reunion of Federal and Confederate veterans.

at the junction of the Manassas Gap and Orange and Alexandria Railroads, which is what made this an important objective during the war. Across Prince William Street from the museum was the depot, site of an enormous supply complex of warehouses, sheds, tents, and sidings filled with hundreds of railcars crowded with supplies. The Confederates destroyed their vast stores here when Johnston evacuated in March 1862, and in August Jackson spectacularly burned a much larger stockpile of Union supplies. Three hundred yards to the west was a high mound topped by a large fort that Jackson's men stormed on August 26 to take Manassas Junction. It was destroyed in the early 1940s.

Behind Old Town Hall were rail sidings, train repair shops, and an engine turntable, all destroyed by Johnston. Also listed is the site of the world's first military railroad, constructed in the winter of 1861–62 to connect the Virginia Central with the Confederate position at Centreville. It was composed of rails Jackson liberated from the Baltimore and Ohio near Harpers Ferry. The Federals returned the rails when they dismantled the six-mile-long line.

Two very important possessions of the city museum are the Mayfield and Cannon Branch Forts, which are currently being cleared of vegetation and prepared for visitors. Hiking trails, interpretive signs, and reproduction cannon will be added to the eleven-acre site to be opened in late 2000. Mayfield may receive a Quaker Gun, a popular Confederate ruse. The guns were large timbers painted black to resemble heavy cannon to distant Federals, which discouraged attacks.

The Mayfield Fort was one of twelve works, connected by trenches, ordered built by Lee in May 1861 to protect Manassas Junction from Union attacks. Erected on the Mayfield farm, the open-ended circular work is two hundred feet in diameter and would have been manned by a company of soldiers and two cannon. Local historians believe part of the crews were sailors serving naval guns seized at the Norfolk Navy Yard. It was abandoned in March 1862.

Four miles away, on the opposite side of Manassas, is Cannon Branch Fort, one of a string of works constructed by Meade during 1863–64 to protect the supply depot and Orange and Alexandria Railroad

The Battle of Bristoe Station

Bristoe Station played a prominent role in a Civil War campaign a year after Stonewall Jackson seized it during the Second Manassas campaign. Following the battle of Gettysburg, Robert E. Lee withdrew to Culpeper and sent Longstreet's corps west, where it was used decisively at Chickamauga, Georgia. Union Gen. George Gordon Meade countered by dispatching his Eleventh and Twelfth Corps to reinforce William Rosecrans in Chattanooga. To prevent Meade from sending additional reinforcements, Lee crossed the Rapidan River in an attempt to sever Meade's supply route back to Manassas, much as he had done to Pope a year earlier. Meade skillfully pulled back with Lee in close pursuit.

A mile north of Broad Run, near Bristoe, on October 14, 1863, the

lead Confederates, under A. P. Hill, encountered what he thought was Meade's rear. Without reconnaissance or communicating with his superiors, Hill ordered Brig. Gen. Henry Heth's division to attack. Finding large numbers of Union troops marching parallel with the railroad on his right, Heth, with Hill's permission, turned to face the danger on his flank.

The Federal troops were the division of Brig. Gen. Alexander Webb. Detecting the Confederates at the same time as the Southerners saw them, Webb formed a battle line behind the railroad embankment from Broad Run to Bristoe Station and the Brentsville road. Maj. Gen. Gouverneur K. Warren's Second Corps soon appeared and extended Webb's position with the divisions of Brig. Gens. Alexander Hays and John

C. Caldwell. Artillery was deployed on high ground behind them.

At 3 P.M. Heth sent the four thousand men of his North Carolina brigade to either side of the Brentsville road at the railroad embankment. They suffered heavy casualties but seized a portion of the embankment before they were blasted by Union artillery. Many stunned Confederates surrendered; the remainder hastily retreated.

During this assault Confederate Maj. Gen. Richard H Anderson's division arrived. Two of his brigades joined Heth's survivors in a second attack, which was again repulsed. In support, Anderson's chief of artillery, Maj. David McIntosh, deployed seven guns on a rise only five hundred yards from the Federals. When the Confederates withdrew, Webb surged

forward and captured the cannon, dragging five into the Union lines.

More Confederates joined the attack as they arrived, but to no better effect. Lee reached the field at 4 P.M. with Lt. Gen. Richard Ewell's Second Corps. A resulting artillery duel was fierce but settled nothing. The day closed with Maj. Gen. Robert E. Rodes unsuccessfully assaulting Caldwell's division near the railroad bridge spanning Broad Run. The Federals withdrew after dark.

Hill attempted to explain his impetuous action as he and Lee rode the battlefield the following day. At length Lee sighed, looking at the debris of battle and said sadly, "Well, well, General. Bury these poor men and let us say no more about it." Confederate casualties totaled 1,300, Union 546.

347

from raiders like Mosby. It is one hundred feet in diameter. The earthworks in both forts average about eight feet in height. Apparently they were never attacked and rarely if ever manned.

Two miles south of the national park on Route 234 is the Ben Lomond Manor House (1837, Ben Lomond Manor House, 10311 Sudley Manor Drive, Manassas, VA 22110, 707-792-7060), which in 1986 was donated to the Prince William County Park Authority. The residents retired to safety with relatives in Richmond when battles loomed, and it is believed that Union soldiers occupied the dwelling before or during Second Manassas, when it may have been a hospital. On plaster walls throughout the house are scrawled names, dates, units, and comments in pencil. The writing is found both at standing height and near the ceiling, which suggests the rooms had been outfitted with bunk beds. The dining room, probably used for surgery, contains no graffiti. One legible name is Wallace Cranston, who won a Medal of Honor at Chancellorsville for rescuing a wounded Confederate officer and transporting him to a field hospital at the Chancellor house. After the war Cranston became a congressman from Kansas. The six-acre site is open for special events and by appointment.

Several surviving historic homes include Willow Green (Balls Ford Road near New Market on Routes 234 and 66), a refuge for civilians during both battles, and Fairview, the Conrad home

(Routes 234 and 66), was a hospital during the fighting. Ewell's Chapel (1847, now Grace Church, on Route 615 west of Route 15 near Hickory Grove) marks the site where Mosby and a band of men were ambushed on June 22, 1863. The Federals fired poorly and Mosby escaped, leading Meade to say, "Thus the prettiest chance in the world to dispose of Mr. Mosby was lost."

Return to Grant and turn right. Turn left onto Route 234 North–Sudley Road, and turn right to the Manassas National Battlefield Visitors Center. There is a twelve-mile, twelve-stop driving tour to important sites on the Second Manassas battlefield.

Peruse the exhibits and fiber-optic map and perhaps take the First Manassas walking tour that begins at the visitors center.

Return to Route 234–Sudley Road and turn right, then left onto U.S. 29. Turn right into Stop No. 1, Battery Heights.

After watching Union troops marching past on the Warrenton turnpike (U.S. 29), Jackson called his men down from their wooded hilltop in the late afternoon of August 28. Their surprise attack against John Gibbon's brigade was met with great bravery from the Federals. A vicious two-hour stand-up fight at a distance of eighty yards occurred

A Tour of the Battle of Bristoe Station

Available from Richmond National Battlefield Park or Manassas National Battlefield Park is another of the excellent mini guided tours of otherwise forgotten battlefields. *The Battle of Bristoe Station, October 14, 1863,* lists only three stops. The first is at the intersection of Chapel Springs Road and Route 619. This was the Old Greenwich road on which A. P. Hill's corps was traveling when it spotted Union Gen. George Sykes's Fifth Corps a half mile ahead at Broad Run. Confederate

artillery unlimbered and opened on the Federals.

The second stop is at Broad Run, on Route 28, which our tour passes after we visit present-day Bristow. There Sykes's men were resting when Hill shelled them. The Federals hurriedly withdrew, pursued briefly by three Confederate brigades—two of which would join the attack.

Stop No. 3 is at Bristoe Station (present Bristow) on the Orange and Alexandria Railroad. Confederates attacked the line of the railroad from

both sides of the road. The strong Federal defense, supported by artillery, extended in a line behind the railroad embankment.

As Sykes retreated, Gouverneur K. Warren's corps advanced along the railroad, pursued by other Confederate units. Upon spotting Warren's force, Hill turned from his pursuit of Sykes and attacked Warren. Seeing the Confederates massing, Warren placed his units in a battle line behind the railroad. The Confederates made a brief breakthrough northeast up the tracks, at the

railroad trestle, which Stuart attempted to burn and which was destroyed by Stonewall Jackson in the Second Manassas campaign, but the Federals beat them back. Here, in the center, Confederate attacks ebbed forty feet from the railroad, and many Rebels surrendered rather than attempt a retreat through the deadly fire. The Federals captured five Confederate cannon abandoned just to the left. Late in the battle Southern reinforcements attacked the left of the Union line, to the southwest, but Federal reinforcements drove them off.

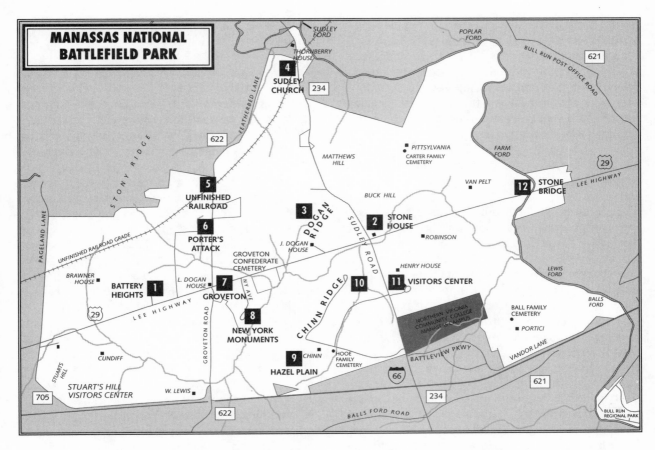

in the fields to your front; the combat ended only when night fell. One-third of the seven thousand soldiers involved fell. Jackson had prevented Pope from proceeding to Washington, where he would have been united with McClellan's Army of the Potomac. A hiking trail leads to the site of Brawner farm. The Dogan house, where Mosby and Union Gen. Edwin H. Stoughton (Mosby's prisoner) ate breakfast, the only surviving house in Groveton, was purchased and restored by the Prince William County Chamber of Commerce in 1949 and donated to the National Park Service.

Turn left onto U.S. 29 to the intersection with Route 234–Manassas-Sudley Road. Turn left here and immediately right to the parking area for Stop No. 2, the Stone House.

This red sandstone structure was owned by Henry Matthew during the Civil War and had seen furious fighting during First Manassas when Federals and Confederates seesawed across the turnpike that separated Buck Hill and Henry Hill. Constructed as a tavern in 1820, the Stone House was used as a hospital during both battles. Union soldiers were paroled here in August 1862. Cannonballs embedded in its walls are re-creations. The house, usually open on summer weekends, has several exhibits inside that describe its history.

Pope's headquarters on August 29–30 were a short distance behind the Stone House on Buck Hill, where the view of the battlefield is as good today as it was then. The ridge to the west across the road was an important artillery position, Dogan Ridge, where Pope concentrated twenty pieces to pound the Confederate line on Stony Ridge beyond.

Turn right from the parking area onto Route 234–Manassas-Sudley Road, then left at the top of the ridge into Stop No. 3, Dogan Ridge.

349

To the front are fields where Pope's men deployed for battle on the morning of August 29. Their long lines marched into the distant woods to attack Jackson's twenty-four-thousand-man corps, which held a two-mile-long line from Sudley Ford to the northeast to the Brawner farm to the southwest. The day-long Federal attacks were fierce but uncoordinated, and each was defeated in turn.

Turn left onto Route 234–Manassas-Sudley Road and turn left again to Stop No. 4, Sudley Church.

The old brick Sudley Methodist Episcopal Church (1814) was so badly damaged through use by both armies as a hospital during the two battles fought here that it was razed following the Civil War. Wounded at First Manassas, Federal Col. John Rice was propped up in a fence corner by his fleeing comrades. When Amos and Margaret Benson found him two days later, his condition was so poor that they feared to move him. They cared for him in place for ten days, then he was moved and nursed back to health in Sudley Church. Rice returned home to Springfield, Massachusetts. Visiting Sudley in 1886, Rice learned that a debt of fifteen hundred dollars remained on the replacement structure, a sum the members could not raise. In appreciation of the kind care he had received in the land of his enemies, Rice took out an advertisement in a Massachusetts newspaper soliciting funds to pay off the debt. That church was burned by a lightning strike in 1918, and Sudley Methodist Church (1922) occupies the historic site today.

The Sudley Springs Hotel was a resort with a medicinal sulfur spring. Occupied during First and Second Manassas by local residents fleeing the fighting, it was used as a hospital following both battles. It burned early in the 1900s. A short trail leads to Sudley Springs Ford, where most of McDowell's army crossed in 1861.

The railroad cut atop Stony Ridge begins near the parking area. The cut and the high hill to the northwest formed the extreme left of Jackson's line, held by Brig. Gen. Maxey Gregg. Throughout August 29 a number of savage Federal assaults struck the knoll to the northwest, but all were turned back. While Pope's attention was focused here, Longstreet arrived on the opposite end of Jackson's line, extending the Confederate right beyond the Federal left. Lee wished to attack at once to relieve the pressure on Jackson, but Longstreet advised him to wait.

Turn left onto Route 234–Manassas-Sudley Road, then turn sharply left onto Route 622 (the historic Groveton-Sudley road and present-day Featherbed Lane), which parallels the railroad cut. Turn left into Stop No. 5, the Unfinished Railroad, which marks the center of the Southern line.

The deep cut running along the spine of Stony Ridge was part of an unfinished railroad that would have connected the Manassas Gap Railroad directly with Alexandria, bypassing the Orange and Alexandria Railroad to the south. Trails lead to the cut on either side of the road, where separate Federal attacks briefly broke Jackson's lines on August 29. Reinforcements rushed from less-threatened points on the line restored the Confederate position.

You may cross the road to the west to enter the Deep Cut, where the Federal Groveton Monument, identical to the one on Henry Hill, was placed by Union veterans in 1865. Here occurred some of the bloodiest fighting of the Civil War on August 30 when Fitz John Porter assaulted the position held by Confederate Gen. William E. Starke. When their ammunition was exhausted, Southerners hurled stone ballast at the Federals in a famous incident.

Turn left onto Route 622 and turn right into Stop No. 6, Porter's Attack.

The deep railroad cut atop Stony Ridge formed a natural breastwork manned by Jackson's men at Second Manassas.

A Confederate flank attack at Chinn Ridge in July 1861 led to the Union rout at First Manassas, and in August 1862 Southern troops again drove Union soldiers from the heights.

Believing Jackson was retreating on August 30, Pope sent Porter's corps in pursuit. Five thousand Federal troops advancing across open fields found the Confederates firmly in place and were decimated by Longstreet's artillery. Porter lost a third of his men before Longstreet loosed his infantry. Rangers lead summer weekend walking tours of the cut.

Continue to U.S. 29 and turn right onto it, noting the small, white frame Dogan house on your right at the intersection.

It is the only surviving structure of vanished Groveton, which was a crossroads community of eight or nine houses. The Dogan house started life as an overseers residence occupied by the family after their home burned in 1860. It is one of two original structures left on the battlefield today.

Turn left onto U.S. 29 for a short distance, then turn left into Stop No. 7, Groveton.

The Groveton Confederate Cemetery contains the remains of 275 to 500 soldiers, only a handful of them identified, killed at First and Second Manassas. A monument honors their sacrifice. Other Confederate casualties of the battles near Manassas are interred at Manassas, Haymarket, and Warrenton. Following the war Union dead were reinterred at Arlington National Cemetery, opposite Washington, D.C.

The Chinn house survived the Civil War but burned to the ground during restoration efforts in the 1950s. Only the foundation remains.

Turn left onto U.S. 29, then almost immediately turn right to Stop No. 8, the New York Monuments.

The monument to the Fourth New York Zouaves is to the right and the others, for the Fifth and Tenth New York units, are on the loop at the end of the road. Hood's Texans destroyed these regiments during the assault on August 30 (123 men of the Fifth New York were killed in five minutes). Longstreet's men continued east across Young's Branch and up Chinn Ridge.

Return to U.S. 29 and turn right. At the intersection with Route 234–Manassas-Sudley Road, turn right onto Route 234. Turn right at the first road. At the next intersection turn right to Stop No. 9, Hazel Plain, where the stone foundation is all that remains of the Chinn House atop Chinn Ridge.

Longstreet's men attacked past here about 5 P.M. Hazel Plain (1809) was used as a hospital; its well reportedly was filled with amputated arms and legs. The large two-story structure survived two battles, but burned down while being restored in the 1950s. Federal troops fought bravely here late on the afternoon of August 30, slowing the Confederate assault before Longstreet's men enveloped both flanks.

Continue down the road to turn around at the loop parking area. Stop No. 10 is Chinn Ridge, a Federal line that stretched for four hundred yards along the hill crest.

Union soldiers here bought time for Pope to assemble a defensive line on the next ridge, Henry Hill. If this attempt had failed, Confederate troops would cut the Warrenton turnpike and trap much of Pope's army, which would be isolated from McClellan's help at Alexandria. A monument on the east side of the loop road notes the spot where Daniel Webster's son, Fletcher, was killed leading the Twelfth Massachusetts.

At the intersection turn left on the park road to Route 234. The park road to the visitors center is nearly opposite.

Most Federals retreated along this route. Enough men, however, had occupied the sunken path (Route 234) and Henry Hill beyond it so that the Confederates attacking over the crest of Chinn Ridge behind you were driven off. This allowed Pope's army to retreat across Bull Run to Centreville, Fairfax, and Washington in some semblance of order. The rout ended here, two miles after it started.

Drive to the visitors center, Stop No. 11.

Troops of McDowell, Porter, Jesse Reno, and Franz Sigel occupied the ridge late in the day and halted the Confederate pursuit, inspired by George Sykes's regular army professionals. After the Confederates had won the first battle of Manassas here, the Federals staved off complete defeat at Second Manassas.

You may proceed to the Stone Bridge, Stop No. 12, if you have not visited it on an earlier tour.

From the visitors center turn right onto Route 234 and right on U.S. 29 to the bridge parking on the left.

The Stone Bridge of First Manassas fame had been destroyed, but Pope crossed here on a wooden replacement.

The battle of Third Manassas was fought a few years ago when developers almost built a huge complex bordering the battlefield. When the smoke had cleared, the NPS had acquired 558 acres of Stuart's Hill, which was Lee's and Longstreet's headquarters during Second Manassas and contains works for twelve cannon. A pullover has been established on Pageland Lane–Route 705, which crosses U.S. 29 from the north and parallels Interstate 66 and intersects Route 622, the Groveton-Sudley road. An exhibit shelter with a large map of the 1862 battlefield and a small, seasonally staffed "Visitors Contact Station" has been erected with exhibits. Weekend walking tours are held during the summer.

Before starting a tour of northern Virginia, consult the Virginia Civil War Trails publication *Northern Virginia: Crossroads of Conflict*. It lists about thirty stops for the battles around Manassas, the activities of Mosby, and preliminary maneuvers in the Gettysburg campaign.

The Atlanta and Gettysburg cycloramas are famous, but the Second Manassas cyclorama has been lost to history. Painted on a twenty thousand square foot canvas in 1886 by Theophile Poilpot and a team of thirteen artists who spent a summer sketching the battlefield, it was displaued in a circular building near the Washington Monument. The canvas was apparently cut up and sold in pieces to satisfy a debt, and little of it has survived.

The Dogan house is the only surviving structure from the tiny community of Groveton, where the battle of Second Mannassas began.

7

The Campaign and Battle of Antietam

T HE PRESENT SEEMS TO be the most propitious time since the commencement of the war for the Confederate Army to enter Maryland," Robert E. Lee wrote from his headquarters at Chantilly on September 3, 1862, after his stunning success at the battle of Second Bull Run. John Pope's army had been badly beaten, but after regrouping within the strong defenses of Washington, it would be united with the remainder of George B. McClellan's army. Lee feared that in a short time he would find himself again on the defensive, attempting to prevent a Federal force twice as large as his own from capturing Richmond. At the same time, he doubted that northern Virginia could sustain his army after a year of war had depleted its resources, and the transportation did not exist to feed his army from Richmond.

Lee hoped that a great victory on Northern soil might gain the Confederacy recognition and assistance from Great Britain or France. It could induce the people of the North to turn against the war and elect congressmen in the November elections who would require Lincoln to end the conflict. Considering the pro-Confederacy riots in Baltimore a year earlier, Marylanders might well throw "off the oppression to which she is now subject," Lee wrote, and join the Confederacy.

Such a diversion would force Lincoln to defend Maryland and prevent a late fall campaign against Richmond. Lee could feed his troops from Maryland's ripe harvest while allowing Virginia's farmers to reap their own crops. Horses could also be secured for the cavalry and worn-out teams.

The Confederate commander knew that his army was in poor condition, informing Davis that the men were "not properly equipped for an invasion of an enemy's territory. It lacks much of the material of war, is feeble in transportation, the animals being much reduced, and the men

On August 31, 1862, Robert E. Lee stood beside his famed mount Traveller, reading a map. When the wind blew the map into Traveller's face, the horse shied. Grabbing for the bridle, Lee stumbled and fell on his hands, breaking a bone in one and severely spraining the other. Doctors splinted and bandaged both hands. Lee, unable to ride, entered Maryland in an ambulance.

James Longstreet spent the campaign limping about in carpet slippers because of a painful blister on one of his heels. Stonewall Jackson, recently thrown by an unfamiliar horse, spent every possible moment resting his strained back in his tent.

Leesburg had been occupied by the enemy for several months when Robert E. Lee arrived, and the civilians gleefully welcomed the Confederates. "Everything that wears crinoline or a pretty face is out, and such shouts and waving of handkerchiefs and hurrahs by the overjoyed gender never emanated from human lips," wrote newspaperman Felix G. De Fontaine.

The Confederates invaded Maryland with two vital generals relieved of their commands for trivial reasons. Brig. Gen. John Bell Hood and Brig. Gen. Nathan Evans had clashed over possession of Union ambulances captured at Second Manassas. Hood was arrested and charged with insubordination.

Maj. Gen. A. P. Hill and his corps commander, prickly Stonewall Jackson, had also conflicted. Jackson noticed that on September 4 Hill's division started their march half an hour late. Once started, Hill rode in front of his men, ignoring heavy straggling at the rear, then he continued the march through a scheduled rest stop. After Jackson halted the column, Hill offered Jackson his sword. "Consider yourself under arrest for neglect of duty," Jackson snapped.

are poorly provided with clothes, and in thousands of instances are destitute of shoes."

That September morning Lee started the Army of Northern Virginia northeast toward Leesburg, twenty-five miles from Chantilly, to fords on the Potomac River. From there he could threaten Washington or Baltimore and force Lincoln to shift his forces north of the Potomac.

It was perhaps the most ragged and hungry invasion army in history. Like Stonewall Jackson's men a week earlier, they lived off the land. "For six days not a morsel of bread or meat had gone in our stomachs," wrote a private. "Our menu consists of apples and corn. We toasted, we burned, we stewed, we boiled, we roasted these two together, and singly, until there was not a man whose form had not caved in, and who had not a bad attack of diarrhea."

Most uniforms had been reduced to tatters, and one in four men was barefooted. Fortunate were the men who had secured new footwear from the Federal dead and prisoners at Manassas Junction.

Thousands of stragglers fell out of the march because of exhaustion and sickness. More, mainly from the Carolinas, were willing to die in defense of their homes but refused to leave Southern soil. Two-thirds of one regiment deserted before reaching the Potomac.

On Thursday, September 4, Lee's Army of Northern Virginia forded the Potomac River and crossed into Maryland. The water was only waist-high in places, and the crossing took four days. Alfred Waud sketched a small group of Union scouts observing a moonlit moment of the invasion while one of their number takes aim on one of the columns.

While Stonewall Jackson's corps was crossing the Potomac River at White's Ferry, a team of mules reached midstream and refused to move. Jackson summoned Maj. John A. Harmon, his chief quartermaster, who addressed the recalcitrant asses in the only language they understood—profanity.

"The ford is clear," Harmon reported to Jackson, who piously refrained from any cursing or blasphemy. "There's only one language that will make mules understand on a hot day that they must get out of the water."

Jackson only grinned.

The morale of the footsore and hungry Confederates swelled as the army crossed the Potomac. Amid the shouting and hurrahing, only one complaint was heard. Lt. William Johnson of South Carolina noted, "We needed a good washing of our bodies, but wading in the water did us no good in that direction."

BATTLES AND LEADERS

Even though Lee lost fifteen thousand troops along the way, three infantry divisions, a cavalry brigade, and his reserve artillery added twenty thousand soldiers to the army, which now numbered fifty thousand.

"None but heros are left," one Confederate bragged. These men had fought from Yorktown to Chantilly in six months, victoriously for the most part, and they were happy to finally take the war to their enemy.

The Confederates were met at Leesburg with food and water on September 4. "The Lord bless your dirty, ragged souls!" one old lady shouted as they passed.

The division of Maj. Gen. Daniel Harvey Hill led the way across the Potomac at White's Ford. Ragged Rebels shucked pants and shoes to wade across the half-mile-wide river, waist deep in late summer, as bands played "Maryland, My Maryland."

Surprised by the Confederate invasion of Union territory, a cabinet member wrote, "The War Department is bewildered, knows but little, does nothing, proposes nothing."

Maryland, My Maryland ■ By James Ryder Randall

The despot's heel is on thy shore,
Maryland!
His torch is at thy temple door,
Maryland!
Avenge the patriotic gore
That flecked the streets of Baltimore,
And be the battle-queen of yore,
Maryland, my Maryland!

Hark to an exiled son's appeal,
Maryland!
My Mother State, to thee I kneel,
Maryland!
For life and death, for woe and weal,
Thy peerless chivalry reveal,
And gird thy beauteous limbs with steel,
Maryland, my Maryland!

Thou wilt not cower in the dust,
Maryland!
Thy beaming sword shall never rust,

Maryland!
Remember Carroll's sacred trust,
Remember Howard's warlike thrust,
And all thy slumberers with the just,
Maryland, my Maryland!

Come! 'Tis the red dawn of the day,
Maryland!
Come with thy panoplied array,
Maryland!
With Ringgold's spirit for the fray,
With Watson's blood at Monterey,
With fearless Lowe and dashing May,
Maryland, my Maryland!

Come, for thy shield is bright and strong,
Maryland!
Come, for thy dalliance does thee wrong,
Maryland!
Come to thine own heroic throng,

That walks with liberty along,
And chant thy dauntless slogan-song,
Maryland! My Maryland!

Dear Mother, burst the tyrant's chain,
Maryland!
Virginia should not call in vain,
Maryland!
She meets her sisters on the plain,—
"Sic semper!" 'Tis the proud refrain
That baffles minions back again,
Maryland, my Maryland!

I see the blush upon thy cheek,
Maryland!
For thou wast ever bravely meek,
Maryland!
But lo! there surges forth a shriek
From hill to hill, from creek to creek,—
Potomac calls to Chesapeake,
Maryland, my Maryland!

Thou wilt not yield the Vandal toll,
Maryland!
Thou wilt not crook to his control,
Maryland!
Better the fire upon thee roll,
Better the blade, the shot, the bowl,
Than crucifixion of the soul,
Maryland, my Maryland!

I hear the distant thunder-hum
Maryland!
The Old Line's bugle, fife and drum
Maryland!
She is not dead, nor deaf, nor dumb,
Huzza! She spurns the Northern scum!
She breathes! She burns! She's come!
She'll come!
Maryland, my Maryland!

Lee erred in decreeing that sick, wounded, and barefoot soldiers would accompany the wagons to Winchester. Many soldiers were observed throwing their shoes away. "This idiotic proclamation cost us 10,000 men," a private complained.

"It was a noble spectacle," an officer wrote. A trooper agreed, noting, "There were few moments, perhaps, from the beginning to the close of the war, of excitement more intense, of exhilaration more delightful."

By September 7 the Army of Northern Virginia was in Union territory, concentrated around Frederick, Maryland. It had been a long summer of crisis in Washington, and the situation grew rapidly worse. In the West, Braxton Bragg's Army of Tennessee was near the Ohio River. Then, on September 4, a Maryland farmer rode down Pennsylvania Avenue shouting that the Confederates were coming.

Federal forces in Washington remained in disorder as gunboats patroled the Potomac and government employees again took up arms. Two days earlier Lincoln had restored McClellan to command "the fortifications of Washington, and all the troops for the defense of the capital."

The populace of every community, Southern and Union, anxiously maneuvered for a glimpse of Robert E. Lee, Stonewall Jackson, James Longstreet, Jeb Stuart, and other Confederate heroes. While Jackson wrote dispatches in the Everett house in Martinsburg, Virginia, civilians opened the windows and littered the floor with bouquets of roses.

McClellan proved his genius for organization a second time by combining Pope's Army of Virginia with his own Army of the Potomac. By September 5 McClellan was on the march, leaving two corps under Maj. Gens. Samuel Heintzelman and Franz Sigel to protect Washington. McClellan's other six corps, totaling eighty-four thousand men, marched to a base at Rockville, Maryland, twenty-five miles northwest of Lee.

In Frederick, Lee was disappointed to receive only a lukewarm welcome. There were few Southern sympathizers here, unlike eastern Maryland and Baltimore, but the citizens thronged the streets to view this legendary force.

Lee's Proclamation to the People of Maryland

Headquarters Army of
Northern Virginia
Near Fredericktown,
September 8, 1862

To the people of Maryland:
It is right that you should know the purpose that brought the Army under my command within the limits of your State, so far as that purpose concerns yourselves. The people of the Confederate States have long watched with the deepest sympathy the wrongs and outrages that have been inflicted upon the citizens of a commonwealth allied to the States of the South by the strongest social, political, and commercial ties. They have seen with profound indignation their sister State deprived of every

right, and reduced to the condition of a conquered province.
Under the pretense of supporting the Constitution, but in violation of its most valuable provisions, your citizens have been arrested and imprisoned upon no charge and contrary to all forms of law. The faithful and manly protest against this outrage made by the venerable and illustrious Marylander, to whom in better days, no citizens appealed for right in vain, was treated with scorn and contempt; the government of your chief city has been usurped by armed strangers; your legislature has been dissolved by the unlawful arrest of its members; freedom of the press and of speech has been suppressed; words have been declared offenses

by an arbitrary decree of the Federal Executive, and citizens ordered to be tried by a military commission for what they may dare to speak.
Believing that the people of Maryland possessed a spirit too lofty to submit to such a government, the people of the south have long wished to aid you in throwing off this foreign yoke, to enable you again to enjoy the inalienable rights of freemen, and restore independence and sovereignty to your State. In obedience to this wish, our army has come among you, and is prepared to assist you with the power of its arms in regaining the rights of which you have been despoiled.
This, citizens of Maryland, is our mission, so far as you are concerned.

No constraint upon your free will is intended; no intimidation will be allowed within the limits of his army, at least. Marylanders shall once more enjoy their ancient freedom of thought and speech. We know no enemies among you, and will protect all, of every opinion. It is for you to decide your destiny freely and without constraint. This army will respect your choice, whatever it may be; and while the Southern people will rejoice to welcome you to your natural position among them, they will only welcome you when you come of your own free will.
R. E. Lee,
General.

THE ANTIETAM CAMPAIGN
PRELIMINARY MOVEMENTS
September 3–17, 1862

Robert E. Lee and many other Confederates expected to be welcomed in Maryland as liberators, but few civilians cheered. There were "little symptoms of 'secesh'" in Buckeystown, wrote Lt. William Johnston. Buildings were shuttered, and people on the street seemed sorrowful that the Confederates had come.

"We were not received with cheers or songs or other evidence of approbation," Johnston continued, "but instead they looked on us in self-evident pity."

"I do not anticipate any general rising of the people in our behalf," Lee informed Jefferson Davis on September 7.

"A dirtier, filthier, more unsavory set of human beings never *strolled* through a town," wrote Dr. Lewis H. Steiner of the Southerners' entrance into Frederick. "Marching it could not be called without doing violence to the word."

One resident wrote of her humiliation "that this horde of ragamuffins could set our grand army of the Union at defiance." She noted their cheerfulness and dedication, though she labeled them "poor, misguided wretches."

Maryland civilians universally disdained the dirty and barely clothed condition of the Rebels, but one spotted something significant: "Just look at their guns. Ain't they bright and polished, and don't they glisten in the sun?"

"Why, John," a local woman exclaimed to a former neighbor who now marched with the Confederates, "how can such a dirty, filthy set of soldiers defeat the neatly dressed boys of the Army of the Potomac? Such clothes! All ragged and filthy."

"Bessie," he replied, "we don't put our best clothes on to kill hogs."

"I asked myself in amazement," wrote one loyal citizen, "were these dirty, lank, ugly specimens of humanity the men that had driven back again and again our splendid legions with their fine discipline, their martial show and colour? I felt humiliated at the thought that this horde of ragamuffins could set our grand army of the Union at defiance. Oh! They are so dirty! I don't think the Potomac River could wash them clean." Another noted, "They were the dirtiest men I ever saw, a most ragged, lean and hungry set of wolves. Yet there was a dash about them that the northern men lacked." Most observers were dismayed by the sight.

Lee had issued strict orders banning destruction and seizure of civilian property. Soldiers were required to pay for everything taken in foraging. The Confederates behaved as expected, and the people of Maryland responded in kind.

"To the People of Maryland," Lee proclaimed, his men had come "to assist you with the power of its arms in regaining the rights of which you have been despoiled. It is for you to decide your destiny freely and without

When Robert E. Lee's orders for the move against Harpers Ferry arrived, James Longstreet outstripped Stonewall Jackson's legendary secrecy by memorizing the orders and eating them. For his part, Jackson instructed his officers to ask local residents for a map of Chambersburg, Pennsylvania, and started that way via the National Road before veering off toward Harpers Ferry.

Abraham Lincoln had no illusions about George B. McClellan's capabilities. Returning him to command, the president knew, was like "curing the bite with the hair of the dog." However, he told John Hay: "We must use what tools we have. There is no man in the Army who can man these fortifications and lick these troops of ours into shape half as well as he. If he can't fight himself, he excels in making others ready to fight."

The Southerners could forage for food in Maryland, but they were low on munitions. Lee proposed to solve the problem by sending Jackson to seize the ordnance and supplies then stockpiled at Harpers Ferry.

constraint. This army will respect your choice, whatever it may be."

But there were few converts to the Confederacy. Only two hundred locals joined the army. Realizing that there would be no popular uprising, Lee continued his campaign.

Lee decided to march twenty-five miles west, across Catoctin and South Mountains to Hagerstown, then follow the Cumberland Valley, an extension of the Shenandoah Valley, twenty miles northeast to capture Pennsylvania's capital, Harrisburg. The destruction of a nearby railroad bridge over the Susquehanna River would disrupt an important east-west supply route for the Federals. From there Lee reportedly could have attacked Philadelphia, Baltimore, or Washington.

Before this ambitious plan could be executed, Lee would have to shift his vulnerable supply lines west of the Blue Ridge Mountains to the Shenandoah to protect against Federal cavalry raids. To accomplish this two Union garrisons had to be eliminated. At strategic Harpers Ferry, situ-

Jackson had first occupied Harpers Ferry during the early weeks of the war. He abandoned it in June 1861, and a Federal garrison had been in residence shortly afterward. The geography of the area made the town indefensible. Stonewall had once said he would rather "take the place forty times than undertake to defend it once."

Lee's plan required all avenues of escape from Harpers Ferry to be sealed off by having his men occupy the high ground: Loudon, Maryland, and Bolivar Heights. This image shows Gen. John Walker's view from Loudon Heights of the Federal camps across the river on Maryland Heights.

BATTLES AND LEADERS

ated where the Shenandoah River enters the Potomac, were twelve thousand Federals. North of that was Martinsburg, held by twenty-five hundred soldiers. Lee had expected that the two positions, isolated by his move across the Potomac, would be evacuated. In fact, McClellan had ordered the withdrawals, but the War Department had overruled him.

Lee, ever daring, split his army into four columns. James Longstreet—with three divisions, the supply trains, and reserve artillery—would march straight to Hagerstown via Boonsboro. Jackson, also with three divisions, would move through Boonsboro and on to Williamsport to cross the Potomac River there and seize Martinsburg from the north. He would then circle back east to invest Harpers Ferry north of the Shenandoah

Shoot If You Must, This Old Gray Head

As Confederate troops marched through Frederick, Maryland, on September 10, 1862, ninety-five-year-old resident Barbara Fritchie (also spelled Frietchie), thinking them Federals, took her American flag and stepped to her second-story window to wave it at the troops. Finding Rebels instead, she waved defiantly to taunts from the soldiers.

"Go on, Granny," an officer called to her. "Wave your flag as much as you please."

The legend grew that the officer was Stonewall Jackson and that he had prevented his men from shooting the intrepid lady. John Greenleaf Whittier wrote a poem that instantly immortalized the incident. In response to critics who maintained the incident was purely fiction, in 1886 he wrote, "I had no reason to doubt its accuracy then, and I am still constrained to believe that it had a foundation in truth."

Up from the meadows rich with corn,
Clear in the cool September morn,
The clustered spires of Frederick stand
Green-walled by the hills of Maryland.
Round about them orchards sweep,
Apple and peach tree fruited deep,
Fair as a garden of the Lord
To the eyes of the famished rebel
   horde,
On that pleasant morn of the early fall
When Lee marched over the
   mountain-wall,
Over the mountains winding down,
Horse and foot, into Frederick town.
Forty flags with their silver stars,
Forty flags with their crimson bars,
Flapped in the morning wind; the sun
Of noon looked down, and saw not
   one.
Up rose old Barbara Frietchie then,
Bowed with her fourscore years and
   ten;
Bravest of all in Frederick town,
She took up the flag the men hauled
   down;

In her attic window the staff she set,
To show that one heart was loyal yet.
Up the street came the rebel tread,
Stonewall Jackson riding ahead.
Under his slouched hat left and right
He glanced; the old flag met his sight.
"Halt!"—the dust-brown ranks stood
   fast;
"Fire!"—out blazed the rifle blast.
It shivered the window, pane and
   sash;
It rent the banner with seam and gash.
Quick, as it fell, from the broken staff
Dame Barbara snatched the silken
   scarf;
She leaned far out on the window-sill,
And shook it forth with a royal will.
"Shoot, if you must, this old gray
   head,
But spare your country's flag," she
   said.
A shade of sadness, a blush of shame,
Over the face of the leader came;
The nobler nature within him stirred
To life at that woman's deed and word;

"Who touches a hair on yon gray
   head
Dies like a dog! March on!" he said.
All day long through Frederick Street
Sounded the tread of marching feet;
All day long that free flag tost
Over the heads of the rebel host.
Ever its torn folds rose and fell
On the loyal winds that loved it well;
And through the hill-gaps sunset light
Shone over it with a warm good-
   night.
Barbara Frietchie's work is o'er,
And the Rebel rides on his raids no
   more.
Honor to her! And let a tear
Fall, for her sake, on Stonewall's bier.
Over Barbara Frietchie's grave,
Flag of Freedom and Union, wave!
Peace and order and beauty draw
Round thy symbol of light and law;
And ever the stars above look down
On thy stars below in Fredericktown!

At Frederick a party of six ladies, including Henry Kyd Douglas's mother, and a gentleman escort arrived to meet the reknown Confederate leaders. They gave flowers to James Longstreet and Stonewall Jackson, but Douglas, an aide on Jackson's staff, refused to disturb Robert E. Lee on their behalf.

Overhearing the conversation, Lee stepped out of his tent, offering an apology for Douglas's manners and reprimanding him with a smile. He later told Mrs. Douglas that this was "the only time I ever knew your son to fail in the performance of his duty, as General Jackson can testify."

All the ladies wanted to shake Lee's hands, which were still bandaged. "Touch them gently, ladies," he ordered, and they did.

River. Maj. Gen. Lafayette McLaws, with two divisions, approached Harpers Ferry from the Maryland side of the Potomac through Jefferson, Burkittsville, and Brownsville. Brig. Gen. John G. Walker's division retraced Lee's invasion route to Licksville before turning west to parallel the Potomac and cross it above Licksville, then marched west to Harpers Ferry via Hillsboro. After seizing Harpers Ferry, the six divisions would march north to join Longstreet and Lee.

Longstreet opposed the plan, telling Lee the men were "in no condition to divide in the enemy's country."

This complex plan, transcribed as Special Orders No. 191, was issued on September 9 to each commander. Jackson personally copied his order and sent it to D. H. Hill, who never realized that his copy from Lee never arrived. A Confederate staff officer, known only to himself, wrapped three cigars in that order and pocketed them.

The next morning Lee's scarecrows, rested and fed, marched out in good humor, bands playing and men singing. Stuart, operating from Urbanna to the east, informed Lee that McClellan was advancing from Washington to Frederick along three different routes. Lee dismissed the

Lee's Lost Dispatch

Special Orders, No. 191
Hdqrs. Army Of Northern Virginia
September 9, 1862

I. The citizens of Fredericktown being unwilling, while overrun by members of this army, to open their stores, in order to give them confidence, and to secure to officers and men purchasing supplies for benefit of this command, all officers and men of this army are strictly prohibited from visiting Fredericktown except on business, in which cases they will bear evidence of this in writing from division commanders. The provost-marshal in Fredericktown will see that his guard rigidly enforces this order.

II. Major Taylor will proceed to Leesburg, Va. And arrange for transportation of the sick and those unable to walk to Winchester, securing the transportation of the country for this purpose. The route between this and Culpeper Court-House east of the mountains being unsafe, will

no longer be traveled. Those on the way to this army already across the river will move up promptly; all others will proceed to Winchester collectively and under command of the officers, at which point, being the general depot of this army, its movements will be known and instructions given by commanding officer regulating further movements.

III. The army will resume its march to-morrow, taking the Hagerstown road. General Jackson's command will form the advance, and, after passing Middletown, with such portion as he may select, take the route toward Sharpsburg, cross the Potomac at the most convenient point, and by Friday morning take possession of the Baltimore and Ohio Railroad, capture such of them as may be at Martinsburg, and intercept such as may attempt to escape from Harper's Ferry.

IV. General Longstreet's command will pursue the same road as far as Boonsborough, where it will halt,

with reserve, supply, and baggage trains of the army.

V. General McLaws, with his own division and that of General R. H. Anderson, will follow General Longstreet. On reaching Middletown will take the route to Harper's Ferry, and by Friday morning possess himself of the Maryland Heights and endeavor to capture the enemy at Harper's Ferry and vicinity.

VI. General Walker, with his division, after accomplishing the object in which he is now engaged, will cross the Potomac at Cheek's ford, ascend its right bank to Lovettsville, take possession of Loudoun Heights, if practicable, by Friday morning. Key's Ford on his left, and the road between the end of the mountain and the Potomac on his right. He will, as far as practicable, co-operate with Generals McLaws and Jackson, and intercept retreat of the enemy.

VII. General D. H. Hill's division will form the rear guard of the army, pur-

suing the road taken by the main body. The reserve artillery, ordnance, and supply trains, &c., will precede General Hill.

VIII. General Stuart will detach a squadron of cavalry to accompany the commands of Generals Longstreet, Jackson, and McLaws, and, with the main body of the cavalry, will cover the route of the army, bringing up all stragglers that may have been left behind.

IX. The commands of Generals Jackson, McLaws, and Walker, after accomplishing the objects for which they have been detached, will join the main body of the army at Boonsborough or Hagerstown.

X. Each regiment on the march will habitually carry its axes in the regimental ordnance-wagons, for use of the men at their encampments, to procure wood &c.

By command of
General R. E. Lee;
R. H. Chilton, Assistant Adjutant-General.

threat, telling Walker that McClellan "is an able general but a very cautious one. His army is in a very demoralized and chaotic condition, and will not be prepared for offensive operations—or he will not think it so—for three or four weeks. Before that time I hope to be on the Susquehanna." Lee, remembered for his insights into the thoughts of his opponents, was wrong in every respect on this occasion.

McClellan was fifteen miles southeast of Frederick on September 11, making six miles a day. He could have marched much faster but for his innate caution. His trusted chief of intelligence, Allan Pinkerton, believed Lee had 200,000 soldiers in Maryland. His adjutant general reported more than 100,000. McClellan, once again seeking reinforcements, reported to Washington that "not less than 120,000" men faced him.

The Federal commander was also ignorant of Lee's position and intent, thanks to Stuart's inspired screening. McClellan did not know Lee had been in Frederick until he occupied the town. In Washington, Henry W. Halleck feared Lee's invasion was a feint. "It may be the enemy's object," he suggested, "to draw off the mass of our forces and then attempt to attack from the Virginia side of the Potomac."

Prior to marching against Lee, McClellan had reorganized the expanded fifteen-division Army of the Potomac into three wings. Brig. Gen. Alfred Pleasonton led with the cavalry. Maj. Gen. Edwin Sumner marched in the center along the National Road through Rockville,

Jeb Stuart's cavalry frustrated all efforts by Federal horsemen to scout the position of the Confederates on both sides of the Potomac. Southern troopers also briefly detained war artist Alfred Waud, who sketched them and noted how well mounted and armed they were with materiel captured from their Union counterparts—and for whom they showed only contempt.

LIBRARY OF CONGRESS

McClellan Reports the Capture of Lee's Orders

Head-quarters, Frederick,
September 13, 1862, 12 P.M.

To the President:

I have the whole rebel force in front of me, but am confident, and no time shall be lost. I have a difficult task to perform, but with God's blessing will accomplish it. I think Lee has made a gross mistake, and that he will be severely punished for it. The army is in motion as rapidly as possible. I hope for a great success if the plans of the rebels remain unchanged. . . . I have all the plans of the rebels, and will catch them in their trap if my men are equal to the emergency. . . . Received most enthusiastically by the ladies. Will send you trophies. All well, with God's blessing will accomplish it.

Geo. B. McClellan.

Confederate troops, on orders to display their best behavior in Maryland, were camped outside Frederick to prevent incidents. The only problem in Frederick occurred when Secessionist residents, emboldened by Lee's presence, stormed the offices of two Unionist newspapers. Southern troops stopped the attack, sent the offenders to jail, and helped clean up the debris.

The Federal army entered the town of Frederick, Maryland, on Friday, September 12, as the last elements of Lee's troops departed. Command of the Union army had only recently been restored to George B. McClellan, and he appeared on the town streets on Saturday and was thronged by well-wishers. Men reached out to shake his hand, women held babies up for him to kiss, and youngsters decorated his horse with garlands of flowers.

In Frederick an old, portly German immigrant woman snatched a Union lieutenant off his feet and bearhugged him nearly into unconsciousness as his men shouted with delight.

A beautiful girl stepped out of the crowd and said she was so happy the Federals had come that she could kiss the entire regiment. After a burly sergeant suggested she start with him, the young lass quickly disappeared into the mob.

Gaithersburg, Hyattstown, and Urbana. Maj. Gen. Ambrose E. Burnside led the right wing along the Baltimore and Ohio Railroad, and Maj. Gen. William Franklin followed the Potomac River on the left. The twenty-five-mile-wide front protected both Washington and Baltimore and allowed the wings to concentrate if necessary.

The Federal troops enjoyed the pleasures of campaigning in their own country. Civilians, particularly young women, brought out food and lemonade for them. "It was cheering to see their pleasant faces," a major wrote, comparing them to his experience in Virginia, "where the few women have ruined their faces by looking sour."

Learning on the night of September 11 that Lee had departed Frederick, McClellan rushed Burnside forward. Confederate cavalry under Brig. Gen. Wade Hampton commanded a rear guard just east of the Monocacy River and was driven back quickly by Brig. Gen. Jacob D. Cox's division. Yet when Col. Augustus Moor, one of Cox's brigade commanders, raced into Frederick with one cannon and a troop of cavalry, Hampton bushwhacked the unit and captured Moor.

Northerners gave Cox's division a raucous welcome, "ladies waving their handkerchiefs and national flags," wrote Cox, "whilst the men came to the column with fruits and refreshments."

McClellan bragged that he was "nearly pulled to pieces" when he arrived on September 12 by civilians who kissed his uniform, hugged his great mount Dan Webster, and covered both with flowers.

On the following day, September 13, two Indiana soldiers were lounging just outside town in a meadow that had been a Confederate camp two days earlier. Cpl. Barton W. Mitchell felt fortunate to find three cigars but was astonished by its wrapping. The document shot up the chain of command and was authenticated by Adj. Gen. Samuel E. Pittman, who recognized the handwriting of Lee's adjutant general, Robert H. Chilton, an old army friend. Pittman raced to McClellan's headquarters and demanded an immediate audience.

"Now I know what to do!" McClellan exclaimed after reading the order. He telegraphed Lincoln within the hour, saying: "I have the whole rebel force in front of me, but I am confident, and no time shall be lost. I think Lee has made a gross mistake, and that he will be severely punished for it. I have all the plans of the rebels, and will catch them in their own trap if my men are equal to the emergency. Will send you trophies."

To one of his commanders, McClellan bragged, "Here is a paper with which if I cannot whip Bobbie Lee, I will be willing to go home."

If McClellan could strike Longstreet before Harpers Ferry was captured, he could cut the enemy in two and defeat him in detail.

Unknown to the Federal commander, on September 10 Lee had further divided his force, sending ten thousand of Longstreet's men on to Hagerstown to face a reported Union threat from Pennsylvania. He left five thousand men, D. H. Hill's lone division, at Boonsboro as a rear guard.

Col. Dixon S. Miles, thirty-eight years in service and one of the top thirty officers in the army when the war started, commanded the Union garrison at Harpers Ferry because of a drinking problem. After a court of inquiry had found him guilty of being drunk while leading his division at

While Confederates largely refrained from unauthorized foraging, the Federals felt less restraint. Spotting a flock of sheep grazing beside the road, Federal Col. Edward E. Cross called to one of his officers, Lt. Thomas Livermore, "Mr. Livermore, don't you on any account let two of your men go out and get one of those sheep for supper."

"No, sir!" Livermore replied, then sent two privates to grab a sheep apiece and carry them into the woods. "I sent iron kettles to them," Livermore recalled, "which were soon returned filled with mutton and nicely covered with green leaves. I sent one kettle to the colonel with my compliments, telling him that it contained rations I had drawn. He returned his thanks and caution against leaving any part of them in sight."

After Maj. Gen. Jesse L. Reno scolded his men for taking straw for a bed, Lt. Col. Rutherford B. Hayes, a future president, replied, "Well, I trust our generals will exhibit the same energy in dealing with our foes that they do in the treatment of our friends."

One of Hayes's sergeants in the Twenty-third Ohio was another future president, William McKinley.

The Georgia Feud ■ Lafayette McLaws

Born in Augusta, Georgia, on January 15, 1821, Lafayette McLaws graduated in the U.S. Military Academy class of 1842 with James Longstreet, a fellow Georgian. He won no brevets in Mexico in 1846 and resigned from the army on March 23, 1861. He became colonel of the Tenth Georgia, then a brigadier on September 25, 1861, and major

general on May 23, 1862, for ably leading a division on the peninsula. He fought in the Seven Days and helped capture Harpers Ferry before seeing action at Antietam.

McLaws fought well at Fredericksburg, Chancellorsville, and Gettysburg and was transferred west with Longstreet. He missed the battle of Chickamauga, and after the failed

attack against Knoxville, Longstreet relieved him of command on December 17, 1863, charging him with having no confidence in the assault and making insufficient preparations for it. A court-martial on May 4, 1864, found McLaws guilty of some charges, but Jefferson Davis rejected the findings.

The bitterness between McLaws and Longstreet continued. When

Longstreet threatened to resign, McLaws was sent to Georgia.

After the war McLaws entered the insurance business in Augusta and was postmaster and a tax agent in Savannah, where he died on July 24, 1897. He is buried there in Bonaventure Cemetery.

Eccentric Col. Dixon S. Miles often wore two hats, one on top of the other.

First Manassas, Miles was shipped off to the upper Potomac. Jackson's approach motivated the garrison at Martinsburg to retreat to Harpers Ferry on September 11, giving Miles fourteen thousand men, many with no combat experience. The last orders from Halleck were to hold to "the latest moment."

Harpers Ferry changed hands a dozen times during the Civil War because the post was indefensible, surrounded as it is by high mountains. To the north across the Potomac River is the dominant position, 1,476-foot-high Maryland Heights, the southern end of twelve-mile-long Elk Ridge.

Across the Shenandoah River to the south is 1,180-foot-high Loudoun Heights. West is Bolivar Heights, its 668-foot elevation extending from the

The Sad Saga of Dixon S. Miles

At First Manassas, fifty-seven-year-old Col. Dixon S. Miles commanded a division under Irwin McDowell. Despite the fact that Miles had a long-standing problem with alcohol, only hours before the battle his doctor prescribed brandy for an ailment that had bothered Miles for several days.

Fortunately, Miles's division was kept in reserve. The colonel drank steadily throughout the day and skirmished only with his subordinates. Drunk by the time the Federal troops fled the field, Miles would not accept the news. When his troops complained of his drunkenness during their withdrawal to Centreville, Irwin McDowell ordered Col. Israel B. Richardson to relieve Miles, but the inebriated officer argued and threatened Richardson with arrest.

Charged with drunkenness, Miles was brought up before a court of inquiry on August 21. He was found guilty, but because of his illness and the prescription, Miles was not court-martialed.

In the wake of the fall of Harpers Ferry just before the battle of Antietam, Miles (who was mortally wounded and died shortly after surrendering Harpers Ferry) was naturally suspected of being drunk again. The fact that he was a Maryland native also contributed to groundless rumors that he was guilty of treason.

First Manassas, Ball's Bluff, and Second Manassas had been embarrassing enough defeats, but the mass surrender of American troops at Harpers Ferry, not surpassed until Corregidor fell to the Japanese eighty years later, was too much for the public to bear. The people, press, government, and military demanded to know why the disaster had occurred, and they all wanted a scapegoat on whom to place the blame.

The defense of Harpers Ferry had been criminal: Loudoun Heights left undefended, successive strong positions atop Maryland Heights abandoned, and Bolivar Heights unfortified until hours before Stonewall Jackson's arrival. Artillery ammunition had been squandered, infantry was not utilized to slow Jackson's advance, and no escape had been attempted. Confederate prisoners had also been released during the siege, and they took valuable intelligence to the attackers. The most important questions to be answered were, Why had the garrison surrendered so quickly? Could McClellan have lifted the siege?

The War Department ordered a special commission to investigate the situation eight days after the surrender, and it convened five days later, on October 4, 1862. The six-man panel

was led by Maj. Gen. David Hunter, who would soon court-martial Fitz John Porter and would try the Lincoln conspirators in two and a half years.

On trial were the deceased Miles; his second in command, Brig. Gen. Julius White; Col. Thomas H. Ford, who commanded atop Maryland Heights; and the other three brigade commanders. Fifteen days of testimony by forty-four witnesses who were asked eighteen hundred questions filled nine hundred printed pages. No officer would accept any responsibility for the debacle, and everyone defended his actions and placed the blame on others. Truth, as usual, was the first casualty.

The commission deliberated only two days. On November 3 it delivered its decisions. Recognizing that Miles "cannot appear before any earthly tribunal," the commission felt he was entitled "to the tenderest and most careful investigation." So it was with "extreme reluctance" that the deceased colonel was condemned. They found that Miles's "incapacity, amounting to almost imbecility, led to the shameful surrender of this important post." White was applauded for his "capability and courage," and the three brigade commanders escaped censure.

Ford became the scapegoat. The board found that he "conducted the

defense without ability, and abandoned his position without sufficient cause, and has shown throughout such a lack of military capacity as to disqualify him . . . for a command in the service."

Gen. John E. Wool was criticized for placing Miles in command of the vital position. McClellan, the commission thought, "could and should have relieved and protected Harper's Ferry."

"Had the garrison been slower to surrender or the Army of the Potomac swifter to march, the enemy would have been forced to raise the siege or have been taken in detail," the board concluded.

Ford was a typical political officer. He had led a company to Mexico in 1846, had practiced law, and had been elected Ohio's lieutenant governor in 1855, serving as a Republican under Gov. Salmon P. Chase, soon to be Lincoln's treasury secretary. When the Civil War began he raised a regiment.

After his dismissal, Ford practiced law in Washington, became superintendent of public printing, and died in 1868. Lawyers who had known Ford before the war considered him skillful, but most of the time found him "indolent and careless," according to one, and "most times inactive and useless," added another.

NATIONAL ARCHIVES

The garrison of more than ten thousand troops at Harpers Ferry was little more than a railroad guard tasked with the responsibility of protecting the Baltimore and Ohio from Confederate raiders. While there were sufficient troops and fortifications to address this need, they were woefully untrained to withstand a full-scale attack.

Potomac River to the south. Losing the high ground would leave the Northerners defending "a well bottom," one soldier wrote.

Miles concentrated on defending Bolivar Heights, approached by a gradual rise, which he expected to be the main Confederate avenue of attack. Only two thousand men were placed on Maryland Heights, and none at Loudoun Heights.

McLaws's eight thousand men arrived at Brownsville on the night of September 11. They were in Pleasant Valley, six miles northeast of Harpers Ferry, with Elk Ridge to the west and South Mountain on the east. On September 12 McLaws detailed three thousand men to cut off the Federal escape route to the east. Another three thousand watched his rear at Brownsville Gap in South Mountain. The remainder, two brigades under Brig. Gens. Joseph Kershaw and William Barksdale, gained Elk Ridge at Solomon's Gap and marched south for four miles down a rugged trail on the narrow elevation toward Maryland Heights. Encountering enemy fire from behind an abatis at 6 P.M., they were stopped for the night.

At sunrise the advance continued. The Confederates drove the Federals from the first position only to find a more extensive barrier four hundred yards beyond. Behind it were hastily constructed breastworks of logs and stone, defended by seventeen hundred Northerners. One of four Federal regiments facing them, the 126th New York, raised only three weeks earlier, held the center of the line. The seven Union guns, including two huge 10-inch Dahlgrens, which protected Harpers Ferry from attack to the south and west, were useless against the assault from the north.

Col. Benjamin F. Davis, who led the Federal cavalry out of Harpers Ferry, had been born in Alabama and raised in Mississippi. Jeb Stuart had been a West Point classmate.

One of his squadrons, known as the "college cavaliers," consisted almost entirely of three-month volunteers from Dartmouth College or Norwich University. Their commander, Maj. Augustus W. Corliss, announced that by morning they would be "in Pennsylvania, on the way to Richmond or in Hell!"—free, captured, or dead.

The escaping cavalry had turned onto a road leading to Hagerstown near dawn when they heard a Confederate wagon train coming toward them—it turned out to be James Longstreet's reserve ammunition. Davis secreted his men in the woods and stopped the lead wagon. His Southern accent and the darkness concealed his identify as he told the driver that Federal cavalry were prowling, and the train would have to take the next right turn. The teamsters did as ordered, heading north to Greencastle, Pennsylvania.

When the wagon train's cavalry escort rode up to investigate the diversion, the Union troopers drove them off. "A change of governments was probably never more quietly or speedily effected," one Federal asserted.

The wagon drivers were confused until the sun rose and revealed the Yankee uniforms.

Asked by a Confederate what regiment he was with, Pvt. Henry Norton replied, "The Eighth New York!"

"The hell you say!" the driver responded.

By 9 A.M. Davis was in Pennsylvania without losing a man and with forty wagons loaded with enemy ammunition. It was one of the few early Northern cavalry triumphs in the war. "The boys thought soldiering wasn't so bad after all," Norton observed.

"Their shells at first fell far wide of the mark and we laughed at them," said one Federal trooper of the opening artillery shots at Harpers Ferry, "but they soon got the range and plumped shell after shell among us, killing a few horses and causing a rush for cover."

"The infernal screech owls came hissing and singing, then bursting," another soldier wrote, "plowing great holes in the earth, filling our eyes with dust, and tearing many giant trees to atoms."

LIBRARY OF CONGRESS

Shortly after Jackson fell upon Harpers Ferry, these men of the Twenty-second New York Militia were photographed at drill on the heights overlooking the town. Few of their beleaguered predecessors had any combat experience, and some had not yet mastered the nine-step drill for loading their weapons.

After Dixon S. Miles was mortally wounded, Brig. Gen. Julius White surrendered to the Confederates decked out in his dress uniform and riding a finely appointed horse. Henry Kyd Douglas wrote that White "must have been somewhat astonished to find in General Jackson the worst dressed, worst mounted, most faded and dingy looking general he had ever seen anyone surrender to."

Beginning at 6:30 A.M. Kershaw twice attacked the position directly but was thrown back with heavy losses. The Federals had taken heart from their commander, Col. Eliakim Sherrill, whose reckless leadership inspired the raw soldiers. He fearlessly jumped atop the works when a third charge started, was wounded, and was carried from the field.

Barksdale's brigade had worked its way around the entanglements and breastworks to attack from the flank. The shaken New Yorkers chose to believe the rumor of an ordered withdrawal and started scrambling down the southern slope of Maryland Heights.

Claiming illness, Col. Thomas H. Ford, commanding the force on Maryland Heights, had remained two miles behind the line. He sent his aide, Maj. Sylvester Hewitt, to supervise the withdrawal to a position farther down the ridge. Miles finally arrived from Harpers Ferry to stop the retreat, but he neglected to commit a nine-hundred-man reserve that waited nearby.

At 3:30 Ford ordered a retreat into Harpers Ferry. The cannon were spiked, several were pushed over the slope, and by 4:30 the Federals had crossed a pontoon bridge and entered Harpers Ferry. Although he maintained that he followed Miles's orders, a court of inquiry later found that Ford had "abandoned his position without sufficient cause."

At 10 A.M. that morning Walker's 3,400 soldiers arrived below Loudoun Heights to find it unoccupied. An hour later Jackson reached the scene and placed his 11,500 men several miles west of Bolivar Heights, facing the primary Union line.

Miles's defense of Harpers Ferry was literal and passive. On the night of September 13, when his officers urged him to recapture Maryland

366

Heights, he refused, maintaining that he had to defend Harpers Ferry, not the ridges around it. "I am ordered to hold this place and God damn my soul to hell if I don't," he thundered.

Miles also sent a party of ten troopers, led by Capt. Charles Russell, to slip out of Harpers Ferry and find McClellan, twenty miles to the northeast. Miles announced that he could hold out for two days but would then be required to surrender.

Throughout the morning of September 14 Jackson tightened his siege of Harpers Ferry, bringing his guns closer and closer to the Union line. A narrow path was cut up the slope of Maryland Heights and eight hundred men used ropes to drag four Parrott rifles to the top. Walker grew tired of waiting for orders from Jackson, who wanted to open on Harpers Ferry with all his guns simultaneously. At 1 P.M. he fired from Loudoun Heights, soon joined by other batteries.

In the late afternoon Jackson advanced to an attack position near Bolivar Heights. A. P. Hill was sent along the west bank of the Shenandoah River to assault the Federal left flank at the heights in the morning. By dark Hill had seized a rise on the southern edge of Bolivar Heights and readied two brigades to take the Northerners from the rear along the river.

In a message that failed to penetrate Confederate lines, McClellan urged Miles to "hold out to the last extremity. If it is possible, reoccupy Maryland Heights with your whole force. If you can do that, I will certainly be able to relieve you."

It was wise counsel, for only a single Confederate regiment held the ridge. McLaws had shifted the remainder north to defend Crampton's Gap, which was heavily pressed by McClellan.

Despite the perilous situation, Miles took no action. His subordinates questioned his sobriety and sanity, then they discussed mutiny.

Col. Benjamin F. Davis asked Miles to allow him to lead the Union cavalry, fourteen hundred strong, to break out of the trap. They would be of

A Federal prisoner watching Stonewall Jackson ride out of Harpers Ferry on September 9 remarked, "Boys, he is not much for looks, but if he had been in command of us we would not have been caught in this trap."

Stonewall's Narrow Escape

When Federal cavalry surprised Stonewall Jackson and his staff in Boonsboro, Col. Basset French was eating supper in the United States Hotel. Responding to the attack, French ran out and saw his horse killed. So he ran back into the hotel, where a free black worker took him to the cellar and directed him to leap into a heap of foul-smelling garbage.

As Henry Kyd Douglas, one of Jackson's aides, raced to safety, a Federal bullet plucked his ostrich plumed hat, newly presented by a lady in Frederick, from his head.

While Jackson sought safety, he lost his gloves.

Afterward the general sourly complimented Douglas on his fast horse. Douglas made no reply but topped Jackson by handing him the gloves he had lost.

A Private Green, who had helped run the Federals out of town, excitedly approached Jackson and said, "General, we drove them out."

"That was good," Jackson answered.

"General, we captured some," the private continued.

"And that is better."

"And killed and wounded others."

"That is better still."

At that moment Colonel French joined the exchange, saying, "General, was it not a gallant thing for the small squad of Black Horse to charge so large a force and save you from capture?"

"Very gallant, Colonel, very gallant," Jackson replied.

"General, how would you have felt if the Yankees had captured you?" French pressed.

"Very bad, Colonel," Jackson shot back, "especially if they had found me in a dark cellar with a negro standing guard over me."

Days before Stonewall Jackson captured Harpers Ferry, its commander, Dixon Miles, received the following order: "The position on the heights ought to enable you to punish the enemy passing up the road in the direction of Harpers Ferry. Have your wits about you, and do all you can to annoy the rebels should they advance on you. Activity, energy, and discretion must be used. You will not abandon Harpers Ferry without defending it to the last extremity."

little assistance against a Confederate infantry attack, and their escape would deny the enemy good mounts, he argued. Miles initially refused, calling the scheme "wild and impractical," but he authorized it when he realized that Davis would proceed with or without his approval.

The cavalry gathered on Shenandoah Street after dark. At 9 P.M. they rode slowly and silently across the pontoon bridge. There was no moon as they skirted the base of Maryland Heights and started north for Sharpsburg without being detected. Davis maintained a "killing pace," said one man. They rode through woods and fields to avoid Confederates retreating from the combat that had been going on in the gaps of South Mountain. The Union horsemen quietly captured forty wagons filled with Confederate ammunition and arrived safely in Greencastle, Pennsylvania, around 9 A.M.

Not long after the Federal cavalry escaped, Jackson, to support A. P. Hill, positioned ten guns at the base of Loudoun Heights to enfilade the rear of the Federals holding Bolivar Heights.

When the mist burned off on the morning of September 14, Jackson opened with fifty artillery pieces. Col. William H. Trimble of Ohio claimed there was "not a place where you could lay the palm of your hand and say it was safe."

At 8 A.M. Miles informed his officers that their artillery ammunition was depleted and there was no sign of relief from McClellan. They all agreed to surrender.

For the Confederates, the first crisis of the campaign was the arrival of the vanguard of three Federal corps at South Mountain, an imposing and rugged ridge that extended fifty miles across Maryland to Pennsylvania. It could only be crossed through a small number of passes, and Lee had left the task of guarding these passes to a single division.

Stonewall Jackson reinstated A. P. Hill to command before the fighting at Harpers Ferry. As Hill's men started up South Mountain to stem the Federal flood through Turner's Gap, they spied Robert E. Lee, once again mounted on Traveller.

"Give us Hill!" they shouted.

"You shall have him, gentlemen," Lee replied with a wave of his hat.

When Hill arrived, Lee asked if he would apologize for the conflict with Evans. Despite Hill's refusal, Lee said, "I will suspend your arrest till the impending battle is decided."

BATTLES AND LEADERS

Confederate fire diminished as white flags sprouted around the defensive perimeter. One of the last shells exploded behind Miles, almost severing his leg. Some believed it was a Federal shell, fired as punishment for Miles's incredible incompetence. He died the following day.

The Southerners captured 73 guns, 13,000 rifles, and paroled 12,500 men. It remains the second largest surrender of American troops, eclipsed only by the 1942 capitulation of Baatan in the Philippines during World War II. That night columns of Confederates marched through the streets of Harpers Ferry for Sharpsburg, twelve miles north. An urgent message from Lee prompted Jackson to rejoin the army with all possible speed. Their march "was a weird, uncanny sight," one Federal remembered, "and drove sleep from my eyes. They were silent as ghosts; ruthless and rushing in their speed; ragged, earth-colored, disheveled and devilish, as though keen on the scent of blood. . . . The spectral picture will never be effaced from my memory."

McClellan still believed Lee had 120,000 men and was not aware that Longstreet was at Hagerstown, thirteen miles from D. H. Hill at Boonsboro. By the afternoon of September 13 the Federal commander knew that Harpers Ferry was besieged, and he made immediate plans to relieve the garrison and destroy Lee in pieces. The Union army had to pass over Catoctin Mountain and the more formidable South Mountain, a sixteen-hundred-foot-high ridge extending fifty miles from Pennsylvania to the Potomac River. The two primary passes across the mountain were Turner's Gap, where the National Road crossed between Frederick and Boonsboro, and the much-less-traveled Fox's Gap, a mile south of Turner's Gap. Six miles south of Fox's Gap was Crampton's Gap, where the Burkittsville road entered Pleasant Valley, a natural route to Harpers Ferry.

McClellan's main force, seventy-nine thousand men, would march west from Middletown, between Catoctin and South Mountains, and cross Turner's Gap to attack what the Federal commander thought would be the largest part of Lee's army at Boonsboro.

Maj. Gen. William Franklin's twelve thousand men at Buckeystown, halfway between the Potomac River and Frederick, and Maj. Gen. Darius Couch's seventy-two hundred men on the Potomac River at Licksville

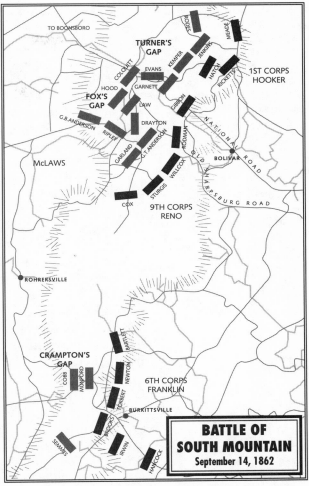

BATTLE OF SOUTH MOUNTAIN
September 14, 1862

As Union troops lay behind a wall at South Mountain waiting for orders, a rattlesnake appeared and slithered among the men, who froze in place. One private could not bear the agony and leaped to his feet to kill the snake, then dove to the ground before Confederates could shoot him.

After Ohioan Samuel Compton gave water to a wounded Confederate, the soldier asked him to relay a message: "Tell my mother it's her fault I'm here."

There were no water sources for thirsty soldiers atop South Mountain, and Union officers seemed to have filled their canteens with liquor. Samuel Compton chanced upon Col. Carr B. White, who asked for directions to his unit. Noticing two canteens hanging from White's shoulder, Compton asked for a drink of water. White gave Compton one, then watched in amusement as he took a big swig, then suddenly spit it out, gasping for air.

"You prohibitionist," White laughed at him, "taking down whiskey like an old toper."

"Colonel," Compton said, "be a gentleman, give me a drink of water!"

"I would if I had it," the colonel replied, indicating his second canteen. "The other is brandy."

As the Twenty-first New York started up South Mountain to Turner's Gap, an old lady fleeing the battle warned Federal soldiers, "Don't you go up there. There are hundreds of 'em up there. Don't you go. *Some of you will be hurt!*"

would cross South Mountain at Crampton's Gap to raise the Confederate siege of Harpers Ferry.

When McClellan received the copy of Lee's orders, a Southern sympathizer at Frederick deduced that the Federals now had important intelligence concerning Lee and sent word to Stuart. In the meantime, D. H. Hill reported a score of Union campfires seen at Middletown, only four miles east of Turner's Gap. The Confederate commander knew he was in danger.

Lee immediately ordered Jackson and McLaws to seize Harpers Ferry quickly and warned them that McClellan was trying to split the Confederate force and relieve the Federal garrison there.

To buy time for the Harpers Ferry operation, D. H. Hill's division was detailed to help Stuart hold Turner's Gap. "The gap must be held at all hazards," Lee ordered his cavalry chief. Longstreet was instructed to leave Hagerstown at dawn with eight of his nine brigades and reinforce Hill.

Jacob Cox was still leading the Army of the Potomac along the National Road as he started for Turner's Gap at 6 A.M. on September 14. His three thousand men were scheduled to support Pleasanton's cavalry in reconnaissance of the gap, but that mission changed when he encountered Col. Augustus Moor, who had been captured days earlier. Moor had been paroled on conditions that he not rejoin the fighting until a Confederate of equal rank had been paroled and that he not reveal any information he had learned while in Confederate hands.

Told that Cox was heading to Turner's Gap, Moor exclaimed, "My God! Be careful!" then refused to comment further.

On the strength of Moor's revelation, Cox called up his other brigades and informed Ninth Corps commander Maj. Gen. Jesse Reno. In Bolivar, at the base of South Mountain, Cox and Pleasanton felt it wiser for them to flank the Confederates waiting in Turner's Gap by ascending the mountain along the old Sharpsburg road through Fox's Gap.

A Promising Career Cut Short ■ Jesse Lee Reno

Jesse Lee Reno was born on June 20, 1823, at Wheeling, West Virginia (then Virginia), but moved to Pennsylvania at age nine. He graduated from West Point in 1846, eighth in a class that included George B. McClellan, Stonewall Jackson, and George E. Pickett. Until the start of the Civil War, Reno taught ordnance at West Point and served on ordnance boards and with the topographical survey. He was breveted lieutenant and captain for gallantry at Cerro Gordo and Chapultepec

during the war with Mexico. After serving as Albert Sidney Johnston's chief of ordnance in Utah, Reno was forced to surrender the Mount Vernon arsenal to Alabama state authorities in January 1861.

Promoted to brigadier of volunteers on November 12, 1861, Reno led a brigade under Ambrose E. Burnside at the capture of Roanoke Island, New Bern, and Camden, North Carolina. On April 8, 1862, he had a division in North Carolina and was commissioned major general on

August 20. He led the Ninth Corps under John Pope on the Rappahannock River, fought well at Second Manassas and Chantilly, and retreated to Washington with the rest of the Army of Virginia. Leading his corps west in pursuit of Lee, Reno was killed in action at Fox's Gap atop South Mountain on September 14, 1862. Originally buried at Trinity Church in Boston, in 1867 his body was reinterred in Oak Hill Cemetery in Georgetown, Virginia, in 1867.

LIBRARY OF CONGRESS

The battle of South Mountain began shortly after dawn on September 14. Ohio units from Jesse Reno's Ninth Corps were dispatched to Fox's Gap to outflank the Confederates defending the main pass at Turner's Gap. They engaged in a bitter two-hour fight with North Carolina troops under Samuel Garland, dislodging the defenders but thwarted in the move on the critical mountain pass by the sudden arrival of reinforcements from Longstreet's command.

Before going into combat, Lt. William M. Carter approached Capt. Cyrus L. Conner and said, "Captain, I know I shall be shot."

"Nonsense," Conner replied.

"But I will," Carter insisted. "I am an unlucky mortal. I was shot while on the peninsula almost the first chance I got . . . today I will be killed. I know it."

"Come now, Lieutenant," Conner scolded Carter, "it's only a foolish notion that has got into your head; get rid of it; cheer up, you will come out all right."

"I wish I could think so," Carter said in resignation. "I will fall doing my duty."

The two were crossing a stone wall in pursuit of fleeing Confederates when a bullet hit Carter square in the head and he fell backward, instantly dead.

At 9 A.M. the Federals encountered a force of one thousand men, Brig. Gen. Samuel Garland's brigade and two hundred cavalry crouched behind a stone wall near the summit beside a road that connected Turner's and Fox's Gaps.

As the two sides exchanged a brisk fire, Federal Col. Eliakim Scammon led his brigade around the Confederate right flank. After successfully executing that move, Scammon brought up two guns to blast canister into the Southern ranks from only forty yards. This threat allowed another of Cox's brigades to charge the stone wall, resulting in hand-to-hand combat. While discussing the desperate situation, Col. Thomas Ruffin, commanding the Thirteenth North Carolina, was seriously wounded and Garland was killed. The Confederate defense collapsed at 11 A.M., and two hundred prisoners were taken. Cox continued north along the ridge-top road toward Turner's Gap.

At Turner's Gap, D. H. Hill scaled an observation tower near South Mountain Inn and was astonished by the sight of McClellan's army surging through the valley below. With Garland dead and his brigade routed, Hill had only one brigade to hold against a threat from two directions. His

Charles Stamp, an aggressive Federal flag-bearer, ran in front of his regiment and urged the men to join him. The words were barely spoken before Stamp was dead from a head wound, leading the regimental historian to later write that Stamp "was mustered out of the army militant and mustered into the army triumphant."

An old woman atop the mountain adamantly refused to leave her one-room cabin even as the fighting approached. John B. Gordon courteously saluted the lady and attempted to reason with her, saying, "My dear madam, fighting will begin in five minutes. Your life and that of your children are in imminent peril. You must leave here at once."

"I know what you want, you thieving Rebels!" she thundered, hands on her hips. "You want to get me out of my house and come and steal all I've got. I won't go there! I'll die first!"

Gordon's men goaded the woman on, shouting, "Go it, old lady!" "Hold the fort!" and "Bully for you!"

other three brigades were en route, and Longstreet was far behind them. "I do not remember ever to have experienced a feeling of greater *loneliness,*" Hill wrote.

In desperation Hill deployed two cannon to face the Fox Gap road and lined up "dismounted staff-officers, couriers, teamsters and cooks" in a firing line. This audacious display halted Cox until a Confederate brigade came up and drove the Federals back to Fox's Gap.

Meanwhile, McClellan spent the morning in Frederick confident there would be no action until after his right wing had crossed South Mountain. Alerted to the battle, he rode to the base of the ridge and, amid the cheers of his troops, joined Burnside.

The Federals made slow progress, each column a "monstrous, crawling blue-black snake miles long," a witness testified. Three hours passed before the first reinforcements, the division of Brig. Gen. Orlando Willcox, reached Cox in Fox's Gap.

Hill was sorely pressed, fighting alone from 9 A.M. until 3 P.M. His men were near to collapsing, their fears fed by the impressive sight of the massive Federal force approaching through the valley below. Longstreet appeared at 3:30, his men having marched thirteen rugged miles in nineteen hours.

John Bell Hood's division arrived at the last moment to fill a gap in Hill's line, and the Confederates beat back several assaults through the afternoon. While he was scouting the front at dusk, Reno was killed by Confederate fire near the spot where Garland had died at the start of this long day.

At 4 P.M. McClellan finally attacked Turner's Gap with Maj. Gen. Joseph Hooker's First Corps, which was exhausted from an all-day march. One brigade, that of Brig. Gen. John Gibbon, of Second Bull Run fame, was sent to attack Turner's Gap head-on up the National Road. His men advanced

The key to the breakthrough at Fox's Gap had been a bayonet charge against an inexperienced regiment. Unnerved by the attack, the Southern regiment fell back and created a break and confusion in the line. The sheer weight of numbers overcame the determined defense of the veteran soldiers on both ends of the gap.

Union Gen. Jesse Reno died as game as he had lived. Carried off the field at Fox's Gap, he cheerfully yelled to Brig. Gen. Samuel Sturgis, "Hallo, Sam, I'm dead!" Sturgis could not believe he was badly wounded, but Reno died within minutes.

D. H. Hill considered Reno "a renegade Virginian killed by a happy shot."

BATTLES AND LEADERS

steadily in the face of increasing rifle and artillery fire, displaying a bravery praised by McClellan. Around dusk the Federals met the main Confederate line, manned by a five-regiment brigade of Georgians commanded by Brig. Gen. Alfred Colquitt. The Southerners were crouching in a ditch behind a stone wall north of the road and in woods to the south. When Gibbons's men were only forty yards away, the Georgians rose and unleashed a volley. As darkness fell, men fired at the flashes of enemy guns.

The Confederates repulsed an attack against their right flank to shouts of "Hurrah for Georgia!" from Hill's staff. The contest sputtered out at 9 P.M. Gibbon had lost a fourth of his brigade, 318 men. One hundred Georgians had fallen.

To the left, a twelve-hundred-man brigade of Alabamians under Brig. Gen. Robert Rodes defended a mountain spur north of the National Road, a steep ravine through which the old Hagerstown road had run, and a commanding peak a mile away. Four of Rodes's regiments defended the peak, and the fifth held the ravine, which left a gap between them that would be covered by three of Longstreet's brigades, provided they arrived in time.

Two of Hooker's divisions started up the slope around 4 P.M., driving Rodes's skirmishers and overlapping both Confederate flanks by half a mile. A savage battle erupted in a cornfield near the summit. Brig. Gen. John Hatch, leading his division against the Confederates, was badly wounded. His replacement, Brig. Gen. Abner Doubleday, thought a ruse might be effective. He instructed his men to lie down behind the fence and cease firing. The Confederates, thinking the Federals had retreated, raced forward and were decimated by Union fire.

To the north, Brig. Gen. George Gordon Meade pressed a determined attack against the Confederate left flank. By nightfall Rodes had been pushed back half a mile to Turner's Gap. He had lost 422 men, a

After examining the bodies of Confederates on the field, one troubled Federal approached Capt. Henry Pleasants and asked, "Captain, isn't them men?"

Pleasants was confused by the comment, so the soldier continued, "By my soul every one of them has a third eye in his head."

Understanding now, Pleasants was consumed by laughter. Recovering, he indicated the stone wall. "The enemy was behind it when we were engaged and in order to fire on us they had to take aim over the stone fence and consequently they got shot by our men somewhere between the shoulders and head and that is the reason so many of them is shot in the head."

Another Federal came upon a Confederate lieutenant who had been shot in the left arm eighteen times. He also noted a number of ramrods stuck in trees behind Union lines, fired accidentally by Southerners in the heat of battle.

One Confederate skirmisher pushed his luck by staying too long to get off a final shot. Nearly an entire Union company fired as he scrambled away, felling the man with thirty-six bullets.

Defender of Fox's Gap ■ Samuel Garland Jr.

Samuel Garland Jr., born on December 16, 1830, at Lynchburg, Virginia, was a collateral descendant of James Madison, the fourth president of the United States. Garland was graduated from the Virginia Military Institute in 1849 and the University of Virginia Law School in 1851. After practicing law in Lynchburg, he entered Confederate service as colonel of the Eleventh Virginia.

He participated in First Manassas, Dranesville, and Williamsburg, where he sustained a wound.

Appointed brigadier on May 23, 1862, he led a brigade under D. H. Hill with distinction at the battles of Seven Pines, the Seven Days, and Second Manassas.

On September 14, 1862, while defending Fox's Gap on South Mountain, he led a force of one thousand men against vastly superior forces.

Col. Thomas Ruffin admonished him, "General, why do you stay here? You are in great danger."

"I may as well be here as yourself," was the response.

Garland was killed moments after Ruffin was seriously wounded.

Garland is buried in Lynchburg. A modest monument to his sacrifice was erected atop South Mountain at Fox's Gap, near the Reno Monument. It was dedicated on September 11, 1993.

BATTLES AND LEADERS

At Crampton's Gap a Federal fell into a crevice to find it occupied by a Confederate. They stared for a moment, then the Rebel laughed. "We're both in a fix," he said. "You can't gobble me, and I can't gobble you. Let's wait till the shooting is over, and if your side wins I'm your prisoner, and if we win you're my prisoner." The Confederate lost.

The fight for South Mountain ended around 10 P.M. with the Federals in possession of the high ground. Around midnight the exhausted Confederates withdrew and marched toward Sharpsburg, where Lee hoped to regroup his army and retreat into Virginia. When he received news from Jackson that Harpers Ferry had capitulated, he rethought his plans.

third of his strength. Longstreet's brigades, assaulted as they came into line, were forced to withdraw.

Six miles to the south, the advance against Crampton's Gap had developed slowly. Franklin waited several hours for his third division to arrive from Buckeystown, but it did not appear until 10 P.M. It was noon before Franklin approached Burkittsville, a mile east of the gap, where his men were fired upon. A Federal major recalled that "cannon balls crashed among the houses, and the women, young and old, with great coolness, waved their handkerchiefs and flags at us."

On the lower slopes of South Mountain, Col. Thomas T. Munford commanded one thousand Confederates, mainly dismounted cavalry, and two light batteries. The sight of twelve thousand Federals marching through the valley was unsettling. One Southerner thought they "were so numerous that it looked as if they were creeping up out of the ground." He also noted that they were extremely cautious, like "a lion, making exceedingly careful preparations to spring on a plucky little mouse."

The advance did not start until 3 P.M., but it covered a mile-wide front. While Maj. Gen. Howard Slocum's division attacked along the Burkittsville road, the two brigades of Maj. Gen. William F. Smith's division flanked the Confederate right, to the south. The Northerners advanced fiercely, driving the Southerners back steadily from the base of the mountain. When Phil Kearny's old brigade stormed the summit shouting his name, the Confederate defenders broke and ran down the western slope of the mountain, leaving a number of prisoners behind.

The Confederates reached Sharpsburg starving and chewing straws, one remembered, "merely to keep their jaws from rusting and stiffening entirely."

"They nearly worried us to death asking for something to eat," a resident wrote. "They were half famished and they looked like tramps."

Confederate Brig. Gen. Howell Cobb arrived with his thirteen-hundred-man brigade only to see his men join the rout. Cobb tried desperately to rally his troops, waving a regimental flag until a bullet broke the staff. By 6 P.M. the Federals had lost 500 men to the Confederates' 750.

The Southerners' panic ended half a mile beyond Crampton's Gap in Pleasant Valley, where McLaws stood with seven regiments. He incorporated the routed Confederates into his line, which was probed by the Federals. Franklin could have pressed on and relieved Harpers Ferry, only six miles distant, but he elected to withdraw to the mountain.

McClellan described the battle at South Mountain as a "glorious victory," and Lincoln telegraphed, "God bless you and all with you. Destroy the rebel army if possible."

From headquarters near Boonsboro, Lee decided to abandon Turner's Gap before it was overrun at daylight. During the night D. H. Hill and Longstreet withdrew to the village of Sharpsburg, six miles west. Lee had lost 2,700 of 18,000 men; McClellan 1,800 of 28,000 committed.

At 8 P.M. Lee decided his position was hopeless. "The day has gone against us," he wrote McLaws. He would retreat past Sharpsburg to cross the Potomac into Virginia. McLaws was to abandon the siege of Harpers Ferry and march along the Potomac northwest to find a crossing. Lee changed his plans later that night after Jackson informed him that Harpers Ferry would soon be forced to capitulate.

Many theories have been proposed to explain Robert E. Lee's decision to fight against such numbers and with his back against the Potomac River, but Lee put the speculation to rest in an 1868 interview. "I went into Maryland to give battle," was his simple statement.

McClellan pursued Lee cautiously. The first Union divisions appeared east of the Antietam on the afternoon of Monday, September 15, but the bulk of the Army of the Potomac was not in the area until evening. The Federal commander personally supervised every detail of positioning his force on the field, and while he was methodical there was no sense of urgency about his task or the execution of his orders.

LESLIE'S

George B. McClellan's rapid move from Frederick caught the Confederate commander by surprise. "I thought I knew McClellan, but this movement of his puzzles me," Robert E. Lee wrote. However, McClellan's deployment at Antietam was so slow that his men grew bored. Two officers of Brig. Gen. Thomas Meagher's brigade, Capt. Jack Gossom and surgeon Frances Reynolds, challenged each other to a horse race. They sped across the fields, leaping ditches and fences, to the thunderous cheers of Federal observers. They rode through Union lines and near the Confederates, who shouted just as enthusiastically.

During the night of September 16 even the animals sensed impending battle. A line of horses broke their picket ropes and stampeded, almost running down their sleeping Union masters.

James Longstreet's corps was thinly spread as the men watched McClellan's huge army deploy. They were anxious as the afternoon of September 16 passed slowly, then they learned the troops from Harpers Ferry were arriving. One tattered man approached Henry Kyd Douglas and asked if it were true that Stonewall Jackson was up.

"That's he," Kyd said, pointing, "the man with the big boots on."

"It is? Well, bless my eyes! Thankee, Captain," the man said, then shouted to his company, "Boys, it's all right!"

The Confederates marched southwest through the night and entered Sharpsburg on the morning of September 15. Pointing to a low ridge on the eastern edge of town, between Antietam Creek and the Potomac River, Lee said, "We will make our stand on those hills."

The Confederate defensive position would not rely on Antietam Creek, which was fordable in many places. The creek was no more than one hundred feet wide and crossed by a series of three stone bridges placed a mile apart. The ridge paralleling the creek was the prominent defensive feature. To the east were cornfields and pastures, broken by small stands of timber. Each lot was neatly enclosed with split-rail or stone fences, and these, along with large outcroppings of limestone and hundreds of undulations in the land, presented good fighting positions for infantry. There were also a number of elevations for the advantageous placement of artillery.

Lee's line was thin, counting only eighteen thousand men from Longstreet's two divisions and D. H. Hill's single division, which had sustained considerable loss a few hours earlier. To the north, near the Potomac River, Stuart's cavalry covered the left flank. Steep bluffs commanded the creek to the south, particularly where the last stone bridge crossed. Near the center of the position was an old sunken road that formed a natural defensive work.

Just behind the line ran the Hagerstown turnpike, which provided good interior lines, enabling Lee to shift soldiers quickly from one part of the battlefield to another.

Lee told a concerned officer that McClellan would not attempt to attack that day or the next. When a messenger arrived from Harpers Ferry with news of the Federal surrender, the Confederate commander exclaimed, "This is indeed good news. Let it be announced to the troops."

McClellan established his headquarters on the grounds of Philip Pry's house (below left), which was on the high ground east of the Antietam. Lee set up his headquarters in a cluster of trees just west of Sharpsburg, near the home of Jacob Grove (below right).

BATTLES AND LEADERS

After an exchange of artillery, the first combat of the battle began in the cornfield of David R. Miller. At 6 A.M. eleven hundred men began to advance through the head-high corn. One of Stonewall's stalwarts noted, "The sunbeams falling on their well polished guns and bayonets gave a glamor and a show at once fearful and entrancing."

Lee might have been convincing himself that making a stand here was wise. But if this sparse line broke, the Potomac River was not far in his rear. The Army of Northern Virginia would be readily destroyed. Lee's attitude was summed up by an officer who wrote, "I do not think General Lee wanted to leave Maryland without a fight.

The first Federals appeared before Sharpsburg during the afternoon, and the entire army arrived by dark. "Nobody seemed to be in a hurry," wrote a member of McClellan's staff. "Corps and divisions moved as languidly to the places assigned them as if they were getting ready for a grand review instead of a decisive battle." McClellan personally scouted the Confederate dispositions, then placed each of his divisions. At one point a Southern battery fired on him.

As the afternoon passed slowly, three of Jackson's divisions arrived, having marched since dusk the previous evening. Lee was now only outnumbered two to one, and an officer found him "calm, dignified, and ever cheerful. If he had had a well-equipped army of a hundred thousand veterans at his back, he would not have appeared more composed and confident." Jackson held the left, to the north, and Longstreet the right.

Lee's prediction proved correct. McClellan was not satisfied with his position and plan of attack until 2 P.M. on September 16. Because the southern bridge over the Antietam was dominated by high bluffs and the center

A number of local women and children had taken shelter in a stout stone house on the Confederate left, where the day's battle began. Terrified by the tremendous artillery duel that screamed over the house, the women ran out into the battle "like a flock of birds," wrote Confederate Capt. William W. Blackford, with their "hair streaming in the wind and children of all ages stretched behind." They wallowed across a plowed field, which caused many to lose their balance and fall, and "the rest thought it was the result of a cannon shot and ran the faster."

Blackford laughed at the scene as he rode out to pluck several children up and deposit them behind his saddle, then he led the group to a safer place. Confederate chivalry was equaled by Northern civility as the Federals ceased fire until the innocents were off the field.

A Union shell exploded beneath a Confederate cannon, miraculously causing no casualties, but it ignited the fuse of a shell held by a loader. He smothered the fuse with his hand, saving his comrades from a unique death.

While the fighting raged in the cornfield, four Union regiments under Gen. John Gibbon moved south, paralleling the Hagerstown turnpike. They encountered two brigades of Confederate infantry, who fired from behind a rail fence bordering the roadway.

During the early fighting at Antietam, Joseph Hooker sent newsman George Smalley of the *New York Tribune* to order an attack by one of his colonels. When the officer refused to accept orders from a civilian, Smalley replied, "Very good, I will report to General Hooker that you decline to accept his authority."

"Oh, for God's sake don't do that!" the colonel hastily replied. "The Rebels are too many for us, but I had rather face them than Hooker."

bridge was commanded by Confederate artillery, McClellan decided to cross half his army over the upper bridge to smash Lee's left. Two corps would attack, with support from two others. A fifth corps would demonstrate on the Confederate right, and any success would send McClellan's reserves crashing into Lee's center.

McClellan redesigned his newly redesigned command system, dissolving the three-wings concept and placing each of his six corps directly under his personal control. Not only would he direct the battle himself, McClellan sent each commander orders only for that unit. No one but he understood the battle plan, making coordination, already complicated by the terrain, nearly impossible.

Hooker's First Corps would initiate the attack at dawn. At 4 P.M. his three divisions crossed Antietam Creek on the upper bridge and fords. As they passed what would become known as the East Woods, Hood's skirmishers opened up, sparking a severe skirmish that inflicted heavy casualties on the Federals. Hooker's men bedded down near the Hagerstown turnpike on the Poffenberger farm. A reporter heard Hooker say, "Tomorrow we fight the battle that will decide the fate of the Republic."

To meet the threat, Lee oriented his left toward Hooker and sent dispatches urging McLaws's two

Federal gunners raked the Confederate ranks with case shot, and Gibbon's men managed to outmaneuver the Southerners. They fired into the flank and rear of the Confederate position along the Hagerstown turnpike, leaving behind this grim image of the fighting on the left of Lee's line.

divisions in Pleasant Valley and A. P. Hill's division, still in Harpers Ferry, to join him immediately.

McClellan ordered Maj. Gen. Joseph Mansfield's Twelfth Corps to cross Antietam Creek to support Hooker, and Sumner's Second Corps was to be ready to move before daylight. Franklin, still in Pleasant Valley, was to leave Maj. Gen. Darius Cook's division to occupy Maryland Heights at Harpers Ferry and bring his other two divisions to Antietam.

On the field McClellan's seventy thousand soldiers outnumbered Lee's forty thousand, and although Lee's two hundred artillery pieces held commanding heights, McClellan counted three hundred superior guns.

McClellan commanded from the Pry house across Antietam Creek near the center of the line, while Lee established his headquarters just west of Sharpsburg.

The fifteen hundred citizens of Sharpsburg knew a storm was about to break over them. Most left for neighboring communities or retired to cellars, but two hundred or more entered caves along the Potomac River.

Before dawn Hooker rose and rode through the North Woods to observe his objective, the high ground where the Smoketown road intercepted the Hagerstown turnpike near a simple Dunker church. The Confederate line extended north from the church to the West Woods. The Federal line started at the North Woods on the turnpike and ran to the East Woods. Between the lines was the Miller farm, mainly open pasture except for a cornfield in the center.

Facing Hooker were Jackson's three divisions. On the left was Brig. Gen. John R. Jones's division, formally Jackson's, posted in the West Woods and fields to the pike. Brig. Gen. Alexander Lawton's division continued from the pike through the pastureland and the East Woods, crossing the Smoketown road and the Mumma farm. In reserve behind the Dunker

While fighting in the cornfield, Isaac Hill of the Ninety-seventh New York remembered seeing a Confederate marksman who stood in full view and killed a comrade named Gleason. "There is the man who killed my brother," said another man, "and he is taking aim now against that tree." The second Gleason was immediately killed.

"Men I can not say fell," wrote Maj. Rufus Dawes of the fighting in the cornfield. "They were knocked out of the ranks by dozens." When his fourth color-bearer fell, Dawes picked it up himself, later writing, "When I took that color in my hand, I gave up all hope of life." He survived and remembered the men of the Sixth Wisconsin "loading and firing with demonical fury" while "shouting and laughing hysterically" as they neared the Dunker church.

Bushwhacked ■ Joseph King Fenno Mansfield

Born in New Haven, Connecticut, on December 22, 1803, Joseph King Fenno Mansfield was thirteen when he entered the U.S. Military Academy and graduated second in the class of 1822. An engineer, he built coastal forts in the South and became Zachary Taylor's chief of staff in Mexico, where he won three brevets. As inspector general of the army (a post recommended by Secretary of War Jefferson Davis), Mansfield toured military installations until 1861, when he was

appointed a regular army brigadier and assigned the defense of Washington and the protection of Abraham Lincoln.

Mansfield seized the Virginia side of the Potomac River and started the massive ring of fortifications that eventually surrounded the capital. Transferred to the peninsula, he commanded occupied Newport News and watched the *Virginia-Monitor* clash. After Second Manassas, Mansfield received command of the Twelfth Corps under George B. McClellan.

After only two days in command, he foolishly led his corps into the inferno of Antietam without knowledge of the situation and was mortally wounded. He died the following day, September 18, 1862, and was posthumously promoted to major general of volunteers. He is buried in Indian Hill Cemetery at Middleton, Connecticut.

LIBRARY OF CONGRESS

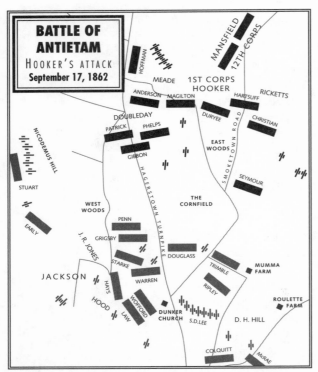

BATTLE OF ANTIETAM
HOOKER'S ATTACK
September 17, 1862

John Bell Hood's men had fought the previous evening as Joseph Hooker moved into position. Tired and hungry, they went into reserve behind the Dunker church and were preparing their first hot meal in days when Stonewall Jackson was forced to send them into battle at 7 A.M. Their hunger and anger at being disturbed while cooking their food sent the irate Confederates crashing into the Union line.

A Confederate courier, Pvt. William Hood, was seen riding with the high staff barefooted but wearing spurs on his ankles.

church was Hood, on loan from Longstreet. It was a strong defensive position held by seventy-seven hundred men, only a thousand less than the initial attacking force.

At 5:30 A.M. Hooker advanced with three divisions along a half-mile front, with Doubleday's to the right and through the North Woods, Meade's in the center, and Brig. Gen. James Ricketts's on the left and through the East Woods. As Doubleday left the North Woods, twenty guns belonging to Stuart and Jackson opened from a rise half a mile west of the pike. They were accompanied by four batteries of Col. Stephen D. Lee's battalion, firing from the high ground near the Dunker church.

Hooker had deployed nine batteries on a ridge near the Poffenberger farm, which answered immediately and were soon joined by four batteries of powerful 20-pounder Parrott rifles sited two miles east of Antietam Creek. The twenty-four rifles fired a shell a second, according to one correspondent. A Pennsylvania colonel noticed that individual shots grew into "one prolonged roar." A Confederate called it "artillery hell."

The Fifth Pennsylvania Regiment of Brig. Gen. Truman Seymour reached the Smoketown road before Confederate Col. James A. Walker's brigade drove it back into the East Woods. As Hooker rode to the front to direct his corps' attack against heavy Confederate resistance, he saw the sun glint off the bayonets of Southern soldiers lurking in a cornfield. He immediately diverted his infantry toward the movement and called up four artillery batteries, which peppered the cornfield and killed many Confederates. Hooker wrote that within moments "every stalk of corn in the northern and greater part of the field was cut as closely as could have been done with a knife, and the slain lay in rows precisely as they had stood in their ranks a few moments before."

Hooker ordered Brig. Gen. Abram Duryee's brigade, one of Ricketts's units, to advance from the East Woods. Leaving "the Cornfield," the Union regiments were blasted by a Georgia brigade under Col. Marcellus Douglas. A fierce exchange occurred from two hundred yards as the Confederates were reinforced with three regiments of Walker's brigade and the Federals received a brigade from Meade in the East Woods.

The combat continued "till the lines melted away like wax," one man observed. At 6:45 A.M. Walker's Confederates were driven back by the Union fire, which inflicted 228 casualties on the 700-man unit, but the Georgians fought on, losing Douglas, five of six regimental commanders, and 50 percent of their men. As the Southerners wavered, the five fierce regiments of the Louisiana Brigade, the famed Tigers, arrived and charged, forcing the Federals through the cornfield and delivering "the most deadly fire of the war," thought Massachusetts Capt. Benjamin F. Cook. "Rifles are shot to pieces in the hands of the soldiers, canteens and haversacks are riddled with bullets, the dead and wounded go down in scores."

Hooker stemmed the drive with a battery of 3-inch ordnance rifles, halting the Louisianans with point-blank fire. Ricketts's final brigade gained the field at 7 A.M., and the exchange of charges continued without a decisive outcome. The Tigers lost 323 of 500 men; the Twelfth Massachusetts 224 of 344.

Doubleday's division, led by John Gibbon's four regiments, advanced west from the north, with the turnpike on their right. At 6 A.M. they came under fire around the Miller farmhouse from Douglas in front and Jones to the right. Deploying two regiments to protect his right and six guns firing case shot forward, Gibbon entered the West Woods with a brigade sent up by Doubleday.

Two of Gibbon's regiments were advancing through the cornfield when a Confederate regiment rose out of the tall grass of a pasture. "Simultaneously, the hostile battle lines opened a tremendous fire upon each other," recalled Wisconsin Maj. Rufus Dawes:

The scene of the fighting in and around the cornfield and the West Wood was obscured from general view by powder smoke from rifles and artillery, exploding shells, and at the southeast edge of the cornfield, the blazing Mumma farm buildings. Confederates had been positioned here at the beginning of the battle, and once the Southerners had withdraw, D. H. Hill ordered the property torched to prevent its use by Federal sharpshooters

Federals retreating past the cornfield before John Bell Hood's attack were rallied by a boy private who waved his hat and shouted, "Rally, boys, rally! Die like men, don't run like dogs!"

LIBRARY OF CONGRESS

The man who had found the copy of Lee's Order 191 four days earlier, Cpl. Barton Mitchell, and his buddy, Sgt. John Bloss, were both wounded in the cornfield, and Capt. Peter Koop, to whom they had taken the papers, was killed.

A Union veteran of the battle, James Hope, produced a series of paintings to depict the fighting at Antietam. He condensed several stages of the combat in each. Above he depicted Stephen D. Lee's gunners in front of the Dunker Church as they fought off the Federal advance under John Sedgwick. Other veterans generally approved of the images, although one observed that the artist omitted the vast numbers of dead and wounded men on the field. Some have also pointed out that at the time of Sedgwick's advance, Lee's artillery had been withdrawn.

Confederate Col. Stephen D. Lee called Antietam "artillery hell."

Men were knocked out of the ranks by dozens. But we jumped over the fence, and pushed on, loading, firing, and shouting as we advanced. There was, on the part of the men, great hysterical excitement, eagerness to go forward, and a reckless disregard of life, of everything but victory. Now is the pinch. Men and officers of New York and Wisconsin are fused into a common mass, in the frantic struggle to shoot fast. Everybody tears cartridges, loads, passes guns, or shoots. Men are falling in their places or running back into the corn. The soldier who is shooting is furious in his energy. The soldier who is shot looks around for help with an imploring agony of death on his face.

The Confederates were driven back several hundred yards toward the Dunker Church, but at 6:45 A.M. two Southern brigades led by Brig. Gen. William E. Starke deployed along a fence bordering the turnpike and fired from thirty yards away. Within minutes two regiments of Federals from the West Woods were laying down fire on the Confederate rear and flank, and a battery from the Miller farm fired canister and case shot at the Confederates. The dead and wounded piled up behind the fence. The Southerners soon withdrew, and Starke was mortally wounded. The Federals advanced toward the Dunker Church, "loading and firing with demonical fury, shouting and laughing hysterically," Dawes recalled.

Georgians of Alfred Colquitt's brigade spotted six cows stampeding away from artillery fire and straight for them. "I remember I was more afraid just then of being run over by a cow than of being hit by a bullet," one soldier recalled.

Jackson's two divisions under Jones and Lawton had been mauled with a heavy loss of officers. At this critical moment Jackson committed his last reserve, the twenty-three hundred men of John Bell Hood who, three months earlier, had broken the Federal line at Gaines's Mill. With their breakfast disrupted at 7 A.M., the Confederates charged angrily, wildly shouting the Rebel yell. Their first volley was "like a slaughter" wrote Dawes, turning the Federal advance into a rout through the cornfield. Hood, however, was soon overextended, sending word to Jackson, "Unless I get reinforcements I must be forced back, but I am going on while I can!"

D. H. Hill moved his three brigades to Hood's right. On the far Confederate left, Lawton's last brigade, under Brig. Gen. Jubal Early, supporting Stuart on the flank, closed on the West Woods. A dozen guns were also moved up behind the West Woods.

Hood drove the Federals from the cornfield and into the East Woods, but two of Meade's brigades counterattacked and reached the cornfield, where the Confederates rallied in turn and stopped Meade.

Heavy fighting developed along the turnpike as six Federal guns fired quickly to stop Hood's Texans and Early's brigade with canister. Forty of the batteries' gunners fell, but other men filled their places. The Confederate attack ebbed fifteen yards from the muzzles, stopped by guns firing double canister. Running low on ammunition after repulsing three charges, Gibbon ordered the guns back.

Many of the Federal casualties at Antietam were inflicted by "buck and ball" rounds fired by the Confederates. The typical bullet was accompanied by three pieces of buckshot. With one man killed for every eleven hit, many wounds were not serious.

After the attack through the cornfield had been thrown back by John Bell Hood's Texas Brigade, Edwin Sumner's corps advanced on the West Woods. His attack was rushed and uncoordinated, his men too close to one another, but the worst of his problem was his collision with reinforcements hurried by Lee to shore up the Confederate line. The left flank of Sumner's line was exposed to a murderous fire, and his men fell in ranks, carpeting the floor of the forest.

LIBRARY OF CONGRESS

Confederate Pvt. B. H. Witcher hunkered down in the cornfield amid ranks of prone comrades. A friend shouted for him to join the retreat, explaining that the Confederates who surrounded him were dead. Witcher was confused until the friend fired a shot into one of the bodies. Then he understood the situation and ran for live support.

"I have heard of the 'dead lying in heaps,'" wrote Federal Capt. Emory Upton, "but never saw it till at this battle. Whole ranks fell together."

The Texas Brigade advanced fifty yards beyond other Confederate units until they were surprised by one of Meade's brigades lying on the ground and firing from behind a fence. The Rebels found themselves trapped in a crossfire that cost the First Texas 186 of 226 men—82 percent, the greatest losses suffered by any regiment in the Civil War. Nine color-bearers were lost and their flags captured.

With great sacrifice Hood had broken Hooker's attack. After ninety minutes, twenty-six hundred Federals were casualties and the remainder of the nine thousand in disarray. Hood called his half-hour solo attack "the most terrific clash of arms, by far, that has occurred during the war."

But now Mansfield's Twelfth Corps took the field with 7,200 men, half of them green recruits. Mansfield, an engineer who had never directed a large force before, had received the command only two days earlier. Despite these shortcomings the Twelfth Corps cost Hood an additional 1,380 men. The survivors, nearly out of ammunition, withdrew to the West Woods. When Hood was later asked where his division was, the general replied, "Dead on the field."

Mansfield reached the battleground in a mass formation ten ranks deep instead of two. Concerned that the raw soldiers would run if not kept under tight control, he presented a wonderful target to the Confederates in the East Woods. While trying to decide if his men were shooting Confederates or their comrades, Mansfield was shot in the chest and killed. Brig. Gen. Alpheus S. Williams took command. "If all the stone and brick houses of Broadway should tumble at once," he wrote, "the roar and rattle could hardly be greater."

The lines faced off as they had at 6 A.M., and the battle soon reached another crescendo with Mansfield's corps facing D. H. Hill, Lawton, and Jones in the West Woods, the cornfield, and parts of the East Woods.

The cornfield, an area 400 yards wide and 250 yards deep, was already covered with hundreds of dead and wounded Confederates and Federals as fresh troops marched up to renew the struggle. Possession of the cornfield changed fifteen times or more on this day.

On the Confederate right was one of D. H. Hill's brigades, the North Carolinians routed at Fox's Gap following Garland's death and now under Col. Duncan McRae. Seeing Brig. Gen. George Greene's Federal division advancing on their flank, the Confederates broke in what McRae called "the most unutterable stampede. The whole line vanished, and a brigade famous for its previous and subsequent conduct, fled in panic from the field."

Greene immediately exploited the breach, leading the seventeen hundred men of two brigades through the gap. His flank attack caused Confederate casualties to "literally fall upon and across each other," a Union colonel observed, and the action drove the survivors back through the cornfield.

Greene's last brigade swung around the Confederate right and emerged at the Smoketown road behind the East Woods and close to the Dunker Church. His assault forced Stephen Lee's four Confederate bat-

The savage fighting during the early morning at Antietam unnerved even the normally unflappable Robert E. Lee. He failed to recognize his son Robert E. Lee Jr., serving in an artillery crew, whose gun had been withdrawn from the field for ammunition replenishment.

The young Lee, blackened with burnt gunpowder, approached his father and saluted. Noting the general's confused look, he introduced himself and asked, "General, are you going to send us in again?"

"Yes, my son," Lee replied. "You all must do what you can to help drive those people back."

LIBRARY OF CONGRESS

A small whitewashed building in a patch of woods guided the attacking Federals toward their goal: the raised open field to the east of the Hagerstown turnpike. Many soldiers believed the building was a schoolhouse, but it was the meeting place for a small group of German Baptist Brethren, known as pacifists and by the nickname of Dunker. The abandoned caisson to the far left of the image marks the farthest point of Federal advance during this first phase of the fighting.

teries to abandon the high ground that Hooker had striven for since dawn. Other scattered Federal units were also in the area.

Hooker reorganized his First Corps for a renewed attack, but a marksman wounded him in the foot. Faint from loss of blood, shock, and pain, Hooker was carried off the field, leaving no corps commander with authority to initiate an attack. Hooker later believed his men were able at that point "to drive the rebel army into the Potomac or to destroy it."

Greene was forced to stop two hundred yards from the Dunker Church and send for ammunition. Under fire from the West Woods, his advance ground to a halt.

Twelfth Corps had lost one man in four. In less than four hours eight thousand soldiers had become casualties in the first part of the battle of Antietam. It was only 9 A.M.

Lee spent the morning close to the front, castigating shirkers and shifting reinforcements from his right to Jackson on the left as they were needed. These consisted of Brig. Gen. John Walker's division and Col. George "Tige" Anderson's brigade from the south and McLaws's and Maj. Gen. Richard H. Anderson's divisions, which had marched onto the field

The simple Dunker Church, a single-story whitewashed brick building, belonged to the German Baptist Brethren. Its members, dubbed Dunkers for their practice of total-immersion baptism, dressed plainly and believed steeples were a sign of vanity.

The skillful Federal advance that reached the Dunker Church was led by Brig. Gen. George S. Greene, whose son was Lt. Dana Greene, executive officer aboard the *Monitor* when she fought the *Virginia*.

This view of the fighting was sketched from a hill behind McClellan's headquarters at the Pry house, which is visible on the smaller hill in the midforeground and to the left. Sumner's advance occupies the center of the image. The column of smoke in the center marks the Mumma farm, and the East Woods are to the right, where the fighting between Jackson and Mansfield is ongoing. Dominating the image is the clear terrain, which afforded little cover for the attacking Federals. Also apparent is the limited perspective McClellan had of the battlefield; he could clearly see the right side of his line but not the center and left, where the heaviest fighting was to occur as the battle expanded.

Maj. Gen. Edwin Sumner commanded the Union Second Corps at Antietam. When he noticed the colors of his lead regiment were still in their cases, he shouted, "In God's name, what are you fighting for! Unfurl those colors!"

from Harpers Ferry only a few hours earlier. They were approaching the battlefield as the attack by the Union First and Twelfth Corps sputtered out.

McClellan remained at the Pry house with Fifth Corps commander Maj. Gen. Fitz John Porter, watching the battle a mile to the east through telescopes. Burnside had yet to divert Confederate attention to their right, and Sumner's Second Corps had not been sent in to support Hooker and Mansfield. Ready to advance since before dawn, Sumner waited nearly two hours to speak with McClellan. Only as Hood's counterattack could be seen rolling back Hooker did McClellan dispatch Sumner at 7:20

"Tige" ■ George Thomas Anderson

Born February 3, 1824, in Covington, Georgia, George Thomas Anderson left Emory College to fight with Stephen W. Kearny in the Mexican War. He received a regular army commission in 1855 and served with the First Cavalry before resigning in 1858. In 1861 Anderson became colonel of the Eleventh Georgia and received a brigade after fighting at the Seven Days, Second Manassas, and Antietam. Known as Tige, short for "Tiger," he fought at Fredericksburg, Suffolk, and Gettysburg, where he was seriously wounded.

Briefly transferred to the western theater with James Longstreet, Anderson fought at Knoxville and returned to Virginia for the battles of Grant's Overland campaign, from the Wilderness to Appomattox, where he surrendered.

Anderson was chief of police in Atlanta, Georgia, and Anniston, Alabama, dying in the latter on April 4, 1901, where he is buried in Edgemont Cemetery.

A.M., and even then he allowed only two divisions to be sent forward. Maj. Gen. Israel Richardson's division was to remain in reserve until replaced by one of Porter's.

An hour and a half passed before Sumner reached the battlefield a mile and a half away. He forded the Antietam two thousand yards east of the Dunker Church and deployed near the East Woods. Maj. Gen. John Sedgwick's three brigades were formed in three lines five hundred yards across. With this tight formation, Sumner expected to roll over the Confederates in the West Woods, crush Lee's left, and seize Sharpsburg to the south.

Sumner raced his men through the disorganized First and Twelfth Corps without seeking information about the situation or waiting for support from them. He moved so quickly he left his second division behind. Following twenty minutes behind Sedgwick, Brig. Gen. William H. French saw only Greene's men and took his division to their left, leaving Sumner with only one division totaling fifty-four hundred men.

Sumner, whose appropriate nickname "Bull" had been bestowed after a round bounced off his head in Mexico, barreled on without sending out skirmishers or flankers. He emerged from the West Woods to encounter Stuart's artillery and some scattered infantry near the Poffenberger farm to the west.

As Sumner's front brigade, led by Brig. Gen. Willis Gorman, engaged them at 9 A.M., McLaws's division, Anderson's brigade, and Early with Lawton's division, slammed into the unsupported and unsuspecting left flank of Sumner from the south.

George B. McClellan and Fitz John Porter set up shop beside the Philip Pry house on high ground east of Antietam Creek. Soldiers brought parlor chairs from the house, drove stakes in the ground to rest telescopes on, and stacked fence rails around the position for protection against stray Confederate shells. There the generals smoked and murmured quietly together as McClellan received dispatches and issued orders.

Robert E. Lee encountered a straggler who had killed a pig and was making for the rear to prepare it. Lee's notably even temper was lost, and he ordered Stonewall Jackson to shoot the man. Jackson had better use for the miscreant, sending him back into battle where he fought bravely, thereby "losing his pig," an officer noted, "but saving his bacon."

The lasting images of the Antietam battlefield were made by two of Mathew Brady's cameramen, Alexander Gardner and James F. Gibson, who were on the scene as early as September 18. Their photographs of the corpses on the battlefield—the first images of American dead on American battlefields—shocked the public when they were displayed in October in Brady's New York gallery. Part of this exhibit included the wreckage of war near the Dunker Church (below left) and a line of approximately twenty-five bodies on the Mumma farm awaiting burial (below right).

LIBRARY OF CONGRESS

LIBRARY OF CONGRESS

Confusion reigned when Confederates bushwhacked Edwin V. Sumner's corps from several directions. One company commander with the Twentieth Massachusetts, Capt. Oliver Wendell Holmes, knocked down one of his own soldiers with the flat of his sword for firing to the rear before realizing Confederates were attacking from that direction also.

Holmes received an ugly wound through his neck and fell helplessly to the ground. A chaplain knelt beside him and asked, "You're a Christian, aren't you?" To Holmes's nod, the chaplain replied, "Well, then *that's* all right!" and he left, believing the captain to be fatally wounded.

During the night another Union officer, Capt. William G. LaDuc, found Holmes wandering across the battlefield and tended his wound. Unable to procure the services of a surgeon, LaDuc treated Holmes as best he could. "I'm glad, LaDuc," Holmes managed to say, "it ain't a case for amputation." Holmes survived to become one of America's most respected Supreme Court justices.

Lt. Col. Wilder Dwight of the Twentieth Massachusetts had started a letter before dawn that day. Lying mortally wounded on the field, he took the unfinished letter from a pocket and wrote: "Dearest Mother, I am wounded so as to be helpless. Good by, if so it must be. I think I die in victory. God defend our country." The blood-stained letter was mailed to his home.

"Where the line stood the ground was covered in blue," a Georgian wrote. "I could have walked on them without putting my feet on the ground."

"My God!" shouted Sumner, who with the remainder of his army had been facing west, "we must get out of this."

Three Union regiments crumbled before Sumner could reorient his division to face the threat. In minutes Brig. Gen. Oliver O. Howard, recovered from the loss of his arm at Fair Oaks, lost 545 men of his Philadelphia Brigade. "Quicker than I can write the words," he wrote, "my men faced about and took the back track."

The Federals who remained were too closely packed to return fire, "so near together that a rifle bullet would often cross them all and disable five or six men at a time," Howard remembered. Regiments in the center fired on their comrades to the front. One of those regiments sustained 344 casualties, the largest number of any at Antietam. One regiment in the center lost 60 men before it could fire a shot. Sedgwick left the field after his third wound and one of his brigadiers, Napoleon J. T. Dana, was severely wounded. Dana would remember the fire as "the most terrific I ever witnessed," coming from three directions as Confederates gained the Union rear. Stuart also advanced his artillery and added canister to the carnage. "In less time than it takes to tell it," recalled an officer from Massachusetts, "the ground was strewn with the bodies of the dead and wounded."

The fighting in the West Woods subsided as the battle shifted to the center of the Confederate line, prompted by the movement of William French's division in that direction. Rather than follow Sedgwick's division toward the woods, French's men mistakenly veered toward the farmstead of William Roulette and a thin line of Confederates, which was James Longstreet's corps.

BATTLES AND LEADERS

Soldiers fighting on the Roulette farm were attacked by hundreds of thousands of bees enraged after artillery shells destroyed their hives.

The middle of Lee's line was dangerously thin, having supplied most of the reinforcements for the fighting in the woods. All that remained were the ravaged remnants of the units that had fought at South Mountain, but the strongest brigades held the central position and occupied a well-worn country lane that connected the Hagerstown and Boonsboro turnpikes. It was known as the sunken road, and it made an excellent rifle pit and would become infamous as Bloody Lane.

Panic developed in the Federal ranks as most regiments took flight, while a few steady ones withdrew in some order. After twenty minutes Sedgwick had lost half of his division—2,255 men led to the slaughter.

At 9:45 A.M. the exuberant Confederates raced through the woods and encountered dozens of cannon from the Second and Twelfth Corps placed in a continuous line. McLaws rapidly lost a third of his division before they could regain the woods.

When the fighting petered out on the Confederate left, battered Rebel artillery withdrew for repairs and ammunition. Confederate Capt. William W. Blackford noted that wounded horses, cut from the traces, faithfully hobbled along behind their guns. One horse seemed to be dragging a rider until it neared. "To my horror I discovered that the horse was dragging his own entrails from the gaping wound of a cannonball." Blackford shot the horse and "the poor brute fell dead with a piercing scream."

"Fighting Dick" ■ Israel Bush Richardson

Also known as "Greasy Dick," Israel Bush Richardson was born December 26, 1815, in Fairfax, Vermont. He was a descendant of Revolutionary War hero Israel Putnam. Richardson was graduated thirty-eighth in the U.S. Military Academy class of 1841, which provided the Civil War with twenty-three generals (of the fifty-two graduates, fourteen had died before the war). Richardson fought the Seminoles and won two brevets for gallantry in Mexico——at Contreras, Churubusco, and Chapultepec.

He retired in 1855 to farm in Pontiac, Michigan, but raised a regiment early in 1861 and was appointed its colonel on May 5, 1861, thus participating in his third war.

Richardson saw little action at First Manassas, but his Second Michigan withdrew in an orderly fashion. He attained the rank of brigadier on August 9 and spent the winter skillfully training recruits. Richardson took a division to the peninsula, fighting at Yorktown, Seven Pines, and the Seven Days, and was

appointed major general on July 5, 1862. He gained a reputation for the organization and discipline of his troops as well as for his own personal bravery.

At Antietam, Richardson attacked vigorously and captured the Bloody Lane from D. H. Hill. Wounded by Confederate artillery fire, he was borne to George B. McClellan's headquarters, the Pry house, where he died on November 3, 1862. He is buried at Pontiac.

Clara Barton arrived during the battle and worked for three straight days. At one point a bullet passed through her sleeve and killed the man whom she was tending.

The Confederates opened a murderous fire on French's men, devastating the front ranks and blunting several assaults. Federal casualties were taken to the ruins of the Mumma farm, where Union artillery continued to duel with Southern batteries near the Dunker Church.

"We were in the very maelstrom of the battle," remembered Pennsylvania Lt. Frederick L. Hitchcock. "Men were falling every moment. The horrible noise was incessant and almost deafening. Except that my mind was absorbed in my duties, I do not know how I could have endured the strain."

At 10 A.M. two Federal regiments of Brig. Gen. George H. Gordon's brigade of Twelfth Corps left the East Woods to assist Sumner, but they were stopped at the fence along the turnpike by Confederates in the West Woods.

Greene, resupplied with ammunition and supported by six cannon, repulsed two assaults at the Dunker Church then counterattacked Walker's

"Old Bull Head" ■ Edwin Vose Sumner

Edwin Vose Sumner, the oldest corps commander in the Civil War, was born January 30, 1797, in Boston. He received a brevet commission into the army in 1819, made captain in 1833, major in 1846 while serving in the West, and was breveted lieutenant colonel and colonel in Mexico, where he was wounded. He received the regular army rank of lieutenant colonel in 1848. Sumner led the First Cavalry in 1855 as a colonel before serving in Bleeding Kansas from Fort Leavenworth. In his long service, Sumner had led infantry, dra-

goons, and cavalry. As war loomed in 1861, he became one of only four regular army brigadiers. Gen. Winfield Scott had previously selected him to accompany Abraham Lincoln on the hazardous journey from Illinois to Washington for the inauguration in 1861.

Sumner led George B. McClellan's Second Corps on the peninsula, where he was wounded and praised by his superior. Breveted major general for Seven Pines, "Old Bull Head," nicknamed for an incident in which a bullet had bounced off his

head, covered John Pope's withdrawal from Second Manassas but was criticized for charging blindly into the battle of Antietam. After leading two corps against Mayre's Heights at Fredericksburg, Sumner asked for relief rather than serve under Joseph Hooker.

En route to command the Department of Missouri, Sumner died at Syracuse, New York, on March 21, 1863, and is buried there in Oakwood Cemetery. Two sons fought in the Civil War as Union officers, but one son-in-law directed Stuart's

artillery and became secretary to Robert E. Lee, and another was related to Joseph E. Johnston.

three regiments and drove them two hundred yards beyond the church. Greene requested reinforcements, but none were forthcoming.

"The Federals have done their worst," Jackson predicted at 11 A.M., having crushed six Union divisions in five hours.

The action now shifted to a half mile east of the Dunker Church, where French had veered off two hours earlier. Skirting the Mumma farm, his three brigades encountered the Confederate center just beyond the Roulette farm at 9:30 as a courier arrived from Sumner to explain the disaster. He urgently requested a diversion against the Confederate center to relieve the pressure on the Union right.

French had blundered into the exact position where Sumner needed him. Although seven of his ten regiments were green, French attacked immediately toward the south, parallel to the turnpike.

Five hundred yards south of the Roulette farm, one hundred yards beyond the crest of a gently sloping hill, was Longstreet with only D. H. Hill's five-brigade division, a total of twenty-five hundred men. Three brigades had fought earlier in the day, but the two fresh ones held a sunken road, soon to be called Bloody Lane. This farm path, occupied by Brig. Gens. Robert Rodes and George Anderson, ran from the turnpike a third of a mile south of the Dunker Church and wandered between the Roulette and Piper farms to the Boonsboro road. Confederates crouched in a half-mile section and piled fence rails to their front, which faced French's division.

At the top of the ridge, one hundred yards forward, the Federals stopped to straighten their line. Col. John Gordon, a Georgian commanding Alabamians in the road, described the scene:

> Soon they were so close that we might have seen the eagles on their buttons; but my brave and eager boys still waited for the order. Now the front rank was within a few rods of where I stood. It would not do to wait another second and with all my lung power I shouted, "Fire!"
>
> My rifles flamed and roared in the Federals' faces like a blinding blaze of lightning accompanied by the quick and deadly thunderbolt. The effect was appalling. The entire front line, with few exceptions, went down in the consuming blast. Before his rear lines could recover from the terrific shock, my exultant men were on their feet, devouring them with successive volleys.

Federal Brig. Gen. Max Weber's brigade was ambushed from a distance of twenty yards. After five minutes his brigade withdrew behind

A dead Confederate was found kneeling in his firing position in the sunken road, frozen in place.

One Federal recalled that "the Confederate dead lay three deep for half a mile" along Bloody Lane.

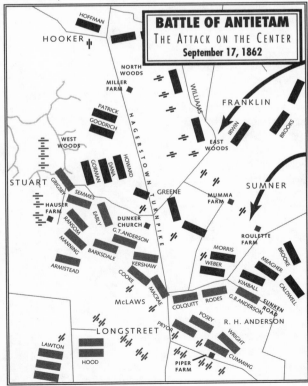

BATTLE OF ANTIETAM
THE ATTACK ON THE CENTER
September 17, 1862

As the battle started at the sunken road, Robert E. Lee, James Longstreet, and D. H. Hill observed the battle from a hill. Lee and Longstreet dismounted, but Hill remained on his horse. "If you insist on riding up there and drawing their fire," Longstreet complained, "give us a little interval," but Hill remained on his horse.

Seconds later a Federal shell took off both of the horses's forelegs, but the animal remained upright. "Hill was in a most ludicrous position," Longstreet remembered. "With one foot in the stirrup he made several efforts to get the other leg over the croup, but failed. Finally, we prevailed upon him to try the other end of the horse, and he got down."

Col. John B. Gordon was one of the bravest or stubbornest officers in the Confederate army. "These men are going to stay here, General, till the sun goes down or victory is won!" he had promised Robert E. Lee. As he stalked the sunken road encouraging his men, Gordon was wounded twice in the right leg, once in the left arm, and once in the shoulder. Undeterred by the wounds and loss of blood, he continued directing the battle until hit a fifth time in the face.

"I fell forward and lay unconscious with my face in my cap," Gordon wrote years later. "I might have been smothered by the blood running into my cap from this last wound but for the act of some Yankee, who had at a previous hour during the battle, shot a hole through the cap, which let the blood out."

Earlier Gordon had found two soldiers, father and son, lying beside each other in the Bloody Lane. "The son was dead, the father mortally wounded. The gray-haired hero called and said: 'Here we are. My boy is dead, and I shall go soon; but it is all right.'"

the hill, leaving 450 casualties on the field. Col. Dwight Morris's brigade followed, three raw regiments that also soon retreated. French's last brigade, veterans under Brig. Gen. Nathan Kimball, marched forward with no more success. One private knelt on the ground, fascinated to observe that "every blade of glass is moving. For some time I supposed that this is caused by the merry crickets; and it is not until I have made a remark to that effect to one of our boys near me and notice him laugh, that I know it is the bullets that are falling thickly around us!" Within an hour French lost half his division in front of Bloody Lane.

During the fight Hill was reinforced by thirty-four hundred men, the two-brigade division of Richard Anderson who marched past the Piper farm, behind the sunken road, and extended Hill's line to the right.

As the Confederate reinforcements prepared to attack French's left flank, Israel Richardson, with Sumner's withheld division, arrived to strengthen that portion of the Union line. Without hesitation, Richardson attacked with the Irish Brigade, under Brig. Gen. Thomas F. Meagher. The Irish were staggered by Confederate fire from the sunken road, losing eight color-bearers in a few minutes. The brigade fought bravely until ammunition ran low, then withdrew, having suffered 540 casualties.

Brig. Gen. John C. Caldwell's brigade replaced the Irish. Hearing that Caldwell himself was hiding in the rear behind a haystack, Richardson

There was a weakness to the Confederate position in the sunken road, at an elbow in the lane where the road turned southeast. Two Federal regiments found a ridge near here that looked down the length of the roadway and unleashed an enfilading fire that decimated the Confederate ranks. Compounding Southern misfortunes, an inexperienced officer unwittingly ordered a retreat, and his brigade abandoned the lane. Union soldiers occupied the roadway and ventured into the cornfield beyond. They were stalled by desperate counterattacks and artillery, fell back, and then ordered to hold their position by a cautious commander.

The carnage in the sunken road was recorded by Gardner and Gibson. In the four hours' of combat centered on the deadly lane, there were more than three thousand Federal casualties and twenty-six hundred Confederate. Lee's army was ravaged, but fortunately for him, McClellan was not intent on victory, only saving his army and avoiding defeat.

damned him loudly and personally and led the brigade to within thirty yards of the Confederate position.

The two-hour-long battle had also piled up Confederate casualties in Bloody Lane. George Anderson had taken a mortal wound, as did his second in command. One of his regiments lost every officer. Gordon was finally knocked out of the fight by his fifth serious wound. Richard Anderson's reinforcements contributed little to the defense after their commander was seriously wounded.

Federal Col. Francis C. Barlow now noticed that a hill overlooked a bend in the road where the lane was shallowest. Taking two regiments to

Union Col. Francis C. Barlow carried the biggest sword available for swatting malingerers. At Antietam he tied his skittish drummer boys to his sash to keep them in the battle.

An Achilles Heel ■ George Burgwyn Anderson

Born on April 12, 1831, near Hillsboro, North Carolina, George Burgwyn Anderson attended the University of North Carolina and West Point, graduating from the academy in 1852.

A cavalryman on the frontier and in Kansas, he resigned April 25, 1861, and led the Fourth North Carolina to Manassas as its colonel. He just missed the battle of First Manassas, but commanded the garrison there until it was evacuated in March 1862.

Ordered south to participate in the rear-guard action following the evacuation of Yorktown, Anderson led his brigade at Williamsburg on the peninsula with such conspicuous valor that Jefferson Davis made him a brigadier on June 9, 1862.

The Fourth North Carolina served with distinction during the fighting at Seven Pines and the Seven Days, where Anderson was wounded at Malvern Hill. His wounding prevented his participation in the Second Manassas campaign, but he returned to duty to lead his regiment in the Maryland campaign.

He fought with D. H. Hill at South Mountain and alone held part of the Confederate line in the sunken road at Antietam. During the second assault on that position, he was wounded in the foot.

He received rudimentary treatment, but when the wound refused to heal, Anderson was sent to Raleigh, where the foot was amputated. He died of complications on October 16, 1862. He is buried there.

A private in the 108th New York captured a Confederate flag and was running to the rear with it when an officer from another regiment warned he could be accidentally shot by his comrades. The man gave the flag to the officer, not realizing he had been had.

the rise, they opened fire on the exposed Confederates below. "We were shooting them like sheep in a pen," wrote a New York sergeant. "If a bullet missed the mark at first it was liable to strike the farther bank, angle back, and take them secondarily."

Then the fog of battle descended on the Confederates. General Rodes ordered Lt. Col. James N. Lightfoot to wheel part of the Sixth Alabama to face the threat. Instead, Lightfoot ordered the entire regiment to "about face" and march to the rear. Maj. Edwin L. Hobson of the Fifth Alabama, the next regiment in line, saw the move and asked if the entire brigade was withdrawing. Assured that it was, all five brigades abandoned Bloody Lane. A serious wound distracted Rodes's attention for a few minutes. Looking up, he was horrified to see the Confederate line retreating to the Hagerstown turnpike.

Barlow's 350 men raced down the rise and captured 300 Confederates. The tables had turned. Soon Federals controlled the lane, firing from its protection at the retreating Southerners. Two Confederate regiments under Col. John R. Cooke marched to attack the Federal left flank, passing the Dunker Church and the Mumma farmhouse, burned earlier by retreating Confederates. Union reserves from the sunken road engaged them at a distance of two hundred yards, forcing Cooke to retreat. He left behind half his 675 men as casualties.

Artillery fire at Antietam was so devastating that many men developed the "cannon quickstep," a hasty race for the rear.

While D. H. Hill, who had lost three horses that day, rallied his disorganized division, Longstreet gathered artillery to slow the Federal pursuit with canister. At the Piper farm, three hundred yards from the sunken

Shunted Aside ■ William Buel Franklin

William Buel Franklin, born at York, Pennsylvania, on February 27, 1823, graduated first in the West Point class of 1843 (Ulysses S. Grant was twenty-first). As a topographical engineer he helped survey the Great Lakes and the Rocky Mountains then was breveted for gallantry in Mexico. Until the Civil War he supervised construction of the Treasury building in Washington and the new dome for the Capitol.

Franklin became a colonel on May 14 and a brigadier of volunteers on May 17. His brigade fought at First Manassas, although one regiment, the Fourth Pennsylvania, had claimed its discharge only hours before the battle. He commanded a

division in Washington's defenses during the fall and winter and led the Sixth Corps on the peninsula, where it fought well. Franklin's men slowly seized Crampton's Gap at South Mountain in September 1862 and ventured no farther. He led the Grand Left Division, consisting of two corps, at the battle of Fredericksburg. One of his divisions, under George Gordon Meade, broke through Stonewall Jackson's lines but Franklin failed to reinforce this success. After the battle Franklin and William F. Smith wrote a letter to Washington condemning Ambrose E. Burnside's campaign and proposing one of their own. Burnside claimed Franklin was responsible for the disaster and demanded that Lin-

coln either fire Franklin and others or himself. Lincoln chose to relieve and reassign both Burnside and Franklin.

Months later orders finally arrived that sent Franklin west with the Nineteenth Corps, where he was wounded in Nathaniel Banks's doomed Red River campaign in 1864. The train carrying the injured Franklin was captured by partisan rangers, but the general managed to escape. Finding himself relegated to obscure boards, he resigned as a major general in the regular army and moved into more successful fields. Franklin managed the Colt firearms plant in Hartford, Connecticut, for twenty-two years, constructed the Connecticut capitol, and became the U.S. commissioner

general to the Paris Exposition in 1888. Franklin died in Hartford on March 8, 1903, and is buried in York, Pennsylvania.

road, the "little battery shot harder and faster, as though it realized that it was to hold the thousands of Federals at bay or the battle was lost," Longstreet recalled.

Hill collected two hundred men and advanced to attack the Federal left flank, running instead into Col. Edward E. Cross's Fifth New Hampshire. "You have never disgraced your state," Cross told his troops. "I hope you won't this time. If any man runs I want the file closers to shoot him; if they don't, I shall myself."

One volley drove the tiny Confederate force back, where Hill discovered another two hundred men led by his officers. He renewed the battle but was beaten off with the help of the Eighty-first Pennsylvania.

By this time Longstreet had assembled twenty cannon that halted the Federal advance at 12:30 P.M., six hundred yards south of Bloody Lane at the Piper farm. Hooker's goal had nearly been met—Sharpsburg was half a mile down the pike. But Barlow had been seriously wounded by canister, one of Israel Richardson's one thousand casualties.

Around Bloody Lane, Lee had lost twenty-six hundred soldiers. The bottom of the road was carpeted with bodies piled two or three deep. The Confederate left was fatigued and disorganized, its ammunition nearly exhausted. One more attack would crack the Confederate center and the Army of Northern Virginia would be destroyed in pieces, its back against

Three bridges spanned the Antietam, but Lee chose to defend only one. Ambrose E. Burnside's corps was to have crossed it and attacked the southern segment of the Confederate line at the same time that Hooker's men were attacking the West Woods. When he did attack in the late morning, he funneled his men across the bridge and sent another group to ford the creek a half mile downstream.

As Confederate Col. John R. Cooke, whose sister was married to Jeb Stuart and whose father, Brig. Gen. Philip St. George Cooke, commanded Federal cavalry, prepared to advance his brigade, a barber-fiddler from Arkansas asked, "Sir, would it be all right if I kinda give the boys a tune as they move out? I got my fiddle with me."

Cooke acquiesced, and the men marched into battle to the tune of "Granny, Will Your Dog Bite? Hellfire, No!"

Cooke told his energetic color-bearer that the troops could not keep up with him. "Colonel," the man replied, indicating another regiment, "I can't let that Arkansas fellow get ahead of me."

BATTLES AND LEADERS

Fighting D. H. Hill's counterattack, Col. Edward E. Cross of the Fifth New York shouted to his men: "Put on the war paint!" and his men ripped cartridges open and smeared gunpowder across their faces.

"Give them the war whoop!" Cross yelled next. Then, roaring at the tops of their lungs, the Federals attacked and scattered the Confederates.

"It is General Burnside's special request that the two Fifty-firsts take that bridge," said Col. Edward Ferrero to the Fifty-first Pennsylvania and the Fifty-first New York. "Will you do it?"

The Pennsylvanians remained quiet, remembering that Ferrero had recently disciplined them by suspending their daily shot of whiskey.

"Will you give us our whiskey, Colonel, if we take it?" asked Cpl. Louis Patterson.

"Yes, by God," Ferrero shouted, "you shall have as much as you want!"

For the successful assault Ferrero was promoted to brigadier general. At the promotion ceremony a corporal reminded Ferrero of his promise by shouting, "How about that whiskey?"

They finally got their barrel.

the Potomac River. "We were already badly whipped," Longstreet wrote, "and were only holding our ground by sheer force of desperation."

Israel Richardson withdrew behind the sunken road to reorganize his division and that of French and to bring up artillery to silence Longstreet's guns. He was only able to assemble eight of McClellan's three hundred pieces. During the ensuing artillery duel, Richardson was mortally wounded by a shell. His place was taken by Brig. Gen. Winfield S. Hancock, but momentum on that part of the battlefield had been lost.

McClellan could have committed twenty-eight thousand men to the center: Porter's Fifth Corps, only a mile from Bloody Lane at the middle bridge; Franklin's Sixth Corps, just arriving from Pleasant Valley, which McClellan had sent to reinforce the West Woods; and more than thirty-five hundred cavalry.

At 1 P.M. Franklin prepared to renew the attack on the West Woods, but Sumner, Franklin's senior, canceled it. Another defeat would endanger the Federal right, he believed. At about the same time McClellan sent a dispatch suggesting that while the Sixth Corps attacked, Sumner could defend the right flank. The commanding general seemed to agree with Franklin, but Sumner thundered at the courier, "Go back, young man, and tell General McClellan I have no command!"

At last McClellan crossed Antietam Creek to meet with his generals. After hearing them both out, McClellan supported Sumner, saying "it would be unsafe to risk everything on the right." Sumner, Franklin, and Hancock were ordered to "hold their position." Porter and the cavalry were held in reserve.

At the southern end of the battle line was the lower bridge spanning Antietam Creek. It was called Rohrbach's Bridge but soon came to be known as Burnside's Bridge, named for the commander of Eleventh Corps, Maj. Gen. Ambrose E. Burnside. When Hooker began his attack that morning, Burnside followed McClellan's instructions to prepare his men to attack the 125-foot-long span. His eleven thousand men and fifty cannon occupied hills overlooking the bridge from the eastern bank.

Burnside, twice criticized by McClellan for his slow pace, had lost command of one corps under the new command structure. Petulantly, he refused to command his own corps, instead relaying orders to Brig. Gen. Jacob Cox. Burnside "shrank from responsibility with sincere modesty," Cox later wrote.

Neither general bothered to inspect a ford discovered a day earlier by McClellan's engi-

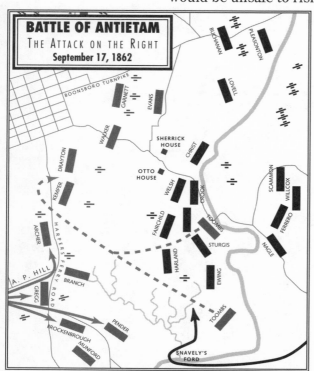

BATTLE OF ANTIETAM
The Attack on the Right
September 17, 1862

LIBRARY OF CONGRESS

Burnside's corps secured the bridge after three separate attacks. None dislodged the Confederates directly. The Southerners on the heights overlooking the crossing withdrew after exhausting their ammunition. They had succeeded, however, in delaying the attack on Lee's southern flank for three hours. The image above is one of James Hope's paintings of the battle.

neers, apparently intent on following their orders to the letter by crossing eleven thousand men across the fifty-foot-wide bridge. Burnside and Cox spent the morning watching the battle to their north. At 9 A.M. they saw Walker's Confederate division march from the bridge to the West Woods, leaving only the five small brigades of Maj. Gen. David R. Jones's two-thousand-man division to defend the mile north to Sharpsburg. Four of

Attacking Burnside's Bridge was Federal Col. Henry W. Kingsburg of the Eleventh Connecticut, who was married to the sister of Confederate Gen. Simon B. Buckner, and Union Lt. George W. Whitman, brother of poet Walt Whitman.

The Elephant Man ■ John Sedgwick

Born at Cornwall Hollow, Connecticut, on September 13, 1813, John Sedgwick received a local education and taught two years before entering West Point. He graduated in the class of 1837 with Braxton Bragg, Joseph Hooker, Jubal Early, and John C. Pemberton. Sedgwick fought the Seminoles, helped remove the Cherokee Indians from Georgia, and stood garrison duty. He won two brevets in Mexico and became major of the First Cavalry; his superiors were Col. Robert E. Lee and Lt. Col. William Joseph Hardee. He served in Bleeding Kansas and on the Mormon expedition, then fought Indians. When Lee and Hardee resigned, Sedgwick became colonel of the regiment in 1861. He was appointed brigadier on August 31, 1861.

Sedgwick was given command of Charles P. Stone's division when Stone was arrested following the Ball's Bluff disaster and led it on the peninsula, fighting at Yorktown, Seven Pines, and the Seven Days, where he was wounded at Glendale. Promoted to major general, he returned to duty and fought at Antietam, where his brave conduct was noted when his command was fired on from three sides. Sedgwick received three wounds. He led the Sixth Corps under Joseph Hooker, which in 1863 was assigned to capture Marye's Heights at Fredericksburg while the main body of the Army of the Potomac fought at Chancellorsville. After Lee defeated Hooker, he fought Sedgwick to a draw at Salem Church, forcing the Federals to withdraw. Sedgwick was in reserve at Gettysburg, but late in the year skillfully stormed a Confederate position on the Rappahannock River, capturing seventeen hundred prisoners.

Sedgwick's steady leadership continued through the Wilderness to Spotyslvania on May 9, 1864, where he dismissed the threat of Confederate marksmen with the remark, "They couldn't hit an elephant at this distance." He fell seconds later with a bullet to the head, one of three Union corps commanders to be killed during the Civil War. Known as "Uncle John," Sedgwick was one of the most beloved men in the Union army. He is buried at Cornwall Hollow, Connecticut.

At 3 P.M., following a two-hour lull in the fighting, the assault began on the right side of the Confederate line anchored in Sharpsburg. Eight thousand men advanced along a front three-quarters of a mile wide. The Ninth New York, a Zouave regiment, dislodged two determined Virginia brigades from a stone-and-rail fence within sight of the town (above). Only the timely arrival of A. P. Hill's Light Division, three thousand strong, blunted the attack and preserved Lee's army.

the brigades manned high ridges near town, leaving Brig. Gen. Robert Toombs covering the six hundred yards of high ground overlooking the bridge and fords. Toombs, a Georgia politician who hated the army, swore that the day after he fought a great battle, "I will retire if I live through it." He was about to get his chance.

Toombs's 550 Georgians faced the Ninth Corps, most of them from atop a one-hundred-foot-high wooded bluff that towered directly over the span and behind stone walls paralleling the creek. The last quarter mile of the road leading to the bridge from the eastern bank was also dominated by the Georgians, who were supported by twelve guns on a ridge behind Toombs, near Sharpsburg.

Just after nine, with Hooker and Mansfield repulsed, Sumner attacking, and Franklin approaching from Pleasant Valley, McClellan ordered

In the midst of battle, Martin Eakle, a miller in Keedyville, loaded his carriage with biscuits and ham and crossed the middle bridge to distribute them to Capt. William Graham's battery. Eakle then filled the carriage with a load of wounded, carried them to a field hospital, and returned for another load.

The Quaker Soldier ■ Isaac Peace Rodman

Born in South Kingstown, Rhode Island, on August 18, 1822, Isaac Peace Rodman had a successful business and political career before becoming a captain in the Second Rhode Island on June 6, 1861, part of Ambrose E. Burnside's brigade

that lost 362 men at First Manassas. Rodman became the colonel of the Fourth Rhode Island in October and fought at Roanoke Island, New Bern, and Fort Macon, North Carolina. Burnside recommended Rodman for a brigadier rank, which was

approved while the Quaker recuperated from typhoid fever at home.

Returning during the campaign, Rodham was given a division. He crossed Antietam Creek at Snavely's Ford, near Burnside Bridge, as A. P. Hill attacked. Rodham's men fought well,

but one green regiment crumbled as he brought up reinforcements. Rodman was mortally wounded, dying September 30, 1862. He is buried in the family cemetery at Peace Dale, Rhode Island.

Burnside's advance to draw off Confederate strength from the massive Confederate counterattack he expected to fall on the right at any moment.

At 10 A.M. Burnside relayed the order to Cox, who set their plan in operation: to simultaneously attack the bridge and then ford the creek half a mile downstream. A division under Brig. Gen. Isaac Peace Rodman, a Quaker, and another brigade headed for the reported ford.

The bridge would be attacked by the Eleventh Connecticut acting as skirmishers, to be followed by a brigade of Ohioans led by Brig. Gen. George Crook, who had fought well at South Mountain. When the Eleventh Connecticut breasted a ridge two hundred yards from the bridge, most of the regiment was immediately pinned down, but two companies reached the road and advanced slowly toward the bridge. Their commander, Col. Henry W. Kingsbury, was shot four times and killed. A company led by Capt. John R. Griswold made it to the creek and started to ford, but they were driven back with Griswold mortally wounded. In fifteen minutes a third of the regiment, 139 men, went down.

Behind Kingsbury, Crook's men suffered for his failure to scout the terrain during the previous two days. They blundered into woods and reached the road a quarter mile from the bridge, where they stopped.

Rodman located the ford, but finding its banks too steep he started downstream for what locals told him was Snavely's Ford.

A second assault of four regiments from Brig. Gen. Samuel D. Sturgis's division pushed directly down the road toward the bridge in a narrow column four men wide, but it was soon stopped by Confederate fire.

Two hours had passed, and an impatient McClellan sent repeated orders for Burnside to advance. "Tell him if it costs 10,000 men he must

As Robert Toombs pulled his Confederates back from Burnside's Bridge, Lt. Col. William R. Holmes refused to withdraw. The commander of the Second Georgia ran down to the creek to take on the Federal hordes with his sword. He was instantly killed.

Toombs, whose one great battle was Antietam, despised graduates of the U.S. Military Academy. The epitaph of the Confederacy, he claimed, should be "Died of West Point." Many officials in Washington, D.C., shared that feeling.

The people of Antietam had endured a three-day occupation by Confederate troops and cowered in their cellars all day as the fighting raged around them. When Federal troops approached late in the day, one girl, watching from her attic, remembered, "On all the distant hills around were the blue uniforms and shining bayonets of our men and I thought it was the prettiest sight I ever saw in my life."

Prior to the arrival of Hill's troops, a few Federal soldiers had ventured into the streets of Sharpsburg. They were pulled back when it was feared that Lee had even more reserves to call upon. By 5:30 P.M. a relative quiet fell on Hall Street (below left) after almost twelve hours of fighting in the nearby countryside. St. Paul's Lutheran Church on Main Street (below right) was damaged by the artillery of both armies. Confederates used it as a signal station, and after the fighting it served as a hospital.

"The day had been a long one," recalled Lt. James A. Graham of North Carolina, "but the evening seemed longer; the sun seemed almost to go backwards, and it appeared as if night would never come."

Soldiers wandered the battlefield wondering at the debris of battle. "One poor fellow had one leg shot off and was hobbling along with two guns for crutches," a Federal noted.

"In the midst of all this carrion," a Union officer observed, "our troops sat cooking, eating, jabbering, and smoking; sleeping among the corpses so that but for the color of the skin it was difficult to distinguish the living from the dead."

A Sharpsburg resident wrote afterward that the wounded "filled every building and overflowed into the country round, into farm-houses, barns, corn-cribs, cabins,—wherever four walls and a roof were brought together."

After the savage battle a correspondent described the town of Antietam as "one vast hospital."

Connecticut soldier Samuel Fiske wrote that "there are hundreds of horses, too, all mangled and petrifying, scattered everywhere! Then there are the broken gun-carriages, the wagons, and thousands of muskets, and all sorts of equipments, and clothing all torn and bloody, and cartridges and cannon-shot, and pieces of shell, the trees torn with shot and scarred with bullets, the farm-houses and barns knocked to pieces and burned down, the crops trampled and wasted, the whole country forlorn and desolate."

One Federal noted Confederates who looked as if they were just out of the cradle or ready for the grave. Further, "There was not to the best of my knowledge in all that was buried two dressed alike."

go now," McClellan instructed one courier. The next courier was Col. Delos B. Sackett, McClellan's inspector general, who relayed the latest instruction "to push forward the troops without a moment's delay." Sackett was to remain until the attack succeeded, which outraged Burnside. "McClellan appears to think I am not trying my best to carry this bridge," he told Sackett. "You are the third or fourth one who has been to me this morning with similar orders."

Burnside detailed the four-regiment brigade of Col. Edward Ferrero, part of Sturgis's division, for the task. Motivated by Ferrero's promise to restore their whiskey ration and supported by two batteries that enfiladed the Confederate position, at 12:15 P.M. the Fifty-first New York and Fifty-first Pennsylvania fixed bayonets and started over the ridge at the double quick to race down the road for the bridge. Federal casualties rapidly mounted as Confederates fired from behind stone fences, trees, boulders, and even tree limbs. Both regiments sought cover only twenty-five yards from the bridge, pausing to return fire. "The way we showered the lead across that creek was nobody's business," wrote Walt Whitman's brother, Lt. George W. Whitman.

The Fifty-first Pennsylvania's commander, Col. John F. Hartrantf, waved his hat at his men, rasping, "Come on, boys, for I can't halloo any more." One of his captains, William Allebaugh, was the first on the bridge, followed by his color guard. Inspired, the men of both regiments leaped to their feet and raced across the span.

Although one Federal thought the Confederates "scattered and scampered over the hills like a huge drove of scared sheep," Toombs's men

Throughout the next day, September 18, while Lee waited for McClellan to attack, informal truces were arranged between the combatants to retrieve their wounded and bury the dead.

Out of every four men engaged in the fighting, one was a casualty. Amputated limbs were piled several feet deep around some field hospitals. Civilians were also called upon to aid in the treatment of the wounded. One of the most noteworthy of these was Clara Barton, a clerk in the patent office in Washington, who arrived with a wagonload of medical supplies while the fighting was ongoing.

were out of ammunition, and Rodman's division and attached brigade had waded the creek at Snavely's Ford. The Confederates had inflicted 500 casualties and delayed Burnside three hours, while losing only 160 men. It was 1 P.M.

Sturgis's division crossed the bridge, soon joined by Rodman and Crook's brigade, which forded the creek north of the bridge. Lee's right flank had been stripped to hold the left and center, and McClellan had five hours of daylight remaining to exploit this breakthrough.

Cox sanctioned a delay by allowing Sturgis to withdraw, his division exhausted and low on ammunition. Brig. Gen. Orlando B. Willcox replaced him; however, he had to march from a position one mile east of the creek

He Knew His Limitations ■ Ambrose Everett Burnside

Although born in Indiana in 1824, Ambrose Everett Burnside was the son of a South Carolina slave owner who freed his slaves upon moving north. He was briefly a tailor's apprentice before attending West Point, from which he graduated in 1847. Burnside saw garrison duty during the Mexican War, was wounded by Apaches, and left the military for a business career in 1853. He developed an innovative breechloading rifle and started a company in Rhode Island to manufacture them, but the enterprise failed.

Burnside reentered the army when war threatened. He led a brigade at First Manassas and successfully directed an amphibious operation on the North Carolina coast, which gave the Union a strategic base of operations on the Southern coast. Always a favorite of Abraham Lincoln, Burnside was appointed major general and reportedly twice declined appointment to command the Army of the Potomac in 1862. He led two corps at Antietam, and although he captured an important bridge that bears his name, he took his orders too literally and required three hours to seize it from a mere five hundred Confederates. His delay probably saved Robert E. Lee's army from destruction.

When Lincoln relieved George B. McClellan in November, he again called upon Burnside to lead his foremost army. Burnside did not believe he was capable of commanding such a large force, but accepted the job, knowing that the next candidate was his arch rival, Joseph Hooker. Burnside immediately started living down to his expectations. Things began well enough when a move against Richmond almost succeeded. The Federals stole a march on Robert E. Lee and reached the Rappahannock River, opposite Fredericksburg, unopposed, but the army had to wait for pontoon bridges. When Burnside finally crossed the river, Lee was strongly entrenched on a ridge commanding the town. In a series of senseless attacks on December 13, 1862, the Federals lost thirteen thousand men. A month later Burnside made another feeble attempt to reach Richmond, but the rancorous aftermath of the infamous "Mud March" forced his removal.

Burnside received command of the Department of Ohio in March 1863 and captured Knoxville, Tennessee, holding it against a siege and assault by James Longstreet in November and December 1863. He left the army in April 1865.

Burnside embarked on a number of business endeavors after the war.

He was elected governor of Rhode Island three times and served in the U.S. Senate before his death in 1881. He is buried in Providence. Burnside is best remembered for the luxurious muttonchops he sported during the Civil War, which have ever since been called "sideburns."

The desperate work in the field hospitals was moved to barns, churches, and homes—anywhere a man could be laid out. More than seventeen thousand wounded overwhelmed the resources of the medical corps of both armies. These images were made of the facilities given over to the medical task at the farm of Otho Smith, near Keedysville, two miles northeast of Sharpsburg.

During the informal truce to attend the wounded and bury the dead on September 18, Federal Col. Norman J. Hall praised a wounded Confederate, "You fought and stood well."

"Yes," the soldier responded, "and here we lie."

John B. Gordon's wife, Fanny, accompanied him on every campaign. Hearing of his grievous wounds at Antietam, she sought him out in a field hospital. "My face was black and shapeless," Gordon wrote, "so swollen that one eye was entirely hidden and the other nearly so. My right leg and left arm and shoulder were bandaged and propped with pillows. I knew she would be greatly shocked. As she reached the door and looked, I saw at once that I must reassure her. Summoning all my strength, I said: 'Here's your handsome husband, been to an Irish wedding.'"

Fanny suppressed a scream and faithfully attended him. "The doctors told Mrs. Gordon to paint my arm above the wound three or four times a day with iodine," Gordon remembered. "She obeyed the doctors by painting it, I think, three or four hundred times a day."

and cross the bridge, still under artillery fire and crowded with artillery, caissons, and wagons filled with ammunition.

While this transpired, Lee acted to forestall what would be a disastrous attack against his center and to draw off Federals from the right. He sent Stuart's cavalry and what units Jackson could assemble to swing around the Federal right to the northeast.

At the edge of the West Woods, Jackson sent a private up a tree to determine Federal strength.

"How many troops are over there?" Jackson asked.

"Oceans of them!" the boy shouted excitedly.

"Count the flags, sir!" Jackson replied.

After the count hit thirty-nine, Jackson said, "That will do. Come down, sir." Each regiment had two flags. Despite the overwhelming Federal force, estimated at twenty or more fresh regiments, Jackson proceeded with the advance until it was stopped at the Poffenberger farm by Union artillery parked hub to hub.

Lee assembled every artillery piece he could spare to slow the Federal advance from Burnside's Bridge, but if Jackson's last division did not arrive soon from Harpers Ferry, the Confederate line would break.

At 6:30 that morning, A. P. Hill had received an urgent summons from Lee. Leaving one brigade to secure captured equipment, Hill donned his red flannel battle shirt and started five brigades up the road traveled earlier by Jackson. They followed the south bank of the Potomac River to cross at Boteler's Ford, two miles west of Sharpsburg, where they arrived at 2 P.M., still two miles from the battlefield. They had accomplished a fifteen-mile forced march.

When Hill arrived at 2:30 P.M. ahead of his division, the largest of the Army of Northern Virginia and its most experienced, Lee's concern betrayed his calm pose as he embraced the general.

Burnside's delay of an hour and a half brought McClellan's aide, Col. Thomas Key, with orders to replace Burnside with Brig. Gen. George Morell if the attack was not launched immediately. Key found Burnside directing traffic at the bridge, getting the last of his corps across Antietam Creek at 3 P.M. Burnside's plan was to cut off Lee's line of retreat from Sharpsburg to Boteler's Ford.

Willcox's division advanced on the right, with Rodman on the left, and Crook's brigade and a brigade of Ohioans in reserve, a force totaling eight thousand, supported by twenty-two guns.

"The earth," wrote one Confederate officer in Sharpsburg, "seemed to tremble beneath their tread."

The Federals marched over open terrain broken by steep hills and hollows, the road bordered by stone fences and haystacks that concealed numerous Southern skirmishers and sharpshooters. Confederate guns on the heights to their right kept up a continuous shelling. A Southern brigade on Cemetery Hill attacked Willcox's lead regiment, the Seventy-ninth New York, near the Sherrick farmhouse, but two guns and a bayonet charge rooted the Confederates out of an apple orchard. As Willcox advanced closer to Sharpsburg, he was supported by Porter's Fifth Corps, which had crossed the middle bridge on the Boonsboro pike, where two six-gun Federal batteries had deployed. Both moves threatened Southern artillery and infantry on Cemetery Ridge, which was forced to withdraw into the village.

As Willcox paused to resupply with ammunition, Rodman was to the south, approaching the Harpers Ferry road. A dozen Confederate cannon sited on a ridge ahead of them slowed the advance and inflicted an increasing number of casualties. The steady Federal march, however, forced the

Wounded Confederates were cared for in tents in Smith's fields. Below Dr. Anson Hurd, regimental surgeon of the Fourteenth Indiana, poses among his Southern patients.

LIBRARY OF CONGRESS

At midnight Stonewall Jackson's aide Henry Kyd Douglas rode through the North Woods. In his memoirs of the war, he described the aftermath of the battle of Antietam:

The dead and dying lay as thick over it as harvest sheaves. The pitiable cries for water and appeals for help were much more horrible to listen to than the deadliest sounds of battle. Silent were the dead, and motionless. But here and there were raised stiffened arms; heads made a last effort to lift themselves from the ground; prayers were mingled with oaths, the oaths of delirium; men were wriggling over the earth; and midnight hid all distinction between the blue and the grey.

My horse trembled under me in terror, looking down at the ground, sniffing the scent of blood, stepping falteringly as a horse will over or by the side of human flesh; afraid to stand still, hesitating to go on, his animal instinct shuddering at this cruel human mystery. Once his foot slid into a little shallow filled with blood and spurted a little stream on his legs and my boots. I had had a surfeit of blood that day and I couldn't stand this. I dismounted and giving the reins to my courier I started on foot into the wood of Dunker Church.

"The spectacle yesterday was the grandest I could conceive of," George B. McClellan wrote his wife, Ellen, the day after the battle. "Nothing could be more sublime."

Two days after the battle, Gardner and Gibson came upon this scene in the West Woods: a recent grave with a makeshift marker and a Confederate corpse. The grave was that of 1st Lt. John A. Clark of the Seventh Michigan. His family later claimed the body, which was reburied in Monroe, Michigan. The unburied Southerner was likely from either North Carolina or Louisiana.

LIBRARY OF CONGRESS

two batteries to limber up and retreat, leaving two understrength brigades waiting behind a stone wall and rail fence. The Confederates fired on the Northerners from fifty feet away, but the Federals stood their ground and returned the fire, losing eight color-bearers, then charged and broke the Confederates in hand-to-hand fighting. "Oh, how I ran!" said one Virginian. "I was afraid of being struck in the *back,* and I frequently turned around in running, so as to avoid if possible so disgraceful a wound."

Union shells exploded in the streets of Sharpsburg, which were filled with Confederate stragglers. Willcox was two hundred yards from the town, his skirmishers almost in Sharpsburg, and Rodman's advance was less than a mile from Lee's retreat route to the Potomac. Jones's division had been mauled except for Toombs's brigade, reinforced to seven hundred men, who were the last remaining organized Confederate defenders on the Southern right. They faced the far Federal left, a half mile south of Sharpsburg on the Harpers Ferry road.

Anxiously Lee watched for A. P. Hill's appearance. At 3:30 P.M. he spotted two columns of men marching to his right. The Confederate comman-

"Don't let any of your friends sing 'My Maryland,'" Maj. Walter H. Taylor wrote his sister, "not 'my Western Maryland' anyhow."

The Last General Casualty ■ Ambrose Powell Hill

BATTLES AND LEADERS

Ambrose Powell Hill, born on November 9, 1825, in Culpeper, Virginia, was a member of the U.S. Military Academy class of 1847. He fought the Mexicans and Seminoles before leaving the U.S. army in March 1861. Hill, a brigadier when 1862 began and a major general when it ended, fought his division well at Williamsburg on the peninsula and heroically at Mechanicsville, Gaines's Mill, and Glendale during the Seven Days. His command, designated a "light division," meaning it marched swiftly and lightly, saw heavy combat at Cedar Mountain and Second Manassas. After he helped capture Harpers Ferry, Hill's last-

second appearance at Antietam saved the Army of Northern Virginia from destruction.

Hill served under Stonewall Jackson at Fredericksburg and Chancellorsville, where he was seriously wounded soon after receiving command of the corps following Jackson's wounding. Hill recovered physically but was never the same commander. His leadership grew erratic as he succumbed to psychosomatic illnesses. Hill led the Third Corps as a lieutenant general, and his men fought the first day's battle at Gettysburg, but he was in an ambu-

lance some distance away. Later in 1863 he attacked a strong enemy position at Bristoe Station without reconnaissance or orders, losing thirteen hundred men.

Hill served through the rest of the war in 1864 and 1865 from the Wilderness to Petersburg. On April 2, 1865, as Ulysses S. Grant broke Robert E. Lee's lines at Petersburg, Hill was killed while attempting to capture Federal stragglers. He is buried in Richmond. Hill's brothers-in-law included Confederate generals John H. Morgan and Basil Duke.

Burial crews were kept busy for quite some time. Some companies made up their own teams to find, bury, and mark the graves of their dead (above left). One day after the battle, the Army of Northern Virginia left behind its dead and critically wounded and began the long march home, piling the wounded in wagons and ambulances (above right). The crossing of the Potomac as the men returned to Virginia was not as invigorating as it had been two weeks prior, when they had entered Maryland.

der stopped Lt. John A. Ramsey, an artillery officer with a telescope, pointed to one of the lines of troops, and asked him to identify them.

"They are flying the United States flag."

He indicated the second column. "What are those?"

"They are flying the Virginia and Confederate flags."

"It is A. P. Hill from Harpers Ferry," Lee stated calmly.

Hill's Light Division only numbered three thousand—hundreds had fallen out on the eight-hour, seventeen-mile march, but he directed the troops cross-country toward the Harpers Ferry road. Two brigades were deployed to protect his right flank, and the other three extended Toombs's right. It was a perfect position on the vulnerable Federal left. Two of Col. Edward Harland's regiments, of Rodman's southernmost brigade, the Sixteenth Connecticut and Fourth Rhode Island, had lagged behind the advance, leaving a wide gap for Hill to exploit.

Rodman, seeing Hill's men in the distance, was galloping to warn his brigade when a Confederate marksman mortally wounded him.

At 3:40 P.M. Hill's advance troops, Brig. Gen. Maxey Gregg's South Carolinians, crashed into the green Sixteenth Connecticut, in service only three weeks, in John Otto's cornfield. After a few minutes the Sixteenth Connecticut had lost 185 men as "volley after volley in quick succession was hurled into our midst," remembered one, and the regiment dissolved. The Fourth Rhode Island was next, decimated in the tall corn from a distance of thirty yards. Further confusion resulted from the blue uniforms Hill's men wore, seized at Harpers Ferry, and a South Carolina regimental flag that resembled the national colors. The Federals ceased fire and went forward to investigate. From twenty feet the Confederates fired so quickly that powder fouled their rifles. Men were "obliged to use stones to hammer the charges down," a Southern colonel reported.

Killed at Antietam, Brig. Gen. William E. Starke was buried in Richmond beside his son, mortally wounded at Seven Pines four months earlier.

On September 22 Confederate Brig. Gen. Dorsey Pender wrote, "Some of the Army have a fight nearly every day, and the more we fight, the less we like it."

Lee's army waded across the river at Boteler's Ford and entered Shepherdstown on the Virginia side. In the evening, cavalrymen were posted with torches to mark the way for the steady parade of wagons, ambulances, and caissons.

BATTLES AND LEADERS

These Federals also fled for the rear, leaving Harland's last regiment, the Eighth Connecticut, advanced and alone. Hill and Toombs broke the Eighth, recapturing three guns Toombs had just lost. Cox sent the Kanawha Brigade to seal the gap, but it was met by all of Hill's strength and driven back.

While Hill paused to give his attack some order, Cox withdrew all his brigades, including a regiment looking down on Sharpsburg from a hill. Burnside continued the retreat all the way to Antietam Creek, having lost 20 percent of his Ninth Corps, and asked McClellan for reinforcements.

McClellan sent a battery, stating, "I can do nothing more. I have no infantry." That was manifestly untrue, for Porter's Fifth Corps remained

The Emancipation Proclamation

For the first year of the Civil War Abraham Lincoln managed a shaky coalition of Republicans and Democrats. Each party was composed of factions that variously supported the war, wanted peace under different conditions, desired to abolish or not to abolish slavery, or wanted to abolish it under varying criteria. The president himself opposed slavery, but his first goal was to preserve the Union—with slaves if that were the only option.

In July 1862 Lincoln told Sen. Charles Sumner that he would free the slaves "if I were not afraid that half the officers would fling down their arms and three states would rise." After ciphering that the gradual ending of slavery through government compensation of owners would only cost the same as eighty-two days of fighting the current war, Lincoln suggested to representatives from the Border States that the offer was preferable to ending the institu-

tion "by the mere incident of war," leaving them with nothing.

A mood of emancipation was slowing working through Congress, which abolished slavery in Washington, D.C., and the territories, then prohibited the army from returning runaway slaves to their owners.

Later in July 1862, Lincoln was visiting the telegraph office in the War Department when he asked Thomas T. Eckert for some paper, saying that "he wanted to write something special." Lincoln returned on a number of days to work on his document. "He would look out the window a while and put his pen to paper," Eckert remembered, "but he did not write much at once. He would study between times and when he made up his mind he would put down a line or two." Each day Eckert watched the president carefully revise what he had written, "studying carefully every sentence."

To avoid constitutional questions, Lincoln called the decree a "necessary military measure" issued by the commander in chief. Cautioning that he would listen to comments but was determined to carry out the plan, Lincoln read the paper to his cabinet on July 22, ending with the declaration that slaves would "forever be free."

When he was finished, cabinet members raised practical political considerations. Postmaster General Montgomery Blair feared the effect such a pronouncement would have on the coming elections in the Border States. Secretary of the Treasury Salmon P. Chase feared slave revolts in the South that would generate opposition in Europe, and, of course, in the seceded states. Secretary of State William Seward questioned the timing, citing recent and continuing military defeats. He worried that the proclamation would be taken as "the last measure of an exhausted Government . . . our last shriek on the retreat."

Lincoln agreed to issue the Emancipation Proclamation only after an important Union victory.

The president seemed to be backpedaling in August when, in response to Horace Greeley's demand for an end to slavery in his *New York Tribune*, Lincoln wrote: "If I could save the Union without freeing *any* slave I would do it, and if I could save it by freeing *all* the slaves I would do it; and if I could save it by freeing some and leaving others alone I would also do that."

According to Secretary of the Navy Gideon Welles, Lincoln had said before Antietam, "If God gave us the victory in the approaching battle, he would consider it an indication of Divine Will" to end slavery.

After the battle, on September 22, Lincoln again summoned the cabinet. He opened in a curious manner by reading a chapter of humor by Artemus Wood. Then, according to Welles, he announced, "God had

McClellan kept an eye on the retreating Southerners from signal stations, such as this one at Elk Mountain, just as they had monitored Lee's army during the battle. Yet the Federal commander chose not to pursue his quarry aggressively.

largely in reserve and Franklin's Sixth Corps had remained on the defensive. But McClellan still feared a massive counterattack, which seemed to be developing on his left, and the magnitude of the day's losses appalled him. He was too afraid of losing to win a great victory.

"We were so badly crushed," Longstreet later wrote, "that at the close of the day ten thousand fresh troops could have come in and taken Lee's army and everything in it."

Only one brigade defended the Boonsboro pike into Sharpsburg, and some Federals realized it. Union Capt. Hiram Dyer peered into the village and urged an immediate attack on the Confederate center. Brig. Gen. George Sykes, his divisional commander, took the suggestion to McClellan

decided this question in favor of the slaves." The revised Emancipation Proclamation was again read to the assembled men. Unless the rebellious states rejoined the Union by January 1, 1863, all slaves there would be "thenceforth, and forever free." He would tell Congress: "In *giving* freedom to the *slave*, we *assure* freedom to the *free*—honorable alike in what we give, and what we preserve. We shall nobly save, or meanly lose, the last, best hope of earth."

Newspapers received copies of the document the following day, and fifteen thousand copies of it were distributed to Federal troops. To complement this dramatic move, Lincoln issued another decree that suspended the writ of habeas corpus to those guilty of "discouraging volunteer enlistments, resisting militia drafts, or guilty of any disloyal practice, affording aid and comfort to Rebels."

Senator Sumner claimed "the skies are brighter and the air is purer," and newspaperman Greeley editorialized that this was "the beginning of the end of the rebellion; the beginning of the new life of the nation." Other papers condemned the action as unconstitutional.

Government officials were concerned about the reaction of the military to the Emancipation Proclamation. In the fall of 1861 George B. McClellan had made it quite clear that he believed the war should be fought to "preserve the integrity of the Union," and for "no other use." It was a theme he would return to frequently.

McClellan had threatened that emancipation would dissolve his army. Fitz John Porter now wrote to a newspaper, stating that the proclamation "was resented in the army,—caused disgust, discontent, and expressions of disloyalty." Some generals seemed to believe that the document would induce the Confederates to fight even harder than before. They also feared that common soldiers would reject the suggestion that they were fighting for slaves, who were hated by many Northerners simply for being of a different race and for the economic competition they would provide as free workers. The widespread belief was that the enlisted ranks would fight only to destroy the rebellion and restore the Union. In reality, the soldiers did not seem much concerned about the proclamation, and the feared revolt in the ranks of officers, who, according to some, would march the army against Washington and overthrow the administration, never materialized.

McClellan counseled with his political supporters and close military advisers to determine his public stance on the issue. They wisely told McClellan that he should accept the development, explaining that the soldiers were not as upset over the issue as he might have thought.

McClellan accepted their view and kept silent concerning his opposition.

Bowing to political reality, on October 7 McClellan issued a general order explaining that civil authority was superior to that of the military. The general informed his soldiers that if they did not approve of this new policy, the alternative was the ballot box.

The Confederate retreat at Antietam reversed the pro-Southern views of British prime minister Henry Palmerton, who told his ministers on October 22 that "at present we could take no step" to recognize or give assistance to the Confederacy.

"I cannot imagine that any European power would dare to recognize and aid the Southern Confederacy," Lincoln had written nearly a year earlier, in January 1862, "if it became clear that the Confederacy stands for slavery and the Union for freedom." He was correct.

and Porter. Sykes remembered McClellan's favoring the plan, but he deferred to Porter who said, "Remember, General, I command the last reserve of the last army of the Republic."

By 5:30 P.M. the twelve hours of slaughter known as the battle of Antietam had ended. Perhaps the best that could be said of that day was that Lee had not been destroyed. McClellan gained little, for the Confederates had been prepared to withdraw into Virginia before the battle.

Federal losses totaled 12,411—2,108 killed, 9,550 wounded, and 753 missing. Lee's casualties were 10,316—1,546 killed, 7,752 wounded, and 1,018 missing. Each side lost three generals killed or mortally wounded, and another six were seriously injured. Total losses were 22,727. It was the largest one-day loss of American soldiers in our history.

The Emancipation Proclamation

By the President of the United States of America
A Proclamation.
Whereas, on the twenty-second day of September, in the year of our Lord one thousand eight hundred and sixty-two, a proclamation was issued by the President of the United States, containing, among other things, the following, to wit:

That on the 1st day of January, in the year of our Lord one thousand eight hundred and sixty-three, all persons held as slaves within any State or designated part of a State the people whereof shall then be in rebellion against the United States shall be then, thenceforward, and forever free; and the executive government of the United States, including the military and naval authority thereof, will recognize and maintain the freedom of such persons and will do no act or acts to repress such persons, or any of them, in any efforts they may make for their actual freedom.

That the executive will, on the first day of January aforesaid, by proclamation, designate the States and parts of States, if any, in which the people thereof, respectively, shall then be in rebellion against the United States; and the fact that any

State, or the people thereof shall on that day be in good faith represented in the Congress of the United States by members chosen thereto at elections wherein a majority of the qualified voters of such States shall have participated shall, in the absence of strong countervailing testimony, be deemed conclusive evidence that such State and the people thereof are not then in rebellion against the United States.

Now, therefore, I, Abraham Lincoln, President for the United States, by virtue of the power in me vested as Commander-In-Chief of the Army and Navy of the United States in time of actual armed rebellion against the authority and government of the United States, and as a fit and necessary war measure for suppressing said rebellion, do, on this first day of January, in the year of our Lord one thousand eight hundred and sixty-three, and in accordance with my purpose so to do, publicly proclaimed for the full period of one hundred days from the first day above mentioned, order and designate as the States and parts of States wherein the people thereof, respectively, are this day in rebellion against the United States the following, to wit:

Arkansas, Texas, Louisiana (except the parishes of St. Bernard, Plaquemines, Jefferson, St. John, St. Charles, St. James, Ascension, Assumption, Terrebonne, Lafourche, St. Mary, St. Martin, and Orleans, including the city of New Orleans), Mississippi, Alabama, Florida, Georgia, South Carolina, North Carolina, and Virginia (except the forty-eight counties designated as West Virginia, and also the counties of Berkeley, Accomac, Northampton, Elizabeth City, York, Princess Anne, and Norfolk, including the cities of Norfolk and Portsmouth), and which excepted parts are for the present left precisely as if this proclamation were not issued.

And by virtue of the power and for the purpose aforesaid, I do order and declare that all persons held as slaves within said designated States, and parts of States are, and henceforward shall be, free; and that the Executive Government of the United States, including the military and naval authorities thereof, will recognize and maintain the freedom of said persons.

And I hereby enjoin upon the people so declared to be free to abstain from all violence, unless in

necessary self-defense; and I recommend to them that, in all cases where allowed, they labor faithfully for reasonable wages.

And I further declare and make known that such persons of suitable condition will be received into the armed service of the United States to garrison forts, positions, stations, and other places, and to man vessels of all sorts in said service.

And upon this act, sincerely believed to be an act of justice, warranted by the Constitution upon military necessity, I invoke the considerate judgment of mankind and the gracious favor of Almighty God.

In witness whereof, I have hereunto set my hand and caused the seal of the United States to be affixed.

Done at the City of Washington, the first day of January, in the year of our Lord one thousand eight hundred and sixty-three, and of the independence of the United States of America the eighty-seventh.
By the President:
Abraham Lincoln
William H. Seward,
Secretary of State

The battle was not resumed on September 18; both sides were seemingly stunned by the carnage. Tens of thousands of men littered the battlefield. An informal truce allowed the wounded to be taken to dozens of makeshift hospitals, which were soon surrounded by heaps of amputated limbs. The fields were strewn with the debris of war—abandoned rifles, haversacks, canteens, broken caissons and wagons, and dismounted cannon.

Worst of all were the thousands of dead bloating in the late summer sun. "Many were as black as Negroes," remembered a Union officer, "heads and faces hideously swelled, covered with dust until they looked like clods. Their attitudes were wild and frightful."

"Most troublesome," added Oliver O. Howard, "was the atmosphere that arose from the swollen bodies of the dead horses. We tried piling rails and loose limbs of trees upon them and setting the heap on fire. This made the stench only increase in volume."

Despite having received additional divisions during the night—fourteen thousand men under Brig. Gen. Andrew Humphrey from Frederick and Brig. Gen. Darius Couch from Pleasant Valley—McClellan thought "the success of an attack was not certain." Should he lose, McClellan pompously declared, "Lee's army might then have marched as it pleased on Washington, Baltimore, Philadelphia, or New York."

Always aggressive, Lee considered attacking the Federal right but realized it would be disastrous. As darkness fell, supply wagons loaded with the booty from Harpers Ferry and a long line of ambulances rolled three miles southwest to Boteler's Ford on the Potomac. The seriously wounded were

On October 1 the president arrived unexpectedly at McClellan's headquarters on the Antietam battlefield. He remained for three days, reviewing the troops, visiting the hospitals, and touring the areas of the fighting. Lincoln was photographed with the general's staff—McClellan facing him, Fitz John Porter behind the president (with his hand on his sword), and to the far right, a young staff officer, George Armstrong Custer. Porter observed that visitations of this kind "have always been followed by injury. So look out—another proclamation or war order." Undoubtedly, McClellan was wary.

Primarily, Lincoln was there to meet with his general. No record of their conversations exist, but apparently the men parted with different impressions of the counsel. The president believed he had spurred McClellan into action, but the general had only heard his president praise his conduct of the campaign. When the army did nothing in the following weeks, Lincoln decided that the time had come to replace McClellan.

left behind for Federal care. The infantry followed, wading across by the light of torches held by cavalrymen. Soldiers shouted down "Maryland, My Maryland" being played by a band and insisted on "Carry Me Back to Old Virginny."

Lee, fearing pursuit, waited at the ford and with great relief watched Walker's division cross near dawn. "Thank God!" he intoned. To guard against pursuit, he deployed forty-four guns and two brigades of infantry, six hundred men, commanded by his chief of artillery, Brig. Gen. William N. Pendleton, on the bluffs overlooking the Potomac from the Virginia side of the river.

The Federals heard the rumble of wheels and the stamp of troops, but McClellan did not follow until after daylight, when he sent Porter's Fifth

McClellan Gets Canned

On September 18, 1862, George B. McClellan informed Henry W. Halleck, "The battle will probably be renewed to-day," but it was not. On October 15 he explained that failure by writing that he did not see "any reasonable certainty of success if I renewed the attack without re-enforcing columns."

McClellan's ego again surfaced in a letter to his wife, Ellen: "I have the satisfaction of knowing that God has, in His mercy, a second time made me the instrument for saving the nation."

The general also seemed to believe that Antietam had given him considerable bargaining power. On September 20 he bragged to former Ohio governor William Dennison, "I have insisted that Stanton shall be removed & that Halleck shall give way to me as Comdr in Chief. I will not serve under him—for he is an incompetent fool."

McClellan's reports after the battle were long on bombast but short on facts. His communiqués were "seldom clear or satisfactory," Secretary of the Navy Gideon Welles complained. "[He] 'behaved splendidly,' 'performed handsomely,' but what was accomplished is never told and our anxiety is intense."

While refusing to advance and misinforming his superiors, McClellan continued his attacks against official Washington. He wrote, "Stanton is as great a villain as ever & Halleck as great a fool."

After Lincoln visited Antietam in October, McClellan wrote his wife: "I incline to think that the real purpose of his visit is to push me into a premature advance into Virginia. The president was very kind personally, told me he was convinced I was the best general in the country, etc, etc."

Lincoln told John Hay, "[I] went up to the field to try to get him to move & came back thinking he would move at once. But when I got home he began to argue why he ought not to move."

Judge David Davis heard Lincoln state that he had tried to convince McClellan "that he wd be a ruined man if he did not move forward, move rapidly & effectively."

McClellan's good feelings toward Lincoln soon soured again. The general called Lincoln's advisers "men whom I know to be greatly my inferior socially, intellectually & morally!" Of Lincoln, he continued, "There never was a truer epithet applied to a certain individual than that of the 'Gorilla,'" McClellan's earlier term for the president.

On October 6 Halleck informed McClellan that the president was "very desirous that your army move as soon

as possible." The general's continued resistance led Halleck to write: "There is an immobility here that exceeds all that any man can conceive of. It requires the lever of Archimedes to move this inert mass. I have tried my best, but without success."

Jeb Stuart's second circuit of the Army of the Potomac disturbed Welles, who wrote on October 13, "It is . . . humiliating, disgraceful . . . it is not a pleasant fact to know that we are clothing, mounting and subsisting not only our troops but the Rebels also."

That same day Lincoln wrote to McClellan: "You remember my speaking to you of what I called your over-cautiousness. Are you not over-cautious when you assume that you can not do what the enemy is constantly doing? Should you not claim to be at least his equal in prowess, and act upon the claim?"

Corps forward. Union cavalry reached Boteler's at 8 A.M. and dueled Pendleton's artillery with eighteen guns. Shortly after noon, sharpshooters took positions in the dry Chesapeake and Ohio Canal and began felling Confederate gunners. At dusk, Pendleton withdrew, but a force of five hundred Federals captured four of his guns.

It was Pendleton's first field command. He panicked, waking Lee after midnight and fearfully reporting the loss of all his guns.

"All?" Lee asked.

The shocking news rattled Lee's staff, but the general remained calm. Rest, Lee told Pendleton, we will deal with this after dawn.

On his own initiative Jackson ordered A. P. Hill to take his division to the ford at daylight. It proved to be a wise move because at 7 A.M. McClellan sent three brigades across the Potomac. Encountering Hill a mile beyond the river, the first two brigades withdrew at Porter's orders. Unfortunately, the third brigade, led by Col. James Barnes, had also crossed the Potomac but turned to the right, past an old dam and cement mill. In the lead was a new regiment, the 118th Pennsylvania, which scaled an eighty-foot-high cliff through a ravine. The men deployed across the cliff top just as Hill's five thousand veterans arrived in a line three brigades wide.

Since Robert E. Lee was reported to have a bigger army and was subsisting it without a rail line, why, Lincoln inquired, did McClellan need time to build a railroad supply line before he moved? The general's policy "ignores the question of *time,* which can not, and must not be ignored."

The president continued with this advice: "I would press closely to [Lee], fight him if a favorable opportunity should present, and, at least try to beat him to Richmond on the inside track. I say 'try'; if we never try, we shall never succeed."

"Lincoln is down on me," McClellan told a subordinate, and lamented, "I expect to be relieved from the Army of the Potomac" and exiled to a post in the West, a fate that had just befallen John Pope.

McClellan informed Lincoln that he would advance when the men and horses had shoes, then expressed a fear that Braxton Bragg's Army of Tennessee was "now at liberty" to join Lee, a ludicrous notion. Of the state of his horses, called "absolutely broken down from fatigue and want of flesh," Lincoln replied snappishly, "Will you pardon me for asking what the horses of your army have done since the battle of Antietam that fatigues anything?"

A newspaper correspondent remarked that a growing number of army officers "fear that the country is dying of McClellan." Lincoln told a Republican candidate that he doubted "that George would move after all. Said he'd got tired of his excuses, said *he'd remove him at once but for the elections.*"

To Montgomery Blair, Lincoln confided that he "had tried long enough to bore with an auger too dull to take hold." When the president finally removed McClellan, he told John Hay, "I began to fear he was playing false—that he did not want to hurt the enemy. . . . If he lets them get away I would remove him. He did so & I relieved him." To a *New York Tribune* reporter Lincoln said McClellan's delay in crossing the Potomac was "the last grain of sand which broke the camel's back. I relieved McClellan at once."

"Of course I was much surprised," McClellan wrote Ellen, "but . . . I am sure that not the slightest expression of feeling was visible on my face. . . . They shall not have that triumph. They have made a great mistake. Alas for my poor country!" At the end of the letter he concluded, "I have done the best I could for my country."

McClellan magnified the sorrow that his men manifested at his relief. "In parting from you I cannot express the love and gratitude I bear to you," his farewell message read. "As an army you have grown up under my care. The battles you have fought under my command will proudly live in our Nation's history." He boasted to a staffer that the Army of the Potomac was "my army as much as any army ever belonged to the man who created it." Of the final review of *his* army on November 11, he wrote, "I never before had to exercise so much self-control."

Many Union soldiers were upset by McClellan's removal. One man wrote, "I am so mad that I can hardly write. The God-d— abolitionists of the North have succeeded in their hellish work of removing Little Mac." Six drunken officers attacked *Tribune* correspondent Albert Richardson, blaming the Northern press for McClellan's downfall.

Barnes withdrew his brigade, shouting the orders up the cliff to the 118th's commander, Col. Charles E. Provost, who bristled at the breach of protocol. "I do not receive orders in that way," he replied. "If Colonel Barnes has any order to give me, let his aide come to me."

Hill was slowed by Union artillery fire from the Maryland shore, but still the Confederates opened on the Federals. As they attempted to return fire, the Pennsylvanians discovered that half their muskets did not work. Flanked on the right, part of the Federals shifted to meet the threat, but their comrades in the center thought they were withdrawing. The regiment started to break, and Provost's attempt at a rally was ended by a wound. Lt. Col. James Gwyn fought on for half an hour, when formal orders to withdraw arrived. It was Ball's Bluff on a smaller scale as men tumbled down the cliff while Confederates laid down a hail of fire into the ravine. Hill's men continued to fire at men struggling in the river and crossing over an old dam, while sharpshooters in the cement mill pinned down many Federals. Soldiers hiding in the ruins were victimized by the Union batteries across the river.

The combat died out by 2 P.M., leaving 269 of the regiment's 750 soldiers casualties at what became known as the battle of Shepherdstown. Hill

McClellan and the 1864 Presidential Campaign

Having given up his house in Washington, D.C., George B. McClellan was homeless when he was relieved of command. He was directed to Trenton, New Jersey, where his wife, Ellen, lived at her parents' home. The people of Trenton treated McClellan as a wronged hero, greeting him with bands, speeches, and a large reception on November 13. But the general refused to accept exile.

Within a week McClellan was staying in New York City at the Fifth Avenue Hotel, where his reception was even more boisterous. He attended balls, dinner parties, and theatric and operatic performances and associated closely with the highest Democratic Party officials in the most Democratic state in the North. He cultivated relationships with the editors of Democratic newspapers and was accepted by the great financial leaders such as John Jacob Astor. His patrons soon favored him with a four-story, fully furnished home in a fashionable neighborhood.

McClellan's new associates were so conservative that they were considered Copperheads and even traitors in some political quarters. At the same time, McClellan believed he had become such a serious threat to the Radical Republicans that their agents followed him wherever he went and opened his mail.

In January 1863 McClellan visited prominent conservative Democrats in Boston, where he made the rounds of concerts, balls, and dinners. More than ten thousand people crowded a public reception held in his honor. The former general entered the political arena that October, endorsing the Democratic candidate for governor of Pennsylvania, who promptly lost— hardly an auspicious start to McClellan's political career. He publicly stated that the objects of the war should be restoring the country's unity, preserving the Constitution, and enforcing national law.

McClellan debated whether to resign his major general's commis-

sion in the army, which paid six thousand dollars a year, an idea made feasible when friends included him in a railroad deal that netted him twenty thousand dollars within the year. He also wrote a number of articles analyzing the military situation.

The closer the election of 1864 came, the more vicious were the attacks aimed against McClellan. There were charges that he had offered to fight for the Confederacy, that he had cowered aboard a gunboat during the fighting at Malvern Hill, that he had met with Lee at Antietam and agreed to let the Confederates escape. As famed newspaper editor Horace Greeley openly admitted, "I hate McClellan."

Although the Democratic Party performed poorly in the 1863 gubernatorial elections, the events of 1864 brightened the party's prospects. By late August, Ulysses S. Grant's three-pronged offensive seemed to be a bloody failure. William T. Sherman was stymied before Atlanta, the Red

River campaign was a total fiasco, and Grant was deadlocked at Petersburg after suffering massive casualties at the Wilderness, Spotsylvania, and Cold Harbor. The Union had endured ninety thousand casualties, and a call had gone out for half a million additional soldiers. By July, when Jubal Early appeared near the capital itself, the country was weary of the war, the draft, the government's suspension of the right of habeas corpus, seemingly arbitrary arrests, and the censoring of several Democratic newspapers.

As conditions became grimmer, cries for a McClellan candidacy increased. Many Democrats believed only he could repair the rifts that had split the party in 1860. The problem, however, was the rabid "peace at any price" wing of the party. McClellan and his supporters hoped to emphasize peace after reunion by pursuing "a war for Union and Constitution" but not to end slavery.

While Secretary of War Edwin Stanton grew increasingly hostile

called it "the most terrible slaughter that this war has yet witnessed. The broad surface of the Potomac was blue with the floating bodies of our foe."

Incredibly, Lee contemplated crossing the Potomac again at Williamsport, then wisely reconsidered, informing Jefferson Davis that his men were in no condition for the effort. The Confederates withdrew through Martinsburg to Winchester, thirty miles southwest of Sharpsburg.

McClellan reoccupied Harpers Ferry but remained at Antietam to reorganize, rest, and resupply his army. "Those in whose judgment I rely tell me that I fought the battle splendidly and that it was a masterpiece of art," he wrote to his wife. He wired Halleck: "Our victory was complete. The enemy is driven back into Virginia. Maryland and Pennsylvania are now safe."

After McClellan failed to pursue the shattered Army of Northern Virginia, Lincoln traveled to Antietam on October 1 and spent the next three days urging McClellan to follow Lee into Virginia. On an early morning during the visit Lincoln and Ozias M. Hatch stood on a hill. The president, gazing at the vast Federal camp, said, "Hatch, Hatch, what is all of this?"

"Why, Mr. Lincoln," Hatch replied, "this is the Army of the Potomac."

"No, Hatch, no," Lincoln said sadly. "This is McClellan's bodyguard."

---

toward the former Federal commander, Francis P. Blair met informally with McClellan and expressed confidence that if McClellan rejected the Democratic nomination, the general would be placed in command of the force being raised to defend Washington and the Shenandoah Valley in the wake of Early's raid or to replace George Gordon Meade as commander of the Army of the Potomac (but under Grant's direction). McClellan seemed open to the proposal but refused to ask Lincoln for the post. The general stated that he was not actively seeking the Democratic nomination, but he allowed "that no true man should refuse it." Lincoln and Grant discussed the matter at Fort Monroe on July 31, but the job in the Shenandoah went to Philip H. Sheridan, who won acclaim for his campaign there, and Meade was retained.

In a famous note written on August 23, Lincoln confessed that "it seems exceedingly probable" that he would

not be reelected. He considered a proposal, in case of political defeat, to cooperate with McClellan to raise troops and win the war before his term expired in March.

Lincoln had two hopes. The first was that the war news would improve by November—which it did. The second lay with the radical peace element among the Democrats. "They must nominate a Peace Democrat on a war platform, or a War Democrat on a peace platform," Lincoln stated. This also occurred.

The Democratic Convention opened in Chicago on August 29. McClellan, a War Democrat, won the nomination on the first vote, and the peace element forced through a platform that declared the four-year-old war a failure and included a "demand that immediate efforts be made for a cessation of hostilities." The convention also handicapped McClellan with a vehement peace-at-any-price vice presidential candidate, George H. Pendleton.

At home in Orange, New Jersey, McClellan accepted the nomination but rejected the peace platform in his speech to the convention, stating, "The Union is the one condition of peace."

On the war front, Adm. David Farragut had captured Mobile Bay earlier in the month, and Sherman marched into Atlanta the day after McClellan's nomination. In the fall Sheridan destroyed the Rebel threat in the Shenandoah. It seemed likely that the Confederacy would not long survive.

McClellan remained in New Jersey during the campaign, making only two appearances and issuing no statements. The Republicans berated him, his platform, and his running mate unmercifully. The general was shocked when he learned that the common soldier, who had recently worshiped at his feet, overwhelmingly rejected him at the ballot box.

McClellan had brief hopes that a third-party candidacy by John C. Frémont, the Republican Party's first

presidential candidate in 1856, would take the Radical Republican vote away from Lincoln. Frémont, however, withdrew from the race on September 22. An overture from the Frémont campaign proposing that if he or McClellan won the presidency, they would appoint the other general in chief, McClellan termed "strange."

Just before the November 8 election McClellan thought he could squeak out a victory, and Lincoln estimated the electoral vote would be only 120 to 114 in his favor. In fact Lincoln won 212 to 21 and took 55 percent of the popular vote—four hundred thousand more than McClellan. The president received 79 percent of the votes cast by soldiers on active duty. They knew who was winning the war.

Lincoln returned to Washington on October 4. Two days later he had Halleck wire McClellan: "The President directs that you cross the Potomac and give battle to the enemy or drive him south. Your army must move now while the roads are good."

McClellan reverted to form, refusing to advance and demanding more reinforcements and supplies. His force was in poor shape for a Northern army, but vastly better fitted than the Confederates, particularly immediately after Lee's retreat. By October 10 many Confederates had rejoined Lee at Winchester, doubling his post-Antietam strength to 64,275 men.

One day earlier Jeb Stuart had led eighteen hundred troopers on a reconnaissance north across the Potomac through Maryland and Pennsylvania, which circled McClellan's army for the second time in six months.

On October 13, the day after Stuart completed his circuit, an irate Lincoln explained to McClellan that Lee, west of the Blue Ridge in the Shenandoah Valley, was farther from Richmond than he was. Unless "you admit that he is more than your equal on a march," Lincoln goaded, McClellan could reach Richmond first or intercept the Confederate army en route. As Lincoln explained to John Hay, he secretly made this a test. "If he lets them get away I would remove him," the president said. To Lincoln, this failure would indicate that McClellan "did not want to hurt the enemy."

It required nearly two weeks for McClellan to move. On October 26 the 110,000-man-strong Army of the Potomac crossed the river for which

McClellan's Life after the Presidential Election

George B. McClellan had resigned his six-thousand-dollar-a-year commission in the U.S. Army to run for president. His Democratic notoriety, however, cost him business opportunities after the election, "merely because a great & honest party chose to make me their leader," he groused. Taking a biblical allusion, McClellan elected to "shake the dust off my shoes & go elsewhere." He considered offering his talents to the French puppet ruler Maximilian in Mexico or the Russian czar, Alexander, but then he determined to tour Europe.

McClellan and family left America on January 25, 1865, intending to "remain abroad until the expiration of Uncle Abraham's term of service." Nevertheless, three months later, the general expressed "unmingled horror & regret" at the president's assassination.

McClellan remained in Europe for three and a half years. In November 1865 Ellen gave birth to a son, George Jr. Although Democrats considered running McClellan again in 1868, the idea was shelved when Ulysses S. Grant was chosen by the Republicans. On September 29, 1868, McClellan returned home.

McClellan had lived on his investments while in Europe and returned to work in the United States. He earned twelve thousand dollars hawking a floating ironclad battery intended for harbor defense, which was never completed. In July 1870 he became chief engineer for the New York City Department of Docks, then he was named trustee and later president of the Atlantic and Great Western Railroad. He earned twenty thousand dollars in 1870 and grew increasingly wealthy.

That same year he moved into Maywood, a large home on Orange Mountain, New Jersey.

In 1873 McClellan organized his own company—George B. McClellan and Company, Consulting Engineers & Accountants—which represented European investors in American railroad securities. The former general again sailed for Europe in October, staying for three years this time. On his travels he encountered Charles P. Stone, who had been destroyed by Edwin Stanton and the Radical Republicans in the Joint Committee on the Conduct of the War for the debacle at Ball's Bluff. Stone served the khedive of Egypt as chief of staff and seemed "very well & is happy," McClellan observed.

McClellan wrote extensively of his travels and military matters and

worked on his memoirs, which were started in 1866. In 1877 he was elected to a three-year term as New Jersey's governor. Although he commuted to Trenton only one day a week, McClellan cut the state budget by 23 percent, ended direct state taxes, reorganized the state militia, and advanced education and industry. In 1881 he returned from six months in Europe to find that the only copy of his memoirs had been destroyed by fire. McClellan stated that he did not have the heart to rewrite it.

The McClellan family lived at Maywood, wintering in New York City, where they participated in a lively social life, and summering in the mountains of New England. McClellan became involved with many companies and owned considerable

it was named five miles east of Harpers Ferry, over a pontoon bridge constructed beside the ruined railroad bridge at Berlin. The Federal commander intended to concentrate his army at Warrenton before intercepting the Confederates.

Lee beat McClellan, who had a two-day lead. Leaving Jackson in the Valley, Lee and Longstreet quickly marched sixty miles southeast through mountain gaps and reached Culpeper Court House, twenty miles southwest of Winchester, before McClellan reached his objective.

"He has got the slows," said Lincoln, decribing McClellan to Frances P. Blair. The president issued orders removing McClellan from command. His replacement would be Ambrose E. Burnside.

Stanton worried that McClellan would refuse to obey the orders or that the army would mutiny. Chartering a special train, he sent his assistant, Brig. Gen. Catharinus P. Buckingham, to ensure a quiet turnover in command.

Buckingham stopped first at Salem on the night of November 7 to pick up Burnside. The general who never believed he was suited to command an army had twice refused this appointment. Burnside only accepted it now because if he turned it down, Joseph Hooker, a hated rival, would receive the job.

At 11 P.M. Buckingham and Burnside arrived at McClellan's headquarters in Rectortown. Despite the secrecy involved in this operation,

---

stocks and bonds. After campaigning for Grover Cleveland in 1884, he hoped to be appointed secretary of war, but political considerations prevented it.

In May 1885 McClellan returned to Antietam for the first time and attended a tour conducted by local resident Henry Kyd Douglas, who had served on the staff of Stonewall Jackson during the battle. In early October McClellan had an angina attack. He seemed to recover quickly, but on the night of October 28 his chest pains returned. At 3 A.M. on October 29 he said, "I feel easy now. Thank you," and died. He was fifty-eight years old.

McClellan's death surprised the nation and elicited considerable news coverage and reexamination of his military legacy. His New York City funeral was attended by Joseph E. Johnston, Fitz John Porter, Winfield Scott Hancock, and many other former Federal and Confederate leaders. He was buried at Riverview Cemetery in Trenton, New Jersey.

McClellan's beloved wife, Ellen, lived most of her remaining years in Europe, dying in 1915 in Nice, France, aged seventy-nine. She had been visiting her daughter May, who had married a French diplomat. May died in 1945 at her Nice estate, appropriately named Villa Antietam. Son George Jr., called Max, spent eight years in the U.S. Congress and served as mayor of New York for six years. Neither May nor Max had children.

Reluctantly, McClellan had begun to rewrite his memoirs in the 1880s, but his death left the manuscript unfinished. The writing ends just before the fateful battle of Seven Pines. The Seven Days, Second Manassas, and Antietam were not mentioned, nor the continuing controversies that accompanied these events and their aftermath. Publishers, however, were frantic for any account of the general's campaigns. Under intense pressure, William C. Prine, executor of McClellan's estate, carelessly slapped one together. He incorporated large sections of McClellan's self-serving wartime reports—which ran to 756 manuscript pages, not including the 263 reports written by his subordinates—parts of articles the general had written for magazines, notes and rough drafts from McClellan's first memoirs, and portions of 250 letters the general had written to Ellen. Prine also censored McClellan's criticisms and characterization of Lincoln, then a martyred hero, and altered other portions of the writings.

Most critics excoriated *McClellan's Own Story* for gross inaccuracies and the general's inability to accept any responsibility for his actions. McClellan had heaped his failures upon Lincoln, Stanton, McDowell, Burnside, and others. At the same time, the government had begun publishing the *Official Records of the Union and Confederate Armies,* and many contemporary reports belied McClellan's accounts. *McClellan's Own Story* is considered the worst of many revisionist memoirs produced after the war. It appeared that even in death McClellan continued to campaign against his enemies.

When Union troops left Sharpsburg, every animal had been slaughtered for food—cows, sheep, chickens, even dogs. "When night came," a local resident wrote, "I was so lonesome that I could see I didn't know what lonesome was before. It was a curious silent world."

While McClellan was still it's commander, the Army of the Potomac finally left its camps around Sharpsburg on October 26, six weeks after the battle. The following day the first elements of the army entered Virginia to renew the pursuit of Lee. McClellan, however, was to be removed from command in November. In this sketch of his dramatic farewell to his troops around Warrenton on November 10, he doffs his cap to the soldiers he trained to fight the war.

McClellan had known the meaning of the mystery train. "They have made a great mistake," McClellan wrote his wife. "Alas for my poor country! I know in my inmost heart she never had a truer servant."

Burnside and McClellan were old friends, but the Young Napoleon was shocked by Burnside's ascension to command, writing that Ambrose was "not fit to command more than a regiment." Although McClellan was ordered immediately to his home in New Jersey, Burnside asked him to remain several days to smooth the transition.

McClellan had taken great care of his soldiers' welfare, ensuring they were well fed, clothed, and housed, and avoiding costly battles. The men worshiped him and considered his removal a crime. At McClellan's final review of his army on November 10, soldiers wept in "despair, as a mourner looks down into the grave of a dearly loved friend," noted Col. Charles Wainwright.

Officers shared the sentiment. "Thunderstruck!" is how Gen. John Gibbon described his reaction to McClellan's removal. He felt "the government has gone mad."

"If McClellan wished to establish himself Supreme Dictator today," wrote Lt. Edgar Newcomb of Massachusetts, "the army in the heat of their resentment of this wrong would be with him."

Leaving his army on November 11 from Warrenton Junction, McClellan told his distraught honor guard, "Stand by General Burnside as you have stood by me, and all will be well. Good-by lads."

McClellan would never again command troops. In a little more than a year he would enter the world of politics.

A Tour of the Antietam Campaign

BECAUSE OF the capriciousness of Civil War geography, two other tours are incorporated into the Antietam campaign tour. Lee's route passes the site of the battle of Ball's Bluff, so it is included early in the Antietam campaign tour even though it occurred a year before. On the northern bank of the Potomac we will also explore the battle of Monocacy, which took place two years after Antietam.

From the Manassas National Battlefield Park Visitors Center, turn right onto Route 234–Sudley Road. Drive straight across the intersection with U.S. 29–211, then turn right onto Gum Springs Road–Route 659 to U.S. 50–Lee-Jackson Memorial Highway. We are following Stonewall Jackson's flanking move around Pope. Drive through Chantilly to turn right onto Route 608–West Ox Road, then turn right onto Monument, and the small memorial and parking are on the left.

A simpler but less historic route is to leave the Manassas visitors center by turning right onto Route 234–Sudley Road, then right onto U.S. 29–211. Pass through Centreville and turn left onto Route 608–West Ox Road. Turn left onto Monument Avenue to the park on the left.

The monuments to Gens. Philip Kearny and Isaac I. Stevens, erected in 1915 by Federal veterans, are on the slope above the parking area. This is one of the most developed of all Civil War battlefields, with only 5 acres of the 250-acre battlefield preserved. The Confederates were to the north, just south of the Little River Turnpike, with A. P. Hill on the right, Alexander Lawton in the center, and William E. Starke on the left. Stevens attacked from the south at 5 P.M., falling near the monuments, and Kearny was killed leading his division to the left of Stevens at 6 P.M.

Pope's rear-guard action after Second Manassas prevented Robert E. Lee from destroying the Army of Virginia and enabled the Federals to withdraw behind strong entrenchments at Centreville. The Confederate commander, however, refused to end the campaign without inflicting all possible damage to Pope, or at least chasing him into Washington's defenses, where McClellan waited to reinforce him. Lee determined to slip around the Federal right to the Little River turnpike, which led through Chantilly and Germantown to Fairfax Court House, eight miles behind Centreville. Jackson started his three divisions north on the Gum Springs road to the Little River turnpike, where he turned east. Longstreet followed half a

Twin monuments honor Union Gens. Philip Kearney and Isaac I. Stevens, who were killed during the confused battle at Chantilly, following Second Manassas.

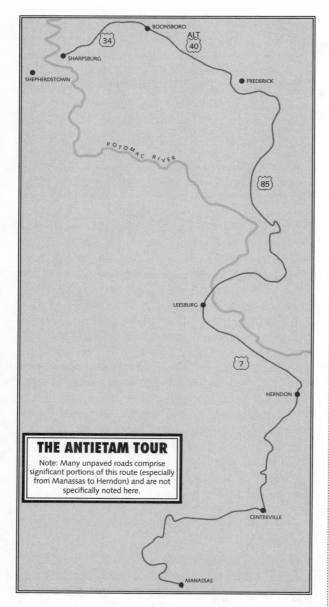

THE ANTIETAM TOUR

Note: Many unpaved roads comprise significant portions of this route (especially from Manassas to Herndon) and are not specifically noted here.

town, Pope sent Reno's Ninth Corps to take up a blocking position to protect the Federal retreat to Fairfax. Stevens directed the Ninth for the ailing Reno, and the Third Corps was ordered to assist the Ninth.

Stevens attacked at 4 P.M. to halt the Confederate march on the Little River turnpike and hit Lawton in the center of the Confederate line. When the Union assault faltered, Stevens grabbed the colors of the Seventy-ninth New York and led a charge until killed by a bullet in the brain. His son had been wounded minutes earlier.

Kearny's division, leading Heintzelman's Third Corps, attacked Hill on the Confederate right. Unable to motivate a regiment to attack, Kearny rode forward into a cornfield occupied by Confederate troops, who killed the general as he attempted to escape. Southern losses were 83 killed and 138 wounded; the Federals lost 83 killed and 418 wounded. More importantly, Pope and Halleck were induced to leave northern Virginia, leaving the route to Maryland open.

The battle was noteworthy for an apocalyptic thunderstorm that enveloped the field, changing day into night, drowning out the roar of cannon, and soaking gunpowder so throughly that muskets were rendered useless.

On March 23, 1863, John S. Mosby and fifty-three partisan rangers were retreating through Chantilly when they turned and attacked one hundred Federals pursuing them. Five Yankees were killed, a number wounded, and thirty-six captured. Lt. Col. Robert "Outhouse" Johnstone was relieved of command for the debacle.

Drive back on Monument Avenue to Route 608–West Ox Road and turn left. Remain on Route 608–West Ox Road and cross U.S. 50, where Lee turned north for Dranesville and Leesburg on September 3.

West Ox Road snakes across suburban Washington, so pay close attention to signs and turn left onto West Ox Road as Route 602 goes straight. At the intersection with Route 657–Centreville Road, turn right onto it, shortly passing historic Frying Pan Church on the right, frequently visited by cavalry during the war.

day later. Bad weather and fatigued men, exhausted from a strenuous campaign and battle, slowed the Confederates and gave Pope time to react by concentrating around Germantown. Jeb Stuart encountered Joseph Hooker, advancing west from Fairfax as Irwin McDowell and Edwin Sumner marched directly to Germantown on the Warrenton turnpike, while Jesse Reno and Samuel Heintzelman marched cross-country toward Chantilly. As the Federal army concentrated at German-

On August 31, 1862, Brig. Gen. Jacob Cox passed through. Stuart's cavalry was in transit on December 28. Mosby used the church as a meeting place for his men, and one of them, Mortimer Lane, is buried here. At nearby Herndon Railroad Station (Route 657–Elden Street), Mosby's men captured all forty Union soldiers in a picket post. Across the street is the Printz house (727 Elden Street) where four Federal officers hid to escape Mosby in the home of Union sympathizer Nat Hannah. Noticing four horses hitched in front of the house, Confederates entered and demanded the men come down from their hiding place in the attic. To hurry them along, a Rebel fired a pistol into the loft. In their haste, one of the Federals, Maj. William Wells, fell through the plaster ceiling. Past Dulles Fall Road this route becomes Route 228–Elden Street.

Turn left to follow Route 228, which first is Monroe, then Park Avenue, and then Dranesville Road, but always follow the signs for Route 228. At Route 7–Leesburg Pike turn right to Dranesville Tavern, which will be on your right.

Dranesville Tavern (1720), long an important stage stop, was moved a mile east of its original position to prevent destruction by development. The battle of Dranesville occurred on December 20, 1861, when a Confederate supply train, protected by Stuart with 2,500 men and four guns, was riding through. Union Brig. Gen. Edward O. C. Ord left 5,000 men at Clovin Mill farther south to protect his flank and attacked with another 5,000. During the battle Ord thought the Confederates would cut him off, and Stuart feared his wagons would be captured. After a clash that caused 68 Federal and 194 Confederate casualties, they both withdrew, the Federals proclaiming victory. Half of Stuart's losses resulted from friendly fire.

A month earlier Brig. Gen. George A. McCall advanced his division here as part of the Ball's Bluff campaign, inducing Nathan Evans to withdraw from Leesburg and shift his sick and baggage to Oatlands Plantation before the Federals withdrew. In June 1863 the Union army passed here on its way to Gettysburg.

Turn right onto Route 7–Leesburg Pike but take the first opportunity to reverse direction and head northwest on Route 7–Leesburg Pike to Leesburg.

Historic Dranesville Tavern witnessed much Civil War history, including a battle fought in 1861.

At the U.S. 15 bypass a right will take you to a few sites of the Ball's Bluff campaign, but there is little to see. Edwards Ferry Road leads past the site of a masked Confederate battery that discouraged a Union advance. Earthworks exist on either side of the road, which is blocked before the ferry site is reached. Just before the blockade turn right onto California Road. A water tower marks the site of fortifications constructed by D. H. Hill after Ball's Bluff, and in another half mile is a historical marker for Fort Evans. All the earthworks are on private property.

Ignore the U.S. 15 bypass and continue straight into Leesburg on Route 7 Business–East Market Street. At the sign for the Loudoun Museum, turn left onto Loudoun and the museum is on the right.

The Loudoun Museum (mid-1800s, 16 Loudoun Street SW) serves as a county museum and information center. It illustrates two hundred years of local history with an emphasis on the battle of Ball's Bluff and other conflicts of the Civil War in the area. It contains artifacts from Ball's Bluff and displays concerning local military units, particularly the Eighth Virginia and Thirty-fifth Battalion, and the divided loyalties among its citizens. In the region of northern Virginia it was often a brother-versus-brother situation. A Virginia Civil War Trail sign, which has recently been erected outside the museum, describes significant Civil War activity in the city. A downtown walking tour is also being prepared.

On March 6, 1862, Brig. Gen. D. H. Hill was ordered to abandon Leesburg. He destroyed forage, mills, barns, and haystacks, and burned bridges to discourage pursuit. Union Brig. Gen. John Geary took control of the courthouse, banks, and public buildings, and occupied Forts Evans, Beauregard, and Johnston.

Confederate cavalry entered Leesburg on September 2, 1862, and drove out Maryland cavalry and one unit of local Unionist cavalry, the Loudoun Rangers, capturing thirty prisoners. D. H. Hill followed with the vanguard of the Army of Northern Virginia. Jackson arrived on September 4 and Longstreet on September 5. All crossed the Potomac River at White's Ford, where Stuart returned after his October 1862 Chambersburg raid with twelve hundred captured horses and Longstreet's reserve ammunition train, captured earlier by Federal cavalry escaping Harpers Ferry, just before Antietam. Jubal Early reentered Virginia at White's Ford in 1864 after his famous raid on Washington and spent two days at Leesburg.

Potomac River sites on the southern edge of the county were involved in several Civil War episodes. After a cavalry battle at Upperville on June 27, 1863, Stuart fought a skirmish at Dranesville as he turned to cross the Potomac River the next day at Rowser's Ferry, near Riley's Lock on the C&O Canal, to ride around Meade during the Gettysburg campaign. He captured 120 Union wagons at Rockville, Maryland. At McCoy's Ferry, Confederates attempted to capture the ferry boat on May 23, 1861. The Union Clear Spring Guard, however, opened fire, forcing the Southerners to abandon the boat in midstream. It floated downriver and was recovered by the Federals. In October 1862 at the start of the Chambersburg raid, Stuart crossed from Virginia into Maryland there. In September 1862 Confederate soldiers damaged Lock 27 near Spink's Ferry.

Leesburg was occupied by Federal soldiers for most of the last two years of the war. When occupation forces arrived, George K. Fox Jr. saved the county records.

Lee's headquarters as he prepared to cross the Potomac River in September 1862 was Harrison Hall (North King Street). There he, Longstreet, Jackson, and Stuart conferred. The Patterson house (1761, 1 Loudoun Street) has drawings on attic walls left by Hessian prisoners during the

Leesburg, Virginia, near the Potomac River, was occupied by Union forces for most of the war, but Confederate armies invading the North passed through twice.

American Revolution. During the Civil War a Unionist emerged here and found a Confederate leaving the Fendall house across the street. Shots were fired that left large chips in the wooden wall of the Fendall house. Orr house (early 1800s, 7 Cornwall Street NE) was home of Leesburg's Civil War mayor, John M. Orr. Supposedly there was a secret tunnel connecting his home with the courthouse in which Confederate soldiers were hidden. The Janney house (1780, 10 Cornwall Street NE) was the home of John Janney, elected February 13, 1861, to be president of the Virginia Secession Convention in Richmond. He presented a sword to Robert E. Lee when the general received command of state forces in the capital.

Off Union Street is the Leesburg Cemetery, where a tall monument marks the grave of Col. Elijah V. "Lige" White, who fought at Ball's Bluff as a private and later led a cavalry company named the Comanches, because of their fierce fighting spirit in battles at Brandy Station and Gettysburg. Confederate dead from Ball's Bluff and one of Mosby's rangers rest here. A Civil War Trails sign at Mile Hill in Morven Park, north of Leesburg, describes a rout of Federal forces on September 2, 1862, by Col. Thomas Munford.

The magnificent mansion Oatlands (1803) is found on U.S. 15 east of Leesburg. Here Evans sent his sick for safekeeping during the crisis at Ball's Bluff. Armies frequently camped on the estate, and Federal soldiers cut all the trees and dismantled fencing for their fires, drove off all the horses, and ate the cattle, sheep, chickens, and grain. The area was generally devastated, particularly late in the war when Union forces attempted to quell Mosby's activities by making the civilian population suffer.

This is the center of Virginia's horse country. Appropriately, cavalry reenactments are held here to support the restoration of Oatlands and the purchase of the Brandy Station battlefield, scene of America's largest cavalry clash.

In Loudoun County near the intersection of Route 868–Broad Run Drive and Route 815–Daisy Lane, Mosby was surrounded and surprised by 150 Federals on the morning of April 1, 1863. The Confederates fought fiercely and turned the battle, killing 8 Federals and capturing 87 others and 95 horses. Mosby's losses were 1 killed, 3 wounded. Another skirmish occurred in the streets of Leesburg on April 28, 1864, when 18 of Mosby's men and several wagons filled with grain were surrounded by Federals.

The western half of Loudoun County, between the Blue Ridge and Bull Run–Catoctin Mountains, important for pre-Gettysburg cavalry clashes and Mosby's operations, will be examined in the next book in this series, *The Storm Tide.*

Turn right here onto Wirt and then right onto West Market.

On the left is the Loudoun County Courthouse (1894), guarded by a Confederate memorial, an unusual copper soldier with rifle held in front, ready for action. The work of F. William Sievers, it was dedicated on May 28, 1908.

Carefully continue straight onto Edward's Ferry Road where the road veers off to the right. Turn left onto the U.S. 17 bypass, then turn right onto Battlefield Parkway at the sign for Ball's Bluff National Cemetery. Turn left at the sign for Ball's Bluff Regional Park onto Ball's Bluff Road. Where the road turns right is the area where Federal scouts mistook haystacks for a Confederate camp.

A Federal probe under Col. Charles Devens advanced down this road in the opposite direction and was surprised by Confederates guarding Smart's Mill Ford just upstream. The incident led the Federals to abandon Brig. Gen. Charles P. Stone's original plan, which was to cross the Potomac at Smart's Mill, where the river channel was narrow and the men could have walked across from Harrison's Island. Instead they started the disastrous ferrying operation at Ball's Bluff. Some Federals, led by Capt. William F. Bartlett, retreated upstream and crossed safely.

Curve right and park in the lot, then take the short hike to Ball's Bluff National Cemetery in the center of the battlefield.

The clearing here was much larger in 1861, and the Federal's 12-pounder James rifle was deployed on the cemetery site. One of the two monuments notes the spot where Baker was killed (he is buried at the Presidio in San Francisco), and the second indicates

The tiny cemetery at Ball's Bluff marks the center of the battle, a Union disaster.

where Clinton Hatcher, the color-bearer of the Eighth Virginia, was killed. It was placed by members of the Twentieth Massachusetts, who had killed Hatcher. The tiny national cemetery, surrounded by a stone wall, contains fifty-four graves. Only one, that of James Allen, is identified.

Twelve interpretive markers, which have been located along the three-quarter-mile loop trail through the woods and down the steep bluff to the riverbank, explain each phase of the battle and describe the soldiers and their leaders. A position on the high bluffs affords good views of the Potomac and Harrison's Island, which splits the Potomac River into two channels. The wider channel flows beyond the island. From the banks of the Potomac, look up and imagine Union soldiers tumbling down the slope, even jumping, often onto the soldiers and their bayonets below. Confederate soldiers shouted

Although Union Col. Edward D. Baker, a close friend of Abraham Lincoln, has a gravestone at Ball's Bluff, he is actually buried at the Presidio in San Francisco.

demonically as they loaded and fired at Federals here and those struggling through the river. Many who escaped Rebel bullets drowned, their bodies floating as far downstream as Washington, D.C. The Northern Virginia Regional Park Authority owns 168 acres, or about two-thirds of the battlefield, and hopes to purchase the rest.

Return to U.S. 15 and turn right. Turn right onto Route 655 to White's Ferry and take the four-minute journey across the Potomac.

This is the sole survivor of the one hundred ferries that once plied these waters. The 112-foot-long barge runs on a steel cable anchored on each bank with tons of concrete. The present fifteen-car capacity ferry is named for Jubal Early, although that general crossed to Virginia upstream at the old White's Ford in July 1864. White's Ferry was Conrad's Ferry (established 1836) during the Civil War. During 1861–62 this was the site of a Union camp of observation, which was quiet on most nights along the Potomac. On December 11, 1862, Capt. Lige White paroled a number of Federal soldiers he had captured at Poolesville. The name of the ferry was changed soon after the Civil War for new owner E. W. White, who led the Thirty-fifth Virginia at Gettysburg.

Cross the canal and note the ruins of grain warehouses built along it. A canal boat was wrestled out of the canal for use in ferrying troops to Ball's Bluff. Edward's Ferry, which operated until 1936, is only accessible from the Maryland shore. For a side trip to it, turn right onto River Road, passing the Maryland departure site of Federals bound for Harrison's Island and Ball's Bluff, to the intersection with Edward's Ferry Road, then turn right to the C&O Canal, Lock 25, a restored lockhouse. Beside it is an abandoned building that was once a store. At this important site Joseph Hooker and the Army of the Potomac crossed on two pontoon bridges, one on each side of Goose Creek on the Virginia shore, in June 1863 on their way to Gettysburg.

It was here that Stone received erroneous reports of the activity at Ball's Bluff and set in motion the chain of tragic events that brought on the Federal disaster, including dispatching Col. Edward D. Baker to take charge at Ball's Bluff. As part of Stone's feint, Federal troops crossed here and

White's Ferry, the only one still functioning along the Potomac River, is near a number of fords used by the Confederate army to invade the North.

upstream at Ball's Bluff. Stone maintained his headquarters here, which was equidistant between Baker upstream at Ball's Bluff and Brig. Gen. George A. McCall downstream at Dranesville Tavern. Confederate Brig. Gen. Willis Gorman crossed here and demonstrated against Brig. Gen. Nathan G. Evans who, having learned of Stone's plan from a captured courier, sent all but the Thirteenth Mississippi to Ball's Bluff. Although considerably outnumbered by Col. Willis A. Gorman's forty-five hundred men, the Confederates attacked the next day, persuading the Federals to withdraw to Maryland that night. On August 27, 1863, Lige White damaged the canal here and skirmished nearby with the Eleventh New York cavalry.

To reach shallow White's Ford (people endlessly confuse it with modern White's Ferry), from White's Ferry turn left onto White's Ferry Road toward Poolesville, passing Annington (1800), where Baker ate his last meal. Take a left on Martinsburg Road and the first left after the bridge, following signs to Dickinson Conservation Park, to the parking area near the Potomac. Walk upstream along the canal towpath from Lock 26 to the wartime site of White's Ford.

Access from the Virginia shore is extremely difficult. Here most of Lee's Army of Northern Virginia crossed into Maryland on September 5, 1862, and Early returned after his 1864 raid on Washington. On

October 12, 1862, Stuart fought with pursuing Federals between the Monocacy River and this point to cross into Virginia after his Chambersburg raid. The John Pelham Historical Association has just placed a marker at White's Ford, where Pelham's famed horse artillery heroically held back determined Union cavalry until Stuart's rear guard had passed safely.

This close to the Confederacy, Lincoln and Union authorities in general suspected local inhabitants of treason and collusion with the enemy. By the fall of 1861, fifteen thousand soldiers held the area, where the president had declared martial law and suspended the writ of habeas corpus, thus allowing citizens to be held without trial. Many area men did serve the Confederacy, and Federal troops treated locals harshly, confiscating and destroying much private property. Local resident Lige White led the Twenty-eighth Virginia Cavalry and operated extensively in his home territory.

Take a left from Dickinson Conservation Park and bear left onto Martinsburg Road at the stone wall. Turn left onto West Route 28.

To the right is Poolesville, where the unique town hall seems to stand in the center of the street. Behind it is the restored John Poole house (1793, 19923 Fisher Avenue, south side of Main Street near Willard Road, 301-972-8588), which features

The Chesapeake and Ohio Canal, originally intended to connect the Potomac and Ohio Rivers, was often involved in Civil War actions.

collections of Civil War relics and local history displays. Stone camped in Poolesville prior to Ball's Bluff, and his body was prepared for burial in the building at the intersection of Route 107 and Willard Road. Stone's corps of observation, twelve thousand strong, camped here from June 1861 until march 1862. A cavalry skirmish occurred on September 8, 1862, and on December 14 Confederates captured a number of Federals while they worshiped at the Presbyterian church. At the intersection of Edward's Ferry Road and Route 107, between the community and the Potomac River, was Camp Heintzelman, a large Union encampment during the winter of 1862–63. Skirmishes were fought here on September 9 and 11, 1862, and in July 1864. While pursuing Lee in 1863, Hooker established his headquarters here.

North of Poolesville is Monocacy Chapel (1915), off Route 28 on West Hunter Road in Beallsville. It replaces a chapel destroyed by Union troops who used the pews and woodwork for fires and stabled horses inside. The churchyard contains many Confederate graves, including that of Capt. Benjamin White, a local scout for Stuart. In the October 1862 Chambersburg raid, White's knowledge of the area allowed the Confederates to elude Union pursuers sent out to intercept them. On September 9, 1862, the Twelfth Virginia Cavalry was driven from Beallsville toward Sugarloaf by Federal troopers led by Col. John Farnsworth. In the cemetery is a memorial (1911) to the town's Confederate veterans, dedicated in front of seven hundred spectators by Col. Robert E. Lee, Robert E. Lee's grandson.

Turn left onto Mouth of Monocacy Road, then turn left at the sign for Aqueduct Park.

The Monocacy was the largest tributary of the Potomac River that the path of the C&O Canal encountered. The C&O was elevated above the Monocacy on an aqueduct of white and pink granite quarried from Sugarloaf Mountain, four miles away, and transported here via a temporary rail system. Four years and 235 workers were required to construct the 516-foot-long aqueduct, which has seven beautiful 54-foot spans. This engineering feat, the largest aqueduct in the United States, was completed in 1833.

Several attempts by Confederates to destroy the Monocacy Aqueduct were unsuccessful. The entire length of the Chesapeake and Ohio is now a national historical park.

To disrupt coal supplies from the west and the transfer of all manner of supplies in both directions, Lee ordered D. H. Hill to destroy the Monocacy Aqueduct immediately after invading Maryland. Thomas Walter, a lockkeeper, talked Hill out of destroying the aqueduct. Instead, the Confederates damaged a lock, destroyed a culvert, drained the canal, leveled the towpath, and built a log road over it to cross artillery and supply wagons.

A week later Confederate Brig. Gen. John Walker was ordered to destroy the aqueduct as he marched for Harpers Ferry. Because the solid structure defeated his drills, Walker could not bore holes for explosives and was forced to abandon the enterprise as he hurried to help Jackson capture Harpers Ferry. Walker reported, with frank admiration, that the structure was "virtually a solid mass of granite. Not a seam or crevice" could be exploited and "the attempt had to be abandoned."

Lockkeeper Walter was arrested by Union authorities on charges of collaboration with the enemy, but his neighbors convinced the government that he had saved the valuable aqueduct. His lock house and Lock 27 survive a mile downstream of the structure.

A flood in the early 1970s bent the aqueduct, nearly destroying it. A network of steel and wooden braces stabilizes the structure, but repairs will cost more money than the government is ever likely to appropriate.

Return to Route 28–Dickerson Road and turn left.

Note Sugarloaf Mountain on the right, a monadnock of very hard, erosion-resistant quartzite. When the surrounding terrain eroded, this 1,283-foot-high feature was left looming 700 feet above the countryside, much like Georgia's famed Stone Mountain. As part of McClellan's reorganization following First Manassas, he established a Signal Corps under Maj. Albert J. Myer, which utilized the telegraph, flags, and torch signals to rapidly transmit intelligence of Confederate activity. The Federal government was most concerned about Rebel moves along the Potomac River. As a result, on August 31, 1861, the first field training center for signalers was established at Sugarloaf Mountain, which provided grand views of a very vulnerable sector of the Federal line. Union observers, and on several occasions Confederates, operated from signal towers here. During the Civil War they could see the Bull Run Mountains to the south, the Catoctin Mountains and South Mountain to the north, and a number of crossings of the Potomac River, including Noland's Ferry, Conrad's Ferry, Spinks Ferry, Point of Rocks, and the Monocacy Aqueduct. A string of Federal signal stations—built at Fairview Pass at Braddock Heights, High Knob, South Mountain, and Carrick Knob at Emmitsburg—gave Union authorities news of Confederate moves threatening the North. Observers watched the moves that led to Ball's Bluff in November 1861 and kept McClellan and George Gordon Meade informed during the Antietam and Gettysburg campaigns. Lee's crossing at White's Ford was observed from here in September 1862, and that of Jubal Early in July 1864, as well as occasional cavalry raids. Confederates captured the signal station on September 5, 1862, after the two officers there had informed Washington of Lee's crossing. On September 10 the Sixth U.S. Cavalry assaulted the Confederates here but were driven off by Confederate infantry and artillery. Union infantry under Winfield S. Hancock secured the position on the following day.

In 1922 Gordon Strong purchased the property and constructed a mansion on the mountain. After visiting Strong's facility, Franklin D. Roosevelt wanted it as a presidential retreat but settled instead for ten thousand acres of South Mountain near Thurmont, which Dwight D. Eisenhower named for his five-year-old grandson David. A nonprofit organization maintains trails and roads at Sugarloaf that are open to the public. The trails atop the mountain are steep, rocky, and strenuous, but the views are worthwhile. Two scenic overlooks, with parking areas, may be reached by car. A small, white log cabin at the foot of the mountain was used as a military hospital.

Washington and the Valley ■ Jubal Anderson Early

Born on November 3, 1816, in Franklin County, Virginia, Jubal Anderson Early graduated from West Point in 1837 but resigned after fighting the Seminoles. He practiced law and entered state politics before leading Virginia volunteers to Mexico in 1846. Early opposed secession but entered Confederate service as colonel of the Twenty-fourth Virginia, which fought at First Manassas.

A brigadier by the end of July 1861, Early participated in every Virginia campaign through 1863, leading a division at Williamsburg, where he was wounded, and returning to service for Malvern Hill, Cedar Mountain, and Second Manassas. Gaining a division at Antietam, he led it at Fredericksburg, Chancellorsville, Gettysburg, and the Wilderness, after which he temporarily directed A. P. Hill's Third Corps at Spotsylvania, then Richard Ewell's Second Corps at Cold Harbor. He was made a lieutenant general at the end of May 1864. Early's greatest claim to fame, however, came when Robert E. Lee sent him to divert Federal strength away from Petersburg with a strike through the Shenandoah Valley and into the North. He moved rapidly, defeating Lew Wallace at Monocacy and reaching the fortifications of Washington, where Ulysses S. Grant had been forced to dispatch reinforcements.

Early's star quickly fell. He withdrew into the Shenandoah Valley after ordering Chambersburg, Pennsylvania, burned as retaliation against Federal atrocities in the Valley. Grant sent Philip H. Sheridan after Early, who suffered a series of defeats at Third Winchester, Fisher Hill, and Cedar Creek in 1864 and at Waynesborough in March 1865. Lee relieved Early from command just weeks before he fled to Canada when the war ended. Early was soon back in Virginia, practicing law, writing his autobiography, serving as the first president of the Southern Historical Society, and supervising the Louisiana lottery.

The irascible Early feuded until his death with James Longstreet, blaming the Georgian for the defeat at Gettysburg in an effort to defend Lee's reputation. Early died at Lynchburg, Virginia, on March 2, 1894, and is buried there.

Southeast of Sugarloaf is Barnesville. The town changed hands five times on September 9, 1862, as the cavalry of Stuart, Fitzhugh Lee, and Wade Hampton fought Union troopers. One resident claimed the Confederates placed a big log on two wagon wheels and used it to keep the Federals at bay for a while. Wounded soldiers were cared for in town, and several Southerners who died are buried in the Methodist Church cemetery south of town.

In the Monocacy Natural Resources Area, near Route 28, is Rock Hall (early 1800s), site of Confederate and Federal camps in September 1862.

Go straight on Route 85 when Route 28 veers off.

If you remain on Route 28, a right turn onto Noland's Ferry Road will take you to the site of Noland's Ferry, one of the oldest (1750) on the Potomac. Sev-

The Battle of Monocacy

With Ulysses S. Grant hammering away relentlessly at Petersburg with ever-increasing strength, Robert E. Lee desperately needed to relieve the pressure in the summer of 1864. To accomplish this goal, the Confederate commander sent Jubal Early through the Shenandoah Valley to cross the Potomac River and threaten Washington, D.C. Grant would be forced to send substantial reinforcements to protect the nation's capital.

Early swept north from Winchester, threatened Harpers Ferry, then waded the Potomac near Shepherdstown on July 5. His force passed through Sharpsburg and Boonsboro, crossed South Mountain, and entered Frederick on July 8, where he collected a two-hundred-thousand-dollar ransom. His cavalry ransomed Hagerstown, to the north, for twenty thousand dollars.

The North was suitably alarmed. Closest to Early was Maj. Gen. Lew Wallace with twenty-three hundred men. Headquartered in Baltimore, his quiet military sector was largely used for training new recruits. Most of them had never seen combat. Racing to join Wallace was James B. Ricketts's five-thousand-man division, which left Petersburg for Washington on July 6. The full corps of H. G. Wright followed several days later.

Several miles southeast of Frederick was a transportation bottle-neck called Monocacy or Frederick Junction. Just north of an iron railroad bridge that carried the Baltimore and Ohio line across the Monocacy River, a spur line split off north. Beside the railroad bridge was a wooden covered bridge carrying the Georgetown pike to the capital. This area was defended by two large blockhouses, one placed on either side of the river. Early's objective was unclear, for from this position he could attack either Washington or Baltimore. The National Road to the latter crossed the Monocacy several miles upstream of the junction. Including a number of fords upstream and downstream from the railroad bridge, Wallace's defensive line covered six miles. He recognized this as the only location where he might stand and delay the numerically superior Confederate veterans, or at least discover Early's target.

Wallace, with Ricketts increasing his strength, deployed along the Monocacy River's higher eastern bank on July 9. Union soldiers manned the blockhouses, hurriedly dug trenches, or simply took cover behind fencerows.

The Confederate division of Robert Rodes faced Federal Gen. Erastus B. Tyler on the National Road, while Stephen D. Ramseur's division found Ricketts astride the Georgetown pike

at the railroad bridge, which Wallace thought would be the main axis of Confederate attack. Rather than assault prepared defensive positions, Early sent John McCausland's cavalry south on the Buckeystown road to flank Wallace at the Worthington-McKinney Ford. The cavalry overran a Union battery, but veteran Federal infantry pushed the Southern horsemen back across the river. Close behind the cavalry was John C. Breckenridge's division, with John B. Gordon's brigade leading, which struck Wallace's left flank. Severe fighting erupted when they encountered Ricketts's men at a fence between the Worthington and Thomas farms. Ricketts was almost able to shift his front before being overwhelmed and forced to retreat, which left the railroad bridge uncovered for Ramseur to cross.

Fighting also developed on the National Road and Georgetown pike as Breckinridge's division launched a three-pronged attack on the Federal flank with the brigades of William Terry, Zebulon York, and Clement A. Evans. After a game fight throughout the day, Early's eighteen thousand men finally put Wallace's smaller command to flight. The Federals withdrew in disorder toward Baltimore, suffering sixteen hundred casualties, including one thousand

captured or missing, to Early's seven hundred to thirteen hundred.

The Confederates continued their march on July 10, reaching Washington the following day. Early watched as Grant's battle-hardened troops streamed into the capital's forts, then satisfied himself with a demonstration against Fort Stevens before withdrawing. He reentered Virginia at White's Ford on July 14, having accomplished all that could be expected.

Wallace would proclaim that his men "died to save the National Capital, and they did save it." Early acknowledged that the forced fight at the Monocacy cost him a day. Grant, who had been disappointed in Wallace's lackluster showing at Shiloh two years earlier, agreed, writing, "If Early had been but one day earlier he might have entered the capital before the arrival of the reinforcements I had sent." Wallace contributed more by his defeat, Grant continued, than most generals did "by means of a victory."

After the Civil War, Wallace served on the military commission that tried the Lincoln conspirators and Henry Wirz, commandant of the Confederate prison camp at Andersonville, Georgia. He later gained fame by writing the novel *Ben Hur: A Tale of the Christ.*

426

eral Civil War crossings occurred here, including A. P. Hill's in September 1862 on his way to join Lee around Frederick. If you take this side trip, continue on Route 28 to U.S. 15 and turn left to Point of Rocks, which is described in detail at the end of the Harpers Ferry tour.

Continue through historic Buckeystown on Route 85, a road frequently traveled by Civil War armies.

The forty-five-room mansion Arcadia (1780, 4721 Buckeystown Pike–Route 85) was used as a hospital that treated the wounded of both armies during the battle of Monocacy. The head surgeon, Dr. David McKinney, bought the place following the war. Lee's headquarters was nearby on September 7, 1862, and Franklin's Sixth Corps camped here September 13–14. Early's flanking column at Monocacy took the Buckeystown road to a spot near Arcadia, then turned east to cross the Monocacy River.

On the outskirts of Frederick turn right through the mall to Route 355–Georgetown Pike or drive a little farther to the intersection with that highway and turn right onto it. Watch for the pullover on the right beside two monuments about a mile north of the railroad bridge.

Confederate Gen. Stephen D. Ramseur attacked in this area and placed a battery near the monuments and another to the east, near the railroad, when he assaulted Monocacy Junction directly.

These first two battlefield memorials might be called dueling monuments. The Confederate monument, placed by the UDC in 1914, the fiftieth anniversary of the battle, praises the Southern soldiers who won a great victory here. The adjacent monument, dedicated on July 9, 1964, the one-hundredth anniversary of the battle, by the state of Maryland, contends that this was a "temporary victory" for the Confederates but saved Washington from capture. Behind and left of these monuments is the Best farm, owned by the National Park Service, which leases it out for farming. Two Confederate batteries, eight guns, deployed on the Best farm to bombard the defenders at Monocacy Junction, and Southern troops used the fields as a staging area for their attack. Federal artillery fired in response and destroyed the barn, grain, hay, tools, and other farm-

ing equipment. In September 1862 this ground was used first for a vast Confederate campground, then a Federal one. It was there that Lee's Special Orders No. 191 was found by Union soldiers. At this spot in 1864, attacking Southerners encountered their first resistance from Illinois cavalry. The Rebels then deployed four cannon to shell Monocacy Junction, which was held by Federal infantry. Additional artillery fired from the Best farm.

This was the center of Lew Wallace's skirmish line, 350 infantry, guarding a covered highway bridge, a steel railroad bridge, and Monocacy Junction. The *Y* of the junction is visible beneath the highway bridge. Wallace's initial battle line was behind the river.

Jubal Early wisely elected to avoid a frontal attack, sending Brig. Gen. John McCausland's cavalry to find a river crossing to his right, with Maj. Gen. John B. Gordon's division following to cross the river at the Worthington-McKinney Ford, near Route 85–Buckeystown Road. This forced Wallace to shift the bulk of his force to his left and to burn the wooden bridge here, isolating his skirmishers to the north. Later in the afternoon Confederate Gen. Stephen D. Ramseur attacked and carried this position.

Continue south on Route 355. Just across the railroad bridge but before the river bridge, turn right to the Fourteenth New Jersey Monument, twenty-four-feet high and topped by a granite soldier.

The monument was unveiled on July 11, 1907, in front of 180 survivors of the unit known as the Monocacy Regiment, which fought at the Thomas farm. There is an excellent overlook here of much of the battlefield. The Best farm is in the background. Visible from an overlook are the two bridge sites and Monocacy Junction, consisting in 1864 of a railroad station, telegraph office, warehouses, and homes. When the Federals torched the wooden highway bridge, 350 skirmishers were cut off on the southern bank. As a third Confederate charge bore in, they walked across the ties on the railroad tracks. Their commander, Lt. George E. Davis, received the Medal of Honor for his service here.

An interesting artifact dating to the Civil War is found upstream of Monocacy Junction, near where New Route 40–National Road crosses the river. The tollhouse still stands near the remains of the Jug Bridge, which is abandoned and partially dismantled in the woods, but beside the park-and-ride lot on East Patrick Street are the remains of a stone pillar with one of the original stone demijohn (jug) ornaments. There Confederate Gen. Robert E. Rodes attacked Union Gen. Erastus B. Tyler.

Continue south on Route 355 across the river and turn left to the Monocacy Battlefield Visitors Center in the stone Gambrill's Mill (1830), a field hospital. Union Gen. Lew Wallace's headquarters, near the vanished blockhouses, burned several years ago.

The mill was used as a Federal field hospital. A Union battle line formed here, and the building was shelled. Yielding the field to Early's attackers, the Northerners retreated past the mill en route to Baltimore as the Confederates camped here for a few hours' rest before continuing toward Washington. The visitors center, opened in 1991 at the mill, contains an electronic map that helps to explain the sixteen-hundred-acre site. The park is still under development but contains artifacts, including Early's camp chair, and other interpretive displays. A brook here was tinted red by blood during the battle. A half-mile loop trail, soon to be expanded, leads to Federal rifle pits.

Monocacy is the newest Civil War site in the National Park Service. Established in July 1991 it has only recently gained possession of all five monuments and can now repair them, maintain the grounds, and prosecute vandals in federal court. The park hopes to obtain funds that will enable it to move the visitors center from the Gambrill mill—so

close to the Monocacy that it flooded twice in one year and was forced to close for expensive repairs—to a barn on the Best farm, which will minimize modern intrusions to the site. In 1864 skirmishing occurred on these grounds as the armies fought for possession of the Georgetown pike. An expanded walking tour is planned to the Best farm and Worthington house, the site of Wallace's headquarters, field works, and the site of the blockhouse where the Tenth Vermont made a stand before retreating across the railroad bridge. The nearby Gambrill house (1872) may house a training center for the National Park Service.

Monocacy Junction and the sites of the blockhouses are just north of Gambrill's mill and east of the highway from the New Jersey Monument. This junction was an important site because the railroad and major roads leading to Baltimore and Washington crossed the Monocacy River here and intersected in Frederick.

Carefully turn left to resume driving south on Route 355. Turn right in a short distance on Araby Church Road (the wartime Georgetown Pike) to the Pennsylvania Monument on your left. The Vermont Monument is to the right. Stand behind the monument to view the battlefield and the Thomas farm.

More than 250 veterans of three Pennsylvania regiments, the 67th, 87th, and 138th, which fought here, were present on November 24, 1908, when the twelve-ton, eight-thousand-dollar monument, a polished ball perched atop a thirty-five-foot-high granite shaft, was dedicated. The Vermont Monument, a granite slab erected in 1915, honors the Tenth Vermont. Behind it

The Writing General ■ Lew Wallace

Lew Wallace, born in 1827 in Indiana, volunteered for service in Mexico then became a lawyer-politician in his home state. Commissioned a brigadier when the Civil War began, Wallace started his undistinguished military career at Fort Donelson, where he led a brigade ineffectively. Commanding a division at Shiloh, he was expected to march rapidly to the relief of Ulysses S. Grant, but his column became lost and only arrived after dark. With the North clamoring for a scapegoat for this near disaster, Wallace seemed a good candidate. He was sent home.

Indiana Gov. Oliver P. Morton gave Wallace another regiment, and he commanded the defenses of Cincinnati when Confederates invaded Kentucky in late 1862. He sat on military boards until 1864, then commanded troops at Monocacy, Maryland, on July 9, 1864, where he delayed a Confederate attack on Washington, D.C.

Wallace served on the kangaroo courts that convicted the Lincoln conspirators and later sentenced Henry Wirz, commandant of the Confederate prison camp at Andersonville, to death. He continued in government service as a diplomat and administrator, and wrote a number of books. His best-known work was *Ben Hur: A Tale of the Christ.*

The Gambrill Mill, currently the visitors center at Monocacy National Battlefield Park, was used as a hospital for Federal soldiers in 1864.

The Ohio Monument honors soldiers from that state who were engaged in the July 9, 1864, battle of Monocacy. It is one of five state-unit monuments in the park.

is the privately owned Thomas farm known as Araby, where much of the heaviest fighting occurred. Union sharpshooters operating from the house and grounds slowed the Confederates who advanced from the west after crossing the Monocacy. The Confederates swept around the Union left and advanced toward Gambrill's mill. At either Araby or the nearby Worthington house, Ulysses S. Grant met with Philip H. Sheridan on August 6, 1864, to plan the destructive Valley campaign of 1864, which decisively defeated Early's force and devastated the Shenandoah Valley.

Turn right at the Vermont Monument onto Baker Valley Road for a closer view of the Thomas house and the Worthington farm. Just past the Interstate 20 underpass, turn right to the parking area for the Worthington Farm Trail.

The Thomas farm, also known as Araby (1780, privately owned), was occupied by Federal sharpshooters and changed hands several times during the battle (the Thomas family hid in the cellar). A Confederate cannon at Worthington caused considerable damage to the building. Three hundred Union soldiers were buried here after the fighting and were later reinterred at Antietam. Several months after the battle U. S. Grant and Philip H. Sheridan conferred here. Earlier in 1863, en route to Gettysburg, Maj. Gen. Winfield Scott Hancock had his headquarters here for three days.

From here the ford where Confederate generals John McCausland and John C. Breckinridge crossed the Monocacy River is visible. At the fence line Union Gen. James B. Ricketts's veterans lay, then rose, and decimated overconfident Confederate cavalry. Fighting raged around the house, used by Breckinridge as headquarters. Six-year-old Glenn Worthington, who later wrote the first history of this battle, *Fighting for Time,* watched the battle with his family from the barricaded cellar. The Confederates massed in the woods nearby and attacked to gain control of the high ground. Their fourth attack caused the Federals to retreat in disorder.

Worthington (1851), a brick Federal-style structure with six large rooms and 278 surrounding acres, was purchased by John T. Worthington in 1862. Acquired by the National Park Service in 1982, it is being restored to its 1864 appearance. The heaviest fighting at Monocacy started here as Confederate troops formed up four times to assault the Union line at the Thomas house. Maj. Gen. John C. Breckinridge supervised the attack from this site, and artillery deployed in support of the action. Two loop trails totaling 3.5 miles have four Civil War–related stops. Stop No. 2 is the fence line. McCausland's cavalry and Gordon's division waded the river at the Worthington-McKinley Ford, which is Stop No. 9. They deployed in the fields and marched across Brooks Hill (Stop No. 4), where the battlefield can best be appreciated. The Southerners continued east, past modern-day Interstate 270, and encountered firm resistance from Brig. Gen. James Ricketts's veterans. Wallace had shift most of his men from Monocacy Junction west to this point. The Confederate battle line stretched from the river on the right to the Baker Valley road. Stop No. 7 is a stretch of original sunken roadway, which was used to shelter a brigade of Gordon's men during their march over the hill.

There are good views of the Best and Worthington farms from a scenic overlook on Interstate 270, which cuts through the heart of the battlefield.

Return to Route 355 and turn right, then right again on Urbanna Church Road to the ruins of Zion Episcopal Church (1802).

The church burned in 1861, three years before ministers administered "baptisms in extremis" to the dying from Monocacy. On July 9 Federal cavalry covering Wallace's withdrawal ambushed pursuing Confederates, killing Maj. Frederick F. Smith and Lt. Col. William C. Tavenner, both Virginians who are buried here.

In nearby Urbanna, at the intersection of Route 355 and Route 80, is Statham Hall. Originally built in Fredericksburg, Virginia, then disassembled and shipped here for use as a private girls school then a boys' military academy, this was Stuart's headquarters while he screened Lee, camped to the northwest in Frederick, against Federal probes approaching from the east. His skillful work prevented McClellan from divining the Confederates' location, strength, and purpose. Statham Hall was the empty schoolhouse where Stuart held his legendary "sabers and roses" ball on September 8, 1862. When the dance was interrupted by a Federal raid at Hyattstown, the Confederates snatched their weapons from the wall and rode off into the night, returning with several casualties who received care from the ladies attending the ball. Stuart was here as Federals approached on September 11 and shelled the town. The Confederates withdrew, but reportedly Stuart staged a second ball at his new headquarters on the Monocacy River. Stuart returned here briefly on October 12 after the Chambersburg raid to visit Anne Cockey, a Northern Confederate sympathizer he called the "New York Rebel." During

the battle of Monocacy the Eighth Illinois Cavalry clashed with the Seventeenth Virginia Cavalry here.

Return to Route 355 and drive toward Frederick, where the road rejoins Route 85 and becomes Market Street. Turn left into Mount Olivet Cemetery (established 1852, 515 South Market), which contains two legendary figures involving the American flag.

The Francis Scott Key Monument at the entrance is fifteen feet high, forty-five feet around, and over nine feet high. Key, who seems to be reading a draft of his famous poem, "The Star-Spangled Banner" and pointing toward Fort McHenry, is buried beneath the memorial.

Turn right inside the cemetery and drive on the outer road. A long line of Confederate gravestones,

Confederate dead from the battle of Monocacy and hospitals around Frederick are buried in Mount Olivet Cemetery, where they are also memorialized by several monuments.

low and simple, appear to the right, marking the mass graves of Confederate remains gathered by the UDC in 1880. Soon after the Civil War ended, Frederick residents organized an association that gathered 409 Confederate dead from Monocacy, South Mountain, Antietam, and church cemeteries where the hospital dead were buried and reinterred them here. The 304 headstones, 29 unknown, run from the northeast to the southwest. The first grave, added in 1907, is out of order, but the others are arranged chronologically in order of death from the various battlefields and hospitals. At the end of the line are two monuments. One, a nearly illegible marble slab mounted on a brick base (June 2, 1881), honors the 409 Confederate dead. The other, sponsored by Glenn H. Worthington in 1936, has a bronze tablet containing the names of 220 men from Frederick County who fought for the Confederacy.

Francis Scott Key is buried at Frederick's Mount Olivet Cemetery. His grandson was imprisoned in Fort McHenry during the Civil War for seditious opinions.

Mount Olivet Cemetery contains at least eight hundred Civil War graves. In 1870 Maryland funded the establishment of Confederate cemeteries here and at Hagerstown. Before removal to the cemetery on the battlefield, the Federal casualties from Antietam who died here were buried in rows seven feet wide and twenty to thirty feet long. Those that remain, about one hundred, were local Union veterans who died after the war. Confederates were buried in a different section of the cemetery.

The grounds in this section seem guarded by a statue of a Confederate soldier at parade rest. Made of Carrara marble and designed by Carl Conards of Connecticut, it was dedicated by Confederate Gen. Bradley T. Johnson, a native of Frederick.

When one of the Confederate monuments was dedicated, the local newspaper wrote: "Twenty years ago it was wrong for the Southern States to go into rebellion against the national authority; it is just as wrong now, to say it was right then."

From the Confederate section keep going straight on the outside road. Turn left at area NN, and Barbara Fritchie's grave (she died at age ninety-five) will be on the right with (naturally) a U.S. flag in front. An eight-foot-high granite monument, with her likeness embossed on a bronze plaque, contains the entire text of Whitter's poem "Barbara Frietchie." Prominent is the date of her alleged adventure, September 10, 1862, and the legend, "Shoot if you must, this old gray head, but spare your country's flag." When this monument was unveiled on September 9, 1914, the local UDC chapter protested.

Confederate Lt. Col. Thomas C. Watkins, killed at South Mountain, rests here. Union Brig. Gen. James Cooper is buried in Section A, Grave No. 46. Commandant of the infamous Federal prison Camp Chase in Ohio, he himself succumbed to disease there in 1863.

In 1997 a unique new monument was dedicated in Mount Olivet. The small memorial, with an engraved dedication and a drummer boy effigy, honors all the children who served and died in the Civil War as drummer boys and couriers and those who lied about their ages in order to serve in the ranks.

Frederick's position near the Shenandoah Valley on the north bank of the Potomac River placed it in a natural invasion route between North

Barbara Fritchie is buried in Mount Olivet. John Greenleaf Whittier's poem is reproduced on the marker for her grave.

and South. In 1862 the Army of Northern Virginia and the Army of the Potomac occupied the city before passing through to Antietam. In 1863 the Army of the Potomac returned en route to Gettysburg, and in 1864 Confederate forces, this time under Jubal Early, returned, ransoming the town and fighting a battle just south at Monocacy. Frederick was both a hospital and a supply center for the Union during much of the war.

Return to Route 85–Market Street and turn left.

Note the Tyler house to your right at 108 West Church Street, notable for the cast-iron dog on the front stoop. Modeled after Guess, the pet of Dr. John Tyler, America's first ophthalmologist, it was appropriated by Confederates in 1862, presumably for melting down for munitions. The unwieldy statue was abandoned in a field near Antietam and a resi-

dent of Hagerstown recognized the pooch from a newspaper account and returned it.

Several streets to the right are the Hessian Barracks (1777, 101 Clarke Place), on the grounds of the Maryland School for the Deaf. The barracks housed German mercenaries and British soldiers captured at Bennington and Saratoga during the American Revolution. From 1801 to 1803 Meriwether Lewis and William Clark prepared there for their famous expedition into the area gained via the Louisiana Purchase. When Union casualties began flowing north in 1862 from battles with Stonewall Jackson in the Shenandoah Valley, the government used the barracks and the school for the deaf as a Union hospital. The complex encompassed four acres and eight buildings, including one stone structure used as George Washington's headquarters during the French and Indian War as he campaigned with Edward Braddock. By June 1862 the hospitals had 690 patients, and additional buildings were constructed to accommodate 200 additional men. It was considered one of the largest and best run military hospitals in the country, supervised by Dr. R. F. Wier. At one time four thousand wounded soldiers received care in seventeen Frederick hospitals. As in the South, local women contributed a great deal of care for the men. The barracks displays Revolutionary and Civil War relics.

To the right at 100 South Market is the Frederick County Community Center, which was the old B&O Railroad station during the Civil War. Returning from his tour of the Antietam battlefield on October 4, 1862, Lincoln spoke to the citizens assembled here before starting back for Washington: "I also return thanks, not only to the good men, women, and children in this land of ours, for their devotion in the glorious cause, and I say this with no malice in my heart to those who have done otherwise." It sounds much like Lincoln's second inaugural speech. With Lincoln was John McClernand, a political general who would cause Ulysses S. Grant much grief around Vicksburg.

Turn right onto Church.

The building on the corner to your right is Kemp Hall (1860, 4 East Church Street). One of Lincoln's greatest worries early in the war was the possible secession of Maryland. The state legislature was dominated by Secessionists from eastern Maryland, but Gov. Thomas H. Hicks was a Unionist. Lincoln convinced Hicks to relocate the legislature from Annapolis, in a Secessionist portion of the state, to Frederick, a solidly Unionist area. The delegates met at Frederick County Courthouse on March 26, 1861, then moved here, where the Ordinance of Secession failed. To ensure their loyalty, in mid-September Lincoln ordered the arrest of thirty-one Secessionist legislators and imprisoned them at Fort McHenry until after the November elections.

As you turn right onto Church Street, the Evangelical Reformed Church (1848, 15 West Church Street) is on the northwest corner of Market and Church. Finding no services at the Presbyterian Church on Sunday night, September 7, 1862, Stonewall Jackson and Henry Kyd Douglas attended church here. As usual Jackson dozed off, missing a sermon about the importance of preserving the Union that was pointedly aimed at the Confederate visitors. The minister, Dr. Daniel Zacharias, presumably was amused at the end of the service when Jackson complimented him on the message. Barbara Fritchie was a member of the congregation. After the battle of Antietam, boards covered the pews, and the sanctuary was transformed into a hospital.

Jackson had ridden first to the Presbyterian Church (1825, 115 West Second Street) to hear his old friend J. B. Ross speak. As the Confederate army left Frederick, Jackson and Douglas rode to Ross's home, but the minister was sleeping. Jackson left him a note and rode west, never approaching Fritchie's house, according to Douglas.

Less than a block farther up North Market Street, from the turn onto Church Street, at 124, is the Greater Freedom Development, which was the Frederick city hall in 1864. As reprisal for the recent destruction of civilian property by Union forces in the Shenandoah Valley, on July 9, 1864, Early demanded a $200,000 ransom or the equivalent in supplies from Mayor William G. Cole. Otherwise the city would be burned. Frederick's banks quickly raised the sum. The Frederickstown Bank gave $64,000, nearly a fourth of its capital; Farmers and Mechanics Bank donated $28,000; Franklin Savings Bank offered $31,000; Central Bank gave $44,000; and Frederick City Bank found $33,000. The greenbacks were delivered to Early in baskets as the Confederates left to battle Lew Wallace at the Monocacy River. Frederick's citizens approved a bond issue in 1868 to pay off half the debt, which was not retired until 1957. The remainder of the debt was refunded by a reduction of city taxes on the banks until 1896. Despite repeated requests, the federal government has not reimbursed the city.

The Frederick County Visitors Center (19 East Church) is on the left. Stop for maps, brochures, and all manner of information about this very historic city. Guided walking tours of the Frederick Historic District start at the visitors center on weekends from April through December. The local historical society is just up the street on the right.

Continue straight on Church, then turn right onto Chapel Alley–Carroll Street. At the first intersection turn right onto Patrick Street. The National Museum of Civil War Medicine is on the left (48 East Patrick Street).

This is the perfect location for the unique and recently opened museum, which was sponsored by all the banks that cooperated to save the city 135 years earlier. At least seventeen hospitals operated here after the battles of Antietam, Gettysburg, and Monocacy. The building (1830), James Whitehill's factory, is thought to have been a hospital and legend

This cast-iron dog was stolen by Lee's soldiers when they passed through Frederick. It was found and returned following the battle of Antietam.

has Maj. Gen. Jesse Reno, killed at Fox's Gap while leading his Ninth Corps, and other soldiers being embalmed here.

Medical science was primitive at the start of the Civil War. Neither government was prepared to deal with the hundreds of thousands of combat casualties or the ill and diseased who tripled the number of deaths in the war. Wounds to limbs usually resulted in amputation, with instruments and operating tables "cleaned" occasionally with buckets of water splashed over them. Infection killed many who survived the surgery. Wounds to the chest and belly were normally fatal. Battlefield hospitals operated in tents, sometimes in churches, schools, and homes, but too often in fields shielded only by hastily rigged canvas. The germ theory and antiseptics were unknown. Because the vast, crowded army camps provided poor sanitation, bad food, and worse water, epidemics of disease were common. Medical science improved by necessity during the war. Large hospital complexes developed in the North and the South, and casualties received quicker care.

The National Museum of Civil War Medicine interprets medical practices during the war and explores the plight of patients and the work of doctors, matrons, stewards, nurses, and civilian volunteers. Female nurses became common in America for the first time through the work of women such as Clara Barton and Phoebe Yates Pember. Numerous medical subjects—including anesthesia, triage, ambulance corps, and hospital ships—are examined. Exhibits include a military field hospital set in a barn with stretchers, a four-wheeled ambulance, and medical equipment; a ward in a pavilion general hospital (a more sanitary environment for convalescence); a surgeon's tent in camp and a mural illustrating life there; and a Victorian parlor (where women cared for soldiers, rolled bandages, and knit clothing) with a holding coffin in which embalmed soldiers were transported to their families. Videos, including one about amputations, help tell the story. The museum has more than three thousand artifacts and sponsors special programs and exhibits.

Continue on East Patrick, which becomes West Patrick.

Confederate and Federal cavalry skirmished on this street as Lee withdrew and McClellan entered. A rare photo of Confederate troops was taken as they marched out of town on Patrick Street in 1862. To the left (192 West Patrick) is the Barbara Fritchie house. This is a replica (1927)—the original was destroyed during a flood—but much of the original material was used in the reconstruction, and the house contains many of Fritchie's possessions, including the bed in which she died. Fritchie was a controversial woman for her day, a successful businesswoman who at age forty married a twenty-six-year-old man, whom she outlived by thirty years. Born December 3, 1766, she lent her china to the town for a reception held for George Washington. One display contains material relating to Whittier.

The Fritchie legend has spread around the world. After World War II Winston Churchill visited the Fritchie house, where he awed an audience with a spirited rendition of Whitter's poem. According to Henry Kyd Douglas, the general never passed this way, riding through on Mill Alley (present Bentz Street). He is the only authority on the subject; the two principles of the story were soon dead—Fritchie of natural causes and Jackson at Chancellorsville by friendly fire—before either could record specifics of the incident. History supports Douglas's version, but it's a great story.

Legend has Jesse Reno asking Barbara Fritchie to allow him to carry the flag she waved into battle. Reportedly she refused but gave the general a larger one that was found on his body and sent to his family in Massachusetts. In the museum is a desk where Reno wrote his wife while the Union army paused in Frederick.

Several streets north is the Ramsey house (119 Record Street). On October 1 Lincoln traveled from Washington to Frederick to visit McClellan and inspect the Army of the Potomac at Antietam thirteen days after the battle. After viewing the battlefields of South Mountain on October 4, Lincoln returned to Frederick. He stopped here to visit his friend Brig. Gen. George C. Hartsuff, wounded at Antietam and recuperating here. He felt obligated to speak briefly to the people who gathered outside, hoping for a glimpse of a president who had received only 103 of the 7,329 votes cast in 1860 in Frederick County. (He finished fourth in a four-man race.) Lincoln then continued to the B&O Railroad Station, where he again made a short speech.

Several streets south is the Roger Brooke Taney house–Francis Scott Key Museum (1799, 121 South Bentz Street). Taney served as Andrew Jackson's attorney general and secretary of the treasury, then became Chief Justice of the U.S. Supreme Court from 1836 until his death in 1864. He swore in seven presidents, the last being Lincoln, but is best remembered for the Dred Scott decision in 1857. Abolitionists brought suit hoping to restrict slavery in the territories, but Taney's court ruled that slaves were constitutionally protected property that could be taken anywhere in the country. This interpretation of the Constitution implied that there could be no restrictions on slavery, a legal perspective that doomed the Missouri Compromise and other legislation that had postponed the outbreak of war for decades. The decision hardened feelings on both sides of the thorny issue and perhaps hurried the split between North and South.

In 1861 Taney clashed with Lincoln after the president suspended the writ of habeas corpus in Maryland and arrested and imprisoned people without trial.

Taney married Key's sister, and the brothers-in-law practiced law together in Frederick. Ironically, one of Key's grandsons, Frank Key, a Baltimore newspaper editor, was arrested and imprisoned at Fort McHenry for expressing Southern sentiments.

The museum displays Taney family heirlooms and collections of artifacts associated with Taney and Key. A bust of Taney (1931) is at the Frederick County Courthouse (Court and Church Streets), and a full-sized statue stands at Annapolis.

Taney died October 12, 1864, at eighty-seven and is buried at Saint John's Catholic Cemetery (established 1845, entrance at East Third and East Fourth Streets, near East Street). Also buried here are forty-eight Federals and Confederates, many of them local citizens who died after the Civil War. One is Pvt. George Washington, a black Union soldier who enlisted in 1864 at age nineteen and died here at age seventy-six. Another Federal, Pvt. John Lanaham of Pennsylvania, enlisted on August 26, 1861, murdered an officer on September 22, 1861, and was hanged here on December 24, 1861.

Saint John's Catholic Church (1837, 116 East Second Street) was constructed by the same Irish stone masons who built the C&O Canal. The high, thick walls led authorities to use it as a prison for Confederates. Inmates carved their names, initials, and in one case a diary, on the walls of the consistory and behind the altar.

All Saints Episcopal Church (1856) and the Parish house (1814, 108 West Church Street) were both used as hospitals. A former rector was Brig. Gen. William N. Pendleton, the head of Lee's artillery who panicked after Federals captured four guns protecting Boteler's Ford following the retreat from Antietam.

The Frederick Academy of the Visitation (1846, 200 East Second Street) was also a hospital. The Ross-Mathias Mansion (1816, 105 Council Street) was home to Union Brig. Gen. James Cooper.

A year after Antietam, an important event occurred a little southwest of Frederick at Prospect Hill (1855, at the intersection of Route 180–Jefferson Pike and Butterfly Lane). On June 27, 1863, Lincoln ordered Hooker replaced as commander of the Army of the Potomac by George Gordon Meade. Brig. Gen.

Barbara Fritchie's house was reconstructed when the original was destroyed in a flood. It is now a museum.

James A. Hardie, chief of staff to Secretary of War Edwin Stanton and former judge advocate general under Hooker, traveled to Frederick, where the Union forces had concentrated. He found Meade at 3 A.M. on June 28 in a tent on the grounds of Prospect Hill. Hardie woke him, and Meade feared he was being arrested for some unknown crime. The two men informed Hooker of the change in command. Three days later Meade commanded the greatest battle ever fought in the Americas. Prospect Hall is now Saint Joseph Literary Institute, a school. Call for conditions to visit.

Reportedly President James Buchanan first learned of John Brown's actions at Harpers Ferry from John Ritchie, son-in-law of Prospect Hill's owner, Col. William P. Maulsey, who led militia to help quell the uprising. Confederate Col. Bradley Johnson's regiment camped here in September 1862, and Maulsey accompanied the troops who captured Harpers Ferry several days later. Other Confederate and Union forces bivouacked here, and we are assured that all were received hospitably, including Federals Nathaniel P. Banks, John J. Abercrombie, Francis E. Patterson, and Fletcher Webster, son of Daniel Webster.

The site of Meade's camp is marked by a granite boulder, transported from the Devil's Den at Gettysburg, with two bronze plaques (1930).

Pass the shopping centers and Interstate 70 congestion west of Frederick and turn left onto Alternate U.S. 40 to cross Catoctin Mountain at Braddock Heights, where Stuart and Federal cavalry clashed as McClellan pursued Lee.

There is a scenic pullover atop Braddock Heights that affords a good view of South Mountain. At the base of the ridge is Middletown, between Frederick and South Mountain. A large portion of the Confederate army marched through Middletown in September 1862 followed by the bulk of McClellan's army, who were largely funneled along the National Road (Alternate U.S. 40) to Turner's Gap and Fox's Gap and farther west to Antietam Creek. Others took Route 17–Burkittstown Road to Crampton's Gap. Two years later Early passed from the opposite direction and demanded a five-thousand-dollar ransom from Middletown to prevent his torching the town.

One of the most active preservation groups in the nation is the Central Maryland Heritage League (CMHL), which is purchasing considerable property along South Mountain. The organization has secured the Lamar Sanitarium in Middletown, which retains extensive medical equipment from the time it served as a hospital during the battles at South Mountain and Antietam. The building, which has a grand view of South Mountain, contains displays exploring the Civil War in Frederick County. In the carriage house is a hearse and display of period funeral science. Guided tours are available by appointment. Available locally is a self-guided tour brochure with eighteen sites prepared by the Central Maryland Heritage League that starts with Middletown's four hospitals, winds through three gaps, and ends at the site of Mount Tabor Church, which was Joseph Hooker's headquarters.

The Middletown Valley Historical Society has recently received the original ransom note Early wrote demanding five thousand dollars from the community. He collected fifteen hundred dollars before leaving to fight at Monocacy. For 135 years the note was used as a bookmark.

To the left on Route 17–South Church Street is Christ Reformed Church (simply the Reformed Church during the 1860s). From the steeple Federals observed the advance of their armies and the attacks against the gaps in South Mountain. The church suffered extensive damage during its use as a hospital. On May 30, 1863, the United States recompensed the congregation seventy-eight dollars. They have since billed the government for more but without response.

Continue through Middletown on Alternate U.S. 40. Just past the intersection with Route 17 is Zion Lutheran Church (corner of West Main Street and North Jefferson Street) to the right. The military took over the church and used it as a hospital for a year, forcing the congregation to meet in a nearby lecture hall. For damages sustained by the church the government paid fifteen hundred dollars.

Just west of Zion Church and on the opposite side of the road is the Crouse house (204 West Main Street), which has a version of a familiar tale. As Confederate cavalry trailed Lee through town, a squad of troopers noticed that seventeen-year-old Nancy Crouse had draped a large U.S. flag across her second-story balcony. It had reportedly hung unmolested for several days, but now a dozen cavalrymen stomped up the stairs to confront Crouse and her friend Effie Titlow. When Crouse politely inquired as to the purpose of their visit, the leader demanded, "Take down that damned Yankee rag!"

When Crouse refused, a trooper placed his revolver against her head and repeated the demand. At this point she acquiesced. The Confederate wrapped the banner around his horse's head as he rode off, but Federal cavalry soon captured the band and returned the flag to the plucky Crouse. Local poet Thomas C. Harbaught penned verse honoring the fair maiden, but it never gained the fame that Whitter's poem did.

A little farther west, on the north side of the road, is the Shank house (504 West Main Street). Future president Rutherford B. Hayes, a lieutenant colonel leading the Twenty-third Ohio Regiment, was brought here to recuperate from wounds suffered at Fox's Gap on September 14, 1862. His wife, Lucy, soon arrived to nurse him back to health.

Hayes, wounded six times during the war, reached the rank of brigadier general. Moving to politics, he served in the U.S. Congress and as Ohio's governor before running for president as the Republican Party candidate in 1876. He lost the popular vote by two hundred thousand and was nineteen electoral votes behind Democrat Samuel Tilden, but corrupt Reconstruction politics left twenty disputed votes in several southern states. A committee, containing one more Republican than Democrats, gave all the questionable votes to Hayes. To reduce Democratic anger, Hayes agreed to end Reconstruction in the South.

Hayes succeeded Grant. During the war one of Hayes's sergeants was William McKinley, another future president.

Continue toward South Mountain, a long ridge of resistant quartzite that extends in a north-south direction from the Pennsylvania line through Maryland to the borders of Virginia and West Virginia at the Potomac River.

The famed presidential retreat Camp David is located here, sharing space with a ten-thousand-acre Maryland state park. Farther north (12625 Catoctin Furnace Road near Thurmont) is Catoctin Furnace, where legend claims that iron plate used in the *Monitor's* construction was manufactured. Across the street from the ironworks is the Episcopal church where the father of A. S. "Sandie" Pendleton, of Jackson's staff, was a rector. Federals marched past on their way to intercept Lee at Gettysburg.

McClellan hoped to cross the mountain quickly and destroy the isolated segments of Lee's army, thought to be dispersed from Hagerstown (Longstreet) to the north and Harpers Ferry (Jackson) to the south, with D. H. Hill at Boonsboro at the western base of South Mountain.

The Confederate line on the northern sector of South Mountain stretched for four miles from a position one-half mile south of Reno Monument Road at Fox's Gap through Turner's Gap and a half mile beyond Frosttown Road, north of South Mountain Inn.

Near the base of South Mountain, the National Road was intersected by two roads. Our route will be roughly that of the Union army, as taken by Reno's Ninth Corps, on the old Sharpsburg road, which ran southwest to Fox's Gap. From there a ridge-top farm road led north from Fox's Gap to Turner's Gap.

The second road intersecting the National Road was the old Hagerstown road that turned north then west to rejoin the National Road atop the mountain. This was the main focus of McClellan's attack. While Reno flanked Turner's Gap via Fox's Gap and John Gibbon fixed Southern attention along the National Road directly to Turner's Gap, most of the Federal assaulting force swung right to attack the Confederate line north of Turner's Gap. Union artillery deployed at Bolivar near the eastern base of the mountain to support the Federal attacks.

Between Bolivar and Turner's Gap on Alternate U.S. 40–Old National Road, at the base of South Mountain, we turn left onto Fox's Gap Road.

On the right as you turn is White House Inn, a stone inn and tavern constructed in 1809. It is often confused with South Mountain Inn–Mountain House, which is farther west at the summit of South

Mountain in Turner's Gap. The CMHL has purchased the historic tavern and eighteen acres where Gibbon's Iron Brigade began its assault up the National Road here. This was the center of the Federal assault up South Mountain. After the battle it was a field hospital for the Iron Brigade.

Because Turner's Gap posed such a formidable position, Reno's lead Ninth Corps division, Brig. Gen. Jacob Cox's three thousand men, marched northwest from Middletown and turned southwest down the Bolivar road, then turned northwest to labor up the old Sharpsburg road (today's Reno Monument Road) to Fox's Gap in order to outflank Turner's Gap. At 9 A.M. Cox found Samuel Garland's one thousand Confederates defending the gap from behind stone walls just north of the present Reno Monument. When Garland was killed around 11 A.M., the Rebels retreated on a summit road to Turner's Gap.

After Garland's death, Confederate reinforcements led by George T. Anderson attacked the Union line south of Fox's Gap but were repulsed. The Federals then advanced toward Turner's Gap on the Ridge road, which no longer exists. Fighting occurred along rocky ledges on both sides of the road while D. H. Hill desperately deployed several cannon and a shaky battle line composed of staff officers, couriers, teamsters, and cooks. The Federals paused before this thin line and awaited reinforcements, which allowed Lee the time he needed to rush additional units to Turner's Gap. After the remainder of the Ninth Corps arrived, the battle resumed, Reno was killed on the ridge top, and the battle closed with nightfall. At the same time Hooker assaulted to the north against the Confederate left.

Among those fighting in the Kanawha Division was Sgt. William McKinley, who as president was assassinated on the thirty-ninth anniversary of the battle of South Mountain, and Lt. Rutherford B. Hayes, both of the Twenty-third Ohio. In the Thirtieth Ohio was Hugh Ewing, William T. Sherman's foster brother and brother-in-law.

At the intersection turn right onto Reno Monument Road and turn left beside the Reno Monument to park.

Reno swung farther to the south and emerged here. This monument, dedicated on September 14, 1889,

South Mountain Inn was used as D. H. Hill's headquarters as he struggled to hold Fox's and Turner's Gaps.

by one hundred comrades from the Ninth Corps and nine hundred others, who arrived on a special train from Philadelphia, is a tapered granite shaft six feet high, occupying a forty-foot plot surrounded by a concrete wall with an iron gate. The speaker was Maj. Gen. Orlando B. Willcox, commander of the First Division at Fox's Gap. The memorial was rededicated in 1989.

As you face the Reno Monument, the Wise farm and well were to the right, where over nine acres of Wise's field have been preserved. Note the small monument to Garland, unveiled on September 11, 1993.

On September 15, 1862, Daniel Wise, with his son and daughter, abandoned their mountaintop farmhouse (torn down in 1919) and returned to find dead Confederate and Union soldiers strewn across their fields and behind the stone walls. One angle, which held fourteen dead Rebels, was dubbed Dead Man's Corner. Their home had been used as a field hospital. A common story has Wise accepting a dollar per Confederate body he buried. For convenience he dumped fifty-eight into an abandoned sixty-foot-deep well and sealed it with rocks. Other stories claim Federal soldiers started the process and Wise finished it. The truth is that Northern burial teams did the entire deed themselves and Wise was not paid a penny. Some authorities even doubt the event occurred, but records from the Hagerstown Confederate Cemetery make note of fifty-eight bodies collected from one site at Fox's Gap, where they had apparently been excavated from Wise's well. One hundred Federals and seventy Confederates were buried in Wise's fields, the work performed by the men of a regiment who had angered their commander.

In front of the Reno Monument, across Reno Monument Road at the corner of the stone wall, is a large historical marker honoring the Seventeenth Michigan. The path leading north was the Ridge Road–Wood Road, on which Federals pursued the retreating Confederates after Garland was killed. It is now the Appalachian Trail. Confederates fought from behind the natural breastworks formed by stone walls right of the old Sharpsburg road and the sunken wagon trail. South Mountain will recive its first dramatic monument in a few years when a memorial is dedicated to thirteen North Carolina regiments that fought at Fox's Gap. The bronze statue is being prepared by Gary Casteel and

Union Gen. Jesse Reno was killed at the battle of South Mountain. This monument was erected on the site.

depicts a dying Tarheel struggling to raise a Confederate banner.

Over the past ten years the CMHL and Maryland Department of Natural Resources have purchased a number of lots around South Mountain, particularly at Fox's and Turner's Gaps and several historic structures. They hope to secure a total of five hundred acres linked by a two-mile trail that will follow the path of the Federal attack from Fox's Gap to Turner's Gap. Maryland is considering establishing it first Civil War state park here.

Continue west on Reno Monument Road, the old Sharpsburg road, which continues down the mountain to Pleasant Valley. Turn right onto Moser Road, the current ridge-top road, which is very hilly and curvy.

Moser Road parallels the Ridge Road–Appalachian Trai–Wood Roadl to the east. Fighting occurred along this route to your right as Confederates withdrew from Fox's Gap.

At Alternate U.S. 40–Old National Road turn right to the South Mountain Inn on your right.

Turner's Gap, whose elevation is just under one thousand feet, is the lowest in the Blue Ridge and unusually broad, two miles in width. It was relatively easy for the numerically superior Federals to outflank the Confederate defenders.

South Mountain Inn–Mountain House (1755) was built on the National Road in 1755. Visited by Henry Clay, Daniel Webster, and other notables, it was purchased in 1876 for thirty-five hundred dollars by Madeleine Vinto Dahlgren. She was the widow of U.S. Adm. John Dahlgren, an ordnance expert who designed powerful artillery during the Civil War, and mother of Ulric Dahlgren, killed outside Richmond during a controversial cavalry raid whose purposes might have included the assassination of Jefferson Davis and other leading Confederates, the burning of Richmond, and the release of thousands of Union prisoners imprisoned throughout the city. Dahlgren used the structure as a summer home, which she named Sky Farm.

Across the highway and a short distance to the east is Dahlgren Chapel, constructed in 1881 by Madeleine, a devout Catholic. Intended not only as a place of worship, it was meant to serve as a memorial to her husband and son and as a family crypt. She was temporarily interred there before the Dahlgren family sold the property in 1922.

In 1995 the CMHL purchased 2.5 acres in Turner's Gap abutting the chapel. The 6 cast-iron two-hundred-pound tablets were part of 250 cast at a Hagerstown foundry in 1896. Most of the others were placed on the Antietam battlefield. Dangerously close to the highway only here, they were recently restored and moved to a safer location thirty feet off the road on CMHL property. Additional signage has been added.

On September 14 South Mountain Inn was the headquarters of D. H. Hill. Garland's body was laid on the porch. From this superb vantage point D. H. Hill watched the approaching Federals in the valley below with awe and fear. At 4 P.M. one Northern brigade attacked straight up South Mountain but was repulsed by Southerners fighting from behind a stone wall below the ridge crest. Meanwhile, the largest Union force, under Hooker, climbed to the north and attacked the Confederate left from the area now known as George Washington Monument State Park and toward Turner's Gap on Washington Monument Road. The Southerners were driven back in bitter fighting but still controlled the gap. Lee withdrew to Antietam during the night, having won a respite but at the cost of twenty-eight hundred casualties to McClellan's eighteen hundred.

From South Mountain Inn turn right onto Alternative U.S. 40–Old National Road past the Dahlgren Chapel, and turn left onto Washington Monument Road to George Washington State Park.

Washington County, Maryland, claims to be the first named for George Washington. On July 4, 1827, the people of nearby Boonsboro, five hundred strong, decided to build a monument to the president at absolutely no cost. Meeting at the square, they marched up to the summit of the mountain and started laying a circular, dry, native-stone tower shaped like a jug. They left it half completed, fifteen feet high and twenty-four feet in diameter, and returned after the crops were in to double its height. The Civil War, vandalism, and the elements crumbled the mortarless structure, but it was rebuilt and rededi-

cated in 1882 in a ceremony witnessed by three thousand people. From 1934 to 1936 the Civilian Conservation Corps repaired the edifice. The monument is reached via a short, steep trail. Thirty-four steps lead to a great view of three states and the Potomac River. In the visitors center is a taped history of the site and Civil War artifacts. On September 14 Federal soldiers cleared trees from the summit here and established a signal station that could be seen from the valley below. The Appalachian Trail passes through the park.

Return on Washington Monument Road to Alternate U.S. 40.

Hooker attacked Hill and reinforcements from Longstreet arrived along this route. Robert E. Rodes's Alabama Brigade held off George Gordon Meade's division along Dahlgren Road.

Turn right onto Alternate U.S. 40 and descend South Mountain to Boonsboro. Continue past Route 17 and the sign for Antietam Battlefield to the Boonsborough Museum of History, on the right at 133 North Main Street–Alternate U.S. 40, just past Potomac Street.

This museum dedicates considerable space to Civil War material, primarily artifacts collected locally in the gaps of South Mountain and at Antietam and Harpers Ferry. One bullet-riddled piece of fence from the Bloody Lane at Antietam was presented by a Union sergeant who won the Medal of Honor and was shot in both legs. Displayed is the large pulpit Bible

Union soldiers cleared the summit of South Mountain at the Washington Monument for use as a signal station.

This is the view of South Mountain from Pleasant Valley, which runs south to Harpers Ferry and west to Sharpsburg and Antietam Creek.

removed from the Sharpsburg Lutheran Church during the battle of Antietam, Confederate money spent in Boonsboro, and Mrs. Dahlgren's rolltop desk used at Mountain House, where she wrote *South Mountain Magic.* There is extensive material about Henry Kyd Douglas, one of Jackson's staff officers who lived on the Potomac River at Ferry Hill, now headquarters of the C&O Canal National Historical Park. Included is a letter Douglas wrote to his father on captured Federal stationary, his diary, Bowie knife, and original orders signed by Jackson. One display case contains material relating to John Brown's Harpers Ferry raid of 1859. A highlight of the offerings is a collection of weapons, including cannon, muskets, a sharpshooter's rifle, and five thousand edged weapons. Other objects include a belt buckle that stopped a bullet, a flower from Abraham Lincoln's coffin, hardtack, a fifteen-inch solid shot weighing four hundred pounds, wooden legs worn by Civil War amputees, a Bible reportedly kissed by ten thousand Confederate soldiers, and personal possessions of soldiers such as games, musical instruments, tobacco products, currency, and writing material. Most unusual is a collection of carvings by soldiers from soft lead bullets—chessmen, checkers, poker chips, and bottle stoppers.

Jackson was almost captured in Boonsboro when he was surprised by Federal cavalry. With members of his staff, the general was walking Little Sorrel when the skirmish began. The Confederates leaped into their saddles and began an undignified "skedaddle" to avoid capture. A probably apocryphal story has the Federals chased off when the Confederate officers shouted orders to nonexistent troops in the woods. Trapped in the Boonsboro Hotel, Col. Bassett French hid in a pile of garbage in the basement.

Nearly the entire Confederate army marched through Boonsboro. A Confederate cavalry regiment covered Lee's rear in Boonsboro on September 15. They fought a lively skirmish with Federal troopers on Main Street before withdrawing with twenty casualties.

At 6524 Main Street is the John Murdock house. Jackson stopped here and set up his headquarters tent in a field across the street. The Boonsboro Museum contains a trunk given to Murdock by Confederates in appreciation of his hospitality.

North of Boonsboro off Alternate U.S. 40 are several interesting Civil War sites worth a side trip. Near the intersection with Benevala Church Road is Beaver Creek Bridge, one of thirty scenic stone bridges constructed in Washington County between 1819 and 1863. Shadowed by Federals, the Confederates passed through after Gettysburg, July 9–14, as Lee retreated to Williamsport, eight miles away. A cavalry skirmish occurred on July 8 between the Sixth and Eleventh Virginia and Union forces. George Gordon Meade established his headquarters nearby on July 9. Local legend claims that a resident had painted an American flag on an exterior wall of his home but whitewashed it out when the Confederates approached.

On Route 68, which branches off to the northwest from Alternate U.S. 40 a short distance north of Boonsboro, is the Devils Backbone Bridge, a one-arch span built in 1824 over Antietam Creek. Jackson traveled this route in 1862 as his corps marched to Williamsport at the start of the campaign to seize Harpers Ferry. On July 10, 1863, the Army of the Potomac passed through in pursuit of Lee, who established a defensive perimeter around Williamsport while waiting for the water level of the Potomac River to subside. Meade's headquarters was set up nearby on July 10–14, 1863.

Farther up Route 68, at the intersection with Route 65, which leads south to the Antietam battlefield and north to Hagerstown, is James Crossroads, where Meade's reserves—the Second, Third, and Twelfth Corps—camped and skirmished with Confederates.

Before starting the tour of the Antietam battlefield, you have the option of touring Crampton's Gap, the southernmost pass in South Mountain, and Pleasant Valley. The simple route is to drive on Route 67 south from Boonsboro, but for those who are serious about retracing Civil War campaigns, backtrack along Alternate U.S. 40 across South Mountain to Middletown and turn right to take Route 17 to Burkittsville, a scenic and historic community of fifty-eight structures little changed since the Civil War.

The good citizens of Burkittsville have suffered of late because the movie *The Blair Witch Project* (1999) was set and filmed here. The story is entirely fictional, and Burkittsville is proud of its extensive and real legends and lore. The community has developed a Civil War walking tour.

In Burkittsville turn left onto East Main Street to the United Church of Christ (1829, 3 East Main Street; the German Reformed Church during the Civil War) and Saint Paul's Lutheran Church (1859, 5 East Main Street). Wounded from both armies received care in the churches and in most other structures in town. Despite persistent tradition, Lincoln probably never visited either hospital in October 1862 as he passed through Burkittsville when returning to Frederick from Antietam. Confederates shelled the Federals as they passed through Burkittsville. Saint Paul's remains an active church while the United Church of Christ now houses the local Heritage Society. The Union cemetery between the churches offers a good view of Crampton's Gap. Winfield Scott's brigade was held in reserve and watched the battle from here.

The Tailor Shop (1821, 3 East Main Street) was a Confederate headquarters; the Michael Wiener house (1830, 108 West Main Street) is alleged to have hosted Lee, Lincoln, McClellan, and Burnside. From the Wiener tannery (110 West Main Street) Confederate cavalry under Col. Thomas Munford appropriated wagons, wheels, saddles, harnesses, and kegs of nails. The Dr. John E. Garrott house (101 East Main Street) was used as a hospital, and Garrott also volunteered his services. Federal troops attacked Crampton's Gap across the David Arnold farm (house, 1790, 108 West Main Street) and the lawn of the Otho F. Harley house (1849, 6633 Gapland Road). Union Gen. William B. Franklin's headquarters was in the yard of the Schafer house (corner of Catholic Church Road and Jefferson Pike). The Federals hugged the south side of Main Street, where buildings protected them from a Confederate shelling.

McClellan's wife and mother-in-law visited him in October, staying near his headquarters at Needmore, a mile from Burkittsville.

At the Rebel Yell estate in the area are the marked graves of eight Georgia and Virginia soldiers killed in a skirmish.

Franklin's Fourth Corps marched from Buckeystown south of Frederick to Jefferson, at the base of Catoctin Mountain, and Burkittsville, then he attacked through Crampton's Gap to Pleasant Valley. Lafayette McLaws had crossed South Mountain at

Stone walls like these at Crampton's Gap played an important role in the struggles fought atop South Mountain here and at Fox's and Turner's Gaps.

Crampton's and Brownsville Gap, a few miles farther south, into Pleasant Valley, then ascended Elk Ridge at Solomon Gap, a little northeast of Crampton's Gap, and advanced to Maryland Heights. He left a small force in Crampton's Gap and artillery at Brownsville Gap as he moved against Harpers Ferry. Learning of Franklin's approach through Middletown, McLaws dispatched three cavalry regiments under Col. Thomas Munford to Crampton's.

To follow Franklin's actual route to Crampton's Gap, return northeast on Route 17 and turn left on Picnic Woods Road, then left onto Arnoldstown Road, and left onto Mountain Church Road, where the Federals started up the mountain. Earlier, on September 13, 1862, Federal Brig. Gen. Alfred Pleasonton's cavalry and Stuart's Southern troopers had clashed at Braddock Gap, Catoctin Creek Bridge, and Middletown. As Stuart's wagons started for Crampton's Gap, the Eighth Illinois under Maj. William H. Medill started in pursuit, but it was ambushed by Wade Hampton. Fighting swirled around Quebec Schoolhouse, now a garage for a private home on Marker Road near the intersection with Quebec Schoolhouse Road, just to the north off Mountain Church Road.

At the next intersection turn right onto Gapland Road. At this intersection the stone walls to the north constituted the first Confederate line of defense, primarily manned by dismounted cavalry. At 3 P.M. one Federal division advanced north of the road and two attacked to the south on a mile-wide front. Outnumbered by ten thousand, the Confederates retreated to meet Brig. Gen. Howell Cobb's thirteen-hundred-man brigade rushing from Pleasant Valley. Despite his best efforts to stop them, Cobb's infantry joined the dash to the rear. For no discernable reason Franklin halted near Crampton's Gap and McLaws threw together a new line across Pleasant Valley to the south.

Continue on Gapland Road to the War Correspondents Arch at the summit of South Mountain. As you face the monument, the Confederates retreated along the road to the left, while Federal forces approached from both directions. Two Confederate cannon fired from the intersection here.

The National Park Service owns the arch and a plot of land surrounding it, and the Maryland Department of Natural Resources owns Gathland

State Park and the battlefield. A number of historical markers describe the battle that occurred here. Dominating the gap, which has a low elevation but is quite narrow, is the War Correspondents Arch (1896), constructed on the estate of George Alfred Townsend (whose pen name Gath came from his three initials; the *h* refers to 2 Samuel 1:20: "Tell it not in Gath, / publish it not in the streets of Ashkelon"). He was a renowned journalist and newspaperman during the Civil War. Inscribed on the fieldstone monument are the names of 157 correspondents and artists who "thrilled the fireside" and "educated the provinces" in the early 1860s. Sixty feet high and fifty feet wide, the monument has a sixteen-foot Moorish arch and three Roman arches, with square crenelated towers. Inspiration for the arch came from the B&O Railroad Depot at Sharpsburg and Fire Company No. 2 in Hagerstown. Among the symbols on the arch is a horse, representing speed; electricity, for the telegraph; and the Greek god Mercury, denoting speedy communication. The zinc statue in the niche represents Pheidippides, who delivered the news of the great military victory from Marathon to Athens and then fell dead. War correspondents from the ancient Greek wars to post–Civil War conflicts are quoted on the monument. Donations to meet the five-thousand-dollar cost came from many people, including Joseph Pulitzer and Thomas Edison. The donors' names are inscribed on the monument.

Townsend covered the Peninsula campaign and the early phases of Second Manassas, then left the country for a lecture tour in England, returning in time for Appomattox. In 1865 he published a book titled *Campaigns of a Non-combatant.* Townsend was also a novelist, poet, and playwright, said to have written up to eighteen thousand words a day. While researching *Katy of Catoctin,* a novel about John Brown's Harpers Ferry raid, he fell in love with this area. Townsend purchased one hundred acres and constructed nine major buildings with fifty rooms, which he designed, including homes for himself and his wife and their children, plus a stable, barn, library, and guest houses. He summered here, where many prominent visitors were entertained. Although he built a tomb for himself here, with the inscription "Good Night" engraved on it, Townsend left, never to return, when his wife died in 1905. He died in 1914 in New York City and is buried in Philadelphia.

The complex of Gathland has been owned by a church, civic groups, and the state, but has been too expensive to upkeep. The monument has been rededicated in 1946, 1962, and 1995. It is an occasional state park when Maryland can find the funding. The site is always open, with a walking tour available to the ruins, and a museum with Civil War relics located in Gapland Hall (1885), which is sometimes open. The Appalachian Trail passes through the gap.

Drive down South Mountain to Route 67 and turn left (south). The stone house passed on the descent belonged to Dr. Joseph Claggett, a surgeon under Longstreet who was captured at Winchester. After the war he lost the place and moved to West Virginia. The Holiness Church a mile or so south on Route 67 marks McLaws's final defensive line, which stretched across Pleasant Valley from South Mountain to Elk Ridge. Continue south and turn left on Boteler Road, originally the Pleasant Valley pike. Turn right onto Brownsville Pass Road beside the historical marker. The road is paved to a point where it becomes a driveway for several houses and then peters out to a goat path. It was a rough route during the Civil War. McLaws entered Pleasant Valley here and stationed artillery to defend it against Union attackers. Saint Luke's Church in Brownsville was McLaws's headquarters on September 13–14 and doubled as a hospital.

Return to Route 67 and turn left to continue south. On the right is Yarrowsburg Road, used by two of McLaws's brigades, under Joseph B. Kershaw and William Barksdale, to reach Solomon's Gap. There they gained the crest of Elk Ridge and swept down the narrow spine to Maryland Heights, its southern extension. Continue south on Route 67 and turn right on Garrett's Mill Road, then left onto Valley Road. Cross Israel's Creek on a beautiful, narrow stone bridge like the ones around Antietam. McLaws crossed this bridge. Continue south on Valley Road to Grist Mill Road on the right. The battle of Maryland Heights, between McLaws's brigades and Federal defenders atop the ridge, occurred on the mountain opposite this point. Continue south on Valley Road to Grist Mill Road on the right. McLaws used that

The War Correspondents Arch was erected by a noted newspaperman of the Civil War era. It stands on the battle gound of Crampton's Gap.

road to manhandle his artillery to the top of Maryland Heights. Continue south on Valley Road to U.S. 340 or return to Route 67. A right on U.S. 340 takes you to Harpers Ferry, a left to Frederick. Turning off at Route 478 takes you to Brunswick (wartime Berlin), where McClellan crossed the Potomac River after Antietam.

The Confederates at Harpers Ferry would have been seriously challenged to resist an attack by Franklin. Jackson's siege could have been lifted and a large Federal force would have been on the south bank of the Potomac River with Lee dangerously isolated twelve miles to the north. Franklin allowed the Confederates to hold both approaches to Harpers Ferry, here and across Elk Ridge to the west on the Harpers Ferry road. He remained in Pleasant Valley until September 17, when he slowly started north for Antietam along the path now of Route 67 to the north, skirting Elk Ridge and Red Hill instead of crossing Red Hill to the Burnside Bridge.

A right on Route 67 leads to Rohrersville, which witnessed the passage of Lincoln in October 1862 as he traveled to Antietam from Harpers Ferry. A mile west was Solomon's Gap near the intersection of Trego Road and Chestnut Grove Road, where McLaws ascended Elk Ridge and drove down it to Maryland Heights overlooking Harpers Ferry.

If you have taken this side trip and wish to return to the tour of the Antietam battlefield, return north on Route 67 past Brownsville. In Boonsboro turn left onto Alternate U.S. 40, then turn left onto Route 17 at the sign for the Antietam battlefield.

A Tour of the Battle of Antietam

From the parking lot of the Boonsborough Museum of History, turn left onto Main, then right onto Route 34 toward Sharpsburg and Antietam National Battlefield Park.

YOU WILL pass through Keedysville, three miles east of Antietam Creek, where a number of Federal hospitals were established. In mid-September most of Robert E. Lee's army and all of George B. McClellan's army marched through town from the passes of South Mountain. The Samuel Keedy house (1836, 42 South Main Street, at the corner of Main and Dogstreet Roads) has a well used by many soldiers. Before the battle of Antietam, McClellan ate at the Jacob Hess house (1801, 17 Main Street). The two brick buildings at the Wyand house (3–5 North Main Street), though unfinished in 1862, were used as hospitals that cared for two hundred wounded Federals. The Christian Keedy house (1870, 41 North Main Street) replaces a log house where Capt. Oliver Wendell Holmes Jr. received care for his wounds before being transferred to Hagerstown, where he was met and cared for by his famed physician-poet father. Holmes Sr. traveled to Keedysville and paid Margaret Kitzmiller for attending his son. The Geeting house (Geeting Road near Red Hill Road) was a large hospital that accommodated four hundred seriously wounded men. The structure, now a dairy farm, had a convenient large spring.

Just south of Keedysville a choice can be made to explore the route of the Union army as it marched to attack the Confederate left and center, or you can return after exploring the Antietam battlefield for this side trip. Assuming you will first take this detour, turn right onto Keedysville Road to the Upper Bridge. Just before reaching it, the Jacob Cost farm is to the right and the Samuel Pry mill to the left. Both are private homes; the Cost house was a Federal hospital.

The one-lane upper bridge (also known as Hitt's, Pry's, or Hooker's Bridge) is the original, a three archer with an unusually high center. Constructed in 1830 at a cost of $1,413.66, it stands at the site where British Gen. Edward Braddock crossed the creek in 1765. Late on the evening of September 17, Joseph Hooker's First Corps passed to encounter fierce resistance from Confederates in the woods to the west. Early on the following morning, Edwin Sumner crossed the creek, and just downstream at Pry Ford the divisions of John Sedgwick and William French waded across later in the day. They assaulted the Confederates through the North Woods, the East Woods, the Cornfield, and farther south at the Sunken Road.

McClellan decided to attack Lee's left because the upper bridge was in his possession and Confederate artillery could not reach it. The attack was spearheaded by Hooker's corps of eighty-five hundred men. They were supported by Joseph K. F. Mansfield's Twelfth Corps, with Fitz John Porter's Fifth Corps and forty-three hundred cavalry commanded by Brig. Gen. Alfred Pierson reserved to exploit offensive breakthroughs or to cover the army's retreat if necessary.

Across the bridge is an intersection; to the right on Keedysville Road is the Hoffman farm; to the left, Joseph Mansfield Road leads to the spot where Mansfield was mortally wounded, but it will be seen on the regular tour. Return to Route 34 and turn right.

446

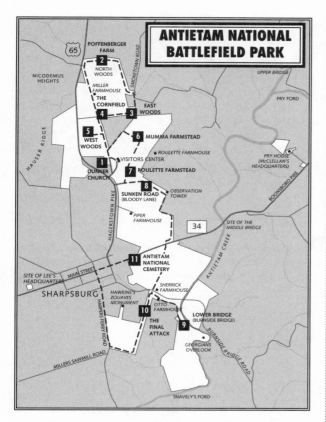

At the small sign for the Philip Pry farm (McClellan's headquarters), turn right to the house.

The house is owned by the National Park Service. The exterior and grounds are open to the public; the interior is not. The Pry family fled the approaching battle and took shelter in Keedysville.

This was McClellan's command center during the battle, a mile east of the Antietam National Battlefield's Visitors Center. Soldiers carried chairs from the house to the ridgetop to the west, where McClellan and Porter, commanding the Federal reserves, sat and smoked cigars during the fighting, observing the action through telescopes and talking quietly. McClellan, seeing John Bell Hood's counterattack, dispatched the Third Corps, which was the only contribution the commanding general made once the battle started. An overlook northwest of the house affords good views of the North Woods and the Sunken Road. Federal artillery was deployed along this ridge, far outnumbering the Confederate guns and markedly supe-

rior in range and accuracy. Throughout the battle, these cannon fired across Antietam Creek and created havoc within Confederate lines.

Hooker's wound was tended at the Pry house, and mortally wounded Brig. Gen. Israel Richardson was also brought here. Lincoln visited Richardson here before the general died on November 3.

Return to Route 34 and turn right.

To the left is Porterstown Road, which provides an interesting side trip, particularly in late fall and winter when the leaves have fallen from the trees. At the intersection turn left on Red Hill Road and ascend Elk Ridge. Near the top is a cleared area with a good view of the Antietam battlefield. A Federal signal station, photographed by Mathew Brady's cameramen, was here during the battle. The Pry farm is two miles to the north.

In a few years visitors nearing the site of the Middle Bridge, at Shepherdstown Pike and Richardson Avenue, may encounter a grouping of bronze equestrian statues depicting Confederate heroes of Antietam: Lee, Jackson, and Stuart. A businessman has purchased land here and wishes to add Southern monuments—Antietam has only two. Most monuments were erected in the decades immediately following the war, a time when Southern states were destitute. In the intervening years the National Park Service has declared a moratorium on new monuments. Texas sculptor Ron Moore is to produce the figures, and they will be interpreted by markers.

The stone gatehouse at Antietam National Cemetery marks the entry to burial ground for Federal soldiers killed at Antietam.

447

Return to Route 34 and turn left to the national cemetery on the right.

The dead were buried haphazardly, particularly the Confederates, who were left until last, when they were in an advanced state of decay. Federal soldiers always swore that Southern soldiers turned black and decayed faster than their own dead and attributed it to poor diet, lack of salt, or a combination of whiskey and gunpowder they supposedly drank before entering battle to make them fierce. The real reason was certainly that they were the last to be buried. The exhausted Federal burial details, after interring their comrades, had no affection for Southerners, alive or dead. They were also often drunks, stragglers, and petty thieves. Three-fourths of the Confederate dead at Antietam were buried unidentified, and arms, legs, and even heads were often found protruding through the soil, sometimes covered only with fence rails. Hogs soon rooted at the bodies and buzzards also fed. In the following years most farmers went about their business, plowing through graves and toppling wooden headboards.

In March 1864 the Maryland legislature decided to establish a cemetery for the dead of Antietam, but on March 23, 1865, just weeks before Appomattox, it elected to bury Confederates separately. A board of trustees established to implement the program, however, refused to deal with the Southern dead. More than ninety thousand dollars, raised from nineteen Northern states, was used to establish what became a national cemetery.

A canvass of local residents and veterans provided a list of burial sites, and in October 1866 sixty men started the work of exhuming and reinterring remains. A thousand coffins were delivered, and a wagon train brought provisions for the expedition, which camped near the cemetery. By November 22 they had located twelve hundred graves, two-thirds of them identified, mainly those who lay in undisturbed churchyards and those who had been buried with photos of family or notes in bottles on them. One body that seemed too heavy for its size was found to have a twelve-pound cannonball embedded in it. The reburial party received kind cooperation from most of the population, which was stoutly Unionist, but two residents denied that soldiers were buried on their property. One of them was found to

The number of casualties incurred during the one-day battle of Antietam was staggering. This image invites reflection on the sacrifices of the individual soldier.

be raising cabbages among the dead, and another had constructed a farm road over a trench grave.

As work progressed it was decided to bury all Federal dead in Maryland at Antietam. Remains were gathered from South Mountain and Monocacy, more from Virginia's Shenandoah Valley, and eleven from Pennsylvania. The work, which was completed by September 1867, produced 4,695 Federals—2,903 known and 1,792 unidentified. A third of the graves were dug, or rather carved, out of limestone. Officers rest in one section of the cemetery; enlisted men in a separate area. The wall surrounding the cemetery, made with local stone and cement, the iron entrance gate, and the attractive lodge house were added later.

The cemetery was dedicated on September 17, the fifth anniversary of the bloodiest day in American history. The crowd numbered ten to fifteen thousand, and the guests included President Andrew Johnson, Gens. Ulysses S. Grant and Ambrose E. Burnside, Pennsylvania Gov. John W. Geary, and the current and a former governor of Maryland. The Maryland governors were poorly received by the Union veterans and their families, and President Johnson, a native Tennessean and Democrat, whose impeachment was imminent, was virtually ignored.

This burial ground became a national cemetery on August 30, 1890, the second in the United States. It passed into the hands of the War Department before being transferred to the National Park Service in 1933. Lack of space closed the cemetery to further veteran burials in 1953, but bones continue to be found on the battlefield. In 1989 the remains of four Irish Brigade members, discovered near Bloody Lane, received a full military burial and they rest beneath a monument in the New York section.

The Forty-eighth Pennsylvania Infantry Monument on the battlefield depicts Sgt. George Simpson carrying the regimental colors. George was killed, his brother Randolph wounded, and two hundred other comrades fell. The Simpsons' sister Annie unveiled the monument on September 17, 1904.

For more than forty years Pennsylvania Pvt. Henry Struble placed flowers at his own grave. Lying wounded after the battle of South Mountain, he lent his canteen to a thirsty comrade who died with it in his possession. A burial party saw the

An accident sent part of "Simon," a monumental statue at Antietam, to the bottom of the Potomac River.

name on the canteen and buried the man as Henry Struble. The real Struble survived until 1912, becoming mayor of Youngwood, Pennsylvania. He sent flowers every Memorial Day to the grave of the unknown man in his grave.

The monumental statue here was designed by George Keller, who also produced the Gettysburg Soldier Monument, and was executed by J. G. Batterson of Hartford, Connecticut. Completed in 1874 at the substantial expense of thirty-five thousand dollars, the giant figure was exhibited at the 1876 Centennial Exposition in Philadelphia, then transported by boat to Washington, D.C., in two large pieces. The dedication was delayed one year when a segment accidentally fell into the Potomac River and had to be retrieved. The 250-ton statue was transported to the site on wooden rollers pulled by twenty-six to forty-six horses and oxen. It is twenty-one and a half feet high and stands on a base twenty-two and a half feet tall. When the giant memorial was dedicated on September 17, 1880, the temporary wooden headboards in the cemetery had been replaced by the present headstones. The figure is affectionately known as "Old Simon," from a nineteenth-century hero called Simon Pure. The simple inscription reads, "Not for themselves, but for their country."

When trees were cleared from the cemetery site, a large limestone boulder was discovered. Instantly rumors started that Robert E. Lee had stood atop the stone to watch the progress of the battle. Visitors did not seem to care that the stone was not known in 1862 or that trees would have cut visibility to yards. They flocked to "Lee's Rock" and chiseled off pieces as souvenirs. Unable to tolerate a site associated with the Rebel general that attracted southerners to the Union cemetery, the stone "was broken up, dug up, scattered, [and] obliterated," according to Henry Kyd Douglas. The site, in the Pennsylvania section, is today occupied by the grave of Elizabeth Bryant, wife of a former superintendent. Lee did direct part of the battle from this area, but forty-five Confederate artillery pieces were stationed here. With cannon positioned in the Old Sharpsburg Cemetery across Route 34, Southern artillerists shelled Federals crossing the lower bridge and middle bridge and advancing on the Boonsboro road. Hills north and south of Sharpsburg were also used as Confederate artillery sites.

Hundreds of horses were killed at Antietam, and their bloated, maggot-riddled carcasses were dealt with by contracts to farmers. The animals were collected and burned, which created such a stench that residents for ten miles around closed up their houses.

Continue straight on Route 34 and enter Sharpsburg.

This is the oldest community in Washington County, established in 1763 and named for an early Maryland governor. A walking tour of the historic community can be taken before or after visiting the battlefield. Most buildings in town stood during the Civil War, and a number of missing stones from walls were caused by Federal artillery, which rained projectiles onto the town. Historic homes are marked by small bronze plaques near the front door that read "Antietam 1862," and larger signs mark most structures used as hospitals or headquarters.

One of the most prominent landmarks pictured in photos and drawings during the Civil War was Calvary Lutheran Church. Damaged by Union cannon fire while used as a Confederate signal station and used as a Federal hospital after the battle, it was demolished in 1864. It stood west of the national cemetery, its site marked by the adjacent cemetery on the south side of the road. The present Lutheran Church, the third, was constructed in 1944. It contains several memorial windows.

Christ Reformed Church (117 West Main Street) retains its 1862 appearance. After the Confederates withdrew, its pews were covered with boards, then hay and blankets were added to form hospital beds. During remodeling in 1890 veterans of the Sixteenth Connecticut, decimated nearby in Sherrick's cornfield and treated here, dedicated a memorial window. It was rededicated on September 19, 1995.

Confederate and Federal flags were flown over Saint Peter's Roman Catholic Church (1833) to prevent damage during the Civil War. Saint Paul's Episcopal Church (1833), now a ruin, was struck repeatedly by Federal artillery.

The southwest corner of Main and Mechanic Streets (100–101 West Main Street), the site marked by a plaque, was the Jacob Grove house. At dusk Lee met there with his generals to discuss the condition of the army. At the council of war James Longstreet, Stonewall Jackson, and others advocated a retreat across the Potomac River into Virginia. Lee elected to remain on the field, ready to fight if McClellan attacked the following day. Damaged by a number of artillery rounds, the house was torn down.

The John Kretzer house (128 East Main Street), a stout stone structure, became a refuge for more than two hundred men, women, and children who crowded into the basement. "Every time the firing began extra loud," one of these remembered, "the ladies would cry and the dogs would bark, and some aged old men would break out in prayer." When a Confederate officer ordered Kretzer to take down and burn the U.S. flag that flew over his home, a daughter hid the banner in an ash pile. When the officer returned, the girl truthfully answered that, indeed, the flag was in ashes.

Jacob Miller's log-and-stone home, a stop on the Underground Railroad, stood at 138 East Main Street. The house was demolished in 1957, and the site is now occupied by a gas station. At the southwest corner of Main and Church Streets is an old slave block (or paving stone, depending on your source), marked by a bronze plaque.

The William Chapline house (1790 West Main Street), a limestone structure on the northeast corner of the town square, was home to Dr. A. A. Biggs, who treated the wounded and was instrumental in the creation of the Antietam National

The artillery display in front of the Antietam National Battlefield's visitors center highlights the vital role the big guns played in the fighting.

Rail fences, limestone outcroppings, and artillery were all important components of the battle fought on this ground.

The reconstructed Dunker Church marks the site of some of the war's fiercest fighting.

Cemetery. Artillery fire damaged an eastern gable of the house.

Drive through Sharpsburg and turn right onto Route 65. Turn right at the sign for Antietam National Battlefield Visitors Center and park in the lot to the left.

Antietam is one of the few battlefields that are a pure pleasure to visit. The remote site guarantees that only history enthusiasts will visit. Rarely is the park crowded, and those who arrive are there to explore Civil War history. There is little traffic congestion such as plagues Gettysburg and other battlefield parks. Perhaps the most startling aspect of the area is a complete lack of commercialization. The battlefield is intact, the area preserved as working farms. The only drawback is a nearly complete absence of hotels and restaurants, but Hagerstown and Interstates 70–81 are just up the road.

The sixteen-hundred-acre park (and still expanding through the actions of the National Park Service, the state of Maryland, and private donations) contains 97 statues and stone monuments, 300 metal interpretive markers, and 41 cannon that represent the 500 employed during the battle—270 Federal, 230 Confederate. Because of economic conditions following the Civil War, only two Southern monuments stand on the field, and both were dedicated during the Civil War Centennial. The Georgia Monument, a generic stone memorial placed on a number of battlefields, was unveiled on September 20, 1961, and the Texas Monument, a pink slab also replicated in several parks, was dedicated November 11, 1964.

The visitors center contains a twenty-six-minute orientation film and paintings, displays, and artifacts that help interpret the battle. Each year on the night of September 17, five hundred volunteers arrive for the Memorial Illumination, when 23,600 candles, one for each casualty at Antietam, are lit. It is an awesome and sobering display.

At certain times park rangers give talks at the visitors center and lead battlefield tours. Living history programs are presented during the summer. There is a nine-mile driving tour over paved roads through the battlefield, plus hiking and biking trails. Available in the visitors center are maps and brochures of the battlefield, and a ninety-minute taped driving tour is available for sale. Available for rent are portable tape players that allow visitors to use the tape outside their car at tour stops. The narrative provides a basic overview of the campaign and battle. The eleven stops feature display markers with maps, photos, and quotes. The ubiquitous metal tablets and books and booklets available for sale add as much detail as you can stand.

The Confederates occupied a four-mile-wide front on a ridge west of Antietam Creek. It stretched along the Hagerstown turnpike from the Poffenberger farm to the north to Antietam Creek to the south. The battlefield covers a twelve-square-mile area.

The geography that dictated the action of the battle is clearly visible from the visitors center. The land is composed of rolling hills—short but steep—and fields and woods. Note the limestone outcroppings that sheltered Confederates and the numerous wooden fences that supplied scant protection during the battle. Much of the open areas were wooded in 1862, and a reforestation project has been initiated. In late summer the corn grows as it did in September 1862.

The high ground of the visitors center has a wonderful view of South Mountain, where the armies fought savagely on September 14, and of most of the Antietam battlefield to the north, east, and south.

To the west is the Reel farm (5553 Mondell Road), where Confederate casualties were treated in a barn. After an exploding Union shell set the structure on fire, it burned quickly, killing a number of wounded soldiers. Only the stone foundation of the original barn remains. This was also a staging area for Confederate attacks against the West Woods.

Continue the short distance to Stop No. 1.

The Dunker Church now stands on what was the Hagerstown turnpike in 1862. Nearby are the Maryland, New York, and Ohio Monuments.

The church was constructed in 1852 as a single-room, simply furnished building. During a violent storm on May 21, 1921, the original building collapsed. A historically minded farmer gathered the bricks and stored them until a program was started to reconstruct the church, which was dedicated on September 17, 1962, the one-hundredth anniversary of the battle of Antietam. The structure looks

The area known as the North Woods was cleared a long time ago, but trees were replanted to approximate the appearance of the region during the war.

the same as it did during the battle, but the woods that then surrounded the church are gone. They were replanted in 1995. The Dunker Church was built by the German Baptist Brethren, a pacifist religious group that did not believe in ostentation. Because the building had no steeple, many Federals thought it was a school. The members believed in total immersion baptism, which explains their popular name "Dunkers." Building commissioners were Daniel Miller and Joseph Sherrick, and the land was donated by Samuel Mumma—three family names forever linked to the famous battle. Women entered through the eastern entrance, men the southwestern entrance, and they sat separately. The congregation, which built a new church in Sharpsburg in 1916, meets here once a year, on September 17.

Hit by many bullets and cannonballs, the church was subsequently used as a hospital and morgue. A New York soldier stole the pulpit Bible, which was donated forty-one years later to the Washington County Historical Society in Hagerstown.

Joseph Hooker started the battle with a fierce artillery exchange at 5 A.M., then launched his first attack at 5:30 A.M. The Dunker Church was his objective because of the Confederate artillery concentration. His eighty-five hundred men faced seventy-seven hundred Southerners. Starting from the North Woods and the Poffenberger farm, he fought through the Miller farm, the Cornfield, and the East Woods, before being repulsed at 7 A.M. by John Bell Hood, whose division was resting in reserve behind the church. After advancing through the West Woods and into the Cornfield, Hood was in turn driven back through the East Woods and Cornfield to the Hagerstown turnpike in front of the church by Joseph Mansfield's attack at 7:30 A.M. Maj. Gen. Edward Sumner's Second Corps's attack at 9 A.M. was beaten off by Lafayette McLaws and George B. Anderson. Around 9:30 A.M., after four hours of continuous slaughter, the lines ended up pretty much where they had started. This fighting for two hundred acres of land caused thousands of casualties. The Confederate commander on the left, Stonewall Jackson, remained concerned about another massive Union attack here for a number of hours. Such an effort would certainly have succeeded, but McClellan refused to renew the combat.

In front of the church near the visitors center are a number of artillery pieces that mark the location of a Confederate artillery concentration: four batteries commanded by Col. Stephen D. Lee. The guns unleashed a murderous fire on attacking Federal troops, but in turn Union guns east of the creek exacted a high toll of the gunners, marking one of the Civil War's most terrible artillery duels. Southern artillery was also arrayed west of the Dunker Church and Route 65 on Hauser Ridge.

Note the Maryland Monument, unveiled on Decoration Day, May 30, 1900, in front of a crowd of twenty-five thousand, including President William McKinley, Confederate Gens. James Longstreet and Joseph Wheeler, and Rep. George B. McClellan Jr. Honoring soldiers of both sides, the octagonal Greek temple, topped by a bronze figure of Peace sheathing her weapons, is dedicated to six Federal and two Confederate regiments of Marylanders who fought at Antietam. Four bronze bas reliefs depict scenes from the battle. Beyond it is the New York Monument (1920). The Twentieth New York Monument near the visitors center has a bronze bas relief of the regiment charging into battle. Usually overlooked on the battlefield is the Fifteenth Massachusetts Monument, topped by a mortally wounded but still defiant lion. Created by sculptor Andrew O'Connor, it was dedicated on September 17, 1900.

Continue north up Old Hagerstown Turnpike, following the arrows of the tour, and turn right onto Mansfield Avenue to Stop No. 2.

Before making the turn, to the left (west), across Route 65, is Nicodemus Hill, where fourteen pieces of Jeb Stuart's artillery, commanded by the gallant young Capt. John Pelham and protected by a cavalry regiment, plowed furrows through the flanks of Federal columns advancing from the North Woods. For unknown reasons Hooker left Pelham's guns unmolested. A number of other Confederate artillery batteries along the Hagerstown pike protected the Confederate left flank. A cavalry brigade was also stationed at the southern end of the Confederate line.

From Stop No. 2, the North Woods, Hooker launched his first fierce attack, which Jackson's men stopped in the Cornfield, half a mile south. Hooker's headquarters were to the north at the Joseph Poffenberger farm, which was also a large field hospital where Federal artillery occupying high ground anchored the Union right. Also north of the road is the Clara Barton Monument, a large marble slab erected by the American Red Cross in 1962 to honor their founder, who brought supplies to the battlefield and aided the wounded. It was the famed nurse's first battlefield experience. The monument is misplaced—it should be on the Samuel Poffenberger farm to the southeast. Other monuments here commemorate the Seventh, Fourth, Third, and Eighth Pennsylvania Regiments.

Continue following the tour route to Smoketown Road.

The Twelfth Pennsylvania Cavalry monument is to the left. North, off Smoketown Road, is the George Line farm, a private, working farm where the original house stills stands. Wounded Maj. Gen. Joseph Mansfield, commander of the Twelfth Corps, was taken there, where he died.

Turn right onto Smoketown Road.

Shortly to the left, at the intersection with Mansfield Road, is the Mansfield Monument, a cannon embedded in the ground muzzle first at the spot where Mansfield was hit. It is one of six such monuments that mark the sites where six Union general officers

The East Woods have also been replanted. It was in this area that Union Gen. Joseph Mansfield was mortally wounded.

were killed or mortally wounded at Antietam. Six others were seriously wounded. A stone obelisk honors Mansfield's memory.

Continue to Stop No. 3, the East Woods.

Mansfield's attack here led to his wounding. Coming to the relief of Hooker, to the west in the Cornfield, Mansfield's seven-thousand-man Twelfth Corps raced into the East Woods. Believing his troops were firing on friends, Mansfield rode forward and learned his mistake when a bullet hit him in the chest.

Turn right onto Cornfield Avenue, and proceed to Stop No. 4, the Cornfield.

The avenue is lined with monuments to the First New Jersey Brigade, the 137th, 128th, and 124th Pennsylvania Regiments, and the Texas and Georgia Monuments. The Indiana and New Jersey Monuments are at the end of the road on the Old Hagerstown Pike.

The Cornfield is a thirty-acre plot that was filled with tall corn plants. Here some of the Civil War's most vicious fighting occurred. Twelve or more divisions fought on this ground for three hours as each side committed fresh troops and the two armies advanced and retreated repeatedly through the field. The Cornfield changed hands six times. Artillery and rifle fire lashed the corn from all sides, and thousands of soldiers fell in close, savage fighting. Of his first attack through the Cornfield, Hooker wrote that in seconds "every stalk of corn . . . was cut as closely as could have been done by a knife, and the slain lay in rows precisely as they had stood in their ranks a few moments before."

The farm of David R. Miller, who owned the Cornfield, stands to the north along Old Hagerstown Pike. Now the property of the federal government, the original home and barns are leased out for farming. The structures were used as hospitals during the battle. One patient was George Gordon Meade.

Drive straight to the stop sign at Hagerstown Road.

To the right are the New Jersey and Indiana Monuments, and across the road is the 124th Pennsylvania Monument.

Turn left onto Old Hagerstown Pike and take the next right to the circle at Stop No. 5, the West Woods, where the Philadelphia Brigade Monument stands.

The cannon you passed marks the site where Brig. Gen. William Starke, a rising star in the ranks of the Amry of Northern Virginia and commander of the Louisiana Brigade, was mortally wounded.

When D. H. Hill begged Lee for reinforcements on the left, Hill found a concentration of artillery being established behind the West Woods and Lafayette McLaws's division, hurried from Harpers Ferry, arriving to help. At this time, around 9 A.M., Hooker and Mansfield had both been wounded, and Sumner was hurrying his Second Corps to the battlefield. Finding the East Woods quiet, Sumner raced ahead with one division, Maj. Gen. John Sedgwick's fifty-four hundred men. His other two divisions, under Maj. Gen. William H. French, would follow. Sumner hurried into a trap with McLaws and Walker on the Confederate right, Jackson in the center, and Stuart's guns, transferred to Hauser's Ridge, on the left.

As they crossed the Cornfield, the Federals were again slaughtered by Stuart's artillery on Nicodemus Hill, then all hell broke loose when the Confederates unleashed a devastating fire from three directions. Sedgwick lost 2,350 men, 44 percent of his division, in less than thirty minutes. The Confederate pursuit ended when it again encountered the fierce Union artillery fire covering the Cornfield, but the Federals failed to push beyond the church.

To the south, just north of the Dunker Church, is Confederate Avenue, a hiking trail in what was part of the West Woods. It contains monuments to the 34th New York and 125th Pennsylvania. The latter features the likeness of Color Sgt. George A. Simpson, the only actual person portrayed on a monument at Antietam. Shot through the brain and killed, he was one of eight color-bearers who fell here. This monument was unveiled on September 17, 1904, by his sister, Annie Simpson. George is buried in the Antietam National Cemetery.

Civil War accounts lead one to believe the distance from the North Woods to the Dunker Church to be longer than it actually is, but the area covers only about one thousand acres. The reality is sobering when the cost of the three-hour battle is considered.

Return to Old Hagerstown Pike and turn right, then left onto Smoketown Road and right onto Mumma Lane to Stop No. 6, the Mumma farmstead.

Samuel Mumma fled with his family when the battle started and returned to find his home and outbuildings burned. This was the only property on the battlefield purposely destroyed. Retreating Confederates torched the structures to prevent their use by Union sharpshooters. Note the family cemetery and original well house, where Confederates and Federals drank during the battle. The Mumma house and barn were rebuilt immediately after the battle and are now being restored with the original well house, smokehouse, and chicken house.

Continue to the Roulette farm, Stop No. 7.

On the way is the Old Vermont Brigade Monument. Sumner had impetuously led his first division, Sedgwick's, to disaster in the North Woods. His rapid pace left behind his following two divisions, under French and Israel B. Richardson. Reaching the East Woods, French found no trace of Sedgwick but assumed from the sounds of battle that he was west of his position, to the right. To his left French could see George S. Greene fighting near the Dunker Church. Deciding to take up a position on Greene's left, French started south at 9:30 A.M., taking his six thousand men toward the Sunken Road and away from the Confederate left flank, which could easily have been broken by his and Richardson's divisions. These Federals, advancing across the fields of the Roulette farm found their first enemy in the form of angry bees whose hives had been destroyed by artillery fire.

The pressure was now off Jackson and on Longstreet, who with Lee and D. H. Hill watched the six thousand Federals approaching from a rise on the Piper farm. A Union cannonball took off the front legs of Hill's horse, presenting an entertainingly grisly spectacle for the Confederate high command. Two other horses were shot from under Hill that day.

In 1998 the Mellon Foundation purchased the 179-acre Roulette farm, scene of some of the fiercest fighting at Antietam, and donated it to the NPS. More than ten thousand men assembled on the property to assault the Confederate position in the Sunken Road. The house was used as a Federal signal station and field hospital, and nearly seven hundred Southerners were buried in trenches on the farm. William Roulette and his wife and five children huddled in the basement with stragglers and wounded from both sides. A hiking trail is planned from Bloody Lane to the farm.

The Piper house, behind Bloody Lane and just off the Hagerstown pike a quarter mile south of the visitors center, was Longstreet's headquarters. It is presently a battlefield bed and breakfast.

Continue on the tour route and turn left onto Richardson Avenue to Stop No. 8, the Sunken Road–Bloody Lane.

The 130th Pennsylvania and 5th Maryland (U.S.) Monuments, the George Burgwyn Anderson Mortal Wounding Monument, and the 132d Pennsylvania Monument are passed. The Israel Bush Richardson Mortal Wounding Monument is near the parking area and observation tower.

The Sunken Road, six hundred yards south of the Dunker Church, extended only a mile but made three turns. Eroded by decades of use by farmers taking their grain to be milled, it was a perfect natural breastwork for D. H. Hill's men, who occupied the center of the Confederate line. His three brigades totaled twenty-five hundred men, less than half the number of attackers.

"These men are going to stay here, General," John B. Gordon had assured Lee, and later he added, "Alas! Many of the brave fellows are there now."

Gordon ordered his men to lie still in the road as he counted four lines of infantry approaching, their commander in front and bands playing martial music at the rear. The battlefield here was eerily silent until Gordon bellowed, "Fire!" The first line of Federal troops, only yards away, fell to the ground as the Confederates reloaded and fired, their line looking "like a blinding blaze of lightning," one participant recalled. In minutes French's division was decimated, losing 1,750 men. "God save my poor boys," Union Brig. Gen. Nathan Kimball muttered during the withdrawal.

Richardson's division, led by the famed Irish Brigade, followed. They were also savaged until the fog of war descended on the Confederate ranks.

After an order to redeploy a regiment was mistaken for a general retreat, the Confederates left the protection of the Sunken Road. The Federals now had the advantageous position and shot down scores of Rebels. As the Yankees charged, the Confederate center was pierced. Attacking across the Piper farm toward the Hagerstown pike and Sharpsburg, they threatened to split Lee's army in half.

Desperate situations call for desperate measures. Hill grabbed two hundred men and led them in a desperate counterattack that slowed the Union advance while Longstreet's staff officers manned abandoned pieces of artillery. Longstreet quickly organized a battery of twenty guns that forced the Federals back to a ridge beyond the Sunken Road. Four hours of desperate fighting had left five thousand casualties, including a Confederate and a Federal general dead. It was said that one could have

An observation tower at Bloody Lane affords excellent views of the battlefield and surrounding terrain. In the background is the visitors center and the New York Monument.

walked on corpses for half a mile down Bloody Lane without touching the ground.

There are a few Civil War landmarks that elicit respectful silence. Shiloh's Hornet Nest, the Mule Shoe at Spotsylvania, and the High Water Mark at Gettysburg. The Sunken Road is such a place. Descend into the road and walk its length, thinking of the roadbed carpeted in bodies, or John Gordon being wounded five times before he passed out, nearly dying to keep his word to Lee. The lane is three to six feet deep, and bodies lay three to four deep. Note the dramatic 132nd Pennsylvania Monument, a color-bearer grasping a flag by its broken staff. The incident actually occurred at Fredericksburg three months later, when a record number of color-bearers fell, but the monument was erected here.

The seventy-five-foot-tall observation tower was constructed in the 1890s by the War Department as a teaching tool. Students from the U.S. Army War College, the Military Academy at West Point, and other institutions studied battle tactics here and at other battlefields. A long, steep spiral staircase takes visitors to an observation platform where markers along the wall point out important sites on the battlefield and surrounding areas. The military also erected 236 interpretive metal signs on the battlefield.

Antietam's 104th monument, and according to the National Park Service the last, was dedicated here in October 1997. The ten-foot-high monument, composed of two blocks of granite from County Wicklow, Ireland, honors the Irish Brigade, which was decimated in attacks against the strong Confederate position. Composed mainly of Irish in the Sixty-third, Sixty-ninth, and Eighty-eighth New York and Twenty-ninth Massachusetts, it was organized in February 1862 by Thomas Francis Meagher. The brigade suffered 540 casualties with two regiments losing 60 percent of its men. Named the Forgotten Irish Monument, it weighs fifteen hundred tons. On the front is a bronze bas relief four feet wide and six feet high, which depicts the color guard of the Sixty-ninth New York in battle. As one flag-bearer falls another reaches for the banner. Eight men were killed or wounded carrying the colors. The back of the monument is adorned with a relief of Meagher and his famed medallion.

The Sunken Road approximates its appearance prior to the battle, with lush fields on either side. After the smoke had cleared from the fighting, however, it was carpeted with the bodies of Confederate infantrymen, stacked deep for half a mile.

From the Sunken Road follow the NPS tour across Route 34, with Sharpsburg to your right, and continue on Rodman Avenue past the Fiftieth Pennsylvania Monument. Below the overpass is the Joseph Sherrick farm and Otto house. Turn left to the lower bridge–Burnside Bridge (also known as the Rohrback Bridge) at Stop No. 9.

A trail leads down to the famous bridge and across to the eastern side where Maj. Gen. Ambrose E. Burnside and Brig. Gen. Jacob Cox waited half the day before attacking. Trails also lead to the Georgian Overlook, where Confederate sharpshooters denied the Federals access to the bridge for hours. The Snavely Ford Trail loop takes hikers to the site where a number of Union soldiers crossed the creek, which was fordable at many points.

Note the monuments to the two Fifty-first regiments, one from New York, the other a Pennsylvania unit, and the William McKinley Monument, one of the more unusual Civil War memorials. Future President McKinley, a nineteen-year-old commissary sergeant at Antietam, noted that the men had gone without breakfast and coffee. Under fire, without orders, and at great personal risk, McKinley

produced hot coffee and warm food for every man in his regiment at this spot after they had crossed Antietam Creek. The men cheered lustily, making McKinley the world's most famous commissary sergeant. The surprisingly large monument, thirty-three feet high and nine feet wide, was conceived just months after the popular president had been assassinated. When the state of Ohio allocated money for monuments at Antietam, each regiment received five hundred dollars. The McKinley memorial was given five thousand dollars. Another Ohio president, Rutherford B. Hayes, absent from Antietam because of wounds suffered at South Mountain, was not present, although he claimed that McKinley's exploit was "a thing that has never occurred under similar circumstances in any other army in the world."

In a battle filled with controversy and "what ifs," the largest question lies with the situation at the extreme southern end of the battle line, anchored here on Antietam Creek. The Federal Ninth Corps was commanded by Burnside who, angry at McClellan, was reluctant to give orders to Cox. Their orders were vague—to cross the lower bridge and threaten the Confederate right flank with their

12,500 men. A major mystery is when Burnside was ordered to advance. After the Civil War, McClellan revised his account to an earlier hour, which placed the blame on Burnside. Regardless of the time, Burnside dallied for hours, watching as enemy units marched off to shore up the endangered Confederate left. At length the Confederates had only five hundred men, the Second and Twentieth Georgia, under Brig. Gen. Robert Toombs, a near president of the Confederacy who was sick of army life. These men acted as sharpshooters, hidden behind stone walls, trees, and quarry pits on the crest of the ridge. Their fire was supplemented by five batteries of artillery to the rear and north, on hills around Sharpsburg.

When McClellan directly ordered an attack at 10 A.M., Burnside sent the Eleventh Connecticut to the creek, which quickly lost a third of its men. They were followed by Col. George Crook's brigade, which was also repulsed. At the same time Brig. Gen. Israel Rodman headed downstream looking for a suitable ford. In the previous two days neither McClellan nor Burnside nor Cox had scouted the terrain.

At 1 P.M. Burnside finally stormed the bridge with the Fifty-first Pennsylvania and Fifty-first New York. Meanwhile, Rodman crossed his thirty-two-hundred-man division at Snavely's Ford, one mile downstream, threatening to cut off the Confederate line of retreat. Toombs withdrew as the Federals loudly cheered their triumph. Another two hours passed before they advanced again.

Burnside Bridge is another of Montgomery County's stout stone bridges. A three spanner, 125 feet long and only 12 feet wide, it presented quite a bottleneck for soldiers attempting to cross under a deadly rifle fire. It was built in 1836 by John Weaver for twenty-three hundred dollars. The bridge has been fully restored, including a unique feature, wooden coping on top of the walls.

After the Federals organized and supplied themselves on the western bank of Antietam Creek, they started northwest through these hills toward Sharpsburg to attack the rear of the Army of Northern Virginia and sever its access to Boteler's Ford.

Retrace your path to Stop No. 10, the Final Attack, which is near the overpass, on a hill overlooking the

Union Gen. Ambrose E. Burnside wasted hours taking the bridge that now bears his name. The delay allowed A. P. Hill sufficient time to reinforce Lee from Harpers Ferry.

Sherrick farmhouse to the north and the Otto farm across the road to the south.

As fighting neared, both families fled. Joseph Sherrick secreted three thousand dollars in gold in a stone wall and retrieved it later. The few Confederates remaining in the area fought stubbornly from behind haystacks and stone walls, but they were driven back by the relentlessly advancing Federal force. Artillery batteries on this hill were limbered up and raced away to avoid capture. The red-brick Sherrick house (1830s) and wood-frame Otto house (late 1700s) are currently being restored, and orchards and other landscaping are being re-created.

Fighting occurred around the farmhouses and stone mill in the ravine below, which were prominently mentioned in accounts of the battle. Along the road are monuments to the Forty-fourth, One Hundredth, Fifty-first, and Forty-eighth Pennsylvania, the Twenty-eighth and Twenty-third Ohio, and Durrell's Battery, and the Lawrence O'Bryan Branch Death Monument.

This is the end of the NPS tour, but not ours. Continue straight on Branch Avenue to the Harpers Ferry Road–Mechanic Street and turn right. Watch closely for the small parking area to the right, then climb the footpath to the top of the hill to the Ninth New York Hawkins Zouave Regiment Monument and the Isaac Peace Rodman Mortal Wounding Monument.

After Burnside finally crossed the bridge, he advanced northwest toward Sharpsburg. This marks the farthest advance of the Federals on September 17, close to the Harpers Ferry road, which would have turned Lee's right flank and blocked his withdrawal to Boteler's Ford. As eighty-five hundred Federals marched steadily toward Sharpsburg, an anxious Lee rode atop a hill and desperately searched the horizon to the south. He spotted two bodies of troops approaching—one flying the U.S. flag, the other marching under Virginia and Confederate flags. "It is A. P. Hill from Harpers Ferry," he announced calmly.

During the previous seven hours, Hill's three-thousand-man corps had made a forced march of seventeen miles from Harpers Ferry. They crossed the Potomac at Boteler's Ford and marched southeast on Sawmill Road to encounter the Federal left flank. Hill had stripped off his coat to reveal his red-flannel battle shirt and directed his men from their marching column into line of battle without pause. The veteran Confederates ripped into the flank of the Fourth Rhode Island and Sixteenth Connecticut, raw troops barely familiar with their rifles. The Federals fled, Burnside ordered his corps to retreat, and the longest day of the Civil War ended.

When returns for Lee's thirty-five thousand soldiers came in, he had lost 10,316 men—1,546 killed outright. Of McClellan's 75,000, 12,411 had been killed, wounded, or were missing. The most

From his headquarters in a grove of trees, Robert E. Lee skillfully deployed and shifted his army to counter the overwhelming numbers commanded by George B. McClellan.

significant figure was the 20,000 troops he had failed to commit to battle. McClellan could have easily won the battle by reinforcing the three attacks against the Confederate left, the breakthrough at the Sunken Road in the center, or Burnside's advance on the Confederate right.

This is a fine observation point for the National Cemetery, Burnside Bridge, and Elk Ridge, the Federal signal station. The upended cannon marks where Rodman was killed and a monument honors the Sixteenth Connecticut, a group of college students armed only three days. The Sixteenth lost 226 men.

Continue north on Mechanic Street to Main. The corner to the left was the site of the Grove house. Turn left onto Main and pass Saint Paul's Episcopal Church on the right. A side trip leads to two interesting sites. A right from Main onto Potomac Street, followed by a left onto Chapline Street, and a right on Snyder's Landing Road leads to Barron's C&O Canal Museum and Country Store (301-432-8726), where artifacts and photos explore local heritage and the history of the canal.

A mile downstream of Snyder's Landing, at Mile 176 on the C&O Towpath, is Killiansburg Cave, one of several in the area. The shallow cave, 20 feet high, 30 feet wide, and 35 feet deep, is found 50 feet up a steep, 75-foot-high cliff that towers over the Potomac River. Citizens east of Antietam Creek, in Boonsboro and Keedysville, not threatened by cannon fire, crowded hilltops to observe the battle, but those west of the creek, particularly in Sharpsburg, were endangered by the long-range Federal artillery. Civilians huddled in stone basements or these caves.

Continue straight on Route 34 and pull over to the right at the site of Lee's headquarters.

Walk up the path to the stone slab with a bronze plaque, placed on September 19, 1936. This was an oak grove when Lee and his staff set up headquarters here on September 15–19, 1862. From the high ground to the rear Lee could observe the action along the Hagerstown pike. Nearby was a hill, on which the national cemetery now rests, where Lee could observe the rest of his line. From this central location he dispatched troops arriving from Harpers Ferry, including A. P. Hill's.

Continue west on Route 34 toward Shepherdstown. On the left (17201 Sharpsburg Pike–Route 34) is the Steven Grove farm–Mount Airy (1820), an impressive mansion marked by interpretive signs.

When Lincoln visited McClellan to urge an immediate advance into Virginia, he met with the general here, where Alexander Gardner photographed the pair on October 3. Fitz John Porter and others were also present. The farm was the headquarters of Porter and a hospital following the battle. Lincoln visited the wounded and shook hands with Confederates as well as Federal casualties, "with no malice," a witness reported. It was a touching moment that left many in tears. Because Confederates had retreated across the rear of the property, the estate is also known as Retreat Glen. The state of Maryland and Save Historic Antietam Foundation have recently preserved ninety-two acres of the property and have established a parking area and signage.

To the right of the road was the railroad station of the Shenandoah Valley Railroad, established in 1880 and now the Norfolk and Southern line. It was constructed originally to accommodate visitors to the battlefield. Veterans were welcomed by a monument consisting of eight artillery tubes arranged in a pyramid with a platform made of cannonballs on top. A gravel path, with a curb of local slate, led to the national cemetery. The monument was dismantled in the 1960s and only the cement base remains. The slate, however, is incorporated in walls on both sides of Main Street and in the benches along the walk.

Continue west on Route 34. Just before the Potomac River Bridge turn left onto Canal Road beside the historical markers describing Boteler's Ford. Turn right into the C&O parking area, cross the canal, and make your way down to the Potomac River.

Boteler's Ford is just downstream, where A. P. Hill crossed on September 17 and the entire Confederate army departed on September 19. At Mile 70.8 on the towpath is Miller's Sawmill and Turning Basin, powered by canal water. During the battle of Antietam, Lee's chief engineer was stationed in a stone house

there to monitor the water level of the Potomac in case the Confederates were forced to withdraw.

As a side trip you may retrace A. P. Hill's route by continuing down Canal Road and turning left onto Miller's Sawmill Road, a black snake of a road, then turning left at the Harpers Ferry Road–Mechanic Street to the Zouave Monument on the right.

Return to Route 34 and turn left. On the right is Ferry Hill Place (1812), now headquarters for the C&O Canal Park.

Henry Kyd Douglas was born in Shepherdstown but grew up here on a plantation where a mix of slaves and hired help grew wheat and corn. On September 14, 1862, Douglas, staff officer to Stonewall Jackson, secured his superior's permission to leave Halltown, just outside Harpers Ferry during the Confederate siege, and visit his parents here. One month later Douglas's father was arrested on false charges of spying and communicating with Confederate forces. He was incarcerated in Baltimore's Fort McHenry for six weeks. During the march to Gettysburg, Confederate Gen. Edward "Allegheny" Johnston established his headquarters here, and Douglas visited again, finding the plantation trashed and outbuildings torched by Federal occupiers. Union troops returned on June 18, 1863, and confined the family to the home.

Because of his intimate knowledge of the area, on September 16, the day before the battle of Antietam, Jackson tasked Douglas with siting the artillery of his corps and establishing routes for resupplying and shifting them.

Continue on Route 34 and cross the Potomac River. A covered bridge stood here until Confederates burned it in 1861. In West Virginia this highway becomes Route 480 and passes Shepherdstown College.

Shepherdstown is the oldest inhabited community in West Virginia, founded in 1734. A fort built during the French and Indian War stood at the site of the college, which owns McMurran Hall (King Street, 1859). Constructed as the town hall and library, it was used as a Civil War hospital and the Jefferson County Courthouse (1866–67) until the official one in Charles Town could be rebuilt. To honor her father, who was a Civil War enthusiast, actress Mary Tyler Moore donated the Conrad Shindler house to the college to serve as the George Tyler Moore Center for the Study of the Civil War. The Moores are direct descendants of Shindler, who built the house.

The Entler Hotel (1793, corner of King and German Streets, 304-876-0910) now houses the headquarters of the Historic Shepherdstown Historical Commission and a museum containing Civil War artifacts. During the Civil War it sheltered troops from both sides. In a one-room museum behind the Entler is housed a replica of the Ramsey steamboat, which James Ramsey built in 1786, twenty years before Robert Fulton built his. At the Sheets house (northwest corner of German and King Streets) rifle stocks were produced for the Harpers Ferry Armory. When it was destroyed during the war, the owner of this house constructed a picket fence around his property with surplus stocks. Elmwood (1797, near town off Route 17) was a Civil War hospital.

The towering monument along the Potomac River honors Ramsey. Shepherdstown also has one of the largest overshot waterwheels in the country.

At the intersection turn left onto German Street. Past the courthouse and through the historic downtown, the route becomes River Road.

Several miles downstream is the ford variously known as Pack Horse, Boteler's, Blackford's, Shepherdstown, and Swearingman's. First used in the 1720s, it was the best ford between Harpers Ferry and Williamsport to the west and saw extensive use until the covered bridge was erected at Shepherdstown in 1850. During September 16–17 five divisions under Jackson arrived from Harpers Ferry and forded here, the last of A. P. Hill's men near the end of the battle. Lee's entire army waded the Potomac River here into Virginia on September 20, covered by forty-four cannon and two depleted companies on the cliffs above. Cavalry sat astride their horses in the river holding torches aloft and an anxious Lee kept watch through the night as ambulances, supply wagons, walking wounded, infantry, and cavalry crossed, exclaiming at the end, "Thank God!" When a band started playing "Maryland, My

The ruins of the mill at Boteler's Ford can be found along the Potomac River, near Shepherdstown, West Virginia. The ground was a battlefield two days after the fighting at Sharpsburg, when McClellan mounted a timid pursuit of Lee's army.

Maryland," weary soldiers shouted it down, demanding "Carry Me Back to Old Virginny." Civil War armies used this ford at least ten times during the war.

Perched on the riverbank to the left and the cliff to the right of the road are the extensive ruins of an old mill. Erected as a flour mill in 1826, it was converted to a cement mill in 1829 to supply the heavy requirements of C&O Canal construction. Known as Botelers Hydraulic Lime Cement Mill, Federals burned the works on August 19, 1861. On September 20, the day after Lee withdrew across the ford, three Union brigades pursued up the bluff. Most withdrew, but one regiment stubbornly refused to retreat and was decimated. Union soldiers were sheltered in the arched kilns during the battle of Cement Mill, also known as the battle of Shepherdstown. Union artillery deployed on the heights across the Potomac River bombarded Confederate and Federal alike as Yankee soldiers tumbled down the sheer cliff in a scene reminiscent of Ball's Bluff. The Federals, the 118th Pennsylvania, also known as the Corn Exchange Regiment, of Fitz John Porter's corps, were largely armed with defective rifles. The white water upstream marks the dam that provided water power for the mill. The Federals recrossed there, where the water is three feet deep, but as they forded the river Confederate sharpshooters plagued them from the cover of the cement mill. The mill was rebuilt after the war and destroyed by flood in 1889.

In July 1864 Franz Sigel's Federals evacuated Martinsburg and crossed here to reach Harpers Ferry; they were followed by John B. Gordon's Confederates.

Five historical markers describing the Civil War fording and fighting here once stood at the nearby intersection of River Road and Trough Road, but they have been removed.

The gravel Trough Road is where A. P. Hill's division arrived from Harpers Ferry after a forced march of seventeen miles. The usual twelve-mile route between Harpers Ferry and Sharpsburg lay on the northern bank of the Potomac via the Harpers Ferry road, but Federal troops were swarming in that area. Directions for following Hill's route from Harpers Ferry are given at the end of the Harpers Ferry tour guide. Although there is nothing to be seen, some of us get a thrill just from riding historic trails.

Return to Route 480 in Shepherdstown and turn left to Elmwood Cemetery, which appears on the right.

At the front is the Confederate section containing 106 known Confederates and 56 unknowns from eight Southern states. Another 90 Confederate veterans, primarily locals who served in cavalry units, are buried elsewhere in the cemetery.

When Lee retreated through Shepherdstown, many of his most seriously wounded were left behind, and the town became a vast hospital. Add Shepherdstown to the long list of Southern communities who claim to have observed the first Memorial Day. Theirs, called Confederate Decoration Day, was first held in October 1862 only weeks after Antietam. In 1868 the Southern Soldiers Memorial Association purchased this land and reinterred those who had died locally and a number of Confederate dead from the battlefield at Antietam. Other Confederate dead were buried in Frederick and 2,447 in Hagerstown (for details of the latter, see *The Storm Tide,* the next volume in this series). The soldiers cemetery was dedicated on June 6, 1870, in front of thirty-five hundred people. The 144 headstones were added in 1884.

Behind the graves and up the slope is a memorial honoring local Confederate dead, a draped obelisk dedicated by the Sons of Confederate Veterans in September 1937. Also there is a monument to the Stonewall Brigade, composed of long concrete slabs on which are mounted five bronze plaques listing 577 men who served in the famed unit.

Near the rear of the cemetery is the large gravestone of Henry Kyd Douglas, who grew up just across the Potomac at Ferry Hill, attended John Brown's trial, and became Jackson's youngest staff officer. Jackson's assistant inspector general at Antietam, Douglas used his knowledge of local geography to place Jackson's artillery advantageously. He was twice wounded then captured at Gettysburg. Exchanged, he raided Washington with Jubal Early in 1864 and commanded A. P. Hill's Light Brigade before surrendering with Lee at Appomattox. After the Civil War, Douglas was arrested in Washington for having his photograph taken in Confederate uniform. He testified at the trial of the Lincoln conspirators before moving to Hagerstown, where he practiced law and served as a judge. Like Confederate Gen. Joseph Wheeler, Douglas was appointed a brigadier general during the Spanish-American War but poor health prevented his active participation. When George McClellan was the featured speaker at Antietam in 1885, he and Douglas walked the battlefield together. McClellan died less than a year later. Douglas never married and died in 1903.

On the left as you approach Douglas's marker is the grave of Alexander R. Boteler, a U.S. and a Confederate congressman and designer of the Great Seal of the Confederacy. He owned the cement mill on the Potomac River that figured prominently in the battle at the ford bearing his name. Federal Maj. Gen. David Hunter later burned his house.

Across from Douglas's grave is that of Edmund Lee, a relative of Robert E. Lee. After Hunter burned their house, Lee's wife wrote him a letter and warned:

> Your name will stand on History's pages as the Hunter of weak women, and innocent children; the Hunter to destroy defenseless villages and beautiful homes—to torture afresh the agonized hearts of widows . . . the Hunter with the relentless heart of a wild

beast, the face of a fiend, and the form of a man. Oh, Earth, behold the monster! Can I say "God forgive you"? No prayer can be offered for you! Were it possible for human lips to raise your name heavenward, angels would thrust the foul thing back again, and demons claim their own. The curse of thousands, the scorn of the manly and upright and the hatred of the true and honorable, will follow you and yours through all time, and brand your name infamy! Infamy!

Also buried in Elmwood is Confederate Brig. Gen. William W. Kirkland, born February 13, 1833, at Hillsboro, North Carolina. He was a West Point dropout thrice wounded while fighting at First Manassas, in the Valley campaign, at Gettysburg, Bristoe Station, Cold Harbor, Fort Fisher, and Bentonville. After living in Savannah, New York City (where his daughter Odette Tyler was a famous actress on Broadway), and Shepherdstown, he died at a soldiers home in Washington, D.C., on May 12, 1915. Four Confederate colonels are also buried here.

A Tour of Harpers Ferry and John Brown's Raid

ALTHOUGH STONEWALL JACKSON and A. P. Hill marched from Harpers Ferry to Antietam, our tour reverses the process and takes a different route, along the northern bank of the Potomac River to visit the Kennedy farm, John Brown's operational base, and to follow his route to Harpers Ferry. After examining the historic sites and natural wonders of Harpers Ferry, we continue to Charles Town to explore the imprisonment, trial, and execution of Brown.

To reach Harpers Ferry the traditional way, from the Antietam National Battlefield Park Visitors Center, return on Route 65 to Main Street–Route 34 and turn right onto Main. Turn left onto Mechanic Street, which becomes Harpers Ferry Road. Hang on for a rolling, twisting ride and pay close attention to stay on Harpers Ferry Road. Pass the Hawkins-Zouave Monument on the left and Miller's Sawmill Road on the right. Three miles south of Sharpsburg the road crosses Antietam Creek on another historic stone bridge, Antietam Iron Works Bridge, a graceful four-arch span built in 1832 by John Weaver. The Harpers Ferry Road turns left past the substantial remains of several lime kilns.

This is the village of Antietam, site of a forge established in 1750. Water backed up by a twenty-foot-high dam provided the power to one of America's first ironworks, organized in 1765. A bed of iron ore is nearby. Local hardwoods were cooked into charcoal, and area limestone provided the flux. A water wheel twenty feet across and four feet wide ran the operation. Iron produced here was used during the American Revolution and in James Ramsey's steamboat. By the Civil War fifty tons of pig iron were pro-

duced weekly, and a dozen other mills had been built—rolling, grist, spinning, woolen, slitting, flour, saw, hemp, shingle, cooperage, sheet iron, and paddle. One facility produced stoves, and a nail factory produced five hundred kegs weekly. By the

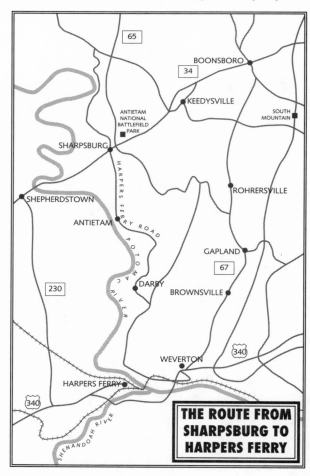

THE ROUTE FROM SHARPSBURG TO HARPERS FERRY

Antietam Village was an industrial center before the Civil War. These are the massive remains of the ironworks.

John Brown launched his raid on Harpers Ferry from the Kennedy farm in southern Maryland.

1880s eight to ten tons of cast iron were produced daily in works that employed fifty laborers.

The Federal Ninth Corps camped here after Antietam. During the Monocacy campaign John B. Gordon's Confederates camped nearby and swam in the mill pond. Antietam Creek, which flows into the Potomac River nearby, four miles downstream of Shepherdstown, crosses the C&O Canal on a three-arch stone aqueduct. A cholera epidemic here killed hundreds of Irish workmen during its construction.

Continue south on Harpers Ferry Road, which winds along the flank of Elk Ridge to the left. Pleasant Valley separates it from South Mountain (a part of the Blue Ridge Mountains, farther to the left, which is east). At the intersection with Chestnut Grove Road, turn left to the Kennedy farm, on the left.

This rustic, two-story log-and-stone structure was rented for nine months at a cost of thirty-five dollars on July 3, 1859, by Isaac Smith, the alias used by John Brown in the guise of a mineral prospector. During the following months twenty-one men filtered in by night. Brown's group aroused local curiosity because it included blacks, but most of the men were concealed in the attic during daylight and no visitors were allowed. While Brown plotted the raid, his daughter Annie cooked for the group. His son John Jr. raised money and bought arms in the North. Weapons were shipped to Chambersburg, Pennsylvania, where Brown picked them up in a

wagon. The raiding party of nineteen left for Harpers Ferry at 8 P.M. on October 16, 1859, rifles hidden beneath their coats and two hundred rifles, one thousand pikes, and sledgehammers and crowbars covered in a wagon.

The house, which has recently been restored and furnished with period furnishings listed on an inventory made immediately after Brown's arrest, is open for tours. Lifelike figures of Brown and his raiders re-create the scene. The new owner and others believe the farm is haunted. They hear snoring, muttering, and thumping from the attic, and visitors report a strong sense of being watched.

The Chestnut Grove road was the route taken by Federal Col. Benjamin F. Davis and 1,510 cavalry to escape Jackson's trap at Harpers Ferry. Lafayette McLaws crossed South Mountain at Brownsville and Crampton's Gaps into Pleasant Valley, then ascended Elk Ridge at Solomon's Gap, across the ridge and farther south. The two Confederate brigades made slow progress along the narrow wilderness trail. On September 13 they dislodged the Federals at the southern end of Elk Ridge, which is Maryland Heights and dominates Harpers Ferry.

Return to the Harpers Ferry Road and turn left onto it.

This approach to Harpers Ferry was used by the Federals following Antietam. Jackson and A. P. Hill came to Harpers Ferry south of the Potomac River and marched to Antietam along the south bank of the Potomac, crossing the river at Boteler's Ford just below Shepherdstown.

At the base of the ridge on the right is the Potomac River and limited parking for the C&O Canal towpath at Lock 33. Along the towpath are the remains of canal locks, dams, crossover bridges, and iron-ore quarries. Trails lead up onto Maryland Heights, which towers to the left. To the right across the Potomac is Harpers Ferry and the site of bridges destroyed repeatedly during the Civil War. Today only a railroad bridge and a pedestrian footspan cross the river there, and we must take a very round-about route to Harpers Ferry.

There are four separate battery sites on the slopes of Maryland Heights, which rises to a 1,448-foot summit. All can be reached via NPS hiking trails, which were military roads built in 1862. Note that these trails are steep and strenuous, and portions of the fortifications will be covered with vegetation much of the year; however, wonderful views of the surrounding natural beauty presented by the ridges and the river confluence six hundred feet below can always be enjoyed.

First, in order, is the naval battery, then the six-gun or 30-pounder battery, the 100-pounder battery, and the stone fort ruins. The naval battery, established in May 1862 in reaction to Jackson's Shenandoah Valley rampage, was initially manned by a detail of three hundred sailors and marines from the Washington Naval Yard. It contained three coastal guns, two 9-inch Dahlgrens and a 50-pounder, and four 12-pounder howitzers. The battery commanded Loudoun Heights and Bolivar Heights to the south and west. Originally protected by sandbags, the three-sided earthwork was added in July 1863. Here and at other places on the mountain are the remains of magazines. These storage areas for gunpowder and ammunition were eight-foot-deep, twenty-by-thirty-foot excavations covered with heavy timber and a foot or more of soil. The battery existed when Jackson besieged Harpers Ferry and was commanded by Union Capt. Eugene McGrath, but the big guns could not be brought to bear on the Confederates advancing from the north.

The six-gun 30-pounder battery contained six 30-pounder Parrott rifles and twelve 24-pounder siege pieces. Long lines of trenches and stone breastworks supported this position.

The 100-pounder, a huge 9,700-pound 9-inch Dahlgren, was replaced by a 5-ton Parrott rifle, the largest at Harpers Ferry. It was sited here in June 1863 and fired 100-pound shells with a range of more than two miles. This cannon, mounted on iron runners so it could fire in any direction, was trained on Early during his three-day demonstration in early July 1864. The work, started in October 1862, made Harpers Ferry more secure. Union soldiers camped on the ridge from November 1863 until the end of the war.

In the months following Antietam, the most extensive work atop Maryland Heights, the stone fort, was added. A new artillery battery, mounting nine 30-pounder Parrott rifles and six other guns, covered Loudoun Heights, Bolivar Heights, and the rear of Elk Ridge to prevent an attack from the north, like McLaws's successful assault in September 1862. An infantry blockhouse, measuring forty by one hundred feet, occupied the summit. It was protected by an exterior fort consisting of a double line of rifle pits, which measured ten feet high, with a wide exterior ditch. To prevent a flanking maneuver like the one that enabled the Confederates to seize the Union fortifications on Maryland Heights, a stone breastwork was extended five hundred feet down the ridge to the west.

Overlooks provide dramatic panoramic views of Harpers Ferry, the river below, and the surrounding ridges. The trails are steep, not much improved from the time Lincoln visited the mountain on October 2, 1862. His lieutenant guide claimed "Abraham backed out" when the path became nearly vertical.

A poor trail from Lock 36 leads up to Fort Duncan, an earthwork established in 1864 on Huckleberry Hill. It had a fifteen-foot-high wall, a wide exterior ditch, sixteen cannon, and three ammunition magazines. This was the last defense added at Harpers Ferry, part of a master plan designed a year earlier by Brig. Gen. John G. Barnard, who constructed the extensive and intricate defenses of Washington, D.C. Fort Duncan protected the right flank of the Maryland Heights defenses and was connected to the other works by a chain of breastworks and infantry trenches. The National Park Service, which owns three hundred acres of the area, has recently cleared vegetation from the land and established interpretive trails to Fort Duncan.

After McClellan occupied Harpers Ferry in the fall of 1862, his engineers surveyed and mapped the ridges surrounding Harpers Ferry and set out strong supporting defenses. Thousands of men and contrabands began fortifying key heights to the point of invincibility. They cleared trees from the slopes, constructed earthworks, dry moats, and magazines and built roads. Several dozen siege guns were emplaced, pulled into position by forty mules and horses and one hundred to two hundred men. The strength of the fortifications might have influenced Lee to start for Gettysburg by crossing the river at Williamsport rather than here.

Digging graves in the thin, rocky soil around Harpers Ferry was nearly impossible. After the 1862 siege Federal soldiers buried their dead in a mass grave placed in a depression atop Maryland Heights. According to reports, they cremated Confederate casualties.

In July 1864 Confederate Lt. Gen. Jubal Early took the Second Corps of the Army of Northern Virginia up the Shenandoah Valley to divert Union troops from Petersburg. As he neared Harpers Ferry on July 4, the Federals withdrew across the Potomac to these strong defensive positions on Maryland Heights, destroying the railroad and wagon bridges in their wake. Federal Brig. Gen. Max Weber—reinforced when his theater commander, Maj. Gen. Franz Sigel, arrived from Martinsburg—commanded thirty-five hundred men, six regiments, and forty big guns atop the ridge. Early had no thought of assaulting the Federals, satisfying himself with looting the vast Union supply depot and marching up the Potomac River to Boteler's Ford, as A. P. Hill had done two years earlier. He marched east across South Mountain and through Frederick, fighting the battle of Monocacy on July 9, before being turned away on July 12 by Fort Stevens at Washington, D.C.

On the north bank of the Potomac River, between Harpers Ferry and Fort Duncan, is John Brown's Cave, where legend but certainly not reality maintains that Brown and his men plotted their attack.

Continue in the same direction of travel, and Harpers Ferry Road becomes Sandy Hook Road as it passes through that community on an extremely narrow road sandwiched on a ledge between the cliffs of Maryland Heights and the highway, canal, and river. Pass under U.S. 340, and at the stop sign, turn left onto Keep Tryst Road. At the next stop sign turn left onto U.S. 340 West to Harpers Ferry. After you cross the Potomac River, Loudoun Heights will loom to your left and a parking area is to the right.

John Brown and three of his men lived in Sandy Hook before moving to the Kennedy farm. The marines sent to capture him disembarked from the railroad there on October 16, 1859.

Military roads had been cut up the slopes of Loudoun Heights thirty years before the Civil War, and half the timber had been harvested for the charcoal used in the factories and for heating buildings and homes. The ridge was covered by a heavy growth of underbrush and young trees when Jackson cleared an area twelve hundred yards long and three hundred yards wide near the summit and constructed three log blockhouses in 1861. In 1862 Confederate Gen. John Walker marched through Frederick and Licksville, crossed the Potomac downstream at Hillsboro, east of Point of Rocks, gained access to the summit by the old timber roads, and found the ridge undefended. He quickly dragged cannon up the steep mountain to shell the Federals in the town below. Most of the guns were on a rocky shelf halfway up the slope, but a few were hauled to the crest. On September 14 Walker was the first to open fire on Harpers Ferry.

Between September 22 and December 11, 1862, after the Federals had reoccupied Harpers Ferry, the Second Division of the Twelfth Corps completely cleared the ridge of trees, improved the roads, and built a series of thirty-five stone fortifications and numerous rifle pits along the crest, where a signal station was also established. The division camped here. The only Confederate threat occurred on January 10, 1864, when John S. Mosby unsuccessfully attacked a Union cavalry camp.

A trail from Harpers Ferry crosses the Shenandoah River on the U.S. 340 bridge and extends up Loudoun Heights. There is limited parking at two locations along U.S. 340 at the base of the ridge.

Three overlooks provide panoramic views of Harpers Ferry, the river, and surrounding ridges. Stone works remain scattered across the summit. The Appalachian Trail follows the Virginia–West Virginia border along Loudoun Heights.

Continue toward Harpers Ferry on U.S. 340 across the Shenandoah River and past the entrance to Harpers Ferry National Park. Turn right to Harpers Ferry at the sign, and the local visitors center will be to your left.

This is Whitman Avenue. Turn left onto Prospect Street at a sign that reads "1862 Surrender Site Bolivar Heights," and drive to the parking area for Bolivar Heights on the left.

Jackson was at Harpers Ferry three times during the Civil War. He briefly commanded Confederate troops here from April 28, 1861, just ten days after the Federals abandoned the place, until Joseph Johnston arrived. He remained to train a number of troops during the next six weeks. From one of the many trains his men stopped here, Jackson found his famous mount, Little Sorrel. Raised by Noah Collins in Somers, Connecticut, the horse had been sold to the U.S. Army in 1861 and seized in September by the Southerners. Jackson had intended to send the horse to his wife, Mary Anna, as a gift, but he decided to keep it after he noted its calm nature. The reddish brown gelding "could eat a ton of hay or live on cobs," Henry Kyd Douglas wrote. Jackson was shot from Little Sorrel at Chancellorsville in May 1863. The horse joined Jackson's widow at the Morrison farm in North Carolina and lived to the age of thirty-six. The hide was stuffed and mounted on a frame that is still displayed at the Virginia Military Institute, and the bones were only recently buried beside Jackson's statue there. On one sheer side of Stone Mountain near Atlanta, Georgia, Jackson rides Little Sorrel forever.

After battles at McDowell, Front Royal, and Winchester, Jackson returned to Harpers Ferry on May 29, 1862, with seventeen thousand men. He withdrew when three separate Union armies approached the Shenandoah Valley behind him, but he continued his famous Valley campaign, which included the battles of Cross Keys and Port Republic.

In September 1862 Jackson rapidly marched his command from Frederick to Boonsboro and crossed the Potomac into Virginia at Williamsport, then occupied abandoned Martinsburg and approached Harpers Ferry from the west.

From the parking area an asphalt trail leads half a mile along earthworks and interpretive markers to a six-gun battery. When Maj. Gen. Philip H. Sheridan arrived at Harpers Ferry in August 1864, his troops built a two-mile-long earthwork to connect infantry trenches with the artillery redoubt. There are grand views of the surrounding ridges. Face Harpers Ferry as Jackson did. Loudoun Heights, occupied by Walker, is on the right, southeast across the Shenandoah River; McLaws held Maryland Heights, on the left, to the north across the Potomac River; and Jackson was behind to the west on the next elevation, Schoolhouse Ridge. A. P. Hill secured an advanced position on the Federal

In 1862 these earthworks at Bolivar Heights (below left) provided little defense for the Union garrison at Harpers Ferry, which surrendered after a day's bombardment. The view from the heights (below right) includes Maryland Heights to the left, Loudon Heights to the right, and the confluence of the Potomac and Shenandoah Rivers in the center, beyond Harpers Ferry.

left near the Shenandoah River from which he prepared to launch the assault.

Most of Dixon S. Miles's troops occupied earthworks here on Bolivar Heights and cowered behind them or in gullies as artillery fire rained down from the three ridges surrounding Harpers Ferry. There was no escape from the shelling; shots arced over Harpers Ferry and plunged down on Bolivar Heights. Although the only practical direction of attack was from the west, this important position was not fortified until days before the Confederates arrived. On September 13 Jackson, with the largest Confederate force, faced Miles directly. The bombardment started September 14, and on the following morning Miles and his officers assembled here and unanimously agreed to surrender at 9 A.M., just before he was killed. A short surrender ceremony was held here on September 15. A. P. Hill paroled eleven thousand Federals, which was the largest surrender of U.S. troops until Corregidor fell during World War II. Also seized were 73 cannon; 12,693 rifles, carbines, and pistols; 200 wagons; and vast stores of supplies. Federal losses included 44 killed and 173 wounded. Confederate casualties totaled 283.

Several weeks later Abraham Lincoln reviewed part of McClellan's army, sixty thousand men, at this site. A year earlier, on October 16, 1861, Confederate Lt. Turner Ashby's five hundred men fought an equal number of Union troops under Col. John Geary on this property and in the streets below before withdrawing after the battle of Bolivar Heights.

On August 6, 1864, Sheridan accepted command of the Union forces gathered in Harpers Ferry. By September he led fifty-seven thousand men against Lt. Gen. Jubal Early's thirteen thousand. Ordered to make the Shenandoah Valley "a desert," Sheridan complied, burning two thousand barns and twelve hundred flour mills and destroying hundreds of miles of railroad, not to mention staggering quantities of food and uncounted livestock. The estimated damage was thirty-five million dollars.

Return to Whitman and turn left onto it. Whitman becomes Washington and then High Street as the road wends down to the Point.

On Washington Street in Bolivar is Jackson's headquarters, now a private home, and Bolivar Methodist

The Point in Harpers Ferry offers this view of the joining of the Potomac and Shenandoah Rivers. This water was harnessed to provide the power for the area's industries.

Church, a Civil War hospital. The site of Miles's mortal wounding is near Bolivar Junior High School. The Barbour house (1848) hosted Miles and Second Corps commander Edwin V. Sumner.

From Washington, a right on Jackson leads to Camp Hill, between Bolivar Heights and Harpers Ferry. It is the site of armory buildings, Civil War training fields, Union occupation facilities, and the campus of Storer College. Many of the buildings were severely damaged. Stop and read the interpretive markers there and throughout the Harpers Ferry area. The north wing of Anthony Hall is Building No. 25 (1847), where the superintendent of the armory lived. While it was being used as headquarters by the Second Corps following Antietam, Lincoln spent the night of October 1, 1862.

Outside Anthony Hall on May 30, 1881, the fourteenth anniversary of Storer College, Frederick Douglass spoke on the subject of John Brown. One attendee was Andrew Hunter, who had successfully prosecuted Brown. Here on August 17, 1906, the one hundredth anniversary of Brown's birth, were Louis Douglass, Frederick's son; Henrietta Leary Evans, whose brother and nephew died during Brown's raid; and W. E. B. DeBois. In 1903 Storer College raised funds to purchase John Brown's "fort," which was then neglected and decaying at a site overlooking the Shenandoah River three miles from Harpers Ferry. From 1909 until 1968 the building, housing a museum, was near Anthony Hall.

From the parking area turn right onto Fillmore, then left in front of Anthony Hall. A right back onto Fillmore leads past three more armory buildings. First is the Morrell house (1858), Building No. 30, constructed as quarters for the paymaster's clerk. Next is the Brackett house (1858), Building No. 31, quarters for the superintendent's clerk, a two-story, eleven-room brick house used today by the NPS. It was occupied by Union troops before September 1862, and the recent removal of layers of paint and wallpaper has revealed numerous signatures, dates, and a sketch of a Zouave soldier in his unique uniform on the original plaster wall. Executed in pencil and simple fireplace charcoal, the drawings are found up to the twelve-foot ceiling. Additional graffiti is believed to be in every room. A sample of the artwork is preserved under plexiglas in the master armorer's house in the lower town. Finally is the Lockwood house (1847), the paymaster's quarters. The four buildings are now used by the National Park Service. Until recently the Mather Training School for NPS workers was headquartered here. It has since moved to the Monocacy National Battlefield Park. Federal Brig. Gen. Henry H. Lock-

wood lived here in 1863, and it became Sheridan's headquarters in August 1864. Neglect, abuse, and shelling at several times during the war had ravaged the structure, leaving only the battered walls, but the building saw further service. When the Civil War ended, there were an estimated fifty thousand freed slaves in the Shenandoah Valley. Many had gathered in Harpers Ferry for the safety provided by Union forces. Church groups fed and clothed them, tasks assumed after the war by the Freedmen's Bureau. Late in 1864 Julia Mann started a school for runaway slaves in the Lockwood house. After the war the government donated the four buildings—Lockwood house, Brackett house, Morell house, and Anthony Hall—to help establish Storer College, which educated African Americans for forty-eight years.

Return to Washington-High Street via Columbia, Gilmore, McDowell, or Jackson Streets, and turn right onto Washington-High.

Near the intersection of High Street and Shenandoah Street at the Point, note the John Brown Wax Museum

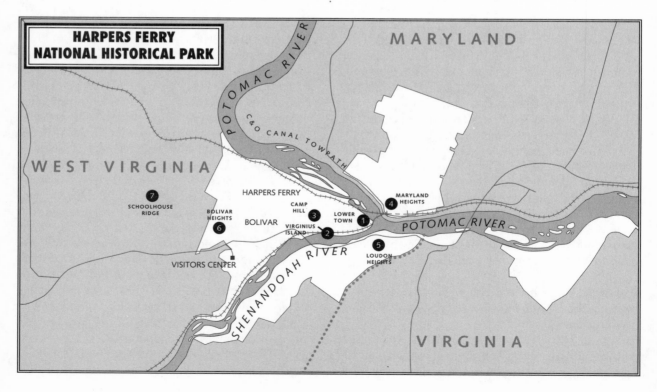

to the left, a Civil War museum (Nichols-Williams Building, 1896) and an African-American museum to the right and the Storer College Museum (1840) to the left. You may return to the ones that interest you. At the stop sign turn left onto Shenandoah Street, where local resident Thomas Boerly was killed by Brown's men on October 17, 1859. Note the John Brown Museum on your left before turning left onto Potomac Street. The original site of John Brown's Fort, then known as the armory engine house, was to the right at the entrance to the armory. Note the Hayward Shepherd Monument on the left, a source of continuing controversy. Erected in 1931 by the UDC and SCV, the large stone honors the black man killed at the start of John Brown's raid. Find a parking space along Potomac Street.

If you have picked the right time, early or on a weekday, you will probably find parking near the Point. If it is a heavy traffic time, continue to the Point and turn right to follow Shenandoah Street past the industrial works on Virginius Island on the left and follow the signs for Harpers Ferry National Historical Park to the visitors center and take the shuttle into Harpers Ferry. The visitors center has a number of historical markers that point out important geographical points in the area and a seven-minute orientation film.

A new visitors center here in the lower town also has a film and interactive displays. On High Street is an even newer museum devoted to the September 1864 siege and surrender of Harpers Ferry.

The U.S. Armory grounds contained eighteen structures—rolling mills, boring mills, grinding mills, shops, storehouses, and other buildings. After Congress established a national armory at Springfield, Massachusetts, President George Washington established a second one here, where the confluence of the Potomac and Shenandoah Rivers supplied limitless water power. Harpers Ferry also occupied a secure inland location near supplies of iron ore and trees for conversion into charcoal, and it was sited along a major river near Washington, D.C. The natural gap cut through the Blue Ridge Mountains by the rivers, and its position at the head of the Shenandoah Valley made this a transportation locus that early attracted a canal and railroad.

In 1796 the U.S. government purchased 125 acres on the Potomac side of the peninsula formed by the rivers. Three years later construction started on what was called the U.S. Armory and Arsenal at Harpers Ferry. The first weapons were produced in 1802, and by 1810 ten thousand rifles, muskets, and pistols were being produced annually. Between 1845 and 1854 the facility was expanded and modernized, with stout buildings of cast-iron frames and brick constructed on stone foundations. Between 1799 and 1861 factories, manned by up to four hundred workers, turned out six hundred thousand firearms. On June 16, 1861, withdrawing Confederates burned the principal buildings and two railroad bridges. By the end of the Civil War, only the engine house remained. Over a century ago the area was raised with twenty feet of earth embankments to accommodate the B&O railroad, obliterating all traces of the armory.

There were two other important components to the armory. Along the Shenandoah River near the Point was the arsenal, where manufactured goods were stored, and Hall's Island. John Brown's Fort is located beside Arsenal Square, where the foundations of two U.S. Arsenal buildings, burned by retreating Federals, remain. On April 18, 1861, the day following Virginia's secession, Federal Lt. Roger Jones torched the buildings to prevent Confederates from seizing fifteen thousand new rifles.

Harpers Ferry is one vast historical park. Many of the historic sites are restored, and there are indoor and outdoor exhibits, museums, intriguing ruins, and awe-inspiring views. Visitors may take self-guided or park-conducted tours along miles of interpretive trails, which have dozens of descriptive markers. Lectures and special programs are regularly scheduled.

Visit the museums of your choice on High and Shenandoah Streets. At the intersection of these streets, John Brown's men killed two townspeople.

The John Brown Wax Museum (304-535-6321) has eighty-six life-sized and lifelike wax figures that dramatically recreate the career of Brown from cradle to gallows. A light, sound, and animatronic show illustrates the planning and execution of the Harpers Ferry Raid and Brown's trial and execution in nearby Charles Town. The Civil War Museum houses exhibits about the war and its impact on civilians and soldiers here. Exhibits at Storer College (1840) describe the founding and history of this early black school. Next door to it is the Wetlands

The Point in Harpers Ferry affords this view of the confluence of the Shenandoah and Potomac Rivers (left) as well as this tranquil scene of the bridge that connects the area to the mainland (right).

Museum. The Black Voices Museum (1804, the John T. Rieley Building) explores the history of slavery, its end, and the lives of freedmen. The John Brown Museum (1846, the John C. Unself Building), across the street from John Brown's Fort, features a ten-minute slide program, a twenty-six-minute film *To Do Battle in the Land,* interactive displays, and historic artifacts (including pikes, carbines, and pieces of the battered engine house door) that illuminate Brown's life. The role of Brown's five black raiders is interpreted upstairs.

Walk down to the Point, which is one of those sites that everyone intrigued by the Civil War must visit. It is on a point of land where the Potomac River to the left and the Shenandoah River to the right converge. Three states can be seen: Maryland Heights across the Potomac in Maryland, Loudoun Heights across the Shenandoah in Virginia, and the land under your feet is West Virginia. Bolivar Heights is to your rear. The sight of the fast streams flowing over rock beds is inspiring, and it was this water power that made possible the early industries established here. Read the five historical markers describing Stonewall Jackson's capture of Harpers Ferry in September 1862.

In 1861 Harpers Ferry was a community of three thousand, an important arms-producing center, and a rail and canal transportation link between east and west. Located at the head of the Shenandoah Valley, it was an obvious invasion route both into Virginia and Maryland-Pennsylvania. Virginia had scarcely

seceded before Gov. John Letcher sent militia forces to occupy Harpers Ferry, which was partially destroyed by retreating Union forces. Difficult to defend because of its unique geography, Harpers Ferry changed hands a number of times before becoming a base of operations against Confederate forces in the Shenandoah Valley late in the war. An important component of the Antietam campaign was Jackson's capture of the Federal garrison in 1862. Early occupied the town and skirmished with the garrison on Maryland Heights in 1864.

At the beginning of the war, the stone piers in the Potomac—28 feet high, 30 feet wide, and 10 feet thick at the base—supported the Baltimore and Ohio Railroad bridge and a covered wagon bridge (which was used by Brown and his raiders to enter the town on the night of October 16, 1859). All the bridges were destroyed by Confederates at 4 A.M. on June 14, 1861, as they withdrew for the first time. The railroad bridge was rebuilt and destroyed eight times during the war. One constructed in 1864 stood until a 1927 flood. The pedestrian footbridge crosses the Potomac River and leads across the C&O Canal and Harpers Ferry Road to trails leading up Maryland Heights. The B&O Railroad, started in 1828, reached the Potomac River opposite Harpers Ferry in 1834, beating the C&O Canal by several years.

The piers to the right supported a post–Civil War (1882) bridge across the Shenandoah River, which replaced a covered bridge three hundred yards upstream before the war. Three of John Brown's men were shot down as they attempted to escape over the rocks; their bodies were used for target practice.

A close examination of the area north of the Point, upstream near the present railroad bridge, will reveal a steep path cut down to the Potomac River. This was the site of the pontoon bridge that connected Harpers Ferry with Maryland Heights during the Civil War. Ring bolts used to anchor the bridge remain embedded in the walls. Federal soldiers abandoning Maryland Heights in 1862 retreated across it, and Union cavalry made their escape a day later. Northern troops destroyed the span in July 1864 when Early threatened. During the Civil War the railroad crossed the Potomac here and ran through Sandy Hook, where the highway is today. The railroad is now funneled through the tunnel, which can be see at the base of Maryland Heights.

The Point was originally the Ferry Lot Reservation, which contained depots for the B&O and Winchester and Potomac River Railroads and a number of stores. Federals torched the area on February 7, 1862, to deny cover to Confederate sharpshooters who had recently killed a Union soldier.

John Brown's Fort (1848), originally at the entrance to the U.S. Armory, housed a fire engine and watchman's office. Under siege from militia units, Brown ordered his raiders, including five free blacks, which he called the Provisional Army of the United States, to barricade themselves in the small brick structure on October 17, 1859. After Brown rejected a final surrender demand brought by Lt. Jeb Stuart on October 18, Col. Robert E. Lee ordered the building stormed by a party of twelve marines led by Lt. Israel Green, who quickly broke in and subdued the raiders. One marine was killed and another wounded. Of the eighteen men who accompanied Brown, ten were killed, four escaped, and four captured. Two of the dead were Brown's sons. Five civilians were also killed in the fighting. It is estimated that two thousand people, locals and area militia who rushed to the town, witnessed the assault.

Lincoln visited the engine house on October 1, 1862. Despite vandalism inflicted by Confederate soldiers and pieces taken as souvenirs by Union soldiers, this was the only armory structure to survive the Civil War. In the following years the curious came to gawk at this relic of what many considered the beginning of the war. It was dismantled in 1892 and re-created at the Chicago World's Columbia Exposition in 1894, but it proved to be a financial disappointment. In ten days of exhibition, the historic structure attracted only ten paying visitors. The engine house would have been sold for brick except for the efforts of journalist-actress Kate Field, who raised funds for the purchase of the building. It was returned to Harpers Ferry but displayed at a remote site, Alexander Murphy's farm. Ignored and decaying for years, it was purchased by Storer College and moved to the

The bridge piers in the foreground (below left) supported spans for railroad and wagon traffic during the Civil War. Union pontoon bridges were constructed nearby. In the background is Maryland Heights, which the Federals reoccupied after the Confederate withdrawal following the battle of Antietam. The stone piers (below right) mark the site of a bridge that once crossed the Shenandoah River from Harpers Ferry.

This building was the engine house for the U.S. Armory at Harpers Ferry. Ever since the October 1859 raid, it has been known as John Brown's Fort.

Harpers Ferry campus in 1910. After the school closed, the National Park Service acquired the building and moved it here in 1968. Its original location is marked above Potomac Street by a small white pyramid visible on the raised railroad embankment to the north. It was erected by the B&O in 1895.

Behind John Brown's Fort was Arsenal Square, which by 1861 consisted of two brick buildings surrounded by a stone wall and high fence. The Small Arsenal (1806), 36 by 68 feet and two stories tall, contained fifteen thousand firearms and was torched on April 18, 1861, by Roger Jones as he abandoned the town. The Large Arsenal (1799), 125 feet by 32 feet, was in poor shape and contained only supplies and housed a company of troops who arrived following Brown's raid to guard the facilities here. In January 1861 armory superintendent Alfred M. Barbour informed the War Department that he felt the armory was threatened by Virginia militia gathering in the Shenandoah Valley. On April 17 Virginia seceded, and the situation here became critical. One day later, at 10 P.M., Jones, with fifty soldiers and fifteen civilians, torched the Small Armory and withdrew over the Potomac River bridge into Maryland. The people of Harpers Ferry turned out to fight the fires and saved some buildings, but the arsenal was destroyed along with fifteen thousand weapons.

On the night of September 14, 1862, Federal cavalry under Benjamin Davis gathered on Shenandoah Street and crossed the Potomac River on a pontoon bridge, passing quietly beneath Maryland Heights just hours before Jackson thought to post troops there. The Federals took the Harpers Ferry road to Sharpsburg then the Hagerstown turnpike to the Boonsboro-Williamsport turnpike and detoured off the road to avoid Confederates retreating from South Mountain. They captured a munitions train and escaped to Greencastle, Pennsylvania.

The first structure behind Arsenal Square is the New Master Armorer's House (1858), ordered constructed by Secretary of War Jefferson Davis. It was the home of the chief gunsmith at the armory and was occupied in 1859 by John E. P. Daingerfie, a paymaster's clerk taken hostage by Brown. It is now the information center for the park and contains general exhibits about Harpers Ferry. Next is the Old Master Armorer's House (1812). After a company of soldiers arrived to guard Harpers Ferry, this became a recruiting station. It was also used as a headquarters by the Confederates in 1861 and was occupied by various Federal officials during the war, including Gen. John Stevenson in 1865. It served as a school, town hall, post office, and home before the U.S. government purchased it and restored the structure to its 1859 appearance. The first floor re-creates a typical dry goods store of the mid-nineteenth century, and the second floor houses two exhibits. In one a Civil War officer's quarters has been recreated and the other is called the James Taylor Room, arranged as the quarters of the sketch artist for *Frank Leslie's Illustrated Weekly,* who lived here from August until December 1864.

Beside the Old Master Armorer's House is the Provost Marshal's Office (1882), which replicates the facility from which order was maintained in the town during the military occupation. Union authorities based here issued passes to anyone entering or leaving Harpers Ferry, regulated prices, read mail, searched for contraband, and administered the oath of allegiance to civilians.

Walk down Shenandoah Street and cross to the last building, where the Harpers Ferry Historical Association runs a bookstore in the Stage Coach Inn–John G. Wilson Building (1825), a Federal barracks and warehouse. It contains an extensive inventory of books concerning the Civil War and the bountiful natural attractions of the region.

Up the street in the direction from which we came is the McCabe-Marmion Building (1845),

Harpers Ferry, John Brown, and the Civil War

The geography that made peacetime Harpers Ferry an economic and transportation hub transformed it in wartime to a strategically important position. Situated at the confluence of the Potomac and Shenandoah Rivers, the site was perfect for harnessing water power for nineteenth-century industry. It was a natural transportation locus because the surrounding mountains squeezed roads, railroads, and a canal into a narrow defile. Harpers Ferry was also on the politically sensitive Virginia-Maryland border and at the head of the Shenandoah Valley, which quickly became a natural invasion route into both Virginia and the North, including Washington, D.C. The community was condemned to suffer constant military activity when the Civil War started.

After he first visited Harpers Ferry in 1785, George Washington promoted the location for construction of a U.S. armory. The government purchased 125 acres in 1796, and a dam to channel water was started a year later. By 1802 workshops, workers barracks, and an arsenal for storing weapons had been built. An extensive armory was eventually constructed north of the confluence along the Potomac River. The arsenal was to the south, near the confluence along the Shenandoah River, and Hall's Rifle Works was farther up the Shenandoah on Virginius Island. By 1860 the army had manufactured 522,938 firearms at Harpers Ferry.

John Brown was born in Farmington, Connecticut, on May 9, 1800. He lost his mother at age eight, his first wife after eleven years of marriage, and four children of dysentery within a month. Added to these tragedies was a long string of financial reverses. When abolitionist Elijah Lovejoy was murdered by a mob in 1837, Brown dedicated his life to ending slavery.

In 1847 Brown revealed his plans for destroying America's "peculiar institution" to Frederick Douglass, who opposed his violent ideas. In 1851 Brown founded the League of Gileadites, an organization of black abolitionists, to combat the Fugitive Slave Law, which required the return of escaped slaves. In 1855, a year after the Kansas-Nebraska Act opened the western territories to possible slavery, Brown followed his five sons to Kansas. Within a year he had organized a band of abolitionist guerrillas who murdered five proslavery settlers along Pottawatomie Creek in reprisal for an earlier raid against Lawrence, Kansas.

Brown's abolitionist activities continued to accelerate and become more radical as he gained support throughout New England. A raid into Missouri in 1858 freed eleven slaves. On July 3, 1859, Brown arrived in Harpers Ferry, then continued north five miles into Maryland the next day to rent the Kennedy farmhouse.

At 8 A.M. on October 16, Brown and eighteen followers started for Harpers Ferry, leaving three men on guard in Maryland. They crossed the Potomac River bridge and seized the U.S. Armory and Arsenal and Hall's Rifle Works. Brown captured two prominent citizens and their slaves and armory employees as they arrived for work. After halting a train on the Baltimore and Ohio Railroad, Brown allowed it to continue, spreading the alarm throughout the nation. The first casualty at Harpers Ferry had been a free black man, Hayward Shepherd, the station baggage master, mortally wounded on the railroad bridge by Brown's men.

By daylight townspeople had grabbed their weapons and were firing on Brown's party, who returned fire, inflicting casualties on both sides. At 10 A.M. the militia unit the Jefferson Guards seized the Potomac River bridge, leading Brown to ask for negotiation. Two white flags from the abolitionists resulted in two dead raiders and one captured, and a fourth was killed trying to escape across the Potomac.

By early afternoon Robert E. Lee and Jeb Stuart, leading ninety marines, were traveling by rail from Washington, but local citizens had taken matters into their own hands by recapturing Hall's Rifle Works. Three more raiders were killed or captured, but the mayor of Harpers Ferry was also killed. Enraged, the populace stormed a house and killed another raider, then threw his body into the Potomac. By 3 P.M. many of Brown's prisoners had been liberated and the raiders driven into the brick engine house at the arsenal. The men who had remained in Maryland to guard supplies escaped north through the mountains.

Another of Brown's men was killed and three others escaped before Lee arrived. Harpers Ferry was in an uproar throughout the night as more militia and hordes of the curious, most of them drinking heavily, descended upon the town.

After Brown refused to receive Lee's surrender demand, offered by Stuart, the future cavalier stepped aside at 7 A.M. on October 18 and the marines stormed the engine house. They battered open the door with a heavy ladder, then used their bayonets to avoid hurting hostages with gunfire. The marines suffered one killed and one wounded, but after three minutes two raiders were dead and the remainder were wounded and captured. Brown suffered sword wounds, and two of his sons were dead. A total of ten raiders had been killed, five were captured, and four escaped. Five civilians had been killed. The surviving raiders were taken to Charles Town on October 19 and jailed. Before Christmas, Brown had been convicted and executed there.

Brown's image—Christ to many in the North, the antichrist for most Southerners—became an issue that further polarized the United States.

Within hours of Virginia's secession on April 17, 1861, a considerable number of militia were marching on Harpers Ferry. At 10 P.M. the next morning, U.S. Lt. Roger Jones and his forty-four men hurriedly fired two arsenal buildings, where fifteen thousand rifles were stored, and several rifle factories, then crossed the Potomac River to Maryland on their way to Pennsylvania. Civilians immediately began to fight the flames, which limited the damage to weapons-producing machinery.

Virginia and Confederate authorities occupied Harpers Ferry from April 18 until June 15, 1861. They stripped 78 government buildings of 432 machines used to manufacture weapons, 57,000 tools, and any other materiel thought useful to the Southern war effort. The salvage was shipped to armories in Richmond and Fayetteville, North Carolina.

During this period, government housing, churches, and private residences quartered the many Confederate troops who were drilled in Harpers Ferry. Private property was

John Brown

confiscated, and those suspected of Unionist sympathies were jailed without trial. Some residents would be treated rudely by both contending governments.

During the Confederate withdrawal the B&O Railroad bridge and wagon bridge over the Potomac River was destroyed, in addition to many government buildings spared by the Federals. Confederates returned two weeks later, June 28, and torched the buildings of Hall's Rifle Works and the bridge spanning the Shenandoah River.

Union troops occupied Harpers Ferry on July 21, but on August 17, following the battle of First Manassas, they withdrew, leaving the town in a no man's land between the lines. On October 16, five hundred Confederate cavalry under Col. Turner Ashby fought six hundred Federals under Col. John Geary at Bolivar Heights. Both forces retreated, each claiming victory. Confederate and Federal authorities alike recognized the difficulty of defending the town.

In October, after an invitation from a Unionist owner, Federal troops confiscated a large amount of wheat from a mill on Virginius Island. Confederates promptly raided Harpers Ferry and burned the mill, which was the last surviving industry in Harpers Ferry.

The first private citizen of Harpers Ferry was killed on July 4 when a Federal soldier on Maryland Heights killed businessman Frederick Roeder. After Confederate sharpshooters killed

a Union scout on the Maryland side of the Potomac on February 7, 1862, Union troops torched Harpers Ferry's commercial district, an area of stores and hotels located at the Point.

Because the North needed the B&O Railroad, C&O Canal, and the wagon road between Frederick and Winchester to be operational, Harpers Ferry could not be left permanently undefended. The town was reoccupied on February 25, and on March 29 Col. Dixon S. Miles arrived to command the fourteen-thousand-man Railroad Brigade.

Following the capture of Harpers Ferry and the battle of Antietam, McClellan entered the town on September 20. Troops were placed on Maryland Heights, Loudoun Heights, Bolivar Heights, and Camp Hill. More than sixty thousand troops were camped here by October 1, when Lincoln reviewed their ranks at Bolivar Heights. Maryland Heights was cleared of trees and a series of strong stone forts were built across the ridge, supplemented by a number of batteries and rifle pits.

These formidable works were one reason why Lee crossed the Potomac River upstream in June 1863 as he headed toward Gettysburg. The Federal garrison withdrew anyway, first to the works atop Maryland Heights on June 29, then they abandoned the position completely on July 1 and withdrew to Frederick. They returned to Maryland Heights on July 7 and descended into Harpers Ferry on July 14.

Quiet returned to Harpers Ferry for a year, but in early July 1864 the last Confederate invasion of the North occurred. When Jubal Early approached with twenty thousand men on June 4, Federal Brig. Gen. Max Weber wisely withdrew to Maryland Heights, burning the railroad and pontoon bridges behind him. He was reinforced to sixty-five hundred men with the arrival of Maj. Gen. Franz Sigel, and an additional twenty-eight hundred men and three batteries were dispatched from Washington.

Early arrived on July 5 but satisfied himself with pillaging Union supplies and feasting on the bounty warehoused in Harpers Ferry before he burned the remainder. He skirmished with Federal troops, who for the only time fired their huge siege guns in earnest. The Confederates withdrew on July 7 to cross the Potomac River at Boteler's Ford, near Shepherdstown. After ensuring that Early was truly gone, Weber came down from the mountain into Harpers Ferry the following day.

To eliminate Confederate forces in and the invasion threat from the Shenandoah Valley, in August 1864 Ulysses S. Grant sent Philip H. Sheridan to clear the region. Enormous quantities of supplies and thousands of soldiers arrived at Harpers Ferry, which became the supply center for the effort. Great trains numbering up to one thousand wagons started here for the Shenandoah. The burned-out industrial buildings were reroofed to serve as vast warehouses. In Novem-

Thomas Jonathan Jackson

ber the Federals rebuilt the destroyed railroad between Harpers Ferry and Bunker Hill, five miles north of Winchester, and six hundred men operated 13 engines and 75 cars on the short line. Between December and June 1865 they ran 2,236 trains, which delivered two hundred thousand men and thousands of tons of ammunition, food, and supplies to Sheridan, then transferred the men back to Grant when Early was neutralized. Thousands of Confederate prisoners were processed through Harpers Ferry.

When the war ended, the U.S. government decided against rebuilding the armory and arsenal and disposed of the property. Harpers Ferry became a ghost town, devastated repeatedly by floods. Today much of the community is a national park, and much of the rest caters to tourists. The history and natural beauty of the region also attracts many visitors.

John Brown's Body (and Others)

John Brown's second wife, Mary Ann, visited him in jail on December 2, 1859, and after his execution took the body for burial to their home in North Elba, New York. She was buried in Madronia Cemetery in Saratoga, California, after her death on February 29, 1884, at age sixty-seven. Her

grave was marked by a large headstone with the inscription, "Wife of John Brown of Harpers Ferry."

Brown's fifth child, Frederick, born December 31, 1830, was killed by proslavery forces at Ossawatomie, Kansas, and was buried there on August 30, 1856.

Two of Brown's sons died of wounds received at Harpers Ferry. The body of Watson Brown, aged twenty-four, was taken to Winchester Medical College, where the skeleton was preserved. In 1882 the remains were reinterred beside his father. Watson had married only two months before Harpers Ferry.

Oliver Brown, aged twenty, had been married for eight months. He was buried beside the Shenandoah River. His body and those of the other raiders were exhumed in 1899 and taken to North Elba.

where the operations of water power and armory machinery are explained. Farther up the block the Restoration Museum (Tearney Building, 1844) describes how alterations, additions, and uses of historic structures are traced.

Looming over Shenandoah Street are sheer rock walls and Saint Peter's Catholic Church (original 1830; present 1896). Other historic sites up the hill are the Harper house (1782) and Saint John's Episcopal Church (1851), which saw service as a hospital and Confederate barracks and guardhouse. Civil War activity severely damaged the church, which was rebuilt in 1882. It has been abandoned for nearly a century. Also there is Jefferson Rock, where Thomas Jefferson stood in 1785, writing later that it was "one of the most stupendous scenes in Nature. This scene is worth a voyage across the Atlantic."

Continue down Shenandoah Street. On Shenandoah Street below the Point was Bridge Street, which led to the Shenandoah River bridge, destroyed by Confederates in June 1861.

The Virginius Island hiking trail leads past the ruins of Herr's Mill, a three-and-a-half-story gristmill that measured ninety-six feet long and forty-eight feet wide. In 1860 it produced thirty-two thousand barrels of flour. It was owned by Unionist Abraham Herr who in October 1861 invited Federals in Maryland to cross the Potomac and take a large amount of grain he held. The Thirteenth Massachusetts and Third Wisconsin did, and in retaliation Confederates burned the mill. Note the Winchester and Potomac River Railroad (now a CSX line). Established in 1836, it ran thirty-two miles to Winchester. Confederates used it in early 1861 to ship hundreds of armory machines and tools to Richmond and Fayetteville, North Carolina. From the fall of 1864 to the end of the war, Sheridan transported troops and supplies on it to support his operations in the Shenandoah Valley.

By 1857 thirteen-acre Virginius Island held three dozen mills and factories and twenty-eight homes, but the industrial complex was substantially destroyed by floods in the 1870s. In 1861 Confederates seized the U.S. Rifle Factory here with 132 machines and countless tools and spare parts.

The trail continues to Lower Hall Island. In 1819 John H. Hall, who had patented a breechloading flintlock rifle, contracted to manufacture them for

In Harpers Ferry, the ground rises very sharply behind Shenandoah Street to the site of a Catholic church, which was occupied by Federals during the Civil War.

the U.S. government. Before ceasing production in 1840, Hall had produced twenty thousand rifles. In 1844 the government demolished the buildings of Hall's Rifle Works and constructed the U.S. Rifle Factory, composed of three iron-framed brick buildings with machinery powered by four turbine waterwheels. It was briefly occupied by John Brown's men. The facility made U.S. Model 1841 rifles until the Federals abandoned Harpers Ferry in April 1861. Confederates torched the complex during their first withdrawal.

Federal forces occupied this area from February 1862 until February 1866. The Cotton Factory and other buildings were utilized as hospitals, barracks, stables, corrals, workshops, and warehouses.

Many other industrial ruins and displays are scattered across Virginius Island and Lower Hall Island.

A variety of self-guided walking tours are available to historic Harpers Ferry, its extensive ruins and industrial works, and Civil War fortifications on the surrounding heights.

Drive down Shenandoah Street to U.S. 340 and turn right toward Charles Town.

The KOA Campground on U.S. 340 contains earthworks. To the right, Shipley Elementary School still occupies Schoolhouse Ridge, from which Jackson bombarded Harpers Ferry while A. P. Hill secured a position on the Union left flank near the Shenandoah River from which he prepared to attack. Through the Civil War Trust the NPS has secured fifty-six acres of the one-thousand-acre area atop Schoolhouse Ridge. Inquire at the visitors center.

If you are a serious student of the Civil War, you will want to trace A. P. Hill's route to Antietam. In response to an urgent summons from Lee, Jackson hurried to Antietam while Hill organized the captured booty and paroled the large number of prisoners at Harpers Ferry. Hill left on the morning of September 17, the day of the battle at Antietam. The usual route was the twelve-mile trip via the Harpers Ferry road, but with considerable Federal strength in Pleasant Valley marching west toward Sharpsburg on the north bank of the Potomac River, Hill directed his division along the southern bank to Boteler's Ford at Shepherdstown, a longer but more secure seventeen-mile trip.

To follow Hill's path, turn right off U.S. 340 onto Route 27–Bakerton Road. After the railroad underpass turn left onto Route 28–Old Furnace–Moler Road to parallel the Potomac River. At the intersection with Route 31 there are two options. A right onto Route 31–2 and left onto Route 17–Cement Mill Road leads to Boteler's Ford on the right and the cement mill on both sides of the road. The historically accurate route involves a short left onto Route 31 to Moler Crossroads (where a cavalry skirmish occurred on July 15, 1863, between the Twelfth Virginia and the Eighth Pennsylvania) and a right onto Route 31. To the right at the top of a hill is an unmarked gravel road known as Trough Road, which is a rough avenue that meets Route 17–Cement Mill Road at Boteler's Ford.

Assuming you will skip this side trip, continue on U.S. 340 toward Charles Town. In Halltown, off U.S. 304 between Harpers Ferry and Charles Town, is Rion Hall (1836), home to Judge Daniel B. Lucas, a captain in Wise's Legion, a friend of John Yates Beall, and author of *The Land Where We Were Dreaming*. Saber slashes on the woodwork attest to the presence of Sheridan and his staff, who established their headquarters here. A mile north, off Route 24, is Beallair, home of Col. Lewis Washington, one of John Brown's hostages. When captured, Brown had a sword taken from Beallair that had belonged to George Washington.

On Route 27 west of Harpers Ferry is the Strider farm, where Confederate batteries and troops were positioned during the 1862 siege. In 1864 Union Gen. Horatio G. Wright placed his headquarters there as Sheridan's Shenandoah campaign opened.

At the outskirts of Charles Town, when U.S. 340 turns to the right, continue straight on Route 51, which becomes Washington Street.

To the left at 417 East Washington Street is the Stribling house. As Sheridan prepared his destructive campaign, Grant conferred with him at his headquarters here.

Continue down Washington.

On the right is the Presbyterian Church (1851), the only church in town not extensively damaged during the war because both armies used it as a hospital.

Continue down Washington. On the right is the Jefferson County Library and Museum; the latter is downstairs.

This museum is one of the most delightful small facilities in the country, with an emphasis on John Brown. Exhibited here is a re-creation of his jail cell, the cot on which he lay during the trial, the wagon on which he rode to be hanged, lengths of rope from the noose and pieces of the scaffold, the pistols and documents Brown had on him when captured—including a constitution for his black state and a certificate making one of his men a captain in the "Provisional Army of the United States," and the papers of Col. John T. Gibson, the officer in charge of the execution. Of Civil

War note are the battle flag of Stuart's Horse Artillery (made by local women) and the effects of its commander, Col. Roger Preston Chew, who is reputed to have used two hundred troopers to bluff George A. Custer away from the community. His sword, which disappeared in 1865, was returned anonymously by mail fifty years later.

Continue down Washington. On the right at Washington and George Streets is the Jefferson County Courthouse (1837), where Brown and four of his party were brought the day after their capture, October 19, 1859.

Brown was shortly tried for treason, murder, and conspiracy to incite a slave rebellion. The wounded Brown lay on a cot during the trial, refusing an attempt by friends to have him declared insane and ignoring the two local lawyers appointed to represent him. He denied no charges, showed no fear or remorse, and was convicted on all counts after the jury deliberated for only forty-five minutes on November 2. Brown declined to appeal his case. During the trial Brown stated: "I deny everything but what I have all along admitted; of a design on my part to free slaves. . . . Now, if it is deemed necessary that I should forfeit my life for the furtherance of the ends of justice and mingle my blood further with the blood of my children and with the blood of millions in this slave country whose rights are disregarded by wicked, cruel, and unjust enactments, I say, let it be done."

Industrial ruins abound on and around Virginius Island, where thousands of rifles were manufactured by the U.S. Armory before the Civil War.

This was the nineteenth century's "trial of the century." The people packed the town and crowded into the courthouse to observe every detail. A horde of newspaper correspondents telegraphed stories to their papers, which were read throughout the country. One witness was arch-Secessionist Edmund Ruffin; another was actor John Wilkes Booth. Hundreds of soldiers with bayoneted muskets and two cannon guarded the courthouse, and roads leading to Charles Town were picketed by troops.

The courtroom has been divided into several offices, but one contains some relics of the trial—a window and railings from the courtroom. During the war legal records were moved to Winchester for safekeeping. Federal soldiers used the building as a barracks, and it was reduced to a shell by Confederate and Union artillery bombardments. Across the street from the courthouse is the post office, which was the jail site (1801–1922) where Brown was hanged.

Nothing remains of the execution site. The gallows where Brown was hanged on December 2, 1859, stood on the property of the Gibson-Todd house (1892, 515 South Samuel Street, corner of Samuel and Hunter), which was then a field on the Rebecca Hunter farm, just north of the present home. The house was constructed by Col. John Gibson, who protected the trial with the Fifty-fifth Virginia Militia. Just before his execution, Brown passed the following message to a guard: "I, John Brown, am now quite certain that the crimes of this guilty land will never be purged away without very much bloodshed." Four of his companions were convicted and executed later.

Gibson surrounded the execution site with eight hundred troops, including a detachment from the Virginia Military Institute and two cannon under Thomas J. Jackson. Martial law edicts prevented the public from witnessing the hanging, but civilians crowded into surrounding houses, including the Riddle-Murphy-Hunter house (1858, 534 South Samuel Street) and the Green-Timberlake house (pre–Civil War, 203 South George Street), home of Thomas C. Claiborne, Charles Town's mayor and one of the two appointed lawyers for Brown. Claiborne's wife, Mary, observed the hanging from the attic. A later owner, Richard Tim, had been a juror.

The people of the North protested Brown's execution by firing cannon, ringing bells, and holding prayer services. They made him a martyr, often equating him with Christ. In response Southerners joined militias and recalled their children who were being educated in the North, while their state legislatures organized armories and expanded their armed forces.

The Chew house (early 1800s, 514 South George Street) was the home of Col. Roger Chew, who served with Turner Ashby and Jeb Stuart. Iron rings in the basement of the Sheetz house (1797, southeast corner of Liberty and Lawrence Streets) suggest that horses were hidden there during the war. Charles Washington Hall (1874, 100 West Washington Street) replaced the structure burned during the war when ammunition stored there exploded. During the trial, John Wilkes Booth gave dramatic readings at the Episcopal Lecture Room (1833, northeast corner of Liberty and Lawrence). The Sadler Building (1830, 106 West Congress Street) housed Sadler Brothers, the furniture company that built Brown's coffin and supplied the wagon and team that transported him to the gallows. The first program on February 11, 1911, at the Old Opera House (northwest corner of George and Liberty Streets) was produced by the UDC to benefit indigent Confederate veterans.

The original Hunter house (northwest corner of Washington and Samuel Streets, replaced by a later building) was owned by Andrew Hunter, prosecutor of John Brown. In 1864 his cousin, Union Gen. David Hunter, ordered it burned without allowing anything to be removed. Jailed without trial, Andrew no doubt reflected bitterly upon his gold ring, a present years earlier from David, complete with the inscription "As evidence of his affection."

Federal troops quartered in Zion Episcopal Church (1851, Congress Street, between Mildred and Church Streets) caused extensive destruction. In the churchyard rests John Yates Beall, who constructed the stone-and-brick wall surrounding the property. Beall entertained his college friend, John Wilkes Booth, during Brown's trial. Wounded while serving with Turner Ashby's cavalry at First Manassas, Beall then joined the Confederate navy. While participating in raids against Federal shipping on Chesapeake Bay, he was captured and exchanged. In 1864 Beall traveled to Canada as part of a plot to release Confederate prisoners held at Johnson's Island, Ohio, on Lake Erie. Recaptured on December 16, 1864, by Niagara police after derailing a train near

Buffalo, New York, he was tried as a spy. Beall was convicted and ordered executed by the commandant of military courts, Gen. John A. Dix. The sentence was carried out on Governor's Island in New York City on February 18, 1865, making him the first spy executed in that military district since Maj. John André, Benedict Arnold's British contact during the American Revolution. In rejecting pleas for clemency, Lincoln wrote, "There had to be an example—I had to stand firm—I can't get the distress out of mind yet." Also buried here is Col. Robert P. Chew and S. Howell Brown, Robert E. Lee's cartographer.

In the Confederate section at Edge Hill Cemetery in Charles Town is a monument to local Confederate dead, an urn atop an obelisk, dedicated on April 26, 1871, Confederate Memorial Day.

On May 28, 1862, during Jackson's Valley campaign, Confederate Brig. Gen. Charles S. Winter routed Union troops in Harpers Ferry. On October

John Brown was tried, convicted, and sentenced to death for treason at the Charles County Courthouse in Charles Town.

18, 1863, Brig. Gen. John D. Imboden's cavalry rode forty-eight miles to capture four hundred Federals stationed here. Other Union occupiers were driven out by artillery fire, which unfortunately destroyed or damaged a number of buildings. Whenever Federal troops marched through Charles Town, they habitually sang "John Brown's Body" very loudly just to annoy the residents.

Early's troops camped on the grounds of Richwood (1820, off U.S. 51 near Charles Town) during the 1864 battle of Cameron's Depot. On U.S. 51 three miles west of Charles Town is Locust Hill (1840), which suffered battle damage in 1864. Blakeley (1820, off Route 13–3) was home to John Augustine Washington III, killed at Elkwater in 1861 while on Robert E. Lee's staff. It was later owned by Robert P. Chew.

Five miles east of Charles Town, near Leetown, on Route 1.1, is the Bower, where Stuart's cavalry rested for three weeks after the battle of Antietam.

After crossing the Potomac River following Antietam, Lee camped near Martinsburg on Opequon Creek, then continued on to Bunker Hill and Winchester before passing with James Longstreet through the Blue Ridge gaps to concentrate at Culpeper; Jackson remained in the valley. McClellan immediately sent forces to occupy Harpers Ferry then tarried a month before crossing one corps there and three others over a pontoon bridge constructed at Berlin. They advanced east of the Blue Ridge and marched south, covering successive mountain passes to the west while heading to Warrenton. McClellan's headquarters was at Rectorstown when he was replaced by Ambrose E. Burnside, who was at Salem (Orlean).

The tour now examines McClellan's movements following the battle of Antietam.

When finished in Charles Town, or if you forgo Charles Town, drive east on U.S. 340 past Harpers Ferry, across the Shenandoah River, beneath Loudoun Heights, and cross the Potomac River. On the right is the community of Weverton, where trails lead to locks, impressive stone headgates of the C&O Canal, ruins of large flour mills (used as Federal barracks), and dramatic cliffs.

Exit right off U.S. 340 onto Route 17 toward Brunswick. At the intersection turn right to Brunswick (to the left is Burkittsville). To avoid prematurely crossing the Potomac River on Route 17 (Route 87 in

Virginia), in Brunswick turn left onto Maryland Street at the sign for the Brunswick Museum, which is ahead on the left at the corner of Maryland Street and West Potomac.

The town of Brunswick is listed on the National Register of Historic Places as a prime example of an 1800s railroad community. The museum contains three floors of historical exhibits illustrating the area's heritage. The third floor is filled with an ever-expanding model railroad that strives to reproduce accurately the area between Washington, D.C., and Brunswick.

This was called Berlin during the war. In early June 1861 Lee ordered Jackson, commanding Virginia militia in Harpers Ferry, to destroy the Potomac River bridges at Berlin and Point of Rocks. The spans, including a two-way covered bridge here, were destroyed with kerosene and gunpowder by cavalry on June 9. All remains of the bridge, constructed in 1858, have disappeared, including eight stone piers. When McClellan finally pushed himself into motion following Antietam, he built an eleven-hundred-foot-long pontoon bridge here. From October 26 to November 1, he crossed most of his 120,000-man army, 40,000 horses and mules, and thousands of artillery pieces, supply wagons, and ambulances. In June 1863 part of Joseph Hooker's army pursued Lee into Maryland on the pontoon bridge. Days later he was replaced by George Gordon Meade in Frederick. After the battle of Gettysburg, Meade recrossed elements of the Army of the Potomac into Virginia at this point.

Brunswick-Berlin is the starting point for the next book in this series, *The Storm Tide,* which will take Route 17 across the Potomac River into Virginia to Warrenton, then explore the campaigns and battles of Fredericksburg, Chancellorsville, and Gettysburg.

We conclude with a side trip to Point of Rocks (also an option during the Antietam campaign tour between the Potomac River and Frederick) that can be made from Brunswick. From Brunswick backtrack on Route 17 to Rosemont and turn right to follow Souder Road–Route 464 to Point of Rocks. At the stop sign turn right onto U.S. 15 South, then left onto Clay Street and almost immediately right down the first street that almost parallels the Potomac River. At the sign for the C&O Canal Historical Park turn right carefully over the one-lane bridge spanning the canal. Drive under the towering supports of the U.S. 15 bridge and note the original B&O Railroad tunnel through Catoctin Mountain on the right.

The bridge spanning the Potomac River at Point of Rocks was destroyed by Confederates in June 1861. Raiders, scouts, spies, and smugglers prowled both sides of the Potomac River in this area throughout the Civil War. After crossing the Potomac on June 4, 1864, Mosby crossed the canal over the pivot bridge near Lock 28, half a mile upriver from the U.S. 15 highway bridge, and drove 150 Union cavalry and militia out of Point of Rocks. Mosby returned and clashed nearby with the Eighth Illinois Cavalry on July 6 as Early invaded Maryland farther to the west. Lock 28 had been destroyed by Confederates in 1862. The river, narrow and shallow here, could usually be forded. The B&O Railroad, C&O Canal, and a road hugged a narrow ledge that separated the north bank of the Potomac from the Catoctin Mountains. In the early 1830s, a lawsuit over the limited space resulted in the railroad's excavating the tunnel through the mountain.

The Point of Rocks railroad station, a Victorian gem from the late nineteenth century, is still used today.

CONCLUSION

W HEN THE EASTERN ARMIES took to the field during the summer of 1861, the troops of both sides, Confederate and Federal, were poorly trained for serious combat and unprepared for sustained campaigning. Their leaders were similarly inexperienced—few officers in the country's brief military history had led forces as large as a Civil War brigade. George Washington's largest Revolutionary War command totaled only one-sixth of George B. McClellan's massive Army of the Potomac.

All parties, save General-in-Chief Winfield Scott, expected a short conflict that would be decided by one or a few battles, where the combat would be relatively bloodless but filled with deeds of valor. A joyous war hysteria consumed the soldiers and civilians of the two sections. The confused slaughter of First Manassas shocked both. Early assumptions about the conflict had to be reevaluated, forcing political and military leaders to initiate strategic planning.

The first full year of the war, 1862, provided a seemingly endless series of threats and triumphs. The Confederate retreat from Centreville-Manassas alarmed the South and heartened the North. In Hampton Roads, within the space of two days, the battles of the first ironclads ensured the end of the Federal naval blockade, the destruction of Washington, D.C., and New York City, and a return to the status quo. When McClellan drove up the peninsula to the outskirts of Richmond, the end of the war in the East seemed in sight. Robert E. Lee's stunning Seven Days' battles shattered that illusion. McClellan's withdrawal and John Pope's defeat at Second Manassas brought the Southerners back to the periphery of Washington, D.C., and made possible the first Confederate invasion of Northern territory. Lee's repulse at Antietam ended the danger, but there were few expectations of an early end to the war.

From March until November 1862, more than a quarter of a million troops had marched and fought savage battles across Virginia, from Chesapeake Bay to the Shenandoah Valley, from Hampton Roads into Maryland. A number of generals had proven themselves in battle, others were found wanting, and some promising leaders were cut down in battle.

Most soldiers discovered that they could stand and fight. Appalled by the carnage they experienced on the field, they found the motivation to continue. Although the soldiers and their leaders had been inexperienced when the war began, by the fall of 1862, after sixteen months of combat, they had been forged by fire into formidable armies.

As the Army of Northern Virginia and the Army of the Potomac drifted back to the banks of the Rappahannock River, the unofficial border between the Union and the Confederacy, it was clear that this would be an extended conflict, expensive in terms of lives and property. So much had been sacrificed that the possibility of compromise seemed to have vanished. This war would be prosecuted to a bloody conclusion, leaving one of the contenders in ruins. Few would have believed that the tragic events of the coming year would surpass the horror witnessed from First Manassas to Antietam.

APPENDIXES

A: Chronology
B: Resources

BIBLIOGRAPHY
INDEX

APPENDIX A

CHRONOLOGY

1860

November 6. Abraham Lincoln is elected president of the United States.

December 20. South Carolina secedes from the Union.

December 26. Maj. Robert Anderson abandons Fort Moultrie to occupy Fort Sumter in Charleston Harbor.

December 30. President James Buchanan refuses to surrender Fort Sumter.

1861

January 9. Mississippi leaves the Union. The *Star of the West* turns back from Fort Sumter after being fired on.

January 10. Florida and Alabama leave the Union.

January 19. Georgia secedes.

January 21. Southern senators and congressmen deliver their farewell addresses to the Congress.

January 26. Louisiana leaves the Union.

February 1. Texas leaves the Union.

February 4. The seceded states meet at Montgomery, Alabama, to form the Confederate States of America.

March 3. Abraham Lincoln is inaugurated.

April 10. P. G. T. Beauregard delivers an ultimatum demanding the surrender of Fort Sumter.

April 12. Confederate forces open fire on Fort Sumter.

April 13. Fort Sumter surrenders.

April 16. Lincoln calls for seventy-five thousand volunteers to suppress the revolt of the Southern states.

April 17. Virginia secedes.

April 18. Union forces abandon the U.S. Armory and Arsenal at Harpers Ferry, which is quickly occupied by Virginia's military forces. Robert E. Lee declines an offer to command the forces of the United States.

April 19. Union troops and the citizens of Baltimore engage in a street battle. Thomas J. Jackson arrives to command Confederate forces in Harpers Ferry but is replaced within a week by Joseph E. Johnston.

April 20. Lincoln declares a blockade of Southern ports.

April 20. The Union navy abandons the vital naval facility at Gosport, near Norfolk, leaving valuable facilities, heavy artillery, and the burned hulk of the USS *Merrimack* in Confederate hands.

May 1. Tennessee joins Confederate ranks and secedes on June 8.

May 6. Arkansas joins the Confederacy. Jefferson Davis appoints Lee his chief military adviser.

May 11. Confederates raise the *Merrimack* and start transforming her into an ironclad, a process that continues until March 1862.

May 13. Benjamin Butler seizes Baltimore.

May 16. North Carolina leaves the Union.

May 24. A day after Virginia's voters ratify the state's ordinance of secession, Union troops occupy the west bank of the Potomac River.

May 29. The Confederate Congress votes to move the capital from Montgomery to Richmond.

May 31. Beauregard is appointed commander of Confederate forces gathering at Manassas Junction. Johnston receives command of Southern troops in the Shenandoah Valley.

June 10. John B. Magruder's Confederate forces defeat Butler's troops at Big Bethel on the peninsula.

July 16. Under intense pressure from his superiors, Irwin McDowell marches his Union forces toward Manassas.

July 17. Fighting breaks out along the banks of Bull Run.

July 18. After an all-day battle, Union troops are routed at the battle of First Manassas when Beauregard is reinforced by Johnston's Shenandoah Valley army.

July 22. Lincoln appoints George B. McClellan to command Union forces in Virginia, which he names the Army of the Potomac.

August 3. Congress approves the construction of three prototype ironclads for the Union navy.

September 15. The design for the *Monitor* is approved.

September 27. Johnston abandons the outskirts of Washington, D.C., for Fairfax Court House.

October 17. Johnston withdraws to Centreville.

October 20. Union forces under Edward D. Baker initiate a battle at Ball's Bluff that ends in a catastrophic loss to Confederate Nathan Evans.

October 25. The keel of the *Monitor* is laid on Long Island, New York.

November 1. Scott is replaced as general in chief of Federal forces by McClellan and is forced into retirement.

November 8. Confederate officials aboard the British vessel *Trent* are seized, leading the United States to a dangerous diplomatic crisis with London.

Fall-Winter. McClellan slowly builds a massive army around Washington, D.C., but adamantly refuses to campaign against Confederate forces that are close to the capital and blockading the Potomac River. McClellan formulates a plan to bypass Confederate defenses at Centreville-Manassas by taking the Army of the Potomac by ship down the Potomac River to land at Urbanna, on the Rappahannock River, and advance on Richmond.

1862

February 25. The *Monitor* is commissioned. She starts for Hampton Roads on March 6.

February 27. Without consultation with higher authorities, McClellan cancels a two-pronged maneuver to open the Potomac.

March 7–9. Without informing his superiors, Johnston abandons Centreville-Manassas and withdraws behind the Rappahannock. Bad weather and McClellan's temperament prevent an effective Union pursuit.

March 8. McClellan receives conditional approval of the Urbanna operation, but is removed as general in chief. The Confederate ironclad *Virginia* steams into Hampton Roads and destroys two Union frigates, the *Cumberland* and *Congress*. The *Monitor* arrives that night.

March 9. The *Virginia* and *Monitor* fight to a draw in Hampton Roads, initiating a revolution in naval warfare and resulting in the salvation of the Union navy, its blockade, and McClellan's revised Peninsula campaign, which will drive up the peninsula formed by the James and York Rivers.

March 17. The Army of the Potomac begins embarking at Alexandria for Fort Monroe, an operation that requires three weeks.

April 2. McClellan reaches Fort Monroe, expecting to seize Yorktown in three days.

April 4. The Peninsula campaign starts, then stalls along the Warwick River, short of Yorktown. A month-long standoff results between McClellan and Magruder, joined later by Johnston.

April 16. Union troops breach the Warwick line at Burnt Chimneys–Dam No. 1, but McClellan fails to reinforce the success and the Federals are driven back.

April. On several occasions the *Virginia* and *Monitor* venture into Hampton Roads, but neither is willing to fight on the other's terms.

May 3. On the eve of McClellan's planned great bombardment of Yorktown, Johnston quietly retreats. The Federals tardily pursue.

May 4–5. A sizable battle occurs at Confederate works below Williamsburg, centered around Fort Magruder, as Johnston attempts to delay McClellan's pursuit to ensure the safety of his trains. The Confederates safely withdraw.

May 7. Union troops landing at West Point on the York River attempt to intercept Johnston, but John Bell Hood drives them back to the river. McClellan concentrates his troops there.

Early May. While Confederates quietly evacuate Norfolk and Portsmouth, Lincoln arrives at Fort Monroe to speed up Union occupation of those cities.

May 9. Union troops land east of Norfolk and occupy the city the following morning.

May 10. McClellan resumes his advance, concentrating at White House Landing and Cumberland Landing on the Pamunkey as Johnston withdraws first to the Chickahominy River, then to the outskirts of Richmond.

May 11. Unable to ascend the James River to Richmond, the *Virginia* is destroyed by her crew.

May 15. A Union flotilla led by the ironclads *Galena* and *Monitor* unsuccessfully attack Confederate fortifications at Drewry's Bluff, the only James River defenses guarding the Southern capital.

May 31. McClellan faces Richmond, the two wings of his army separated by the rain-swollen Chickahominy. Johnston launches a savage but tardy, confused, and uncoordinated assault at Seven Pines against the left wing. McClellan's left is driven back but saved by reinforcements from north of the river. At the close of the battle Johnston is severely wounded.

June 1. Sputtering Confederate attacks ordered by Gustavus Smith around Fair Oaks are soundly repulsed. President Davis appoints Lee to replace Johnston. Lee renames his force the Army of Northern Virginia.

Early June. McClellan digs in for a siege of Richmond, bringing up his heavy guns. Lee digs in facing the Federals, planning to hold them south of the Chickahominy while attacking the isolated right wing north of the river.

June 12–15. Jeb Stuart circles McClellan's army, gathering intelligence that indicates the Union right is "up in the air"—unsupported and vulnerable to attack.

June 16. Stonewall Jackson's army in the Shenandoah Valley starts marching east to participate in Lee's assault against McClellan.

June 25. McClellan makes a tentative move against Richmond to seize Old Tavern, advancing closer to Richmond in the battle of Oak Grove. This is the beginning of the Seven Days' battles.

June 26. Jackson's assault, which would open an attack against Fitz John Porter at Mechanicsville, north of the Chickahominy, fails to materialize. A. P. Hill's attacks at Beaver Dam Creek–Ellerson's Mill are repulsed with losses.

June 27. During the night Porter retreats to a strong position at Gaines's Mill–Boatswain's Creek. Lee commits his entire force against the Union line. Confederate casualties are horrendous, but at dusk the Federal line is pierced and McClellan's right is broken. Federal units stream across the Chickahominy.

June 28. McClellan initiates his "change of base." The entire Army of the Potomac begins withdrawing across the peninsula to Harrison's Landing on the James River. Lee sends out scouts to gather information on McClellan's next move.

June 29. Lee splits his army into four columns to pursue McClellan in an attempt to destroy the Federals as they pass through White Oak Swamp. Jackson stops at the Chickahominy while Magruder futilely attacks the large Union rear guard at Savage's Station, where mountains of supplies are torched.

June 30. Jackson stops to rebuild a bridge at White Oak Swamp, and Magruder and Benjamin Huger also halt short of their objectives. James Longstreet and A. P. Hill savagely attack the Union rear guard at Glendale–Frayser's farm. Because only half the Confederate army participates, the assault is beaten back.

July 1. To protect the last stage of his retreat, McClellan positions 250 artillery pieces and two infantry corps on Malvern Hill. As a result of a series of misadventures, the Confederates attack and suffer terrible losses. McClellan reaches Harrison's Landing and the Seven Days end.

July. McClellan regroups at Harrison's Landing while Lincoln forms a new Union force, the Army of Virginia, to operate between Washington, D.C., and Richmond. It is commanded by John Pope.

July 12. Believing McClellan will not stir, Lee dispatches Jackson's corps to contest Pope's advance.

July 29. Pope arrives in the field to command his force, which is arriving around Culpeper from Washington, the Shenandoah Valley, and Fredericksburg.

August 9. At Cedar Mountain, Jackson attacks part of Pope's army under Nathaniel Banks. Despite an early reverse, Jackson rallies his men and drives the Federals back to Culpeper.

Mid-August. Learning that McClellan, who refuses to resume an overland offensive against Richmond, has been recalled to Washington, Lee concentrates his army at the Rapidan River south of Culpeper.

August 20. Captured dispatches inform Pope that Lee is planning to flank him. The Federals retreat to a safe position behind the Rappahannock River, where they wait for reinforcements from Washington and Fredericksburg.

August 25. After a raid by Stuart alerts Lee to Pope's approaching reinforcements, Jackson is dispatched around the Union right flank to force the Federals to retreat closer to Washington, D.C.

August 26. Jackson severs Pope's railroad supply line at Bristoe Station, then sacks and destroys a vast supply depot at Manassas.

August 27. Jackson disappears, taking up a position on Stony Ridge, near Bull Run, as Pope marches his troops across northern Virginia in vain pursuit.

August 28. To prevent Pope's escape to Washington, Jackson attacks the rear of the Union columns at Groveton, on the Warrenton turnpike below Stony Ridge.

August 29. Throughout the day Pope launches fierce but piecemeal assaults against Stony Ridge. Jackson is pressed to the breaking point but holds. Longstreet arrives, having followed Jackson, but convinces Lee to wait before committing his corps to battle.

August 30. At a point where Jackson is sorely pressed and the entire Federal army is focused on Stony Ridge, Longstreet strikes the exposed Union left flank in one of the greatest surprise attacks of the war. The Federals are driven several miles before they can make an effective stand, and they withdraw to Fairfax Court House.

August 31. In an attempt to dislodge Pope from Centreville-Fairfax and drive him into Washington's defenses, Lee starts Jackson, followed by Longstreet, around the Union right. At the confused battle at Chantilly on the following day, Pope is induced to withdraw.

September 3. Hoping to take advantage of the confusion in Federal ranks and move the war into Union territory, Lee marches the Army of Northern Virginia to Leesburg. They reach the Potomac River and cross by September 7, to concentrate at Frederick, Maryland. McClellan, returned to command the combined Federal forces in Washington, pursues on September 5 to a base around Rockville, Maryland.

September 9. Finding little support among Maryland's civilians, Lee issues orders to continue his invasion into Pennsylvania. His army is divided to capture Harpers Ferry and advance through Hagerstown, Maryland, to Harrisburg, Pennsylvania.

September 13. Occupying Frederick in Lee's wake, Union troops discover a copy of the Confederate commander's plans. McClellan pursues, hoping to destroy the Southerners in detail.

September 13–15. Confederates under Jackson take three ridges surrounding Harpers Ferry and open a devastating bombardment of the Union garrison, which surrenders.

September 14. Throughout the day McClellan attacks Confederate positions in three gaps on South Mountain—Fox's, Turner's, and Crampton's. The badly outnumbered Confederates fight desperately, but as night falls they are forced to withdraw. Lee decides to concentrate the army along Antietam Creek, near Sharpsburg.

September 15–16. McClellan slowly positions his forces opposite Lee as Confederate troops stream in from Harpers Ferry.

September 17. On the bloodiest day in American history, Union and Confederate soldiers fight from dawn until dusk. Because McClellan refuses to commit large reserves, the battle of Antietam is a draw, but the Army of Northern Virginia is decimated.

September 19. During the night Lee's army retreats across the Potomac into Virginia at Boteler's Ford. Pursuing Federal troops are routed at the battle of Shepherdstown. McClellan declines to follow Lee, who withdraws into the Shenandoah Valley.

October 2. Lincoln visits McClellan, but fails to motivate him to take the offensive for another month.

November 11. After cautiously crossing the Potomac at Berlin, McClellan concentrates his troops around Warrenton Junction. Losing patience, the president replaces McClellan with Ambrose E. Burnside.

APPENDIX B

RESOURCES

BASIC STATE RESOURCES

VIRGINIA

Virginia Tourism Corporation, 901 East Byrd Street, Richmond VA 23219 (804) 786-2051; fax (804) 786-1919. Web site: www.Virginia.org
For a current copy of *Virginia Is for Lovers* magazine, which contains full information on most attractions in the state, call (800) VISITVA (847-4882).

Virginia Civil War Trails (publishers of detailed guides to four campaigns), 550 East Marshall Street, Richmond VA 23219. (888) CIVIL WAR. Web site: www.civilwar—va.org

Page One Inc. (publishers of the outstanding annual newspaper *Civil War Traveler*), P.O. Box 4232, 2211 West Grace Street, Richmond VA 23220 (804) 359-8732.

Department of Conservation and Recreation, Division of State Parks, 203 Governor Street, Suite 306, Richmond VA 23219-2010 (804) 786-2132; fax (804) 786-6141.

MARYLAND

Maryland Office of Tourist Development, 217 East Redwood Street, Baltimore MD 21248-6349. (800) 634-7386. Web site: www.mdisfun.org (800) 543-1036.

Maryland Tourism Council, P.O. Box 180, Severna Park MD 21146. (410) 974-4472.

WEST VIRGINIA

Travel West Virginia, Building 6, Room 564B, State Capitol, Charleston, WV 25305 (800) CALL-WVA. Web site: www.callwva.com. Contact for a West Virginia Civil War sites brochure.

PRESERVATIONIST ORGANIZATIONS

The Association for the Preservation of Civil War Sites (APCWS), Public Square, Suite 200, Hagerstown MD 21740. (301) 665-1400; fax (301) 665-1416.

MAP RESOURCES

There are a number of good combination maps available for the Portsmouth, Norfolk, Hampton, Newport News, and lower peninsula metropolitan areas. A comprehensive and recent map of the city of Richmond is also essential. Maps to the various cities and towns encountered are available from local chambers of commerce or visitors centers or bureaus.

Adventurous travelers should secure county maps from the states. These maps will be invaluable if you decide to stray off the tour route or accidentally zig when you should have zagged.

County maps needed for the First Manassas Tour are Fairfax and Prince William; for the peninsula—New Kent, Hanover, Henrico, and Charles City; for the Seven Days—New Kent, Hanover, Henrico, and Charles City; for Second Manassas—Hanover, Louisa, Orange, Culpeper, Rappahannock, Fauquier, and Prince William; for Antietam—Fairfax and Loudoun in Virginia and Frederick and Washington in Maryland; for Harpers Ferry–John Brown—Washington in Maryland and Jefferson in West Virginia.

County maps for Virginia are available from the Department of Transportation, Administrative Services—Information Desk—Old Building, 1401 East Broad Street, Richmond VA 23219 (804) 786-2838; (804) 786-2801. Maryland county maps, which are the best I have encountered, may be purchased from the Cartographic Section, Maryland State Highway Administration, 2323 West Joppa Road, Brooklandville MD 21022 (301) 321-3518. West Virginia county maps can be ordered from West Virginia Department of Transportation, 1900 Kanawha Boulecard East, Building 5, Charleston WV 25305-0430; (304) 348-3505.

RESOURCES FOR A TOUR OF THE FIRST MANASSAS CAMPAIGN

Each resource appears in the order in which it is needed on the tour.

Alexandria Visitors Center, 221 King Street (Ramsey House), Alexandria VA 22314-3209 (703) 838-4200; (800) 388-9119; fax (703) 838-4683. Web site: www.funside.com

Stabler Leadbeater Apothecary Museum, 105-107 South Fairfax Street, Alexandria VA 22314 (703) 836-3713.

The Lyceum, Alexandria's History Museum, 201 South Washington Street, Alexandria VA 22314 (703) 838-4994; fax (703) 838-4997. Web site: http://ci.alexandria.va.us/oha/lyceum

Christ Church, 118 North Washington Street, Alexandria VA 22314 (703) 549-1450; fax (703) 683-2677.

Lee-Fendall House, 614 Oronco Street, Alexandria VA 22314 (703) 548-1784.

Alexandria National Cemetery, 1450 Wilkes Street, Alexandria VA 22314 (703) 690-2217.

Fort Ward Museum and Historic Site, 4301 West Braddock Road, Alexandria VA 22304-1008 (703) 838-4848; fax (703) 671-7350. Web site: http://ci.alexandria.va.us/oha/fortward

Greater Falls Church Chamber of Commerce, 417 West Broad Street (P.O. Box 491), Falls Church VA 22040-0491 (703) 532-1050.

Fairfax Museum and Visitors Center, 10209 Main Street, Fairfax VA 22030-2403 (703) 385-8414; (800) 545-7950. Web site: www.cvb.co.fairfax.va.us

Fairfax Station Railroad Museum, 11200 Fairfax Station Road, Fairfax Station VA 22039 (703) 425-9225.

Fairfax County Courthouse, 4000 Chain Bridge Road, Fairfax VA 22030.

The William Gunnell House, 10520 Main Street, Fairfax VA 22032 (open on walking tours).

Joshua Gunnell House (bed and breakfast), 4023 Chain Bridge Road, Fairfax VA 22030 (800) 366-7666.

Fairfax County Office of Touruism and Visitors Services, Tysons Corner, 8300 Boone Boulevard, Suite 450, Vienna VA 22182 (703) 790-0660; fax (703) 893-1269.

The Manassas Museum, 9101 Prince William Street, P.O. Box 560, Manassas VA 22110 (703) 368-1873; fax (703) 257-8406.

Historic Manassas Visitors Center, 9431 West Street, Manassas VA 20110 (703) 361-6599.

Historic Manassas, Inc., 9025 Center Street, Manassas VA 20110 (703) 361-6599; fax (703) 361-6942.

Manassas National Battlefield Park, P.O. Box 1830, 6511 Sudley Road, Manassas VA 22110 (703) 361-1339; (703) 361-1339.

Manassas Welcome Center, Virginia Tourism Corporation, I-66 between U.S. 29 and Route 234.

Prince William County—Manassas Visitors Center, 200 Mill Street, P.O. Box 123, Occoquan VA 22125 (703) 491-4045; (800) 432-1792.

Prince William County-Manassas Conference and Visitors Bureau, 14420 Bristow Road, Manassas VA 22112-3933 (703) 792-4254; (800) 432-1792; fax (703) 792-4219. Web site: www.visitpwc.com

Historic Prince William, P.O. Box 1758, Prince William VA 22193.

Pohich Episcopal Church, 9301 Richmond Highway, Lorton VA 22029 (703) 339-6572.

George Washington's Mount Vernon, Mount Vernon VA 22121 (703) 780-2000; fax (703) 794-8698. Web site: www.mountvernon.org

Historic Occoquan, P.O. Box 606, Occoquan VA 22125 (800) SHOPS-TOO.

Mill House Museum, P.O. Box 65, 413 Mill Street, Occoquan VA 22125 (703) 491-7525.

Weems Botts, Dumfries Regional Museum, Box 26, Dumfries VA 22026 (703) 221-3346; fax (703) 221-3544.

Leesylvania State Park, 16236 Neabsco Road, Woodbridge VA 22191-4504 (703) 670-0372; fax (703) 730-6232.

RESOURCES FOR A TOUR OF HAMPTON ROADS AND *VIRGINIA-MONITOR* SITES

Each resource appears in the order in which it is needed on the tour.

Riddick's Folly, Inc., 510 North Main Street (P.O. Box 1722), Suffolk VA 23434 (757) 934-1390.

Suffolk-Nansemond Historical Society, P.O. Box 1255, Suffolk VA 23434.

Isle of Wight Visitors Center, Old Courthouse Building, 130 Main Street, P.O. Box 37, Smithfield VA 23430 (757) 357-5182; (800) 365-9339. E-mail: smfdtour@visi.net

The Isle of Wight County Museum, 103 Main Street, Smithfield VA 23430 (757) 357-7459.

Fort Boykin Historic Park, 7410 Fort Boykin Trail (Route 2, Box 4), Smithfield VA 23430 (757) 357-5182.

Portsmouth Visitors Information Center, 6 Crawford Parkway, Portsmouth VA 23704 (757) 393-5111; (800) PORTSVA. Web site: www.ci.portsmouth.va.us

Portsmouth Convention and Visitors Bureau, 505 Crawford Street, Suite 2, Portsmouth VA 23704-3805 (757) 393-5327; fax (757) 393-5330; (800) PORTS-VA. Web site: www.ci.portsmouth.va.us

Portsmouth Naval Shipyard Museum, 2 High Street, P.O. Box 850, Portsmouth VA 23704 (757) 393-8591; fax (757) 393-5228.

Museum of Military History, 701 Court Street, Portsmouth VA 23704 (757) 393-2773; fax (757) 399-2562.

Norfolk Convention and Visitors Bureau, 232 East Main Street, Norfolk VA 23510 (757) 664-6620; (800) 368-3097. Web site: www.norfolk.va.us

Norfolk Visitors Information Center, Fourth View Street, Norfolk VA 23503 (800) 368-3097. Web site: www.norfolk.va.us

Norfolk on the Waterfront, 232 East Main Street, Norfolk VA 23510 (757) 664-6620; (757) 441-1852.

Nauticus, The National Maritime Center, One Waterside Drive (P.O. Box 3310), Norfolk VA 23510-1607 (757) 664-1000; (800) 664-1080; fax (757) 623-1287; Web site: www.nauticus.org; Hampton Roads Naval Museum, (757) 444-8971; fax (757) 445-1876.

Fort Norfolk, Norfolk Historical Society, P.O. Box 6367, Norfolk VA 23508-0367 (757) 625-1720.

Hampton Visitors Center, 710 Settlers Landing Road, Hampton VA 23669 (757) 727-1102; (800) 800-2202; www.hampton.va.us/tourism. Same for Fort Wool (800) 487-8778.

Casemate Museum/Fort Monroe, P.O. Box 341, Fort Monroe VA 23651 (757) 727-3391; fax (757) 727-3886.

Virginia Air and Space Center and Hampton Roads History Center, 600 Settlers Landing Road (P.O. Box 1883), Hampton VA 23669 (757) 727-0900; (800) 296-0800. Web site: www.vasc.org

Hampton National Cemetery, Cemetery Road at Marshall Avenue, Virginia Medical Center, Hampton VA 23669 (757) 727-0900.

Hampton University Museum, Hampton University, Hampton VA 23669 (757) 727-5308.

Saint John's Church, 100 West Queens Way, Hampton VA 23669 (757) 722-2567.

Virginia Peninsula Tourism and Conference Bureau, 8 San Jose Drive, Suite 3-B, Newport News VA 23606 (757) 873-0092; 727-1102; (800) 333-7787.

Monitor/Merrimack Center, 917 Jefferson Avenue, Newport News VA 23607 (757) 245-1522; fax (757) 245-2813.

Newport News Tourist Information Center, 13560 Jefferson Avenue (U.S. 60), at entrance to Newport News Park, Newport News VA 23603 (757) 886-7777; fax (757) 886-7981; (888) 493-7386. Web site: www.newport-news.org

Brochure: *Guide to Newport News Civil War Sites—Young's Mill, Lee's Mill, Dam No. 1, and Skiffes Creek* (757) 247-8523; fax (757) 247-8627; (888) 493-7386.

Virginia War Museum, 9285 Warwick Boulevard (U.S. 60), Huntington Park, Newport News VA 23607 (757) 247-8523; fax (757) 247-8627; (888) 493-7386.

The Mariners' Museum, 100 Museum Drive, Newport News VA 23606-2222 (757) 596-2222; (800) 581-SAIL; fax (757) 591-7320. Web site: www.mariner.org

RESOURCES FOR A TOUR OF THE PENINSULA CAMPAIGN TO SEVEN PINES

Each resource appears in the order in which it is needed on the tour.

Virginia Peninsula Tourism and Conference Bureau, 8 San Jose Drive, Suite 3-B, Newport News VA 23606 (757) 873-0092; (757) 873-1102; (800) 333-7787.

Newport News Tourist Information Center, 13560 Jefferson Avenue (U.S. 60 at entrance to Newport News Park), Newport News VA 23603 (757) 886-7777; fax (757) 886-7981; (888) 493-7386. Web site: www.newport-news.org

Brochure: *Guide to Newport News Civil War Sites—Young's Mill, Lee's Mill, Dam No. 1, and Skiffes Creek* (757) 247-8523; fax (757) 247-8627; (888) 493-7386.

Newport News Park, 13564 Jefferson Avenue, Newport News VA 23603 (757) 888-3333; fax (757) 886-7981; Historical Interpretive Center (757) 886-2843; (800) 203-8322.

Lee Hall Mansion, 163 Yorktown Road, Newport News VA 23603 (757) 888-3377; fax (757) 888-3373.

Endview Plantation, 362 Yorktown Road, Newport News VA 23604 (757) 887-1862; fax (757) 888-3369. Web site: www.endview.org

U.S. Army Transportation Museum, Washington Boulevard, Building 300, Besson Hall, Fort Eustis VA 23604-5259 (757) 878-1182; fax (757) 878-5656.

Colonial National Historical Park (Yorktown Battlefield and Jamestown Historic Site), P.O. Box 210, Yorktown VA 23690-0210. National Park Service Visitors Center (Yorktown) (757) 898-3400; (Jamestown) (757) 229-1733. Web site: www.nps.gov/colo/

The Williamsburg Area Convention and Visitors Bureau, 201 Penniman Road (P.O. Box 3585), Williamsburg VA 23187-3585 (757) 253-0192; (800) 368-6511; fax (757) 229-2047. Web site: www.visitwilliamsburg.com

Courthouse Historic District, 6504 Main Street, Gloucester VA 23061 (804) 693-2355; fax (804) 693-1263. Web site: www.co.gloucester.va.us

Williamsburg Civil War Round Table, 28 Banister Drive, Hampton VA 23666.

Colonial Williamsburg, P.O. Box 1776, Williamsburg VA 23187-1776 (757) 220-7645; (800) HISTORY.

Jamestown Colonial National Historic Park, P.O. Box 210, Yorktown VA 23690 (757) 229-1733.

Middlesex-Urbanna Chamber of Commerce, Drawer C, Urbanna VA 23175 (804) 758-5540.

Urbanna Historic District, P.O. Box 179, 45 Cross Street, Urbanna VA 23175 (804) 758-2613; (800) 635-0857. Web site: www.urbanna.com

West Point Historic District, c/o West Point Chamber of Commerce, 925 Main Street, West Point VA 23181 (804) 843-4620.

Seven Pines National Cemetery, 400 East Williamsburg Road, Sandston VA 23150 (804) 222-1490.

Richmond National Cemetery, 1701 Williamsburg Road, Richmond VA 23231 (804) 222-1490.

Richmond National Battlefield Park, Chimborazo Visitors Center, 3215 East Broad Street, Richmond VA 23223 (804) 226-1981. Web site: www.nps.gov/rich

RESOURCES FOR A TOUR OF CIVIL WAR RICHMOND

Each resource appears in the order in which it is needed on the tour.

Richmond National Battlefield Park, Chimborazo Visitors Center, 3215 East Broad Street, Richmond VA 23223 (804) 226-1981. Web site: www.nps.gov/rich

Metropolitan Richmond Convention and Visitors Bureau, 550 East Marshall Street, Richmond VA 23219 (804) 780-2577; 358-5511; (888) RICHMOND. Web site: www.richmondva.org

Richmond Metro Visitors Center, 1710 Robin Hood Road, Richmond VA 23220 (800) 370-9004; (804) 358-5511; fax (804) 257-5571. Web site: www.erols.com/richmond

Convention and Visitors Bureau, Sixth Street Marketplace, 550 East Marshall Street, Richmond VA 23219 (804) 782-2777; (800) 365-7272.

The Museum and White House of the Confederacy, 1201 East Clay Street, Richmond VA 23219 (804) 649-1861; fax (804) 644-7150. Web site: www.moc.org

Capitol of Virginia, Ninth and Grace Streets, Richmond VA 23219 (804) 698-1788.

The Valentine Riverside Museum, 550 East Marshall Street, Richmond VA 23219 (804) 649-0711; (800) 365-7272.

Hollywood Cemetery, 412 South Cherry Street, Richmond VA 23220 (804) 648-8501.

Virginia Historical Society/The Museum of Virginia History, The Battle Abbey, 428 North Boulevard (P.O. Box 7311), Richmond VA 23220 (804) 358-4901; fax (804) 355-2399. Web site: www.vahistorical.org

The Valentine, the Museum of the History of Richmond, 1015 East Clay Street, Richmond VA 23219 (804) 649-0711; fax (804) 643-3510. Web site: www.valentinemuseum.org

The American Historical Foundation Museums, 1142 West Grace Street, Richmond VA 23220 (804) 353-1812.

The Library of Virginia, 800 East Broad Street, Richmond VA 23219-1905 (804) 692-3500.

Historic Richmond Foundation Tours, 707-A East Franklin Street, Richmond VA 23219 (804) 780-0171; fax (804) 788-4244.

Historic Downtown Richmond Tours, 1201 East Clay Street, Richmond VA 23219 (804) 649-1861.

RESOURCES FOR A TOUR OF THE SEVEN DAYS' BATTLES

Each resource appears in the order in which it is needed on the tour.

Richmond National Battlefield Park, Chimborazo Visitors Center, 3215 East Broad Street, Richmond VA 23223 (804) 226-1981. Web site: www.nps.org/rich

Historic Richmond Foundation Tours, 707-A East Franklin Street, Richmond VA 23219 (804) 780-0107; fax (804) 788-4244.

Glendale National Cemetery, 8301 Willis Church Road, Richmond VA 23231 (804) 222-1490.

Berkeley Plantation, 12602 Harrison Landing Road (Route 2, Box 390), Charles City VA 23030 (804) 829-6018; (800) 473-5075; fax (804) 829-6757.

Westover, 7000 Westover Road, Charles City VA 23030 (804) 829-2882.

Evelynton Plantation, 6701 John Tyler Memorial Highway, Charles City VA 23030 (804) 829-5075; (800) 473-5075.

Shirley Plantation, 501 Shirley Plantation Road, Charles City VA 23030 (804) 829-5121 (800) 232-1613. Web site: www.shirleyplantation.com

North Bend Plantation, 12200 Weyanoke Road, Route 2, Box 290, Charles City VA 23030 (804) 829-5176; (800) 841-1479. Web site: www.ontheline.com/nbbb

Edgewood Plantation, 4800 John Tyler Memorial Highway, Charles City VA 23030 (804) 829-2962.

James River Plantations, P.O. 150, Charles City VA 23030 (800) 704-5423. Web site: www.jamesriverplantations.org for information about Berkeley, Evelynton, Sherwood Forest, and Shirley Plantations.

Charles City County Tourism Board, 501 Shirley Plantation Road, Charles City VA 23030 (804) 829-5121.

RESOURCES FOR A TOUR OF THE SECOND MANASSAS CAMPAIGN

Each resource appears in the order in which it is needed on the tour.

Ashland-Hanover County Visitors Center, 112 North Railroad Avenue, Hanover VA 23005 (804) 752-6766; (800) 897-1479. Web site: www.town.ashland.va.us

Hanover County Historical Society, P.O. Box 91, Hanover VA 23069.

The Hanover Tavern Foundation, P.O. Box 487, Hanover VA 23069.

Orange County Visitors Center, 122 East Main Street (Train Station), P.O. Box 133, Orange VA 22960 (540) 672-1653; fax (540) 672-1746; (877) 222-8072. Web site: www.visitocva.com

Orange County Historical Society, 130 Caroline Street, Orange VA 22960-1533 (540) 672-5366. Web site: www.kclark.net/ochs/

Trevilian Station Battlefield Foundation, P.O. Box 124, Trevilians VA 23170.

Exchange Hotel Civil War Museum, 400 South Main Street, Gordonsville VA 22942 (540) 832-2944. Web site: www.gemlink.com/~exchange-hotel

Saint Thomas Episcopal Church, 119 Caroline Street, Orange VA 22960 (540) 672-3761.

Louisa County Historical Society, P.O. Box 1172, Louisa VA 23093

Central Virginia Battlefields Trust, 604-A William Street, Suite 1, Fredericksburg VA 22401. Web site: www.cvbt.org

Friends of the Fredericksburg Area Battlefields, 13100 Wilderness Park Srive, Spotsylvania VA 22553-8220

Madison Chamber of Commerce, P.O. Box 373, Madison VA 22727 (540) 948-4455.

Culpeper Chamber of Commerce, 133 West Davis Street, Culpeper VA 22701 (540) 825-8628. Web site: www.co.culpeper.va.us

Museum of Culpeper History, 140 East Davis Street, Culpeper VA 22701 (540) 829-1749.

Culpeper National Cemetery, 305 U.S. Avenue, Culpeper VA 22701 (540) 825-0027.

The Culpeper Historical Society, Inc., P.O. Box 785, Culpeper VA 22701.

Madison County Champer of Commerce (information on the battles of James City and Jack's Shop), P.O. Box 373, 124 North Main Street, Madison VA 22727 (540) 948-4455; fax (540) 948-3174.

Kemper Residence (call for appointment), P.O. Box 467, Madison VA 22727 (540) 923-4464; fax (540) 948-3174.

Warrenton-Fauquier County Visitors Center, P.O. Box 27, 183-A Keith Street, Warrenton VA 20186 (540) 347-4414; (800) 820-1021.

Fauquier Heritage Society, P.O. Box 548, East Main Street, Marshall VA 20115 (540) 364-3440.

Foothills Travel Association of Virginia, 37 Beekman Street, Warrenton VA 22186 (703) 347-4414.

Turn the Mill Around Foundation, P.O. Box 207, Broad Run VA 20137.

Prince William County/Manassas Conference and Visitors Bureau, 14420 Bristow Road, Manassas VA 22112-3933 (703) 792-4254; (800) 432-1792. Web site: www.pwcweb.com/rec

The Manassas Museum, 9101 Prince William Street, P.O. Box 560, Manassas VA 22110 (703) 368-1873; fax (703) 257-8406.

Historic Manassas, Inc., 9025 Center Street, Manassas VA 22110 (703) 361-6599; fax (703) 361-6942.

Manassas National Battlefield Park, 6511 Sudley Road, Manassas VA 22110 (703) 361-1339; (703) 361-7075.

Manassas Welcome Center, Virginia Tourism Corporation, 9915 Vandor Lane, Manassas VA 20109 (I-66 between U.S. 29 and Route 234.) (703) 361-2134; fax (703) 361-4800.

Ben Lomond Manor House, 10501 Copeland Drive, Manassas VA 20109 (703) 792-7060.

Historic Prince William, P.O. Box 1758, Prince William VA 22193.

RESOURCES FOR A TOUR OF THE ANTIETAM CAMPAIGN

Each resource appears in the order in which it is needed on the tour.

Frying Pan Church, 2709 West Ox Road; Dranesville Tavern, 11919 Leesburg Pike; both administered by Fairfax County Parks Department (703) 324-8588.

Loudoun County Tourist Information Center, 108-D South Street SE, Leesburg VA 22075-3732 (703) 777-2167; (800) 752-6118; fax (703) 771-4973. Web site: www.visitloudoun.org

The Loudoun Museum, 14-16 West Loudoun Street SW, Leesburg VA 22175 (703) 777-7427.

Ball's Bluff National Cemetery, Leesburg VA 22075 (703) 825-0027 (Culpeper National Cemetery). Ball's Bluff Regional Park, Leesburg VA 22039 (703) 779-9372.

Northern Virginia Regional Park Authority Headquarters, 5400 Ox Road, Fairfax Station VA 22039 (703) 352-5900; fax (703) 273-0905. E-mail: info@nvrpa.org

Oatlands Plantation, 20850 Oatlands Plantation Lane, Leesburg VA 20175 (703) 777-3174.

White's Ferry, 24801 White's Ford Road, Dickerson MD 20842 (301) 349-5200.

Montgomery County Conference and Visitors Bureau, 12900 Middlebrook Road, Suite 1400, Germantown MD 20874-2616 (301) 428-9702 (800) 925-0880; fax (301) 428-9705. Web site: www.cvbmontco.com

Mongomery County Historical Society, 111, West Montgomery Avenue, Rockville MD 20850-4212 (301) 340-2825; fax (301) 340-2871. Web site: www.montgomeryhistory.org

Poolesville Chamber of Commerce, P.O. Box 256, Poolesville MD 20837 (301) 349-5753; fax (301) 349-0777

John Pool House, 19923 Fisher Avenue, Poolesville MD 20837 (301) 972-8588.

Seneca Schoolhouse Museum, 16800 River Road, Poolesville MD 20832 (301) 977-2430.

Point of Rocks Railroad Station, Point of Rocks MD 21777 (800) 325-7245.

Monocacy National Battlefield, 4801 Urbana Pike, Frederick MD 21704-7307 (301) 662-3515; fax (301) 662-3430. Web site: www.nps.gov/mono

Friends of Monocacy Battlefield, Inc., P.O. Box 4101, Frederick MD 21705-4101.

Landon House, 3401 Urbanna Pike, Frederick MD 21704 (301) 874-3914; fax (301) 831-8558; Web site: www.landonhouse.com; see also www.sabersandroses.com

Mount Olivet Cemetery, P.O. Box 565, 515 South Market Street, Frederick MD 21701 (301) 662-1164; fax (301) 620-8809.

Tourism Council of Frederick County, Inc., 19 East Church Street, Frederick MD 21701 (301) 663-8687; (800) 999-3613; to request a brochure (800) 800-9699. Web site: www.visitfrederick.org

The Historical Society of Frederick County, Inc., 24 East Church Street, Frederick MD 21701 (301) 663-1188; fax (301) 663-0526. Web site: www.fwp.net/hsfc

National Museum of Civil War Medicine, 48 East Patrick Street (P.O. Box 470), Frederick MD 21705-0470 (301) 695-1864; (800) 564-1864; fax (301) 695-6823. Web site: www.civilwarmed.org

Barbara Fitchie House and Museum, 154 West Patrick Street, Frederick MD 21701 (301) 698-0630.

Roger Brooke Taney Home and Frances Scott Key Museum, 121 South Bentz Street, Frederick MD 21701 (301) 663-8687.

Hessian Barracks, P.O. Box 250, 101 Clarke Place, Frederick MD 21701 (301) 662-4159.

Saint John's Cemetery, P.O. Box 189, East Third and East Fourth Streets, Frederick MD 21705 (301) 663-8687.

Prospect Hall Mansion, 889 Butterfly Lane, Frederick MD (301) 662-4210.

Middletown Valley Historical Society, 305 West Main Street, Middletown MD 21769 (301) 371-7582; fax (301) 371-7582.

Central Maryland Heritage League, Inc., P.O. Box 721, 200 West Main Street (Lamar House), Middletown MD 21769 (301) 371-7090. E-mail: infor@cmhl.org

South Mountain Heritage Society, Inc., P.O. Box 59, Burkittsville MD 21718 (301) 834-7064.

Washington Monument State Park, Route 1, Box 147, Middletown MD 21769 (301) 791-4767.

Gathland State Park, 900 Arnoldstown Road, Jefferson MD, and Washington Monument State Park, both c/o Greenbrier State Park, 21843 National Pike, Boonsboro MD 21713-9535 (301) 791-4767.

Friends of Gathland State Park, P.O. Box 192, Burkittsville MD 21718. Web site: www.gathland.org

The Old South Mountain Inn, 6132 Old National Pike, Boonsboro MD 21713 (301) 371-5400; (301) 432-6155.

Hagerstown/Washington County Convention and Visitors Bureau, 16 Public Square, Hagerstown MD 21740 (301) 791-3246; (301) 791-3130; (800) 228-STAY (7829); fax (301) 791-2601.

Washington County Historical Society, P.O. Box 1281, Hagerstown MD 21741-1281 (301) 797-8782.

Boonsborough Museum of History, 113 North Main Street, Boonsboro MD 21713-1007 (301) 432-6969; (301) 432-5151 (always call ahead).

RESOURCES FOR A TOUR OF THE BATTLE OF ANTIETAM

Each resource appears in the order in which it is needed on the tour.

Antietam National Battlefield and Cemetery, P.O. Box 158, Sharpsburg MD 21782-0158 (301) 432-5124. Web site: www.nps.gov/anti

Save Historic Antietam Foundation (SHAF), P.O. Box 550, Sharpsburg MD 21782.

C&O Canal National Historical Park, P.O. Box 4, 16500 Shepherdstown Pike, Sharpsburg MD 21782 (301) 739-4200. Web site: www.nps.gov/choh

Historic Shepherdstown Commission, P.O. Box 1786, Shepherdstown WV 25443. Historic Shepherdstown Museum-Entler Hotel, German and Princess Streets, Shepherdstown MD 25443 (304) 876-0910.

George Tyler Moore Center for the Study of the Civil War, Shepherd College, Shepherdstown WV 25443 (304) 876-5429

RESOURCES FOR A TOUR OF HARPERS FERRY AND JOHN BROWN'S RAID

Each resource appears in the order in which it is needed on the tour.

Kennedy Farmhouse, 2406 Chestnut Grove Road, Sharpsburg MD 21783 (301) 432-2666; (301) 791-3130.

Jefferson County Convention and Visitors Bureau, P.O. Box A, Harpers Ferry WV 25425 (304) 535-2627; (800) 848-TOUR. E-mail: visitors@jeffersoncounty.com

Jefferson County Chamber of Commerce, 201 Frontage Road (P.O. Box 426), Charles Town WV 25414 (304) 725-2055.

Jefferson County Museum, 200 East Washington Street (P.O. Box 992), Charles Town WV 25414 (304) 725-8628.

Harpers Ferry National Historical Park, P.O. Box 65, Harpers Ferry WV 25425 (304) 535-6371; (304) 535-6298; 535-6223.

John Brown Wax Museum, High Street, Harpers Ferry WV 25425 (304) 535-6342; (304) 535-2792.

Brunswick Railroad Museum, 40 West Potomac Street, Brunswick MD 21716 (301) 834-7100.
Web site: www.artcom.com/museums/nv/af/21716-11.htm

A FINAL NOTE ON TOURING

Information technology has changed dramatically since I launched this series in the late 1980s. Now, instead of writing for information from federal, state, and local sources, an E-mail or telephone call will suffice. Also check Web sites for the latest information—new tours or recently opened areas for visiting, hours and seasons when attractions are open, and developing issues concerning historic sites. A growing number of city and county Web pages feature driving and walking tours of their communities, and these usually include fascinating bits of local lore that generally elude most visitors.

A number of organizations sponsor guided bus, steamboat, and train excursions to explore campaigns, regions, battles, and issues of the war. Most are several days in length, and housing and dining are prearranged. Perhaps their most appealing attractions are the high quality of their guides and lecturers—recognized experts in particular fields. Another benefit is that an organized group may be allowed to visit areas that are inacessible to individual visitors.

If you prefer exploring history on your own terms and pace, be a lone wolf. Personally, I avoid crowds. I try to arrive at historical sites early in the morning, late in the afternoon, and early in the week when the crowds are generally small. Note that many state and local parks and areas are closed on Mondays, so check ahead. If my explorations direct me to a large city, I try to visit the area on a weekend, so as to avoid commuter and business traffic.

BIBLIOGRAPHY

Alexander, Bevin. *Lost Victories: The Military Genius of Stonewall Jackson.* New York: Henry Holt and Co., 1992.

Amadon, George F. *Rise of the Ironclads.* Missoula, Mont.: Pictorial Histories Publishing Co., 1988.

Ambrose, Stephen E. *Halleck: Lincoln's Chief of Staff.* Baton Rouge: Louisiana State University Press, 1996.

Anders, Curt. *Fighting Confederates.* New York: Dorset Press, 1990.

Barber, James G. *Alexandria in the Civil War.* Lynchburg, Va.: H. E. Howard, 1988.

Bailey, Ronald H. *The Bloodiest Day: The Battle of Antietam.* Alexandria, Va.: Time-Life Books, 1984.

———. *Forward to Richmond: McClellan's Peninsula Campaign.* Alexandria, Va.: Time-Life Books, 1983.

Barron, Lee, and Barbara Barron. *The History of Sharpsburg, Maryland.* Sharpsburg, Md.: Barbara and Lee Barron, 1972.

Bauer, K. Jack, ed. *Soldiering: The Civil War Diary of Rice C. Bull.* New York: Berkley Books, 1988.

Baxter, James P. *The Introduction of the Ironclad Warship.* Cambridge, Mass.: Archon Books, 1968.

Bishop, Chris, Ian Drury, and Tony Gibbons. *1400 Days: The Civil War Day by Day.* New York: Gallery Books, 1990.

Black, Donald O. *Virginia's Civil War: A Self-Guided Tour.* Virginia Beach, Va.: Genesis Media, 1996.

Boatner, Mark M. III. *The Civil War Dictionary.* New York: Vintage Books, 1991.

Guide to Haunted Places of the Civil War. Columbus, Ohio: Blue and Gray Magazine, 1996.

Bowe, John. *Adventuring in the Chesapeake Bay Area.* San Francisco: Sierra Club Books, 1990.

Brooke, George M., Jr. *John M. Brooke: Naval Scientist and Educator.* Charlottesville: University Press of Virginia, 1980.

Clark, David A. *Fortress America: The Corps of Engineers, Hampton Roads, and United States Coastal Defense.* Charlottesville: University Press of Virginia, 1990.

Colbert, Judy, and Ed Colbert. *Maryland: Off the Beaten Path.* Chester, Conn.: Globe Pequot Press, 1990.

Commager, Henry S. *The Blue and the Gray.* New York: Fairfax Press, 1982.

Cormier, Steven A. *The Siege of Suffolk: The Forgotten Campaign, April 11–May 4, 1863.* Lynchburg, Va.: H. E. Howard, 1989.

Cottingham, David T. *Bridges: Our Legacy in Stone.* Hagerstown, Md.: Washington County Board of County Commissioners, 1977.

Cromie, Alice. *A Tour Guide to the Civil War.* Nashville, Tenn.: Rutledge Hill Press, 1990.

Davis, Burke. *Gray Fox: Robert E. Lee and the Civil War.* New York: Rinehart and Winston, 1956.

——. *Jeb Stuart: The Last Cavalier.* New York: Fairfax Press, 1988.

——. *They Called Him Stonewall: A Life of Lt. General T. J. Jackson, C.S.A.* New York: Fairfax Press, 1988.

Davis, William C. *Battle at Bull Run.* Baton Rouge: Louisiana State University Press, 1977.

——. *Duel Between the First Ironclads.* Baton Rouge: Louisiana State University Press, 1975.

——. *Jefferson Davis: The Man and His Hour, A Biography.* New York: HarperCollins, 1991.

Divine, John, et al. *Loudoun County and the Civil War: A History and Guide.* Leesburg, Va.: County of Loudoun, 1961.

Donald, David Herbert. *Lincoln.* London: Jonathan Cape, 1995.

Douglas, Henry Kyd. *I Rode with Stonewall.* Marietta, Ga.: Mockingbird Books, 1995.

Dowdey, Clifford, and Louis H. Manarin, eds. *The Wartime Papers of R. E. Lee.* New York: Bramhall House, 1961.

Durkin, Joseph T. *Confederate Naval Chief: Stephen R. Mallory.* Columbia: University of South Carolina Press, 1987.

Dyer, John P. *The Gallant Hood.* New York: Smithmark, 1995.

Early, Jubal A. *The Memoirs of General Jubal A. Early.* New York: Konecky & Konecky, 1994.

Evans, Thomas J., and James M. Moyer. *Mosby's Confederacy: A Guide to the Roads and Sites of Colonel John Singleton Mosby.* Shippensburg, Pa.: White Mane, 1991.

Farwell, Byron. *Ball's Bluff.* McLean, Va.: EPM, 1990.

Flanders, Alan B. *The Merrimack.* Privately punished, 1982.

Foote, Shelby. *The Civil War, A Narrative: Fort Sumter to Perryville.* New York: Random House, 1958.

Frome, Michael. *Mid-Atlantic National Parks: Five-Tour Guidebook.* National Parks Mid-Atlantic Council, 1987.

Frye, Keith. *Roadside Geology of Virginia.* Missoula, Mont.: Mountain Press Publishing, 1991.

Gibbons, Tony. *Warships and Naval Battles of the Civil War.* New York: Gallery Books, 1989.

Gilbert, Dave. *A Walker's Guide to Harpers Ferry, West Virginia.* Harpers Ferry, W.V.: Harpers Ferry Historical Association, 1992.

Gleason, Michael P. *The Insider's Guide to the Civil War: The Eastern Theater.* Richmond, Va.: The Insider's Guide, 1993.

Gordon, John Brown. *Reminiscences of the Civil War.* Dayton, Ohio: Morningside, 1985.

Govan, Gilbert, and James Livingwood. *General Joseph E. Johnston, C.S.A.: A Different Valor.* New York: Bobbs-Merrill, 1956.

Greene, A. Wilson, and Gary W. Gallagher. *National Geographic Guide to the Civil War National Battlefield Parks.* Washington, D.C.: National Geographic Society, 1992.

Hart, Allen de. *The Trails of Virginia: Hiking the Old Dominion.* Chapel Hill: University of North Carolina Press, 1995.

Hassler, William Woods. *Colonel John Pelham: Lee's Boy Artillerist.* Chapel Hill: University of North Carolina Press, 1960.

Hastings, Earl C., Jr., and David Hastings. *A Pitiless Rain: The Battle of Williamsburg, 1862.* Shippensburg, Pa.: White Mane, 1997.

Hicks, Roger W., and Frances E. Schultz. *Battlefields of the Civil War.* Topsfield, Mass.: Salem House Publishers, 1989.

Hill, Lois, ed. *Poems and Songs of the Civil War.* New York: Gramercy Books, 1990.

Historic Culpeper. Culpeper, Va.: Culpeper Historical Society, 1974.

Howard, Blair. *Battlefields of the Civil War: A Guide for Travelers.* 2 vols. Edison, N.J.: Hunter Publishing, 1994–85.

Hudson, Carson O., Jr. *Civil War Williamsburg.* Williamsburg, Va.: Williamsburg Foundation, 1997.

Hudson, Patricia L., and Sandra L. Ballard. *The Smithsonian Guide to Historic America, the Carolinas and the Appalachian States.* New York: Stewart, Tabori & Chang, 1989.

Hunt, Harrison. *Hallowed Ground: Battlefields of the Civil War.* New York: Mallard Press, 1990.

John Brown's Raid. Harpers Ferry, W.V.: U.S. National Park Service, 1974.

Johnson, Clint. *Touring Virginia's and West Virginia's Civil War Sites.* Winston-Salem, N.C.: John F. Blair, 1999.

Johnson, Robert U., and Clarence C. Buel, eds. *Battles and Leaders of the Civil War.* 4 vols. New York: Castle Books, 1956.

Johnston, Joseph E. *Narrative of Military Operations During the Civil War.* New York: D. Appleton, 1874.

Jones, Ray. *Harpers Ferry.* Gretna, La.: Pelican, 1992.

Jones, Katharine M. *Heroines of Dixie.* New York: Smithmark, 1995.

Jones, Virgil Carrington. *Gray Ghosts and Rebel Raiders.* McLean, Va.: EPM, 1984.

———. *Ranger Mosby.* McLean, Va.: EPM, 1972.

Judge, Joseph. *Season of Fire: The Confederate Strike on Washington*. Berryville, Va.: Rockbridge Publishing Co., 1994.

Keller, S. Roger. *Events of the Civil War in Washington County, Maryland*. Shippensburg, Pa.: White Mane, 1995.

Kennedy, Frances H., ed. *The Civil War Battlefield Guide: The Conservation Fund*. Boston: Houghton Mifflin, 1990.

Krick, Robert K. *Stonewall Jackson at Cedar Mountain*. Chapel Hill: University of North Carolina Press, 1990.

Lawliss, Chuck. *In Search of Robert E. Lee*. Conshohocken, Pa.: Combined Books, 1996.

Lee Takes Command: From Seven Days to Second Bull Run. Alexandria, Va.: Time-Life Books, 1984.

Leech, Margaret. *Reveille in Washington, 1860–1865*. New York: Darroll & Graf, 1991.

Long, E. B., and Barbara Long. *The Civil War Day by Day: An Almanac 1861–1865*. New York: Da Capo Press, 1971.

Longstreet, James. *From Manassas to Appomattox*. New York: Mallard Press, 1991.

Lord, Suzanne, and Jon Metzger. *The West Virginia One-Day Trip Book*. McLean, Va.: EPM, 1993.

Luvaas, Jay, and Harold W. Nelson, eds. *The U.S. Army War College Guide to the Battle of Antietam, the Maryland Campaign of 1862*. Carlisle, Pa.: South Mountain Press, 1987.

MacKay, Bryan. *Hiking, Cycling, and Canoeing in Maryland*. Baltimore, Md.: Johns Hopkins University Press, 1995

Martin, David G. *The Peninsula Campaign March—July 1862*. Conshohocken, Pa.: Combined Books, 1992.

Marvel, William. *Burnside*. Chapel Hill: University of North Carolina Press, 1991.

Melton, Maurice. *The Confederate Ironclads*. South Brunswick, N.J.: T. Yoseloff, 1968.

Miller, William J. *Mapping for Stonewall: The Civil War Service of Jed Hotchkiss*. Washington, D.C.: Elliott & Clark Publishing, 1993.

Moore, Samuel J. T., Jr. *Moore's Complete Civil War Guide to Richmond*. Richmond: Privately published, 1978.

Morris, Shirley. *The Pelican Guide to Virginia*. Gretna, La.: Pelican Publishing, 1990.

Mulligan, Kate. *Towns Along the Towpath*. Washington, D.C.: Wakefield Press, 1996.

Mumma, Wilmer M. *Antietam: The Aftermath*. Sharpsburg, Md.: Wilmer M. Mumma, 1993.

———. *Out of the Past*. Sharpsburg, Md.: Wilmer M. Mumma, 1993.

———. *Out of the Past II*. Sharpsburg, Md.: Wilmer M. Mumma, 1995.

Murfin, James V. *The Gleam of Bayonets: The Battle of Antietam and Robert E. Lee's Maryland Campaign, September 1862*. Baton Rouge: Louisiana State University Press, 1989.

Nesbitt, Mark. *Rebel Rivers: A Guide to Civil War Sites on the Potomac, Rappahannock, York, and James*. Mechanicsburg, Pa.: Stackpole Books, 1993.

Niven, John. *Gideon Welles: Lincoln's Secretary of the Navy.* Baton Rouge: Louisiana State University Press, 1973.

O'Donald, Mike. *At Manassas: Reunions, Maneuvers, Reenactments.* Mechanicsville, Va.: Rapidan Press, 1986.

Oman, Anne. *25 Bicycle Tours in Maryland.* Woodstock, Vt.: Backcountry Publications, 1994.

O'Shea, Richard. *American Heritage Battle Maps of the Civil War.* Tulsa, Okla.: Council Oak Books, 1992.

Osborne, Charles. *Jubal: The Life and Times of General Jubal A. Early, CSA, Defender of the Lost Cause.* Baton Rouge: Louisiana State University Press, 1992.

Parker, William H. *Recollections of a Naval Officer, 1841–1865.* Annapolis, Md.: Naval Institute Press, 1985.

Peters, John O., and Margaret T. *Virginia's Historic Courthouses.* Charlottesville: University Press of Virginia, 1995.

Piston, William Garrett. *Lee's Tarnished Lieutenant: James Longstreet and His Place in Southern History.* Athens: University of Georgia Press, 1987.

Reed, Rowena. *Combined Operations in the Civil War.* Annapolis, Md.: Naval Institute Press, 1978.

Porter, David D. *Naval History of the Civil War.* Secaucus, N.J.: Castle, 1984.

Priest, John Michael. *Before Antietam: The Battle for South Mountain.* Shippensburg, Pa.: White Mane, 1992.

Riggs, David F. *Embattled Shrine: Jamestown in the Civil War.* Shippensburg, Pa.: White Mane, 1997.

Roberts, Bruce. *Plantation Homes of the James River.* Chapel Hill: University of North Carolina Press, 1990.

Robertson, James I., Jr. *Civil War Sites in Virginia.* Charlottesville: University Press of Virginia, 1991.

———. *Stonewall Jackson: The Man, the Soldier, the Legend.* New York: Macmillian, 1997.

Ropes, John C. *Campaigns of the Civil War: The Army Under Pope.* New York: Jack Brussel, n.d.

Rosenburg, R. B. *Living Monuments: Confederate Soldiers' Homes in The New South.* Chapel Hill: University of North Carolina Press, 1993.

Salmon, John S., comp. *A Guidebook to Virginia's Historical Markers, Revised and Expanded Edition.* Charlottesville: University Press of Virginia, 1994.

Scheel, Eugene M. *The Civil War in Fauquier.* Waterford, Va.: Privately published, 1995.

Schildt, John W. *Drums Along the Monocacy.* Chewsville, Md.: Antietam Publications, 1991.

———. *Four Days in October.* Chewsville, Md.: John W. Schildt, 1978.

Sears, Stephen W. *George B. McClellan: The Young Napoleon.* New York: Ticknor & Fields, 1988.

———. *Landscape Turned Red: The Battle of Antietam.* New York: Ticknor & Fields, 1983.

Seldon, W. Lynn. *Country Roads of Virginia*. Castine, Maine: Country Roads Press, 1994.

Selfridge, Thomas O., Jr. *What Finer Tradition: The Memoirs of Thomas O. Selfridge Jr., Rear Admiral, U.S.N.* Columbia: University of South Carolina Press, 1987.

Semmes, Raphael. *Memoirs of Service Afloat During the War Between the States*. Baton Rouge: Louisiana State University Press, 1996.

Sherman, William T. *Memoirs of General William T. Sherman*. New York: Da Capo Press, 1984.

Sifakis, Stewart. *Who Was Who in the Confederacy*. New York: Facts on File, 1988.

———. *Who Was Who in the Union*. New York: Facts on File, 1988.

Silverstone, Paul H. *Warships of the Civil War Navies*. Annapolis, Md.: Naval Institute Press, 1989.

Smith, Jane O. *The Maryland One-Day Trip Book*. McLean, Va.: EPM, 1988.

———. *One-Day Trips Through History: 200 Excursions Within 150 Miles of Washington, D.C.* McLean, Va.: EPM, 1982.

———. *The Virginia One-Day Trip Book*. McLean, Va.: EPM, 1986.

Soderberg, Susan Cooke. *Lest We Forget: A Guide to Civil War Monuments in Maryland*. Shippensburg, Pa.: White Mane, 1995.

———. *A Guide to Civil War Sites in Maryland*. Shippensburg, Pa.: White Mane, 1998.

Sorrel, G. Moxley. *Recollections of a Confederate Staff Officer*. New York: Konecky & Konecky, 1994.

Stember, Sol. *The Bicentennial Guide to the American Revolution*. Volume 3: *The War in the South*. New York: Saturday Review Press, 1974.

Stevens, Joseph E. *America's National Battlefield Parks: A Guide*. Norman: University of Oklahoma Press, 1990.

Still, William N., Jr. *Confederate Shipbuilding*. Columbia: University of South Carolina Press, 1987.

———. *Iron Afloat: The Story of the Confederate Armorclads*. Columbia: University of South Carolina Press, 1971.

Stotelmyer, Steven R. *The Bivouacs of the Dead*. Baltimore: Toomey Press, 1992.

Swank, Walbrook Davis. *Battle of Trevilian Station: The Civil War's Greatest and Bloodiest All Cavalry Battle*. Shippensburg, Pa.: Burd Street Press, 1994.

Symonds, Craig L. *A Battlefield Atlas of the Civil War*. Baltimore, Md.: Nautical and Aviation Publishing Company of America, 1983.

Taylor, Walter H. *Four Years with General Lee*. Bloomington: Indiana University Press, 1996.

The Civil War Trust's Official Guide to the Civil War Discovery Trail. New York: Macmillan Travel, 1996.

The Rappahannock River. Alexandria, Va.: Virginia Heritage Publications, 1994.

Thomas, Emory M. *Robert E. Lee: A Biography*. New York: Norton, 1995.

———. *Travels to Hallowed Ground: A Historian's Journey to the American Civil War*. Columbia: University of South Carolina Press, 1987.

Thompson, Bryce D. *Military Living's U.S. Military Museums, Historic Sites and Exhibits.* Falls Church, Va.: Military Living Publications, 1989.

Toomey, Daniel Carroll. *The Civil War in Maryland.* Baltimore, Md.: Toomey Press, 1988.

Trudell, Clyde E. *Colonial Yorktown.* Gettysburg, Pa.: Thomas Publications, 1971.

Turner, Fitzhugh, ed. *Loudoun County and the Civil War: A History and Guide.* Leesburg, Va.: Potomac Press, 1961.

Warinner, N. E., comp. *A Register of Military Events in Virginia, 1861-1865.* Richmond, Va.: Virginia Civil War Commission, 1959.

Warner, Ezra J. *Generals in Blue.* Baton Rouge: Louisiana State University Press, 1964.

———. *Generals in Gray.* Baton Rouge: Louisiana State University Press, 1959.

Waugh, John C. *The Class of 1846.* New York: Warner Books, 1994.

Weil, Tom. *Civil War Sites: Your Complete Companion to Over 1,300 Civil War Sites.* New York: Hippocrene Books, 1994.

Wertz, Jay, and Edwin C. Bearss. *Smithsonian's Great Battles and Battlefields of the Civil War.* New York: Morrow, 1997.

Wheeler, Richard. *Lee's Terrible Swift Sword: From Antietam to Chancellorsville, An Eyewitness History.* New York: HarperCollins, 1992.

———. *A Rising Thunder.* New York: Harper-Perennial, 1995.

———. *Sword over Richmond.* New York: Fairfax Press, 1986.

Wieneck, Henry. *The Smithsonian Guide to Historic America: Virginia and the Capital Region.* New York: Stewart, Tabori & Chang, 1989.

Williams, T. Harry. *P. G. T. Beauregard: Napoleon in Gray.* Baton Rouge: Louisiana State University Press, 1989.

Wills, Mary Alice. *The Confederate Blockade of Washington, D.C., 1861–1862.* Prince William, Va.: Prince William County Historical Commission, 1997.

Wright, Mike. *City Under Siege: Richmond in the Civil War.* New York: Madison Books, 1995.

INDEX